Classless Politics

Columbia Studies in Middle East Politics

Columbia Studies in Middle East Politics

MARC LYNCH, SERIES EDITOR

Columbia Studies in Middle East Politics presents academically rigorous, well-written, relevant, and accessible books on the rapidly transforming politics of the Middle East for an interested academic and policy audience.

Classless Politics

Islamist Movements, the Left,
and Authoritarian Legacies
in Egypt

HESHAM SALLAM

Columbia

University

Press

New York

Columbia University Press
Publishers Since 1893
New York   Chichester, West Sussex
cup.columbia.edu

Library of Congress Cataloging-in-Publication Data
Names: Sallam, Hesham, author.
Title: Classless politics : Islamist movements, the left, and authoritarian
    legacies in Egypt / Hesham Sallam.
Description: New York : Columbia University Press, 2022. |
    Series: Columbia studies in Middle East politics |
    Includes bibliographical references and index.
Identifiers: LCCN 2021060324 | ISBN 9780231203241 (hardback) |
    ISBN 9780231203258 (trade paperback) | ISBN 9780231554947 (ebook)
Subjects: LCSH: Political participation—Egypt. | Right and left (Political
    science)—Egypt. | Islam and politics—Egypt. | Identity politics—Egypt. |
    Egypt—Social policy. | Egypt—Politics and government—20th century. |
    Egypt—Politics and government—21st century.
Classification: LCC JQ3881 .S249 2022 | DDC 320.9621—dc23/eng/20220308
LC record available at https://lccn.loc.gov/2021060324

Cover design: Elliott S. Cairns
Cover image: Sahm Doherty / The Chronicle Collection via Getty Images

To all of Egypt's prisoners of conscience,
including those we lost too soon.

Contents

Acknowledgments

T his book was the product of an unusually long journey involving numerous intellectual, logistical, and personal challenges, none of which I could have managed without the kindness, generosity, and patience of my colleagues, collaborators, friends, and family. I apologize to anyone whose name I have omitted. Any errors in the book are my sole responsibility. The views presented herein do not reflect the opinions of the individuals who supported my research.

This book is based primarily on my PhD dissertation research, which would not have been possible without the immense support and thoughtful mentorship of my committee chair Dan Brumberg, and committee members Steve Heydemann and Marc Howard. Throughout my academic career, Dan has been my principal mentor, standing by me every step of the way. Throughout the years, I have benefited from Dan's vast knowledge, his sharp insights, and, on many difficult days, his uplifting humor. Working with a scholar of Steve's caliber is the most intellectually rewarding experience a graduate student can hope for. I have learned a great deal from his thoughtful critiques, which taught me to be my own harshest critic and motivated me to improve as a scholar. Much of what I know about the study of regime types and political change originated in conversations with Marc at his Georgetown research seminars. Marc has also served as a role model (albeit difficult to emulate) to all scholars who aspire to place their intellectual labor in the service of progressive social change. Words alone cannot capture the gratitude I have for these three individuals and their support as I developed and executed this project.

I would also like to express my utmost gratitude to all those who commented on earlier drafts of this book or chapters of it, including Reem Abou-El-Fadl, Amr Adly, Abdullah Al-Arian, Joel Beinin, Nathan Brown, Frank Fukuyama, Gennaro Gervasio, Nate Grubman, Hanan Hammad, Nancy Okail, and Chris Toensing.

In addition to commenting extensively on this manuscript, Joel Beinin has been incredibly influential in the way I think about Egyptian politics. He and his wife Miriam have also been a second family to me at Stanford. I am truly fortunate to have Joel as a colleague and a friend.

Whether in Cairo or at Stanford, Amr Adly has been my intellectual companion for much of the journey that produced this book. There are absolutely no words to describe the wealth of knowledge Amr has shared with me in our conversations about this project. I am genuinely humbled by his generosity.

I am immeasurably indebted to Kevin Martin for the numerous hours he spent on multiple readings of this manuscript in its entirety, for his invaluable editorial input, and for consistently pushing me to make my ideas clearer and my language accessible to all readers.

I would like to express my deep appreciation for the editors and staff at Columbia University Press, particularly Global History and Politics Editor Caelyn Cobb and Columbia Studies in Middle East Politics Series Editor Marc Lynch, for their unflagging efforts to make this book a reality. I would also like to thank the two anonymous reviewers, whose incisive feedback was instrumental in helping me improve and refine this study. I am truly grateful to Ben Kolstad and his team at KnowledgeWorks Global for all the incredible work they have done to prepare this manuscript for publication.

Completing this book would have been impossible without the support of my employer, the Program on Arab Reform and Democracy (ARD) at Stanford University's Center on Democracy, Development, and the Rule of Law (CDDRL). I am immensely grateful to ARD Faculty Director Larry Diamond for granting me the time and mental space to prioritize working on this book, while temporarily setting aside many of my competing responsibilities at CDDRL. This project's completion is in no small part the result of Larry's patience and understanding. I would also like to thank the leadership of CDDRL and its parent institution, the Freeman Spogli Institute (FSI), especially Frank Fukuyama, who until recently served as the CDDRL Mosbacher director, the current CDDRL Mosbacher director Kathryn Stoner, and FSI Director Mike McFaul for all their support and encouragement over the years. I am equally grateful to Hicham Alaoui for all he does to nurture ARD's vibrant intellectual space dedicated to the growth and development of research on the Arab world, including my own.

Research for this book was supported by the Social Science Research Council's (SSRC) Dissertation Proposal Development Fellowship (DPDF) (2010), the Georgetown University Department of Government's Jill Hopper Memorial Fellowship (2010–2011), the United States Institute of Peace's Peace Scholar Fellowship (2011–2012), and CDDRL's Pre-Doctoral Fellowship (2013–2014).

I would like to extend my thanks to the participants at the 2010 SSRC-DPDF workshop "After Secularization" for their incisive comments on my research proposal, especially Kristen Kao, Hikmet Kocamaner, and James MacEwan, as well as workshop leaders Vincent Pecora and Jonathan Sheehan.

I would like to recognize those who commented on my project proposal in its formative stages, especially Andy Bennett, Jason Brownlee, Desha Girod, Amaney Jamal, Hans Noel, and Jim Vreeland, as well as participants at the 2010 session of the Institute for Qualitative and Multi-Method Research, including Dina Bishara, Matt Buehler, Igor Logvinenko, Pete Moore, Leila Piran, and Zeki Sarigil. I was also fortunate to receive helpful feedback from various colleagues at Georgetown University's Department of Government, especially David Buckley, Anjali Dayal, Jennifer Dresden, Devin Finn, Yu-Ming Liou, Luis Felipe Mantilla, Meghan McConaughey, Beth Mercurio, Yoni Morse, Paul Musgrave, Fouad Pervez, Zacc Ritter, Peter Rozic, Meir Walters, Michael Weintraub, and Sarah Yerkes.

I would like to acknowledge the valuable comments and suggestions this project received at various seminars and workshops. These commenters include Alex Blackman, Lisa Blaydes, and Steve Stedman at the 2015 CDDRL research seminar series, Jennifer McCoy and Murat Sommers at the 2016 "Polarized Polities Workshop," and Steven Brooke, Nathan Brown, Marc Lynch, Elizabeth Nugent, and Jillian Schwedler at the Project on Middle East Political Science's 2016 workshop entitled "Evolving Methodologies in the Study of Islamist Politics." I would also like to extend my thanks to Kate

Wahl and Sean Yom for generously sharing their thoughtful feedback on my book proposal in its earliest stages.

I would like to acknowledge the many individuals who supported my research during my fieldwork in Egypt. Sadly, many of them have since passed away, in a few notable cases because of the reprehensible medical negligence they experienced as prisoners of conscience. Others remain behind bars under inhumane conditions, solely for voicing opinions that unsettled the fragile egos of those ruling over the country.

I am immensely grateful to the following individuals for going beyond the call of duty in supporting my research in Egypt: Fouad Allam, Kotb El-Araby, Abdel-Hamid Barakat, Farag Al-Durry, Hany Enan, the late Kamal El-Ganzoury, Talaat Hammad, Ismail Hassan, Magdy Hussein, Mohamed Farag, Mostafa El-Feki, Abul-Ela Madi, the late Mahmoud Mohamed, the late Khaled Mohieddin, the late Mohamed Morsi, the late Mohamed Mounir, the late Mustafa Abdel-Qader, Mamduh Qenawy, Samir Ragab, the late Rifaat El-Said, Abdel-Hafiz El-Sawi, the late Shawki El-Sayyid, and Essam Sultan.

I would also like to acknowledge all individuals who shared ideas or insights that contributed to my research, including Mahmoud Abaza, Khaled Abd El-Hameed, Mounir Fakhri Abdel-Nour, Abdel-Moneim Aboul-Fotouh, Gamal Abu-Zekry, the late Ahmed Kamal Abul-Magd, Abdel-Reheem Aly, Zakariya Azmi, the late Essam El-Erian, the late El-Badri Farghali, the late Samir Fayyad, the late Nomaan Gomaa, the late Ahmed El-Gweily, Kamal Habib, the late Mostafa Hussein, the late Abdel-Ghaffar Shokr, the late Wahid Al-Uqsory, Magdy Qurqur, Fatma Ramadan, Khalid Tallima, the late Abbas El-Tarabili, and the late Yousef Wali.

While in the field, I benefited from the generosity of a very welcoming community of Egyptian academics, who have graciously shared their expertise and advice with me, including the late Mona Abaza, Samer Atallah, Gehad Auda, Samiha Fawzy, Salwa Sharawi Gomaa, Aly Eddin Helal, Mustapha Kamel Al-Sayyid, Amr El-Shobaki, and Dina Shehata.

I am enormously grateful to Sami Sharaf and Yahia Al-Shaer for facilitating my access to the electronic version of Sami Sharaf's memoirs and for all the valuable insights they thoughtfully shared with me.

I would like to recognize the wealth of knowledge Belal Fadl generously bestowed upon me in our various conversations about Egyptian politics and journalism. His deep, encyclopedic knowledge often revealed important nuances that greatly sharpened my understanding of issues central to this study.

Executing my ambitious research plan would have proved impossible without the support and assistance of Mamdouh Abbas and Aly Al-Qammash. This book is in large part the product of their vast generosity. I am also grateful to Ibrahim Hafiz and the late Mohamed Sehsah for their assistance while I conducted research for this project in Cairo. I also extend my thanks to Kaylan Geiger and the late DeWalt Stewart for proofreading an earlier version of this manuscript.

The final chapter of this book benefited from knowledge I gained from the 2011–2012 *Jadaliyya-Ahram Online* joint project entitled "Egypt Elections Watch." I must acknowledge the many insights I learned from my incredible project coleaders: Fouad Mansour, Dina Samak, the late Hani Shukrallah, Mohamed Waked, and project manager Mary Mourad Shenouda, as well as from the project's amazing team of researchers, including Mahienour El-Massry, Osman El-Sharnoubi, Salma Shukrallah, Sherif Tarek, and Lilian Wagdy.

Much of my understanding of the nuances of Egyptian politics was informed by the exchanges and conversations I had in the field with fellow academics, researchers, journalists, writers, and analysts. These include Zeinab Abul-Magd, Holger Albrecht, Amro Ali, Omar Ashour, Lina Attalah, Ahmed Badawi, Dina Bishara, Karim Ennarah, Wael Eskandar, Mohammed Ezzeldin, Mohamed Gad, Wael Gamal, Mostafa Hefny, Ibrahim El Houdaiby, Dina Hussein, Salma Hussein, Tim Kaldes, Nada El-Kouny, Heba Morayef, Marten Pettersson, Aly El-Raggal, Philip Rizk, Ahmed Shokr, and Julia Simon.

This project also benefited from intellectual engagement with the North American and European communities of Egypt scholars and researchers, including Paul Amar, Khalil al-Anani, Jason Brownlee, the late Ellis Goldberg, Hanan Hammad, Amr Hamzawy, H. A. Hellyer, Marc Lynch, Abdel-Rahman Mansour, Tarek Masoud, Nancy Okail, and Robert Springborg. I must also thank my fellow participants at Georgetown University's 2013 "Egyptian Revolution Working Group," including Holger Albrecht, Mona Atia, Dina Bishara, Nathan Brown, Elliott Colla, Matthew Hall, Adel Iskandar, Mohamed El-Menshawy, Ahmed Morsy, Paul Sedra, Heba Shams, Samer Shehata, Diane Singerman, Joshua Stacher, and Alanna Van Antwerp.

Finishing this project would have been impossible if not for my supportive colleagues at Stanford University, especially Ayça Alemdaroğlu, Joel Beinin, Lisa Blaydes, Amr Hamzawy, Burçak Keskin Kozat, Didi Kuo, and Kharis Templeman. I am equally grateful to my fellow coeditors and teammates at *Jadaliyya*, whose assuring and encouraging words helped me endure the long writing phase of this project, especially Ziad Abu-Rish, Muriam Haleh Davis, Bassam Haddad, and Sherene Seikaly.

During the various stages of writing this book I was consistently uplifted by an incredible network of caring and empathetic friends, most of whom probably hope I never speak of this book again. They include Mark Baller, Lindsey Hincks, Mythri Jegathesan, Ally and Todd Mortensen, Dena Takruri, Jill Tanem, and many more.

I am tremendously grateful for the support I received from family members during my fieldwork in Egypt, especially the late Sanaa Sallam and Rawhiyya Eteiba. Here in the United States, I am indebted to my brothers Tamer and Karim and my sisters-in-law Tannaz and Jocelyn for their never-ending stream of love and encouragement. Above all, I must acknowledge the support of my parents: Ismail Sallam and Wafia Eteiba. Words could not possibly convey the sacrifices they have made so I could pursue my self-indulgent scholarly passions—including this modest book—while seeking nothing in return but my happiness and self-fulfillment.

My greatest thanks go to my partner and closest friend Mari Fukutomi, who calmly and bravely endured the years-long emotional toll this project imposed on our lives and made me feel both loved and cared for throughout the process.

My final words go to Aidan, Laila, Adam, and Noah. By the time you are old enough to read this book, I hope that the somber stories it tells will have reached a happier conclusion—one that involves an inclusive Egypt that embraces and cares for all its people equally without exception; that has an abundance of "bread, freedom, and social justice"; and that makes you feel even prouder of being Egyptian.

Hesham Sallam
Stanford, California, September 28, 2021

A Note on Transliteration

My Arabic transliterations are based on a modified version of the *International Journal for Middle East Studies* (*IJMES*) system, while omitting diacritics, except for the *ayn* (denoted as ʿ) and *hamza* (denoted as ʾ). Arabic names of individuals and organizations appearing in the text generally follow the conventional spellings used in the English language press. As a result, the same name may appear in different spellings, depending on the identity of the person under discussion (e.g., *Osman* Ahmed *Osman* versus Mohamed *Othman* Ismail). Also, the Arabic letter *jim* is often transliterated as "g" in Egyptian names, per the Cairene dialect (e.g., Gamal as opposed to Jamal). Names of organizations are sometimes transliterated from Arabic contractions and abbreviations instead of the full, translated English-language names (e.g., Hadeto, as opposed to Democratic Movement for National Liberation; or Al-Tagammu rather than the Nationalist Progressive Unionist Rally Party).

Classless Politics

Introduction

More Identity, Less Class: Paths to Classless Politics

A meeting was scheduled to begin at the ruins of the Egyptian left in downtown Cairo in July 2010. Within these ruins, otherwise known as Al-Tagammu Party headquarters,[1] I was hoping to find some clues as to how an opposition party that was a thorn in the side of Anwar Al-Sadat throughout the 1970s eventually turned into little more than a state-sponsored prison designed to encapsulate and contain leftist political activism.[2] The strange irony is that Al-Tagammu's decline coincided with the height of economic liberalization, a process through which the state was retreating from its commitments to protect social and economic rights. Yet, as these changes were taking place, the field of opposition politics was dominated not by the traditional advocate of these rights (i.e., the left) but by the Muslim Brotherhood, which brought a different set of priorities to the political stage.

Khaled's Portrait

The huge portrait of a smiling Khaled Mohieddin hanging in the conference room stood as a constant reminder for visitors of Al-Tagammu's political lineage. Mohieddin, who cofounded the party in the 1970s, was once a member of the Free Officers movement that deposed the monarchy in 1952 and paved the way for Gamal Abdel-Nasser's formal acquisition of power two years later. Mohieddin was known to many as the Red Major,[3] a reference to his strong leftist leanings and ties to underground communist organizations before 1952.[4] Although initially opposed to Abdel-Nasser's ascent in 1954 and the Free Officers' repressive tactics, Mohieddin eventually made an uneasy peace with Nasser and assumed high-ranking positions in the state-owned press and the ruling Arab Socialist Union (ASU).

In many ways, Al-Tagammu, as led by Mohieddin, was home to an important protagonist in the story of modern Egyptian politics. Once a significant player in Nasser's ruling coalition, this powerful leftist current was eventually marginalized and captured inside Al-Tagammu. Many scholars assert that post-independence regimes in the Arab region were based on an authoritarian bargain. According to this argument, Arab populations tolerated their rulers' restrictions on political rights in return for state-sponsored economic and social benefits.[5] In the context of Egypt, Mohieddin and his party symbolized those who reluctantly accepted Nasser's crackdown on political freedoms and whom the late president was only able to win over through a commitment to redistribution and the protection of social and economic rights. Unsurprisingly, that political community was largely alienated after Nasser's death, as Egypt's economy was steered away from "state socialism"[6] and toward a free-market orientation, accompanied by modest openings in the political arena.

On a certain level, Mohieddin and Al-Tagammu epitomized the burden inherited by Nasser's successor, Anwar Al-Sadat. The new president's policies—effectively, a withdrawal from the state's commitments to the economic tenets of Nasserism and the redistributive initiatives they once promised—constituted a rejection of this burden. The conception of Al-Tagammu as Sadat's inherited burden is reinforced not only by Mohieddin's former association with the late president but also by the fact that Al-Tagammu was, in effect, a splinter party from Nasser's ASU.[7] Al-Tagammu housed, among others, a large community of leftist leaders and activists from the ASU, whom Sadat abandoned following the political housecleaning of the ruling coalition that he implemented shortly after assuming power.

Nasser's orphans within the Al-Tagammu Party, along with other leftists, did in fact fight back against Sadat and his successor Hosni Mubarak. In particular, they protested the breakdown of the so-called authoritarian bargain, as the Egyptian state was no longer able to support the distributive schemes that once justified its chronic transgressions against political rights. For more than a decade, Al-Tagammu came to represent an important voice inside the opposition and a formidable opponent to the economic liberalization measures the Egyptian state adopted during the 1970s and 1980s.

Two decades later, Al-Tagammu became one of the most notable members of the loyal opposition under Mubarak's rule. In the early 1990s, party leader Rifaat Al-Said coined the term *al-asquf al-munkhafidah* ("lowered ceilings") to summarize Al-Tagammu's new, pragmatic orientation toward the regime and its retreats from supporting antisystem popular mobilization.[8] For almost two decades its coopted leaders silenced antiregime voices among its activists and crushed them under its lowered ceilings on the grounds that the party's major battle was with its ideological adversaries within the Islamist opposition and not with the ruling party. Khaled Mohieddin's Al-Tagammu Party, which Sadat lost in the 1970s, was back under the regime's influence.

The rapprochement between Al-Tagammu and the ruling establishment spoke to broader transformations occurring in Egyptian politics during Sadat and Mubarak's rule as a result of the deepening of Islamist groups' engagement in politics. The ideological rivalries and culture wars between Islamist and leftist groups brought the latter closer to a regime they had once opposed, even at times when the government's economic policies were inimical to their professed mission. The story of these transformations is also the story of the ruling party's ability to sustain its rule despite its failure to deliver on the long-standing authoritarian bargain that began to disintegrate in the 1970s. In other words, this story is about how the regime turned itself into an indispensable arbiter of social conflict.

The immediate objective of this study is to theorize the determinants of Islamist groups' entry into formal political life[9] and examine how their participation shapes the politics of neoliberal economic reforms[10] under authoritarianism. Specifically, the book addresses two related questions: Why do autocrats provide Islamist groups political space? And, once they do, how does the participation of Islamists in politics affect opposition to economic liberalization schemes? To answer these questions, the study relies on the post-1970 political history of Egypt.[11] Its findings, however, are relevant to more than just the Egyptian context.

"More Identity, Less Class": Global Perspectives

At its core, Al-Tagammu's story is part of a global phenomenon: the waning of class conflict from national politics in the face of religious revival, ethno-nationalism, and culture wars—that is, the story of "more identity, less class."[12] As a traditional representative of class-based demands, the left, unsurprisingly, was among the first casualties of this transformation. In recent decades, leftist parties struggled to maintain their relevance and vitality as issues of national identity, immigration, and religious pluralism increasingly shaped the contours of national political debates. In Europe, Sheri Berman writes, identity politics, or "the politics of recognition," have sidelined "the politics of redistribution," to the detriment of center-left parties.[13] Writing in 2018, Francis Fukuyama finds that class-based left-wing parties throughout the world have lost ground to nationalist and religious parties as primary interlocutors of political conflict.[14]

Such trends have challenged scholars and observers struggling to understand how leftist parties and class-based voting are on the decline at a time when economic disparities have grown considerably, especially in advanced industrial countries.[15] With the advent of the Great Recession of 2007–2009 and the resulting proliferation of economic grievances, one would have intuitively expected to witness an expanding role for leftist parties, class politics, and advocates of the welfare state and social protections. Instead, the result was the rise of "right-wing populist nationalist forces across many parts of the developed world," notably at the expense of the left.[16] Nowhere was the drift toward right-wing populism more shocking than in the United States, where the victory of Donald Trump in the 2016 presidential election inaugurated an era of white nationalism and increasing polarization around issues of race and immigration.

These trends have motivated scholarly interest in investigating the roots of right-wing populism,[17] particularly how it managed to rise to prominence in a period of economic decline conventionally viewed as political prime time for leftist mobilization. Many posited answers focus on the transformations that the left underwent in advanced industrial democracies in recent decades, experiences that drove many of its former supporters to the extreme right. Ronald Inglehart and Pippa Norris present the resurgence of right-wing populism as a backlash against the left's recent turn to postmaterialism, or its prioritization of nonmaterial concerns pertaining to such issues as personal autonomy, environmental protection, and gender equality. "The new non-economic issues intro-duced by Postmaterialists," they explain, "overshadowed the classic Left-Right economic issues, drawing attention away from redistribution to cultural issues."[18] Within that political climate, they continue, extreme right-wing movements have been able to capitalize on widespread "anxi-ety that pervasive cultural changes and an influx of foreigners are eroding the cultural norms one knew since childhood."[19]

Also emphasizing the decline of the left in recent decades, Berman argues that right-wing populism is the symptom of the left's failure to offer clear solutions to socioeconomic problems in advanced industrial democracies.[20] Since the 1990s, she argues, traditional leftist political leaders have come to embrace neoliberal economics in ways that made them virtually indistinguishable from right-wing parties on questions of redistribution and social protections. In the absence of clear alternatives on economic policies among mainstream parties, issues like immigration and the threat of cultural encroachment, which tend to dominate the platforms of the extreme right, became front and center in national poli-tics. The increasing prominence of such concerns has allowed populist right-wing parties to credibly claim that they present "the real alterna-tive to the status quo, thereby increasingly becoming the choice of those dissatisfied with it."[21]

Analyses of public support for populist right-wing parties in Europe show that the diminishing salience of redistributive issues is indeed a key element in their electoral success stories.[22] Significantly, the primacy of identity and culture over the economy enabled populist right parties to draw support from an unlikely demographic—working-class voters with economic interests that do not necessarily align with such parties.[23]

The rising emphasis on immigration and threats to national iden-tity, moreover, has made it possible for extreme right parties to capture support from voting blocs with varying, if not contradictory, economic preferences, such as blue-collar workers and small-business owners.[24] The diversity of economic interests within right-wing populism's vot-ing blocs has brought renewed attention to long-standing claims that culture wars disrupt economic coalitions by compelling people to vote against their own economic interests.[25] Outside of Western democracies, the idea that identity politics can disrupt economic voting blocs and create new dynamics of competition that sideline economic affairs finds similar resonance.[26]

To recap, relevant global trends in recent decades have coalesced around a clear narrative: class politics and leftist parties are in decline at a time when mounting inequality and economic grievances suggest they "should" be on the ascendance. Meanwhile, identity politics are on the rise, albeit under different subheadings depending on the local and regional context: ethno-nationalism, right-wing populism, ethnic polarization, religious revival, and culture wars. Analyses seem to suggest that the two developments—decline in class politics and rise of identity politics—are intertwined.[27] The failures of the left may help us understand why advocates of identity politics have risen to prominence in recent decades. In turn, the effects and dynamics of identity politics may offer insight into why markers of class politics have declined in relevance. These two developments, moreover, are happening against the backdrop of important structural changes and exogenous shocks. These include economic downturns, regional integration, immigration, cultural change, globalization, and increasing pressures, especially from international financial institutions (IFIs), to adopt neoliberal economic policies or reforms.

That broader narrative, however, omits some critical questions that warrant a pause and contemplation. The first concerns the boundaries between structural factors and human choice. For instance, some theories attribute identity politics' apparent subsuming of class conflict to strategies and choices that political parties and elites adopt in response to crises, structural conditions, and outside pressures. Yet, as it stands, the dominant narrative is largely devoid of specific examples of such choices or of the process by which they are made. The causal mechanisms at the individual level are, for the most part, obscure. Therein lies one of the important contributions of this book. It offers detailed, micro-level insight into how the rise of identity politics and culture wars has sidelined redistributive agendas commonly associated with class-informed politics. It gives readers a chance to identify the individual protagonists in this story, along with the choices and significant junctures that gave rise to this phenomenon, albeit in a specific context. By doing so, this work delineates the boundaries between the structural conditions and the individual choices that gave way to the politics of "more identity, less class."

To be clear, the book does not offer a generalizable argument about the interplay between class-based demands and identity conflicts, nor does it embrace the assumption that such a theory can exist. It is, after all, first and foremost a book about Egypt that is by no means oriented toward grand theorization. In advancing the story of Egypt with all its fascinating idiosyncrasies and contextual peculiarities, the book aspires to build an understanding of one possible path leading to an outcome of "more identity, less class."[28] In doing so, it broadens the horizons of the discussion on the interplay between identity and class in national politics. Such discussions have been largely confined to democratic contexts, wherein electoral contests and unencumbered multiparty politics define the terms and scope of analysis. This book expands that discussion to include nondemocratic settings, where political contestation is expressed in less conventional forms and sites and where the politics of redistribution are fought in distinct policy spheres.[29]

In moving the discussion to nondemocratic contexts, the book offers an alternative viewpoint to election-centric theories that simplify the interplay between class and identity to the problem of the "duped voter" making choices against his/her own objective material self-interest. This line of hyper-rationalist reasoning fails to engage adequately with structural factors and institutional legacies shaping how politics evolves in relationship to identity and economic social conflicts. The story, this book shows, is less about Islamists duping voters and more about how regime survival strategies—as well as the structural pressures that inform them—contribute to a type of politics that has given political Islam the upper hand. Put simply, we learn from this study that narratives emphasizing the clouding of a voter's perception overly simplify the structural and institutional factors at play. Such narratives also flatten the complex interplay between identity and class in the experiences of various political actors, reducing the tension between the two to a simple trade-off as opposed to an interaction in which identity modifies and remolds class-based demands.

Logically, at this point, the reader might wonder, how does the global story of "more identity, less class" map out in the context of Egypt?

Egypt's Road to "More Identity, Less Class": Economic Liberalization, Islamist Ascendancy, and Leftist Decline

FOOTING REDA'S BILL

The 1993–1994 Egyptian national football season proved to be a memorable one, leaving spectators from all walks of life in shock. Nothing was exceptionally remarkable about the tournament itself. As expected, the championship title went to one of the wealthiest teams in the country, Al-Ahly, as it did the following six seasons. Still, something was unforgettable about that particular season. Months before the opening game, news media reported that longtime Zamalek Club midfielder Reda Abdel-Aal was preparing to put on the famous red jersey and start playing for Al-Ahly. Indeed, it was quite unusual for a player to switch allegiance from one of these two Cairene teams to the other, particularly given the historic rivalry between them. But what was more jaw-dropping was the inordinate cost of the deal: 625,000 Egyptian pounds. This cost came at a time when no football player had ever made more than 45,000 pounds annually. Unaware that any of their fellow citizens was wealthy enough to make such a transaction, most Egyptians were astonished. Slowly but surely, they were coming to terms with the extent of the social transformations and imbalances that swept the country as a result of the economic trajectory Egypt had embarked on in the 1970s. Sponsoring the Abdel-Aal deal, it was rumored, was a business tycoon whose family managed to accumulate a huge fortune in the wake of state-led economic liberalization in the prior decades.

In the mid-1970s, the government of Anwar Al-Sadat pursued economic liberalization policies under the heading of *infitah* ("opening"), which aimed to overcome deepening fiscal and economic crises by attracting foreign investments.[30] The emergence of these policies spoke to shifts inside the ruling coalition in response to poor economic performance, military defeats, and changing international alliances. These developments empowered advocates and would-be beneficiaries of economic liberalization inside the ruling establishment, setting the political conditions for infitah.

In practice, however, the lifting of restrictions on investments and imports failed to draw foreign capital into productive sectors and instead created opportunities for an enterprising few to make quick profits in construction, trade, and imports.[31] Thus, during that period, Egypt witnessed the rise of a new cadre of wealthy business people who enjoyed ties to previously powerful landowners and influential bureaucrats. With it grew visible displays of wealth rarely seen in prior decades.

Footing the bill for the cost of these transformations was a host of social forces that lost a great deal as a consequence of these reforms. Among them were state employees who, as fixed-income earners, now had to struggle to make ends meet for their families in the face of rising prices. More was at stake for those who worked at state-owned enterprises, whose once-protected rights now came under threat. Significantly for them, Sadat's policies waived labor protection codes for foreign investors if they entered into joint ventures with state enterprises.[32] Additional risks loomed large for these employees as the future of the public sector as a whole became uncertain. Although infitah was not explicitly aimed at dissolving the public sector, it effectively constrained its profitability.[33] That simply made state-owned enterprises all the more vulnerable to the chorus of elites who were cheering on the government to dismantle the allegedly costly and unprofitable public sector. Also losing from economic liberalization were small tenant farmers, who, under Sadat's reforms, lost Nasser-era protections against evictions.

Sadat's path of liberalization reversed many of the distributive commitments the state had taken on during the reign of Nasser and was gradually eroding the government's role as the guarantor of social and economic rights. The pushback from aggrieved stakeholders was apparent throughout the 1970s, most memorably in January 1977, when price increases, prompted by International Monetary Fund (IMF) pressures to slash subsidies, provoked a popular uprising.

Sadat's assassination in 1981 and the transition to the Mubarak presidency brought to power a new leadership that sought to slow down the pace of reform and limit its scope in large part to avert an encore of 1977. Mubarak pledged to direct infitah away from consumption and toward productive sectors, placed limits on imports, and vowed to protect the public sector from privatization.[34] Yet, as the pressures for reform mounted during Mubarak's first decade in office, the government scrambled to address rising unemployment and inflation.[35] With sources of rents dwindling by the mid-1980s, the government cut subsidy spending and resorted to "inflation tax" measures.[36] In a desperate attempt to limit employment in the public sector, the government also modified its guaranteed employment program to prolong the waiting period for college graduates seeking state jobs.[37] Unable to service its debt and unwilling to succumb to IMF pressures to lift energy subsidies and trade barriers and limit state spending, Egypt was at a serious impasse by late 1980s.[38] It emerged from that crisis miraculously.

In return for its support for the U.S.-led coalition in the first Gulf War in 1990, Washington and its allies forgave half of Egypt's debts.[39] Debt relief, however, came at a price: enacting the same economic reform measures the government had been averting for decades. Thus, in 1991, Egypt signed an agreement with the IMF committing to privatizing public sector enterprises, reducing government spending, and cutting subsidies.[40] A subsequent agreement was signed in 1993, initiating even more contentious reforms, including the removal of rent controls.[41] This was an important inflection point, as it marked the beginning of an era that witnessed serious economic liberalization and a clear-cut departure from the distributive commitments the state had assumed during the Nasser era. Thus, the state adopted policy objectives that seemed unthinkable decades prior: letting go of large swaths of the public sector,[42] slashing subsidies,[43] raising prices,[44] and removing social protections, such as rent controls.[45] These changes laid the groundwork for a more aggressive series of economic liberalization measures that were enacted in the 2000s under the leadership of a cabinet more closely linked to business and more ideologically committed to the neoliberal foundations rationalizing these reforms.[46] As the state was bracing to reorient the economy away from the traditional priorities of safeguarding social and economic rights, how did the political opposition react?

"OVER HERE, MAHMOUD"

"Mahmoud? What is this, Mahmoud?" This seemingly innocuous phrase made headlines in Egypt, becoming the subject of controversy in parliament just as the country's 1990s experiment with economic liberalization was about to take off. Bringing that phrase to fame was a furniture store commercial in which a woman, presumably astonished at the quality of the store's products, asks her companion repeatedly: "Mahmoud? What is this, Mahmoud?" For some legislators, however, the phrase and the playful tone in which it was uttered rendered the ad unsuitable for family viewing, because it allegedly evoked a sexual innuendo. Thus, given its "inappropriate" undertones, some legislators stood in the parliamentary chamber demanding that the commercial be taken off the air. This memorable incident captured the extent to which state media and cultural institutions had become a defining battleground in Egyptian politics, creating a space in which to contest the identity of the state in relation to Islam and to define the appropriate role of government in regulating public morality in accordance with Islamic values.

Setting the tone for that incident was a series of 1980s political debates propelled by the Muslim Brotherhood as the organization's public profile and engagement in parliamentary life expanded. By the early 1990s, the question of national identity, and the culture wars it encompassed, came to dominate the political scene. Meanwhile, the leftist coalition that once pushed back against economic liberalization under Sadat took a backseat to the Muslim Brotherhood as the most prominent voice of oppositionist politics. The identity conflicts Islamists brought to the political arena had significant implications for the evolution of the left. They shifted the focus of leftist politicians from advocating a just redistribution of wealth to protecting religious pluralism and equal citizenship from the perceived threat of the Islamist agenda. That is, just as the state was reneging on its distributive commitments, significant parts of the Egyptian left morphed into a "cultural left" with a nominal resemblance to Europe's so-called postmaterialist left.[47] Put simply, Egypt had arrived at the politics of "more identity, less class" well before it became a fashionable subject of inquiry.

When we examine how this happened, it is tempting to frame the rise of "more identity, less class" in Egypt exclusively within the shortcomings of the left and its failure to channel and amplify class-based demands. As many observers of Egypt would say, if only leftist activists would overcome their elitism, ideological self-righteousness, and detachment from the "masses" to put some honest work into organizing themselves, they would have fared much better in electoral contests with Islamists. This discourse became especially popular in the aftermath of Mubarak's downfall, when the left repeatedly failed to overcome the Muslim Brotherhood's dominance in successive elections. Certainly, the left's growing stagnancy is a key chapter in this story, as scholars of advanced industrial democracies have suggested in their research on the rise of culture wars at the expense of class-conscious politics. Yet, in the context of Egypt, the internal deterioration of the left is in no way the starting point of the story. This is exactly where the Egyptian experience offers new theoretical insight on the processes by which identity wars have come to overpower class politics in the contemporary moment. In Egypt, the so-called failure of the left is a symptom of a broader process of transformation, in which state responses to pressures for economic reform have created winners and losers among economic stakeholders and political actors alike.

It is pertinent that economic liberalization was not the only endeavor Sadat pursued in the 1970s. In parallel, he opened political space to Islamist leaders and activists in an attempt to counteract leftist opponents of his economic reforms. That political space, as this book explains, afforded Islamist currents the opportunity to organize politically, elevate their position, and expand their networks in important social spheres. It was in that environment that the Muslim Brotherhood, following decades of exclusion and state repression, reemerged on the political scene as an influential, autonomous organization that was not beholden to the regime's largesse. During that same formative period, the left remained marginalized and constrained under an overbearing legal framework that undermined its autonomy and its ability to forge meaningful ties with the very same stakeholders that lost privileges and rights because of economic liberalization. The conflicts over state identity that rose to prominence in the wake of Islamists' political ascendancy under Sadat, moreover, sidelined demands for redistribution, created divisions within the left, and pushed many of its activists to the embrace of the ruling party. These dynamics, in the long run, materialized into "more identity, less class."[48] And just as the state was about to pull the trigger on privatization, subsidy cuts, price hikes, and such, the leadership of the Egyptian left was looking the other way.

Thus, Egypt's experience teaches us that the pressures that generate the impetus for adopting neoliberal economic policies are also the same pressures that push political leaders and elites to empower advocates of identity politics. Put simply, neoliberalization is implicated in Egypt's road to "more identity, less class."[49] The findings of this study, therefore, leave us pondering the idea that the correspondence between the neoliberal moment—when principles of neoclassical economics became a dominant force in defining the orientation of Western economies and the blueprints of IFIs for emerging economies—and the global surge in identity conflicts at the expense of class politics is anything but coincidental.

In short, understanding Egypt's road to "more identity, less class" motivates this book's interest in examining the interplay between the pressures for economic liberalization in the country and the state's orientation toward Islamists' participation in politics. This interest is also reflected in the theoretical questions framing this study, as the following section explains.

Islamist Movements and the Politics of Economic Liberalization

Two questions are at the heart of understanding how Egypt arrived at "more identity, less class": Why do some autocrats allow Islamist groups entry into political life, whereas others choose to exclude them? And, once Islamists are granted political space, how does their participation in politics affect opposition to economic liberalization schemes?

The first question speaks to the field's long-standing interest in the roots of political Islam and its emergence as a dominant force in the Arab world. A well-known line of reasoning characterizes it as a reflection of cultural dispositions in Arab societies, such as rejecting Western modernity,[50] a perspective widely criticized as essentialist.[51] Many observers attribute the rise of Islamist politics to the ideological vacuum left by the discrediting of Arab nationalism in the wake of the 1967 Arab–Israeli War.[52] In contrast, structurally informed perspectives tie the ascendance of political Islam to widespread grievances fueled by poor economic performance and elite corruption.[53] That is, advocates of political Islam cultivate support by either offering a compelling narrative that posits Islam as the solution for the problems secular governments have failed to address or directly providing goods and services to those who have been overlooked by the state.[54]

More recent work has focused on the origins of the "Islamist advantage," asking why have Islamists scored large gains in elections, whether under authoritarianism in the 1990s and 2000s, or in the aftermath of the Arab Uprisings, notably in Egypt and Tunisia?[55] This body of literature highlights various strategies and conditions that help Islamist groups mobilize public support. First, they are persistent and never take no for an answer. Whenever shut out of formal politics, Islamists direct their outreach to less regulated social spheres, or what Carrie Wickham refers to as the "periphery" of political life.[56] Second, their outreach is carefully crafted. As Steven Brooke argues, Islamists specifically target their social services at likely supporters, while tactfully avoiding overtly transactional forms of vote-buying that could alienate middle-class voters.[57] Third, they excel at navigating the red lines. Islamists, Nathan Brown explains, seize opportunities to expand politically, but they do so in ways that avert the wrath of authoritarian rulers.[58] Fourth, they use their connections to their advantage. Their "superior embeddedness in Islamic social networks," to cite the argument of Tarek Masoud, allows them to mobilize voters more effectively than any other group.[59] Finally, they run a tight ship. As studies of the internal workings of Islamist movements show, their careful strategies of recruitment, internal organization, and ideological socialization all contribute to their efficacy as political players.[60]

This study complements these contributions by focusing on an often-overlooked question that arguably defines the opportunities Islamist movements face, shaping the prospects for their success, namely why do regimes choose to include them in political life in the first place?[61] Many acknowledge that regimes mediate the political participation of Islamists,[62] but state policy on whether to include or exclude them from political competition is rarely a primary subject of theorization.[63] This book argues that studying a regime's decision to include or exclude Islamists is important not only because it constitutes a critical precondition for their participation in politics but also, and equally significantly, because regime policies have long-term effects that can structure the political field in favor of Islamists. In other words, the so-called Islamist advantage cannot be fully understood without a systematic study of how a regime's orientation toward Islamist currents in prior decades shaped their political fortunes in the contemporary moment.

The second way this book contributes to this body of literature is by putting the Islamist experience in a systemic comparison with that of leftist currents. Such comparisons are often merely implicit in studies analyzing the Islamist advantage. When such comparisons are explicitly made, they usually focus on the left's alleged shortcomings relative to their Islamist counterparts, and they largely ignore the left's actual experience.[64] This book breaks the mold by digging deep into the history of the Egyptian left and its evolution, including the internal conflicts and ideological debates that molded its fate. In doing so, it highlights how state policies toward leftists and Islamists in prior decades have put the two currents on divergent trajectories of institutional development—trajectories that shed much light on the origins of the power asymmetries displayed in recent decades.

The second question the book addresses—how Islamist political participation affects opposition to economic liberalization policies—builds on a broader literature on the politics of economic reform. That process is conventionally thought of as a struggle between competing distributive coalitions working to advance or block reforms according to their respective economic interests.[65] In practice, as Steven Heydemann notes, the actors contesting economic reforms rarely fit into these neatly delineated coalitions.[66] Complicating that picture even further is the fact that political institutions can distort the dynamics of competition between these coalitions. For instance, scholars show that conflicts over economic reform are subject to the influence of political institutional design,[67] party systems,[68] electoral contests,[69] the structure of democratic transitions,[70] and IFI interventions.[71] Outside democratic settings, autocrats often introduce similar distortions by adjusting the pace and sequencing of reforms,[72] reconfiguring the ruling coalition,[73] modifying the rules of political contestation,[74] and buying off potential opponents.[75]

The book's analysis engages with the literature by shedding light on another important factor that also can distort competition over economic reform and, by implication, define trajectories of economic liberalization under authoritarian settings: identity politics.[76] This study elucidates how the rise of identity politics in Egypt has tempered opposition to economic liberalization policies, adding new empirical depths to our understanding of how economic liberalization manifests under Arab authoritarianism. It shows that the story of economic reform in the Arab world is more than just the story of the rise of state-allied crony capitalism[77] or the containment of labor demands by force and cooptation.[78] It is equally, as this book shows, the story of how battles over state identity have reconfigured, defused, and tamed political opposition to economic liberalization. Toward that end, the book connects discussions on the trend I have described as "more identity, less class" in advanced industrial democracies with debates on the politics of economic liberalization in the developing world.

Notably, much has been written about the specific positions and the platforms Islamist groups have adopted on economic and social policies.[79] A vast amount of literature has also been published on Islamic economics, analyzing how Islamic divine texts and traditions inform economic practices and orientations.[80] Chapter 2 of this study touches on these questions in the course of making sense of the ambiguities surrounding the Muslim Brotherhood's positions on economic liberalization, but they are not the driving interest of this study. Instead, the book focuses on how Islamists' entry into politics and the agendas they bring to the fore affect the ways economic conflicts are pursued and prioritized in national politics. Islamists' positions on economic issues are only one element of that story. After all, as chapters 2 and 5 explain, the official economic positions of the Muslim Brotherhood do not always align with its actions, and they rarely indicate the extent to which such positions are prioritized (or de-prioritized) in practice.

Finally, it is necessary to acknowledge that Egypt's experience with political liberalization since the Sadat years has been closely examined by a variety of studies and perspectives. Generally speaking, we know that the regime advanced various political openings as part of its broader survival strategy to contain dissent prompted by its destabilizing economic reform policies and to alleviate external pressures for political change. What previous scholarship has been less attentive to, however, are two critical ideas that this study brings into focus. First, the pursuit of political liberalization was deliberately structured in a discriminatory manner to empower some opposition political forces and to marginalize others.[81] This book demonstrates this argument clearly through its examination of firsthand accounts from regime insiders who were at the forefront of these so-called political liberalization initiatives. Second, the legacies of Sadat's political liberalization had an enduring impact on politics for decades to come with respect to political alignments, the content of politics, and the distribution of power among contending political forces.

The Argument in Brief

This book argues that economic liberalization and the Egyptian state's support for Islamists' political ascendancy during the 1970s were entwined.[82] Sadat's decision to open political space toward Islamist currents, or what the book describes as "Islamist incorporation" policies, was tied to the state's growing inability to adhere to the "Nasserist social pact" or the distributive commitments it took on during the Nasser era. As the state struggled to meet these expectations in the early 1970s, Sadat resorted to economic liberalization in an attempt to free the state from the role of safeguarding social and economic rights. The tide of opposition to the president's infitah policies appeared unstoppable, despite his best efforts to contain and isolate opponents of his reforms by purging the ruling coalition and enacting various political changes. Ultimately, Sadat opted to enlist the support of Islamist currents in the hope that, once they entered the political arena, they would counterbalance and marginalize leftist opponents of de-Nasserization within the student movement and elsewhere. Stated differently, Islamist incorporation was Sadat's attempt at orchestrating an escape from the costly social pact forged by his predecessor.

Reaping the benefits of Sadat's Islamist incorporation policies and the favorable conditions they created, the Muslim Brotherhood was able to reconstitute itself and reemerge as an influential political organization at a moment when its future was anything but certain. During that same formative period, communities of leftist activists confronted a much less hospitable environment for political organization, which impeded their once-promising efforts to rally under an effective, credible, organizational umbrella. That is, at the backdrop of Sadat's political responses to address pressures for economic liberalization, Islamist currents won and the left lost.

The legacies of Islamist incorporation policies, however, outlived Sadat and endured even after the ruling elite chose to reverse these measures because of rising competition between the Muslim Brotherhood and the ruling party. These legacies played themselves out in two important respects.

First, legacies of Islamist incorporation affected the politics of economic liberalization by creating a political field that was structured around identity politics to the detriment of those making distributional demands inimical to the objectives of new state-led economic reforms. The agendas that Islamist actors brought to the political stage in the wake of Islamist incorporation policies focused on contesting the religious identity of the state, thereby reducing the salience of distributional demands relative to newly emergent identity conflicts. The advent of conflicts over state identity, moreover, facilitated splits within antireform coalitions across the Islamist–secular divide, as the experience of the Socialist Labor Party demonstrates. These dynamics were evidently taking hold during the late 1980s, just as Egypt's experiment with economic liberalization was about to intensify. Put simply, right as the state was inaugurating an era of far-reaching economic liberalization, the political arena was structured in a way that largely preempted the emergence of serious opposition to these policies. By that point, Egypt was deeply ingrained in the realities of "more identity, less class."

Second, legacies of Islamist incorporation contributed to the asymmetries of power between Islamist and leftist currents—asymmetries that were most evident during moments of political liberalization, especially after Mubarak's downfall in 2011. Among the distinctive features of Sadat's Islamist incorporation policies is that they afforded the Muslim Brotherhood—and its would-be members inside the Islamist student movement—state support without compromising their organizational autonomy. That set the Islamist movement on a different trajectory from that of Egypt's communist movement and of its successors, who did not enjoy such autonomy and remained organizationally subordinate to the state as a result of two interventions. The first was Nasser's success in pressuring the communists to dissolve their parties in 1965 and take on a junior role in the ruling ASU. The second was the decision of former communists and their allies to agree to operate under the constraints of the legal–political environment, which paved the way for various forms of chronic state interference, as the experience of Al-Tagammu Party illustrates. The Muslim Brotherhood, in contrast, neither agreed to operate under the umbrella of the ruling party nor accepted the state's offers for legal status. That is, Sadat was not able to wrest from the Brotherhood what Nasser had taken from the communists in the prior decade, namely their autonomy. It is within that historical context that one can best understand the contemporary imbalances between Islamist and leftist political forces in Egypt.

In articulating the legacies of Islamist incorporation policies that were adopted in the 1970s and their impact on the structure and ideological character of political conflict in later periods, the book is informed by the tradition of historical institutionalism. That is apparent in three respects. The book's findings uphold the view that institutions, formal and informal, "constrain and refract" politics and influence outcomes even if "they are never the sole 'cause.'"[83] Its argument acknowledges the power of "critical junctures," or short moments of elevated contingency when the largely unencumbered choice of political actors generate momentous (and possibly unintended) consequences.[84] Finally, the legacies examined in this book follow the logic of "path-dependence," or "a historical sequence in which contingent events set into motion institutional patterns or event chains that have deterministic properties."[85]

Research Design, Methods, and Sources

The book develops its argument inductively based on a systematic examination of relevant historical records in a single case study, or what George and Bennett would characterize as a "heuristic case study" aimed at developing new theory and understanding casual mechanisms.[86] In layman's terms, this is a book about Egypt that tries to make useful observations about the workings of politics more generally.

Scholars have warned that case-study research could lend itself to methodological pitfalls, such as selection bias, if employed as grounds for testing and evaluating existing theories and hypotheses.[87] Put differently, some might argue that studying Egypt by itself cannot prove or disprove any theories. This book, however, is not testing any theories, but rather is developing a theory about a complex subject we do not fully understand. In scholarly terms, there is wide consensus on the advantages case-study research offers to generate new theories and hypotheses and elucidate complex causal mechanisms.[88] Given the interest of this project in theorizing inadequately studied phenomena, a single heuristic case study is a logical choice for a research design.[89]

We select Egypt, partly because it has long been at the center of salient debates—academic and nonacademic—on political Islam, democratization, and economic reform. From a methodological standpoint, Egypt exhibits variation in patterns of Islamist incorporation and exclusion over the past five decades, which facilitates our understanding of this phenomenon's origins. The fact that Islamists were deeply incorporated into political life at times and excluded at others suggests that the case has experienced "extreme values on the dependent variable" and thus offers promising opportunities for understanding the determinants of this phenomenon and the relevant causal mechanisms.[90] Egypt also has had a rich experience with economic liberalization schemes, and, therefore, it provides an ideal case for understanding the interplay between Islamist activism and the politics of economic reform.

This book's contribution is enhanced by its focus on the spoken words of political leaders, conveyed in their public statements or in firsthand accounts of private discussions and meetings. This approach provides deep insight into the conditions that shaped their major decisions and actions—actions that structured patterns of political conflict and, thereby, the developmental trajectories of opposition groups. Thus, the book relies on firsthand testimonies of political leaders and activists, including former government officials, presidential aides, security leaders, activists from various political groups, journalists, and academics.[91] The study also relies on evidence generated through analyses of a variety of primary documents, including publications, and documents produced by political parties and groups under study. Wherever relevant, each chapter explains the significance and merits of key sources and how they have informed pertinent findings. In constructing its historical narrative, this study relies on "process-tracing"[92] analysis and adopts "triangulation methods"[93] to adjudicate between competing historical narratives.

Book Outline

The rest of the book is organized as follows. Chapter 1 analyzes the context of Islamist incorporation policies and the conditions that contributed to their emergence. It examines the rise of the Nasserist social pact and the structural challenges that undermined its long-term viability and shifted the balance of power inside the ruling coalition. It describes the political and economic steps that President Sadat took to relieve the state of the costly distributive commitments it inherited from the Nasserist era. It also explains the emergence of opposition to Sadat's de-Nasserization policies in formal politics, university activism, and the labor movement. Chapter 2 describes Sadat's Islamist incorporation policies and situates them in his efforts to marginalize and counterbalance leftist opponents of de-Nasserization initiatives.

Chapters 3–5 explain the long-term implications of Islamist incorporation policies. They contrast Islamist incorporation policies under Sadat (chapter 3) with the more adversarial relationship the left had with both Sadat and his predecessor (chapter 4). Islamist incorporation policies have set leftist and Islamist political currents on two different trajectories of institutional development, in ways that have affected the long-term balance of power between the two movements. Chapter 5 examines the impact of Islamist incorporation policies on opposition politics, namely the "splitting" of proponents of redistribution across identity lines and the "crowding out" of conflicts over distribution of wealth by identity politics and culture wars. The concluding chapter recaps the major findings of the book and explains their broader implications for understanding post-Mubarak politics.

1

Inheriting Nasser's Debts
The Rise and Fall of the Nasserist Social Pact

The legacy I had inherited economically was much worse than the political one | . . .| We had, very foolishly, copied the Soviet model as we were pursuing the socialist path, even though we lacked the necessary resources, capabilities, and capital accumulation | . . .| And as a result of this model people became dependent on the state for everything: food, employment, and education. Because the state was now socialist, it had to provide to the citizen all he demanded without any active effort on his part | . . .| And this retrenchment was the beginning of our downward fall into the abyss.

—ANWAR AL-SADAT, *AL-BAHTH ʿAN AL-DHAAT*

"Oh Gamal, one who is loved by the masses, we are walking on your path," chanted Egypt's iconic singer Abdel-Halim Hafez in 1958 in praise of President Gamal Abdel-Nasser on the sixth anniversary of the July 23 Revolution of 1952. In the summer of 2010, the song seemed to follow me everywhere in Cairo.

It was rather unusual in Hosni Mubarak's Egypt for public radio to feature tracks praising former leaders. Presumably, the powers that be felt that playing songs honoring past presidents could be a veiled insult to the current one. That summer, however, someone felt the need to make an exception and give a shout-out to the new Gamal in town—the man who was desperately vying for people's support and admiration.

At the time, it was no secret that Egypt was quickly approaching the finale of the regime's years long "succession theatrical production," whose closing act would feature Hosni Mubarak handing over the presidency to his son Gamal: that is, before the army decided to go "off script" in February 2011 and forced the elder Mubarak to step down.

Still, however, something seemed rather peculiar—perhaps even distasteful—about the choice of song. The new Gamal was neither loved by the masses, nor was he taking Egypt anywhere near the path of the old Gamal. If anything, he was steering the country in the opposite direction, with a declared commitment to deepening economic liberalization in ways that inevitably would curtail the economic and social rights consecrated under Nasser's rule decades earlier.

On some level, the curious reappearance of this song embodies a goal of successive Egyptian leaders since 1970: convincing people that the state had not strayed from Nasser's path, when, in reality, it was doing everything it could to efface it. In fact, it is no exaggeration to say that post-1970 Egyptian politics is the story of a state that has scrambled to find political and economic solutions to manage the costs of the distributive commitments it acquired during the Nasserist era. It is also the story of a state unable to articulate or mobilize support for an alternative social pact that would permit it to abandon the Nasserist obligations that continue to haunt it. This predicament provides the lens through which one can identify and comprehend the major ebbs and flows of Egyptian politics over the past five decades. As this book argues, the tentative and distorted nature of the transition away from the Nasserist social pact shaped the ruling elite's strategies of Islamist incorporation.

This chapter develops a clear understanding of the major features of the Nasserist social pact, a concept central to this book's argument.[1] The first section provides a summary of the pact's economic tenets and an overview of the political context in which it arose. Specifically, it examines the emergence and institutionalization of the state's distributive responsibilities, and the concurrent appropriation of political rights and sidelining of preexisting political organizations, most notably the Muslim Brotherhood. The second section explains the economic challenges Egypt confronted during the second half of the 1960s and examines how these challenges limited the government's ability to honor the distributive commitments of the social pact. It also describes the shifting balance of power inside the ruling coalition and the impact this shift had on mounting pressures for economic liberalization. The third section recaps the political and economic steps Nasser's successor undertook to ease the burdens of the pact. As he advanced the infitah agenda, Anwar Al-Sadat enacted institutional reforms to preempt potential opposition from the pact's former beneficiaries. Nevertheless, he still faced stiff opposition to de-Nasserization policies in various political and social spheres. The final section highlights the extent to which the leftist opposition came to present a serious threat to the Sadat regime, thereby paving the way for the Islamist incorporation policies detailed in chapter 2.

The Rise of the Nasserist Social Pact, 1952–1966

THE RISE OF THE FREE OFFICERS AND THE DEVELOPMENT OF DISTRIBUTIVE COMMITMENTS

The Free Officers movement's 1952 overthrow of King Farouk I and the abolition of the monarchy in 1953 set the stage for Abdel-Nasser's rise to power and his formal ascendancy to the presidency in 1956. Proclaiming social justice as one of its major objectives, the Revolutionary Command Council (RCC), a military-controlled body that ruled between 1952 and 1954, announced a set of far-reaching land reforms.[2] Seeking to curb the influence of the landowning elite, the new law capped the amount of land a single individual could own at 200 feddans (208 acres) and 300 feddans (312 acres) for families with two or more children.[3] The law was seen as favorable to small tenant farmers, because it established rent control and made their eviction practically impossible.[4]

As private capital failed to deliver the type of economic growth and industrial expansion Egypt's new leaders were eager to see,[5] the government eventually embarked upon state-led industrialization measures.[6] In July 1956, Nasser nationalized the foreign-owned Suez Canal Company to fund the Aswan Dam project. The latter initiative was meant to help the state manage irrigation and generate hydroelectricity at levels conducive to industrialization schemes. The decision to nationalize the Canal Company happened against the backdrop of souring relations

with the West, as Egypt's deepening ties with the Eastern bloc provoked the United States to withdraw its offer to fund the Aswan Dam
initiative.[7]

Coinciding with these developments were Egypt's first efforts at central economic planning, with the establishment of the Council on National
Planning in 1955 and the initiation of an industrialization plan in 1957. By
the late 1950s, restrictions on private enterprise were prevalent. Authorities took steps to regulate the establishment, expansion, and closure of
industries, and implemented some nationalization measures with the aim
of "Egyptianizing" foreign-controlled enterprises.[8]

State involvement in the economy deepened in 1961, when Nasser
declared the start of a so-called socialist transformation. He nationalized
major import and export sectors, banks, and insurance companies, along
with hundreds of industrial and trading establishments. He also issued
laws that capped individual shareholdings in nationalized companies, limited workdays to seven hours, and mandated that companies distribute
a quarter of their profits to workers. The public sector began expanding
markedly and was tasked with 80 percent of the goals included in the 1961
five-year plan.[9]

The Nasserist era also witnessed a noticeable increase in the scope and
reach of state-sponsored social services. Nasser widened access to free
education, as part of a growing state commitment to social equity in educational opportunities that would cause mushrooming enrollment rates.[10]
Per capita state spending on education increased eightfold between 1951
and 1964, and between 1952 and Nasser's death in 1970 primary school
enrollment more than doubled. By 1970, one hundred and sixty thousand
individuals were enrolled at public universities, compared with but fifty-
one thousand at the outset of the July 23 Revolution. In 1964, the government committed to guaranteeing employment for all university and
technical institute graduates. Per capita healthcare spending more than
tripled between 1952 and 1965,[11] and the constitution of 1964 guaranteed
free health care for all Egyptians. As part of the state's effort to control
consumer goods prices, this period also witnessed a marked expansion in
state subsidization of basic goods and services, including food, water, transportation, energy, housing, and other products, such as cigarettes.[12] Real
estate rents were reduced through various government decrees between
1952 and 1961 and were placed under strict state regulation in 1962.[13]

The rapid development of these distributive commitments would set the tone for state-society relations in Egypt for decades to come, even when the state lacked the resources to deliver on its end of the bargain.

APPROPRIATION OF POLITICAL RIGHTS AND THE END OF MULTIPARTY POLITICS

The emergence of distributive social and economic policies under Nasser coincided with the state's appropriation of political rights and closure of the limited political space that had existed under the monarchy. Scholars have characterized this region-wide trend as an "authoritarian bargain," in which important social groups presumably tolerated (if not wholly accepted) limitations on political rights in return for state-provided economic and social benefits.[14]

Political party life was officially absent during the Nasser years, after the dissolution and banning of all existing parties, including Al-Wafd,[15] in 1953, and the revolutionary show trials, prison sentences, and house arrests that rendered pre-1952 political leaders impotent.[16] "The Free Officers," writes Reem Abou El-Fadl, "retained a deep-seated belief that opening up the political system would restore the *ancien régime*."[17] Nasser's policies reflected this fear. Thus, Egypt remained a one-party state until Sadat decided to resurrect multiparty life, albeit with serious limitations, in the mid-1970s.

Initially, RCC members launched the "Liberation Rally" in 1953 as a means of mobilizing political support for the policies of Egypt's new military rulers, although the structure and ideological content of the organization remained undeveloped.[18] After consolidating power and sidelining rival officers inside the RCC, Nasser announced in January 1956 a new constitution, which paved the way for his election for president that same year. The National Union (NU) became the country's de facto ruling party, providing a broad organizational umbrella for vetting and managing Egypt's new governing elite. In 1961, it was disbanded and relaunched under a new name: the Arab Socialist Union (ASU). The ASU displayed a stronger socialist bent than the NU, as its founding coincided with Egypt's nominal experiment with state socialism. Under single-party rule, the country witnessed repeated crackdowns against political dissidents, enhanced state surveillance and coercion,[19] and complete state control over the media and press.[20] The state swiftly repressed labor mobilization after the July 23 Revolution,[21] and established a monopoly over workers' represen- tation, beginning in 1957.[22]

MARGINALIZATION OF THE MUSLIM BROTHERHOOD

It was in this context that the Muslim Brotherhood, Egypt's largest Islamist movement, suffered political marginalization, resulting in its complete disappearance from public life after decades of largely open political and social activism since the group's 1928 founding. Initially, the Muslim Brotherhood was allied with the Free Officers movement in the lead-up to and in the immediate aftermath of King Farouk's ouster, and some mem- bers of the Free Officers had ties with the organization under the monar- chy.[23] After assuming power, the Officers ordered the release of imprisoned Brotherhood activists and prosecuted former security officials suspected of involvement in the 1949 assassination of the group's founder Hassan Al-Banna. In addition, the Brotherhood was the only political organization exempted from a 1953 decree dissolving political parties.

Within a year, conflict emerged between the Officers and the Brother- hood. In a dramatic turn of events, the RCC issued a statement in January 1954 announcing the dissolution of the Brotherhood, citing, among other reasons, unauthorized meetings between the group and British officials. The RCC also alleged a Brotherhood plot to overthrow the existing politi- cal system.[24] Later that same year, Nasser accused the Brotherhood of try- ing to assassinate him at a public appearance in Alexandria. Thousands of Muslim Brotherhood members were either rounded up or fled the country, and its leaders, including General Guide Hassan Al-Houdaiby, were handed death sentences, although these executions were never carried out.[25] With its senior figures in exile or serving long prison sentences, recently freed junior members of the Brotherhood made an attempt to reform the orga- nization during the late 1950s and early 1960s.[26] This initiative became known as the "Organization of 1965," and enjoyed the spiritual and intel- lectual guidance of Sayyid Qutb, an imprisoned Brotherhood member whose writings would inspire antisystem Islamist activism for decades to come.[27] Having detected these efforts in 1965, authorities launched a new wave of arrests and prosecutions against Brotherhood affiliates, includ- ing Qutb, who had been released from prison in 1964. Along with six other

Brotherhood activists, Qutb was found guilty of plotting to overthrow the regime. He was sentenced to death and executed in 1966.[28]

Some say that the Officers and the Brotherhood fell out because the Muslim Brotherhood did not take kindly to the Officers' land reform measures, weak stances against British presence in Egypt, and reluctance to implement Islamic law. The Officers, another story goes, were indignant at the Brotherhood's decision to bar its members from joining the Liberation Rally. Others say the Muslim Brotherhood fell from grace because it clashed with the Officers over which Brotherhood members could serve in government.[29]

Thus, many narratives take at face value the seemingly circumstantial character of the clash between the Officers and the Brotherhood, implying that it was the result of a random series of events or of miscommunication. Egyptian political scientist Wahid Abdel-Meguid, however, argues that the fallout between the two groups was unavoidable. As both groups were using the other to get to power, he contends, it was only a matter of time before the two parties would realize that they were pursuing the same objective and thus were locked in a zero-sum game.[30] In some ways, Abdel-Meguid's observations regarding the structural factors that led to the collapse of the Free Officers–Brotherhood alliance speak to a pattern that would recur in subsequent decades: pursuing limited strategic gains, the ruling party opens political space for the Brothers until their competition with the regime provokes a crackdown. This scenario is echoed in the events of the early 1990s, when the Muslim Brotherhood, having used the political space it enjoyed in the 1970s and 1980s to expand its representation in parliament and professional syndicates, suffered a wave of arrests and military trials. A similar pattern recurred in 2006 when Brotherhood officials were prosecuted shortly after winning enough seats in the 2005 legislative election to become the largest opposition bloc in parliament—a political victory that evidently provoked the wrath of their rivals inside the ruling party.

The Pact and Pressures for Change: 1966–1970

By the end of the first five-year plan in 1965, Egypt was entering into a period of serious economic stagnation. At that point, the state posted successive annual budget deficits without the resources to support its expanding bureaucracy and public sector, its costly social services, and its ambitious industrialization plans. State-led industrialization schemes were losing steam and growth rates were declining.[31] By then, the government had expended the resources it acquired through nationalization and was confronting low savings and investments in light of high consumer spending.[32] With exports falling behind increasing imports,[33] a balance of payments crisis ensued, resulting in the suspension of raw material imports for many public sector companies. Eventually, the government was forced to resort to external borrowing and entered into negotiations with the International Monetary Fund (IMF) in 1966. It ultimately rejected the IMF's proposed stabilization program, which mandated spending limits, price hikes, and currency devaluation.[34]

Exacerbating these conditions were regional and international developments that not only added greater strain to Egypt's fiscal crisis but also made it extremely difficult for Nasser to secure the flow of foreign aid at previous levels. By the early 1960s, Nasser had succeeded in devising a sophisticated foreign policy that exploited Cold War rivalries between the United States and the Soviet Union, increasing Egypt's leverage in relation to the two superpowers.[35] Playing the two sides against each other under the banner of "nonalignment," Nasser was able to secure aid and support from both Washington and Moscow.[36] Thus, as the Soviet Union financed the Aswan Dam project, the United States helped Egypt maintain its food subsidy system by providing cheap wheat imports through the Food for Peace program (PL-480).[37]

Geopolitical changes during the 1960s severely constrained Nasser's ability to maneuver for support from both the United States and the Soviet Union. U.S.–Egyptian relations soured as Nasser began adopting more aggressive policies toward Washington's allies, especially through his 1962 military intervention in North Yemen, which would also impose hefty costs on the state budget for years to come.[38] In 1965, the Lyndon Johnson administration reduced food aid to Egypt, and the administration eventually suspended the program completely in 1966.[39] The fall of Nikita Khrushchev in 1964 marked the end of Soviet generosity toward Egypt, and subsequent Soviet leaders were reluctant to extend further credits to the country or renegotiate its loan repayments. In fact, the Soviets now advocated the same type of fiscal responsibility championed by the IMF, a policy shift that threatened the basic tenets of the Nasserist social pact.[40]

As Nasser confronted a dire economic situation in the summer of 1967, the final blow came in the form of Israel's surprise attack against Egyptian airfields.[41] The attack ignited a multifront war, commonly known as the Third Arab–Israeli War or *Al-Naksah* ("the setback"), which ended with Israel's occupation of Egypt's Sinai Peninsula, the Gaza Strip, the West Bank, and the Syrian Golan Heights. The war left Egypt with fifteen thousand casualties, a destroyed air force, lost territories, and a humiliation that would haunt the national consciousness for years to come. The war imposed further costs on Egypt's ailing economy,[42] including massive increases in defense spending designed to rebuild the country's demolished military capacity, as well as a new defense tax on income.[43]

It may seem rather tempting to blame Nasser's economic misfortunes exclusively on hostile regional and international environments. Yet, a big part of the problem lay in the fact that Egypt was distributively overcommitted and thus was ill prepared to absorb these successive economic shocks.[44] According to Nazih Ayubi, between 1962 and 1970, Egypt's bureaucratic growth (70 percent increase in posts and 123 percent increase in salaries) exceeded the rate of growth in population, employment, and production.[45] The Nasserist social pact, moreover, tied the state to a host of competing goals that proved irreconcilable in the long run. These included catering to the new middle class's consumption needs, advancing state-led plans for developing heavy industries, promoting export-oriented production, and implementing ambitious employment drives, all without paying sufficient attention to efficiency or inflationary spending.[46]

Many observers associate the onset of economic liberalization policies in the 1970s with Nasser's successor, Anwar Al-Sadat. Yet, even before Nasser's death, the Egyptian state was considering the choices that were later adopted under Sadat.[47] As the late Ghali Shukri noted, there is no small irony in the fact that Sadat's Economic Affairs Minister Abdel-Moneim Al-Kaissouni, an advocate of the government's infamous 1977 subsidy cuts, previously proposed the identical measure under Nasser.[48]

Well before Sadat's ascent to power, the government was showing signs of unease with the costs of the public sector. In 1966, it launched a campaign under the banner "less philosophy, more production" to encourage executive managers of state-owned enterprises to promote greater "productive efficiency" within their organizations.[49] In his March 1968 statement (also known as the March 1968 Program), Nasser pledged to enhance the role of the private sector.[50] Significantly, the idea of attracting foreign capital was already under consideration at that point. According to Gouda Abdel-Khalek, Law 32/1966, allowed, at least in theory, for foreign capital to participate in public sector projects.[51] That same year, the government passed Law 51 providing for the creation, with the participation of foreign capital, of a free-trade zone in Port Said. The law, which included guarantees against nationalization, was never implemented because of the onset of the 1967 War.[52] Finally, eight months before Nasser's death, as Fouad Morsi reports, the government was considering authorizing foreign investments in limited sectors.[53] These developments indicate that the path to infitah had been under construction well before the Sadat presidency.

Meanwhile, the structural realities the state confronted in the 1960s empowered a set of regime insiders and social forces favoring the opening of the economy to private investments, even if at the expense of the public sector and its beneficiaries. And therein lay the seeds of the coalition that would later rally behind infitah and the desire to reverse the Nasserist social pact. Central to that community, as explained later, were special interests that managed to secure privileges either inside or in partnership with the Nasserist bureaucracy. These included military officers, bureaucrats, and public sector leaders who amassed wealth through their prominent positions and powerful connections. Joining them were landed elites who were able to carve out pockets of influence inside the ruling party. Some of these elements used their political networks to shield their wealth from land reforms, whereas others extracted rents through their control of local governance bodies and agricultural cooperatives. This coalition also featured a private industrial sector, which, during Nasser's final years, grew more powerful and more assertive in lobbying the state for exemptions. In construction, the rise of private sector interests happened with the full cooperation of public sector leaders, who used loopholes and corrupt practices to subcontract housing construction projects out to private companies. Similarly, private parties and traders were forging partnerships with public sector officials to circumvent restrictions on imports and exports.[54] On a more general level, Nasser tolerated the survival of some pre-1952 private capitalists, which, once the opportunity arose, jumped on the infitah bandwagon, utilizing not only their own wealth but also their long-standing ties to foreign capital.[55] Epitomizing Nasser's lenience was the experience of business tycoon and future infi-tah (and Sadat) cheerleader Osman Ahmed Osman. After the nationaliza-tion of Osman's construction company, Nasser created legal loopholes to permit Osman to continue managing his former company with an unusual amount of autonomy.[56] In short, the Nasserist establishment was already imbued with social forces vested in the economic project that would take shape under Sadat. "This is how revolution and counter-revolution coex-isted," writes Ghali Shukri.[57]

Clearing the way for these special interests was the disempowerment of those who had a strong incentive to oppose them. As detailed in chap-ter 4, Nasser pressured the communist parties into dissolving themselves and forced many of their leaders into political submission. Throughout the Nasserist era, workers were deprived of the opportunity to organize out-side of state-controlled bodies, in which they were effectively reduced to tools of the ruling party.[58]

That is all to say that the path of economic liberalization Egypt adopted during the 1970s was anything but an arbitrary blunder on the part of Sadat or purely an expression of his personal preferences. Rather, Egypt's economic trajectory in the 1970s was a choice the political leadership had been actively mulling over since Nasser's final years in office and for which many social forces inside and outside of the ruling coalition were lobby-ing. This choice was made more pressing primarily because of a structural environment in which the Nasserist social pact, along with the distributive responsibilities it entailed, was no longer sustainable. As Esmail Hosseinza-deh argues, Sadat simply "made the hard choice Nasir had postponed."[59]

The advent of economic liberalization under Sadat was part of a much broader process that reconfigured the ruling coalition and shifted the state's domestic and international alliances. Nasser's 1970 death from a heart attack came at a moment when the state was no longer able to ful-fill the distributive responsibilities it took on during the 1950s and 1960s. His abrupt demise put Egypt in a difficult position, as the ruling elite was faced with two choices. One choice, which was largely losing its appeal for reasons described next, entailed augmenting Egypt's socialist experi-ment and cultivating greater Soviet support for the exceedingly expen-sive social pact that Nasser had forged. The other choice was reorienting the economy toward free-market principles, while seeking the support of

Washington, as well as that of European and Gulf capital. The latter path required relaxing some, if not all, of the state's distributive commitments and intensifying and expanding the proefficiency initiatives that Nasser had adopted in the 1960s.[60]

Taking a middle path between the two alternatives was not an option for Sadat. With the advent of U.S.–Soviet détente in the early 1970s, Egypt had no room to reinvent Nasser's strategy of playing both sides against each other. The military stalemate in Yemen, followed by the defeat of 1967, demonstrated (and deepened) the costs of economic development under conditions of anti-imperialism, nonalignment, or any political stances deemed threatening to the United States and its conservative regional allies. These pressures shaped President Sadat's major policy changes. Attracting foreign investment required political accommodation with Western powers, which meant forging an alliance with the United States and, by implication, ceasing conflict with Israel. Turning westward also encouraged the ruling class to signal Egypt's supposed embrace of Western-style participatory, inclusive politics by erecting a façade of political liberalization. This same impulse informed Sadat's nominal shift from the ASU's single-party rule to the multiparty authoritarianism as embodied by the experience of the National Democratic Party (NDP).[61] The need for Arab capital necessitated reconciliation with Gulf monarchies, especially Saudi Arabia, which also would lay, in part, the foundation for reconciliation with Muslim Brotherhood leaders who had built political and economic relationships in the Gulf.[62] Domestically, reducing the costs of the Nasserist social pact required marginalizing the left and counterbalancing it with Islamist currents. Admittedly, the tensions between these goals arose in the late 1970s, when, for example, it became apparent that the pursuit of peace with Israel and the promotion of Islamist currents, which opposed normalization with Israel, were difficult to reconcile (see chapter 2). During the early Sadat years, however, these goals evoked the appearance of a cohesive package to the extent that they each marked, in some form, a departure from the Nasserist order.

Thus, Sadat, quite swiftly and decisively, picked the aforementioned second path, as manifested in a number of steps analyzed in greater detail in the following sections. He purged Nasserist loyalists from the top echelons of the ruling elite through the so-called 1971 Corrective Revolution. Sadat realigned Egypt's foreign policy to secure the flow of aid, investments, and other forms of support from Western countries and conservative Arab Gulf States. The president adopted economic liberalization measures that departed from, if not wholly undermined, the distributive commitments the state had assumed under Nasser. Finally, Sadat reconfigured the ruling coalition by restructuring the ASU, creating a limited multiparty system, and increasing state supervision of labor organizations.

The Corrective Revolution and Purging the Governing Elite

Not long after assuming power, Sadat ousted his political rivals within executive bodies and the ASU, collectively known as *marakiz al-quwah* ("the centers of power"). Led by Vice President Aly Sabri, Minister of Interior and ASU Secretary-General Sharawi Gomaa, and Minister of State for Presidential Affairs Sami Sharaf, the members of that camp imagined they would dominate the political scene following Nasser's death, assuming that Sadat was a weak figure who would serve as president in name only. They were mistaken, for Sadat proved to be a formidable opponent. He rebuffed their attempts to impose Gomaa as prime minister and excluded them from critical decisions, including plans to form a federation with Libya and Syria.[63] As differences between the president and marakiz al-quwah reached new heights in May 1971, Sadat made his move, mounting what came to be called the Corrective Revolution. He sacked Vice President Sabri; he then fired Gomaa, Sharaf, and their allies within the bureaucracy and the ASU and tried Sabri and his collaborators for treason.[64] Afterward, Sadat signed into law a new constitution, commonly known as the 1971 Constitution, which remained in effect, albeit with major amendments in 1980, 2005, and 2007, until Hosni Mubarak's ouster in February 2011.

Although the clash between Sadat and marakiz al-quwah cannot be reduced to a conflict over which of the two aforementioned paths Egypt would adopt, the outcome of the showdown helped resolve that particular dilemma. For one, the Corrective Revolution enabled Sadat's consolidation of power by purging the ruling elite of the Nasserist remnants opposed to his plans to reorient Egypt's economic and foreign policies. Many of the individuals who suffered Sadat's wrath in the course of the May 1971 clash were known advocates of stronger Egyptian–Soviet ties who were unlikely to abandon Egypt's "socialist" experiment without a fight. So, in some ways, the Corrective Revolution was a necessary step toward building (or imposing) a consensus on revising the country's foreign and economic policies.

From Nonalighment to the Beginning of a Special Friendship

In his early years as president, Sadat launched a charm offensive on Washington in the hope of winning over its political and economic support. For him, the United States held the key to recovering Egypt's lost territories and to rebuilding its stagnant economy. As for the Soviet Union, Sadat saw it as nothing more than a decaying superpower that had little to offer, as evidenced by Moscow's recurrent failures to deliver on his repeated requests for advanced weaponry.[65] Thus, at the beginning of his first term, Sadat signaled to U.S. officials, through formal and secret channels, his willingness to distance Egypt from the Soviet Union and to turn a new page with the United States. When Washington did not take his initial gestures seriously, Sadat reached the conclusion that the United States would not come to his aid unless he imposed a new strategic reality that compelled the Americans to reassess their support for the regional status quo. These considerations, coupled with domestic pressures to take action that would display Egypt's resolve to recover the Sinai Peninsula, provided the rationale for the October 1973 War.[66]

During the early stages of the war, Egyptian troops breached Israel's defense lines, crossing the Suez Canal into the Sinai Peninsula. Israel eventually succeeded in repelling Egypt's surprise offensive before a cease-fire came into effect. Although Israel's counterattack kept Sinai under its own control, Sadat felt that the war provided him with a political victory. The conflict did lead, eventually, to a U.S.–Egyptian rapprochement and a negotiated settlement recovering the land Egypt lost in the 1967 War.

After the war, Washington and Cairo restored diplomatic relations. The United States' mediation efforts succeeded in brokering two disengagement agreements between Egypt and Israel, one in January 1974 and another in September 1975. These talks were in some ways the stepping-stones for the U.S.-brokered peace negotiations between Egypt and

Israel that yielded a formal peace treaty between the two countries in 1979. It was in this context that Egypt began receiving a generous U.S. aid package (an average of $2 billion annually since 1979), which helped rebuild its decaying infrastructure and continues to subsidize its defense budget today.[67]

The deepening of U.S.–Egyptian relations under Sadat was part of a broader shift in Egyptian foreign policy. Cairo was moving further away from the Soviet camp and abandoned even the appearance of nonalignment, one of the hallmarks of the Nasserist era. In 1972, Sadat ordered Soviet military advisers to leave Egypt. In 1976, he abrogated the Egyptian–Soviet treaty of friendship and cooperation, which he personally signed in 1971. Subsequently, he "suspended cotton exports to the USSR, recalled all Egyptian students and military personnel engaged in studies or training in the Soviet bloc, and finally imposed a unilateral moratorium on debt repayments to Moscow."[68] As he faced strong opposition from what he believed were pro-Soviet leftists, Sadat did not hesitate to criticize the Soviet Union in his public statements. By the end of the 1970s, he was openly talking about the need to cooperate with the United States to contain the alleged Soviet threat. A month before Sadat's 1981 assassination, Cairo–Moscow relations hit rock bottom, as Sadat expelled the Soviet ambassador, six other diplomats, and one thousand Soviet technicians, "accusing them of subversive activity."[69]

Meanwhile, Sadat also enhanced Egypt's ties with conservative Arab Gulf States, especially Saudi Arabia, after two decades of rocky relations under Nasser.[70] Economically, improved relations facilitated the flow of Arab Gulf aid (about $4 billion between 1973 and 1976),[71] which, to some degree, helped the government manage its growing balance of trade deficit and mounting debts.[72] In 1976, Saudi Arabia, Kuwait, the United Arab Emirates, and Qatar formed the Gulf Organization for Development in Egypt to provide direct budgetary support to the Egyptian government.[73] As relations with Arab Gulf States improved, the flow of tourists from these countries into Egypt soared, providing an important source of revenue for its ailing economy.[74] The 1970s oil boom, moreover, encouraged many Egyptians to seek job opportunities in the oil-rich Gulf. Tarek Osman estimates that between 1974 and 1985 three million Egyptians migrated to the Arab Gulf region,[75] during a time when Egypt's population was no more than fifty million. The remittances that these workers sent back home were an important source of income for many Egyptian families, especially as the prices of basic goods were on the rise.[76] Relations with the Gulf States (and the rest of the Arab world at large) declined again in the late 1970s, however, after Sadat's attempted peace treaty with Israel failed to achieve Israel's withdrawal from other occupied territories or to safeguard Palestinian rights.

In short, after two decades of refusing to become a satellite of either the United States or the Soviet Union, Egypt's foreign policies were completely transformed into what Jason Brownlee describes as "one of the most tectonic shifts of the Cold War."[77] Sadat's new foreign policy aimed to build a strong alliance with Washington and secure Western and Gulf political and financial support.

Economic Liberalization: Relaxing the State's Distributive Commitments

Upon assuming office, Sadat tried to show that the era of state encroachment on the private sector was over, hoping that the message would attract foreign capital to Egypt.[78] Both the 1971 Constitution and Law 34[79] (issued that same year) protected private property from nationalization.[80] Additionally, the government took steps to encourage investment from Arab states through Law 65/1971,[81] and in the spring of 1973, it announced in parliament that it would open the Egyptian economy to the outside world.[82] That new orientation was spelled out in the "October Paper," which was ratified in a March 1974 national referendum and asserted the need for further reforms to attract foreign investment and technology transfers. Shortly thereafter, the president tasked Minister of Economy and Finance Abdel-Aziz Hegazy, known for his proreform leanings, to form a new government. Over the following years, the influence of figures partial to economic liberalization policies continued to grow inside the ruling establishment.[83] Prominent among these figures were Sayyid Marei, who served as minister of agriculture and speaker of parliament under Sadat, as well as Osman Ahmed Osman, who served as minister of housing. These leaders not only played a major role in solidifying the government's new economic orientation but also, as explained in chapter 2, in engineering policies of Islamist incorporation.[84]

With Egypt's rapprochement with the United States and its oil-rich Gulf neighbors underway, Sadat began adopting bolder reforms encouraging private investment. In 1974, the state allowed private individuals to represent foreign companies operating in Egypt (Law 39).[85] It also opened the door for foreign investment in almost all sectors, including banking; reduced taxes on private investments and public-private ventures (Law 43/1974);[86] and provided for the formation of free-trade zones.[87] The most contentious aspect of the new reforms was the granting of "private sector" status to public sector enterprises partnering with private investors, thereby exempting them from regulations governing state-owned enterprises. This status meant that such ventures were not subject to "labor laws, stipulation of worker representation on management boards, profit-sharing formulae, and salary ceilings applied to the public sector."[88]

Organized labor saw these moves as threats to the privileges they had secured under Nasser and an attempt by the government to institute legal loopholes that could put them at the mercy of profit-driven private investors or dissolve the public sector in its entirety.[89] Confirming such fears were subsequent measures geared toward reducing state control of public sector companies, as well as relaxing labor protections in these enterprises. For example, Decree 262/1975 and Law 111/1975 authorized the government to sell or liquidate nonprofitable public sector companies, or to put some of their assets up for private subscriptions. Law 111 gave public sector managers greater freedom in hiring and firing workers. It also allowed them to refuse Ministry of Manpower requests to hire college graduates who qualified for state-guaranteed employment. The law also abolished the General Organizations, a state body responsible for overseeing the performance of the public sector and allowed public sector firms to include private sector experts on their management boards.[90]

Many suspected that Sadat was slowly freeing himself of the obligation to act as the guardian of the public sector or the rights of the workers who staffed it, undermining the fundamentals of the Nasserist social pact. Certainly, the official position of the state at the time was that dissolving the public sector was not under consideration and that the Sadat administration was simply trying to "develop" and "modernize" the public sector.[91] By legalizing competition, taking the state out of its operations, and allowing private investments and new technology to flow into it, the argument goes, the government was giving the public sector room to grow and make profits.[92]

Yet, for insiders like former minister of trade Fouad Morsi (1972–1973), the government's position was disingenuous. He believed that those administering infitah never gave the public sector a real chance and that they had been hoping for the sector's failure and eventual privatization since day one.[93] For example, Morsi observes, as early as 1973, Sadat's allies in parliament were already compiling information on public sector companies that posted losses in prior years. The intent, Morsi contends, was to provide ammunition for those claiming that the public sector was a cash drain that needed to be dismantled.[94] Infitah policies, he argues, simply threw the public sector under the bus by forcing it to compete against the private sector on terms that guaranteed its long-term failure. Specifically, right at the outset of infitah, the government broke the public sector's monopoly on imports and on the representation of foreign companies,[95] thereby exposing it immediately to stiff competition from the private sector and reducing its chances of profitability.[96] Sure enough, only a few years into the infitah era, the data revealed public sector decline. Between 1974 and 1978, Heba Handoussa reports, the number of industrial sector state companies[97] incurring losses grew from two to nineteen (out of 104), and those making more than 20 percent profits fell from forty-one to twenty-three.[98]

Regardless of the soundness of infitah policies, the significant point is that the Sadat government was not serious about enabling the success of the public sector and was evidently maneuvering to abandon it. In fact, the minister of finance said at the time that the government was planning to sell state-owned enterprises that repeatedly posted losses on the pretense that they were unnecessary burdens on the state budget.[99] That is, the message the government was sending to the public sector was "profit or perish."[100] Given that infitah made profiting an uphill battle for these already struggling enterprises, perishing was the more likely outcome.[101] As for government pledges that state-owned companies' stocks would not be sold to private investors before being offered first to the companies' own employees, for Morsi, that was all talk because everyone knew that the average worker could never accumulate sufficient capital to buy stocks.[102] Put simply, once infitah took off, the fates of the public sector and its beneficiaries were sealed.

Meanwhile, the state advanced economic liberalization on other fronts. In 1975, the government broke the state's monopoly on the imports–exports sector through Law 118. Further trade liberalization measures were adopted through Law 97/1976, which granted Egyptian companies the right to hold and spend foreign currency without a license. It also allowed them to resort to "parallel markets" to buy foreign currency.[103] These measures opened the door for foreign currency flight, encouraged the development of black markets, and contributed to the rise of "Islamic investment companies" later on. These laws also resulted in imports being directed away from intermediary and capital goods needed for economic growth and toward consumer and luxury products, which tend to be more conducive to quick profits. More generally, by integrating Egypt into the world capitalist economy, infitah exposed the country to the volatility of international prices and made it more vulnerable to global economic downturns.[104] As the late Adel Hussein famously observed in his seminal study, Egypt's deepening relations with the Western bloc through trade, aid, and loans rendered the country's economic development exceedingly dependent on its Western allies.[105]

On the agrarian front, the government succeeded in passing some productivity measures that further weakened the land reforms Nasser had adopted, tilting the balance in favor of landowners. For instance, the government invited foreign and Egyptian investors to participate in land reclamation and in capital-intensive crops, while also trying to liberalize land rents.[106] Law 67/1975 increased rents for small-farm tenants and made it easier for landowners to evict them. The law disbanded landowner–tenant dispute committees—formed in 1966 and known to favor tenants—sending these disputes instead to the regular court system.[107] In practice, that move was detrimental to small tenant farmers, because most lacked the resources to manage complicated and costly legal challenges against wealthy landowners.[108] In 1978, Law 41 imposed additional rent increases of 20 to 25 percent.[109] These measures reinforced the impression that large landowners had garnered considerable influence inside Sadat's ruling establishment. No one conveyed that impression more than Sadat's close associate Sayyid Marei, who hailed from a wealthy landowning family and whose son was married to one of the president's daughters. Marei's alleged role in eroding the post-1952 land reforms earned him a reputation as Sadat's oppressor of humble tenant farmers. One popular chant often heard at antigovernment protests during the 1977 Bread Uprising, a massive revolt against government-increased prices, went as follows: "Sayyid Marei, who is he? He is the thief of *fellahin*."[110]

In addition to large landowners in the countryside, the aftermath of infitah saw many winners, as Samia Imam shows in her study on the evolution of Egypt's economic elite in the 1970s and 1980s. The most obvious winner was the class of traditional capitalists that had been gradually excluded from the post-1952 political order.[111] Infitah laws returned them to the economic scene, enabling them to use their access to Western capital to swiftly set up investments in the services, banking, and consumer products sectors.[112] Another set of winners was the class of bureaucratic bourgeoisie that developed and flourished under the auspices of the Nasserist state. These included ranking military and security officers, technocrats, and public sector leaders who had used their privileged positions to accumulate wealth, both legally and illegally. During infitah, well-connected members of this class captured lucrative licenses to represent foreign companies per Law 39/1974 and garnered a visible role in the external trade and construction sectors by the late 1970s. Among them was Free Officer Wagih Abaza, who became Peugeot's sole agent in Egypt in 1979.[113] Nasser's son-in-law Ashraf Marwan, who once earned a monthly salary of 50 Egyptian pounds in government service, invested more than 1 million pounds in the construction sector by 1980, according to state records.[114] The visible association of political and economic elites, as symbolized by the intermarriage between President Sadat's own family and that of Osman Ahmed Osman, enhanced public perceptions of a deepening alliance between political power and big business. Finally, beyond the gains of traditional capitalists and powerful bureaucrats, a host of other actors succeeded in exploiting the legal loopholes of infitah and their personal connections to the bureaucracy to make fortunes through illicit trade, smuggling, bribery, and commissions.[115]

The military establishment was a key beneficiary of the infitah era. In light of Egypt's peace treaty with Israel, and just as it was about to incur budget cuts, Sadat authorized the military to establish private sector enterprises. Through Presidential Decree 32/1979, Sadat formed the National Service Project Organization, which became the military's "economic arm" and the manager of its for-profit enterprises and joint ventures with the private sector.[116] Sadat is credited with giving the Ministry of Defense vast control over public lands and their allocation to private investors through Law 143/1981 and Decree 531/1981.[117] As Abdel-Fattah Barayez shows, the military was able to use its control over public lands to capture various forms of rents and generate economic returns.[118]

Public sector workers, whose employment and rights were now in question, and constantly being eroded by economic liberalization measures, topped the list of infitah losers. Also losing were university graduates who had to wait for increasingly longer periods to obtain guaranteed state employment or seek jobs in the less regulated and more unpredictable private sector.[119] Fixed-income earners, such as state employees and pension holders, low-income households, and middle-class families dependent on state price controls, all had to contend with soaring inflation, which reached unprecedented levels by the mid-1970s.[120] Permeating these realities were increasing social disparities. Between 1965 and 1976, the poorest 60 percent of the population's share of gross national income (GNI) declined from 28.7 to 19.9 percent. The middle 30 percent saw their share of GNI decline from 40.2 to 21.5 percent, whereas the wealthiest 10 percent increased their share from 31.1 to 58.1 percent.[121]

Perhaps the situation would have been different had the process of economic reform been managed in a way that broadened the base of winners by enacting the institutional changes needed to enable the growth of labor-intensive micro and small private establishments. Yet, that was not a priority in the country's long experiment with economic liberalization, as Amr Adly shows in his breakthrough study on market making in Egypt.[122]

As Egypt sought to manage the costs of these reforms, the state's position was precarious. Infitah policies failed to deliver on the promise of attracting labor-intensive productive investments or technology transfers. Instead, they steered private investments toward construction, trade, and imports—sectors in which quick profits could be reaped with relatively low risk.[123] Because of rapidly increasing imports, the state was facing a serious balance of trade deficit[124] and was drowning in debts by the mid-1970s.[125]

In the winter of 1976, Egypt sought escape from a grave financial crisis by negotiating a standby agreement with the IMF. The Fund's conditions were just as painful as the ones it had tried to impose on Nasser a decade earlier: currency devaluation, subsidy reductions, and spending cuts. What made the situation even more difficult is that creditors among oil-rich Gulf States were demanding similar conditions, and the aid they provided fell well below Sadat's declared expectation of a Gulf-sponsored Marshall Plan for rebuilding Egypt.[126] Eventually, the state caved to IMF demands, but it opted to wait until after the October 1976 legislative election to begin implementing these measures. And once they did, all hell broke loose.

Sadat's decision to lift subsidies on basic commodities was perhaps one of his boldest breaches of the Nasserist social pact. On the night of January 17, the government increased prices of "basic commodities such as sugar, tea, and bottled gas" without public notice or legislative debate, resulting in the 1977 Bread Uprising. According to Mark Cooper, the price hikes resulted in "an increase in the cost of living of roughly 15 percent for someone with an average income."[127] Nationwide protests ensued for two days until the military intervened to restore order. The 1977 Bread Uprising marked the moment at which the state had to face reality: it had failed to engineer a political framework that would enable it to abandon the distributive commitments Nasser had adopted. On a deeper level, it reflected the fragility of the Egyptian state, which, despite its mighty coercive capacity, had failed to renegotiate the terms of a social pact to which it could no longer adhere.

Housecleaning the Ruling Coalition

As it drifted away from the Nasserist social pact, the state restructured the ruling coalition by demoting advocates of the pact inside state institutions. Two relevant developments are worth highlighting. The first is the splitting of the ASU into three separate political organizations, one of which, Al-Tagammu, soon became an instrument to isolate and contain leftist elements, including former affiliates of the ASU. The second is the emergence of intrusive forms of regime control inside the state-sponsored national labor union, the Egyptian Trade Union Federation (ETUF). The regime tried to undermine opponents of economic liberalization inside the unions and to disrupt alliances between them and official opposition parties.

These trends had important, long-lasting implications for how the state-managed political arena evolved under Sadat and Mubarak. Islamist incorporation policies in the 1970s allowed disparate networks of Islamist political activists to unite and to develop meaningful organizational structures away from direct state oversight, specifically under the umbrella of the Muslim Brotherhood (see chapter 2). Meanwhile, leftist activists operating in underground groups or student unions, along with leftist leaders who were pushed out of the ruling party, were denied the political space in which to form a comparable independent organizational structure. Those who sought to influence national politics, as chapter 4 explains, confronted two unappealing alternatives. One was to join the Al-Tagammu Party and work under the serious limitations of the state-managed political arena. The other was to enter the ruling party and resign themselves to the role of a highly disadvantaged pressure group within the political apparatus. State control of national trade unions, moreover, hindered the ability of organized labor to develop meaningful institutional ties to the licensed opposition, leaving them with no option but to lobby the government from within the state-dominated ETUF or the ruling party. Put simply, Islamist currents capitalized on the political space the state had granted during the 1970s to develop organizationally, whereas the left remained fragmented, harassed, constrained by state repression and institutional manipulation, and largely isolated from its logical social bases. This historical context explicates the perplexing asymmetries in opposition politics under Hosni Mubarak: a strong Islamist current that dominates the opposition, operating alongside a weak left that lacked the capacity to do much beyond mounting short-term contentious political actions.

DISMANTLING THE ASU AND REBRANDING THE RULING PARTY

Returning to Sadat's restructuring of the ruling coalition, it is crucial to remember that the ASU was conceived at a moment when Nasser was poised to start Egypt's "socialist" experiment and expand redistributive policies. The ASU, in many respects, was predicated on the notion that it represents what was famously dubbed the "alliance of the working forces" (*itihad al-quwa al-ʿamlah*). The term denotes a broad social base that encompasses workers, *fellahin*, national capitalists, intellectuals, students, and the armed forces. One of the major functions of the ASU, at least in theory, was to contain conflict between competing social groups and to prevent any one of them from dominating the rest.[128]

Given this broader goal of containing class conflict and maintaining social peace, it is not surprising that the rise of the ASU coincided with

Nasser's efforts to coopt underground communist movements into the ruling party, as chapter 4 explains in detail. The state had imprisoned many
communist activists during the late 1950s, but it released them several
years later in an attempt to rally the left behind Egypt's so-called socialist experiment.[129] Faced with state repression and the immense popularity
of Nasser, and perhaps encouraged by his declared commitment to implementing socialist reforms and improving relations with the Soviet Union,
underground communist parties dissolved themselves by the spring of
1965. Meanwhile, many communist leaders were recruited into the ASU's
secret Vanguard Organization, and left-leaning figures assumed important
positions within the ruling party and state-controlled media.[130]

On the basis of the historical context surrounding the ASU's development, one could interpret its restructuring and eventual dissolution
under Sadat as part of a broader initiative to organize the ruling coalition
in accordance with the state's shifting social and economic priorities. In
other words, Sadat's ruling class was adjusting to the reality that it no longer served the social bases that benefited from the state's largesse under
Nasser. In fact, the official proposal for reforming the ASU explicitly justified these measures by claiming that the ruling party was now host to a
variety of competing interests.[131]

The solution that Sadat sought, however, was not forcing the parties
aggrieved by the state's new economic orientation into the arms of the
opposition. Rather it was to dismiss them from positions of influence while
keeping them isolated and contained inside state-controlled organs far
removed from channels of decision-making. Sadat wanted to appropriate
the privileges of former members of the ruling coalition, while denying
them the freedom to defect to the opposition or politicize their grievances
in ways that could challenge the regime. Yet, as explained next, the strategy proved easier said than done.

The dismantling of the ASU began with the August 1974 release of "The
Paper for Developing the Arab Socialist Union." The document consisted
of an official blueprint outlining proposals for reforming the ASU and
explaining the rationale behind these proposals. Accordingly, in July 1975,
the ASU's Third General Congress passed a resolution decreeing the formation of *manabir* ("platforms") that would represent the various currents
inside the ASU. In the spring of 1976, the ASU and parliament approved the
formation of three platforms, now renamed "organizations," representing

the right, the left, and the center. The National Progressive Unionist Rally Organization, headed by Khaled Mohieddin, became the representative of the left. The right was represented by the Liberal Socialists Organization, under the leadership of former free officer Mustafa Kamel Murad. The Egypt Arab Socialist Organization, headed by veteran police officer and Sadat's Prime Minister Mamdouh Salem, became the representative of the center. In November 1976, the president announced that each of the three organizations would become an independent political party, thereby effectively dissolving the ASU.[132] These measures also rendered the Egypt Arab Socialist Party (EASP), the de facto ruling party.[133] As the EASP's members began criticizing Sadat for holding peace talks with Israel, the president opted to form a new ruling party under his own leadership, the NDP,[134] which remained in power from 1978 to Mubarak's ouster in 2011. In retrospect, the NDP was nothing more than the old ASU rebranded with a new name. The primary difference between the two was that the NDP, unlike its predecessor, privileged the new class of state-allied capitalists that ascended in the wake of economic liberalization and marginalized the major beneficiaries of the Nasserist social pact.[135]

Replacing the ASU with the NDP was a delicate endeavor that lent itself to dissent and controversy, because it marked the reconfiguration of the ruling coalition Sadat had inherited and thus promised to create winners and losers. For this reason, Sadat, even as he worked over the course of years to dismantle the ruling party, was keen to emphasize that dissolving the ASU was not his ultimate objective and that his institutional reforms would not in any way undermine the gains of the July 23 Revolution. In reality, Sadat was doing precisely that. Yet he was eager to conceal this reality from the groups that would suffer from the political and economic adjustments the country was undergoing: the beneficiaries of the Nasserist social pact, especially public sector workers and their advocates. Unsurprisingly, therefore, the leaders of ETUF were uncharacteristically vocal in expressing their opposition to talk of dissolving the ASU and replacing it with an official multiparty system.

In response to Sadat's August 1974 paper proposing an overhaul of the ASU, as well as calls from within state-controlled media for its dissolution, ETUF leaders were defiant. Labor leaders told parliament in September that the ASU was "the only arrangement that could achieve national unity," describing calls for dissolving the ruling party as attempts to undermine the alliance of working forces. The ETUF followed up with a statement reiterating the same message, explicitly rejecting any return to multiparty politics or steps to marginalize the role of workers inside the restructured ruling party. It demanded that the formation of *manabir* inside the ASU not endanger the gains of the July 23 Revolution and that it would guarantee labor participation in setting the policies of the party, as well as ensure that no single party faction became predominant. In other words, the statement tacitly acknowledged that changes inside the ruling coalition would empower a new economic elite whose interests were at odds with those of workers.[136]

The outrage among state-controlled labor was so intense that even the pro-Sadat ETUF President Salah Gharib criticized the proposal in public. Less than a month after the proposal's publication, Gharib wrote an op-ed in *Al-ʿUmmal* warning that class conflict would be the result of any moves to dissolve the ASU or otherwise appropriate labor rights. The warning that Gharib was sending to the president, who had handpicked him for this job years earlier, was unmistakable: he would not be able to contain the wrath of workers should Sadat decide to marginalize them within the ruling coalition or toy with their privileges.[137]

When it became public knowledge that the ASU would move ahead with establishing *manabir*, the ETUF released a statement protesting the lack of deliberation surrounding the decision. It also voiced concerns that certain *manabir* had already demonstrated a lack of commitment to the public sector and its future. Ultimately, ETUF supported the establishment of *manabir* on the condition that they would not be turned into full-fledged political parties. When their worst fears were realized in 1976—Sadat declared ASU's *manabir* to be independent parties—some syndicates voiced dissent even though the ETUF was left with no choice but to formally accept the decision.[138]

GROWING STATE INTERVENTION INSIDE THE ETUF

Sadat was not blind to the explosive potential that public sector workers presented, and, as mentioned earlier, he was careful to maintain an assuring tone when attempting to allay their concerns about the possibility of dissolving the ASU and, more significantly, the public sector. At the same time, Sadat knew that it would take a lot more than just a few comforting

words to contain workers' opposition. When rising prices yielded proliferating and increasingly visible strikes and labor unrest in the 1970s, the
state adopted more intrusive management practices at the ETUF to contain expressions of dissent among workers and to disrupt any efforts to
politicize their grievances.

Under Sadat, the state normalized the practice of merging the positions
of the minister of manpower and president of ETUF, which continued to
undermine the independence of the general union.[139] Under Law 35/1976,
the Ministry of Manpower decrees had to obtain ETUF approval before
implementation. Thus, an individual serving in both offices could, as
ETUF president, ratify their own ministerial decrees without meaningful
deliberation with labor leaders.[140] In 1973, a Ministry of Manpower order
reduced the number of general syndicates to sixteen (down from twenty-
seven in 1964) in a move clearly aimed at centralizing control over organized labor.[141] Decree 757/1972 removed many of the responsibilities and
managerial tasks from the syndicates and transferred them to the Ministry
of Manpower.[142]

Shortly after taking over the post of ETUF president, Salah Gharib
moved to contain subversive elements within the labor movement and
to restrict the channels through which they could pressure the government. In 1973, Gharib ousted all the communist leaning members from the
ETUF's executive committee. He also employed a variety of legal tactics
to engineer the candidacy requirements for ETUF leadership posts so that
leftist opponents of Sadat's policies could not run for these positions.[143]
The state's intervention in ETUF affairs became further institutionalized
through Law 35/1976, which afforded the Ministry of Manpower vast discretionary power to regulate the formation and internal management of
trade unions. In 1977, in the wake of growing labor unrest, the government
passed Law 33, which gave the presidentially appointed socialist public
prosecutor the right to disqualify from trade union office elections any
candidate deemed threatening to the country's national security or social
peace.[144] Another example of the regime's efforts to control and coopt the
leadership of organized labor is Decree 352/1979, which rendered all trade
union leaders "advisers to the president" by virtue of their posts.[145]

State intervention grew even bolder when the regime sensed that dissenters inside trade unions were attempting to build alliances with opposition political parties. As Marsha Pripstein Posusney observed, by the time

platforms were formed inside the ASU, thousands of workers among organized labor joined Al-Tagammu, whereas others began voicing support for the formation of an independent workers' party. Thus, in the aftermath of the January 1977 Bread Uprising, Sadat promised to increase wages and expand the unions' involvement in deliberating relevant draft legislation on the condition that union leaders would steer workers toward support of the ruling party and not toward the opposition. It was in that context that many labor leaders cut ties with Al-Tagammu and entered the ruling party's orbit, including Ahmed Al-Amawi and Aisha Abdel-Hadi, both of whom would later serve as ministers of manpower. The state also employed intimidation and a variety of repressive tactics against unionists affiliated with the opposition, and in response, many resigned from Al-Tagammu.[146] The Sadat regime's efforts to keep organized labor as far as possible from the opposition would continue under Mubarak. For example, one Al-Tagammu official has claimed that his party used to enjoy strong support among petroleum-sector workers employed in South Sinai but that many of them left the party in the 1990s because of intimidation by authorities.[147]

In short, as the state began pursuing economic reforms threatening the rights and entitlements workers had gained under Nasser, the pressure for greater intervention in the affairs of organized labor increased. Through a variety of tactics and strategies, Sadat sought to contain opposition to the state's new economic priorities and policies and to subvert any attempt at cultivating ties between organized labor and the opposition.

The Rise of Opposition to De-Nasserization

Sadat's efforts to preempt opposition to de-Nasserization through these institutional and political strategies fell well short of that goal. As opposition to his policies reached its climax in January 1977, the regime was desperately scrambling for its own survival on the two days that came to be known as the Bread Uprising (or, the "Thieves Uprising," as Sadat dubbed it).[148] On the morning of January 18, Egyptians awoke to news of sharp hikes on the price of basic commodities after the government removed subsidies, per the IMF's directive. That previously unannounced decision led to widespread public anger and nationwide protests. Meanwhile, Sadat, who was in Aswan at the time, had to return to Cairo by helicopter

to escape angry crowds. After learning that protesters were overwhelming police forces, the president ordered the army to intervene. Minister
of Defense Abdel-Ghani Al-Gamasy refused to issue the command until
the government reversed the controversial price increases. Sadat obliged,
and within two days military forces were able to reinstate order, but only
after one hundred and sixty deaths, eight thousand injuries, and five
thousand arrests.[149]

The 1977 Bread Uprising was the culmination of growing opposition to
the economic liberalization path that Sadat had adopted after concluding
that the state was no longer equipped to handle the distributive commitments of the Nasserist social pact. Reflecting that reality were the patterns
of mobilization during the uprising. For instance, it was the primary beneficiaries of the Nasserist social pact, public sector workers and university students, who led the earliest protests on the morning of January 18,
1977.[150] Protesters reportedly attacked the residences of senior officials,
including that of the vice president, and one protest was seen heading in
the direction of the president's residence.[151] The most frequent targets of
vandalism were establishments symbolizing the unfettered wealth of the
privileged classes that reaped the benefits of Sadat's reforms: high-end
hotels, nightclubs, and luxury stores.[152]

The resounding chants crowds repeated throughout Egypt were also
quite revealing. They expressed an unmistakable rejection of policies that
fostered social inequalities and rolled back the economic and social rights
acquired under Nasser: "Abdel-Nasser always said, take care of the workers"; "We the students and the workers stand against the capitalist alliance"; "Oh, thieves of infitah, the people are hungry and unhappy"; "We
the people and the workers stand against the government of exploitation";
"Tell the person sleeping in Abdeen [Presidential Palace], the workers are
going to sleep hungry"; "Isn't it enough they made us wear sackcloth, now
they're trying to take the bread from us"; "They drink whiskey and eat
chicken, while the people are fainting from hunger"; "He is wearing the
latest style, while we are living ten people in one room."[153]

On a broader level, the uprising illustrated that even with Sadat's
attempts to erect institutional barriers constraining advocates of the Nasserist social pact who opposed him, opposition to the state's new economic
orientation was relentless. The following sections summarize the major
elements of this opposition within the student movement, the licensed

opposition, and the labor movement. On each of these three intercon-nected fronts, the regime faced strong resistance to its attempts to steer the state toward economic liberalization and, relatedly, a pro-Western for-eign policy. The final section sheds light on the regime's perceptions of the threat posed by its leftist opponents by analyzing the public statements and government memos documenting the state's reaction to the 1977 Bread Uprising.

THE STUDENT MOVEMENT

Student activism had a rich history in Egypt before the July 23 Revolution, but its role throughout much of the Nasserist era was fairly contained. This was partly the result of expanding state surveillance on university campuses after 1954 and efforts to restrict independent political activism within the student body. The state was also relatively successful in con-trolling unions and coopting student leaders into ruling party organiza-tions. Egypt's embarrassing defeat in the 1967 War, however, injected new energy into the student movement and instilled within it a yearning for greater independence and aspirations for more inclusive politics.

In February 1968, popular outrage over the light sentences the court handed to military officials who allegedly bore some responsibility for the 1967 defeat inspired a wave of student protests that spilled out of major universities in Cairo and Alexandria. The protests featured thousands of students and marked the first time since 1954 that students marched out-side of campus walls. In Cairo alone, the uprising resulted in 635 arrests, seventy-seven civilian injuries, and two deaths. Although initially focused on accountability for the 1967 defeat, student demands quickly expanded to include calls for relaxing state restrictions on university activism and greater press freedom in the country.[154] In response, the government agreed to lift censorship of students' "wall magazines,"[155] limit administra-tion and faculty oversight of student unions, and allow for political speech at universities.[156] The government–student standoff set the tone for cam-pus activism in the years that followed and laid the groundwork for unre-lenting university-based opposition to Sadat's policies.

This newly acquired space enabled greater political vibrancy on cam-pus; hence, the formation of a variety of student groups with clear political agendas like the Supporters of the Palestinian Revolution (SPR) at Cairo

University.[157] As part of his attempts to signal a break from the Nasserist past, Sadat removed the notorious university guard shortly after assuming the presidency. Founded by Nasser in the 1950s, the guard consisted of campus security units that reported directly to the Ministry of Interior, rather than university administrators.[158] With the easing of restrictions, student activism became one the most vocal sectors of opposition to Sadat's policies during the early 1970s, at which time Egypt was still officially a one-party state with no formal mechanisms for voicing dissent.

A new era of campus activism kicked off in January 1972 with the advent of what later came to be known as the 1972–1973 student uprising, which exploded in response to Sadat's reluctance to deliver on his pledge to recover Egyptian territories occupied by Israel. On January 13, the president stated in a national address that the time was not ripe for the country to enter the battlefield because of an unfavorable international environment created by the outbreak of hostilities between India and Pakistan. Because there was not enough room in the world for two major wars, he explained, 1972 would not be the year in which Egypt regained control over the lands taken in 1967.[159]

For many students, the president's speech was confused, condescending, and unpersuasive. As criticism of Sadat proliferated in Cairo University, engineering students, under the leadership of SPR, organized public gatherings attacking the president's policy of "no peace, no war." Talk of sit-ins quickly spread around campus. In an attempt to absorb this growing anger, ASU Secretary of Youth Ahmed Kamal Abul-Magd met with the students.[160] Unable to defend the government's position, he told the gathering lightheartedly, "I am but a postman. I relay your point of views to the president, and I return to you with his opinion." Hardly amused by Abul-Magd's self-deprecating humor, the students' tone became more confrontational. One of them told him to leave because "we have no use for a postman with the rank of minister."[161] Meanwhile, criticism of the government grew louder, spreading to other universities, including Ain Shams and Alexandria. Anti-Sadat students began organizing independent from officially sanctioned bodies. For example, Cairo University students elected a campus-wide organization, the Higher National Committee for Students (HNCS) of Cairo University, to communicate their demands and grievances to the government.

With a sit-in taking shape on campus, the HNCS issued a statement listing its demands and delivered it to the president's residence, calling on him to meet with the students and address their concerns and grievances. According to the late Ahmed Abdalla Rozza, one of the leaders of HNCS (subsequently a prominent scholar and human rights defender), the students demanded a decisive plan for recovering Egypt's occupied lands that went beyond superficial statements and empty slogans. They also called for greater democracy, political pluralism, and press freedom. Although the mobilization transcended leftist currents, the students' statements exhibited a leftist orientation,[162] thereby arousing suspicions that underground communists and Sadat's Nasserist rivals had orchestrated the unrest. Students, for example, asked the government to distribute the burden of war efforts fairly across income brackets so that each social class would contribute in proportion to its means. They called for a maximum wage not exceeding ten-times the minimum wage and requested the reduction of excessive stipends paid to senior officials. They also demanded the release of Helwan workers who had been arrested after mobilizing in solidarity with the student movement. Finally, the students protested the recent appointment of Sayyid Marei to the leadership of the ASU's Central Committee on grounds that he came from a "feudal" background.

The president remained silent, and a sit-in continued with the participation of about a thousand students. Eventually, a compromise was reached through Minister of Interior Mamdouh Salem. Specifically, students met with legislators on January 23 and agreed to amend their statement on the condition that it would be published in official newspapers. Members of parliament backtracked on the deal at the last minute, informing the student delegation that the statement would not be published and the president would address the issue in a public meeting soon. Outraged at these developments, students at Cairo University insisted on continuing their sit-in. Hours later in the early morning of January 24, security forces raided the campus with armored vehicles and arrested students. Similar clashes ensued at Ain Shams University. Still furious, and unfazed by the government's crackdown, students protested their colleagues' arrests at Tahrir Square and staged a sit-in, which garnered sympathy and solidarity from bystanders. Eventually, the gathering was dispersed by security forces. By then, the standoff between the state and the students had assumed national significance with various writers and trade syndicates expressing support for the student movement.

On January 25, Sadat responded with an emotionally charged speech. He blamed the unrest on a minority of students espousing "leftist Marxist thought" with ties to the Nasserist "centers of power," which his Corrective Revolution had disrupted the previous year. The president argued that the students' statement was enough to try them for treason, referring to the HNCS as the "national treason committee." He charged that the students' wall magazines were full of insults and obscenities surpassing all acceptable moral bounds and scolded them for disrespecting his emissary Abul-Magd. Most memorably, Sadat argued that there was no place in politics for students and that they should focus instead on their studies. "A student is a student of knowledge, and that's it," he said.[163] Needless to say, the students did not take kindly to these remarks.

Even though the regime tried to deescalate the situation by releasing the arrested students and referring them to university-based disciplinary committees rather than criminal courts, anti-Sadat student mobilization persisted, and criticism of the president grew in intensity. Sadat's own family members were not spared the students' insults on wall magazines.[164] Thus, in December, attempts by faculty members to censor objectionable wall magazines on the Cairo University campus produced additional confrontations.[165] Signaling that he was fed up with the unrest, Sadat said in a speech that he would give the students no more leeway. Police forces arrested students suspected of leading calls for mobilization, which only led to more protests, this time not only at Cairo University but also in Ain Shams, Alexandria, and Assiut. The president, state media, and a parliamentary fact-finding commission all blamed the events on underground leftist organizations plotting to reverse the gains of the 1971 Corrective Revolution. "They want the suppression of liberties, the sequestration of property, the special measures and all those things that we abolished," Sadat said in a January 1973 speech.[166] Unnerved by public sympathy with the students, the ASU started expelling from its membership writers and public figures who voiced support for the movement, banning their articles in the official press. Calm would not return to campuses until October 1973, when Sadat launched a surprise attack against Israel, an act he later claimed as a political victory.

As confrontations between the student movement and authorities continued during the 1972–1973 academic year, the dominance of Nasserist and other leftist currents on university campuses became more apparent.

Some of them were linked to underground communist organizations, like the Workers Communist Party and the January 8 movement (discussed in chapter 4), that were in the process of reconstituting themselves.[167] That said, state media tended to overstate the ideological coherence of the student mobilization, because some officials, Abul-Magd says, were convinced students were taking orders from secret communist groups or remnants of the ASU's disbanded Vanguard Organization.[168] From this consensus, as chapter 2 explains, emerged the idea of empowering Islamist currents on campus to counterbalance the growing leftist opposition inside the student movement.

Even with Sadat's progress toward recovering the country's lost territories, opposition from the student movement persisted against the backdrop of economic liberalization and the deepening of Egypt's alliance with Washington. And thus, leftist activism on campus grew larger and bolder. Embodying that trend were the Club for Progressive Socialist Thought (CPST) and the Club for Nasserist Thought (CNT), which were formed at Cairo University in 1975 and 1976, respectively.[169] It was within the ranks of these clubs that a new generation of Egyptian leftists emerged, including iconic political figures such as two-time presidential candidate Hamdeen Sabbahi and prominent socialist activist Ahmed Bahaaeddin Shaaban. According to Shaaban, dialogue between CPST and CNT at Cairo University played a major role in building bridges and cooperation between Nasserist and socialist youth, allowing them to move past the infamous clashes between the two political currents during the Nasser years.[170] One of the CPST's most memorable accomplishments was organizing the November 25, 1976, march on parliament and submitting a list of political demands to legislators. These included the elimination of restrictions on the formation of political parties, the right to strike, and freedom of assembly. The document rejected infitah policies and the lifting of price subsidies and also called for improving standards of living, raising the minimum wage, and eliminating stipends for high-ranking bureaucrats. On foreign policy, the CPST rejected the U.S.-sponsored disengagement treaties with Israel and requested the government permit Palestinian groups to operate in Egypt and to allow Egyptian citizens to perform volunteer work on their behalf.[171]

When the subsequent 1977 Bread Uprising erupted, Sadat blamed the national unrest on the students and others, describing the CPST march as a "rehearsal" for the January protests.[172] Indeed, accounts of the 1977 Bread Uprising confirm that university students participated visibly in protests in Cairo and Alexandria[173] and that many of them were arrested as a result.[174] At the same time, once protests grew in size, Rozza argues, students were often dwarfed by large crowds and thus lost control over the course of developments.[175] Still, as will be explained, these realities did not ease the ruling establishment's anxiety that leftist student movements were plotting to mobilize popular opposition to the government's economic and foreign policies. It is, therefore, not surprising that the state's management of campus activism became even more ruthless in the aftermath of the 1977 Bread Uprising. Shortly after these events, the university guard reappeared on campuses for the first time in seven years, censorship of wall magazines returned, restrictions on student unions were tightened, and permission of security services was required before students could run for union office.[176]

In short, university campuses were major sites of dissent challenging Sadat's efforts to discard the tenets of the Nasserist social pact. The open, daring approach that student activists adopted in protesting the government's policies only heightened the fears of the ruling establishment.

THE LICENSED OPPOSITION

As pockets of opposition to his rule began appearing on university campuses and among public sector workers, Sadat sought to prevent underground organizations from emerging on the political scene out of fear that they could politicize popular grievances. Law 34/1972, also known as the "Law for the Protection of National Unity," stated that the ASU was the only lawful political organization and that groups working outside of official state bodies were illegal. The law gave authorities wide discretion in jailing any individual engaged in undermining what is vaguely defined as "national unity."[177] Even when the laws were later amended to permit the existence of multiple political parties, the president employed all possible means to keep them on a tight leash.

With the return of multiparty politics under Sadat, most licensed opposition parties largely refrained from serious criticism of the government. Among them were the Liberal Socialists Party (LSP) and the Socialist Labor Party (SLP). Originally founded as the "right" platform of the ASU, the

LSP, under the leadership of Mustafa Kamel Murad, was generally supportive of Sadat's economic policies,[178] and it even endorsed the president's decision to conclude a peace agreement with Israel. The SLP, which
included, among others, affiliates of the pre–July 23 Revolution Misr Al-
Fatat movement, was granted legal status in 1978. Many argue that Sadat
licensed the SLP in the hope that it would become his loyal leftist party,
after Al-Tagammu refused to play that role. It would be years before the
SLP began challenging Sadat in any serious way. Showing some signs of
oppositionist potential, Al-Wafd Party reconstituted itself and managed to
secure legal status in February 1978. The party opted to suspend its activities later that same year to preempt an impending government decision
to dissolve it. In contrast, Al-Tagammu, even with its modest presence in
parliament,[179] quickly became the most credible voice within the licensed
opposition and a thorn in Sadat's side. Within less than a year of its founding, Al-Tagammu was already claiming one hundred and fifty thousand
members.[180]

As previously explained, Sadat initially allowed the formation of platforms inside the ASU (before declaring them independent parties) to
achieve two goals simultaneously. He wanted to push advocates of the Nasserist socialist pact out of the ruling coalition and, at the same time, keep
them under direct state oversight. Thus, by licensing Al-Tagammu, Sadat
thought he had effectively locked its Marxist and Nasserist activists inside
a state-manipulated party lacking the capacity to wage serious challenges
against the ruling establishment. Notably, during the height of his confrontations with university activists, Sadat urged students to join political parties instead of politicizing campus life.[181] Presumably, the president
thought that once they agreed to operate within his carefully crafted legal
framework, opposition parties would become sites for regulating and containing, rather than amplifying, political dissent. A few years later, Sadat's
plan proved too optimistic. Despite all the legal impediments the president
tried to impose on Al-Tagammu, it nonetheless managed to wage formidable opposition to his policies.

Signs of confrontation were immediately apparent following the formation of Al-Tagammu in the spring of 1976. Proregime media began attacking
the group's declared support for workers' rights to strike, per its founding
principles. Meanwhile, Sadat approached Al-Tagammu leader Mohieddin, urging him to delete that particular statement from the program.

Ultimately, Mohieddin refused. That was perhaps the earliest indication that Mohieddin's long personal friendship with the president would have little bearing on his party's official stances.[182] In fact, Al-Tagammu reaffirmed the same position by endorsing a public transportation workers' strike that same year, while faulting the government for failing to meet the strikers' demands.[183]

Al-Tagammu's official positions clearly reflected and amplified organized labor's criticism of economic liberalization policies, a fact that only strained its already tense relationship with the government. For instance, the party's program rejected the major hallmarks of Sadat's infitah policies, such as exempting foreign investors from labor laws and affording managers greater latitude in firing public sector employees.[184] Al-Tagammu also demanded that the state guarantee and protect labor rights in all sectors of the economy and called for increasing the minimum wage and adjusting it for inflation.[185] The party program also blasted the government's agrarian policies, which included rent hikes for small tenant farmers and the disbanding of landowner–tenant dispute committees.[186]

The height of Al-Tagammu's clash with Sadat came in January 1977 with the outbreak of the Bread Uprising. Indeed, Al-Tagammu was careful to avoid the appearance of complicity in the organization of mass disobedience, which would expose the party to prosecution. For example, Al-Tagammu sided with the protesters and criticized the government for raising prices, but it was also careful to denounce and distance itself from the acts of vandalism that occurred in response. This tactic, however, did not temper the regime's suspicions that Al-Tagammu's communist affiliates were somehow involved in the uprising and that the party's seemingly balanced response was mere double-talk. That view was further solidified when ASU officials intercepted a communiqué from Al-Tagammu's leaders to the party's regional offices with language implying support for more protests.[187] Thus, about one hundred and forty Al-Tagammu members were arrested in the aftermath of the uprising,[188] as state media accused party members of vandalism[189] and atheism.[190] Meanwhile, authorities targeted Al-Tagammu affiliates employed by the state, threatening terminations or transfers to remote regions.[191]

Notwithstanding its limited representation in parliament, Al-Tagammu managed to retain a leading oppositionist voice in public debates through its weekly newspaper *Al-Ahaly*. Not long after its first release in February

1978, the paper's circulation grew from 50,000 to 134,000.[192] As it rose to prominence, *Al-Ahaly* became a major forum for promoting critical views of Sadat's infitah reforms as well as his pro-Western foreign policies. *Al-Ahaly*'s editorial committee tended to adopt what many viewed as a "radical Marxist line," an orientation producing criticism of the government that surpassed that of Al-Tagammu's official statements.[193] At some point, the paper went so far as to accuse Sadat's relatives of engaging in inappropriate economic dealings.[194] Many believe that *Al-Ahaly* provided workers with valuable reporting on relevant laws and policy debates, facilitating their efforts to hold government officials and union leaders accountable.[195]

For his part, Sadat did not pull any punches, waging a series of attacks against *Al-Ahaly* a few months after its founding, accusing the paper of "inciting class warfare and threatening social peace." On one occasion, the president expressed regret for not censoring the paper when it was first released:

> Al-Tagammu's newspaper gets published, and you have all read more than sixteen issues of it. And from the first issue it was supposed to be referred to court, but I said freedom is still nascent, so let them be, because we all agree that social peace is the basic cornerstone of the era we are currently experiencing, and that we will manage our relations based on a familial approach and dialogue; and not by pitting social classes against one another, or by inciting the public and exploiting the underlying circumstances.[196]

In an implicit threat to dissolve Al-Tagammu, Sadat told a parliamentary gathering that same month that he was considering referring the party to a disciplinary committee. Soon after, authorities began banning successive issues of *Al-Ahaly*, a practice that persisted into the fall. In October 1978, Al-Tagammu leaders elected to suspend the publication.[197] But even then, the party kept airing its criticism of the government's economic and foreign policies through a weekly news bulletin, which it printed inside its offices and distributed unofficially. At some point, the circulation of the bulletin reached ten thousand copies, which prompted authorities to mount periodic raids of Al-Tagammu's offices and seize its printing equipment.[198]

The government's reprisals against leftist media were not confined to *Al-Ahaly*. After the 1977 Bread Uprising, Sadat turned his attention to other leftist publications that sided with the protesters, notably *Al-Talia*, which was produced by Al-Ahram Publishing House. The head of Al-Ahram Institution and prominent Sadat ally Yousef Al-Sibai intervened to eject the magazine's editor in chief Lotfi Al-Khouli, a leading Marxist intellectual with ties to Al-Tagammu.[199] After a court battle contesting Al-Sibai's decision, Al-Ahram opted to suspend *Al-Talia*. As the newspaper had been founded in the wake of Nasser's initiative to coopt Marxist writers into the state's media establishment, the closure of *Al-Talia* marked the end of an era. Along similar lines, Sadat publicly scolded the editors of *Rose Al-Yousef* magazine for their critical coverage of the government, effectively pressuring its editor in chief Abdel-Rahman Al-Sharqawi to resign. The regime seized that opportunity to install a pro-Sadat editorial team.[200] Ten months after the uprising, Sadat pledged in a parliamentary speech not to allow any atheist to assume a position of power in the country. At the time, the president's frequent references to atheists were widely understood as his way of denigrating those who espoused Marxist views. Not long after, Sadat unveiled a new law banning from public office, as well as positions in state media and trade unions, individuals "promoting doctrines that involve threats to divine laws or are inconsistent with their provisions."[201] Read differently, Sadat sought to purge official bodies of any leftist influence remaining from the Nasserist era while pandering to religious sensibilities.

Thus, when elections were held in 1979, Al-Tagammu lost its few parliamentary seats, making way for a dominant NDP majority (88 percent), alongside some seats for the SLP (8 percent), LSP (0.5 percent), and independents. Al-Tagammu claimed that the regime rigged the vote against its leader Mohieddin in his hometown to punish him for the party's criticism of the president.[202] From that point on, Mohieddin's presence or absence from the legislature became a virtual indicator of Al-Tagammu's relationship with the regime. His reentry into parliament in 1990 occurred against the backdrop of the party's rapprochement with the NDP. Mohieddin lost the seat again in 2005, a few months after refusing the Mubarak regime's request to participate in Egypt's first multiparty presidential election.

In short, the early years of Al-Tagammu's experiment confounded the expectations of all observers. It proved a huge disappointment to regime members who had hoped that the party would serve as an instrument for coopting the radical left. As for radical leftists who initially doubted the party's oppositionist potential, Al-Tagammu was a pleasant surprise. Nothing captures the spirit of Al-Tagammu's founding years more than Rifaat Al-Said's analogy of a bird that was allowed to fly with a rope tied to its legs:

> Sadat freed us like a bird | . . .| He allowed us the freedom to soar but kept
> our legs tied to a rope he held in his hand. We were not stupid, and we
> knew that. But we made a bet—one that we ultimately won—that once
> the bird soars, it will acquire abilities, energies, experiences, and resis-
> tance, betraying the expectations of the person holding the rope. Flying
> in circles—although limited and fixed—was enjoyable and only motivated
> greater soaring and defiance.[203]

THE LABOR MOVEMENT

Despite Sadat's efforts to preempt opposition from workers, various forces within organized labor[204] challenged the government's attempts to roll back the rights they had acquired during the Nasserist era. Indeed, Sadat was relatively successful in cultivating a cadre of politically loyal lead-ers within the upper echelons of the ETUF, as previously described. That certainly did not deter workers from voicing their dissent through other means, including strikes, demonstrations, and, on at least one occasion, legal action.

Well before infitah laws came into effect, workers were showing signs of discontent with declining standards of living. For example, in August 1971, ten thousand workers in Helwan Iron and Steel Company organized a strike demanding production bonuses. Three thousand people were arrested upon the intervention of security forces.[205] At some point, ETUF President Salah Gharib tried to negotiate with the strikers. They detained him over-night and chanted to his face, "You are the regime's guy." Appalled at these developments, Sadat stated in a public address later that month he consid-ered "sit-ins and strikes undemocratic and unacceptable." Also focusing on wages and working conditions, Shubra El-Kheima workers staged a strike in March 1972. Protesting the government's inaction, they threw stones at Prime Minister Aziz Sedky's motorcade as it was proceeding to Shebeen El-Kom.[206] Later in December, six thousand Alexandria Port workers went on strike over unpaid wages. When arrests were made, workers stormed the police stations, forcibly freeing their detained colleagues.[207] Such actions only increased with the advent of infitah.

As Sadat proposed the idea of opening the Egyptian economy to foreign capital and investments, per his 1974 October Paper, the official response of the ETUF was rather guarded. Its leaders expressed conditional support for the idea of infitah, while emphasizing that the government must (1) keep economic policies aligned with socialist principles and national interests; (2) limit foreign investments to productive, rather than consumerist, sectors; (3) protect domestic industries from foreign competition; and (4) refrain from any action that could result in the dissolution the public sector or the curbing of workers' rights. Thus, it is not surprising that the ETUF, even under the leadership of the pro-Sadat Gharib, criticized Law 43/1974 and Law 111/1975 for granting foreign investors—especially those establishing partnerships with public sector companies—exemptions from labor regulations.[208] More generally, the unions feared that these laws would force state workers into the private sector, resulting in the loss of benefits and a decrease in wages, as the private sector had earned a poor record of complying with minimum wage laws.[209]

When workers received news of these reforms in 1974, they were struggling with declining real wages and rising inflation. This only reinforced the perception that the gains they had made under Nasser were now under attack. Thus, signs of labor unrest began expanding markedly. During that year, Defense Factory 36 workers staged a strike in demand of wage increases.[210] In September, workers at the Harir Textile factory in Helwan carried out a sit-in after learning that their paychecks would be slashed by a new mandatory savings deduction. Additionally, workers at the privately owned Tanta Tobacco Company went on strike in protest of pay cuts.[211] In other incidents, privatization measures themselves were the target of labor action. For example, the workers of United Wholesale Textile Trading Company filed a lawsuit against their management for failing to consult with employees before transferring ownership of two factories to a private investor. Realizing that the case could set a dangerous precedent if the court ruled the privatization of public sector enterprises unconstitutional, the regime pressured its union allies to help withdraw the suit.[212]

More labor unrest came in 1975. On January 1, Helwan workers organized a sit-in demanding higher wages and calling for the resignation of Prime Minister Hegazy, whom they described as "the enemy of the workers." In solidarity, textile workers in Shubra El-Kheima staged a strike that was forcibly ended by the police.[213] When five thousand El-Mahalla Textiles workers followed suit in March, the president called upon the army to intervene, leading to a dramatic showdown, two thousand arrests, and thirty-five deaths.[214] In April, sugar factory workers in Nag Hammadi went on strike, after management eliminated their work break. In December, Port Said arsenal workers did the same in protest of low wages and increasing prices.[215]

In response to burgeoning labor activism and what Sadat considered to be a sluggish pace of reform, the president sacked Prime Minister Hegazy, replacing him with Interior Minister Mamdouh Salem. A police officer's assumption of the premiership from an economist symbolized how economic reform, as a result of the popular backlash it provoked, was becoming a national security issue.[216] "When I found slowness and delay," Sadat remarked, "I reshuffled the government and brought in Mamdouh. Today, Mamdouh is breaking all measures and restrictions that impede freedom of economic activities." For his part, Salem stated that infitah was being impeded by "adherence to socialist slogans"—a reference to the rising opposition to economic liberalization measures—and he vowed to remove every constraint on private investments.[217] Meanwhile, domestic intelligence bodies were ordered to submit weekly reports to senior officials and cabinet members on public reactions to price fluctuations.[218]

Even with Salem in charge and security agencies on alert, labor unrest intensified in 1976, just as workers were feeling the pain of rising prices. According to Howaida Adly, between February and May 1976, strikes and worker protests were reported in Cairo, Alexandria, and Tanta, in some cases calling for a return to pre-infitah economic policies. In March, Damietta textile workers protested unpaid wages, prompting police intervention. A few months later, workers seized control of a military factory in Helwan. They called for new management, improved working conditions, payment of their profit shares, and tax exemptions on their bonuses. Eventually, the minister of military production had to negotiate with them in person to deescalate the situation. In June, a labor strike took place in the Nasr Automotive factory after managers reportedly refused to pay workers their share of profits.[219]

Exacerbating the regime's anxiety at these developments were the marked gains leftist forces scored in labor union elections in the summer of 1976.[220] And sure enough, more unrest surfaced in the fall. In September, Cairo was in virtual paralysis for days, when public transportation workers went on strike demanding unpaid holiday wages, seven-hour workdays, and bonuses to offset the rising cost of living. Ironically, the strike began a day after Sadat was elected president with 99 percent support in a national referendum.[221] Although initially defiant, the president eventually agreed to address their grievances.[222]

Trends in labor unrest between 1975 and 1976, along with ETUF leaders' statements, signaled that public sector workers were unable to keep up with rising prices. In December 1976, an ETUF conference concluded that wage policies in Egypt were failing to account for the increasing cost of living, calling on the government to adhere to stricter price controls.[223] Thus, for the ETUF, the government's lifting of subsidies on January 18, 1977, was a slap in the face. Predictably, public sector workers were livid and became visible participants in the Bread Uprising that followed. In fact, sources attribute the beginning of the uprising to anti–price hike demonstrations led by workers at the Misr Helwan Spinning and Weaving Company and the Naval Arsenal in Alexandria.[224] Workers' outrage at the subsidy cuts was serious enough that the otherwise proregime ETUF rejected the measures in a strongly worded statement that was uncharacteristically critical of the government.[225] Even while condemning acts of vandalism that occurred in the course of these events, the ETUF sided with the workers and sponsored visits to those detained in the wake of the uprising.[226]

The regime responded to the 1977 protests with a new raft of repressive measures. It prosecuted one hundred and sixty-seven political and labor figures on charges of inciting riots and vandalism (the court eventually acquitted the defendants of all charges).[227] In addition to cracking down on leftist media, the government made strikes and demonstrations punishable by life in prison through Law 2/1977.[228] Sadat replaced Minister of Interior Al-Sayyid Fahmy with Al-Nabawi Ismail and began augmenting the capacity of the antiriot police. Within a year of the uprising, the size of Central Security Forces, an antiriot paramilitary force, increased threefold, and "its arsenal was upgraded from batons and rifles to tear-gas canisters and armored vehicles."[229]

Realizing the extent of the danger labor unrest posed, Sadat acceded to many workers' demands for raises and offered them some limited concessions through a new labor law (Law 48/1978). In return, Sadat was able get union leaders to support other policies, including his controversial peace talks with Israel, as well as his repressive campaign against leftist elements inside the unions.[230] That same year, the state passed a set of laws that gave authorities great discretion in disqualifying candidates from labor union elections.[231] When the election was convened a year later, leftists' share of seats shrunk from about four thousand to one hundred and twenty.[232] In the aftermath of the uprising, the state also passed a restrictive political parties law, which barred parties from organizing around social class and prohibited activities that threatened "social peace."

Note that heightened state repression against labor activists in the late 1970s failed to reduce workers' pressure on the government. For example, a strike by El-Mahalla Textile workers in 1978 forced the government to rescind an earlier decision to withhold "back-to-school bonuses."[233] In August 1979, about thirty thousand workers went on strike in El-Mahalla demanding better wages while openly airing criticism of infitah policies and Egypt's peace treaty with Israel.[234]

Although the January 1977 events may have convinced Sadat that food subsidies were untouchable (in fact, subsidy spending expanded after-ward),[235] the state did not relent in its effort to rid itself of the increasingly costly public sector. In 1980, it proposed a law that would have allowed the state to relinquish ownership of public sector companies by putting their shares up for private subscription. In the face of intense objections from union leaders, the government dropped the proposal, letting the bill die in parliament.[236] It would be a decade before the state embarked on a full-fledged privatization program, albeit under entirely different political conditions, as explained in chapter 5.

UNDERSTANDING THE REGIME'S PERCEPTIONS OF THREAT: THE CASE OF THE 1977 BREAD UPRISING

This account illustrates how various pockets of opposition developed in response to Sadat's perceived infringements on the Nasserist social pact, along with some of the immediate state responses to these challenges. This section builds a more complete understanding of how the regime interpreted and characterized each of these oppositionist actors as threats to political stability. The section examines the government's offi-cial response to the 1977 Bread Uprising. That response is documented in senior officials' statements on the uprising's causes and origins, as well as in memos and other documents prepared by security officials to build cases against those suspected of inciting or participating in the so-called riots.[237]

One of the liveliest public responses to the uprising came in the parliamentary address of Prime Minister Mamdouh Salem on January 29, 1977.[238] Salem presented the 1977 uprising as part of a years-long struggle between the state and various forces that had been attempting to exploit deteriorating economic conditions for political gain. The prime minister began his speech with an attempt to justify the controversial removal of price subsidies. Salem then asserted that the state's economic reform path was imperative and unavoidable, given the structural problems confronting the Egyptian economy since the 1960s—or what he dubbed Sadat's "heavy inheritance." In a subtle jab at Nasserists, Salem insinuated that Nasser had failed to address these painful truths before the people, resorting instead to temporary solutions that proved ineffective.[239] In contrast, Salem argued, the current government had been open with the public about the need to embark on a different economic course since the 1971 Corrective Revolution. This new course, he stated, necessitated tax and subsidy reforms to reduce the swelling budget deficit and restore investors' confidence in the Egyptian economy. At the same time, Salem declared, the government had done everything in its power to promote social justice, citing as an example the state's nominal increases in public spending on wages.[240] The prime minister then made the case that the adjustment of prices by executive decree—without legislative approval—was legally and constitutionally sound.

Finally, Salem turned to criticizing communist groups, mentioning by name the Workers Communist Party (WCP), the Communist Party of Egypt, and Al-Tagammu. The latter, he alleged, had become a front for communist radicals. He described the WCP as "the most dangerous of these groups," citing slogans from their secret bulletins in evidence,[241] and he further accused the party of exploiting dire economic conditions to overthrow the regime and achieve narrow political ends. These groups, Salem told parliament, were seeking to return Egypt to the pre-1971 period, and reverse the gains of Sadat's May 15 Revolution, like the rule-of-law, social peace and justice, and political rights.[242]

Salem's account displays a distinctive understanding of how popular uprisings come about. Political activists, the narrative goes, build links with members of social groups experiencing economic hardship, stir up their anger, and, at the right moment, prod them to rise up against the regime. Thus, the prime minister made the case that the affiliates of communist groups were not merely guilty of participating in the uprising. They were also responsible for generating the political environment making such an uprising possible in the first place. In making this latter point, the prime minister invoked the curious term *tahyi'at al-manakh al-'am* ("preparing the general climate"),[243] the same phrase that prosecutors and security officers used to frame accusations against suspects in the Bread Uprising cases. This phrase also appears in the testimony of Colonel Fathy Qattah, who headed the task force responsible for monitoring communist activism at the State Security Investigations Service (SSIS).[244] The prosecutor asked Qattah whether he had evidence that Al-Tagammu engaged in subversive or hostile activities during or before the riots. While acknowledging that there was no such evidence, Qattah cited the group's professed support for the right to strike and to peacefully protest as sufficient evidence to indict the party.[245]

An SSIS memo of the period presents this accusation in greater detail. Entitled "On the Secret Communist Plot and Its Responsibility for the Latest Riot Events," the document claims that affiliates of communist organizations "prepared and created the popular climate"[246] for the unrest:

These groups have resorted to an extended, phased approach, especially during the last period. They carefully and gradually designed their activities to establish | . . .| influential presence inside important popular sectors | . . .| especially inside students' and workers' sectors. [Their goal was to] establish focal points within [these sectors], believing that any success in mobilizing them will necessarily present them with their long-awaited opportunity to | . . .| destabilize the domestic front. To this end, [these groups] engaged in agitation and incitement, exaggerated widespread problems, endorsed the demands of specific groups and professional sectors, and exploited the difficulties of everyday life to pit the masses against the regime. They proposed solutions that are impossible to adopt under the serious economic conditions the country is currently experiencing to pretend to be caring for [people's] interests, and to prove that the regime is unable to fulfill the basic demands of the masses such that public confidence in the regime would sink to a point conducive to popular discontent and unrest. At the same time, they sought to push the

masses to adopt pressure methods to achieve their demands and force
authorities to respond to them. This is why [these groups] have raised the
slogan of upholding the right to strike, protest, and sit-ins, [that is,] in
order to take advantage of any crisis situation to achieve their goals and
start a popular revolution that could bring about the political realities
they desire.[247]

The claim that the January 1977 events were linked to the content of leftist
political discourse in the preceding years is pronounced throughout the
SSIS memo. The document's treatment of the uprising's origins focuses on
the publications of leftist groups and the activities that these groups organized in preceding years at universities and among workers. These activities range from CPST-organized lectures at Cairo University[248] to labor
strikes and sit-ins that featured participants affiliated with Al-Tagammu,
WCP, the Revolutionary Current, or the January 8 movement.[249]

In a similar vein, Prime Minister Salem's speech portrayed the road
to the 1977 Bread Uprising as the culmination of a years-long effort by
communist organizations to infiltrate public universities and factories.[250]
These groups, he explained, have had a long history of working to incite
popular unrest. A review of this history "reveals that the organized communist elements, and some of the leaders of Al-Tagammu Party, were all
monitoring the direction of the economic situation with a view | . . .| to
seizing the popular arena and controlling it."[251] The price hikes, he argued,
"were but the zero hour they chose for implementing" their plot.[252] In
support of this claim, Salem drew links between the Bread Uprising and
the 1972–1973 student uprising, as well as the 1976 strike by Cairo public
transportation workers.[253]

In short, the government's own account of the lead-up to the 1977
uprising underscores the extent to which leftist organizations operating inside the licensed opposition, workers unions, underground movements, and student groups had come to present an imminent threat to
regime stability. According to this understanding, these groups were seeking to overthrow the political system by capitalizing on the social grievances resulting from economic reform policies. They, however, absolutely
did not succeed, said Prime Minister Salem in his parliamentary address:
"They thought that they are capable of mobilizing large masses of people,
and this is an honor they are not capable or worthy of | . . .| because, by

virtue of their leanings, they are far from representing the benevolent values of the people." Behind the failure of these subversive elements, he added, were the strong bonds of solidarity between the honorable citizens and their "sons inside the armed forces and the police."[254]

Salem was careful throughout the speech to refute any claims that these groups were able to come between the state and the communities of workers and students. For example, he asserted that most WCP members were not workers. He also alleged that the vast majority of workers and students had dismissed calls by leftist groups to protest against the regime during and before the uprising.[255] In contrast, the reports of domestic intelligence agencies paint a different picture. For instance, the previously cited SISS memo reports that various underground communist groups had succeeded in building a threatening presence inside student and labor movements, not to mention inside Al-Tagammu Party. This memo even credits specific members of underground communist groups, such as the WCP, with organizing the protests that sparked the uprising. Reinforcing that interpretation is the assertion that disparate protests throughout the capital exhibited identical tactics, chants, and slogans, per the testimony of Ahmed Rushdi, head of the Cairo Security Directorate, who would later serve as interior minister under Mubarak.[256]

Conclusion

This chapter has summarized the economic elements of the Nasserist social pact, specifically the distributive commitments they imposed on the Egyptian state. The deepening of the state's role as guarantor of social and economic protections coincided with the appropriation of political rights and the closure of independent channels of political and social representation. That process also entailed the political marginalization of the Muslim Brotherhood and resulted in the group's disappearance from public life. Just as the state's distributive role reached new heights in the mid-1960s, the government began facing a set of structural economic challenges, along with a variety of international and regional political shifts that exacerbated these difficulties. These structural challenges empowered forces inside the ruling coalition that advocated opening the economy to private investment and curtailing the role of the public sector. By the time Nasser passed away in September 1970, the political leadership was in the midst of contemplating options to address the deep economic predicament confronting the country. These challenges, along with the changes they induced inside the ruling coalition, shaped the context in which Nasser's successor sought to reorient Egypt's political, economic, and foreign policies away from the costly commitments of the Nasserist social pact.

In many ways, Sadat's presidency was a struggle to relieve the Egyptian state of the costly burdens it has inherited from Nasser's social pact. It is telling that in his autobiography *In Search of Identity*, Sadat prefaces his narrative of his years as president with an indignant account of Nasser's handling of the economy and the structural difficulties that resulted from these missteps. Thus, upon assuming the presidency, Sadat opted to reorient the Egyptian state by seeking foreign capital and U.S. political support and by purging top leadership circles of powerful Nasserist elements. These steps set the stage for a raft of economic liberalization reforms that gradually weakened the state's commitment to the tenets of Nasser's social pact. On the political side, Sadat sought to purge the ruling coalition in ways that would undermine the influence of the pact's former beneficiaries (particularly organized labor and their advocates) while keeping any potential opposition contained.

Although Sadat was somewhat successful in keeping his leftist opponents on the defensive, the tide of opposition he confronted was unstoppable. Sadat faced a serious challenge from the left, whether in the sphere of licensed party politics, university activism, or the labor movement. Evidence indicates that the political leadership was fearful of the subversive potential posed by leftist movements, in particular, their capacity to mobilize the losers of economic liberalization in opposition to the regime. As the next chapter explains, it was under these conditions that policies of Islamist incorporation came into being.

2

Islamist Incorporation in the State of Science and Faith

The sight of the president in an Islamic appearance—with a rosary and abaya while praying in mosques—dampened the hearts of the Brotherhood.

—SALEH ABU-RUQAYIQ, IN *AL-TAHARUKAT AL-SIYASIYYA LI-L-IKHWAN AL-MUSLIMIN*

I remember, Mr. President, that when I was a student in King Fouad I University, all parties were represented within the student body and had their own leaders. The Muslim Brotherhood enjoyed that too. But because those affiliated with the Muslim Brotherhood believed in their convictions, it was only enough for one of them to say, 'God is Great and Praise Be to Him' and within a second you would find thousands gathered around him, as if the earth was split open and released them—dwarfing the presence of all other parties.

—MOHAMED OTHMAN ISMAIL, IN *MUHAMAD ʿUTHMAN ISMAʿIL YATADHAKAR*

The world was open in front of us.

—ABDEL-MONEIM ABOUL-FOTOUH, IN *SHAHID ʿALA TARIKH AL-HARAKAH AL-ISLAMIYYA FI MISR*

All the officials in Egypt recognized this state of affairs and considered me the person responsible for the Muslim Brotherhood. They met and talked to me in that capacity . . . And I accepted these conditions and based on them I helped out in many situations when the government needed the cooperation of the Muslim Brotherhood. And this was a de facto recognition from the government of the existence of the Brotherhood on the scene.

—OMAR AL-TILMISANI, *DHIKRAYAT LA MUDHAKARAT*

The Islamic Groups are working publicly and openly, and their goals are pure with no ambiguity surrounding them. They reject violence and do not adopt it and they protect Egypt and its youth and do not corrupt them.

—AL-NABAWI ISMAIL, IN *AL-JAMA'AH AL-ISLAMIYYA FI-L-JAMI'AT*

Sometime in 1972, Mohamed Othman Ismail (hereafter MOI), a prime architect of Anwar Al-Sadat's Islamist incorporation policies, prepared to receive a senior Muslim Brotherhood leader at his home. While generally sympathetic to the "Islamist cause," MOI could not help but view the movement with some reservations, which he attributed to one of his earliest encounters with the Brotherhood—an experience that left a bad taste in his mouth. During his first year in college, MOI pulled out a cigarette while chatting with a group of students. An acquaintance, who happened to be a Muslim Brotherhood affiliate, responded judgmentally: "You are a student and yet you smoke a pack of cigarettes that costs sixteen piasters!" As trivial as the incident seems in retrospect, MOI says, the man's remark created an emotional chasm between him and the Muslim Brotherhood.

Some decades later, MOI sat in his home conversing with Omar Al-Tilmisani, one of the Brotherhood's foremost leaders. MOI sought the meeting to convey President Al-Sadat's desire to support the Muslim Brotherhood's activities. MOI knew that smoking in the company of a Brotherhood figure was most likely a faux pas. But he was desperate for a cigarette and could not help himself: "I am sorry, Mr. Omar, but I have to ask for your permission to smoke a cigarette." Al-Tilmisani's response left MOI in shock: "And why not? Hand me a cigarette, too." MOI watched with intrigue as

Al-Tilmisani, much like a rookie, awkwardly blew out the smoke without inhaling. MOI immediately realized that his guest was not a smoker but had asked for the cigarette out of courtesy, hoping to make his host feel more comfortable. He was touched by Al-Tilmisani's diplomatic gesture, and thus the barrier between Sadat's aide and the Muslim Brotherhood was lifted—all with a single cigarette.[1]

MOI and Al-Tilmisani met against the backdrop of escalating tensions as the regime clashed on university campuses with its Nasserist and Marxist opponents, or "communist agitators," as Sadat often labeled them. MOI was leading an effort to undermine these leftist dissidents by encouraging their Islamist rivals to challenge and contain them. This initiative constituted one of the most important strategies the state employed during the 1970s to dismantle the Nasserist social pact and jettison the costs it entailed. In other words, the structural pressures described in chapter 1 generated the impetus for a state policy of opening political space to Islamist activists in the hope of undermining the opponents of economic de-Nasserization. In the long run, as explained in subsequent chapters, that strategy steered Egypt toward the politics of "more identity, less class."

This chapter examines the principal elements of Islamist incorporation policies, exploring the internal regime debates and the underlying considerations that gave rise to these policies. Islamist incorporation emerged in the midst of Sadat's attempts to highlight the Islamic dimensions of Egypt's national identity by displaying a commitment to religious values in government discourse and the legal sphere. That effort was aimed, at least partially, at marginalizing and discrediting leftist ideologies that clashed with the state's shifting economic priorities. Toward the same end, the state began supporting, directly and indirectly, Islamist student activism on university campuses, thereby facilitating the growth of an influential Islamist student movement. It also encouraged the Muslim Brotherhood's return to the political scene, lifting the legal and political restrictions on the group's public engagement.

These policies were crucial to the Muslim Brotherhood's efforts at reconstituting itself and rebuilding its organizational structures after suffering two decades of marginalization under Gamal Abdel-Nasser. The Brotherhood took full advantage of the political space Sadat afforded it. The group also benefited greatly from the president's support for Islamist activism at universities, coopting large swaths of the Islamist student movement that expanded with tacit state support. This new generation of student activists infused the Muslim Brotherhood with vigor at a time when its return to political life was in doubt.

It is critical to contrast the considerable latitude Islamist movements enjoyed as they developed their organizational structures and networks with the state's interventionist, repressive posture toward their leftist counterparts. Various communities of Islamist activists exploited this favorable political climate to organize outside of state structures and, eventually, to find refuge under the umbrella of the Muslim Brotherhood. The leftist opposition, in contrast, faced a more hostile environment, one that impeded its ability to develop sustainable organizational structures autonomously of the state or to forge meaningful links with aggrieved stakeholders in organized labor. Thanks to a variety of state-imposed formal and informal restrictions, Al-Tagammu's once-promising experiment to aggregate these various forces into a coherent, viable organization ended in failure (see chapter 4). Also devastating to Al-Tagammu's development were the long-term effects of Islamist incorporation policies, as explained in chapter 5.

The rest of this chapter is structured as follows. It first describes the political environment in which Islamist incorporation policies took form, one featuring state efforts to project a religious identity in cultural and legal spheres. The next section describes the documents and personal accounts informing our understanding of Islamist incorporation policies and the political circumstances in which these sources were produced. Where relevant, it also presents the new information each account has brought to light. The chapter then examines in detail the regime measures that supported Islamist student activism at public universities and enabled the Muslim Brotherhood's reemergence as an influential political actor. In making sense of the Sadat regime's laissez-faire attitude to the Muslim Brotherhood throughout much of the 1970s, this chapter assesses the major issues animating the movement's political discourse and its criticism of the government. Based on analysis of content from *Al-Dawa*, a Muslim Brotherhood-sponsored monthly magazine,[2] it argues that, because of the anti-Marxist, anti-Nasserist orientations it shared with the regime, the Brotherhood operated without intense state scrutiny for many years. In *Al-Dawa*, the social and economic issues that defined the conflict between the state and opponents of economic de-Nasserization during the 1970s often took a back seat to identity-based issues surrounding the implementation of Islamic law and foreign policy. That orientation, as explained in this chapter's final section, reflects the Brotherhood's long-standing approach to economic issues.

The State of Science and Faith

"We found a strange kind of faith as the Quran adorned the desks of officials," writes Wael Othman, a student activist who helped form an Islamist group at Cairo University: the Youth of Islam. Reflecting on his meetings with Arab Socialist Union (ASU) leaders in early 1973, Othman was surprised by the incongruous expressions of piety he observed at the ruling party's headquarters. "Members of the [Arab] Socialist Union were addressing each other as 'Hagg' [an honorary title awarded to Muslims who conduct pilgrimage to Mecca], as opposed to 'comrade,' the default form of address used during the days of [Abdel-Nasser's ASU Secretary General] Aly Sabri," he reports. "Whenever we visited an official, and he knew that we were from the Youth of Islam group," Othman recounts, "he would quickly prepare for prayer or ask for our permission to perform it in front of us during the discussion . . . and sometimes he would deliberately make a point to show that he had just finished praying."[3]

Othman's recollections capture the spirit of the Sadat era, one in which the government ritualized performative expressions of religiosity and flaunted its Islamic commitments to attract supporters and discredit opponents. Upon assuming the presidency, Sadat pledged that Egypt would become "the state of science and faith." The slogan came to embody a modernizing vision of reviving the country's Islamic heritage and, per the professed goals of *infitah*, infusing its economic development with the latest technological knowledge. The revivalist dimension of this motto was apparent in the clear religious orientation the state media began to project.[4] The press labeled Sadat *al-ra'is al-mu'min* ("the believing president"), while his religious credentials were on constant public display. Meanwhile, Islamic thinkers and preachers gained visible profiles on state television and radio. Exemplifying that trend was writer and opinion-shaper Mustafa Mahmoud. Once a controversial novelist and reputed atheist, Mahmoud reportedly underwent a personal and intellectual transformation that restored his faith and led him to renounce his previous Marxist sympathies.[5] He subsequently became a poster child for religious revivalism and the renunciation of so-called leftist extremism.

It all started in May 1971, when the state-owned weekly *Rose Al-Yousef* ran an article by Mahmoud commending Sadat for sacking his Nasserist foes in the course of the Corrective Revolution. "You are the leader and there is no leader like you . . . You are the man of science and faith," Mahmoud declared. Evidently, this particular passage left a lasting impression on the new president. Sadat not only appropriated the phrase "science and faith," but he also requested that public television launch a show under the same title with Mustafa Mahmoud as its producer. The program became a standby of Egyptian television through the late 1990s, earning Mahmoud much fame and popularity in the process.[6] Mahmoud's entrepreneurial activities were not limited to television, as he became involved in other endeavors, such as building medical centers.[7] With this elevated profile, Mahmoud devoted many of his writings to critiquing Marxist ideas.[8] Memorably, he criticized the 1977 Bread Uprising in an angry tirade in the weekly *Sabah Al-Khair* magazine under the title "It was not an uprising, but rattle and death," writing: "They exploit the economic crisis to provoke opposition and dissent. And then they take advantage of people's pain by telling them that they have the cure . . . communism. And I say, communism is a disease and not a cure. It is the reason for the economic collapse that has occurred."[9]

In many ways, Mahmoud's career neatly captures the Sadat presidency's commitment to private enterprise and its antipathy to leftist ideologies, both advanced under the banner of religious revivalism. There is no small irony in the fact that shortly after Mubarak's 2011 downfall, and years after Mahmoud's death, the entrance to the lavish mosque bearing his name in the nouveau-riche Mohandiseen neighborhood served as a frequent rallying site for right-wing supporters of the former National Democratic Party (NDP).

Undoubtedly, the state's interest in the discourse of religious revivalism was aimed, in part, at discrediting leftist leaders and activists who opposed the president's efforts to reorient Egypt's economic and foreign policies. Toward that end, Sadat enlisted the support of the official religious establishment in his antileftist campaigns. Al-Azhar Grand Imam Mohamed Al-Fahham described the leaders of the 1972–1973 student uprising as unbelievers. His successor Abdel-Halim Mahmoud declared communism inconsistent with Islamic religious traditions,[10] handing the president much-needed ammunition for his battles with the left. Sadat did not shrink from mounting religiously tinged attacks against leftist dissidents, frequently portraying them as social outcasts, whose ideologies were at odds with mainstream pious sensibilities. In a 1977 parliamentary address, Sadat described those who led the 1977 Bread Uprising as Soviet-backed demagogues mobilizing to impose atheism on the rest of society. In that same speech, the president promised that no "atheist" (code word for "leftist") would ever assume a position of influence inside state bodies—a pledge that was later codified through the 1978 Social Peace Law.[11] Reflecting on Sadat's flagrant exploitation of religious discourse to confront the left, Mohamed Hassanein Heikal writes, "It almost appeared as if the regime, in its opposition to communism, was trying to make religiosity a practical example of [Karl] Marx's famous statement that religion is the opium of the people."[12]

Sadat's politicization of religion was not, by any means, novel. Nasser used the religious establishment to propagate the idea that his "socialist reforms" were consistent with Islam,[13] and, much like Sadat, he even accused communists of atheism as he cracked down on their organizations in the late 1950s.[14] The Sadat era was distinctive for the state's recurrent flaunting of rather vague promises (or, viewed differently, threats) to implement Islamic law. Throughout his presidency, Sadat oversaw an effort to infuse the legislative process with Islamic religious principles. For example, the 1971 Constitution declared Islam the religion of the state and Islamic law a source of legislation. In 1979, parliament ordered a committee to reconcile Egypt's various legal codes with Islamic law,[15] and, in 1980, a constitutional amendment made Islamic law the principal source of legislation. Years earlier, Al-Azhar sent to parliament a draft bill rendering apostasy and atheism punishable by execution.[16] Although such proposals never resulted in legislation, officials frequently revisited them whenever Sadat was bent on either threatening his leftist adversaries or deflecting criticism from Islamist allies who questioned the regime's professed Islamic commitments.[17]

Equally significantly, as described next, Sadat's pledges to implement Islamic law presented an opportunity for various Islamist currents to critique the president on his own terms—that is, to demand fulfillment of his pledge to make the state operate in accordance with Islamic principles and norms. It is not surprising, therefore, that once Sadat lost patience with Islamist criticism toward the end of his presidency, he famously declared, "there is no religion in politics, and there is no politics in religion." Ironically, the president made that statement while he was bracing to amend the constitution to make Islamic law the principal source of legislation.[18] Thus, it was embarrassingly obvious that by arguing for the rigid separation of politics and religion, Sadat was, in effect, asserting that he alone was entitled to politicize religion and wield it as a weapon against his opponents. And he certainly did. In this political environment, in which the ruling establishment, perhaps naively, perceived the Islamist movement as a potential weapon to be used against the left, Islamist incorporation policies came into being.

Islamist Incorporation: Politics of Narration, Sources, and Documentation

REGIME PLOT VERSUS POPULAR AWAKENING

Sadat's support for Islamist groups remains a sore subject for many of the era's activists and government officials. Thus, it is critical to address the politics surrounding predominant narratives of that history before proceeding to interpret the evidence. Two competing perceptions inform leading interpretations of Sadat's support for Islamist activism during the 1970s. One presents the resurgence of Islamist activism, especially at university campuses, as nothing more than the product of Sadat's desire to intimidate and antagonize his Nasserist and communist opponents. That perspective is popular among leftist activists who—perhaps conveniently—attribute their own political decline relative to their Islamist rivals to underhanded deals between a devious regime and opportunistic Islamist activists. Such claims are also common in Nasserist and Marxist retrospective critiques of Sadat that usually present his reckless exploitation of religion as the root of contemporary manifestations of "religious radicalism" and sectarian violence.[19]

Another perspective minimizes the state's role in promoting Islamist currents, instead characterizing the ascendancy of the Islamist student movement as an organic expression of a previously repressed popular yearning for political Islam. According to this view, such movements are principally the product of social and cultural changes that have little to do with Sadat's political maneuvering. This account prevails among 1970s Islamist student activists, who are insulted by insinuations that their professed commitments were less than genuine or that they were gullible tools of the regime.[20] Other proponents of this view are Sadat-era officials who cringe at any suggestion of personal connections with 1970s Islamist student activists who were subsequently accused of violence and terrorism.[21]

This book argues that neither interpretation holds up against a rigorous analysis of the evidence. Rather, the firsthand testimonies of relevant regime figures and Islamist activists paint a far more nuanced picture. These accounts demonstrate that the state deliberately promoted Islamist activism on campus with the goal of countering the leftist influences that opposed Sadat's policies. Toward that end, ASU officials launched an initiative to promote the formation of religious groups on university campuses, including offers of material support. That said, the most influential strand of the Islamist student movement at the time, the Islamic Groups at Universities (IGUs), evolved autonomously from state involvement. Even if they were not a state creation, IGUs did in fact benefit greatly from the Sadat regime's receptive orientation toward Islamist activism at public universities, along with the state's efforts to privilege Islamists over leftist currents.

Notably, no evidence suggests that senior regime officials who pursued Islamist incorporation foresaw the fateful consequences of that policy when they first adopted it. That is, they did not realize that the Islamist student movement was central to the Muslim Brotherhood's efforts to rebuild its organization.[22]

MOHAMED OTHMAN ISMAIL AND ISLAMIST INCORPORATION

Most narratives about President Sadat's relationship with Islamist currents revolve around MOI. A principal architect of Islamist incorporation policies, MOI was an adviser to Sadat and ASU's secretary for organizational affairs (*amin shu'un al-tanzim*) in the early 1970s and the governor of Assiut between late 1973 and February 1982. During the 1960s, he served as member of parliament and was a ranking official at the ASU's local party office in his home governorate of Assiut.

The son of a staunchly Wafdist village mayor, MOI epitomized the land-owning elites who, marginalized in the wake of Nasser's land reforms and sequestrations, grudgingly joined the ruling party in the hope of shielding their privileges from further state encroachment.[23] Thus, he was a natural ally of Sadat's de-Nasserization policies. In fact, MOI reveals in his memoirs that his admiration for the future president was kindled years before, when he overheard then member of parliament Sadat say, "I would like to see Egypt the way it used to be . . . Egypt."[24] That phrase was music to MOI's ears, who despised Nasser's disruption of social hierarchies and promotion of "socialist" ideas, which he deemed antithetical to Egyptian society's traditional, religiously conservative sensibilities.[25] Thus, when Sadat forced a showdown with the centers of power in May 1971, MOI took the president's side against Nasserist establishment icons like Aly Sabri and Sharawi Gomaa. In the aftermath of Sadat's triumph, MOI emerged as one of his closest aides, becoming his de facto representative in parliament and at the ASU.[26]

MOI is often portrayed by his adversaries as a vengeful, thuggish figure who did not shy away from extralegal measures, including violence. According to one famous tale, in the midst of Sadat's battle with the centers of power in 1971, MOI used a Kalashnikov rifle to personally secure the entry of Sadat's envoy into the Maspero Television building in anticipation of resistance from elements loyal to the president's rivals.[27] Another story says that during an ASU Central Committee meeting in which Aly Sabri and other Sadat rivals criticized the president, MOI placed a handgun on the conference room table, stating that he was prepared to defend Sadat with his own life.[28] Although MOI never confirmed or denied these tales, his own memoirs suggest that he did not mind playing dirty when confronting the "forces of darkness." For example, when unrest was taking place at Assiut University in 1972, MOI reveals, an old friend acted on his behalf to kidnap a "communist" student leader suspected of inciting protests.[29]

Without question, MOI made numerous enemies during his long political career. Many leftists who lived through the 1970s still despise MOI, citing his role in the state's retaliation against journalists and writers who expressed support for the 1972–1973 student uprising. In his capacity as ASU's secretary for organizational affairs, he disciplined many such writers, either terminating their employment or transferring them from state media organizations to menial public sector jobs.[30] MOI, moreover, appeared to have ruffled one too many feathers inside the security apparatus and admits to having a poor relationship with Mamdouh Salem while serving as minister of interior.[31] As governor of Assiut, he had a tense relationship with some local Coptic Church leaders, as he was perceived as being soft on sectarian violence and partial to Islamist elements that antagonized Christian communities.[32] During his final days in office under Mubarak, MOI openly clashed with Prime Minister Fuad Mohieddin in the presence of other provincial governors.[33]

MOI's contentious reputation, along with the acrimony he generated, make investigating the state's support of Islamist movements in the 1970s a challenging endeavor. Because of the numerous damning allegations about MOI's conduct in office,[34] distinguishing between valid claims and fabrications likely spread by his adversaries requires great care. Thus, accounts of MOI's covert support for Islamist groups in the 1970s must be assessed critically. The next section summarizes the accounts informing this book's interpretation of events and, when necessary, describes the political context and circumstances in which these sources appeared.

SOURCES, ACCOUNTS, AND THE PARABLE OF A BELIEVING PRESIDENT

The earliest mentions of MOI's support for Islamist groups at universities appear in the firsthand accounts of activists involved in the 1970s student movements at Cairo University. In his book *The Secrets of the Student Movement*, first published in 1976, Wael Othman details meetings between officials of the Youth of Islam and the ASU, at which both MOI and Sayyid Marei offered them material support—offers they reportedly declined.[35] Over the years, Muslim Brotherhood affiliates have issued their own insider accounts of the 1970s Islamist student movement. Many acknowledge the ruling party's efforts to set up or sponsor Islamist associations at universities during that period, although they deny that their own organizations were ever coopted by the regime.[36]

The media coverage of the 1983 trials of those suspected of leading a violent insurrection in Assiut, which occurred shortly after Sadat's assassination, brought new evidence to the fore. During court proceedings, prosecutors asked Assiut police officers about alleged meetings between

Islamist student groups and former governor MOI, suggesting that official investigations revealed possible ties between MOI and Islamist activists. Pressed by the prosecution on why authorities refrained from acting against Assiut University's Islamic Group despite being informed of its subversive activities, a police witness said that they were following a high-level political decision to steer clear of the organization.[37] At one court session, a defense lawyer asserted that his client was being scapegoated for a regime-sponsored scheme through which officials ordered the creation of the Islamic Group at Assiut University with the objective of undermining communist students.[38]

Before the Mubarak era, most of what was publicly known about Sadat's support for Islamist groups at universities came from student accounts,[39] with the regime offering little by way of admission or denial.[40] A major breakthrough came in 1983, when former ASU senior leader Mohamed Abdel-Salam Al-Zayyat[41] published in *Al-Ahaly* an account of how Sadat came to the decision to support the formation of Islamist student groups at universities.[42] This was the first time a high-ranking official who directly reported to Sadat acknowledged the initiative's existence and the president's knowledge of and support for it. Al-Zayyat would augment this account in his memoirs, which were published in early 1989.[43]

Al-Zayyat's account of the ASU's support for Islamist groups was part of a wave of extended critiques of the Sadat presidency that emerged in the 1980s.[44] Almost all such writings convey the idea that Sadat fell victim to his own stratagems, as he empowered the same Islamist currents that were responsible for his assassination in October 1981. A classic example of that narrative, or what I call the "Parable of a Believing President," appears in Mohamed Hassanein Heikal's *Autumn of Fury*, published in 1983.[45] Heikal, once editor in chief of *Al-Ahram*, minister of information, and Sadat confidant (before falling out with him), implicated the late president and MOI in promoting Islamist student activism in the 1970s. In addition, Heikal revealed Sadat's efforts to return the Muslim Brotherhood to political life, as well as the role of Osman Ahmed Osman in mediating discussions between the president and the movement's leaders.[46]

Fresh insight about links between the Sadat regime and Islamist currents came in 1990, when the memoirs of former interior minister Hassan Abu-Basha (1982–1984) were published. Abu-Basha had years of experience at the State Security Investigations Service (SSIS), where he served as deputy director (1971–1975) and director (1975–1977). Abu-Basha's memoirs provided the first senior security official's admission that the Sadat regime pursued a policy of supporting Islamist currents to counter the left. In addition to offering an insider's view of the circumstances under which this policy was adopted, Abu-Basha's account inaugurated a new trend in the narration of the Parable of a Believing President.

In propagating and elaborating on the tale of the president who fell victim to the rash bargains he struck with the religious right, Abu-Basha was not merely criticizing Sadat. On a more subtle level, he was also criticizing the existing political leadership for being too sanguine about Islamist currents. As an example, Abu-Basha cites the Muslim Brotherhood's return to the electoral arena in the 1980s, despite the group's questionable commitment to democratic norms.[47] Abu-Basha suggests this was a repeat of Sadat's ill-advised and imprudent deals with Islamists, all of which were to the detriment of national security and long-term stability.[48] Put simply, by narrating Sadat's relationships with Islamists, Abu-Basha was implicitly critiquing what he considered to be the Mubarak regime's carelessly permissive attitude to the Muslim Brotherhood's efforts to form electoral coalitions with licensed opposition parties.[49]

Abu-Basha's sobering message would acquire greater weight in the early 1990s, when the government was battling an Islamist insurgency targeting high-level officials and secular intellectuals. It was also a time, as chapter 5 explains, when numerous leftist opposition leaders were forging alliances with the ruling party, with the aim of resisting Islamist extremism. Alarming many leftist intellectuals was the perception that some Mubarak regime elements still believed they could effectively fight armed Islamists by cooperating with "moderate" alternatives like the Muslim Brotherhood and state-allied religious figures.[50] More concerning were reports suggesting that then minister of interior Abdel-Halim Moussa was a proponent of dialogue with militant groups.[51] Sensing the regime's indecisiveness about confronting political Islam, leftist writers frequently revisited state-Islamist relations under Sadat to warn of the dangers of pursuing appeasement with Islamist currents. Thus, the Parable of a Believing President reappeared in public debates.

In the political context of the early 1990s, the moral of this parable was not simply that Sadat brought about his own destruction, as many of his adversaries had gloated for much of the previous decade. More significantly, the parable also warned that appeasing Islamists was akin to playing with fire and imperiling national security. The most important exemplar of this argument was found in *Rose Al-Yousef* magazine, which refocused attention on Sadat's missteps in propping up the Islamist movement, while linking these errors to the current Islamist insurgency and recent sectarian violence.

A decade after Sadat stripped *Rose Al-Yousef* of its status as a leftist press powerhouse, Mubarak sought to restore the magazine's role as the leftist voice within the state media establishment. In part, this reflected improving relations between the regime and Nasserist and Marxist intellectuals who had suffered Sadat's wrath in the 1970s. Also driving the magazine's revitalization were efforts to cultivate state-managed intellectual spaces for a proregime left that could steal the thunder of opposition parties' publications like *Al-Ahaly*.

In that permissive environment, *Rose Al-Yousef* became a forum for debating issues routinely treated as taboo in other state-controlled media. Among these issues were sectarianism, the Islamist insurgency, and political Islam more generally.[52] And when Islamist militancy in Upper Egypt made headlines, the magazine often returned to the subject of MOI's anticommunist campaigns in the 1970s, asserting that they empowered Islamist groups in Assiut and other "terrorist hotbeds." In July 1992, for example, Aly Salem contributed a lengthy article expounding upon the dangers of Islamist militancy in Upper Egypt. The militants' intellectual advocates, Salem warned, may have duped some statesmen into thinking that these groups could be pacified through "faith-based dialogues," which the author likens to Sadat's and MOI's disastrous alliances with Islamist groups.[53] Interestingly, MOI fired back a month later with a letter to the editor denying that he had any hand in promoting "radicalism" in Upper Egypt.[54]

In mid-1995, as *Rose Al-Yousef* continued its focused coverage of Islamist violence,[55] new events informed the debate. Shortly after the attempted assassination of Mubarak in Addis Ababa, the magazine began publishing the memoirs of former SSIS deputy director Fouad Allam. At the time, *Rose Al-Yousef*'s editorial line asserted that the Muslim Brotherhood secretly supported political violence, just like that targeting the president, and argued that the government must therefore reject Sadat-style Islamist appeasement.[56] Hence, magazine writers sought to call attention to the Brotherhood's alleged history of violence and Sadat's role in encouraging the rise of violent Islamist currents.[57]

Allam's memoirs provided new details about Sadat's and MOI's roles in forming Islamic groups at universities. Allam also identified Mahmoud Gamee, a Sadat friend and associate,[58] as a key interlocutor between the late president and the Muslim Brotherhood in the early 1970s. Allam, who headed the SSIS's Religious Activism Bureau, was responsible for supervising the Muslim Brotherhood's file in various capacities between 1965 and 1985.[59]

Allam's statements sparked much debate and even elicited a response from an otherwise-silent MOI. While contesting many of Allam's claims,[60] MOI did acknowledge that he was involved in forming Islamist groups at university campuses but denied that he ever advocated the use of violence.[61] Other respondents included Mahmoud Gamee, who admitted carrying messages to Muslim Brotherhood leaders on behalf of Sadat. A few years later, Gamee detailed these and other incidents in a book entitled *I Knew Sadat*.[62]

An immense breakthrough in the documentation of Sadat's relationship with Islamists came in 2000 with the publication of MOI's memoirs, edited by longtime *Uktubar* magazine journalist Atef Abdel-Ghany.[63] By that time, however, MOI had passed away, and Sadat's backing of Islamist student groups was, for most observers, old news, as multiple official sources had already confirmed MOI's involvement in these efforts. Thus, the book received only scant attention. Yet it arguably contains, for several reasons, one of the most important eyewitness accounts of Sadat's relations with Islamists.

First, although previous publications documented Sadat's support for Islamist student activism, MOI's account delineates that initiative more clearly. In the process, it dispels the myth that the IGUs operated under state control. As chapter 3 explains, the state's practice of supporting these groups without encroaching on their organizational autonomy was a critical feature, as it contributed to the growth of strong Islamist currents in the following decades.

Second, MOI's insider account, unlike many others that preceded it, makes a distinction between state support for Islamist student activism and support for the Muslim Brotherhood. Because many of the leaders of the 1970s Islamist student movement eventually joined the Brother-hood, observers often assume that Sadat's ultimate aim in backing Islamist student activism was rebuilding the Brotherhood's organization.[64] MOI's testimony refutes that view, adding an important nuance to this study's findings: that the regime's support of the Islamist student movement ulti-mately contributed to the Muslim Brotherhood's organizational resurrec-tion was an unintended consequence of this policy.

Third, MOI provides the only account quoting personal exchanges with Sadat about the ASU's plans to support Islamist currents, thereby offer-ing unique insight into the president's role in formulating this policy, his reasons for adopting it, and his intentions for the Islamist movement.[65] Fourth, the memoir addresses some inaccuracies that appeared in previ-ous accounts.[66] Finally, the book is one of few insider testimonies of the state's support for Islamist groups not authored by one of Sadat's or MOI's adversaries. Thus, it is less hyperbolic and exaggerated.

In the years following the release of MOI's memoirs, discussions of the late-president's assassination yielded more revelations about Sadat's rela-tionship with Islamists. With the proliferation of sensationalist political talk shows in the 2000s, the Sadat assassination became a popular subject of conversation. For example, in 2007, *Al-Mehwar* television aired a mul-tipart interview with Sadat's last Minister of Interior Al-Nabawi Ismail.[67] Although focused on the assassination plot and the events surrounding it, Ismail's interview provided new insight into Sadat's approach toward Islamist leaders and activists.[68]

Around the same time, some Muslim Brotherhood affiliates who par-ticipated in the 1970s Islamist student movement began publishing their own accounts of the period.[69] Shaping their narratives, at least in part, were deepening generational tensions between these activists and their elder leaders (more on that in chapter 3).[70] In other words, the marginal-ization of these younger figures by the Brotherhood leadership may have prompted some of them to speak out about their own contributions to the organization's resurgence during the 1970s and 1980s.[71]

In 2012, one year after Mubarak's ouster, and just as the Muslim Broth-erhood became a dominant force on the political scene, Nasserist journal-ist Hassanein Koroum published a book on the group's ties with the state during the 1970s and 1980s.[72] Notably, the book included the firsthand tes-timony of the late Muslim Brotherhood leader Saleh Abu-Ruqayiq, which details previously unpublicized contacts between the movement's leaders and senior government officials.[73] Abu-Ruqayiq's revelations inform this study's characterization of the choices and pressures the Brotherhood faced when rebuilding its organizational presence after a prolonged absence from the political scene. Specifically, it underscores Sadat's interest in coopting the group's members into the ruling party, as well as prevalent concerns among Brotherhood leaders about potential restrictions accompanying the assumption of legal status.

Finally, files from the U.S. Embassy in Cairo, generated between 1974 and 1979, contain a range of details on Sadat's relationships with Islamists, his support for Islamist groups at universities, and pertinent internal regime deliberations.[74] These documents, which cite conversations with state officials and other political figures, including Sadat and Al-Tilmisani, were declassified and made publicly accessible between 2006 and 2014.[75]

Islamist Incorporation at Public Universities

As described in chapter 1, the idea of promoting Islamist student activism gained currency inside the ruling establishment in 1972 in response to intensifying Nasserist and communist opposition at various universities. Before this development, the political leadership had been considering revitalizing the ASU's Youth Organization (YO) on campuses. The YO's student outreach efforts had been deprioritized toward the end of Nasser's rule, partly because of the domineering role of the ruling party's secret arm, the Vanguard Organization (VO), during that period.[76] Sadat's triumph over the centers of power in 1971, however, led to the dissolution of the VO, prompting the question of what would replace it at universities.

At the center of these discussions was ASU Central Committee head Mohamed Abdel-Salam Al-Zayyat, whom Sadat tasked with reorganizing the ruling party after the purge of the president's Nasserist rivals. Al-Zayyat advocated restoring the YO's role as a channel of ASU outreach within the student body. Sadat resisted this idea vehemently, arguing that the YO was a stronghold of Nasserist remnants: "Every person in that organization is an enemy of mine, they are communists. They are the lackeys of the centers of power." He demanded instead a loyal organization of "fierce youth" who could stand up to his opponents. Al-Zayyat pleaded with the president, warning that arbitrarily dissolving the YO might alienate "fine" elements who could be won over through dialogue. Convinced that the YO was packed with Aly Sabri's loyalists, Sadat was initially adamant. Ultimately, he agreed to Al-Zayyat's proposal, but only after Minister of Interior Mamdouh Salem said he was on board with the plan.[77] Accordingly, Al-Zayyat proceeded to promote YO's activities in the summer of 1971. Soon, however, a major attitude shift occurred in response to the 1972–1973 student uprising. Specifically, Sadat lost patience with the YO's inability to assert itself on campus and thereby effectively oppose the leftist influences challenging him.

RISE OF CONSENSUS AROUND ISLAMIST INCORPORATION

In January 1972, mounting opposition to Sadat at Cairo University and elsewhere confirmed the president's fears that his Nasserist rivals and their Marxist allies were on the verge of destabilizing his rule (see chapter 1). The tipping point for Sadat, explains Hassan Abu-Basha, then deputy director of SSIS, came on January 24, when he witnessed Cairo University students' occupation of Tahrir Square and was informed that underground communist organizations were involved.[78] Realizing that the regime had too few friends among students and that the YO was ineffective at confronting of leftist dissidents,[79] Sadat began entertaining the idea of unleashing Islamist groups against his rebellious opponents on college campuses.[80] "Some proposed to [Sadat] confronting the communist current with a religious current, and from there came the idea of forming Islamic groups," explains Al-Nabawi Ismail, then aide to Minister of Interior Mamdouh Salem.[81] This was the genesis of one important element of Sadat's Islamist incorporation policies.[82]

In January, Sadat took steps to facilitate this change in course, just as student protests were erupting. He removed Al-Zayyat from the ASU's leadership, appointing him to the office of deputy prime minister, a ceremonial role devoid of real influence.[83] Meanwhile, the question of the ASU's presence at universities was passed to Secretary for Organizational Affairs MOI. He convinced Sadat that the ruling party's youth organizations were obsolete and full of opportunists, and that the religious current was the only force capable of opposing Nasserist and Marxist dissidents:

> With the beginning of the year 1972, the communists' activities increased, especially at public universities. They had taken control of the student government body, and by implication, all its related activities. Also, they were expressing themselves visibly in the form of wall-magazines. Not only that, but they were also publishing [wall-] magazine articles containing abusive language and cartoons targeting the president, either personally or the regime he represented. In one of my meetings with the president—and at the time I was his adviser for legislative affairs and [ASU] secretary for organizational affairs—he brought up that subject, and asked me: "Are you aware of what is happening at the universities?" I told him: "I am, Mr. President." He went on to ask: "And where is the role of the political organization [of the ASU]?" I answered: "Does your Excellency actually believe there is a real political organization? This is the organization of political authority. The members of the ASU are the same members of the Liberation Rally and the National Union, meaning these are people who have no conviction ['aqida]." He asked, "What do you mean by conviction?" I told him: "Mr. President, these are organizations that members join just to be close to political authority and benefit [from it]. But deep down, you cannot say that these people believe in any political conviction." I added: "I remember, Mr. President, that when I was a student in King Fouad I University, all parties were represented within the student body and had leaders. The Muslim Brotherhood enjoyed that too. But because those affiliated with the Muslim Brotherhood believed in their convictions, it was only enough for one of them to say, 'God is Great and Praise Be to Him' and within a second you would find thousands gathered around him, as if the earth was split open and released them—dwarfing the presence of all other parties." Once I told that to the president, he, smartly, picked up on something and asked: "What are you trying to say?" I told him: "Actually, Mr. President, I mean the return of the Muslim Brotherhood." I said it directly and added: "This is in your own interest and in the interest of the regime, because nobody can confront this kind of thing [opposition on campuses] except for people who have conviction."[84]

MOI goes on to explain that Sadat agreed to his proposal of granting the movement legal status, but he did so on the conditions that the Brotherhood operate under a different name and that former members of its secret apparatus would not be involved. Using connections he enjoyed through Brotherhood-affiliated entrepreneur Abdel-Azim Luqma, MOI scheduled a meeting with one of the group's senior leaders Omar Al-Tilmisani. According to MOI, Al-Tilmisani politely declined the offer of legal status, refused to change the name of the Brotherhood, and alluded to suspicions that Sadat was trying to exploit the Brotherhood for his own purposes. Fearing a potential conflict between the president and the Brotherhood, MOI declined to report Al-Tilmisani's responses to Sadat and proposed instead that the ASU set up its own Islamist groups at universities:

> The next day I met with the president and told him, "I changed my mind, Mr. President." He said, "Go on." I told him, "Instead of changing the name of the Brotherhood and all that, I suggest we form Islamic groups at the university." He asked me: "And who would undertake this?" I answered: "If you just agree to the idea, I am prepared to execute it myself." He said: "I approve."[85]

MOI proceeded with a plan through which his office would recruit students to establish religious organizations and ask them to counter so-called communist influences on campus. Tasked with identifying potential student recruits, MOI explains, was his senior aide at the ASU, Munir Al-Said:

> I had set with him the principles and guidelines for selection, the first of which was that the young man must enjoy upright ethics and integrity (at least in appearance). Then we would introduce him to the idea by telling him about communist influence at the university and the passivity of the good elements and their reluctance to take part in university activism, etc. If he shows enthusiasm and zeal for religion, then we would tell him about our need to create a group that could counter activities contradicting religion and that are destructive to the nation. If he agrees we would ask the person to introduce us to other colleagues who may show enthusiasm to the same idea. All these activities were conducted in a very open manner. Counselor Munir Al-Said used to receive them at

my office (which also happens to be his own place of work), and as I have already pointed out I never met with them as individuals, but only after they became groups.[86]

MOI claims that they succeeded in setting up groups at Cairo University's School of Engineering, from which they spread to Alexandria University and then to Assiut University.[87] He says that his management of the initiative ended in late 1973 once he became governor of Assiut,[88] where he, nevertheless, continued close engagement with Islamist student activists.[89]

SIGHTINGS OF SADAT'S "FIERCE YOUTH"

MOI's initiative began bearing fruit at Cairo University in the fall of 1972, when self-proclaimed Islamist groups suddenly appeared on campus, flaunting anticommunist rhetoric and physically clashing with leftist students during anti-Sadat demonstrations. Such occurrences were not uncommon at the time. For example, in December 1972, pro-government marchers distributed large numbers of anticommunist leaflets and engaged in physical altercations with anti-Sadat students.[90] Some of the march's participants reportedly attacked their leftist opponents with knives, leaving several injured.[91] After intervening to stop the violence, however, authorities refrained from charging the suspects or investigating the incident.[92]

The question of whether or not state officials endorsed such use of violence is a contentious one. SSIS veteran officer Fouad Allam asserts that MOI used ASU funds to purchase knives and metal chains, presumably for students tasked with intimidating attendees of leftist gatherings and defacing their wall magazines.[93] MOI denies these allegations unequivocally, suggesting that his enemies inside the security establishment circulated such rumors to impugn his character.[94] Other officials tell a different story. Abu-Basha, for example, cites an incident in which MOI revealed prior knowledge of, and perhaps complicity with, upcoming attacks against leftist students. Abu-Basha claims that MOI once asked SSIS leaders to arrange to send as many ambulances as possible to Cairo University, where demonstrations by leftist activists were scheduled to occur later that day. In a chilling comment, MOI said that the ambulances would attend to "injured communists whose blood is going to spill."[95] Ahmed Kamal Abul-Magd, who served as ASU's secretary of youth at the time, acknowledges that some government officials were linked to "the phenomenon of internal violence within the universities," but he stops short of naming MOI.[96] Consistent with these narratives are Sadat's exchanges with Al-Zayyat in late December 1972. When the president remarked that he intended to crush an ongoing student mobilization, Al-Zayyat questioned whether such an escalation was politically wise. Sadat responded:

> I am fed up with your politics and your dialogue . . . I have settled the matter—that we need "real" men who can, hit, attack, and storm, and I have assigned Mohamed Othman Ismail, along with a number of Upper Egyptian Members of Parliament to set up teams of university students, arm them and train them . . . And there is the Muslim Brotherhood who can also stand up to students that exhibit color [meaning students with an ideological leaning—as in communists] |. . . .| It is not possible that these incidents at the universities will end except in this way . . . Violence alone will stop these absurdities and indecencies. I do not have time for dialogue and politics. If you want dialogue, go do it yourself.[97]

MOI also holds that he never spent ASU funds on students, except to subsidize a limited range of activities, such as pilgrimage trips to Mecca.[98] Student accounts paint a different story. As detailed next, Wael Othman, one of the leaders of an Islamist student organization at Cairo University, says that MOI offered his group ASU funding in February 1973.[99] According to Othman, ASU Central Committee First Secretary Sayyid Marei did so as well, stating, "The budget of the Youth Organization amounts to one and a half million pounds, and you are most worthy of it. I would gladly put the resources of the [Arab] Socialist Union at your disposal."[100]

Othman's group, the Youth of Islam (YOI), is often accused of acting under MOI's direction at Cairo University.[101] Othman counters that it was rival student organizations, like those affiliated with the IGUs, that cooperated with the regime.[102] He does acknowledge, however, that the regime may have eventually infiltrated YOI and even succeeded in using it in confrontations with leftist groups:[103] "I realized that the Youth of Islam group was impulsively made to follow those who wanted to use it to silence communist voices and to act swiftly to curtail them."[104]

THE LIMITS OF ASU'S COMMAND-AND-CONTROL AND THE RISE OF IGUs

While the regime's top leadership formulated a strategy to establish and manage Islamist groups at public universities, executing that policy was anything but seamless. When the initiative was first conceived, MOI explains, the plan was to house all of the student recruits in a single complex to provide them with training and organize them around a set of coherent goals and strategies. The plan fell through in the summer of 1972 because of the lack of apartment space.[105] Sensing urgency, MOI swiftly adopted a different approach—one that did not lend itself to the degree of centralized control he had initially envisioned. He began approaching existing Islamist organizations and activists in the hope of coopting them and guiding their efforts toward countering communist influences. Therefore, when the YOI emerged on the scene in the fall of 1972, ASU leaders saw the group as the ideal instrument to accomplish their aims, and thus they sought to win over its leaders: "You were like a spark that spread to almost the entire university," said Sayyid Marei to the YOI's cofounders in January 1973 while proposing that the ASU fund their activities.[106] When the YOI leaders turned down the offer, MOI's office manager begged them to reconsider and, in a tasteless and desperate move, assured them that he had performed a pilgrimage multiple times.[107] So eager was the ASU to attract supporters in the student body that when MOI met with the same students weeks later, he placed his hand on the Quran and swore to them that he was loyal to Islam and that his offer of support was sincere.[108] Despite these repeated, enthusiastic offers, Othman says, the YOI would not accept the regime's support.

Even though the regime was ultimately able to prod the YOI into confrontations with leftist activists, per Sadat's objectives, the effectiveness of that strategy was at best doubtful. The credibility of YOI was always in question. Rival Islamist activists suspected that the group was operating at the behest of the ASU, as its members behaved in ways that violated the basic conservative norms prevalent among committed Islamist activists.[109] In any case, by the 1973–74 academic year, YOI had been overshadowed by other Islamist groups, and by the following year, it ceased to exist.[110] As the center of gravity within Islamist student activism began shifting to other groups, the regime's attention shifted in turn.

As authorities became more receptive to Islamist political activism, a credible grassroots Islamist student movement emerged autonomously from the state: *Al-Gama'at Al-Islamiyya fi-l-Gami'at* (the IGUs).[111] These groups not only enjoyed considerable credibility within the student body but also were genuinely hostile to communist and Nasserist currents, and thus they were primed to confront them without external encouragement or direction. Although MOI's plan had envisaged a set of Islamist organizations the ASU could mobilize on demand, like the YO and VO, these new realities prompted a shift in strategy.

Instead of focusing on forming its own organizations, the regime began extending a helping hand to IGUs, even though that approach would not provide the same degree of control it initially sought.[112] Some in the security establishment were unnerved by ASU's support for Islamist currents.[113] Nevertheless, according to Fouad Allam, the will of the political leadership prevailed, as relevant security bodies were forbidden to interfere with such groups.[114] It is in this context that one can best understand the state's initially welcoming orientation toward IGUs.

MOI reports that following his move to Assiut in late 1973, the Supreme Council on Islamic Affairs (SCIA) took responsibility for promoting Islamist activism at universities.[115] Little is known about the fate of this initiative inside SCIA, save some clues found in U.S. State Department documents made public in recent years. For example, in the spring of 1976, Secretary General of SCIA Tawfiq Oweida told a U.S. Embassy official that he enrolled ten thousand students in a program aimed at promoting "Sadat's moderate views of religion and politics."[116] That said, no evidence indicates that the program had much bearing on campus politics, especially after the IGUs began dominating university activism and student unions. According to Mahmoud Gamee, after losing his position at SCIA because of a corruption scandal in the late 1970s, Oweida was instructed by Sadat to form Islamic groups on campuses that could act as a counterweight to the IGUs.[117] At this point, the IGUs had angered the president by criticizing his foreign policies and causing unrest at Assiut and Al-Minya Universities. Consistent with Gamee's account, Oweida, then head of the religious affairs committee at the ruling NDP, told U.S. officials in September 1979 he planned to "reinvigorate NDP student organizations," to counter the IGUs' opposition.[118] Sadat appeared to be invested in the summer camps Oweida organized for youth recruits,[119] but, as Gamee explains, the campus program never accomplished much as a result of the IGUs' commanding influence.[120]

IGUs IN BRIEF

The IGUs were by far the most influential national student movement of 1970s Egypt. In addition to its central role in altering the dynamics of Egyptian politics during this period, the IGUs movement acquired historical significance for three reasons. First, its leaders and networks were essential to the return of the Muslim Brotherhood as a powerful political organization in the post-Nasser era. Second, some IGU chapters in Middle and Upper Egypt served as breeding grounds for *al-Gamʿa al-Islamiyya* (GI),[121] whose members were implicated in Sadat's 1981 assassination and led an armed struggle against the Mubarak regime until 1997.[122] Third, some IGU affiliates in Alexandria cofounded one of the leading contemporary Salafist groups in Egypt, the Alexandrian Salafist Call movement, which participated in forming—and later took control of—Al-Nour Party.[123]

Cofounders of the IGUs attribute the roots of their movement to small student associations that long promoted religious values on campuses through small-scale, nonpolitical activities like Quranic reading groups. At Cairo University, *al-Gamʿiyya al-Diniyya* (the Religious Society) at the Faculty of Medicine[124] became an important site for these efforts during the early 1970s.[125] Among its early members was a student by the name of Abdel-Moneim Aboul-Fotouh, who would later become an iconic figure in the history of the Muslim Brotherhood and of student activism in Egypt.

Frustrated with the meager funding they received from the leftist-dominated Student Union at the Faculty of Medicine, members of the Religious Society contested the fall 1973 union election, winning a majority of its seats.[126] This was an unusual development, since Nasserist and Marxist currents had long held the upper hand in student union bodies.[127] In that same year, the organization adopted the name the Islamic Group (*Al-Gamaʿah Al-Islamiyya*), which, Aboul-Fotouh says, was inspired by Pakistan's foremost Islamist movement.[128]

With access to the Student Union's budget, the Islamic Group (hereafter referred to as IG) expanded the scale and scope of its activities. The group quickly became a focal point for Islamist student activism at Cairo University, inspiring the formation of chapters in other faculties as well as at other universities. Its occasional lectures turned into regular, high-profile weekly events that brought prominent Islamic thinkers to campus, including those allied with both the regime and the Muslim Brotherhood.

Unlike Marxist and Nasserist union leaders whose efforts focused chiefly on political issues, IG representatives, quite enterprisingly, devoted careful attention to providing services to the student body.[129] With access to the union budget, the IG expanded its social services over time to include selling books at discounted prices, subsidizing pilgrimage trips, and selling Islamic garb to female students.[130] As its profile and outreach expanded, the IG's candidate, Abdel-Moneim Aboul-Fotouh, was elected president of the Student Union of Cairo University in 1975, an event that signaled the left's ceding of ground to the nascent Islamist current. In the same year, the various IG chapters at Cairo University established a joint leadership council composed of all college-level leaders. Elected to head the first such council was a medical student by the name of Essam El-Erian, who would later rise to fame as a leading Muslim Brotherhood figure.[131]

By the mid-1970s, the IG was organizing periodic student camps.[132] Usually held on campus during summer or winter breaks over the course of a few weeks, these retreats brought together thousands of students to study a variety of subjects related to Islamic thought.[133] Featuring speaking engagements by prominent Islamic scholars, these camps provided an easy way to recruit new members en masse and build their intellectual foundation.[134] In addition, they offered Islamist student activists a rare opportunity to network and collaborate with like-minded peers from other academic units or universities. In this setting, the IG's model spread to distant universities, and the Cairo University contingent could collaborate through well-institutionalized, formal bodies with similar groups from across the country.[135]

In 1977, IG chapters nationwide formed a single governing council under the name "The Islamic Group in Egypt." The presidency of the council went to a member of the Cairo University Faculty of Medicine chapter, Helmy Al-Gazzar, who subsequently became a leading figure in the Muslim Brotherhood. With these developments, the IGUs garnered national recognition as a powerful social force, despite the diversity of opinion within the movement. Simultaneously, the IGUs enhanced their legal and political standing in relation to the state, as their expanded presence in student unions throughout the country enabled them to gain control of the national student union.[136]

By the fall of 1978, the control of Islamist currents over university student activism was complete. Islamists came to dominate student union elections at eight out of twelve of Egypt's public universities. Meanwhile, Islamist candidates won a majority of seats in the National Student Union. The post of vice president went to an engineering student from Al-Minya University named Abul-Ela Madi, who would later assume a prominent role in the Muslim Brotherhood, before leaving to form Al-Wasat Party in 1995.[137]

The IGUs were also extremely active in a variety of political and religious spheres outside of university campuses.[138] In the lead up to the 1976 parliamentary election, IGUs took an active role in campaigning on behalf of like-minded candidates.[139] Around that same time, IG chapters in Cairo and Alexandria began organizing Eid prayers in public squares, attended by almost half a million people in the 1980–81 academic year. These prayers were an important public outreach vehicle for IGUs and provided an opportunity to display the popular support they enjoyed.[140]

Without question, the proliferation of IGUs and their expanding power under Sadat completely transformed campus life at many universities. Politically, they tipped the scales against Nasserist and Marxist groups whose intense anti-Sadat demonstrations had dominated university activism throughout the early 1970s. Experiencing these shifting fortunes firsthand was former Islamist student activist Wael Othman, who was shocked in 1974 to witness "communist" students being booed off stage and kicked out of political gatherings, "after they were the ones who used to kick us out of previous student movement [gatherings]."[141] Reflecting on these changes, 1970s student activist Badr Mohamed Badr credits the IGUs for bringing down what he characterizes as indecent wall magazines, promoting "Islamic conduct" among students, and encouraging female students to veil. Badr, later a prominent Muslim Brotherhood figure and journalist, writes that under IGUs' guidance, dormitories became "permanent Islamic camps, in which each student was transformed into a young man committed to Islam in his morals, intellect and dealings."[142]

Other accounts are less sanguine about the IGUs' impact on campus life. Leftist activist Ahmed Bahaaeddin Shaaban asserts that IGUs monopolized student union resources to fund their parochial initiatives and accuses them of violating the personal rights of students through intrusive practices like mandatory gender segregation.[143] Reports of IGUs' transgressions were much more serious at universities in Middle and Upper Egypt,[144] which, to borrow a term coined by sociologist Abdullah Shalaby, turned into "Islamic zones" where IGU affiliates regulated student behavior and disrupted events deemed Islamically objectionable.[145] There is no shortage of allegations of IGUs antagonizing Coptic students and generally behaving in a sectarian manner.[146] "Our enthusiasm surpassed our wisdom, and so our actions were marred by many mistakes," candidly acknowledges Al-Minya University IG leader Mohy Eissa. He admits to enforcing gender segregation through intimidation, vandalizing concerts and alcohol-serving establishments, destroying a church construction site, sabotaging Christian holiday celebrations, and holding Coptic students as hostages in showdowns with security forces.[147] University and state officials' exercise of extraordinary patience with the IGUs despite such grave misconduct prompted accusations that these groups were operating with the support and guidance of the Sadat regime—allegations that the following section addresses.

THE REGIME AND THE GROWTH OF IGUs

Leaders of the Cairo University IG insist that they never struck "deals" with the ruling party or collaborated with it in any formal capacity.[148] "I hereby testify before God that we did not strike any deals with the regime or anyone," says Abdel-Moneim Aboul-Fotouh, declaring that he would have been privy to any such deals.[149] The accounts of IGU affiliates from other regions generally conform to this narrative. Abul-Ela Madi, once a leader of Al-Minya University's IG, asserts that, the YOI aside, Islamist student groups operated independently of the Sadat regime.[150] Salah Hashem, widely recognized as the godfather of the IG at Assiut University, acknowledges that MOI, in his capacity as provincial governor, funded some IG activities, but asserts that the state had no hand in the creation of his group nor did it ever exert control over these activities.[151] Abbas Al-Sisi, an Alexandria-based Muslim Brotherhood leader who was close to the student movement, claims that those who formed the IG at Alexandria University did so of their own free will and without any external support or guidance.[152]

These claims appear credible for three reasons. First, if IGUs were truly under the regime's direction in the late 1970s, their activists would not have intensified criticism of Sadat during this period, especially after it became clear that the government was preparing to sign a peace agreement with Israel. As their clashes with authorities became more heated, Islamist student activists started getting arrested and facing a variety of state-imposed restrictions. These activists' confrontations with the security establishment escalated during this period, a fact that undermines allegations of formal collaboration with the regime. Equally pertinently, Sadat's order to form an Islamic network to counter the IGUs during his final years in office suggests that the regime had not exercised control over these groups through much of the prior period.

Second, the rigidly hierarchical structure of the IGUs appears to have prevented the type of infiltration experienced by the YOI, whose active membership evidently included regime collaborators. For example, in accordance with the principle of al-sam' wa-l-ta'ah ("listen and obey"), student affiliates of the IGUs were required to follow their superiors' orders blindly.[153] With so little room to contest or interpret leaders' directives, any action aimed at disrupting the group from within was detectable. This is in contrast to the YOI, where affiliates often acted independently of their leadership's instructions. Moreover, as Aboul-Fotouh indicates, IGUs insisted that their members rigidly adhere to such conservative social norms that it was difficult for any infiltrator to conform.[154] In fact, many older Muslim Brotherhood leaders found these standards difficult to meet, as they had not been inculcated with the puritanical norms that guided the practices of the newer generations of Islamist activists.[155]

Third, the deep ideological differences between IGU leaders and leftist currents made conflict between the two almost inevitable, with or without the regime's active intervention. As soon as his group began organizing at a small scale, Aboul-Fotouh recalls, it quickly entered into physical clashes with leftist activists who were thought to have mocked or insulted Islamic religious traditions.[156]

IGUs also did their share of ideological combat with their leftist counterparts. They endorsed Al-Azhar Grand Imam Abdel-Halim Mahmoud's statements deeming communism inconsistent with Islam.[157] When the state legalized political parties, the IGUs issued a statement rejecting any party formed on the basis of Marxism, an obvious reference to

Al-Tagammu.[158] In late 1976, the IG of Cairo University refused to participate in Student and Society Week activities and marches to avoid cooperation with Marxist and Nasserist students. The statement read:

> The Islamic Group is well aware that the Islam to which it adheres can
> never meet with Marxism and Nasserism with respect to either the fun-
> damentals, the means, the programs, or values. Thus, we can never coop-
> erate with them or put our hands in theirs, or in those of anyone who
> does not believe in the righteous religion no matter the circumstances.[159]

When the 1977 Bread Uprising occurred weeks later, the IGUs kept their
distance, at least officially. According to Aboul-Fotouh, some movement
affiliates participated in protests as individuals,[160] but the IGUs—as organizations—did not participate or offer support of any kind.[161] During the
same month, a Cairo University IG chapter echoed the regime's characterization of the protests as misguided socialism: "Experience has taught
us that problems arise with the implementation of socialism," the statement read, before asserting that socialism was not a solution to society's
problems.[162]

Mutual antipathies between communist and Islamist currents were
extremely pronounced on college campuses, prompting IGU-leftist clashes
that were, claims Aboul-Fotouh, spontaneous rather than planned or
directed by the regime.[163] That said, the IGUs were well aware that their
role in marginalizing leftist activists was pleasing to the regime, even if
the parties never struck a formal agreement to that effect. Just as Sadat
began publicly attacking IGUs in the spring of 1979, they fired back with
a carefully worded statement that diplomatically, but firmly, reminded
the president what the IGUs had done for him by standing up to his leftist
adversaries at universities:

> The youth of the Islamic Groups believe that Islamism and atheism can
> never meet, and accordingly came the role of Islamic Groups in purifying
> the university of communist and Nasserist thought that were once prom-
> inent . . . And [today] we no longer hear at the university about the clubs
> of communist political thought, and we no longer hear about the meet-
> ings by [clubs of] Nasserist thought and we no longer see the wall maga-
> zines that were filled with the ugliest types of insults and slander directed

at various officials ... That used to be a prominent feature at the universities of Egypt before the rise of Islamic Groups at the Universities.[164]

In other words, with or without a formal agreement, the IGUs were clearly aware that their interests—disempowering and marginalizing leftist groups on campus—converged with those of Sadat. They were by no means oblivious to the fact that the sharing of a common adversary—the left—explained the regime's leniency toward their activities.[165]

Additionally, even if the regime had no hand in forming or managing the IGUs, it evidently welcomed their formation with open arms, allowing these groups to expand and flourish as part of a broader Islamist incorporation strategy. The accounts of Islamist leaders who were active during this period make that point unambiguously. These accounts display a consensus that the political space open to Islamist activism at universities was a product of the regime's desire to counterbalance its leftist adversaries. According to Al-Sayyid Abdel-Sattar Al-Meleegy, criticism from the left impelled Sadat to adopt "the well-known political game of using one political current to undermine another, giving a blind eye for the growing Islamist current in order for it to prevail at universities and replace the communist one."[166] Badr makes a similar argument:

> Political authority did not stand in confrontation with the Islamic Groups at the outset because it hoped to achieve two goals. First, it hoped that Islamic Groups would stand against leftist, Marxist and Nasserist currents, which at the time were controlling the student activism arena and causing many problems for the regime. It needed the presence of another current to clash with these [leftist] currents, contain them, and mitigate the troubles they are causing authorities. Secondly, in the pre-October 1973 era the regime was not prepared to deal with student unrest, and therefore it envisioned that Islamic Groups would enter into conflict and clashes with the other currents such that the university would be too preoccupied with its internal differences to confront the political realities at the time.[167]

Aboul-Fotouh's account echoes this interpretation. The state's enthusiastic support for the expansion of IGUs during this period led him to conclude that Sadat facilitated their activities to undermine leftist dissidents:

I imagine that Sadat found a way to undermine the communist current in a spontaneous manner without any effort on his part, and that is by letting the Islamist current work freely and expand without putting any obstacles in front of it, or without going after it. And the arena was totally conducive to the growth of this current and its natural and spontaneous proliferation. There was no deal or secret agreement as the foes of the Islamist movement have claimed.[168]

In fact, Aboul-Fotouh says that the level of freedom that Islamist currents enjoyed under Sadat was unprecedented and unmatched under Mubarak's rule:

The world was open in front of us. There were none of the obstacles of the Nasserist era or those of the Mubarak regime. I was at the time, as a student leader, able to meet at any time with the President of the University Sufi Abu-Taleb (later speaker of parliament) or Hafez Ghanem, Deputy Prime Minister and Minister of Education, especially when the student movement or the Islamic Groups encountered problems at any Egyptian university. And there was also tolerance or lenience from the state toward the Muslim Brotherhood after they were released from prisons, as they were allowed to exist and work in public, including organizing festivals celebrating the birth of the Prophet in public squares. And the security apparatus never interfered in any of the activities we carried out, whether from nearby or from afar, until the late 1970s when the state moved against Islamists and security interferences became more overt. The Sadat era was notable for a freedom that Egypt had never witnessed since the revolution, and the freedom was real |. . . .| We never heard of anyone during the Sadat era, the 1970s, or that any of us or those of the Muslim Brotherhood ever getting arrested or summoned by security agencies. And he never prevented us from distributing books or publications of any type, and we never saw a single state security agent entering the university and object to any activity of ours . . . with the exception of what happened with the communist organization, and the Military Technical College.[169]

Even while acknowledging state repression of his leftist counterparts, Aboul-Fotouh asserts that the political arena was equally open to all political forces, Islamist and leftist alike.[170] Such a claim, however, can hardly be substantiated by relying exclusively on the accounts of Islamist activists. Central to any such assessment are the accounts of these activists' rivals, the Nasserists and Marxists. Given all of the state-imposed obstacles that leftist activists faced during the period (as detailed in chapter 4), the argument that Sadat was equally lenient with all political currents is tenuous at best.[171] Moreover, evidence suggests that the regime did a lot more to enable Islamist domination of student activism than passively stand on the sidelines.[172]

The state's endorsement of the Islamist student movement was unmistakable. Government figures and leaders of the official religious establishment were featured prominently in the programs of Islamist student camps,[173] and Ministry of Youth officials often presided over the student award ceremonies at these gatherings.[174] It was not unusual to observe at IGUs events senior regime figures speaking alongside Islamist leaders in a collegial fashion. For example, according to Abbas Al-Sisi, Osman Ahmed Osman and then minister of housing Hassaballah Al-Kafrawy spoke alongside Muslim Brotherhood General Guide Omar Al-Tilmisani at Alexandria University in 1980. Speaking before a large audience, Osman praised the general guide while fondly reminiscing about his own past engagement with the Muslim Brotherhood.[175]

Contrary to claims that Sadat opened political space indiscriminately and did the Islamist movement no favors, government officials and state-appointed university administrators often intervened to facilitate the work of these groups. MOI recounts getting the Ministries of Aviation and Endowments to sponsor pilgrimage trips for IGU members.[176] Aboul-Fotouh admits to the extraordinary access he enjoyed to senior university administrators: "Sufi Abu-Taleb who was the Vice President of [Cairo] University until my graduation in 1977 never turned down any of the requests I made as the leader of the Student Union."[177]

Moreover, by the late 1970s, the state not only had recognized the IGUs as an established political entity but also worked with it collaboratively. As the figurehead of the IGUs, Helmy Al-Gazzar reports convening frequently with senior officials like Prime Minister Mamdouh Salem and SSIS Chief Elewa Zaher. On one memorable occasion, he notes, Salem remarked, "I got offices for you all at the Egypt [Arab Socialist] Party," insinuating that IGU leaders should join the ruling party after they graduate. Such meetings, Al-Gazzar states, had a positive impact on the relationship between Islamists and the government and fostered cooperation. For example, Minister of Interior Al-Nabawi Ismail requested the help of IGU national leaders whenever he needed to deescalate contentious situations involving student unrest or cross-confessional conflict.[178] In turn, Ismail came to the IGUs defense when their activities were ruffling feathers and raising eyebrows. In November 1978, Ismail was quoted in *Al-Gumhuria* stating:

> The Islamic Groups [at the Universities] are working publicly and openly, and their goals are pure with no ambiguity around them. They reject violence and do not adopt it and they protect Egypt and its youth and do not corrupt them. The Islamic Groups work for the [greater] good . . . and the regime cares for the [greater] good.[179]

Even in Assiut, where the IG had a rather prickly relationship with authorities, MOI says he often advocated for the group as governor. In one incident, he turned down a request by Prime Minister Mustafa Khalil to intervene against the IG's practice of enforcing gender segregation in university auditoriums. MOI also reports engaging in long dialogues with the group's members, sometimes to deter them from protesting or stirring up unrest.[180] Despite the good rapport he enjoyed with IG members, the former governor contends, these students always acted on their own convictions and not the regime's directives: "The students of the Islamic Groups," MOI states, "were never agents of the regime, but rather loyalists to the Islamic way in the most civilized form of social solidarity and cooperation for the [greater] good."[181]

In addition to the regime's endorsement of the IGUs, the willingness of university administrators and the responsible state authorities to facilitate their activities was arguably indispensable to the success of the Islamist student movement. Note that the IGUs' rise to prominence was predicated on gaining control of student union bodies, thereby securing access to university resources. Both Aboul-Fotouh and El-Erian, who helped build the IG's network at Cairo University's Faculty of Medicine, acknowledge that before securing adequate funding through these means, their group suffered extreme financial constraints.[182] Assuming control of the student union, they explain, provided them with office space, as well as logistical and financial support from the university. Only then, an organization that was barely able to afford printing paper a few years earlier could now print books en masse and sponsor conferences and retreats for thousands of students. The official activities recounted by IG leaders carried costs beyond the capacity of a student organization lacking access to university resources: pilgrimage trips to Saudi Arabia,[183] publishing and printing book series,[184] selling subsidized textbooks to students, sponsoring student trips to Luxor and Aswan,[185] and selling Islamic garb as part of a campaign promoting veiling.[186] Footing the bill for many of these expenses was a receptive university administration.[187] More significantly, the famed student camps that expanded the regional and national networks of IGUs were supervised by the university,[188] which provided housing and meals for hundreds of students for nearly two weeks each year.[189]

In other words, the ability of the university administration to extend or withhold funding for IGUs activities offered the state another channel through which to support (and, at times, curb) Islamist student activism on college campuses. This channel enabled the state to back these groups' efforts without the overt intervention of the regime, just as MOI had initially envisioned in 1972. In fact, MOI appeared to have reverted to that noninterventionist strategy during his tenure as governor of Assiut, where he purportedly funded the IG's university camps from the governorate's budget.[190]

Essam El-Erian is blunt about the patron–client relationship between the university and the student unions during this period. El-Erian recalls that discussions between union leaders and university administrators about issues like the provision of student services and meals involved a great deal of bargaining and "a type of deal-making."[191] It was in this context that the university became the "communication channel" between state authorities and student leaders, according to Islamist lawyer Montasser Al-Zayat, another former member of the student movement at Cairo University.[192]

The vast discretionary power this arrangement afforded the regime in relation to the IGUs became evident after Islamist currents incurred Sadat's wrath. Aboul-Fotouh notes that the cooperative attitude that university administrators had shown Islamist student groups for nearly a decade disappeared in the late 1970s, when IGU affiliates intensified their criticism of Sadat. At that time, administrators began hampering IGUs activities by withholding funding, increasing bureaucratic oversight, tightening regulations governing student housing, limiting services and meals for student events, and, most significant, cancelling student summer camps.[193]

Notably, state support for Islamist activism occurred despite the objections of the security establishment, which was ordered not to interfere with Islamists on campuses and elsewhere. "We even used to camp out with two thousand students in the [Red Sea resort of] Al-Ain Al-Sukhna without any form of intervention from the security apparatus. . . . We used to invite scholars of all Islamist leanings to give lectures without anyone asking us 'why did you bring that person?' Or, 'this person is not allowed,'" recounts Aboul-Fotouh.[194] Moreover, this policy continued in spite of clear signs that some elements of the Islamist movement were mounting violent actions against state targets, as evidenced by the attack against the Military Technical College (MTC) on April 19, 1974.[195] Despite these indications, the regime's policy of promoting Islamist groups on campus continued for a time.

As regime tolerance for dissent waned in the wake of the 1977 Bread Uprising, the state began forcefully cracking down on all oppositionist voices. Although the initial phase of the clampdown was directed primarily at leftists (as described in the previous chapter), the Islamists' dominance of university campuses began to be perceived as a danger to the regime, and thus restrictions on their activities increased. The dramatic turning point came in 1979, when Egypt signed a peace treaty with Israel, thereby provoking the fierce opposition of the IGUs.

As the IGUs became more confrontational with authorities, Sadat started singling them out in his speeches, often expressing disapproval of their behavior at universities and their attempts to politicize religion. In a January 1979 address that specifically cited the activities of religious groups at universities, Sadat declared, "I am against injecting religion in politics or politics in religion. Whoever wants to worship, places of worships are available, and whoever wants to practice politics, the legal channels of political parties are available."[196] Soon thereafter, the dangers of mixing politics and religion became a recurring theme in Sadat's political speeches,[197] which began to feature denunciations of religiously oriented political activists as "groups hiding behind religion."[198]

Sadat's critical tone only angered the IGUs. They responded by issuing an open letter to the president through the national student union they controlled, calling him out for failing to fulfill his promise to bring about a state of science and faith.[199] Further escalation occurred in March, when the IGUs issued another statement in the name of the national student union rejecting the peace treaty with Israel.[200] The IGUs then organized campus protests against the treaty, leading to showdowns with security forces and, in the case Al-Minya University, the arrest of ten IG leaders, including Abul-Ela Madi, the vice president of the National Student Union.[201] Not long after the arrest, the president gave a series of speeches—including a televised address—in which he alleged that the IGUs received foreign funding. And in a provocatively condescending remark typical of the patriarchal style he often adopted, Sadat reported receiving complaints from parents that the IGUs were emboldening students to question and disrespect their elders.[202]

Eventually, Sadat ordered the release of the members of Al-Minya IG who had been arrested in April and, displaying a slight softening of heart, he sent them an envoy conveying the message that "you are all like my children."[203] Yet the president was no longer willing to permit his "children" free reign. That summer, in a move presumably directed at the IGUs, Sadat dissolved existing student unions, issued new bylaws that downsized and reduced the power of elected student bodies, and enhanced university administrators' oversight of these bodies' activities.[204] From that point, the relationship between the state and the IGUs became a security file,[205] as they no longer enjoyed the legally protected status afforded by control of the student union. Nonetheless, the IGUs continued to push back. They voiced opposition to the president's foreign policies, especially his agreement to host the exiled Shah of Iran, an act the IGUs deemed subservient to Western interests and insulting to Iran's Islamic Revolution.[206] Criticism would continue through the fall of 1981, when Sadat, a month before his assassination, ordered the arrest of more than a thousand opposition figures from across the ideological spectrum, including numerous leaders and affiliates of the IGUs.

This crackdown on the IGUs deepened growing discord inside the movement.[207] Once it became clear that the regime wanted a showdown, divisions deepened between IGU members who wanted to challenge the regime through nonviolent political engagement, and those who were prepared to consider more aggressive measures.[208] The former current established a foothold inside the Muslim Brotherhood (as explained in chapter 3), while the latter evolved into *Al-Gamaʿah Al-Islamiyya*, thus embarking on a decades-long armed struggle against the state.[209]

Many characterize the regime's showdown with the IGUs and other opposition forces as a manifestation of Sadat's paranoia, which fueled his fury at the slightest hint of dissent. There is more to the story, however, than an emotionally unstable president. Sadat's falling out with the IGUs— and with Islamist currents more generally—during his final years in office speaks to broader tensions within the coalition he had devised in the early 1970s.

During the early years of de-Nasserization, Islamist currents played a central role in discrediting and marginalizing the leftist opponents of that project. Nonetheless, as the state began to implement the foreign policy elements of de-Nasserization, specifically reorientation toward the West and the pursuit of a settlement with Israel, the Islamists became an obstacle to Sadat's vision. The president could no longer tolerate the harsh criticism Islamist groups and leaders were directing at the regime's foreign policies. Nor could he afford the public relations consequences of foreign reporting about the state's apparent toleration of Islamist sectarian violence,[210] as it undermined the image of modernization and liberalism he sought to convey to his Western allies. In other words, the Islamist current was useful to Sadat when his objective was the marginalization of leftist adversaries, but he could not abide their opposition to his chief foreign policy goal—that is, the deepening of Egypt's Western alliances.

Thus, in reflecting on Sadat's relations with the Islamist student movement, many observers contend that the late president used the IGUs and threw them under the bus once they served his purposes. The long-term outcome of Islamist incorporation policies suggests that Sadat was also being used. The Islamists used the political space he afforded them to rebuild the organizational base of the Muslim Brotherhood, enabling its reemergence as a dominant actor in opposition politics. By the time Sadat began opposing the IGUs in 1979, it was too late to prevent their efforts from bearing fruit: a resurrected and politically robust Muslim Brotherhood. Facilitating this rebirth was the second key element of Sadat's Islamist incorporation policies, permitting the Brotherhood's return to open political activity.

Islamist Incorporation and the Reconstitution of the Muslim Brotherhood

"I am an Egyptian Marxist," said Ismail Sabri Abdallah at a cabinet meeting, shortly before getting interrupted by an angry minister in attendance:

> Marxist? Fine by me. But an Egyptian Marxist? That I do not understand. The word Marxist means blasphemy and atheism. If you are an atheist, that is your business. But an Egyptian atheist? That I cannot fathom, because there is not a single atheist in Egypt among its sons and those who truly belong to it.

Abdallah, a longtime icon of the Egyptian communist movement and then minister of planning, confronted his critic: "You say I am atheist, yet I know God better than you do."

Abdallah's critic exploded in outrage: "I wish that were the case. But is there even such a thing as an atheist who knows God? How could one live such a contradiction?" And just as Abdallah was lighting his cigar, his detractor asked, "And is there such a thing as a communist who smokes cigars and who indulges in this lavish wealth you are enjoying? Or does your communism consist only of handing poverty to the people, and splitting the wealth amongst yourselves?"[211]

The man taunting Abdallah was famed business mogul Osman Ahmed Osman, a close friend of the president and his minister of housing for much of the 1970s. He is best known as the founder of the Arab Contractors, once one of the region's largest construction companies. Osman is an illustrious example of Egyptian capitalists who haggled with the Nasserist establishment to shield their interests inside the state-led economy and who later emerged as a powerful force in the coalition that lobbied for infitah under Sadat. Despite the unusual privileges he enjoyed under Nasser, Osman became an unwavering critic of the late president,[212] and as this exchange illustrates, of Nasser's Marxist allies. The influence Osman gained inside the ruling party in the 1970s epitomized the shift in the state's economic outlook and its embrace of a rising class of business people.[213] His prominence also represented the marriage of political power and private capital, both symbolically and literally, as Osman's son was married to the president's daughter.

In his memoirs, Osman, whose elementary school teacher in Ismailia was none other than Hassan Al-Banna,[214] acknowledges his youthful affiliation with the Muslim Brotherhood, but he claims that his formal ties to the group ended with his graduation from college.[215] Having retained his affinity with the movement, Osman used his influence to shield many Brotherhood members from the wrath of Nasser after their infamous falling out. He offered them employment in his company, especially at its branches in the Arab Gulf, where many exiled Brotherhood figures took refuge during the 1950s and 1960s.[216] His advocacy on behalf of the Muslim Brotherhood continued into the Sadat era, as he became a key player in the regime's rapprochement with the movement.

That Osman was simultaneously a chief advocate of both infitah and the Brotherhood's return to the political arena was by no means coincidental. His role reflected the complementarity of the two sets of policies. Islamist support was central to overcoming the left's opposition to economic liberalization and the reversal of the Nasserist social pact. This dynamic is reflected in the previous exchange, which summarizes the strategies infitah advocates like Osman adopted to counter "Egyptian Marxist" adversaries like Abdallah—that is, they would resort to religious appeals to discredit and defeat leftist political opponents. And that is exactly what Osman did to the extent that he shouldered a good part of the responsibility for making the Brotherhood an ally in Sadat's war against the left.[217] Osman was the perfect man for the job: a pro-infitah, Brotherhood-sympathetic business magnate with strong personal ties to Sadat and an animosity to Nasserists and communists. Osman's entire career is living proof of the affinity between infitah and Islamist incorporation.

Osman's efforts were not, by any means, isolated. They were part of a broader attempt to reset relations with Islamist currents in the hope that they would counterbalance the regime's leftist detractors.[218] Shortly after the 1971 Corrective Revolution, Sadat used the mediation of Saudi King Faisal to meet with Muslim Brotherhood leaders who had fled to the kingdom during Nasser's rule. According to Mohamed Hassanein Heikal, the president told the audience that he was fighting the same elements they clashed with under Nasser, and "that he shares their goals of resisting atheism and communism." Although Sadat expressed willingness to cooperate with the Brotherhood and facilitate its return to public life, according to Heikal, most of the attendees had no authorization to make commitments on behalf of the group and likely were wary of the president's intentions.[219] Nevertheless, the president kept trying.

That same year, Sadat assigned his old friend and confidant Mahmoud Gamee to meet with exiled Muslim Brotherhood leaders and attempt a reconciliation with the group. "We agreed to allow them all back to Egypt, and that those who were fired would be given back their jobs, and they asked that their appropriated political rights be reinstated, for the freedom to preach, and for the release of their prisoners," writes Gamee. He also met with Brotherhood figures serving life sentences in Tora prison, paving the way for their release, as well as that of a host of other senior leaders, including General Guide Hassan Al-Houdaiby and his successor, Omar Al-Tilmisani.[220] More pardons followed, and, by March 1975, the entire Muslim Brotherhood was outside of prison walls.[221] "May God bless you, Sadat, on the path of good deeds and reform," writes Al-Tilmisani in a 1974 *Al-Ahram* editorial praising the president for freeing political prisoners and restoring their jobs and properties.[222]

At the 1972 meeting between MOI and Al-Tilmisani cited earlier, Sadat offered the Muslim Brotherhood a return to public life with two caveats: the organization would operate under a new name, and the offer did not extend to members of the Brotherhood's secret apparatus. When Al-Tilmisani declined, expressing fear that Sadat was trying to use the Brotherhood, MOI countered, "And why don't you use him for the sake of the Islamic *daʿwah*?!"[223] Al-Tilmisani ended up doing just that, although not immediately.

Sadat's offer came before recently released Muslim Brotherhood leaders (many still recovering from the consequences of prolonged incarceration) could act decisively to reestablish their organization. Additionally, as historian Abdullah Al-Arian notes, before 1974, members differed on fundamental issues like the nature of the reformed organization: Would its activities be focused on intellectual production or political activism? Eventually, Al-Tilmisani emerged as the leader of a consensus[224] to revive and expand the Muslim Brotherhood's profile in both the intellectual and political spheres.[225] The regime's representatives were receptive to this idea, albeit with conditions.

The regime's promise of a new relationship with the Brotherhood was tested in the aftermath of the April 1974 Military Technical Institute attack. Once it became known that chief suspect Saleh Sariya acknowledged previous contacts with Muslim Brotherhood members, the group's leaders were certain that Sadat would return them to prison. "Every Brother packed a suitcase for prison," reports Saleh Abu-Ruqayiq, a Brotherhood leader who was summoned for questioning following the attack.[226] Yet, upon meeting with investigators, Abu-Ruqayiq was in shock. Not only did they permit him to leave after questioning, they also treated him in a friendly and courteous manner, something the former inmate had never witnessed during his previous dealings with authorities. The incident convinced Abu-Ruqayiq that the regime was actually sincere about seeking a new relationship with the Brotherhood and that its outreach effort afforded an opportunity that must be seized.

Hoping to develop a channel for dialogue, Abu-Ruqayiq used his connection with Mahmoud Abu-Wafya, First Lady Jehane Al-Sadat's brother-in-law, to secure meetings with Minister of Interior Mamdouh Salem and ASU leader Hafez Ghanem. Soon it became clear that Sadat wanted to limit the Brotherhood's political activity to spaces he could manage and regulate. Thus, through Abu-Wafya, Sadat invited Abu-Ruqayiq and other Muslim Brotherhood leaders to join the ASU, thereby countering communist elements inside the organization. Although his fellow Brotherhood leaders were wary, Abu-Ruqayiq joined the ruling party on an individual basis and served on the committee planning the body's internal restructuring.

Meanwhile, Osman Ahmed Osman initiated another channel of communication between Sadat and the Muslim Brotherhood. Osman asked the group's leaders to prepare a memo for the president summarizing their vision for political and social reform. According to Al-Tilmisani, the nine-page document they submitted led to follow-up meetings with then vice president Hosni Mubarak.[227] On another occasion, Osman arranged for a meeting between the president and another Muslim Brotherhood figure, Helmy Abdel-Meguid. One of Osman's longtime associates at the Arab Contractors, Abdel-Meguid handed Sadat a request to allow the Brotherhood to resume its activities. The president, yet again, stated he would allow this only if the group agreed to operate under a different name. When Abdel-Meguid said that his group would not accede to such a request, Sadat proposed a compromise: the Brotherhood would operate under its own name, but it would do so without a government license.[228]

The spirit of this understanding was apparent throughout the Sadat era, as the Muslim Brotherhood resumed its activities despite lacking legal standing. In 1976, the Brotherhood was permitted to relaunch *Al-Dawa* magazine, which would become an institutional base for its activities. *Al-Dawa* allowed the Muslim Brotherhood to develop a public profile and articulate a distinct voice in national debates. Al-Tilmisani proudly says that *Al-Dawa* was the only magazine at the time that did not have to censor its articles, notwithstanding some occasional objections from the Ministry of Interior.[229] *Al-Dawa* was reportedly printed at state facilities,[230] and a prime minister once offered Al-Tilmisani public funds to support the magazine, an offer that the general guide politely declined.[231] The government's interest in *Al-Dawa* was unsurprising given the anticommunist bent it began displaying soon after its return.[232] In a clear acknowledgment of these realities, in late 1976, Sadat told the U.S. ambassador to Egypt that he was cooperating with the Muslim Brotherhood "for his own purposes."[233]

It is critical to emphasize that the regime not only tolerated the increasing public profile of Brotherhood leaders but also encouraged and amplified it in a way that gave implicit recognition to their movement. In his capacity as the general guide of the Muslim Brotherhood, Al-Tilmisani regularly attended state events and participated in parliamentary hearings:[234]

> All the officials in Egypt recognized this state of affairs and considered me the person responsible for the Muslim Brotherhood. They met and talked to me in that capacity . . . And I accepted these conditions and based on them I contributed to many situations when the government needed the cooperation of the Muslim Brotherhood. And this was a de facto recognition from the government of the existence of the Brotherhood on the scene.[235]

The most important and consequential gift Sadat bestowed on the Muslim Brotherhood was the freedom to participate in intellectual and cultural life on college campuses, where figures like Al-Tilmisani and Mustafa Mashhur were regularly invited to speak and interact with students.[236] In fact, Al-Tilmisani often made these speaking engagements at the request of the minister of interior, who frequently called on the general guide to calm down unruly students and, when necessary, dissuade them from mounting protests.[237] During one such incident in early 1981, Al-Tilmisani cautioned Cairo University students: "I do not approve of a young man who clashes with his professor. And any person who calls upon youth to join protests or engage in vandalism is someone who does not know what is good for him."[238]

This permissive environment enabled recently released Muslim Brotherhood leaders to forge and deepen ties with the Islamist student movement and recruit key Brotherhood figures of the future like Aboul-Fotouh, El-Erian, Al-Gazzar, and Ibrahim Al-Zafarani. As chapter 3 explains, these relationships were critical to the movement's reconstitution and its reemergence as a relevant political actor. Although the political leadership was not initially aware of these developments, according to senior SSIS officer Fouad Allam,[239] it unwittingly contributed to them by relaxing surveillance of Brotherhood activities.[240]

The reemergence of multiparty politics in 1976 appears to have deepened the Muslim Brotherhood's interest in legalizing the de facto political presence it secured through Sadat's informal overtures. For example, Abu-Ruqayiq reports using his influence with Prime Minister Mamdouh Salem to explore the issue. Once plans to create "platforms" at the ASU were underway, Salem invited Abu-Ruqayiq to join him in the centrist platform, or what would later become the ruling Egypt Arab Socialist Party (EASP). He told the prime minister he would do so only if the government permitted the Brotherhood to establish a charitable nongovernmental organization (NGO). According to Abu-Ruqayiq, Salem was receptive to the idea, but the Brotherhood's leadership ultimately chose not to pursue the matter, fearing the potential restrictions that would come with legal status.[241] As for the idea of forming an official party, he explains, the major concern was the Political Parties Law (Law 40/1977), which stipulated that parties could not organize around religion and gave the state considerable discretion in supervising or dissolving licensed parties. In fact, once he saw the draft bill, Abu-Ruqayiq concluded that he had no place at the EASP and withdrew from the party, which he did quietly to avoid jeopardizing his cordial relations with the regime.[242]

To skirt the restrictive Political Parties Law, Al-Tilmisani sought a solution that did not require formal application for a party license. Thus, he filed a lawsuit in October 1977, arguing that the Revolutionary Command Council's 1954 dissolution of the Brotherhood was illegal.[243] This case, which would remain in the courts until 1992, reflected the Muslim Brotherhood's reluctance to submit to Sadat's restrictive legal framework.[244]

Accordingly, the movement was steadfast in its refusal to entertain the legal options Sadat periodically dangled in front of its leaders.

Although the Brotherhood's quest to rectify its tenuous legal status stalled, it did not slow its leaders' efforts to rebuild their organization through a secret partnership with the IGUs. By the late 1970s, they had successfully recruited key IGUs leaders into the Muslim Brotherhood, most notably in Cairo and Alexandria, with somewhat less success in Middle and Upper Egypt. Whereas the Middle and Upper Egyptian contingents grew more resistant, if not plainly hostile, to the Muslim Brotherhood recruitment efforts,[245] the national IGUs' leadership pledged loyalty to Al-Tilmisani and his colleagues.[246] The IGUs' statements, publications, educational materials, book exhibits, and public conferences all reflected the influence of the Muslim Brotherhood.[247] Officially speaking, however, Brotherhood ties with various IG chapters were kept under the radar to avoid Sadat's wrath, as Aboul-Fotouh explains:

> We kept this issue secret for several years out of fear that we could confront repression from the regime, which had cleared the way for Muslim Brotherhood leaders to work but was still not prepared to accept that the Islamic Group [affiliates] | . . . | became members in the Muslim Brotherhood, which Sadat viewed as posing a viable alternative to the regime.[248]

And his worries were not misplaced, as evidenced by the Brotherhood's clashes with Sadat during the final years of his presidency.

Sadat's falling out with the Brotherhood was rooted, as previously explained, in the contradictory nature of their respective goals. That is, the president's de-Nasserization project depended in large part on a strong alliance with Washington and, therefore, on a peace treaty with Israel, whereas many sectors of the Islamist movement opposed such a settlement on ideological grounds. In private, Al-Tilmisani's criticism of the peace treaty was cautious and couched in diplomatic language.[249] In the public realm, Al-Dawa magazine pulled no punches in its criticism of the Camp David Accords and other manifestations of Sadat's pro-Western foreign policy.[250]

In early 1979, Al-Dawa published an article asserting that the United States was pressing the Egyptian government to combat the Islamist movement and the IGUs. The piece was based on an alleged Central Intelligence

Agency (CIA) document that, according to Al-Tilmisani, was mailed to the magazine anonymously.[251] Under pressure from Minister of Interior Al-Nabawi Ismail,[252] *Al-Dawa* immediately published the U.S. Embassy's declaration that the document was a forgery.[253] Although this controversy seemed to dissipate quickly, Sadat would not let it go. From that point on, his public and private attacks on the Brotherhood frequently referenced the article as evidence of the movement's desire to undermine him.[254] In fact, when Ismail begged Sadat to exclude Al-Tilmisani in the notorious September 1981 arrest orders, the president refused by citing this article: "Is he not responsible for *Al-Dawa*, Nabawi, where it was said that there is an Egyptian–American plot to eliminate Islam in Egypt?"[255]

It is not surprising that the article hit a sore spot for Sadat. Authentic or not, the document's claims about Washington's antipathy to the Islamist movement highlighted the tensions between the president's goal of deepening Egypt's alliance with the United States, and his commitment to Islamist constituents who participated his campaign against the left. The article, and *Al-Dawa*'s criticism of Sadat's foreign policies more generally, displayed the contradictions between these two commitments in public. Sadat did not like that one bit.

The Brotherhood's opposition to Sadat's foreign policy aside, evidence shows that the partnership between the Brotherhood and the IGUs rattled Sadat, intensifying his conflict with the movement's leaders. Sadat launched his public attacks against the Muslim Brotherhood in the early months of 1979. During the same period, according to Aboul-Fotouh, the institutional links between the IGUs and the Muslim Brotherhood became known to authorities.[256] Soon, the president's speeches began to feature references to these links, as well as claims that the Muslim Brotherhood's deceitful elders were exploiting otherwise-innocent, modest young students. In a March 1979 public address at Alexandria University, Sadat declared:

> Evil is hateful and can be destructive for your kids, who, under pressure, can fall prey to those who were once part of an old group that is seeking to get to power |. . . .| This is what the Muslim Brothers are all about and I remember them and can tell the story because I am experienced and dealt with Hassan Al-Banna himself |. . . .| They are the ones who are exploiting those youthful students.[257]

In that same speech, Sadat specifically warns students about the dangers of the Muslim Brotherhood, calling on them to steer clear of mixing religion with politics:

> I am repeating it again so my children would hear it, especially my children right here: no religion in politics and no politics in religion. I can tell you later during our discussion all about how the Muslim Brotherhood was formed and how its terrorist, secret apparatus developed |. . . .| Unfortunately the remnants of that line of work have resurfaced and are enrolling the children in da'wah.[258]

In other words, Sadat's public proclamations during this period demonstrated his awareness that the leaders of the Muslim Brotherhood had deceived him and that their ambitions encompassed more than magazine publication and preaching. They were using the student movement the president had nurtured for years—or what he thought of as his own "children"—for their own objectives.

The IGUs' response did not help the situation. When Sadat dissolved the student unions in the summer of 1979, the IGUs issued a statement criticizing the decision and defending the Muslim Brotherhood against Sadat's public accusations. The statement declared that the time had come for young Egyptians to learn about the Muslim Brothers' contributions to the Islamist movement and the sacrifices they had made in defense of Palestine.[259] That latter slip may have dispelled any doubts that the IGUs' leadership was working under the Muslim Brotherhood's direction.[260]

Exacerbating tensions, Sadat and Al-Tilmisani got into a public spat. In an August 1979 address to religious figures and Islamist intellectuals in Ismailia, the president decided to publicly take on the Muslim Brotherhood's general guide, who was seated prominently in the front row of the audience. Preceding this event were months of Brotherhood and other Islamist criticism of the treaty with Israel and a First Lady–sponsored personal status law famously dubbed "Jehane's law,"[261] which some religious figures deemed Islamically objectionable. The IGU-led student unrest in Middle and Upper Egypt only increased the president's ire.

In his speech, Sadat revealed that the Muslim Brotherhood had sent former prime minister Salem a letter stating that it considered its 1954 dissolution by the Revolutionary Command Council invalid and therefore deemed its current status as perfectly legal.[262] The president angrily countered that the Brotherhood had no legal standing and threatened to bring its activities to a halt and force it to reapply for a license. He criticized *Al-Dawa*'s antigovernment coverage and insinuated that the Brotherhood had a hand in the IGUs' transgressions.[263] In a brief public retort at the auditorium, Al-Tilmisani disputed the president's claims, characterizing them as unfair. Perhaps sensing that he may have gone too far, Sadat sent Mansour Hassan and Abdel-Moneim Al-Nimr, ministers of information and endowments, respectively, to meet with Al-Tilmisani and attempt to assuage his anger. The ministers told Al-Tilmisani that the president had not meant any disrespect and that he would meet with him soon to clear the air.[264] The two men eventually met in early December at the presidential residence in Al-Qanatir.

At the meeting, Sadat tried to win the Muslim Brotherhood back to his side—perhaps out of fear that pushing it too far would only force it into the embrace of other opposition actors.[265] With a series of recent issues of *Al-Dawa* in front of him, Sadat complained to the general guide about the magazine's campaign against the Camp David Accords. Al-Tilmisani explained that his opposition to the peace treaty with Israel stemmed from sincere religious convictions and did not involve "what they call international or non-international politics." The president responded approvingly, telling Al-Tilmisani that he had made his point and that he should return to writing. Reflecting on that incident in his memoirs, Al-Tilmisani states, "I will never forget that [gesture] from Sadat for as long as I live, in spite of everything he put me through."[266]

Sadat also proposed a solution for the Brotherhood's chief quandary—its legal status. He suggested that the general guide register the Muslim Brotherhood as an NGO and meet with Minister of Insurance and Social Affairs Amal Othman to work out the details.[267] Al-Tilmisani did not pursue Sadat's offer, because he "realized what he [Sadat] sought was subjecting the Muslim Brotherhood to the authority of the Ministry of Social Affairs." According to Al-Tilmisani, the Brotherhood's leadership refused to go through the steps to legalization, insisting that the 1954 dissolution decree be reversed: "Our demand on which we will not compromise is the return of the group exactly as it was the day it was dissolved."[268] Notwithstanding the lenient attitude Sadat had adopted in his meeting with Al-Tilmisani, the Brotherhood maintained its long-standing position of rejecting the legal restrictions that would accrue from official registration.

Despite the president's efforts to preserve his alliance with the Brotherhood, relations between the two sides kept souring, partly because of the movement's continued opposition to the peace treaty, and partly because Sadat grew exceedingly intolerant of political dissent in any form. The Brotherhood's relationship with the regime reached rock bottom in September 1981, when Sadat found himself at odds with almost the entirety of Egypt's political community. He ordered the suspension of *Al-Dawa* and went on an arrest spree of fifteen hundred political leaders and activists from all ideological currents, including the Muslim Brotherhood's elderly general guide. Al-Nabawi Ismail told Sadat that arresting Al-Tilmisani was unwise because he helped the Ministry of Interior to deescalate sectarian tensions and keep unruly IGU students under control.[269] The president disagreed,[270] maintaining that Al-Tilmisani, along with numerous Brotherhood and IGU members, must be arrested. All would remain in prison until months after Sadat's October 1981 assassination, when new president Hosni Mubarak was sworn into office.

By the time the Muslim Brotherhood and the IGUs fell out of the regime's graces, the Brotherhood's organizational reforms were solidly rooted, as evidenced by the group's continued growth after Sadat's assassination. The nature of the Brotherhood's institutional growth during the 1970s is noteworthy. Despite Sadat's desire to manage the Muslim Brotherhood's political engagement by various means, the Brotherhood refused to play by his rules. Instead, the group elected to practice its activism informally through *Al-Dawa* magazine and its covert partnership with the Islamist student movement. As chapter 3 explains, the Brotherhood's insistence on evading the restrictions that accompanied legal recognition shaped the institutional development of the organization, thereby producing long-term consequences for the balance of power between Islamist and leftist currents.

A question remains: How was the Brotherhood able to maintain cordial relations with the regime, while concealing its ongoing efforts to rebuild its organization for much of the Sadat era? It is important to examine what type of opposition the Muslim Brotherhood projected at that time and why, at least until Sadat's final years in office, it invited less regime scrutiny than other opposition forces. The following section sheds light on this issue by analyzing *Al-Dawa*'s coverage from 1976 to 1981.

Al-Dawa: A Different Kind of Opposition

Following its reemergence on the political scene, the Muslim Brotherhood was quite vocal about its objections to a host of government policies. Yet, until the final years of Sadat's rule, Brotherhood criticism never provoked the regime sufficiently to jeopardize the group's participation in public life.

In understanding the state's relative leniency toward the Muslim Brotherhood during this period, a number of factors loom large. These include the movement's antileftist orientation, its criticism of the Nasserist legacy, and its distance from political activism that overtly threatened the survival of the regime. All these traits, which expressed the Brotherhood's and the regime's shared interest in countering leftists, were evident in *Al-Dawa*'s content during this period.

By way of priorities, *Al-Dawa* avoided many contentious issues over which the regime and the left fought during much of the 1970s. The magazine devoted, at most, cursory attention to social and economic issues like state-led economic liberalization or other regime divergences from the Nasserist social pact. Instead, *Al-Dawa* tended to privilege concerns about state institutions' compliance with Islamic law and the impact of Egyptian foreign policy on Muslim communities abroad.

CRITIQUING LEFTIST CURRENTS AND IDEOLOGIES

During much of the 1970s, the Muslim Brotherhood's criticism of the Sadat regime eschewed the revolutionary bent then prevalent among many on the left. Far-reaching democratic reforms or the reversal of infitah were not on its agenda. Unlike leftist dissidents, the Brotherhood kept its distance from labor unrest and other forms of opposition to economic de-Nasserization. On the contrary, its leaders never missed an opportunity to use the pages of *Al-Dawa* to denounce the leftist ideologies espoused by many of the regime's opponents.

Once Sadat allowed the Muslim Brotherhood to reenter the political arena, *Al-Dawa*[271] quickly became a major forum for critiquing the antireligious views of leftist writers,[272] endorsing, for example, Al-Azhar officials' denunciations of communism.[273] Shortly after its reappearance, *Al-Dawa* published an editorial asking how the state could license what it described as a party that rejects Islam, an obvious reference to the leftist Al-Tagammu.[274] In asserting the moral failings of socialism, the magazine often discussed the antireligious views of Marxist theorists,[275] documented leftist governments' abuse of Muslims,[276] and presented evidence of social decay in socialist countries.[277]

COUNTERING NASSERIST NOSTALGIAS

The Brotherhood also did not advocate abandoning Sadat's path of economic reform in favor of Nasser's state socialism. While workers and leftist students nostalgically chanted Nasser's name, *Al-Dawa* dwelled on the alleged sins of Sadat's predecessor, questioning his character and integrity in the process. The magazine was replete with allegations of Nasser's duplicity in his dealings with the Brotherhood[278] and highlighted numerous accounts of the suffering members endured inside his prisons.[279] To mark the ten-year anniversary of the 1967 defeat, *Al-Dawa* devoted much of its June 1977 issue to exposés of the late president's failings. For example, the issue opened with an article by Omar Al-Tilmisani declaring that the cause of the 1967 disaster could be found in Nasser turning his back on Islam by allying himself with the Soviets and persecuting Islamist groups.[280] *Al-Dawa*'s portrayals of Nasser contradicted predominant perceptions of his legacy at a time when Nasserism, quite alarmingly for Sadat, still resonated with the youth, even those too young to clearly recall the period of Nasser's rule.

DISTANCE FROM ANTIREGIME POLITICS

In contrast to leftist groups, Muslim Brotherhood leaders, before 1979, left no doubt in Sadat's mind that they desired neither political power nor the overthrow of the political system. On that count, a number of factors worked in their favor. Even while paying lip service to terms like "social justice," the Brotherhood showed little interest in building ties with public sector workers or others who were negatively affected by economic liberalization. For example, the movement kept its distance from the 1977 Bread Uprising. Additionally, at this point, the Brotherhood had yet to win the sweeping electoral victories that would earn it a reputation for ruthless political competition. Furthermore, one must not forget that

before 1979, the association of Islamists with large-scale social mobilization was still nascent at best. With no memorable precedent for an Islamic
Revolution, the threat of popular unrest appeared to reside with the radical left rather than with the seemingly innocuous, aging Brotherhood
leaders. If anything, the Brothers showed a clear antipathy for political
confrontation—interestingly, just as Sadat and Al-Tagammu were bicker-
ing over workers' rights to strike—and rejected the radical ideas espoused
by violent Islamist movements.[281]

Islamist incorporation policies were reinforced by the consistently
cordial tone senior Brotherhood leaders maintained when communicating criticism of government policies. For example, Al-Tilmisani frequently framed any such objections with a carefully worded disclaimer
conveying that his group was not competing for political power but was
only voicing its convictions for the sole purpose of advising its rulers. "We
have said over and over again, we are not an opposition. We are just critics and advisors, and that is the least we can do. We are not fans of opposition," he declared.[282] "The Muslim Brotherhood does not seek to rule,
but they are working so [Islamic] doctrines would prevail," Al-Tilmisani
asserted in the spring of 1977 issue of *Al-Dawa*.[283] Two years later, he reiterated this position in an article accusing Western media of trying to create a rift between the Muslim Brotherhood and the regime by focusing
on the group's opposition to the Camp David Accords. The Brotherhood
had raised these concerns, he stressed, not for the sake of embarrassment
or accusation, but out of a sincere concern for the harms that this policy
could cause to Muslims.[284]

ISLAMIC LAW AND PUBLIC INSTITUTIONS

From its return in late 1976 to its suspension in 1981, *Al-Dawa* magazine
repeatedly displayed its abiding interest in a single issue: whether state
institutions were upholding Islamic principles and traditions. Some articles provided broad assessments of the government's progress on insert-
ing Sharia into Egypt's legal framework, including legislation, executive
decrees, legal codes, and regulations governing the conduct of state bureau-
cracies.[285] Many heated debates centered on the 1980 constitutional amendments, the parliamentary committee tasked with Islamizing legal codes, and
the controversial 1979 personal status law, which raised strong objections

from Islamist currents.[286] Within that broader framework, the magazine also featured more specialized articles examining the implementation of Sharia in discrete legal spheres like criminal codes[287] and the court system.[288]

On the question of Islamic values in public institutions, *Al-Dawa* awarded considerable attention to educational reform.[289] Writers often grappled with how Islamic values and teachings could inform curricula in elementary, secondary, and higher education.[290] For example, a 1977 article deplored the Arabic Department of Cairo University's cancellation of a course on divinely inspired texts, attributing this decision to leftist influence in the Faculty of Humanities.[291] Another educational issue frequently addressed in the magazine was public schools' enforcement of gender segregation.[292] Similarly, letters to the editor often featured student reports of instructors or administrators offending Muslim sensibilities or objecting to Islamic practices like gender segregation, growing facial hair, or wearing a headscarf.[293] *Al-Dawa* also devoted much space to discussing reforms that would enhance Al-Azhar's role in informing policy, while maintaining its autonomy from the executive.[294]

Consistent with this broader theme of "Sharia in public institutions," *Al-Dawa* directed a good deal of its criticism at government bodies responsible for cultural and intellectual production. It often faulted the Ministry of Information for failing to censor religiously offensive programming from state-sponsored television channels, especially during the holy month of Ramadan (addressed in detail in chapter 5).[295] Similarly, the Ministry of Culture received a reprimand for permitting movies and plays allegedly offensive to mainstream religious sensibilities to appear in commercial theaters.[296]

FOREIGN POLICY IN RELATION TO MUSLIM COMMUNITIES

Another issue frequently featured in the pages of *Al-Dawa* was the orientation of Egyptian policies toward the Muslim world, specifically countries with Muslim majorities or significant Muslim minorities. Thus, the magazine's contributors often cited "Communism, Crusaderism, and Zionism," that is, the Soviet bloc, the United States and its allies,[297] and Israel, as the chief enemies of Muslims.[298] As noted previously, the magazine devoted considerable space to cataloging incidents of discrimination and persecution suffered by Muslims in socialist countries.

Al-Dawa, however, frequently noted that the Muslim Brotherhood was equally opposed to Western and Soviet dominance. For example, a 1976 editorial responding to a *Christian Science Monitor* reporter who asserted that the Brotherhood was allowed to reenter politics for the sake of countering socialism, declared that the movement rejected any anti-Islamic influence, whether Eastern or Western.[299] And just as it described the threats communism posed to Islam, the magazine turned public attention toward the conversion efforts of Western Christian missionaries, or what it characterized as "modern-day Western Crusaderism."[300] *Al-Dawa* was replete with criticism of U.S. policy,[301] with specific attention given to its support for Israel.[302] Additionally, *Al-Dawa's* portrayals of U.S. society frequently emphasized the theme of moral decline, as depicted in its July 1978 issue, whose cover featured the cartoon image of a cowboy clinking wine glasses with the Statue of Liberty.[303]

The second iteration of *Al-Dawa* (1976–1981) dedicated a regular feature highlighting the plight of Palestinians and other Arabs living under Israeli occupation.[304] Such accounts were accompanied by regular features on the history of the Muslim Brotherhood, which made frequent references to the movement's role in resisting the Zionist presence in Palestine during the 1940s.[305]

The Brotherhood's hostility toward the Soviet Union and its satellites was certainly uncontroversial from the perspective of the government. Soviet–Egyptian relations had suffered a great deal under the presidency of Sadat. Yet, *Al-Dawa's* criticism of both Israel and the United States was at odds with the major elements of Sadat's foreign policy since 1974, which, as described earlier, was predicated on improving relations with Washington, an effort that mandated securing a peace settlement with Israel.

After the president's visit to Jerusalem made headlines in November 1977, Egypt's negotiations, and later treaty, with Israel became one of the most frequently covered issues in *Al-Dawa*, second only to the application of Islamic law.[306] The magazine's contributors often argued that war was the only viable path to recovering Muslim territories, particularly given that peace was not possible with an Israel so bent on expansion and so hostile to Islam.[307] Thus, Sadat's agreements with Israel constituted an issue of great contention between the president and the Muslim Brotherhood. The general guide, as previously explained, tried to defuse Sadat's anger by presenting *Al-Dawa's* criticism of his peace efforts as an expression of religious convictions rather than an attempt to undermine the president politically. Yet, objections to Egyptian–Israeli peace remained a constant cause of tension between the president and all opposition forces, thereby setting the stage for the dramatic September 1981 clampdown.

SOCIAL AND ECONOMIC PROBLEMS: ISLAMIC ECONOMICS IN PRACTICE

Although Al-Dawa did not shy away from covering the government's performance in addressing social and economic problems, such debates usually were overshadowed by other concerns.[308] A case in point is an October 1979 report entitled "Al-Dawa Asks Readers: What Is the Most Dangerous Problem in the Lives of Muslims?" Citing the testimonies of various interviewees, the report's author concludes that the conspicuous absence of Islamic values from laws and everyday life is the most pressing challenge facing Muslims.[309] This message reflects the magazine's long-standing editorial stance that a closer embrace of religious teachings would solve many, if not all, of the country's ills.[310]

Accordingly, many discussions of social and economic problems were broad to the point of ambiguity, aiming primarily at linking these issues to the absence of Islamic practices in society.[311] This theme was obvious in the magazine's depiction of the 1977 Bread Uprising. At a moment when the country's social and economic problems were front and center in public debates, Al-Dawa sought to move the discussion back to the question of Islamic law, as its contributors often implied that such ills could be attributed to the state's delay in implementing the principles of Sharia.[312] Similarly, a March 1977 survey of public views on economic conditions concluded that enforcing the directives of Islamic law, like amputating the hands of convicted thieves, would effectively combat theft and corruption.[313] In the same issue, an article on the need to revive Islamic principles in education cited the 1977 Bread Uprising as an example of the peril that would ensue if society continued to remain alienated from Islam.[314]

In other words, Al-Dawa rarely examined social problems on their own terms, preferring instead to address them in the context of a seemingly more fundamental objective—that is, elevating the role of Islam in policy and public life.[315] This perspective also imbued the magazine's coverage of economic affairs.

The next section elaborates on this point further by moving beyond the content of *Al-Dawa* magazine to analyze persistent features of the Brotherhood's stance on central economic issues. It explains why the Brotherhood's agenda afforded limited significance to demands for social and economic rights. In the process, it sheds light on the role Islamist movements played in the marginalization of distributive demands in national politics since the 1970s, thereby paving the way for the politics of "more identity, less class" in Egypt.

The Muslim Brotherhood and the Economy: Stances and Intellectual Foundations

Sometime in the early 1990s, Saif Al-Islam Hassan Al-Banna, prominent Muslim Brotherhood figure and son of the organization's founder, sought an audience with senior aide to President Mubarak, Mostafa Al-Feki. Seeking to deescalate growing tensions between his group and the regime, Al-Banna asked Al-Feki to relay two requests to his boss. The first request was for Mubarak to publicly lead Brotherhood members in Eid prayers, as a signal that the two sides were ready to open a new chapter in their relationship. The president, Al-Feki relates, flatly rebuffed this request out of security concerns. The second request, that the state divest itself of movie theaters and alcoholic beverage companies on grounds that it must not promote such Islamically objectionable endeavors, amused Mubarak: "Yes. Why not? Let us look into this." He added, "It might be good to get rid of them. And that could be part of the privatization program."[316] Just like that, one man's religious obligation became another's economic liberalization scheme.

Whether or not Mubarak followed through on this request, the incident highlights the extent to which the Muslim Brotherhood's religious agenda and state-led economic liberalization schemes found common ground in recent decades. It also evokes the latent affinity between the economic rationality underlying Mubarak's economic liberalization agenda and the conceptions of Islamic society guiding the Muslim Brotherhood's mission— an affinity Mona Atia describes more broadly as "pious neoliberalism."[317]

This section examines the enduring trends apparent in the Muslim Brotherhood's historical engagement with issues of economic policy and explains why the movement has expressed little serious opposition to economic liberalization policies since the 1970s. It demonstrates that the Brotherhood's conception of Islamic economics reflects the group's abiding prioritization: building a society governed by Islamic principles and practices takes precedence over other goals like economic prosperity. This foundational principle has caused the movement to cultivate a certain ambiguity about its economic positions, ensuring that it appeals to Egyptians across the spectrum of economic policy opinion.[318] At times, that very ambiguity, or what Khalil al-Anani calls "elastic ideology,"[319] also enabled the Brotherhood to obscure its rightist inclinations from supporters with opposing economic interests.

THE MUSLIM BROTHERHOOD'S "ISLAMIC ECONOMY": MORALS FIRST, DEVELOPMENT SECOND

Vital to understanding the Muslim Brotherhood's handling of economic issues—both its specific stances and its subordination of economic affairs to moral ones—is the concept of an "Islamic economy."[320] There is no consensus on the meaning of this term or on the practical economic prescriptions one can derive from divinely inspired Islamic texts and traditions.[321] Although these debates are significant, our focus is the economic stances Muslim Brotherhood leaders sought to justify under the rubric of "Islamic economics" and these leaders' operationalization of that concept.

The late Abdel-Hamid Al-Ghazali, longtime professor of economics at Cairo University, was at the center of the Brotherhood's efforts to formulate an Islamic economic vision. In addition to playing a principal role in articulating the Brotherhood's contemporary economic positions, Al-Ghazali was a key figure in developing the theory and practice of Islamic banking, serving as a senior adviser to a variety of Islamic financial institutions in Egypt and elsewhere in the Arab world.

Active in the Muslim Brotherhood since the 1950s, Al-Ghazali emerged in the 1970s as a key voice in *Al-Dawa* magazine's economy section.[322] In more recent decades, he was an adviser to two successive general guides, Mamoun Al-Houdaiby and Mohamed Mahdi Akef. He served in the group's political office and contested multiple parliamentary electoral races under its banner. It is hardly surprising, therefore, to find a striking correspondence between Al-Ghazali's writings and the language the Muslim Brotherhood has used in various public statements on economic policy

since the 1990s. For example, the same ideas that Al-Ghazali long advocated in his writings are evident in Al-Houdaiby's program for his 2000
parliamentary bid. These proposals also formed the basis for General
Guide Akef's 2004 blueprint entitled "Initiative for Reform in Egypt."[323]
Additionally, the economic reform section of the 2011 Freedom and Justice Party (FJP) program includes verbatim excerpts from Al-Ghazali's previously published work.[324]

The point of departure in Al-Ghazali's writings is the notion that the
microfoundation of an Islamic economy is the devout Muslim who upholds
Islam in every aspect of life. This idea reflects a recurring theme in the
statements of key Muslim Brotherhood figures, starting with Hassan Al-
Banna, who held that without "a reform in ethics," society will fail to
produce individuals capable of generating prosperity.[325] Thus, Mustafa
Mashhur faulted the government for being overly focused on "side issues"
like five-year plans, budgeting, and deficit management, "when the real
issue deserving of attention is raising men and building the virtuous citizen." Reiterating Al-Banna's message, he warned government officials: "Be
cautioned that all your attempts to resolve the economic situation will
result in failure as long as all vices and religious violations remain."[326] In
other words, the first priority is building a society of devout Muslims, from
which will emerge an Islamic economy that can deliver development and
prosperity. This principle shaped Al-Dawa's aforementioned editorial line
that a return to Islam would cure Egypt's economic ills.

Historically, Brotherhood officials have countered accusations that the
group offers no concrete proposals to address salient economic and social
problems, by repeating the argument that society's return to Islam is a sufficient solution to these challenges, and thus the priority must remain the
promotion of Islamic values and principles. A classic example of this tactic
was provided by General Guide Mamoun Al-Houdaiby: "They want us to
drop the question of faith and answer to whether we should grow onions
or cotton! This is not our concern |. . . .| Our concern is with worshipping
God and believing in Islam as one's religion."[327]

ISLAMIC ECONOMICS AND USEFUL AMBIGUITIES

Beyond justifying the Brotherhood's tendency to devalue economic issues,
the idea that a call for Islam is also a call for economic prosperity also

enabled the movement to accommodate contradictory economic orientations within its ranks and among its supporters. That is, it was able to offer
a vision broad enough to satisfy a variety of different opinions about what
role, if any, the state should play in redistributing wealth under an "Islamic
economy."[328]

This fact became increasingly evident in the post-Mubarak era, when
Brotherhood defectors formed parties espousing economic visions contradicting the stated positions of their former leaders.[329] Whenever forced
to articulate a clear position, Brotherhood officials advocated private-
sector development and focused on methods to improve the investment
climate and attract foreign direct investments (FDIs).[330] For example, in
October 2011, Muslim Brotherhood member Hassan Malek argued that the
economic liberalization policies of the Mubarak era were fundamentally
sound, although their implementation was flawed and riddled with corruption.[331] Under the leadership of President Mohamed Morsi, the Egyptian
government took tentative steps to cut subsidies after negotiating a loan
agreement with the International Monetary Fund (IMF).[332] They also made
overtures to big business interests, including those linked to the deposed
Mubarak regime.[333] In contrast, Brotherhood defectors who cofounded the
Egyptian Current Party devised a platform that prioritized state provision
of social services and the reduction of socioeconomic disparities.[334] In the
2011–2012 election, these same activists joined the Revolution Continues
coalition, which openly criticized the Washington Consensus on economic
development, advocated revitalizing the public sector, and proposed some
limited renationalization measures.[335]

The Muslim Brotherhood's ability to house such contradictory economic
orientations demonstrates the degree to which the movement's unifying
spiritual mission had mitigated tensions between competing distributive demands. Nothing delivers that point as clearly as Hassan Al-Banna's
exchange with the future cofounder of Al-Tagammu, Khaled Mohieddin, in
1944. At that time, Mohieddin and Gamal Abdel-Nasser had shown interest in the Muslim Brotherhood and were meeting regularly with fellow
army officers linked to the movement. Mohieddin recounts how he always
pressed the Muslim Brothers about the specifics of their program:

> "What is the program of the group?" He would answer, "Sharia." I used to
> say: "We are all Muslim, and we all believe in Sharia, but what exactly are

> you going to do to liberate the nation; are we going to enter into an armed struggle or accept negotiations? What are we going to offer the people in various fields, in education, housing, agriculture and other social issues?"

Not getting a satisfying answer, a frustrated Mohieddin kept pressing this issue, until his Brotherhood contact arranged for him to meet with Hassan Al-Banna:

> We conversed with [Al-Banna] and he was receptive. I insisted on the importance of announcing a program and said: "You will not be able to win over the people without a clear program that presents practical solutions for people's problems." He answered: "If I were to devise a program, I will end up satisfying some and angering others. I will win some people and lose others. And I do not want that."[336]

Thus, the imperative to satisfy as broad of a coalition of supporters as possible, as Al-Banna described it, must guide any analysis of the Muslim Brotherhood's engagement with economic affairs. This imperative explains the Brotherhood's long-standing practice of eschewing decisive (and perhaps divisive) economic stances, and its framing of social and economic reform issues as secondary components of a much broader Islamic revivalist project.

Certainly, this sort of calculus is not unique to the Muslim Brotherhood, and such "catch-all"[337] tendencies often prevail among parties that constantly attempt to mobilize popular support.[338] What distinguishes the Brotherhood, however, is the religious framing of its mission, which has made the task of building coalitions across social classes more feasible than it otherwise would have been.[339] That point becomes evident when examining the genealogy of one of the Brotherhood's most famous slogans, "Islam is the solution," which was featured in numerous electoral contests over the past three decades.

Although the words "Islam is the solution" have come to define the Muslim Brotherhood's ideology, the individual who proposed the slogan was not actually a member of the organization. It was the brainchild of the late Adel Hussein, one of the most prominent figures in the Socialist Labor Party (SLP).[340] Once a communist activist, Hussein distanced himself from

Marxism during the 1980s, eventually becoming an icon of the Egyptian Islamist movement.[341] During that period, Hussein, to the dismay of his secular comrades, helped orchestrate the Islamist transformation of what used to be a nationalist, socialist-leaning party (see chapter 5). Guiding that move, a fellow SLP associate indicated, was Hussein's dream of uniting all of Egypt's Islamist movements under a single banner.[342] On that basis, the SLP increased its cooperation with the Muslim Brotherhood, agreeing to contest the 1987 legislative election under a single list, the "Islamic Alliance."

The diversity of economic orientations within this alliance was palpable. Traditionally, the SLP had advocated state protection of economic and social rights, maintaining that stance even after adopting an Islamist identity.[343] The Brotherhood was generally unenthusiastic about calls to deepen the state's involvement in the economy and was not opposed to economic liberalization policies in principle. Adding to the diversity of economic orientations was the participation of the Liberal Socialists Party (LSP) as a junior partner in the alliance. The LSP, as chapter 1 explains, was initially formed as the rightist platform of the ASU, and it certainly did not embrace the leftist leanings of the SLP.[344] Thus, as negotiations on the principles of a joint electoral program were underway, the groups differed on economic and social issues, recounts an SLP officer.[345] It was in that context that Adel Hussein proposed the slogan "Islam is the solution" as a unifying banner for the three partners. Under this heading, they devised a program that prioritized their shared interest in promoting the principles of Sharia.

Thus, "Islam is the solution"—a slogan that has come to epitomize the political marketing strategy of the Egyptian Islamist movement—was the product of an effort to build coalitions across divergent economic orientations. It is no wonder that, according to Tarek Masoud, in the 2011–2012 legislative election, "citizens voted for the Muslim Brotherhood's Freedom and Justice Party because they believed it would redistribute wealth and strengthen the welfare state."[346] In other words, the movement was able to obscure its rightist economic positions well enough to secure support from advocates of redistribution.[347] This was not the first time the Muslim Brotherhood successfully obscured its stances on salient economic questions, as the following section explains.

CONCEALING WHAT IS "RIGHT" IN THE BROTHERHOOD'S ISLAMIC ECONOMICS

Another point of departure in Al-Ghazali's account of Islamic economics is the proposition that unrestricted free markets invariably promote moral vices, including various forms of exploitation and injustice. For Al-Ghazali, socialist-inspired modes of state planning have failed to provide a workable alternative to unrestrained capitalism, because such systems tend to foster neglect and incompetence.[348] He argues that Islam, in contrast, offers a viable solution to the shortcomings of both the market and state planning.

How, then, do Islamic economics address the injustices of free markets? Al-Ghazali's answer displays a conception of religion as a restraint on humans' pursuit of material self-interest. That is, in the absence of religion, such pursuits inevitably lead to destructive excesses and abuses.[349] In that context, Islam, Al-Ghazali explains, regulates human choice in ways that preempt potential vices. If everyone fulfills their obligations in accordance with Islamic teachings, the sources of greed, oppression, envy, theft, deceit, and corruption will disappear, thereby paving the way for a society that is not only virtuous but also truly prosperous and socially harmonious. The metatheoretical assumptions underlying this view are significant. This mode of reasoning concludes that vices occurring in free market settings originate in individual choice, not in modes of production or class relations.

Embracing this understanding, successive Muslim Brotherhood leaders have asserted that reforming the individual through proper religious instruction and upbringing must come before any talk of institutional reform. If each person earns a living through honest work without deceit or injustice, pays their dues, and contributes zakat ("a fixed percentage of wealth given to the poor"), exploitation and class conflict will disappear from society. Accordingly, calling for society to return to God must precede any other priority, because the devout, moral individual is the basic building block of the Islamic economy and society.

Al-Ghazali's formulation, furthermore, suggests that divinely inspired texts fulfill a practical function in economic life by placing limits on the on the operation of free market economy, not by posing alternatives to it. The modesty of this prescription belies the popular notion that Islamic traditions mandate an economic order entirely different from Western-style free market economies. Thus, Al-Ghazali's conception of Islamic economics conforms—albeit with limited modifications—to the general line of policies that the Egyptian state has followed since infitah.

Precisely what restrictions does an Islamic economy impose? The most cited one is the prohibition of *ribaa*, most frequently understood as the charging of interest on loans. Al-Ghazali cites the conventional claim that Islam forbids charging interest because, he argues, something is fundamentally unjust about forcing people to pay back more money than they had originally borrowed. This practice extracts value from others without fair compensation, while yielding an effortless profit from the exploitation of others' need.

Given that Islam forbids interest, Al-Ghazali continues, investment financing must be conducted in ways that do not violate divine directives. This perceived imperative has driven Islamic banking's emergence as an important financial sector in many Muslim majority countries, and as a vast field of study in the social sciences. Islamic banks made their debut in the Arab World in the 1970s, appearing in Egypt with the establishment of Faisal Islamic Bank in 1978. An Islamic bank usually advertises its transactions as interest-free and affirms an investment strategy that allots profits and risks among financiers and investors, theoretically permitting no party to profit without effort or risk. Notably, the late 1970s also witnessed the emergence of Islamic investment companies, which advertised interest-free investment portfolios.

Indeed, some claim that Islamic banks and investment companies provide an important service to devout Muslims, allowing them to increase their savings while adhering to the principles of Islam. More cynical observers, however, characterize these institutions as practitioners of false advertising who exploit people's religious sensibilities to attract deposits. Furthermore, these organizations are often accused of hypocrisy, as they charge transaction fees in place of interest and often engage in interest-bearing investments.

The merits of such allegations aside, opposition to interest-bearing banking has been one of the Muslim Brotherhood's most unambiguous and enduring economic positions since the era of Hassan Al-Banna.[350] Thus, the advent of Islamic banking in the late 1970s was met with much acclaim in the pages of *Al-Dawa*, which lauded this development as a major step toward the establishment of an Islamic economy,[351] while it frequently criticized the government's continued support for interest-bearing banking.[352] During the 1980s, the Brotherhood and its publications came to the defense of Islamic investment companies, many of which were facing accusations of fraud and illicit dealings.[353] The same stance was apparent during the presidency of Mohamed Morsi, who, a month before his ouster, signed a law ordering the state to issue Islamic bonds popularly known as *sukuk*.[354]

Conventionally, ribaa has been associated with illicit profits generated through debt service or the exchange of goods and services. Yet, interestingly, Al-Ghazali introduces a more inclusive definition of ribaa, one that encompasses any profit a person accrues at no cost or risk:

> [Understanding the prohibition of] ribaa in all its forms—in light of the texts of the Quran and Sunna—does not require any justification, wisdom, or inference. Besides preventing a person from doing injustice to himself—by depriving himself of participation in economic activities that are productive and that can benefit society and himself—it also prevents him from exploiting his fellow human by taking away money without compensation. This prohibition is consistent with instincts of honesty, proper economic conduct, and sound social sense. Thus, ribaa is a devious profit. Money is simply generating itself, which is not the function it was meant for, that is: as a medium of exchange and a measure of worth [. . . .] Hence, ribaa is an earning made at no economic cost and without any exposure to loss. Accordingly, it presents an unjustifiable burden on those who pay it—whether consumers or producers—and as a result, it poses direct harm to the economy and society.[355]

In other words, Al-Ghazali's definition of ribaa encompassed a wide-range of economic practices falling under the category of "effortless profit." Inquisitive observers might wonder whether such an interpretation could prohibit, in theory, certain forms of state welfare transfers, because they technically fall under effortless earnings. Although Al-Ghazali does not answer this question explicitly, he insists that an Islamic economy is grounded in the principle that "no individual, group, or social class, under this system, can live off the efforts and wealth of others."[356] Simply put, in an Islamic economy, the wealthy are forbidden to exploit the poor, who are, in turn, forbidden to live off the wealth of others. This principle may help explain the apprehension with which the Muslim Brotherhood usually approaches the issue of state welfare provision.

Since its founding, the Brotherhood has proclaimed a strong commitment to social justice, as manifested in its long-standing involvement in various charitable works and its provision of social services to low-income communities.[357] At the same time, the Brotherhood has routinely displayed discomfort with the state acting as guarantor of social justice. Consider, for example, how the group has historically dealt with the issue of social solidarity. In any such discussions, Brotherhood leaders usually pay lip service to the cause of social justice by reminding their audience that Islam requires every capable Muslim to contribute zakat.[358] The Brotherhood's professed support for zakat, however, does not constitute an endorsement of the welfare state model, as a close analysis of the group's public record indicates. The FJP's 2011 platform contends that zakat is central to alleviating poverty, but it never defines the state's role in collecting zakat contributions or distributing their proceeds. Similarly, the document advocates state incentives to encourage private donations to the poor, but it never suggests that such payments should be mandatory.[359] Finally, reiterating Al-Ghazali's previous proposals,[360] the FJP calls for restructuring subsidies and social insurance programs to better target groups in need—language that governments often use to justify cuts in welfare spending.[361]

Regardless of the merits of these proposals, the Brotherhood's privileging of zakat and voluntary contributions as primary instruments of poverty alleviation speaks to the group's preference for confining redistributive schemes to the private sphere and thus moving them outside the reach of state institutions and regulations. In keeping with this attitude, the Muslim Brotherhood has often refrained from endorsing any measures that might deepen the state's involvement in welfare distribution. Consider, for example, the reform proposals that the Brotherhood offered shortly after the July 23 Revolution of 1952. The section entitled "Social Reform" opens by declaring that Islam requires every able-bodied person to work and forbids the extension of aid to people who are capable of working but choose not to. Conversely, a person who cannot find employment or whose income is inadequate is entitled to zakat. If zakat proves insufficient, that person is entitled to financial help from wealthy individuals. In the event that no one provides such assistance, the government must intervene by ordering the wealthy to extend a helping hand.[362] In other words, the document upholds the view that state intervention to redistribute wealth is a last resort—one invoked only out of necessity. These reservations about state-directed welfare are presented in a highly convoluted, roundabout way that is perfectly in keeping with Al-Banna's determination to abstain from adopting decisive positions that might alienate supporters.[363]

Decades later, the Brotherhood's reservations regarding state redistribution of wealth appeared alive and well. The 2011 FJP platform, for example, spoke of the right to participate in economic production and to earn a respectable income, largely eschewing the language of social and economic rights the Egyptian left has long used:

> The party believes that social justice means two dimensions: First, the right of the citizen to participate in the process of production, and second, his right to receive his share of the returns that the process of production creates. Consideration for social solidarity is given to those whose means do not allow them to fulfill their living needs through work, or if they are unable to work. As the Prophet of Allah said in his blessed hadith: "He who sleeps sated while his neighbor is hungry next to him and knows it is one who has not believed in me." And Islam guarantees |...| the right to the basic and primary living needs that ensure one's dignity and freedom, and these are food, drink, clothes, shelter, and means of transportation.[364]

Strikingly, even in post-Mubarak Egypt, when talk of universal economic and social rights seemed unavoidable, the FJP still managed to avoid any talk of enhancing the state's redistributive responsibilities. For one, the document makes access to aid contingent on a variety of criteria, like access to employment and income level.[365] It also avoids any explicit reference to state-sanctioned economic rights, asserting instead that Islam alone guarantees these rights. The authors of the platform subtly reinforce this point by citing a *hadith* (a saying or practice of the Prophet) that calls for social solidarity between neighbors. In other words, the document is adamant that the promotion of social justice is a religious obligation for any practicing Muslim, while ascribing no explicit role in this effort to the state.[366]

For this reason leftist activists have often found the Brotherhood's references to zakat and Islamic justice unsatisfactory and inconsistent with their own conception of social justice as state-guaranteed rights that are not subject to the generosity of devout Muslims. "We are not looking for charity from them or anyone. All we want is to get our rights as citizens of this state," explained an activist from Al-Tagammu when asked to comment on the Muslim Brotherhood's conception of social justice.[367] Heightening these frustrations was the Brotherhood's performance in government, which, for leftist activists, confirmed the long-held fear that "Islamic economics" was nothing more than a pious façade for economic policies indistinguishable from those of the Mubarak regime.[368] Some point out, for example, that despite decades of preaching about the ills of interest and the virtues of Islamic banking, the Muslim Brotherhood voiced no reservations about President Mohamed Morsi's pursuit of an interest-bearing loan agreement with the IMF.[369]

This is all to say the Muslim Brotherhood's treatment of economic issues over time has been ambiguous, often subsuming such issues under a broader vision of religious revivalism. When maintaining such ambiguity proved untenable, the Brotherhood's positions generally adhered to the path of economic liberalization the state had adopted since the 1970s. In other words, the Muslim Brotherhood has not challenged the state's efforts to abandon the distributive commitments of the Nasserist social pact. In fact, the Brotherhood's conception of Islamic economics appears to endorse these policies.

For example, Al-Ghazali's vision of economic development privileged the private sector as the primary engine of growth and employment. Thus, Al-Ghazali proposed measures to expand it and contract the public sector. He also has expressed support, in principle, for Mubarak's efforts at privatization, but faults the regime for poor implementation of this policy. For instance, Al-Ghazali argued that strategic sectors, like utilities, military production, and ports, must remain under the control of the state. He endorsed the sale of state-owned assets, but only through a transparent process that gives priority to Egyptian, Arab, and Muslim investors. It is telling that Al-Ghazali also criticized Mubarak's government for using the revenues accrued from the sale of public sector companies to compensate laid-off workers and reduce the budget deficit. Such resources, he holds, should have been directed toward productive investments.[370]

Consistent with Al-Ghazali's vision, the Muslim Brotherhood expressed general, albeit qualified, support for privatization programs throughout the 1990s. When asked about the Brotherhood's stance on privatization in a 1998 interview, Al-Houdaiby reiterated Al-Ghazali's position that the policy was fundamentally sound but poorly implemented.[371] This stance reflects the Brotherhood's long-standing skepticism toward the public sector. For example, when talk of selling state-owned companies was underway in 1980, *Al-Dawa*'s contributors criticized the government's insistence on retaining the public sector despite massive deficits.[372] In fact, the magazine often attributed Egypt's poor economic performance during the 1970s and 1980s to the legacies of Nasser's state socialism and to the government's unwillingness to abandon a failed economic model.[373]

On agrarian policy, the Muslim Brotherhood has long advocated reversing Nasser-era land reforms and price controls[374] to enhance the efficiency and productivity of the agricultural sector. The Brotherhood was among the most vigorous critics of the land reforms enacted after the July 23 Revolution, on the grounds that the limits on landownership were excessive. Much like some members of Sadat's ruling establishment, senior Brotherhood officials hailed from prominent landowning families, including Mustafa Mashhur and Omar Al-Tilmisani.[375] It remains unclear, however, how, or if, material interests shaped Brotherhood leaders' stances on agrarian reform.

The Brotherhood's professed position on land reform was tested in the 1980s and 1990s, when the government announced plans to remove rent controls on agricultural land. This move marked a major departure from the pro-tenant policies Nasser instituted decades earlier. Officials were aware that the measure was consequential. Although under consideration since the late 1970s, as one former minister explains, the policy was adopted only in 1992 and was not enforced until 1997.[376] "This was a big taboo and we could not move on it until the late 1980s," explains another former cabinet member, adding that the government had to call on religious scholars for support in the anticipated showdown. "[Al-Tagammu leader] Khaled Mohieddin came to me and told me that he will make sure that this law will fail and that he will rally support against it. But at the end nothing happened. All they could do is attack us in their newspapers."[377]

The legislation was a major concern for the SLP, as its founders saw themselves as the intellectual progenitors of Nasser's agrarian reforms. Thus, when the rent controls were actually eliminated in 1997, SLP affiliates faced charges of inciting small tenant farmers to acts of violence.

When the Muslim Brotherhood faced similar accusations, they broke their long silence on the issue, expressing their support for lifting rent controls, while denying any role in the unrest.[378] The Brotherhood initially refrained from taking a decisive stance, explained a member of the group, because senior leaders, while supporting the law in private, feared widespread opposition to the eviction of small tenant farmers.[379] Along similar lines, in 1998, Al-Houdaiby explained that the rent controls were outdated and had to go, but he lamented the lack of government support for evicted tenants. Notwithstanding his reservations, Al-Houdaiby, then the Brotherhood's deputy general guide, argued that Nasser's fundamentally flawed land reforms were the cause of the current crisis: "The Brotherhood had opposed the idea of seizing ownership of people's property and transferring it to others for an unspecified period. And the danger of this measure is evident in | . . .| that it made wealthy landowners poor, and poor tenants who do not own property wealthy."[380]

In addition to supporting privatization and the liberalization of agrarian policies, the Muslim Brotherhood has voiced broad support for greater integration with the global economy. For example, foreign trade and FDIs are central elements of Al-Ghazali's proposed strategy for enhancing economic growth. Citing World Bank data, he stressed the need to improve Egypt's current investment climate to attract sufficient foreign investment.

Once again, Al-Ghazali's position conforms to the professed goals of successive Mubarak governments but with two qualifiers. First, the promotion of FDIs and foreign trade, Al-Ghazali argues, must not undermine productive sectors and local industries.[381] Second, Al-Ghazali advocates prioritizing trade with (and FDIs from) Arab and Muslim countries.[382] While not attributing the latter requirement to "Islamic economics," this caveat resonates with the Brotherhood's long-standing insistence that global economic integration must not entail the contravention of religious traditions. Thus, while acknowledging the centrality of tourism to Egypt's development, Al-Ghazali demands that tourists be required to always respect Egyptians' religious customs.[383] Similarly, during the late 1970s, *Al-Dawa*'s critiques of Sadat's economic reform policies often focused on the "un-Islamic" values and customs that normally accompanied tourism and foreign investments.[384] More significantly, the magazine's critiques of infitah focused on religious values and neglected social justice issues. A case in point is a July 1978 article entitled "Economic Consumerist Infitah

and Morals," which argued that the influx of Western products and services into Egypt has promoted a consumerist culture that has largely disregarded religious norms. The editorial made only passing reference to the
social inequalities wrought by infitah in its closing paragraphs. In other
words, the author found infitah problematic, less for the social disparities
it deepened than for the un-Islamic values it promoted in Egyptian society.

Notwithstanding such concerns about the negative impact of economic
integration on public morals, the Muslim Brotherhood has not objected
to the basic principles of economic liberalization. Some might attribute
this stance exclusively to general ambivalence or to the private financial
interests of Brotherhood leaders who could benefit from such reforms.
Yet, these interests aside, the movement's central mission of "Islamizing
society" is not inherently contradictory to economic reform.

In short, the Muslim Brotherhood has demonstrated a tendency to subordinate social and economic issues to the implementation of Sharia, generally treating such issues as secondary components of a broader project
of religious revival. This inclination reflects the group's professed understanding of Islamic economics, which subsumes the goals of development,
growth, and redistribution within the mission of moralizing the individual.

Moreover, the "constructive ambiguity" (to use Hazem Kandil's terminology) surrounding this conception of Islamic economics has served the
Brotherhood well, enabling it to accommodate contradictory economic
orientations and build support across social classes.[385] This ambiguity
aside, the basic principles underlying the Brotherhood's conception of
Islamic economics demonstrates a practical aversion to a wide range of
state interventions, including welfare payments. Accordingly, the group's
professed ideas about social justice generally advocate pursuing any
necessary redistributive schemes through the private sector. Practically
speaking, the Brotherhood's economic positions have, excepting minor
modifications, not differed from regime policies since the beginning of
the infitah period. Simply put, the Muslim Brotherhood did not oppose
the regime's divergence from the Nasserist social pact and displayed no
ambition to obstruct the process of de-Nasserization. This reality mitigated tensions between the state and the Muslim Brotherhood during
the 1970s and much of the 1980s. This context explains why the regime
allowed the Brotherhood a degree of latitude and space denied to Sadat's
leftist opponents.

It is critical to note that the Muslim Brotherhood's general receptiveness toward market-oriented reforms since the 1970s stands at odds with the positions its intellectuals professed before the July 23 Revolution.[386] Many of their publications explored affinities between Islamic traditions and socialist ideas.[387] This divergence is, in part, a product of the movement's evolution since 1952. The Brotherhood's falling out with Nasser imbued its intellectuals with a general aversion to the economic pillars of his presidency, like state planning and the expansion of the public sector. Moreover, Nasser's crackdown on the Brotherhood entailed barring the group's affiliates from state employment, thereby pushing many into the private sector. This meant that the representation of government employees, who tend to support state-sponsored social protections, diminished inside the movement after 1952.[388] Meanwhile, that same trend engendered the emergence of a large cadre of business people inside the Muslim Brotherhood—ones whose interests aligned with the economic liberalization agenda of the post-Nasser era. Thus, many analysts, most notably the late Hossam Tammam, have attributed the Brotherhood's favorable views of economic reform to the dominance of wealthy business people inside the organization.[389]

Certainly, the path of economic liberalization Egypt has followed since the 1970s contributed to the rise of a Brotherhood-led business community, however diverse, as Angela Joya observes.[390] Sadat's infitah offered Brotherhood members opportunities for engagement in the private sector. Exiled Brotherhood leaders who had accumulated wealth in the Gulf in the 1950s and 1960s returned to Sadat's Egypt, investing in a variety of enterprises.[391] Additionally, by ending the state's monopoly in the financial sector, Sadat paved the way for Islamic banking, through which Brotherhood affiliates asserted considerable economic influence.[392] Sadat's private investment laws also created a legal environment favorable to Islamic investment companies,[393] in which Muslim Brotherhood affiliates invested financial[394] and political[395] capital.

That said, a few caveats are in order. First, the gains that Brotherhood-linked investors and entrepreneurs made in the private sector pale in comparison to the large fortunes amassed by business cronies of the regime. Second, despite their initial success stories, Brotherhood-affiliated business people periodically experienced regime intimidation in the form of arrests, and more recently, sequestration of their assets.[396] Finally, as politically influential as the Brotherhood's business people have become, the movement's economic orientation must not be reduced to a mere expression of their material interests. Such an interpretation fails to account for the ambiguity with which the Brotherhood has consistently articulated its economic stances. If the Brotherhood's economic platform were merely the wish-list of powerful business people, the movement would have enunciated its pro-business stances much more decisively in recent decades. Instead, as explained earlier, the group has usually advanced these positions through ambiguities and apologia, which highlights the internal tensions informing Brotherhood pronouncements on economic questions.

Conclusion

Sadat's Islamist incorporation policies were conceived in a particular environment, one in which the state sought to counter leftist opponents of de-Nasserization through a variety of means, including a religiously couched criticism designed to undermine their credibility. Islamist incorporation entailed two major components. The first was support, direct and indirect, for the Islamist student movement. The second component was encouraging the Muslim Brotherhood's return to political life. Although the regime sought to create an Islamist political arm on university campuses that would operate under ruling party control, that policy proved unwieldy. The Sadat regime, therefore, settled for supporting a more autonomous Islamist student movement, one over which it exerted more limited control. Similarly, Sadat's support for the Brotherhood's return to public life was a stratagem to confine the organization's activists within state-controlled structures and an intrusive legal framework, thereby undermining the group's autonomy. Ultimately, Sadat failed in this endeavor. The Muslim Brotherhood refused to take the regime's bait, electing to channel its public advocacy outside of formal state supervision, through its covert partnership with the IGUs and other informal means, rather than subject itself to the limitations of operating under a legally sanctioned framework. These decisions would have lasting consequences for the group's institutional development in the following decades, as explained in the next chapter. Although Sadat and the Brotherhood differed on a variety of issues, particularly the peace treaty with Israel, the movement's pronouncements on other issues were broadly aligned with the regime's objectives. Specifically, the Brotherhood's attacks on Nasser's legacy and its leftist champions created common ground with Sadat.

The Brotherhood's most salient critiques of government focused on the implementation of Islamic law at public institutions and foreign policy concerns like peace with Israel and relations with the West. Unlike the leftists who loudly decried the state's waning commitment to the Nasserist social pact, the Brotherhood largely eschewed social and economic issues, subordinating them to a broader agenda of religious revival. This order of priorities is consistent with the group's historic tendency to avoid adopting concrete positions on economic and social policies, arguably to accommodate the diverse economic orientations of its members and supporters. Moreover, the movement's reluctance to seriously oppose economic liberalization is equally consistent with the Brotherhood's conception of Islamic economics. This conception exhibits greater commonality with the rhetoric of state-led economic liberalization than with that of its opponents.

3

Sadat's Brothers

Islamist Incorporation and the Autonomous Path

We agreed to pledge allegiance to the Brotherhood and to follow its leaders [. . . .] Since then, [the structure of] the organization of the Islamic Group that we had built in the [different] governorates became [that of the] Muslim Brotherhood.

—ABDEL-MONEIM ABOUL-FOTOUH, IN *SHAHID ʿALA TARIKH AL-HARAKAH AL-ISLAMIYYA FI MISR*

The Muslim Brotherhood is more powerful than the National [Democratic] Party. If we were to hold free elections tomorrow, they would win.

—SENIOR NDP OFFICIAL

The phrase "Stop protesting and go set up a political party" was uttered frequently—albeit in different formulations—in the aftermath of the January 25 Revolution of 2011. Television commentators used it when arguing that the unruly "revolutionary youth" who were taking to the streets needed to demobilize and, like other major political players, join the military-managed political transition. Parents invoked the statement when trying to talk their children out of joining demonstrations, as did drivers when haranguing protesters to spend their time more productively than blocking traffic. Whatever the circumstances, the phrase conveyed an underlying assumption: the leftist protest movements that surfacd in the wake of Hosni Mubarak's downfall were behaving immaturely and losing track of the big battle ahead: elections.

Surely enough, after the Muslim Brotherhood swept successive elections in 2011 and 2012, the same assumption informed a narrative about why so-called secular currents failed to prevent the electoral dominance of their Islamist counterparts. According to this perspective, the leftist revolutionaries and their secular allies were lazy, incompetent, and unwilling to engage constituents outside of their own Cairo-based bubbles. If these youths would only stop protesting and start organizing as political parties and prepare for elections, the argument went, they would have been able to pose a more credible alternative to Islamist currents.

Facticity aside, this perspective ignores a highly salient reality: the arena in which these various political forces competed in the 2011–2012 election did not appear overnight. That is, Islamist electoral successes did not occur in a vacuum. Therefore, these successes cannot be reduced to the short-term failings of secular groups or revolutionary activists. History did not begin on January 25, 2011.

Although this study is not primarily aimed at explaining why Islamist currents dominated the political stage immediately after Mubarak's downfall, it does contribute to this discussion. It does so by examining the divergent paths of institutional development Islamist and leftist political organizations have taken as a result of Anwar Al-Sadat's Islamist incorporation policies. Tracing these divergent paths provides historical context for the contemporary power asymmetries of Egypt's Islamist and leftist forces. A historically informed perspective rejects attributing these disparities exclusively to the strategies and decisions of the political actors who emerged after Mubarak's ouster. Rather, the legacies of Islamist incorporation under authoritarianism shaped the realities of politics in 2011, insofar as they afforded a comparative advantage to some political currents.

This chapter is the first of three examining the long-term effects of the 1970s Islamist incorporation policies on Egyptian politics. In addition to setting Islamist and leftist currents on divergent paths of institutional development (here and in chapter 4), Islamist incorporation also helped configure a political arena more accommodating to conflicts over national identity than those over distributive commitments (chapter 5).

This study describes the combined outcome of these effects as "more identity, less class."

Building on the evidence presented in chapter 2, this chapter explains the mechanisms through which Islamist incorporation policies have affected the contemporary balance of power between leftist and Islamist political forces. Islamist incorporation policies have effectively set Islamist and leftist movements on distinct trajectories of institutional development.

On one hand, Islamist incorporation afforded the Muslim Brotherhood a permissive political environment during the formative period of the 1970s. That leeway allowed it to expand and to join forces with an Islamist student movement that enjoyed a similarly receptive attitude from the regime for much of that decade. It also enabled the Brotherhood to build organizational structures outside of state supervision.

In the following decades, the Muslim Brotherhood was able to preserve its autonomy and avert the consequences of state intervention by limiting itself to informal modes of political participation. Thus, the Brotherhood was not subject to the legal framework that governed other opposition parties—a system that exposed these parties to regime interference and curbed their organizational expansion.

Two factors reinforced these institutional patterns in the post-Sadat era. The first was the Mubarak regime's desire to limit the Muslim Brotherhood's legal privileges and confine its political activities to informal channels. The second was the trajectory of the group's internal conflicts, which empowered a leadership cadre skeptical of any proposals to legalize the Brotherhood's status.

On the other hand, leftist currents (as explained in chapter 4) evolved differently. In contrast to Islamist currents, the left was kept under the tutelage of the state. Many of its leaders submitted to state control during the 1960s, when prominent communist parties dissolved themselves and agreed to support Gamal Abdel-Nasser's ruling party. This decision produced enduring divisions within the communist movement, hindering efforts to organize leftist forces under a unifying political umbrella in the 1970s. Communist cooperation with Nasser's ruling establishment, moreover, fostered channels and norms of collaboration between the two groups.

In the 1970s, Sadat's repression of underground communist groups foreclosed any opportunity to forge strong, independent leftist organizations that could operate outside of the state's legal framework. The regime also worked to preempt alliances between leftist groups and social forces that lost privileges as a result of economic liberalization, especially organized labor.

The left's capitulation to the state was reinforced in the 1970s, when the cofounders of Al-Tagammu, which included affiliates of the communist movement, accepted a formal legal framework that would expose the party to regime intervention and render it dependent on state resources.

What sustained these institutional patterns (as detailed in chapter 5) were the political successes of the Islamist movement during the 1980s and the general intensification of conflict between leftist and Islamist currents. These conditions enabled Al-Tagammu to rationalize its alliance with the ruling party and submission to the Mubarak regime as resisting the "threat" of political Islam.

In other words, Islamist incorporation policies produced an environment in which Islamist currents, unlike their leftist counterparts, were able to develop autonomous political organizations without state resources and thus free from state intervention. This divergence reveals an important, albeit not the only, determinant of Islamists' political dominance in relation to the left in the contemporary era. This factor is also a key element in the story of Egypt's trajectory to the reality of "more identity, less class."

Islamist Incorporation and the Second Founding of the Muslim Brotherhood: The Autonomous Path

"The only chance available for the free Islamist pen is at the university," wrote Wael Othman in 1976. Upon graduation, Othman contended, an Islamist activist lost access to wall-magazines and university-sponsored forums, leaving no venue in which to channel his energy and express his advocacy. Instead, his voice was silenced by newspaper censors and leftist editors or drowned out by the "superficial articles" that frequently consumed space on the religious affairs pages of national newspapers.[1]

Othman's reflections express the difficult realities that Islamist student activists confronted in the mid-1970s. Despite their command of campus politics, the euphoric sense of empowerment they derived from their

university-based activism was transient, fragile, and unsustainable. Graduates who wished to take their activism outside of campus walls faced fairly
grim prospects. In such a highly regulated political environment, credible national political organizations committed to articulating an Islamist
agenda were absent from the political landscape. In addition, because
of student body turnover, the impact these activists had on campus was
always somewhat ephemeral. There was no guarantee that graduating student leaders' replacements would share their predecessors' experience,
commitment, and skill.

Othman published these comments at a historical inflection point
for Islamist activism at universities and beyond: the reemergence of the
Muslim Brotherhood on the political scene. This development produced a
partnership between the group's recently freed elders and large segments
of the Islamist student movement. That partnership was the basis for the
Muslim Brotherhood's second founding. The Brotherhood provided an
institutional umbrella under which the activism of Islamist students could
be organized and sustained. For its part, the student movement infused the
Brotherhood with new life and energy after two decades of marginalization under Nasser had shattered its organizational structures and eroded
its popular following. In other words, the Brotherhood's reemergence
ensured that the skills and energies of Islamist student activists would be
utilized and not go to waste. In return, the leaders of the Islamist student
movement kept the Brotherhood alive.

A critical factor that allowed this partnership to flourish was the relative freedom and openness these groups enjoyed under Sadat's policy of
Islamist incorporation. Another key (and related) element in this story is
autonomy. Despite the Sadat regime's various attempts to coopt the student movement and the Brotherhood within state structures, neither
group seriously entertained these advances. Instead, they chose to operate
independently of the state, thus experiencing a trajectory of institutional
development vastly different from that of most Egyptian political organizations. In subsequent decades, two major factors helped sustain the
institutional patterns that preserved the Muslim Brotherhood's autonomy
from state institutions and control. The first was the Mubarak regime's
increasing fear of the Brotherhood's capacity to compete with the ruling
party in elections. This fear prompted the regime to deny the Brotherhood
a path to legalization and thus an official role in the political process. The

second factor was the course of internal conflicts inside the movement, which consistently empowered a faction advocating reliance on informal modes of political participation. Thus, the Brotherhood maintained a healthy distance from state-managed legal frameworks to protect the movement's autonomy and prevent its infiltration.

ISLAMIST INCORPORATION AND THE MUSLIM BROTHERHOOD–IGU PARTNERSHIP

As detailed in chapter 2, the relative freedom Islamist groups enjoyed in the 1970s thanks to Sadat's Islamist incorporation policies was integral to the resurgence of the Muslim Brotherhood as a dominant force in Egyptian politics. In addition to releasing the organization's members from prison, the president instructed authorities to reinstate these former inmates to their old positions and to relax security surveillance on their activities.[2] Additionally, Sadat permitted the Brotherhood to publish its magazine Al-Dawa, which offered the group an institutional base for its public engagement. This open political environment permitted the Muslim Brotherhood's aging leadership to draw on the dynamism and vitality of the Islamic Groups at Universities (IGUs).

Shortly after his release from prison in 1974, Muslim Brother Kamal Al-Sananiri established contact with Cairo University Islamic Group (IG) leader Abdel-Moneim Aboul-Fotouh.[3] According to Essam El-Erian, at this time the core leaders of the IG began discussing the future of the organization, specifically whether they would remain an independent group or join the Muslim Brotherhood.[4] One of the major reasons they eventually opted to join the Brotherhood, he explains, was the rapport they established with the movement's leaders and preachers, many of whom they often invited to speak at their camps and other sponsored events.[5] Aboul-Fotouh recalled similar experiences: "As our meetings with the Brothers took off and our contacts with them increased by inviting them to [our] lectures and seminars, we found their personalities inspiring, which was the greatest factor that affected our decision to join the Brotherhood later on."[6] Meanwhile, a similar trend was taking hold in Alexandria, where, according to then local IG leader Ibrahim Al-Zafarani, students were forging ties with established Brotherhood figures like Abbas Al-Sisi, Mohamed Hussein Eissa, Mahmoud Shukri, and Gomaa Amin.[7]

By 1975, the top leadership of the Cairo and Alexandria IGs had pledged loyalty to the Muslim Brotherhood, but they kept this affiliation secret for years,[8] primarily to avoid provoking the regime.[9] Despite this secrecy, Brotherhood loyalists within the IG began instilling members and recruits with Brotherhood doctrine, especially at IG camps, which often hosted hundreds of students.[10] With the encouragement of Brotherhood elders,[11] IG chapters at various universities incorporated into a formal, national structure,[12] a move ultimately contributing to the Brotherhood's organizational resurgence.[13] By late 1977, Aboul-Fotouh, El-Erian, and other Brotherhood affiliates inside the IGUs encouraged like-minded IG leaders from other universities to join the Brotherhood.[14] This effort gained momentum in 1979, when ties between the IGUs and the Brotherhood became known to outsiders.[15] In sum, throughout much of the 1970s, Muslim Brotherhood leaders used the IGUs to inject new blood into the movement and rebuild its organizational structures.[16]

Where was the Sadat regime as these developments were underway? Indeed, the extent of government surveillance on the Muslim Brotherhood and the Islamist student movement at that time cannot be precisely measured. But there is little doubt that the regime's decision to relax security service scrutiny of Islamist currents (as described in chapter 2) helped keep the institutional ties between the Brotherhood and the IGUs below the regime's radar, at least until 1979.[17] Additionally, Sadat unwittingly contributed to the Brotherhood's rebuilding efforts by permitting the group to resume publication of *Al-Dawa* in 1976. Sadat thereby provided the Brotherhood with a voice in public affairs and a means to assert the movement's political presence. Throughout the 1970s, *Al-Dawa*'s headquarters served as the de facto home base for the Brotherhood and as the focal point of its political operations.[18] The magazine was one of the major nodes of collaboration between the young student activists and the Muslim Brotherhood's older leaders.[19] Aboul-Fotouh recalls that *Al-Dawa*'s contributions played a key role in convincing him and his colleagues to join the Muslim Brotherhood.[20] *Al-Dawa* launched the careers of many who subsequently became prominent Brotherhood figures in media and journalism. Notable examples include veteran journalists Mohamed Abdel-Quddous and Salah Abdel-Maqsoud, the latter of whom served as minister of information under the presidency of Mohamed Morsi.

RECONSTRUCTING THE ORGANIZATION

Indeed, when IGU affiliates joined the Muslim Brotherhood, they did so as individuals and not as an organizational bloc.[21] Nevertheless, the IGUs provided the building blocks on which the Brotherhood was able to reconstruct its organization.

A common misperception is that the Muslim Brotherhood was in continuous operation since its founding in 1928.[22] Yet, before the leaders of the IGUs entered the Brotherhood in the 1970s, the group had virtually ceased to exist after decades of repression. All that remained of the Brotherhood at that point was a history and a fragmented community of former inmates and exiles whose age, isolation, and personal hardships left them ill-equipped for political activism in a changing and highly volatile political environment. The astounding resurgence of the Muslim Brotherhood as a coherent organization in the 1970s and 1980s was primarily the product of its partnership with the vibrant Islamist student movement. As Abdullah Al-Arian explains, this younger generation of Islamist activists gave the Brotherhood an opportunity to reemerge in Egyptian politics at the moment when the movement's future was in doubt.[23]

Aboul-Fotouh's firsthand account of the history of Egypt's Islamist movement makes this point decisively and is worth quoting at length:

By the time we decided as leaders of the Islamic Group at Universities to enter | . . .| into the Muslim Brotherhood, we had [already] answered the question of [whether or not to form an] organization. We were already an organization before handing [our] structure over to the Muslim Brothers who became [its leaders]. The Brotherhood was an [empty] house that the youth of the Islamic Group filled | . . .| bestowing leadership upon the [heads] of the Brotherhood. We agreed to pledge allegiance to the Brotherhood and to follow its leaders |. . . .| Since then, [the structure of] the organization of the Islamic Group that we had built in the [different] governorates became [that of the] Muslim Brotherhood |. . . .| And after the graduation of the founding leaders of the Islamic Group from the university in 1976, we began asking each graduate to return to his [hometown] to connect with the new [regional] leadership |. . . .| We used to ask Brothers to contact the Islamic Group leader [at their hometown] so he can refer them to the [local Muslim Brotherhood official]. The

Brotherhood's officials in various provinces then received those graduates from the leaders of the Islamic Group. In Alexandria, for example
|...| Ibrahim Al-Zafarani was the leader of the Islamic Group and Abbas
Al-Sisi was the Muslim Brotherhood official responsible for receiving the
new graduates, and so on. Actually, when we pledged loyalty to the Muslim Brotherhood, we were not making a pledge to an established organization that existed in reality. Rather, we pledged loyalty to an idea, a
project, and a history, as there was no actual Brotherhood organization
in the strict sense of the word. Rather, there was a group of individuals or
historic organizers who received from us the leadership of the organization that did in fact exist, and by that, I mean that of the Islamic Group
|....| And thus the organization began to spread throughout the country
and the Brotherhood leaders began rising to its top and asserting control
over it. Most of these [longtime Brotherhood] leaders were individuals
who used to be affiliated with the secret apparatus. They were responsible for communicating with the graduates. They covered almost all the
governorates of the country. Meanwhile, the student organizers (the former affiliates of the Islamic Group) remained in positions of leadership
even after joining the Brotherhood but under the guidance of the Muslim
Brotherhood's leaders.[24]

Abul-Ela Madi makes the same point, although he is less diplomatic regarding the incapacity of the Brotherhood's leaders to manage the logistics of
mobilization and recruitment. At a time when the movement's historic
figures were failing to bring new blood into the group, he claims, student
organizers, such as Aboul-Fotouh and others, were able to recruit thousands of new members.[25]

ROAD TO THE "ISLAMIST ADVANTAGE": MOSQUES AND CHARITIES

The networks and the structures that the Muslim Brotherhood developed during the era of Islamist incorporation formed the foundation from
which the movement could expand into a variety of social spheres. In other
words, the favorable political environment Sadat offered the Brotherhood
yielded numerous benefits, enabling the movement to garner immense
influence in subsequent years.

In fact, the mechanisms scholars have used to explain how the Muslim Brotherhood was able to build its contemporary "Islamist advantage" revolve largely around the organizational expansion the group achieved in the 1970s and 1980s because of Islamist incorporation. For example, it was members of the 1970s student activist generation who led the Muslim Brotherhood into what Carrie Wickham calls the "parallel Islamist sector." The latter term is shorthand for a host of civil society and private sector organizations, including mosques, voluntary associations, charities, and commercial establishments.[26] This same generation of activists established a Brotherhood presence in charity work, thereby laying the foundation for the organization's powerful social services network. That network, as Steven Brooke argues, handed the movement a unique mobilizational advantage during election seasons in the Mubarak era and beyond.[27] Finally, it was in the wake of Islamist incorporation policies that Brotherhood affiliates were able to assert their presence and influence inside mosques. In the long run, this mode of activism endowed the organization with a key element of its electoral success after the January 25 Revolution, namely what Tarek Masoud refers to as its "embeddedness inside religious social infrastructure."[28]

Nothing captures these realities more than the experience of Mohy Eissa, the former IG leader at Al-Minya University. Eissa, who pledged loyalty to the Brotherhood in 1979, describes in his memoirs the role he played in the Brotherhood's creation of an organizational base in Al-Minya during the 1980s. Immediately after his release from prison in 1983, Eissa helped reclaim the Omar Ibn Al-Khattab Mosque (named after the Companion of the Prophet and Second Caliph) as a central node for the organization's outreach in the city,[29] and he succeeded in establishing the Brotherhood's influence over additional mosques in subsequent years.[30] On the social services front, Eissa conceived the idea of forming a charity in Al-Minya also named after Omar Ibn Al-Khattab. This organization ultimately founded the Omar Ibn Al-Khattab Hospital. Eissa's story was not unique. As he details, other Brotherhood affiliates throughout Egypt followed the same strategy, establishing mosque-centered outreach and venues for social service provision.[31]

In other words, the favorable position the Muslim Brotherhood secured as a result of Islamist incorporation policies contributed greatly to the groundwork for the political and electoral gains the movement managed to achieve in the decades that followed.

AUTONOMY FROM THE STATE

Another significant feature of the Muslim Brotherhood's institutional development since the 1970s is the organizational autonomy it secured and maintained in relation to the state. The Brotherhood evaded Sadat's efforts to coopt the organization under a restrictive legal framework and intrusive state controls. Instead, it opted to build its organizational structures outside of state-sanctioned bodies or government regulation. It did so in partnership with the IGUs, a strategy that also permitted the organization to avoid the supervision of the ruling party in the mid-1970s. Following Sadat's assassination in 1981, the Muslim Brotherhood continued rebuilding its organization with comparable autonomy.[32]

Upon their release from prison in the early 1980s, Brotherhood leaders tasked with reviving the organization formed a communication and oversight committee to establish contact with affiliates in various governorates.[33] To that end, they relied on networks the IGUs had built in the 1970s. According to Al-Zafarani, the IGUs' national structure was critical to the Brotherhood's resurrection, as it provided a well-integrated network of experienced activists.[34] Meanwhile, former IGUs affiliates, like Aboul-Fotouh, Al-Gazzar, and Madi, were ordered to build the students' section of the movement. According to Mohy Eissa, this section effectively became the backbone of the Brotherhood's organizational structure given that executive offices and specialized departments had yet to be formed.[35]

In the absence of legal status, the Muslim Brotherhood's leaders ran its operations circumspectly to avoid state oversight and scrutiny. For example, in 1983, the Brotherhood formed a small consulting firm under the name "The Scientific Center for Research and Studies," commonly known as Maʿbad. Publicly, Maʿbad was described as research-support center, but its actual purpose was managing and streamlining the Muslim Brotherhood's university-based activism, including student and faculty outreach.[36]

That same informal approach was evident in the Muslim Brotherhood's engagement in national politics. Because it lacked the necessary license to contest the 1984 election under its own name, the Brotherhood fielded candidates on Al-Wafd Party's electoral lists. It also used this tactic in the 1987 legislative election, when the organization contested races under the banner of the Socialist Labor Party (SLP) and in partnership with the Liberal Socialists Party (LSP). Despite lacking a party license, Brotherhood

candidates won enough seats to form the largest opposition bloc in parliament. The Brotherhood made similar gains inside professional associations, securing significant representation in the physicians, engineers, and
lawyers syndicates.[37]

The Muslim Brotherhood continued to operate on this unofficial basis
throughout the rest of the Mubarak era. This approach was maintained
during moments of relative openness, as well as periods of repression
and marginalization as experienced in the mid-1990s. In other words, the
institutional patterns that emerged during the Sadat era continued until
at least 2011, when the movement established a formal political party.
The following sections explain these institutional patterns' persistence
throughout the Mubarak era.

Two factors were critical to this persistence. First, growing competition
between the ruling party and the Muslim Brotherhood stimulated regime
fears of the organization's growing political influence. Accordingly, the
Mubarak regime continued to deny the Brotherhood legal status, thereby
preserving the institutional patterns formed under Sadat. Second, the
Muslim Brotherhood's intragroup dynamics produced a consensus favoring a cautious approach to political engagement. Thus, the path toward
normalization and legalization was eyed with considerable trepidation.

THE MUBARAK REGIME AND THE PERSISTENCE OF PRIOR INSTITUTIONAL PATTERNS

As the Brotherhood's influence expanded during the Mubarak era, the
regime grew more determined to exclude it from the legal framework governing official parties, thereby limiting its participation in political life to
informal channels. Even though this arrangement exposed the movement
to multiple rounds of repression, it preserved the Muslim Brotherhood's
institutional autonomy from the state.

How did the reversal of Islamist incorporation come about? One could
argue that the Islamist incorporation policies of the 1970s were imbued
with their own demise. Indeed, the Muslim Brotherhood's political gains of
the 1980s—largely enabled by Islamist incorporation—helped the regime
neutralize the leftist opposition to infitah (as analyzed in chapter 5). Paradoxically, however, the Brotherhood's successes, once viewed as beneficial
to the regime, eventually provoked the political leadership to reverse its

Islamist incorporation policies, initiating a process I define as "Islamist de-incorporation." Specifically, increasing competition in multiple political arenas created the perception of a zero-sum game between the Brother-hood and the regime, prompting a host of state-imposed restrictions on the group's political activities.

Before discussing these restrictions, two important points are in order. First, the Mubarak regime's repression effaced many of the Brotherhood's gains in parliamentary elections, professional syndicates, faculty clubs, and student unions. Yet repressive measures did not reverse the organi-zational rebuilding the group had accomplished in the 1970s and 1980s.[38] Second, Mubarak's repression did nothing to compromise the Brother-hood's carefully cultivated autonomy from the state. In fact, the Mubarak regime's actions reinforced this autonomy.

Mubarak began his presidency with an accommodating posture toward the political opposition, allowing them some limited representation in the national legislature. By the end of the 1980s, however, the ruling National Democratic Party (NDP) was displaying discomfort with the regime's rela-tive leniency toward the opposition, especially the Muslim Brotherhood. For example, LSP leader Mustafa Kamel Murad reports that NDP heavy-weights Yousef Wali and Safwat Al-Sherif, along with Minister of Interior Zaki Badr, pressured him to sabotage his party's alliance with the Brother-hood, weeks before the 1987 election. Specifically, they asked him to pub-licly acknowledge that the LSP fielded its candidates on the same electoral list as the SLP. Given that this practice was technically a breach of legal procedures, such a statement would have given authorities a pretext to dis-qualify the entire Islamic Alliance electoral list. In return for his compliant behavior, the officials promised Murad they would guarantee the appoint-ment of LSP leaders to parliament. Murad declined the offer, enabling the Muslim Brotherhood to form the largest opposition bloc in parliament.[39]

Despite regime leaders' concern about the Muslim Brotherhood's growing influence, they shunned opportunities to bring the group under their institutional control, preferring to deny the Brotherhood any form of legal status. A senior NDP leader and government official reveals that Brotherhood affiliates approached him after the 1987 legislative election, proposing that they join the ruling party and end their association with the SLP. The official replied, "As long as I am in charge of this party, this will never happen." The official then explained, "The goal is to keep the

Muslim Brotherhood limited and prevent them from entering any political party."[40] The irony, of course, is that by keeping the Brotherhood outside of the legal political framework, the regime was also forgoing the chance to exert oversight and indirect control over the movement's internal affairs. That institutional arrangement was solidified even more in the 1990s, when regime–Brotherhood confrontations furthered the ruling elite's determination to limit the group's access to formal channels of political participation.

By the early 1990s, the Muslim Brotherhood's impressive electoral gains offered those inside the regime who opposed accommodating the movement new opportunities to change the state's posture toward the Brotherhood. Thanks to the resources the Brotherhood could access through its dominance of professional syndicates,[41] its presence in the political arena expanded to such a degree that it appeared to be a viable alternative to the ruling party. This reality became obvious in October 1992, when a destructive earthquake struck Cairo, leaving hundreds dead and many more homeless. The Muslim Brotherhood played a high-profile role in the provision of disaster relief through professional syndicates and its affiliated nongovernmental organizations (NGOs). These efforts, which received prominent coverage in international media, served as an urgent wake-up call for the regime, revealing the extent of the Brotherhood's organizational empire.[42]

During the same period, Muslim Brotherhood leaders and affiliates also began challenging the ruling establishment on a variety of political issues. One such issue was the legal framework governing the 1990 legislative election, which the Brotherhood found so constraining that it ultimately boycotted the race. The group harshly criticized the government's 1991 support for the U.S.-led coalition against Iraq and refused to endorse Mubarak's nomination for a third presidential term in 1993. Additionally, Brotherhood affiliates were at the center of the infamous 1994 clash between the lawyers syndicate and the Ministry of Interior over the death of an attorney in police custody.[43]

Meanwhile, regime allies began openly attacking the government for its perceived leniency toward political Islam in general, and the Muslim Brotherhood in particular. This opposition came in the aftermath of the assassinations of parliament speaker Rifaat Al-Mahgoub (October 1990) and secular columnist Farag Foda (June 1992), which were attributed to underground Islamist groups. Many secular opinion makers deemed

Islamist commentators complicit in Foda's death, claiming that their slanderous critiques of the late writer and academic made him an apostate,
and thus a legitimate target, in the public's eyes.[44] An *Al-Ahram* editorial on Foda's assassination alleged that the government had planted the
seed for violent extremism by permitting proponents of political Islam
undue influence in the media and public life.[45] Other state-owned publications like *Rose Al-Yousef* adopted a similar editorial line, alleging that the
state had been far too lenient with Islamist sympathizers (see chapter 2,
"Sources, Accounts, and the Parable of a Believing President").

The political leadership was not oblivious to these developments and
began showing signs of alarm. For example, in the aftermath of clashes
between Brotherhood-affiliated students and police forces at Assiut University, Mohamed Habib met with the director of the State Security Investigations Service, who raised firm objections to the Brotherhood's activities
on college campuses: "Is it acceptable for universities to turn into arenas
for ideational conflicts? Is it acceptable for political parties to export these
conflicts to universities? And is it acceptable for the particular intellectual
current of some professors to dominate university faculty through [fac-
ulty] clubs?"[46]

A few months after this meeting, the regime retaliated against the Muslim Brotherhood as part of what became popularly known as the "Salsabeel
case." Salsabeel was an IT company owned by Muslim Brotherhood members Khairat El-Shater and Hassan Malek. Authorities raided Salsabeel's
offices on February 5, 1992, and claimed to have found a Brotherhood blueprint for the seizure of political power.[47] Although the suspects in the case
were eventually released, the document lent temporary credence to the
state media chorus asserting that the Brotherhood was plotting to overthrow the existing political system.[48] According to Al-Sayyid Abdel-Sattar
Al-Meleegy, the most valuable asset authorities seized during the Salsabeel
raid was the Brotherhood's membership roaster,[49] which revealed the massive size of its rebuilt organizational network.[50] As a result, the state's confrontational posture toward the Brotherhood would persist for years.

In 1995, the crackdown against the Muslim Brotherhood escalated to
a degree unseen since the Nasser era.[51] In January, the Brotherhood convened its Shura Council to elect a new Guidance Bureau, a move the regime
considered provocative. Shortly thereafter, authorities launched a wave
of arrests against high-ranking Brotherhood members.[52] Another spate of

arrests followed in July of that same year, leading to a series of military tribunals between 1995 and 2001. These trials resulted in prison sentences of three to five years for dozens of senior Brotherhood leaders, including Khairat El-Shater, Abdel-Moneim Aboul-Fotouh, Mahmoud Ezzat, Essam El-Erian, and Mohamed Habib.[53] The regime also enacted a number of measures effectively suspending the powers of Brotherhood-dominated elected bodies at key professional syndicates.[54] Finally, the security apparatus ensured many Brotherhood losses during the violent, fraudulent[55] parliamentary election of 1995.[56]

In sum, the regime's crackdown on the Muslim Brotherhood during the 1990s locked the group in the institutional arrangement that had long barred it from lawful political competition. As the Brotherhood's increasing influence continued to threaten the Mubarak regime, the confrontation between the two sides severely reduced the possibility of escaping these institutional patterns.

Even during Mubarak's final decade in office, when the government displayed a relative degree of tolerance for the Muslim Brotherhood's limited public presence, it continued to bar the group from institutional participation in electoral politics. For example, in 2000, Brotherhood candidates contested the legislative election as independents, eventually securing seventeen seats in the People's Assembly.[57] The same scenario unfolded in 2005, when the group, despite lacking legal status, became the largest opposition bloc ever formed under Mubarak's rule.

The context of the 2005 election revealed just how the ruling elite's competitive instincts helped preserve the informal institutional patterns that governed the Muslim Brotherhood's activism throughout the Mubarak era. Despite having an evident interest in allowing the Brotherhood to have a visible presence in public life, the regime continued to hamper the group's activities and deny it any form of official recognition. Once again, the familiar dynamics were in operation: by excluding the Brotherhood from the list of licensed parties, the regime denied the movement the means to normalize its political presence. It also, however, denied itself the opportunity to intervene in the group's affairs and, when necessary, disrupt its internal cohesion.

In the lead-up to the 2005 election, the Mubarak regime confronted mounting opposition in the form of proliferating protest movements and public expressions of socioeconomic discontent.[58] Animating these grievances were the adventurist spirit that swept the region in the wake of escalating protests against the U.S.-led war in Iraq and international players' declarations of support for so-called democracy promotion.[59] In response, the regime revived Sadat's strategy of Islamist incorporation, opening limited political space to the Muslim Brotherhood, thereby hoping to arouse liberal and leftist fears of an impending Islamist takeover.

In accordance with an understanding between the regime and the Brotherhood, security forces permitted the group an unusual degree of freedom during the first round of the 2005 legislative election.[60] An NDP leader and aide to President Mubarak explains that the minister of interior had agreed with a Muslim Brotherhood representative that the group would be permitted to win up to twenty seats. In the first round of voting, however, the Brotherhood won thirty-four races, thereby breaking the agreed-upon ceiling. "We were very shaken," Mubarak's aide says.[61] Accordingly, the state intervened forcefully in subsequent phases of voting to limit the Brotherhood's electoral gains. With a lot of sweat and blood (figuratively and literally), the security apparatus held the organization to eighty-eight seats.[62]

The 2005 election repeated a now-familiar pattern: the regime strategically opens political space to the Brotherhood, but then reverses these openings when competition becomes too threatening. The course of the 2005 contest was a classic example of—to borrow the terminology of Nathan Brown—"the cat-and-mouse game" the regime and the Brotherhood have long played.[63] Shortly after the Muslim Brotherhood's electoral victories, its affiliates experienced a fresh wave of arrests and military trials.[64] From this moment until Mubarak's downfall, the Brotherhood was effectively shut out of national elections, including the fraud-ridden 2010 election, which Mona El-Ghobashy has famously dubbed the "liquidation of Egypt's illiberal experiment."[65]

Central to the regime's response was an awareness that the movement was too powerful to be coopted and managed like other established opposition parties.[66] "The Muslim Brotherhood is more powerful than the National [Democratic] Party. If we were to hold free elections tomorrow, they would win," explained the previously quoted Mubarak regime figure, whose prediction came true the following year. Other parties, he indicated, were easier to deal with because "none of them can win seats on their own. We help them win seats."[67]

In short, regime concern about the growing influence of the Muslim Brotherhood made the former more intent on maintaining the latter's exclusion from the legal framework governing the activities of opposition parties. This context explains the regime's efforts to perpetuate the institutional patterns defining the Brotherhood's engagement in political life under Mubarak—patterns that helped the group maintain its autonomy from the state. Yet, the Mubarak regime was not alone in preserving this enduring equilibrium. The Brotherhood's internal dynamics were equally significant.

THE MUSLIM BROTHERHOOD'S INTERNAL DYNAMICS AND BIAS TOWARD INFORMALITY AND AUTONOMY

Another factor reinforcing the pre-existing institutional patterns was the outcome of internal conflicts within the Brotherhood. The trajectory of these disputes since the 1980s has empowered a faction determined to keep the group's political activities under its strict control and beyond the reach of state-imposed regulations.

The history of the Muslim Brotherhood's internal discord is an enormous topic meriting a book-length study.[68] This section, however, focuses exclusively on the aspects of that history that explain, in part, the group's decision to retain its unofficial, unlicensed political activity throughout the Mubarak era. The persistence of these institutional patterns shielded the Muslim Brotherhood from forms of state intervention that compromised and weakened much of the officially recognized opposition. This divergence is key to understanding contemporary power asymmetries between Islamist and leftist forces in Egypt.

Scholars have characterized the Brotherhood's dominant internal division during the 1990s and 2000s as one between *haras qadiym* ("old guard") versus *haras jadid* ("new guard"), *muhafiz* ("conservative") versus *islahy* ("reformist") camp, and *'amal al-'am* ("public engagement") versus *tanzimy* ("organizationalist") current. Each of these binaries bears some explanatory utility, but I characterize the Brotherhood's most relevant internal division as that between adherents of two distinct logics of survival, the *"logic of guardianship"* and the *"logic of institutionalism."*[69] Guiding each of these logics is a set of assumptions about the Brotherhood's proper priorities and survival strategies. The contrast between the two logics, moreover, elucidates major internal disagreements over structuring the movement's political participation and defining its relationship to Egypt's underlying legal framework.

Logic of Guardianship

Predicated on the fear of infiltration and factionalism, the logic of guardianship is an inward-looking survival strategy featuring a preference for informality, opaqueness, and inaccessibility. Survival, according to this logic, necessitates constructing a vanguard of committed, ideologically indoctrinated Brotherhood activists whose work would parallel the movement's official organizational structures. The role of these activists is to informally keep the official leadership in check, and, if necessary, to counter internal or external pressures that could divert the movement from its original mission or even destroy it. Prominent Muslim Brotherhood representatives of this tendency include Mustafa Mashhur, Mahmoud Ezzat, and Khairat El-Shater. Advocates of the logic of guardianship, moreover, tend to emphasize the importance of *tarbiyah* ("indoctrination") and awarding membership, particularly leadership positions, exclusively to those of proven commitment and loyalty. The Brotherhood's opaque, layered membership structure reflects this logic,[70] which Hazem Kandil neatly summarizes with the axiom, "One cannot choose to join the Muslim Brotherhood; one has to be chosen."[71] This cautious approach to recruitment and outreach has produced a movement sufficiently well organized to penetrate wide sectors of society, while being too closed for outsiders to penetrate.

Proponents of the logic of guardianship do not oppose political participation in principle. In fact, as Nathan Brown observes, Brotherhood figures known for such conservative inclinations have supported the group's involvement in politics in the past.[72] What is distinctive about the logic of guardianship is the conception of political engagement as a means to achieve the group's overarching mission rather than as an end in and of itself.[73] Advocates of guardianism are sensitive to the Brotherhood's competing commitments in a variety of social spheres like charity, preaching, religious advocacy, and the economy.[74] Thus, for the guardianists, the movement's involvement in politics must not detract from or threaten the survival of these other endeavors, another argument for managing, monitoring, and, when necessary, restraining the Brotherhood's cadre of ambitious politicians. Finally, the guardianists are skeptical about the Bortherhood's legalization, as it inevitably would expose the group to external pressures and subject it to the mercies of a ruling party that abides by no laws.

Logic of Institutionalism

The logic of institutionalism is an outward-looking survival strategy that prioritizes public engagement and popular mobilization and that tends to favor formality, transparency, and accessibility. Unless the Muslim Brotherhood expands its social base and presence in public life, the argument goes, the group will atrophy even if its cells survive underground. That is, robust organizational structures are useless if the movement has no voice in public debates about popular concerns. To achieve its mission and have a meaningful presence in Egyptian society, the group must revise its rules and practices to make itself more open to the society it is seeking to influence. Thus, proponents of this perspective, as the late Hossam Tammam writes, want to see the movement "transform into a political party in accordance with the laws, framework, and regulations organizing the political process | ... | and that is subject to full legal and financial oversight."[75]

This perspective tends to prevail among those who joined the organization believing it was akin to a political party or an NGO. They include, among others, leaders of the Islamist student movement who pledged loyalty to the Muslim Brotherhood during the 1970s and early 1980s and who have engaged in public service through parliament or professional associations. The most prominent of these figures are Abdel Moneim Aboul-Fotouh, Abul-Ela Madi, Mukhtar Nouh, Mohy Eissa, Ibrahim Al-Zafarani, Mohamed Habib, and Al-Sayyid Abdel-Sattar Al-Meleegy.

The Parallel Organizations

The guardianist camp's rise to power began in the 1980s, when Mustafa Mashhur and Mahmoud Ezzat fled the country to escape Sadat's notorious September 1981 crackdown. Their absence left at the helm those who would form the bulk of the institutionalist camp, namely Omar Al-Tilmisani and former Islamist student leaders. Al-Tilmisani's receptive attitude toward the younger recruits' political aspirations deepened the Muslim Brotherhood's engagement in public life, most visibly in parliament and professional syndicates.[76] In contrast, as the exiled Mashhur labored to construct the Muslim Brotherhood's international network, a community of exiled members and new recruits coalesced around his leadership, initiating the process of the guardianist camp's formation. Meanwhile, Mashhur's faithful deputy Ezzat and Brotherhood entrepreneur Khairat El-Shater formed a partnership while the two were residing in Yemen and London. Decades later, these partners would take effective control of the entire movement, when El-Shater and Ezzat became, as al-Anani describes them, the "king-makers" of the Muslim Brotherhood.[77]

Upon their return to Egypt in the mid-1980s, Mashhur, Ezzat, and El-Shater expanded their collective weight inside the Muslim Brotherhood by awarding positions of influence to trusted associates, drawing primarily from the diaspora network they had built in exile.[78] Among them was Saad Al-Katatni, an employee of El-Shater and recent doctoral graduate recruited into the Brotherhood while he pursued his studies in Germany. Despite having no experience in political organization, Mohy Eissa reports, Al-Katatni joined the Brotherhood's leadership team in Al-Minya,[79] subsequently becoming its chief administrator in that region.[80]

Aiding Mashhur's rise to power was the 1986 passing of General Guide Omar Al-Tilmisani. He was replaced by Mohamed Hamed Abul-Nasr, an aging figurehead who asserted far less leadership and presence than his predecessor. Capitalizing on the weakness of the new general guide, Mashhur expanded his authority to such an extent that many believed he wielded supreme power inside the Brotherhood.[81]

With Al-Tilmisani out of the picture, Mashhur and Ezzat began exercising authority through the tarbiyah department, which became heavily involved in administrative bodies previously led by IGU's alumni.[82] By the late 1980s, the guardianists were able to oust these elements, including Aboul-Fotouh and Al-Meleegy, from the management of the Brotherhood's student department and faculty affairs unit. Replacing them were individuals loyal to the guardianist network, including Ezzat and Rashad Bayoumi,[83] a longtime Brotherhood member who worked in the United Arab Emirates during the early 1980s.[84] Certainly, institutionalists retained some influence, thanks to the Brotherhood's victories in legislative and professional syndicate elections in the 1980s. For example, Aboul-Fotouh, Madi,

Nouh, and Al-Meleegy were tasked with managing the Brotherhood's involvement in various syndicates, while El-Erian and Habib entered parliament in 1987. By ceding the students' department to the guardianists, however, the institutionalists were effectively handing over control of an important channel of recruitment to their opponents, thereby affording them long-term influence over the movement's membership base.[85]

Observers have attributed the guardianist camp's behavior to the movement's long-standing tendency to erect parallel structures that constituted secret, unaccountable centers of power. This interpretation is substantiated by Mustafa Mashhur's former ties with the Brotherhood's "secret apparatus," which was prone to challenging the formal leadership's authority in the 1940s and 1950s.[86] Some assert that Mashhur and many of his collaborators were influenced by the ideas of Sayyid Qutb, specifically the imperative to isolate oneself from the society of nonbelievers in the struggle to achieve a "true" Islamic community.[87] A different and often underappreciated factor is the movement's turbulent experience during the 1970s, which may have reinforced would-be guardianists' belief that greater control was necessary to check the dangerously adventurist inclinations of its newly indoctrinated younger activists. After all, during that period, the Muslim Brotherhood leaders persistently struggled to contain the IGUs' confrontational elements,[88] who not only eschewed the Brotherhood's leadership but also dragged the organization into conflicts with the state.[89]

The Guardianists Strike

The looming competition between the two camps continued into the mid-1990s. A major turning point came in January 1995, when the guardianists won a major victory in the Brotherhood's Shura Council and Guidance Bureau elections.[90] Even with a few seats captured by institutionalists like Aboul-Fotouh and Mohamed Habib, the Guidance Bureau came under the control of guardianists like Mashhur, El-Shater, Ezzat, and Bayoumi. This was the beginning of the end for the institutionalists.

After Abul-Nasr's passing, Mashhur assumed the position of general guide without convening an internal election.[91] From that point forward, the institutionalists were on the defensive, suffering one setback after another. One such setback was on public display in 1996, when former pioneers of the Islamist student movement Abul-Ela Madi and Essam Sultan led a defection of Brotherhood members. This drastic move came in response to Mashhur and his associates' rejection of Madi and Sultan's proposal to establish a political party under the name Al-Wasat.[92] This episode reflected the extent to which the guardianists' victories hardened the Brotherhood's aversion to legalization or any steps that could disrupt the institutional patterns that had long structured its national political activism. Both the Brotherhood's leadership and the regime worked concurrently—albeit on different fronts—to kill the proposal to form Al-Wasat, underscoring their mutual interest in keeping the movement outside of the formal legal framework.

Capital, Coercion, and the Guardianist Triumph

Two factors were key to tilting the balance of power in favor of the guardianists. The first was the intensification of state repression in the mid-1990s. When Mashhur assumed the post of general guide in 1996, many institutionalist figures had been arrested or were serving prison sentences. Among them were Aboul-Fotouh, Habib, El-Erian, Al-Zafarani, Al-Meleegy, and, starting in 2000, Nouh. This development arguably helped Mashhur and his associates tighten their grip on the organization.[93] Also facilitating this task were the regime's efforts to reverse the Brotherhood's electoral victories in professional syndicates. The ruling party also used fraud and violence in the 1995 election to prevent the group from securing representation in the legislature. As the institutionalists' power resided primarily in parliament and professional associations, it is fair to conclude that these regime efforts were more detrimental to the institutionalists than to the guardianists.

The second factor supporting the guardianist camp was the superior access to resources it developed by incorporating a variety of business interests into its networks. This began during the 1980s, when the exiled Mashhur launched an effort to strengthen the Brotherhood's international presence. These efforts solidified Mashhur and his associates' links with wealthy Brotherhood affiliates in the Gulf and Europe, including business figure Youssef Nada. Based in Switzerland, Nada is widely recognized as the principal manager of the Brotherhood's political and financial affairs overseas. He is also the founder of Al-Taqwa, a Bahamas-based bank where

Muslim Brotherhood figures have reportedly invested their money for many years.[94]

Meanwhile, Khairat El-Shater was gaining clout in the business world. Upon his 1985 return to Egypt, El-Shater formed a partnership with Hassan Malek, a young entrepreneur he had befriended years earlier at Alexandria University.[95] They first formed Salsabeel, the computer company at the center of the 1992 state investigation discussed earlier. After dissolving the company in the wake of that fiasco, the partners established other lucrative business endeavors, endowing El-Shater with much wealth and influence.[96]

Indeed, as explained in chapter 2, many Muslim Brotherhood members led successful careers in the private sector, in some cases reaping benefits from the economic liberalization process that began under Sadat. This was especially true for those who had accumulated considerable capital during their exile in oil-rich Gulf countries. Yet, as Tammam notes, El-Shater stood out among Brotherhood business figures in that he possessed both private wealth *and* organizational influence.[97] This unique profile afforded him a great deal of weight within the guardianist camp.[98] It also gave the guardianists an edge over their institutionalist counterparts, who lost access to the resources they had once enjoyed through positions in professional syndicates.

The Flight of the Institutionalists and the Guardianist Utopia

On the eve of the January 25 Revolution, disputes between the guardianist and institutionalist camps were abating, as the former faction appeared to be gaining complete control over the organization's management. Indeed, Mohamed Mahdi Akef, who served as general guide between 2004 and 2010, enjoyed a more cooperative relationship with the institutionalists than his two immediate predecessors, Mashhur and Mamoun Al-Houdaiby. Akef made some concessions to the institutionalists' demand that the Brotherhood "normalize" its presence in the political arena, permitting limited cooperation with non-Islamist political groups and publicly promulgating a vision for political reform.[99] Yet, the institutionalists never regained the upper hand they had lost in the mid-1990s, largely because the guardianists had become far too entrenched in the Brotherhood's management for any rival faction to effectively oppose them. This was evident in the late-2009 power struggle that ended with the removal of Aboul-Fotouh, Habib, and other institutionalists from the Guidance Bureau. Shortly thereafter, Mohamed Badie, a leader with known guardianist sympathies, was named general guide.[100]

Thus, when Mubarak fell in 2011, the Brotherhood's key institutionalists had been marginalized, ousted, or coopted. Now the movement's leadership featured a new cadre that rose through the ranks under guardianist patronage. At the same time, the defection of institutionalists continued. For example, Aboul-Fotouh severed ties with the Brotherhood in 2011 after leaders forbade him from running for president. This incident was potent with symbolism, as the iconic leader of the 1970s Islamist student movement who had done so much to resuscitate the Brotherhood decades earlier was parting ways with the organization.

Beyond the downfall of the institutionalists, the Muslim Brotherhood's conduct in post-Mubarak Egypt reflected its guardianist leaders' abiding interest in minimizing the risks inherent in increasing engagement in politics. They worked around official requirements mandating public transparency and accountability inside legally recognized political organizations. The guardianists also sought to keep Brotherhood-affiliated politicians under tight control to shield the movement from external pressures.

Rather than heeding long-standing internal and external demands to transform the Muslim Brotherhood into a political party, its leaders took a different track. They formed the Freedom and Justice Party (FJP), which remained nominally independent from the Brotherhood. In doing so, the guardianists were deflecting demands to normalize the Brotherhood's status. In other words, they refused to restructure the organization along the lines of lawful political parties, as this would have necessarily entailed increasing its transparency and internal accountability. In effect, the guardianists passed the buck to the FJP. Because the Muslim Brotherhood was technically not contesting elections—the FJP was—the parent organization was not required to restructure itself into a political party or abolish its "secret society traits." This was a significant development, because these secretive practices had long preserved the Brotherhood's autonomy and shielded it from state intervention.

As a result, whereas FJP membership was formally open to all, its parent organization maintained its time-tested practices to keep infiltrators out of its ranks. All Brotherhood members were encouraged to join the FJP and were forbidden to form or join any other party, but FJP membership did not automatically translate into formal affiliation with the Brotherhood. Evoking the image of a movement that penetrates wide sectors of society but remains closed off to external forces, the Brotherhood allowed any person to enter the FJP and lend it support, but kept the Brotherhood inaccessible to outsiders. Moreover, FJP membership was not awarded unconditionally. The party instituted a membership system requiring applicants to serve a probationary period of six to twelve months, during which time their commitment to the party was assessed. In addition, the party's bylaws afforded FJP officers great discretion in determining applicants' fitness for membership.[101]

Most significantly, the FJP reflected the guardianist vision of keeping Brotherhood-affiliated politicians on a tight leash. To that end, the Muslim Brotherhood filled the leadership of the FJP with members of the Guidance Bureau, thereby solidifying its influence over the newly established party. Mohamed Morsi, Essam El-Erian, and Saad Al-Katatni, the president, vice president, and secretary general of the FJP, respectively, were all members of the Bureau before assuming leadership of the FJP. In addition, all three were loyal to the guardianist-dominated leadership.[102] Those who advocated for greater accountability and internal democracy inside the Brotherhood saw these appointments as a major setback, prompting complaints from the group's youth activists. For the guardianists, however, keeping the FJP's leadership in the hands of trusted loyalists was crucial, as it forestalled the possibility of the party's ambitious politicians taking it in unauthorized directions. Additionally, it lessened the potential impact of the external pressures party members would face as elected officials.

Put simply, even under the relative political openness Egypt enjoyed after the January 25 Revolution, the Brotherhood was clearly working to retain its informal channels of political participation and its autonomy from the state, as it had done under Mubarak.

Conclusion

The permissive atmosphere created by the Islamist incorporation policies of the 1970s allowed the Muslim Brotherhood to build anew a truly autonomous political organization. Because this organization developed outside of the legal political framework and therefore independently of state patronage, it did not suffer the same degree of state interference as endured by formal political parties. Even after Sadat's death, the Brotherhood retained its autonomy by limiting its political activities to unofficial channels and declining opportunities to legalize its status. The persistence of these institutional patterns resulted from the confluence of two factors. The first is the Mubarak regime's determination to deny the Brotherhood legal status or any additional privileges that might enhance its capacity to compete with the ruling party. Therefore, the Muslim Brotherhood had to rely on informal channels of political participation. The second is the trajectory of the Brotherhood's internal rivalries since the 1980s, which empowered leaders who were wary of the consequences of legalizing the movement's political engagement. Evidently, this wariness persisted well into the post-Mubarak era.

On the other side of the ideological spectrum, leftist currents pursued a different trajectory of institutional development. Efforts to rally leftist forces under a single banner prompted considerable opposition from a state determined to contain the opponents of de-Nasserization. Just as Sadat's security forces relaxed surveillance on the Muslim Brotherhood and forged cooperative ties with its leaders, leftist activists were struggling to keep regime informants at bay and avoid imprisonment. Brotherhood figures enjoyed the freedom to forge ties with the Islamist student movement and enlist their support, whereas the state closely monitored the left and sought to isolate it from its natural allies among those aggrieved by economic liberalization.

In other words, Islamist incorporation policies yielded a political liberalization process that was highly discriminatory along ideological lines. Thus, Islamist currents were successful in rallying their generationally and ideologically diverse factions within a coherent organization, whereas the left's attempts to mobilize support under a similarly unifying umbrella failed. Leftist currents remained trapped in arrangements that left them dependent on state patronage and highly vulnerable to state intervention. Thus, the characteristic features of Egypt's political liberalization reveal the origins of the power asymmetries displayed by the country's contemporary Islamist and leftist currents. Exploring this context, chapter 4 offers a glimpse into the path not taken by Islamist currents and the institutional constraints they averted, thanks to the Islamist incorporation policies of the 1970s.

4

Nasser's Comrades

State Guardianship and the Dependent Path

Mr. President, by issuing the socialist laws, you have surpassed everything we had aspired for, and, as you may have noticed in our latest
bulletins, we have tried to keep up with the experiment you have been
implementing, because our vision was short-sighted between 1952 and
the issuing of the socialist laws in 1961.

—FOUAD MORSI, IN *SANAWAT WA AYAM MAʿA JAMAL ʿABD AL-NASIR*

Hussein Abdel-Razek, member of the presidential council of Al-Tagammu
Party said that the party will support Field Marshal Abdel-Fattah Al-Sisi
based on the logic of "unity and conflict," "which was used with the late
President Gamal Abdel-Nasser in the 50s and 60s of the last century," indi-
cating that the unity with Field Marshal Al-Sisi is in his war | . . .| against
the terrorism of the Muslim Brotherhood | . . .| and against foreign plots
by the United States of America, Turkey, and Qatar, and some of the coun-
tries of the European Union |. . . .| And Abdel-Razek clarified that "Al-
Tagammu Party will contest the ideas of Field Marshal Al-Sisi on social
justice, rights and liberties, and the achievement of national, independent development."

—*AL-MASRY AL-YOUM*, FEBRUARY 2, 2014

S ometime in late 1964, Gamal Abdel-Nasser prepared to receive a special guest: "Comrade Khaled." The president was seeking the means to build popular support for his recently adopted political line (i.e., state socialism).[1] Nasser's visitor, an underground communist activist, produced a series of secret bulletins that had piqued Nasser's interest when they appeared in routine security briefings. Although the documents bore the penname "Comrade Khaled," Nasser had a hunch about the author's identity. But for good measure, the president had reached out to a friend with ties to the communist movement, asking him flat out who Comrade Khaled was. And as Nasser had suspected, Comrade Khaled turned out to be Fouad Morsi, one of the senior leaders of the Communist Party of Egypt-Al-Raya (CPE-R) and the future cofounder of Al-Tagammu Party.

When summoned to meet with Nasser, the astonished Morsi asked, "Was it the [security] agencies that found this out?"

"No," answered the president, "I have been following and reading what you and others have been writing, and I concluded that you are Comrade Khaled, which is why you were contacted . . . I had suspected it was either you or Dr. Ismail Sabri Abdallah."[2]

This meeting was the prelude to a series of conversations between the regime and the CPE-R that ultimately resulted in the party's formal dissolution in 1965 and the cooptation of the bulk of its leadership into the Arab Socialist Union (ASU). The CPE-R's main rival, the Communist Party of Egypt-Hadeto (CPE-H) followed suit that same year. The communist movement's capitulation to Nasser constituted a grave, long-term injury to Egypt's leftists, as it liquidated their organizational structures and placed large segments of that community under state control. That is, it put leftists on a path of institutional development that compromised their autonomy, in contrast to the "autonomous path" Islamist movements would pursue a decade later under Anwar Al-Sadat (see chapter 3).

The left's state-dependent path was reinforced in the mid-1970s. The repression of underground communist groups limited the chances for strong and independent leftist political organizations to emerge outside of the state's supervision and control. Meanwhile, in the realm of formal politics, the cofounders of Al-Tagammu, including those involved in the dissolution of communist organizations under Nasser, agreed to operate under a legal framework that featured debilitating restrictions. These restrictions solidified and perpetuated the leftists' dependent relation-ship with the state, subsequently exposing the party to new forms of state intervention. In other words, the left's path of institutional development diverged from that of Islamist currents most distinctively with regard to autonomy from the state. Over the course of subsequent decades, this dis-crepancy was repeatedly expressed in the imbalance of power between the two currents.

The remainder of this chapter surveys these state interventions, describes how they hindered the autonomy of leftist political organiza-tions, and contrasts the left's institutional development with that experi-enced by Islamist currents.

The Communist Movement's Capitulation to Nasser

Upon its emergence on the political scene in the mid-1970s, Al-Tagammu's credibility was already suspect among the younger generation of leftists. Unlike Islamist student activists who venerated the old leaders of the Mus-lim Brotherhood and praised them for withstanding Nasser's wrath, left-ist youth had little respect for the "elders" who founded Al-Tagammu. As Rifaat Al-Said recounts, younger Marxists could not forgive Al-Tagammu's senior leaders for handing Nasser the communist movement on a silver platter a decade earlier.[3] That level of distrust would persist for decades. In fact, the communists' submission to Nasser embittered a generation of activists, hindering attempts to organize the left under a single banner throughout the regimes of Sadat and Mubarak. And as will be explained, the surrender to Nasser would push the political forces that coalesced around communist parties onto a path of institutional development that fostered their dependence on the state.

COMMUNIST ACTIVISM ON THE EVE OF STATE SOCIALISM

Communist activism has a long history in Egypt. Communist cells were documented as early as 1894, emerging primarily in the foreign expat communities that formed a considerable segment of Egypt's urban labor force. In 1921, a group of intellectuals, most notably Salama Moussa and Joseph Rosenthal, founded the Egyptian Socialist Party.[4] By 1924, the organization, now renamed the Egyptian Communist Party,[5] claimed several hundred members.[6] In 1923, the party acquired control of the General Union of Workers, an organization of some twenty thousand members. Subsequently, the party's involvement in organizing a strike in Alexandria prompted a major crackdown, resulting in numerous arrests and deportations. By the late 1920s, the party was virtually nonexistent.[7]

The 1940s witnessed the reemergence of communist political organizations.[8] These groups were characterized by chronic disagreement and fragmentation. In 1947, two of the most influential communist organizations, Hameto and Iskra, joined forces to form Hadeto, which would encompass almost 90 percent of the entire communist movement. Hadeto quickly gained prominence by organizing worker and student protests and securing medical services for the poor.[9] Yet, internal divisions appeared during Hadeto's first year of existence, leading to defections and splintering.[10] Hadeto's controversial endorsement of the 1947 United Nations (UN) Palestine Partition Plan also exposed it to internal and external criticism. In addition, the government intensified its repressive campaign against communist activism. In 1950, for example, one of Hadeto's foremost leaders, Henri Curiel, was stripped of his Egyptian citizenship and deported.[11] Despite such unfavorable conditions, communist activism continued to grow.[12] By the early 1950s, Hadeto alone was responsible for six different publications and was succeeding in its efforts to unify disparate labor unions.[13]

Hadeto, which enjoyed some links to members of the Free Officers movement, was initially supportive of the July 23 Revolution of 1952. Yet this support was short-lived. Following the August 1952 crackdown on worker protests, most notably in Kafr El-Dawwar, relations with the country's military leadership deteriorated quickly. By late 1953, Hadeto members were facing arrests and trials. Thus began yet another contentious phase in the communist movement's relationship with the state.

By the mid-1950s, communist activism was focused within three main groups. The first was the Unified Egyptian Communist Party (UECP), which was formed by Hadeto's 1955 merger with several other organizations. The second was Popular Democracy, which was founded in 1949 as a coalition of smaller communist movements.[14] Popular Democracy had approximately one thousand members in 1957, when it was renamed the Workers' and Peasants' Communist Party (WPCP).[15] The third was the Communist Party of Egypt, popularly known as Al-Raya. Formed in 1949, the party included defectors from Hadeto, as well as independent figures like Fouad Morsi and Ismail Sabri Abdallah. Morsi and Abdallah would be founding members of Al-Tagammu in the 1970s.

Issues of collective identity often divided these organizations. The leadership of Hadeto and its constituent elements included a number of Jewish people, many of whom were of non-Egyptian descent.[16] In contrast, Al-Raya's strong nationalist inclinations inspired a commitment to an "authentic" Egyptian identity that excluded Jewish people and others perceived as "foreign."[17] This issue would become a central point of contention, frustrating attempts to forge unity in the late 1950s.[18] Another area of disagreement concerned relations with the post-1952 ruling establishment. In contrast to Hadeto's initial support for the Free Officers, Al-Raya, like most other communist groups, remained critical of Nasser.[19]

By the mid-1950s, communist currents began backtracking from their hostile orientation toward Nasser, whose popularity and anti-imperialist credentials imploded in the aftermath of the 1956 nationalization of the Suez Canal Company and the resulting invasion by the United Kingdom, France, and Israel. Meanwhile, discussions within the communist movement regarding the possibility of unity gained momentum. On January 8, 1958, these three groups announced they would merge into the Communist Party of Egypt (CPE). Because of differences in opinions over the relative share of power among the three factions and persistent disagreements over how to manage relations with Nasser, this unity was short-lived. In January 1959, the Hadeto contingent announced its plan to form a new party.[20]

Against the backdrop of these splits, the state launched a major crackdown on communist organizations, sentencing thousands of activists to prison, where they would remain until the mid-1960s.[21] This wave of repression was partially inspired by communist activists' support for Iraq's president Abdel-Karim Qasim. Such support, which persisted after Qasim refused to join the Egypt-dominated United Arab Republic (UAR), roused Nasser's suspicions of a disloyal third column in Egypt.[22] The beginning of the end for the CPE, however, was denying Nasser's request to instruct its members to join the ruling party.[23] A series of arrests soon followed, effectively erasing the Egyptian communist movement from political life for many years.

STATE SOCIALISM AND NASSER'S WAR AGAINST THE "OPPORTUNISTS"

Nasser revised his posture toward the communists during the early 1960s, releasing many of them from prison and attempting to coopt their leaders into the ruling establishment. Central to Nasser's apparent change of heart was Egypt's turn to so-called state socialism. In the economic sphere, the state's role in planning, investment, and redistribution was expanded through a raft of new land reforms, nationalizations, and welfare programs (see chapter 1). The state also became more assertive in mobilizing public support for the now-revamped ruling party, the ASU.

Nasser's state socialism is best understood as his attempt to grapple with a number of simultaneous challenges to his ruling vision. Chief among these problems was the insufficient investment of private capital in industrialization and long-term development. By the early 1960s, regime officials were blaming Egypt's poor economic performance on capitalists who purportedly had eschewed long-term industrial investment to pursue swift profits, especially in the real estate sector. Thus, the government presented the initial series of nationalization measures of the 1960s as an effort to rectify the poor performance of the private sector.

On the political side, "state socialist" policies were employed to confront and balance against a variety of bureaucratic and private interests that wielded influence within the state apparatus.[24] For example, members of the landed elite leveraged the partnerships they established with government officials during the 1950s to evade legal caps on land ownership and to gain control over provincial ruling party posts.[25] In addition, a wide-range of autonomous, clientelistic networks, enabling bureaucrats, public sector managers, and private capitalists to profit from corruption schemes, presented another challenge to Nasser's authority within the state apparatus.[26] At the heart of these networks was a military establishment that expanded its political weight under the patrimonial leadership of Army Chief Abdel-Hakim Amer, whose influence rivaled Nasser's.[27]

Immediately following a September 1961 military coup, Syria seceded from the UAR, causing that union's effective demise. For Nasser, these events embodied most of the challenges to his rule. On one level, the Syrian coup underscored the subversive potential of capitalists and the landed elite, correctly perceived as the chief proponents of Syria's secession. The coup, as historian Sherif Younis explains, also demonstrated that Nasser's personal popularity was insufficient to protect him from military plotters.[28] Such a concern was by no means far-fetched, given that Nasser's army chief and political rival Amer had just returned to Egypt after a humiliating ouster from the governorship of Syria. Feeding such fears were reports of business people actively lobbying senior officers to "end dictatorship and restore private liberties,"[29] and the ongoing efforts of Western powers and their allies to contain Nasser's regional influence. In such an environment, Nasser could not ensure that the military establishment, private capital, and the landed elite would not join forces and, with the support of external actors, act decisively against him.[30]

The socialist reforms of the early 1960s, along with the initiative to revamp the ruling party and enhance its capacity for popular mobilization, were designed to prevent the Syria scenario from materializing in Egypt. Thus, nationalization schemes and the deepening of land reforms, at least in theory, targeted the influence of private capital and the landed elite. Launching the ASU in the wake of the UAR's dissolution was an attempt to combat the power of private interests within the state apparatus and counter the influence of the military establishment. When analyzing Syria's secession from the UAR, Nasser emphasized in his October 16, 1961, speech the need to reconfigure the ruling party to prevent opponents and special interests from infiltrating it:

> We fell into a huge error that was no less significant than the dangerous illusion that made us lose our bearings. That mistake was the inadequacy of popular organization. Our approach to popular organization was the National Union, established as a framework for [managing] class conflicts. And our mistake was keeping the door open for reactionary forces to enter the National Union. And the result of that mistake was that reactionary forces managed to infiltrate the National Union and were able to debilitate its revolutionary effectiveness |. . . .| Perhaps this phenomenon was most apparent in the fact that those leading the [recent] reactionary, secessionist movement in Syria were [previously] leading the organizations of the National Union. Thus, the most important challenge we face today is rebuilding popular organization so that the National Union could become a revolutionary instrument for the nationalist masses alone.[31]

Most relevant for the imprisoned communist activists was Nasser's interest in combating his rivals by forming a secret, vanguard organization inside the ruling party.[32] This idea eventually led to the establishment of the ASU's "Vanguard Organization" (VO), which became a key instrument through which the president sought to coopt senior communist leaders. Nasser's October 16, 1961 speech laid out the rationale behind an organization like the VO:

> The real path for furthering the struggle without pause or reluctance is expanding the revolution's leadership and [popular] base together and educating the masses through constant, deep awareness to guarantee [the rise of] new leaders for carrying out the popular struggle and [popular] bases that extend to every part of the nation. To that end, labor syndicates, farmer cooperatives, universities, professional associations, and women's groups must all turn into centers for constructive intellectual energy that could advance renewed revolutionary work. Each village, each factory, each college, each school, each professional syndicate council, each man, each woman, each youth, and each child in this nation must become an active, mature revolutionary cell.[33]

The VO and its activities were mentioned in the firsthand accounts of several prominent political figures from the Nasserist era.[34] Yet, our understanding of its scope and its impact has deepened over the past two decades.[35] The 2005 memoirs of Sami Sharaf, a close aide to Nasser and one of the senior leaders of the VO initiative, included a history of the VO's formation and the names of hundreds of its prominent members.[36] In 2007, Egyptian historian Hamada Hosni released a groundbreaking study using primary source documents obtained from former VO affiliates to provide a comprehensive overview of the VO's structure and leadership.[37] Another important breakthrough came in 2016 with the account of Adel Al-Ashwah, who directed Minister of Interior Sharawi Gomaa's ASU office.[38] Al-Ashwah, himself an important interlocutor with the VO, revealed previously unknown details about the VO's internal structures and operations.[39]

Collectively, these sources highlight the extent to which communist activists who submitted to Nasser's authority became part and parcel of the same community of regime collaborators that generated the governing elite for much of the Mubarak era. These sources also reveal that the major protagonists of the official leftist opposition to Mubarak emerged from the VO, a secret intelligence apparatus that fostered covert collaboration with the state, as well as surveillance of the regime's opponents.

STATE SOCIALISM, THE ASU, AND "COMMUNIST INCORPORATION"

The context for the formation of the ASU's VO is revealing. It highlights the similarities between the imperatives that led Nasser to seek the support of the communist movement in the 1960s and those that led Sadat to enlist the help of Islamist currents a decade later. In other words, Nasser encountered the same predicament in 1961 that Sadat would confront in 1972. In each of the two cases, Egypt's ruler contended with the mortality of his own regime while confronting a harsh reality: the existing political order had no organized popular base prepared to fight on its behalf in a crisis.

Just as Sadat would complain to Mohamed Othman Ismail about the virtual absence of a mass organization within the ruling party (see chapter 2), Nasser had been voicing the same concern to close aides since Syria's 1961 succession from the UAR. For example, only weeks after the Syrian coup, Nasser told cabinet members that the ruling party and the state apparatus were hostage to a variety of "bourgeois" and "capitalist" interests. Per the meeting transcript, the president warned that many of those occupying positions of influence inside the ruling establishment displayed opportunistic tendencies and demonstrated little commitment to the state's "socialist reforms."[40] Interestingly enough, the conversation prompting Sadat's decision to seek Islamist support featured strikingly similar judgments, as Mohamed Othman Ismail characterized ASU personnel as unreliable opportunists who lacked "conviction."[41]

The need to create a vanguardist arm inside the ASU received passing mention in a variety of documents, including the 1961 National Charter that officially inaugurated the era of "socialist reforms" in Egypt.[42] Yet, the first real step toward executing the proposal came on September 3, 1963,[43] when Nasser summoned to his home a number of political leaders and advisers to devise a strategy for building a secret organization inside the ruling party. Attendees included Prime Minister Aly Sabri, Deputy Prime Minister Abbas Radwan, *Al-Ahram* editor in chief Mohamed Hassanein

Heikal, head of Misr Bank and former communist activist Ahmed Fouad, and Nasser's senior aide Sami Sharaf.[44] The participants agreed to estab-lish a covert apparatus, named *tali'at al-ishtirakiyyin* (the "Socialists' Van-guard"; also known as *al-tanzim al-tali'y* or the VO), whose motto was "freedom, socialism, and unity." They further resolved to begin recruit-ing a limited number of trusted individuals who would form secret cells.[45] Thus was born Nasser's infamous vanguard, which arguably influenced the structure of the Egyptian political arena for decades to come.

This meeting marked the beginning of Nasser's efforts to coopt members of the communist movement into the ruling party and the state appara-tus.[46] Nasser valued communist groups' organizational agility and ideologi-cal purity, two traits wholly absent from the communities of rent-seekers that traditionally had constituted the bulk of Egypt's ruling establishment. Thus, it was no coincidence that the president told former Hadeto affiliate Ahmed Fouad that he intended "to build a strong organization just like 'the one you all used to have,' meaning communist organizations." Appealing to Fouad's communist sympathies, Nasser indicated that his vision of social and economic affairs did not differ much from Marxist ideas.[47]

Nasser's observations to Fouad were of little substance, because the ruling party instinctively rejected the notion of class struggle, and the president gave no indication that he was prepared to let the working class exercise any meaningful power. Yet Nasser wanted to populate the VO with activists of revolutionary purity or, in other words, individuals who sup-ported the idea of a socialist transformation out of ideological commit-ment, not crass opportunism.[48] For this reason, the president stipulated that each nominated recruit be monitored and vetted to prevent infiltra-tion by opportunist elements lacking "faith in the July revolution and its laws, and in the socialist system."[49]

Consistent with this vision, Nasser delegated the task of forming the VO to individuals who displayed some affinity for leftist ideas. Ahmed Fouad had known former ties to Hadeto, whereas Aly Sabri and Mohamed Has-sanein Heikal, at least from Nasser's perspective, were sympathetic to the principles of "Arab socialism."[50] Unsurprisingly, therefore, the earliest VO cells featured a variety of communist activists, including Hadeto members Ahmed Hamroush, Ahmed Al-Rifai, Zaki Murad, and Fouad Habashi.[51] For his part, Heikal started the first VO cell at *Al-Ahram* with the help of Marxist writers like Ibrahim Saadeddin, Lotfi Al-Khouli, and Mohamed Al-Khafif.[52]

By spring 1964, just months after the VO was launched, all communists detained in 1959 had been released from prison. Meanwhile, Nasser ordered senior officials to facilitate the work of the communist contingent inside the VO, which reached 250 members within a short period of time.[53]

Communists were by no means the dominant force inside the VO, but their presence was quite pronounced, especially during its formative stages. For example, a variety of communist figures served on the VO's General Secretariat, including Hamroush and Mahmoud Amin Al-Alim.[54] A host of individuals within the VO's ranks also had a history of communist ties, including Kamal Abdel-Halim, Mustafa Tiba, and Mohamed Shatta.[55]

The VO arguably advanced the careers of many of the Egyptian left's iconic figures, including, as described next, those who occupied ranking positions at Al-Tagammu and *Al-Ahaly*. Even into the twenty-first century, some surviving former VO affiliates remained visible in political life.[56]

THE DISSOLUTION OF COMMUNIST PARTIES

The president was acutely aware of underground communist activists' participation in the VO initiative. He made repeated attempts to persuade such activists to dissolve their organizations and join the ruling party. Because acceding to Nasser's request had such a debilitating impact on the long-term development of leftist political organizations, it is critical to understand the conditions informing that decision. These decisions can be understood as the confluence of two factors. The first factor was the pressure exerted by the regime to make communist activists obedient "junior partners" in Nasser's program of socialist transformation. The second factor was the internal and external pressure driving the communist movement to augment its nationalist profile and credentials by entering into an alliance with the ruling establishment.

Sharawi Gomaa claims that communists entered the VO of their own free will and denies that they ever struck deals with Nasser,[57] even though the overwhelming evidence suggests otherwise. The testimony of Nasser's close aide Sami Sharaf shows that the president was personally involved in the mid-1960s effort to convince communists to dissolve their organizations and encourage their members to join the ASU.[58] In fact, this was the precise context for Nasser's previously cited meeting with Fouad Morsi (i.e., Comrade Khaled).[59]

At that meeting, Nasser sought Morsi's support for the socialist transformation he had announced years earlier. The president, nonetheless,
asserted that Eastern bloc models of socialism were incompatible with
Egypt's unique conditions. Instead, Nasser explained, his vision of socialism espoused respect for religion and private ownership. Furthermore,
rather than seeking the absolute dominance of a single social class, he
indicated, Egyptian socialism supported the alliance of working forces.[60]
In so many words, Nasser informed Morsi that Marxist visions for social
change were out of the question in Egypt and that his conception of socialist transformation would take precedence over the CPE-R's agenda. Morsi
was nonetheless receptive:

> Mr. President, by issuing the socialist laws, you have surpassed every-
> thing we had aspired for, and, as you may have noticed in our latest
> bulletins, we have tried to keep up with the experiment you have been
> implementing, because our vision was short-sighted between 1952 and
> the issuing of the socialist laws in 1961 |. . . .| Frankly, Mr. President, our
> vision was blocked by a black barrier, as we were concerned that military
> rule will not be able to achieve a social transformation in Egypt along the
> lines of what you are [now] conducting and declaring.[61]

In response, Nasser proposed that Morsi convince his comrades to join the
ruling party:

> Dr. Fouad, I would like to propose an idea for you to think about. And it
> is not binding. All I ask of you is to think [about it] and once you have
> reached a conclusion or decision, my door is open for you to discuss what
> you have reached. And the issue, in very brief terms, is for leftist forces in
> the Egyptian arena to join the people's alliance of working forces one way
> or another. Think about it and offer your suggestions.[62]

This conversation led to a series of follow-up meetings between senior
government officials and CPE-R leaders to discuss the possibility of
recruiting communist activists into the ASU. While some elements of the
CPE-R wanted to retain their organizational structures by joining the ASU
as a bloc, Nasser rejected this proposal, insisting that they join as individuals or not at all.[63] Eventually, the CPE-R complied and dissolved itself in

early 1965. In return, the regime restored the political rights of the CPE-R's previously convicted activists and allowed them to join the ruling party. According to Sami Sharaf:

> The result of all these contacts and meetings was that in early 1965, an agreement was reached, without any pressure, that the CPE would announce its own dissolution. For those who would want to resume or participate in political activities, the doors of the ASU would be open |. . . .| It was also agreed to lift the state sanctions off members of the party, and that each one of them would become a regular citizen without any party affiliation, and that there would be no chain of command, instructions, or directives. And thus, members of communist organizations began entering the units of the ASU as individuals.[64]

On February 4, 1965, the CPE-R's leaders affirmed their acceptance of Nasser's leadership within the framework of the ASU in a letter bearing the signatures of Fouad Morsi, Abu-Sayf Yusuf, Fakhri Labib, Abdel-Moneim Shatla, and Mohamed Helmi Yassin.[65] This event marked the end of the CPE-R, which had once encompassed some of the most significant communist groups of the 1950s. The CPE-R subsequently published a statement in *Al-Ahram* announcing its official dissolution and instructing CPE-R members to join the ASU: "The independent status of the Egyptian Communist Party is terminated, and all its members are directed to apply as individuals for membership of the Arab Socialist Union and to struggle for the formation of a unified socialist party embracing all revolutionary forces in the country."[66]

The other Communist Party of Egypt, which included the Hadeto faction (hereafter, CPE-H), dissolved itself in March. As some individuals formerly in Hadeto's orbit, like Ahmed Fouad, had previously joined the ranks of the VO, one could argue that the CPE-H's road to self-dissolution began earlier than that of the CPE-R. In fact, by the time CPE-H began negotiating its future with the government, half of its former leadership had already defected to the ASU. CPE-H's Ahmed Al-Rifai and Fouad Habashi negotiated a deal whereby the party would join the ASU's VO as a coherent bloc. The regime soon backtracked on this agreement, allegedly because of opposition from Abdel-Hakim Amer. Confronted once more with Nasser's demand to dissolve the party and join the ASU as unaffiliated individuals,

CPE-H eventually obliged.[67] CPE-H's Kamal Abdel-Halim overcame internal opposition to the dissolution, and party members voted to abolish their organization on March 14, 1965. That same day, Abdel-Halim sent Nasser a telegram on behalf of CPE-H. It read:

> The most beautiful thing we present you on this historic occasion is the news that the representatives of the Egyptian Communist Party-[Hadeto] in their meeting held today decided to put an end to their independent organization because of their belief in your call for the unity of all the socialist forces in one revolutionary political organization, and that this one party under your leadership is the substitute for our independent organization. And even though they are barred from political activity and do not have the right to vote, they are sending you their votes and are unanimously electing you president of the republic, leader of the revolution, and the leader of its single, striving political party.[68]

Advocates of the dissolution within the communist movement argued that the decision was an urgent necessity. Refusing to join forces with Nasser after years of imprisonment and torture, they asserted, was not a viable option, especially with the president declaring his commitment to socialism in 1961.[69] Critics countered that no amount of pragmatism could possibly justify these leaders' unilateral decision to deprive the working class of its representation by terminating the communist party.[70] Pragmatism alone seems an unconvincing motivation, given that regime pressure was not the only factor informing the dissolution decision. Rather, the initiative appeared to proceed from a joint consensus between the ruling establishment and certain communist leaders. As the accounts of multiple communist activists indicate, many Marxists, particularly those who had joined the ranks of the ASU before the spring of 1965, exerted pressure on the CPE-R and CPE-H to accept self-dissolution.[71] What then accounts for the enthusiasm of some communist elements for the dissolution proposal, even at the considerable price of ceding organizational autonomy?

THE DISSOLUTION AND THE "TRIUMPH OF NATIONALISM"

Significant political and intellectual transformations that had occurred inside the communist movement a decade earlier were driving, at least in part, the internal momentum for dissolution. Historian Joel Beinin characterizes these developments as the "triumph of nationalism," which he defines as the submission of communist activists to the hegemony of nationalist discourse. In other words, as these movements sought legitimacy by adopting the nationalist rhetoric of those in power, their ability to oppose the ruling class and its policies eroded.[72]

The communists' capitulation to nationalism, and by extension to the ruling party, can be understood as the outcome of two processes. The first process entails communist leaders' changing conception of their historical mission to further a socialist transformation. The second process concerns the internal and external pressures compelling Egyptian communists to assert and substantiate their claims to an "indigenous" identity.

As Sherif Younis notes in his seminal study on the history of Nasserist ideology, the dissolution of communist organizations was partly grounded in an intellectual conviction that Nasser's struggle against imperialism was a fundamental prerequisite for the building of socialism. Such a view is by no means novel and has some theoretical basis in the Marxist concept of "stagism." Socialism, according to this perspective, is the outcome of a two-staged teleological process. The first stage brings the destruction of the feudal society through a national democratic struggle culminating in a bourgeois revolution. By enabling the development of a large working class, the bourgeois revolution sets the necessary preconditions for the next stage, socialist revolution.[73]

In the Egyptian context, many communist intellectuals perceived Nasser's struggle against imperialism as a key component of the first stage of revolution, the national democratic struggle.[74] Specifically, they reasoned that the trajectory of late development locked the Egyptian bourgeoisie into an effective alliance with imperialist interests, reinforcing feudal relations and hindering industrialization. Thus, the Egyptian bourgeoisie was incapable of fulfilling the "historical mission" ascribed to it by Marxist theory, mounting a national democratic revolution.[75] This interpretation prompted many Marxists to detect in Nasser's anti-imperialist, antifeudalist policies the promise of socialist transformation through a different path. Simply put, Nasser's policies were presented as a noncapitalist road to socialism.[76] Communists adopting this view therefore had no reason to oppose the political status quo.

This idea first gained currency in the late 1950s, when the British-French-Israeli "tripartite" invasion of Egypt prompted Nasser to sharpen and clarify his anti-imperialist orientation and thereby attract the support of numerous communists. Nasser's leadership of the effort to liberate Egypt from Western domination caused Marxist intellectuals to inquire if his policies could offer an alternative path to the first stage of socialist transformation. For example, the UECP declared in March 1956:

> The Nasserist government has taken the road toward independent politi-
> cal and economic development of our country, which entails the gradual
> liberation of our country form the imperialist market and the weakening
> of the political power of imperialism and the strengthening of economic,
> political, and cultural links with the socialist camp.[77]

In other words, urgency to resist imperialism and its associated forms of exploitation justified communists' support for actors whose perceived revolutionary commitments were dubious. The significance of this conceptual transformation cannot be overemphasized. Whereas a decade earlier, Al-Raya's leaders had accused Hadeto of excessive focus on the anti-imperialist struggle at the expense of the proletarian revolution,[78] they now began to rationalize the Nasserists' apparent tolerance of the economic status quo. For example, in a 1957 article entitled "Marxism: The Living Theory," Fouad Morsi argued that the emerging alliance between the working class and the bourgeoisie in Egypt could create the preconditions for a nonviolent socialist transformation.[79] In other words, long before the 1961 promulgation of Nasser's so-called socialist reforms, the imperatives of the anti-imperialist struggle were already providing a rationale for the communist movement's dissolution and its submission to the ruling establishment.[80]

To recap, in the 1950s, a consensus emerged among communist intellectuals that Egypt's unique developmental experience made the precepts of classical Marxist theory inapplicable to the country. This conclusion provided the underlying logic for the 1965 dissolution of communist organizations. The idea that Egypt's developmental trajectory diverged from the models informing classical Marxism afforded the communist movement's theorists considerable leeway in justifying their leaders' conservative tendencies. This idea also justified the communists' support for the regime during the 1950s. This intellectual environment subsequently enabled communist leaders to forge an internal consensus that dissolving their own organizations and depriving the working class of representation somehow promoted socialist transformation.[81]

The second process facilitating the communist capitulation to Nasser's nationalist rhetoric is Egyptian leftists' long-term struggle to establish an indigenous identity. As previously noted, communist organizations had contended with the question of identity long before Nasser's political ascendancy. The role of "foreign elements" in the communist movement was a highly contentious issue throughout the 1940s, particularly after communist groups took the extremely controversial step of endorsing the 1947 UN Palestine Partition Plan.[82] Progovernment propaganda accusing communist groups of tacitly supporting the Zionist movement certainly exacerbated these conflicts.[83] The ensuing "identity crisis" drove communist activists to rely increasingly on nationalist vocabulary when expressing their positions.[84]

Egyptian communists' nationalist tendencies became even more pronounced during the 1950s. Coinciding with the rise of Nasser was a growing "Egyptianization" drive within the communist movement. Starting in the late 1940s, this effort was led by a new generation of Egyptian communists, including those who would later form Al-Tagammu.[85] As previously explained, communists believed that Egypt's bourgeoisie was inextricably tied to Western capital and, therefore, unequipped to lead an effective struggle against the imperialist interests obstructing the road to socialism. Thus, the younger cadre of Egyptian communists felt a strong responsibility to assume leadership of the faltering anti-imperialist struggle.[86] As these ideas gained currency within communist organizations, nationalism became more central to the movement's self-professed identity.

Although Nasser's anti-imperialist stances during the 1950s helped improve relations between the government and some communist currents, antagonism and confrontation were the dominant features of the decade's final years. The government's infamous late-1958 crackdown on the communist movement was accompanied by regime officials' relentless attribution of foreign allegiances and treasonous intentions to all Egyptian communists.[87]

Depictions of communists as tools of Soviet influence became prevalent in state propaganda, reflecting the political leadership's conscious effort to defame communist activists. Nasser outlined the contours of that strategy and the rationale behind it in a 1959 handwritten memo.[88] Communists in Egypt and Syria, Nasser asserted, were under Soviet influence, and communists in multiple Arab countries were plotting to seize power. Accordingly, the memo ordered the arrest of members of communist organizations in Egypt and Syria, and it also instructed ruling party officials to counter the influence of communists and uncover their subversive schemes.[89] Thus, Nasser's offensive inaugurated a new era in which state-controlled media and cultural and educational institutions were used to publicly question communists' national loyalty and moral character, thereby undermining their credibility.[90]

Even as Nasser proclaimed the beginning of Egypt's nominal socialist experiment and actively sought the support of communist activists in the VO, the regime repeatedly played the "identity card" to compel the communists' submission. A case in point is a January 29, 1965 article in *Al-Ahram* by then editor in chief Mohamed Hassanein Heikal. The piece came at a time when some communists began voicing objections to the proposed dissolution of their political organizations. Heikal was one of the regime figures involved in negotiating this issue with communist leaders.[91] While ostensibly arguing for a fresh start with Egyptian communists, he sent a less-than-subtle warning to opponents of dissolution. Heikal tacitly directed attention to the weaknesses of communists' negotiating position in relation to the regime by drawing on state depictions of communists as foreign oddities and social deviants. He then argued that any persecution suffered by communists could be attributed to their social alienation, itself a product of the incompatibility of their misguided foreign ways with the Egyptian society's true essence.[92] Heikal sent a clear message to communist dissidents: they had no option but to submit to the regime and its demands, as their alienation from the rest of Egyptian society would always make them an easy target of persecution. Interestingly enough, less than a week after the publication of Heikal's editorial, leaders of the CPE-R pledged loyalty to Nasser in a handwritten letter expressing alarm over media misrepresentations of their intentions and views.[93]

In sum, two important processes underlaid the impetus for the self-dissolution of communist organizations in Egypt. The first process is the evolution of Egyptian Marxist thought during the 1950s, which prompted communists to embrace Nasser's anti-imperialist agenda. According to Joel Beinin, these changes "justified abandoning the struggle for a fundamental alternative to the Nasserist regime, since the Nasserist path would lead to socialism in any case."[94] This line of reasoning was predicated on a growing consensus that Egypt's unusual developmental trajectory rendered the specific prescriptions of Marxist theory inapplicable. This paradigm of "Egyptian exceptionalism" gave communist theorists license to rationalize a host of regime-friendly positions, including the decision to dissolve their own parties. Additionally, the communist movement's conflicted sense of identity—the product of decades-long internal conflicts—made it vulnerable to regime propaganda impugning communists' national allegiance and patriotism. Such attacks put the movement on the defensive and heightened the perceived urgency to comply with Nasser's demand of full political submission and self-dissolution. However compelling this decision may have seemed at the time, its long-term repercussions for communist organizations' autonomy were disastrous.

SELF-DISSOLUTION AT NO RETURN

Leftist activists broadly agree that the communist groups' 1965 dissolution constituted a huge setback for the long-term development of leftist political organizations in Egypt. As noted, the consequences of that controversial measure plagued leftist political groups for decades. For example, in the 1970s, many younger activists refused to join the newly formed Al-Tagammu Party, castigating its founders for dissolving the communist parties in 1965. As Al-Tagammu cofounder Rifaat Al-Said notes, "these youth viewed the establishment of a leftist platform [Al-Tagammu] as the continuation of an old crime; that is, the dissolution of the [communist] party."[95] Among them was Ahmad Bahaaeddin Shabaan, one of the leftist icons of the 1970s student movement:

> I have not joined Al-Tagammu because our generation has taken a negative position toward the older leftists represented by the second generation of Marxist organizations that emerged in the 1940s. We condemned them because of their decision to dissolve themselves |. . . .| We accused them of colluding with the Nasser regime.[96]

In other words, the legacy of the dissolution decision persisted through the 1980s, and, arguably, beyond.[97] It hampered the ability of veteran communist leaders to recruit the younger leftist activists who emerged on university campuses in the wake of Sadat's de-Nasserization initiatives. In its 1981 program, the reconstituted Communist Party of Egypt, acknowledged the disastrous consequences of the 1965 dissolution, recognizing the generational chasm it created within the communist movement:

> [The dissolution created] a great gulf between old-guard communists and the Egyptian youth who began adopting Marxism in the mid-1960s. This produced fragmentation in Marxist circles later. Some exploited that gulf in order to isolate the party from the youth and push the youth toward extreme Marxist groupings that adopt adventurist positions in both policy and organization. No doubt the departure of the old guard from the party and the withdrawal of the youth from it weakened the possibility of our party's transformation into a mass party.[98]

Beyond the internal discord it wrought upon the Egyptian left, the 1965 dissolution of communist parties brought a conclusive end to the movement's organizational independence. That is, the 1965 agreements represented more than a strategic alliance between the ruling party and the communist movement. Rather, it signified a complete annexation, transforming a once-promising political movement into, at best, a subordinate partner inside the ruling establishment or, at worst, a group of underworked bureaucrats. Ahmed Hamroush acknowledged the debilitating impact:

> It was difficult in a practical sense for communist organizations to pursue an opportunity to play a serious role away from the leadership of Nasser during that period [. . . .] But the decision to dissolve the organizations was nonetheless considered, from the Marxist perspective, a huge political error, because it was not up to the party of the working class to dissolve itself and end its role in expressing [the working class'] will and goals [. . .] since it is not possible to profess building socialism in the absence of the leading role of the working class and its communist party. And it may have been possible to reconcile the two imperatives, dissolve the organization but keep its idea alive [. . .] that is, dissolving it practically but while maintaining its idea in theory without liquidation.[99]

A limited number of old guard communists, along with some newer cadres of leftist activists, rejected the dissolution decision, remaining active underground. As detailed next, these cadres displayed considerable potential, building a presence within the student movement of the early 1970s. In contrast to their Islamist counterparts, however, successive waves of state repression during the 1970s and internal divisions prevented these groups from forming enduring political organizations. Additionally, the 1965 experience created deep divisions within these underground groups and hampered the construction of political organizations with the capacity to organize at the mass level.

In contrast, those who accepted the dissolution decision and made their peace with the Nasserist regime found a place inside the ruling establishment's ASU and VO, state media, and cultural institutions. The communists assumed that joining the ruling party would afford them sufficient prominence in leadership circles to advance their agendas from positions of influence. After dissolving their organizations and joining the ASU, the communists soon realized that the regime was determined to subordinate them permanently and exclude them from decision-making positions.

For a while, Marxist perspectives became more prevalent in state media institutions. For example, Al-Ahram Institution launched the magazine *Al-Talia* ("The Vanguard"), which employed a variety of leftist contributors and editors. The rapprochement between Nasser and the communists, as Hamroush notes, "allowed them the opportunity to engage with the masses through the pages of newspapers with greater freedom. And this new intellectual current became an important element in the process of social transformation."[100] Nonetheless, Marxists remained rare in the senior ranks of state media. Certainly, some visible exceptions stood out, such as Mahmoud Amin Al-Alim, who chaired the management board of *Akhbar Al-Youm*, and Ahmed Fouad, who at one point was tasked with chairing the board of *Rose Al-Yousef.* By and large, authority within state media remained in the hands of regime loyalists who were ideologically ambivalent about the socialist ideas their publications professed.[101]

The situation was no different inside the ASU. Notwithstanding the regime's initial interest in recruiting communists into the VO, ruling party Secretary General Aly Sabri never appointed these recruits to influential posts.[102] Outside of decision-making circles, former communists were similarly marginalized. For example, most evidence indicates that the ASU did not welcome them into the party organization proper, confining them instead to the ranks of the VO. Worker cadres of the dissolved communist organizations were largely shut out of the ruling party and public sector

jobs,[103] a practice that subsequently undermined the position of communist activists inside the labor movement under Sadat.

Even in the particular case of the VO, in which the communist presence was supposedly most evident, all power remained in the hands
of the domestic security apparatus, personified by the leadership
of Sharawi Gomaa, who was both head of the VO and interior minister.[104] Unsurprisingly, therefore, the VO came to resemble a domestic
intelligence agency designed to surveil public servants and report on
their political loyalties, rather than a political organization seeking
to advance socialist transformation.[105] Nasser-era officials tend to be
evasive about the VO's clandestine duties.[106] Nevertheless, internal VO
documents disclosed by Adel Al-Ashwah reveal that much of the organization's activities focused on compiling secret reports of potentially
subversive activities and speech.[107]

This evidence underscores the limited role Nasser envisioned for affiliates of the communist movement. He sought to employ them as instruments of state control and propaganda, but he had no intention of ceding
authority or power to the radical left or the social classes it represented.[108]
Nothing captures these realities better than leftist writer Salah Eissa's
weekly exchanges with a senior editor at the newspaper *Al-Gumhuria*.
Each week, the editor would hand Eissa a draft of the lead editorial with
the instruction, "Salah, please spray the article with some socialist touch-
ups [*shwayit tatsh ishtrakiyya*]," shorthand for socialist slogans, which were
apparently unfamiliar to the editor.[109] Ultimately, this is precisely how
Nasser came to see communist intellectuals and activists: as make-up art-
ists employed to apply a cosmetic veneer of socialism on a leadership that
lacked real interest in either empowering them or in socialism altogether.
Much like Salah Eissa's editor, Nasser had no real commitment to socialism
or its advocates. All he sought was a spray of "socialist touch-ups" for the
ruling party.

THE LEGACIES OF THE VANGUARD ORGANIZATION
AND AL-TAGAMMU

Although the VO was officially disbanded in the wake of Sadat's infamous
showdown with the centers of power (see chapter 1), the VO's network survived well into the Mubarak era. Not only did the former VO cadre occupy

important posts inside government and the ruling National Democratic Party (NDP) throughout much of the 1980s and 1990s, they also exerted considerable influence inside opposition groups, including Al-Tagammu. Certainly, the legal framework governing the operations of political parties afforded authorities wide latitude to intervene in the affairs of opposition groups. In addition, the old VO networks that once linked NDP personnel and opposition leaders provided the regime with yet another means to pressure opposition parties into compliance.

The VO left an indelible mark on contemporary Egyptian politics. The VO remains a relatively understudied subject. This is unfortunate, for an entire generation of Egyptian politicians and statesmen—one that came to dominate senior posts within the ruling and opposition parties—began their political careers in the VO. A glimpse at a partial list of former VO affiliates who occupied positions of influence inside the ruling establishment substantiates this reality:[110]

- Mubarak's prime ministers Fuad Mohieddin, Atef Sedky, and Atef Ebeid; and Sadat's prime ministers Aziz Sedky, Abdel-Aziz Hegazy, and Mamdouh Salem
- Senior NDP leaders who managed the ruling party for much of the Mubarak era, including Yousef Wali and Kamal El-Shazly
- Mubarak's parliamentary speakers Mustafa Kamal Helmy, Ahmed Fathi Sorour, and Rifaat Al-Mahgoub
- Mubarak's foreign ministers Amr Moussa and Esmat Abdel-Meguid, and senior foreign policy advisers Mostafa Al-Feki and Osama Al-Baz
- Mubarak's interior ministers Hassan Abu-Basha and Ahmed Rushdi, and Sadat's interior minister Al-Nabawi Ismail
- Education minister Hussein Kamel Bahaaeddin, higher education minister and NDP parliamentary heavyweight Mofeed Shehab, and youth minister Ali Al-Din Hilal
- Mubarak's petroleum ministers Abdel-Hadi Kandil and Ahmed Ezzedin Hilal
- Mubarak's health minister Ragheb Dowidar, and Sadat's health minister Ibrahim Badran
- Hassaballah Al-Kafrawy, who served as minister of housing under both Sadat and Mubarak
- Grand Imam of Al-Azhar under Sadat Abdel-Halim Mahmoud

- Senior officials of the Ministry of Manpower and Egyptian Trade Union Federation Salah Gharib, Abdel-Latif Bultiya, and Ahmed Al-Amawi
- Longtime heads of professional syndicates, including Ahmad Al-Khawaga of the lawyers syndicate, and Hamdi Al-Sayyid of the physicians syndicate.

The influence of the VO network members transcended Mubarak's ruling establishment, featuring in the leadership of opposition parties. By the early 1990s, for example, almost every opposition party was led by a former affiliate of the VO, including the Liberal Socialists Party (Mustafa Kamel Mourad), Al-Tagammu (Khaled Mohieddin), the Socialist Labor Party (SLP) (Ibrahim Shukri), and the Nasserist Party (Diaaeddin Dawoud). In other words, previous VO affiliation became a de facto stamp of approval, indicating that an individual had regime endorsement to assume a leadership post.[111] The VO network was also visible in the editorial boards of opposition newspapers during much of the Mubarak era. It included Gamal Badawi, editor in chief of Al-Wafd daily newspaper during the 1990s, Mahmoud Al-Maraghi who served as editor in chief for both Al-Tagammu's Al-Ahaly and the Nasserist Party's Al-Arabi, Al-Maraghi's successor at Al-Ahaly Philip Gallab, and longtime editor in chief of the SLP's Al-Shaab daily Adel Hussein.[112]

Perhaps the most conspicuous evidence of the VO's enduring impact (a topic meriting its own book-length treatment) is the distinctive character of Egyptian politics in the post-Mubarak era.[113] When a generation of Mubarak-era politicians was swept from the scene, three actors quickly seized control of the political arena. They were the oldest organized bodies that had successfully resisted VO penetration into their ranks: the army, the judiciary, and the Muslim Brotherhood.[114] In other words, only those organizations maintaining some degree of autonomy from the ASU's VO network later proved sufficiently resilient to survive the period following Mubarak's downfall.

Like most of the opposition parties that emerged under Mubarak, Al-Tagammu carried the legacy of its leaders' previous association with the former VO. This is unsurprising, given that its leaders came of age inside the VO's culture of cooperation with the ruling party and security agencies. Many of Al-Tagammu's founding and long-standing leaders had past ties with the VO. For example, Rifaat Al-Said was a member of Khaled Mohieddin's VO cell at Al-Akhbar.[115] Other prominent Al-Tagammu figures who served in the VO include Lotfi Al-Khouli, Amina Shafiq, Philip Gallab, Fouad Morsi, Ismail Sabri Abdallah, Sherif Hetata, Ibrahim Saadeddin, and

Abdel-Ghaffar Shokr.[116] These individuals' primary task was submitting secret reports about activities they deemed to be subversive, especially at their sites of employment. A more cynical assessment would characterize them as spies for the ASU. As explained in chapter 5, the legacy of covert collaboration with the ruling party would haunt Al-Tagammu during the 1980s and facilitate the process by which the regime coopted the party and tempered its oppositionist positions. Many of those who advocated improving relations with the ruling party were former affiliates of the VO, including Ismail Sabri Abdallah, Fouad Morsi, Philip Gallab, and Ibrahim Saadeddin.[117]

THE CAPITULATIONS AND THEIR REVERBERATIONS: A SUMMARY

During the 1940s and 1950s, communist groups had made notable progress toward building their organizations and unifying the movement. In 1959, however, an aggressive state crackdown on leftists halted that progress. Upon releasing them from prison in the mid-1960s, Nasser pressured communist activists to join the ruling party. Despite attempts to retain their organizational structures, the two major communist parties were ordered to disband and to instruct their members to join the ASU as individuals. They obliged, thereby ceding their organizational autonomy to the state. In addition to regime pressure, Nasser's cooptation of communist parties was facilitated by ideological developments within the parties, causing some of their intellectuals to assert a nationalist imperative to cooperate with the president. Communists who joined the ASU were limited to subordinate roles. Equally significantly, they were assigned to the party's VO, where they performed regime-maintenance duties and developed habits of covert cooperation with the state. This would not be the last time descendants of the communist movement capitulated to the ruling establishment, as explained later.

Post-1965 Fragmentation and State Repression: Underground Communist Groups and Sadat

Despite the early 1970s upsurge in leftist activism on university campuses (described in chapter 1), no political force proved capable of translating the energies and abilities of the younger generation into an enduring political organization. In other words, disparate leftist student groups opposing Sadat in the 1970s never found a leftist counterpart to the senior leadership of the Muslim Brotherhood that aggregated and organized the Islamist student movement. For two sets of reasons, a leftist equivalent of the Muslim Brotherhood simply did not exist.

The first set of reasons concerns the major communist parties' afore-mentioned decision to dissolve themselves. This action produced a vac-uum inside the Egyptian left. With communists dispersed throughout the ruling establishment and underground activist circles, or in exile, no political force appeared capable of speaking on behalf of the left and the working class it claimed to represent. The 1965 dissolution also produced great disunity and fragmentation among the remaining communist activ-ists seeking to rebuild their movement under Sadat's rule.

The second set of reasons pertains to the challenges then confronting communists operating underground. Some of these challenges were self-inflicted, as revealed in Gennaro Gervasio's seminal study on communist activism in Egypt after 1967, commonly known as the "third wave" of the Egyptian communist movement. For example, the senior leadership's domineering style and insistence on hierarchical command often alien-ated young activists.[118] Leaders focused on recruiting students, thereby neglecting outreach to workers.[119] At times, some communists were reluc-tant to adopt an aggressive line against the Sadat regime, believing that it harbored progressive elements worthy of engagement.[120] The commu-nists' principal sin, at least for Gervasio, is that they focused on nationalist opposition to Sadat's foreign policies, thereby losing sight of the social and economic issues that concerned large segments of society.[121]

These factors are significant to an analysis of the Egyptian communist movement's general shortcomings. They do not, however, offer a com-pelling explanation for the left's failure *relative to* Islamist currents with respect to generating effective political organizations in the 1970s. Put simply, the Brotherhood did not fare any better than the communists in any of these areas. Indeed, communist leaders may have had strong authoritarian inclinations. Yet, as described in the previous chapter, so did their counterparts in the Muslim Brotherhood. Additionally, the inordi-nate focus on student outreach was not unique to the communists. The Brotherhood's efforts in the 1970s were similarly focused on students. In fact, these efforts subsequently enabled the Brotherhood's revived organization to expand into other social and political spheres. We have no reason to assume that such a path was impossible for the left. If certain communist leaders repeatedly gave the Sadat regime the benefit of the doubt, the Muslim Brotherhood, at least officially, kept an accommodationist posture toward the regime for an entire decade. Finally, nationalism's apparent hegemony over the communist movement's agenda undeniably limited the movement's ability to articulate a platform appealing to socioeconomically aggrieved classes. In fact, this reality arguably has continued to hamper the Egyptian left up to today. At the same time, we should not forget that the second iteration of the Muslim Brotherhood managed to reconstruct an organization and establish a political presence well before it was capable of setting forth a meaningful programmatic vision addressing public concerns and popular aspirations.

What, then, explains the left's inability to replicate the Islamists' success in building enduring political organizations in the aftermath of the Sadat presidency? A large part of the answer lies in state repression of the left when it was trying to rebuild its political organizations in the 1970s.[122] That is, in stark contrast to the permissive conditions engendered by Sadat's Islamist incorporation policies, underground communists were too constrained to expand their political presence and outreach. To be sure, leftists made a variety of poor choices, as many have argued. But the deck was stacked against them. Leftists were frequently targeted, imprisoned, exiled, slandered in state media, and denied access to public forums. Thus, it was virtually impossible for underground communist leaders to replicate the Muslim Brotherhood's organizational successes on university campuses, a fact that becomes clear upon examining the experiences of underground communist organizations during this period.

OVERCOMING FRAGMENTATION AND DIVISION AFTER 1965

After 1965, communist activism continued in the form of small, underground intellectual circles. Although these circles consisted mainly of activists who rejected the self-dissolution decision of 1965, some former proponents of dissolution also became active in the late 1960s. By the time Sadat assumed power, these circles had coalesced around three major groupings. One consisted of old guard communists who joined forces in 1972 to form the Communist Party of Egypt (CPE), which officially announced its existence in 1975. These elements agreed to collaborate only on the condition that participants who had accepted the 1965 dissolution would now condemn it unequivocally. The remaining two groups opposed collaboration with former advocates of the dissolution. From one of these groups emerged the Communist Party of Egypt-January 8 (CPE-January 8), which, like the CPE, declared itself active in 1975. In 1969, the second of the two aforementioned groups formed the Communist Organization of Egypt (COE), which became the Workers Communist Party (WCP) in 1975. The leaders of this organization rejected the 1965 dissolution and the communists who facilitated it, as well as the "accommodationism" they perceived among prominent communists.[123]

Each of these organizations attempted to recruit members of the early 1970s student movement that mobilized in opposition to Sadat's policies. Such efforts, however, were rather unorganized and erratic because of the fragmentation afflicting the communist movement in the wake of the 1965 dissolution. For example, Ahmed Abdalla Rozza, a Cairo University leader of the 1972–1973 student uprising, reported that Marxist intellectuals failed to unite their ranks before engaging with students. As a result, they inculcated student activists with their own conflicts and divisions. For this reason, Rozza argued, leftist activism on campus remained polarized and undeveloped, both ideologically and organizationally.[124]

Their organizational limitations notwithstanding, communist groups maintained sufficient outreach at major universities to recruit a younger generation of activists.[125] According to WCP activist Said Al-Olaimy, by the early 1970s, the party (then known as the COE) had a respectable presence on the campuses of Cairo and Ain Shams Universities.[126] Also in the early 1970s, Al-Istimrar, which would eventually become a component of CPE-January 8, was involved in the Supporters of the Palestinian Revolution, then a focal point of political activism at Cairo University. Years later, CPE-January 8 played a leading role in coordinating the University's Club for Progressive Socialist Thought,[127] which, Ilhamy Al-Mirghani reports, also benefited from the support of Al-Matraqqah, a group that splintered from the CPE in the early 1970s.[128] The groups that established the CPE in 1975 had been active to some extent among university students after 1972, although many ultimately left the party because of strategic disagreements with its older leadership. One such defection led to the formation of Al-Mutammar, which reportedly had a notable presence at Assiut

University, even fielding independent candidates in the Assiut races in the 1979 legislative election.[129]

COERCION, SURVEILLANCE, AND
STUNTED ORGANIZATIONAL DEVELOPMENT

These nominal successes aside, such efforts were severely constrained by the hostile political environment of Sadat's Egypt. Security service surveillance and harassment made visible forms of activism and engagement quite risky. For example, security agency attempts to infiltrate the CPE compelled the organization to abandon its public outreach efforts.[130] Additionally, arrests and imprisonments frequently deprived these groups of their most experienced leaders during critical periods.

The WCP's experience is a case in point.[131] In mid-1973, security agencies arrested and detained its key leaders for almost two years, just as the party (i.e., the COE) was expanding its base and building its organization. Before the crackdown, the WCP had established a presence at major universities like Cairo, Ain Shams, Alexandria, and Assiut, and had played a key role in supporting the 1972–1973 student uprising.[132] The group also had made considerable progress toward developing specialized organizational subunits and committees.[133] It recruited workers from various sites in Alexandria and even formulated a platform specifically addressing workers' demands and calling for curbing state interference in labor organizations.[134] This was no small feat. As the Nasserist establishment had worked to exclude communists from the public sector, and Sadat was similarly keen on keeping communists out of state-sponsored professional organizations, building meaningful ties with labor was already an uphill battle for leftist groups.[135]

According to former WCP activist Salah Al-Amrousy, just as authorities were about to move against them, party leaders initiated a plan to establish secret committees in major textile factories. The idea, Al-Amrousy indicates, was to expand the antistate syndicate movement throughout the entire textile sector from Cairo to Alexandria and, thereby, discredit the official labor unions. Little did the WCP activists know that security personnel already had infiltrated their ranks through the party's labor affiliates.[136] The state's practice of using workers to spy on leftist organizations during the 1970s posed a serious challenge to these groups, making it exceedingly difficult to increase workers' representation within their cadres.[137]

In addition, the agency conducting surveillance on the WCP in the lead-up to the said 1973 arrests was not, per standard practice, a bureau of the Ministry of Interior. Instead, the WCP was targeted by the National Security Authority, a branch of the General Intelligence Service (GIS). As former WCP member Said Al-Olaimny observed, at that time, it was rather unusual for the GIS to pursue a domestic case of this nature. GIS involvement was perhaps evidence of the regime's heightened sense of alarm about communist activism. In fact, the GIS operatives' more advanced surveillance techniques threw off the WCP activists, who routinely adopted measures to protect against standard security surveillance.[138]

In June 1973, security forces arrested eighteen members of the WCP, including its intellectual godfather Ibrahim Fathi, charging seventeen with attempting to overthrow the regime. They would remain imprisoned until April 1975.[139] These arrests, according to Al-Olaimy, were particularly destructive to the party because they targeted key members of its central committee, leaving the WCP's management entirely in the hands of inexperienced student cadres for almost two years. He credits these younger leaders with assuming responsibility and keeping the group alive. Yet, Al-Olaimy also acknowledges that the imprisonments severely damaged the party. In the absence of experienced leadership, there was no clear vision for developing the party organization.[140]

The WCP's experience was a manifestation—albeit an extreme one—of a broader phenomenon: state intervention to isolate leaders from younger activists, thereby interrupting the course of party development. For example, another wave of 1973 arrests imprisoned communists linked to Cairo University, including a host of important communist leaders like Ahmed Nabil Al-Helaly, Adib Dimitri, and Fawzi Habashi.[141] The crackdown forced other prominent movement figures, notably Michel Kamel and Youssef Darwish, into exile.[142] This was just the first of successive waves of repression Sadat inflicted on communists. For example, in early 1975, the state launched major arrest campaigns against communist activists in the wake of labor unrest,[143] and again after the January 1977 Bread Uprising.[144] In the fall of 1979, the state heightened its repression of communist groups,[145] and in 1980, it prosecuted CPE affiliates for allegedly plotting to overthrow the regime.[146] In sum, repression against communists was unrelenting throughout the period of Sadat's rule,[147] greatly undermining their ability to establish a public presence or develop effective organizational structures. It is no surprise, therefore, that by the mid-1980s, many of these underground formations had diminished significantly in size and influence or had disappeared altogether.[148]

INACCESSIBILITY OF PUBLIC FORUMS AND STATE SLANDER

In addition to coercion, the Sadat regime hampered the communist movement's growth by severely limiting or eliminating the presence of communists and that of their sympathizers in the media. For example, ASU leaders—including Islamist incorporation architect Mohamed Othman Ismail—moved swiftly to revoke the party memberships of writers expressing favorable views of the 1972–1973 student uprising; a measure that effectively banned them from publishing in the national press. The situation was not much better for leftists who managed to survive in state-run newspapers. Many of these publications, as Marxist writer Ghali Shukri notes, adopted an unofficial policy of keeping leftist contributors on the payroll, while refusing to print their writings. Moreover, Sadat punished publications that traditionally had afforded Marxist contributors some freedom to express their views. For example, in 1974, the Ministry of Culture took steps to oust dissident voices from *Al-Kateb* magazine, essentially depoliticizing the publication. Not long after the 1977 Bread Uprising, Al-Ahram publishing house discontinued the magazine *Al-Talia*, as detailed in chapter 1. Also in 1977, *Rose Al-Yousef*'s editorial leadership was reshuffled in a move clearly aimed at moderating its anti-regime, leftist orientation.[149] Al-Tagammu Party's *Al-Ahaly* eventually faced a similar fate and was suspended in 1978.[150] Thus, without access to public forums, communist groups had no channels—apart from their secret bulletins—through which they could address the public and mobilize popular support for their agendas.

The exclusion of Marxist voices from mainstream media outlets was a serious handicap, given that the regime constantly slandered and defamed communists in the press and official statements. For example, after the 1977 Bread Uprising, the government declared that the CPE, the WCP, and Al-Tagammu's communist affiliates were guilty of rioting, vandalism, and plotting to overthrow the regime.[151] Even before 1977, the state, as described in chapter 2, had employed rhetoric doubting the national loyalty of Egyptian leftists, and equating communism with atheism.[152] According to Ghali Shukri, Sadat's strategy was "to focus on the left and always portray it as the echo of a foreign voice and not an authentic voice and try to strike it from within by saying that there is a patriotic left and a foreign, client one. And then attempt to incite people against it by weaponizing religion and accusing it of atheism."[153] In such a political climate, the idea that a communist current could cultivate a popular following or expand its organizational presence was unrealistic.[154]

In summary, the underground communist movement faced a variety of challenges limiting its ability to develop effective political organizations during Sadat's rule. These include disagreements and splits resulting from the 1965 dissolution, periodic state repression, the exclusion of its allies from public media, and image problems caused by recurrent slanderous attacks from the regime and state media. Thus, the notion that any of the underground communist organizations could have developed in partnership with student activists, à la the Muslim Brotherhood, was out of the question. Whereas the Brotherhood and its student activist partners found a permissive political climate in Sadat's "state of science and faith," the communists were too constrained to effectively translate leftist student activism or labor discontent into an enduring political organization. Under these circumstances, Al-Tagammu Party became one of the few channels through which leftist activism was able to survive in the post-Sadat era. Yet other obstacles Al-Tagammu encountered pushed it toward a path of institutional development that cemented the party's dependence on the state, rendering it vulnerable to regime interventions.

Al-Tagammu and the Costs of Legal Legitimacy

In 2010, a senior NDP official recounted a joke he frequently shared with the leader of Al-Tagammu Party: "Sometimes I tell Rifaat Al-Said, 'What is that party you keep talking about? Where is this party of yours? Why don't you bring your 'party' and let's all meet at Qasr Al-Neel[155]?' He [Al-Said] just laughs."[156] This official's dark-comedic exchange with Al-Said reflects just how much Al-Tagammu had declined by the end of the Mubarak era. Over the course of decades, it turned from a site of serious regime opposition into a benign entity with barely any followers—at least not nearly enough to form a noticeable crowd in Qasr Al-Neel.

Al-Tagammu's woeful state in the aftermath of the 2005 legislative election was summarized by economist and longtime Al-Tagammu member Ibrahim Al-Issawi:

> Old age has become one of the hallmarks of [Al-Tagammu] Party leaders and cadres, and many entities within it lost their key elements, which paralyzed their ability to act. Its membership has declined. Many left it, either because they disapproved of its policies or its actions [. . . .] The cultural and intellectual capabilities within the community eroded due to the significant decline in training and indoctrination activities. The divisions within the leftist movement increased more broadly, especially because of the inability of Al-Tagammu to form a "democratic left coalition," and the lack of sufficient enthusiasm on the part of its leadership in this regard due its large preoccupation instead with dialogue with the National Democratic Party.[157]

Many observers blamed Rifaat Al-Said for all the party's woes. The prevalence of this opinion is unsurprising. After all, many viewed Al-Said as a Darth Vader–like figure who, after crossing over to the "dark side" of regime collaboration, presided over Al-Tagammu's transformation into a lackey of the NDP in its war against Islamist dissidents. As the face (and enforcer) of Al-Tagammu's alliance with the ruling party during the 1990s and 2000s, Al-Said certainly bore great responsibility for the party's diminishing credibility. That said, by exaggerating the impact of Al-Said's personal preferences, intellectual transformation, or pure opportunism in the tale of Al-Tagammu's decline, the "Vader narrative" omits a significant element of the story.

Specifically, a personalist interpretation overlooks the fact that the conservative tendencies displayed by Al-Said and his collaborators have long resonated within the Egyptian left, during periods of both accommodation with and opposition to the regime. Ever since the Nasser era, a contingent of the left has consistently argued that the state is embedded with progressive elements that must be won over, whether to resist imperialism, build socialism, or fight the "Islamist threat." The question is this: what outside forces empowered accommodationist elements within Al-Tagammu, thus rendering the party susceptible to cooptation? A crucial factor is the institutional context that initially enabled regime intervention in party affairs, thus allowing it to employ Al-Said and others to tame Al-Tagammu. This fact invites us to expand the focus of discussion beyond Al-Said's individual characteristics and interests and to further examine the path of institutional development the party has taken since its founding.

This chapter argues that the formation of Al-Tagammu marked the second capitulation of the left to the ruling establishment, the first being the dissolution of the communist parties in 1965 at the behest of Nasser. The communist activists who founded Al-Tagammu in 1976 made a number of significant concessions by agreeing to participate in national politics through a highly restrictive legal framework. That institutional arrangement ceded the autonomy of the leftist currents housed in Al-Tagammu, fostered their dependence on the state, and made them vulnerable to chronic regime intervention. These conditions also constituted an important divergence from the path of institutional development the Muslim Brotherhood had pursued since the 1970s. The Brotherhood's path, as explained in chapter 3, directed its political participation toward informal channels, thus retaining its autonomy in relation to the state. The left embarked on a qualitatively different track, one defined by formal participation and state dependence.

AL-TAGAMMU AS THE LEFT'S PATH TO LEGALITY

Al-Tagammu, as explained in chapter 1, was conceived in a raft of Sadat-era institutional reforms designed to contain political actors capable of mobilizing aggrieved communities like organized labor. The obvious targets of this policy were Nasserists, whom the president had just demoted from the ruling coalition, and communists, who had been covertly reconstituting their organizations since the late 1960s. Sadat had hoped to coopt these forces and keep them in check through the left *minbar* ("platform") of the ASU, which later became Al-Tagammu Party.[158]

Initially based in the ASU building near Tahrir Square (later the NDP headquarters), Al-Tagammu was formed as a national coalition of a variety of leftist currents, notably communists, Nasserists, and Arab nationalists.[159] Although some CPE elements were critical of the minbar system, especially its prohibition on forming organizations based on social class, the party ended up endorsing Al-Tagammu's experiment, as evidenced by the overlapping membership between the two groups. A considerable part of the communist movement, however, was not on board. That included the WCP and the CPE-January 8, both of which considered Al-Tagammu nothing more than a regime ploy to pacify its opponents.[160] In addition, many younger activists felt antipathy for the party's founders, who were deemed responsible for the 1965 dissolution of communist organizations at Nasser's behest, and who were far too accommodating to Sadat.

To some extent, Al-Tagammu defied popular expectations by mounting a formidable opposition to Sadat, despite its reputation for being too soft on the regime. At the same time, even with the formal protections supposedly accompanying legal recognition, the party was subjected to many of the same constraints imposed on illegal communist groups during the 1970s. Only a few years after its founding, Al-Tagammu's activities and publications faced a variety of restrictions, in addition to the regime's efforts to abort any nascent alliances between the party and the labor movement (see chapter 1). Sadat and senior government officials often singled out Al-Tagammu in public attacks on the left, while regime-allied writers worked to undermine its credibility and foment divisions within its ranks.[161]

Despite these impediments, the party made some important gains during Sadat's presidency. The diverse communities of activists who formed Al-Tagammu succeeded in carving out valuable space for the progressive left within the emergent political arena. Opponents of Sadat's economic policies now had an identifiable home base at Al-Tagammu, even if many activists remained dubious of the organization's credibility.

Remarkably, Al-Tagammu provided this relatively safe haven for leftist activism at a time when the regime vigorously suppressed underground communist groups, all but eliminating the possibility of political engagement outside of legal channels. The late Mohamed Mounir, a longtime leftist activist and journalist, explained that during Mubarak's first decade in office, and after multiple waves of repression, some of the communists who initially rejected Al-Tagammu joined the party in various capacities. Others maintained a long-term commitment to underground activism or steered clear of party politics altogether, pursuing careers in civil society,[162] thereby contributing to the phenomenon Vickie Langohr dubs "too much civil society, too little politics."[163] That is to say, Sadat's repression of communists made Al-Tagammu the de facto address of the Egyptian left in the national political arena.

At the same time, by assuming the role of a formal opposition, the founders of Al-Tagammu accepted a number of institutional constraints that proved devastating in the long run. Submitting to the requirements of legal political participation introduced a variety of obstacles to Al-Tagammu's activism, increased its dependence on the state, and opened the door to state interference. This experience stands in stark contrast to that of the Muslim Brotherhood, which pursued a path of institutional development that secured its continued autonomy from the state. This discrepancy is central to any understanding of how opposition politics evolved under Sadat and Mubarak. This seemingly benign disparity would have enduring implications for the future balance of power between the Muslim Brotherhood and leftist currents.

FORMALITY AND STATE DEPENDENCE: OPPOSITION PARTIES UNDER THE LEGAL FRAMEWORK

Just like any other licensed political party, the founders of Al-Tagammu ceded a great deal of autonomy to the state by agreeing to operate under a highly unfavorable legal framework, particularly Law 40/1977, popularly known as the Political Parties Law.[164] Law 40, as Holger Albrecht writes, "was not created with the aim of inspiring a flourishing party life, but rather of controlling activism through several restrictive regulations that were overseen by a state body."[165] This law effectively gave the state carte blanche to interfere—directly and indirectly—in the affairs of opposition parties. In this respect, one could argue that Al-Tagammu's story is the story of every formal opposition party that existed under Mubarak: all had to operate according to the regime's rules, an arrangement that was not only unfair but also debilitating to the organizational development of opposition groups.

For example, the law, which remained in effect until 2011, required all parties to report their finances to the state's Central Auditing Agency, which in turn was obligated to report them to the Political Parties Committee (PPC) each year. In theory, these are not unreasonable reporting requirements. They offer a mechanism for detecting any unlawful financial dealings, like accepting foreign funding, which was forbidden under

Article 11 of the Political Parties Law. Requiring political parties to maintain some level of transparency, in theory, should ensure that they operate according to the same rules so that no party improperly develops an unfair advantage. Yet in practice, the law was not applied impartially.

First, the state institutions responsible for enforcing such regulations, especially the PPC, were under the control of the "party of the state," that is, the ruling NDP. In fact, throughout much of Mubarak's reign, the head of the PPC was also the secretary general of the NDP. In other words, ruling party officials could monitor the financial activities of their rivals and use such information to intimidate financial contributors to opposition parties.

Second, the Muslim Brotherhood was never subjected to the Political Parties Law because it participated in elections and parliamentary life without an official political party license. This is not to say that the Brotherhood did not suffer from periodic state repression, arrests, and politically motivated trials, as previously detailed. Rather, state repression of the Brotherhood did not include the same disruptive, interventionist tactics employed against legal parties like Al-Tagammu. An organization that participates in politics without a license appears to be at a huge disadvantage, because it is denied the privileges accruing to legal status, like constitutional protections and public financing. In practice, however, the lack of legal status meant the absence of heavy-handed state oversight, especially in the financial sphere. Thus, as a group permitted to participate in politics through informal channels, the Muslim Brotherhood did not have to deal with the same financial reporting requirements that their rivals were subject to. As a result, the state had no obvious mechanism to inspect the Brotherhood's finances or to trace revenue from abroad. In this respect, one could argue that Al-Tagammu's legal status placed it at a severe disadvantage relative to the Muslim Brotherhood. As one Al-Tagammu official observed in 2010:

> The Brothers are at an advantage today because they are not bound to the same legal constraints we deal with. Every year, we have to open our books to two to three government auditors and explain to them how every piaster was obtained and how it was spent, which is something the Brothers do not deal with. No one asks them where they get their money from or how they spend it. No one imposes on them the same spending caps we are bound to. We are the prisoners of legal legitimacy.[166]

This perception, common among opposition party leaders, was perhaps best summarized as follows: "People say that the Brotherhood are banned, when in reality [legal] parties are ones that are banned, not the Brotherhood."[167]

Another instrument through which the PPC exerted influence over the legal opposition—as opposed to the Muslim Brotherhood—was Article 17 of the Political Parties Law. This article empowered the head of the PPC to order the dissolution of a party if it has conducted activities in violation of the constitution or threatened national security or social peace.

Often, the PPC froze the activities and assets of opposition parties and suspended their publications on the pretext that they were experiencing unresolved leadership conflicts.[168] The application of this rule was highly politicized and was exercised only when a party overstepped the bounds of acceptable government criticism.[169] For example, the state used the pretense of "an unresolved struggle over leadership" to suspend the SLP in 2000,[170] just as it intensified its criticism of powerful officials like Agriculture Minister Yousef Wali and Culture Minister Farouk Hosni. The same scenario unfolded in the aftermath of the 2005 presidential election when the state suspended Al-Ghad Party on similar legal grounds.[171] In both cases, it is widely believed that the "power struggles" inside these parties were provoked or manufactured by regime infiltrators operating under the direction of security officials. In short, an inequitable legal framework afforded the regime the authority to suspend the licenses of even the most law-abiding parties. This mechanism constituted a powerful deterrent to legal opposition parties contemplating challenges to the political status quo.

The Mubarak regime imposed an additional stricture on licensed political parties, requiring them to maintain open membership (i.e., grant membership to all applicants). The Political Parties Law stipulated that every party must publicize membership requirements, as well as the grounds and procedures for membership suspension, and prohibited membership criteria based on religion, race, sex, or social class (Article 5). At first glance, these requirements seem rather harmless and uncontroversial. Yet upon closer examination of the context in which opposition parties operated, the open-membership requirement is revealed for what it is: a regime ploy to monitor, weaken, or control the opposition. This open-membership requirement permitted security agencies to infiltrate opposition political parties and install networks of informants.[172]

The legal framework gave parties little or no discretion in admitting new members, thereby rendering them vulnerable to infiltration by security agencies. Unconstrained by these legal restrictions, the Muslim Brotherhood devised rigid membership requirements and procedures, making the task of infiltration extremely difficult (see chapter 3). To become a fully active member of the Brotherhood, one goes through multiple levels of probationary membership. Applicants and probationary members must demonstrate commitment to the organization, its principles, its directives, and its grassroots activities to advance to the next level of membership.

The same cannot be said of most parties operating under the state's legal framework. With lax membership requirements and obligations, it was not uncommon for wealthy individuals to rise rapidly through the ranks of such parties without much prior experience in, or service to, the organization. In fact, the head of one licensed political party admitted that he knew little about the party over which he presided because he was "new to it," describing it as another of his many mashariʿ ("business projects").[173]

This context explains the "closed" nature of the Brotherhood, which has inspired frequent criticism from both opponents and followers. The Brotherhood's opponents liken it to an underground militia plotting behind closed doors to seize power, whereas many of its disgruntled affiliates complain that the group lacks transparency and internal accountability. Both perspectives assume that the Brotherhood's obsession with secrecy and opaqueness is a weakness, one that has alienated many of its sympathizers and isolated it from the rest of society. One could make a strong case, however, that this uncompromising commitment to secrecy and inaccessibility has enabled the group to survive in an environment characterized by persistent security agency attempts to penetrate and disrupt political organizations.

As much as its inaccessibility and hierarchical structure has exposed the Brotherhood to criticism, these very features arguably produced an organizational model that no other political group or movement in Egypt has been able to replicate. The organization has been sufficiently open to occupy and dominate broad sectors of society, yet sufficiently closed off to prevent occupation or domination by external social forces. The same cannot be said of licensed political groups. It is no wonder that obtaining legal status and launching a political party have remained highly contentious topics of debate within the Muslim Brotherhood. Legal status, although potentially advantageous for any political group, carries a high price in Egypt, a degree of transparency and accessibility that enemies, especially the state, can easily exploit. As one SLP leader concluded, "Once a party accepts legal status, it is on the home turf of the regime."[174] The issue of open membership is a case in point.

Finally, throughout the Mubarak era, the state was able to exert pressure over opposition parties through the various constraints it placed on their publications. Almost every party produced a daily or weekly newspaper, a critical instrument to convey its ideas and principles, critique government performance, and conduct outreach to members and potential supporters. Before the proliferation of privately owned newspapers and media outlets in the 1990s and 2000s, these publications represented a rare alternative to state media.

Such publications usually were printed at state-owned printing houses. This enabled the government to block the printing of opposition periodicals without having to resort to formal censorship or to obtain a court order recalling a publication from newsstands. A classic example of this tactic was on display in October 1978. The October 22 issue of Al-Tagammu's *Al-Ahaly* was dedicated exclusively to the texts of ten speeches delivered on the floor of parliament criticizing the then recent Camp David Accords. A court overturned authorities' decision to ban the issue, ruling that it contained nothing legally objectionable, just transcripts of parliamentary sessions as they appeared in official state documents. In desperation, the state ordered the printing house to hold that day's issue of *Al-Ahaly*. The chair of the state-owned Al-Taawon Printing House simply informed Al-Tagammu officials that his workers refused to print the latest *Al-Ahaly* issue because its content deeply offended their patriotic sensibilities.[175] This was the last official *Al-Ahaly* edition to go to print until May 1982, several months after Sadat's assassination.[176]

The advertising departments of opposition newspapers provided another channel through which the state could wield influence over publications. Because the circulation of these papers tended to be fairly limited, they rarely generated sufficient revenue to cover operating costs. Thus, these publications were always eager to increase their modest revenues by selling as much advertising space as possible. Given their limited circulation, demand for advertising space in such publications was scant. Thus, the only organizations willing to consistently purchase advertisements were those not operating on a for-profit business model: state-owned companies and government agencies.

As the major purchasers of advertising space in opposition newspapers, state ministries effectively became the subsidizers of opposition parties. Thus, government officials wielded considerable influence over opposition parties behind the scenes, bestowing or withholding advertising revenue at their discretion. In turn, opposition party newspapers had an incentive to temper criticism of government officials who regularly purchased their advertising spaces and to attack those who deprived them of this much-needed income. One political party chief once implied that his newspaper consistently criticized a particular ministry solely because its senior officials refused to purchase advertising space in the party's newspaper.[177]

In short, by accepting legal status and formally entering Egyptian political life, Al-Tagammu effectively embraced a variety of restrictions and mechanisms through which the state could systematically interfere in its affairs and deter political dissent. In contrast, the Muslim Brotherhood averted these constraints throughout the Sadat and Mubarak eras by retaining its legally undefined status, thereby preserving its organizational integrity and autonomy from state intervention.

Yet, as previously noted, the legal framework and the costs it imposed on Al-Tagammu constitute only half of the story. In the 1980s, the Muslim Brotherhood's political successes prompted internal changes at Al-Tagammu that sustained these institutional patterns. Growing alarm at the expansion of Islamist influence bolstered a consensus that cooperation with the regime was necessary to confront the looming danger of political Islam. Additionally, the intensification of conflict between leftists and Islamists during the 1990s and 2000s pushed Al-Tagammu closer to the regime, preserving the institutional patterns that compromised the party's political autonomy (see chapter 5).

Conclusion

Islamist incorporation policies sent leftist and Islamist political currents down divergent developmental paths, creating a long-term imbalance of power between the two movements. The left's trajectory was characterized by restrictive, repressive policies during the formative period of the

1970s. Following two important events, this trajectory ended in its complete domination by the state. The first such event occurred in the 1960s, when leaders of the communist movement decided to dissolve their political organizations and join the ruling ASU, thereby capitulating to Nasser. This move produced enduring disunity within the progressive left and hampered efforts to forge a credible political organization capable of aggregating and institutionalizing the energies of the leftist student movement that emerged in the early 1970s. It also engendered a practice of communists collaborating with the ruling establishment, further undermining the left's autonomy. The second event occurred when some communist leaders agreed to once again play by the regime's rules and form Al-Tagammu Party, thereby accepting the constraints of formal political contestation and opening the door to multiple forms of state interference.

In contrast, the Muslim Brotherhood averted the fate of the communist movement and its successors, because it denied Sadat the prize Nasser wrested from the leftists: its autonomy. Islamist incorporation policies lifted numerous constraints from the Muslim Brotherhood and its prospective leaders in the Islamist student movement, permitting them to develop their organizations with greater freedom from state interference. That same path was not viable for underground communist groups, which confronted successive waves of repression during the same period.

A number of factors sustained these institutional patterns. Growing competition between the Muslim Brotherhood and the ruling party hardened the regime's determination to deprive the group of any legal privileges. Thus, whenever conditions permitted, the Brotherhood participated in politics through informal channels. Reinforcing that trend were internal conflicts, which empowered a contingent committed to maintaining the informal nature of the Brotherhood's political activities. In the case of Al-Tagammu, the Brotherhood's ascendancy, as explained in the next chapter, propelled the party into the arms of the Mubarak regime, cementing the formal institutional patterns established under Sadat.

5

Islamist Incorporation, National Identity, and the Left

A Tale of Two Comrades

Does it seem surprising that I extend my salutations and respects to Mrs. Suzanne Mubarak, even though I came here as a [member of the] opposition? I think not, for she deserves our fullest respect and appreciation.

—RIFAAT AL-SAID, IN *AL-TAJAMMU' FI-L-BARLAMAN*

I got the intellectuals to enter the barn of the Ministry of Culture.

—MINISTER OF CULTURE FAROUK HOSNI, IN *DONIA AL-WATAN*

Reporters, activists, diplomats, and foreign dignitaries, like Jarallah Omar of the Yemeni Socialist Party, were gathered at Al-Tagammu Party headquarters in early 1995. They breathlessly awaited a public showdown between two intellectual icons. Much of the excitement was generated not by the prospective content of the debate, but by the spectacle of Adel Hussein and Rifaat Al-Said sharing the same stage, as many observers doubted that they could even conduct a civil conversation. Most attending did not realize that Hussein and Al-Said—both imprisoned by Gamal Abdel-Nasser for half a decade—had once been friends and comrades in the same communist organization. In fact, Hussein began his remarks by highlighting this relationship: "I recall that when we left prison together in 1964, we were closer to each other than any of the released prisoners, both on a personal level and in our agreement on all issues."[1] By the winter of 1995, Al-Said and Hussein were at the helm of two utterly incongruous political camps. As secretary general of Al-Tagammu, Al-Said led the charge against political Islam in tacit alliance with the regime. Meanwhile, Hussein, as secretary general of the Labor Party (the former Socialist Labor Party or the SLP), was a principal interlocutor with the Islamist movement, a strong ally of the Muslim Brotherhood, and the target of Al-Said's sharpest critiques. For close observers of Egyptian politics, however, the story of Adel and Rifaat was not unique. Islamist incorporation policies transformed Egyptian politics during the 1970s and 1980s, causing many longtime comrades to find themselves in opposing trenches. The unfolding of these transformations is the topic of this chapter.

This is the third chapter to analyze the impact of Islamist incorporation policies on the Egyptian political arena—that is, the country's journey to a politics of "more identity, less class." Chapters 3 and 4 examined 1970s Islamist incorporation policies' effects on the institutional development of Islamist and leftist political organizations, and these institutional patterns' impact on the relative power of the two currents in subsequent decades. This chapter explains the impact of Islamist incorporation policies on political alignments and the relative salience of identity politics and distributive conflicts. Thus, it brings into focus two significant effects of these policies: "crowding out" and "splitting."

I use the term "crowding out"[2] to designate the process by which identity politics gradually excludes distributive issues from the political arena. It is meant to capture the declining salience of distributive conflicts relative to identity politics, as the latter increasingly defined predominant cleavages in national politics. "Splitting" denotes the emergence of identity-based political cleavages between "old comrades." In other words, it describes how Islamist incorporation policies sharpened identity-based divisions inside coalitions opposed to infitah economic policies.

The first section of the chapter demonstrates how Islamist incorporation policies contributed to the reconfiguration of social conflicts in the political arena. Specifically, Islamist incorporation policies enhanced the salience of identity politics and culture wars relative to issues of wealth distribution, especially as the latter related to Egypt's experience of economic liberalization during the 1980s and 1990s. The tone of this transformative process was set by the issues that the Muslim Brotherhood, then enjoying an expanded public profile because of 1970s-era Islamist incorporation policies, pushed to the center of the political arena throughout the 1980s. By the early 1990s, culture wars, inspired by the issue of national identity, came to dominate the political scene. Meanwhile, the Muslim Brotherhood became the most prominent voice of oppositionist politics, supplanting the leftist coalition that emerged in response to Anwar Al-Sadat's de-Nasserization schemes. The impact of crowding out and the growing salience of identity conflicts were also felt inside Al-Tagammu. An internal battle erupted between proponents of greater cooperation with the ruling party to counter Islamist movements and advocates of continued opposition to the regime's economic policies. Ultimately, the former camp emerged triumphant, paving the way for a tacit alliance between the ruling National Democratic Party (NDP) and Al-Tagammu—an alliance that lasted until Hosni Mubarak's overthrow in 2011. The final section of the chapter focuses on the concept of splitting. It describes the transformations experienced by the SLP during the 1980s and 1990s to illustrate the mechanisms through which Islamist incorporation policies promoted splitting in the ranks of the leftist opposition.

Crowding Out: Politics of Economic Liberalization and Culture Wars

"Crowding out" denotes the process by which the politics of distribution loses salience relative to identity politics, as the latter becomes increasingly central to national debates. In 1980s Egypt, crowding out occurred in the context of the state's continuing struggle to abandon the expensive commitments imposed by the Nasserist social pact. Sadat's successor, Hosni Mubarak, was wary of the social and political costs of infitah. Yet expanding debt and a precarious fiscal situation made retaining the pact untenable, thus increasing pressure for economic liberalization.

The Mubarak regime finally succumbed to these pressures and began proposing economic reform measures once deemed unthinkable, like the privatization of public sector assets. Soon Egypt's political arena appeared calmer and more stable than it had under Sadat. Political opposition to economic liberalization was significantly tempered, as identity politics increasingly defined the terms of political conflict, and as Islamist currents began supplanting the leftist opposition that had emerged during Sadat's reign.

Central to this transformation was the reemergence of the Muslim Brotherhood as a leading opposition actor, a development made possible by the institutional patterns described in chapter 3. Of equal significance were the "crowding out" effects engendered by Islamist incorporation policies. This section examines two manifestations of crowding out. The first pertains to the policy priorities the Muslim Brotherhood pursued in the 1980s, as reflected both in its legislative conduct, and in its impact on the programmatic agendas of political actors outside the Islamist movement. The second manifestation is the transformative impact of the Brotherhood's political victories on the organized left, as epitomized by Al-Tagammu's experience. Al-Tagammu revised its priorities, tempering its opposition to state economic policies to join the ruling party's culture wars against Islamist currents.

THE CONTEXT FOR CROWDING OUT: MUBARAK AND ECONOMIC LIBERALIZATION

Upon assuming office, Mubarak was confronted with the consequences of Sadat's infitah policies, as the unrestrained import of consumer goods had produced chronic trade deficits.[3] Simultaneously, government spending on subsidies continued to rise,[4] contributing to budget deficits each year from 1985 to 1989.[5] Unable to spend within its means, the government resorted to borrowing, leading to further accumulation of debt.[6] By 1987, debt service totaled 40 percent of Egypt's gross domestic product (GDP),[7] and the domestic public debt had grown to 94 percent of GDP, compared with 63 percent in 1981.[8]

In spite of international pressure to resume Sadat's path of economic liberalization, Mubarak signaled his strong desire to revise the terms of economic reform. Eager to distance himself from his predecessor,[9] Mubarak publicly acknowledged the problems caused by infitah and pledged to redirect liberalization efforts to productive sectors. He ordered a series of investigations into Sadat-era business figures suspected of corruption, and he declared his unwillingness to sell public sector assets.[10]

Mubarak's first government displayed a nominal commitment to resuming state planning, announcing a five-year plan in 1982. Meanwhile, the state increased investments in industrial expansion and launched a set of initiatives to revamp the country's decaying infrastructure.[11]

In the early 1980s, temporary upsurges in government revenues somewhat curtailed the urge for further economic liberalization. The slightly improved fiscal situation gave Mubarak some breathing space, enabling him to resist international pressure to deepen his predecessor's reforms. By the mid-1980s, however, a fall in international oil prices produced sharp declines in revenue. The proceeds from Suez Canal customs fees and taxes on the energy sector plunged.[12] In addition, slumping oil prices severely reduced remittances from Egyptians working in the Gulf, a critical source of foreign currency for the government and of income for many families.[13]

Unable to service its foreign debt, the government turned once more to the International Monetary Fund (IMF), hoping that a loan agreement would induce the Paris Club to reschedule Egypt's debt. The IMF, however, insisted on a raft of reform measures that would raise the prices of consumer goods and curtail the state's redistributive capacities. The IMF pressed for currency devaluation, unifying the exchange rate, reducing the budget deficit, and lifting energy subsidies. According to a former presidential aide, "The IMF wanted to push Mubarak to add burdens on poorer classes through currency devaluation and a commitment to a certain margin of debts."[14]

Indeed, Mubarak did show a willingness to consider some reforms. At the same time, as Bessma Momani indicates, officials refused to implement any measures that would increase the price of basic goods, citing the potential "social and political unrest that could result from rapid implementation of the suggested IMF reforms."[15] In the spring of 1987, the IMF and Egypt reached agreement on a $327 million Stand-By Loan. Although this agreement retained many onerous elements, the IMF tempered some conditions in response to pressure from Washington. Thanks to the agreement, the Paris Club rescheduled payment of Egypt's $7 billion debt.

The net effect of IMF pressure on Egyptian economic policy around the time of the 1987 agreement was a series of selectively implemented reforms. The government relaxed restrictions on private sector imports of food products, lifted some tariffs, imposed a new sales tax, and increased the price of rice and cotton.[16] It also committed to a partial revision of the exchange rate and increasing interest rates, although it did so to lower levels than the IMF initially requested.[17]

In managing pressure for economic liberalization, the government appeared keen to avoid provoking the ire of the Nasserist social pact's beneficiaries. For example, when raising the price of some basic commodities by 20 percent in accordance with the 1987 agreement, the government also moved to raise the salaries of state and public sector employees by the same percentage.[18] This move was in keeping with a strategy followed throughout the 1980s and 1990s, offsetting price hikes with raises and bonuses for state employees to avert the wrath of these valuable constituents.[19]

Despite the Paris Club agreement to reschedule Egypt's debt repayment, the government's economic woes persisted. Unable to reduce spending in accordance with the IMF agreement's terms, the government began printing money to finance its deficit,[20] thereby producing unprecedented rates of inflation.[21] The accumulation of annual budget deficits increased pressures to confront the issue that Sadat had failed to address decisively—that is, the fate of a public sector that continued to incur burdensome losses.

Although Mubarak had famously pledged that the public sector would remain untouched, the deepening of Egypt's fiscal crisis, coupled with the pressures of international financial institutions (IFIs), made fulfilling that promise impossible.[22] Thus in 1986, in an effort to enhance public sector efficiency, the government proposed a bill reducing workers' bonuses and share of profits. Because of strong opposition from labor leaders inside the Egyptian Trade Union Federation (ETUF), the draft law was eventually withdrawn. During the same period, minister of tourism and privatization enthusiast Fouad Sultan led efforts to privatize the management of state-owned hotels. The Mubarak regime eventually opted to curtail its highly controversial privatization drive, declining to conclude a number of high-profile sales of large hotel resorts.[23]

By the late 1980s, strong domestic and international pressure caused the president's resistance to the sale of public sector assets to wane. The government's economic situation was precarious. Unable to repay its growing debts, Egypt could not secure sufficient credit to purchase wheat on the international market and was facing the real threat of bankruptcy. In fact, after failing to service its military debts to the United States in 1989, Egypt was threatened with suspension of the country's annual $2 billion aid package.[24] In addition, Egypt's agreement with the IMF collapsed in late 1987 after the government defaulted on its pledge to reduce the deficit, enact tax reform, and liberalize trade.[25] Because of the government's failure to implement IMF recommendations, the U.S. government and the World Bank withheld some aid payments. In addition, the Paris Club began rejecting Egypt's requests to reschedule debt payments.[26]

The Egyptian government faced a much more aggressive negotiating partner when it resumed talks with the IMF in 1988. IMF officials rejected mere stabilization measures, insisting on deeper structural adjustments. Probably aware of Egypt's weak negotiating position, the IMF demanded spending reductions that encompassed eliminating subsidies, dissolving nonprofitable state enterprises, enacting tax reform, raising interest rates, devaluing the currency, and unifying the exchange rate.[27] Because of this immense pressure, the regime could no longer avoid public discussion of privatizing state-owned enterprises.

In mid-1989, not long after assuring skeptics that the public sector was untouchable, Mubarak's position on the question of privatization changed: he dropped his opposition to the sale of loss-incurring state-owned enterprises. Later that year, just as Prime Minister Atef Sedky repeated Mubarak's pledge to protect public sector assets in a parliamentary address, the ruling party started deliberating privatization measures. Meanwhile, state-controlled media began openly discussing the fate of public sector companies incurring massive losses.[28]

The Egyptian government laid the groundwork for a bold privatization drive well before 1991, when it signed its infamous agreement with the IMF and adopted Law 203/1991 authorizing the sale of public sector companies. In 1989, it passed Law 230/1989, which sought to stimulate foreign investment by authorizing foreign ownership of real estate.[29] By mid-1990, the government had formed a task force to privatize companies owned by local governments and had begun selling assets in the tourism sector.[30] Additionally, between 1989 and 1990, the government undertook a host of measures designed to reduce IMF concerns about the slow pace of reform. It proposed a budget that cut the deficit to 10 percent of GDP, increased interest rates, and cut subsidies on the price of electricity, cigarettes, and a variety of consumer goods, including bread.[31]

Nevertheless, Egypt's negotiations with the IMF remained tense, as the fund still demanded a larger hike in interest rates to match the rate of inflation, unification of the exchange rate, and more drastic cuts in subsidies and other government spending. The Gulf crisis of August 1990 and Cairo's participation in the U.S.-led coalition to expel Iraqi forces from Kuwait significantly improved Egypt's negotiating position. Washington pressured the IMF to conclude a loan agreement with Egypt and lobbied the Paris Club to forgive some of the country's debts.[32]

Although still managed and constrained, the process of economic liberalization gathered new momentum in the aftermath of these developments, as the government aggressively dismantled the fundamental elements of the Nasserist social pact. By 1990, the government had effectively suspended the policy of guaranteeing employment to college graduates.[33] In 1992, the government announced it would remove rent controls on agricultural lands within five years.[34] Even the public sector became fair game. In June 1991, the government passed the aforementioned Law 203, which permitted the sale of 314 companies, or 70 percent of the state-owned industrial sector.[35] In 1996, Presidential Decree No. 341 committed the government to relinquishing its shares in joint ventures.[36] By 2002, 190 firms had been privatized, and just two years later, Prime Minister Ahmed Nazif's business–dominated government implemented a more far-reaching series of liquidations.[37]

Law 203 diluted worker representation on company management boards and afforded managers of privatized firms greater discretion to determine workers' wages and benefits. As the law constituted an assault on labor rights long established in law, it inspired fierce opposition from ETUF members.[38] The government, which had frequently asserted that privatization would never undermine labor rights, now claimed that Law 203 forbade owners of newly privatized firms from undertaking mass layoffs.

In practice, however, the implementation of Law 203 did result in massive layoffs and significant cuts in benefits and wages.[39] Left to the mercy of profit seekers, workers at privatized firms lost many of the protections they once enjoyed. Ultimately, workers remaining in the public sector were also stripped of these protections. In 2003, the government adopted the Unified Labor Law (Law 12/2003), which authorized public sector enterprises to hire contracted workers (also known as "temporary workers") for an indefinite period. Temporary workers were not eligible for trade union membership and had no protection from arbitrary dismissal. Previously, the state could not extend such contracts beyond a fixed term, after which it could retain such employees only by awarding them permanent positions providing full benefits and protections. Law 12 effectively ended this requirement, thereby granting public sector managers a means to strip many of their workers of long-standing rights.[40] In simple terms, the state was phasing out jobs that came with meaningful protections, now increasingly replaced by contract positions providing far fewer rights. The law's detrimental effects were revealed in the wake of Mubarak's downfall in 2011, when temporary government workers protested frequently in demand of full-time employment and its accompanying benefits.

All these turbulent developments raise a question: How did the political opposition react when the state toppled the pillars of the Nasserist social pact? This process of economic liberalization proceeded against the backdrop of a transformed political arena. On one hand, dominant Islamist currents, epitomized by the Muslim Brotherhood, brought issues of national identity to the forefront of political debates. These issues competed with, and detracted from the salience of distributive conflicts, especially those engendered by economic liberalization.

On the other hand, the ascendancy of Islamist currents contributed to the transformation of the left—as exemplified by Al-Tagammu—into protagonists in culture wars and identity conflicts. This development promoted an alliance between the ruling party and the leaders of the new "cultural left" that Al-Tagammu came to embody, all in the service of countering Islamist influence. The irony, of course, is that leftist leaders entered the regime's embrace and modified their criticism of the government on the eve of new economic reforms eroding the Nasserist social pact upheld by the left for decades.

In other words, issues of economic reform and its costs were increasingly sidelined in party politics and national debates.[41] The following section examines these dynamics by analyzing the crowding-out effects produced by the Muslim Brotherhood's engagement in national politics and the legislative arena.

THE MUSLIM BROTHERHOOD AND CROWDING OUT

The Muslim Brotherhood constituted a serious challenge for Mubarak during the initial years of his presidency. Many of the group's affiliates were arrested before and after Sadat's assassination, and one of its revered figureheads, Kamal Al-Sananiri, died in police custody.[42] Tensions subsided once Mubarak released imprisoned Brotherhood activists and permitted the return of exiled movement leaders who had fled in the wake of the September 1981 crackdown.

Unlike his predecessor, Mubarak conducted his relations with the Muslim Brotherhood behind closed doors.[43] Yet he left the movement ample space to operate and remain active. This permissive environment (detailed in chapter 3) enabled the group to expand its public presence and to score notable victories in professional syndicate, university faculty club, and student union elections. In the 1984 legislative election, eight of seventeen Muslim Brotherhood candidates running on Al-Wafd Party list won seats in parliament.[44]

Regime relations with all opposition forces deteriorated somewhat in the late 1980s. Interior Minister Zaki Badr, known for his flagrantly confrontational approach to opposition parties, was responsible for much of this acrimony. While Badr's security forces attempted to intimidate and disrupt the Brotherhood, the state did not prevent the movement from increasing its representation in parliament.[45] Through an alliance with the SLP and the Liberal Socialists Party (LSP), the Brotherhood secured thirty-eight seats in the 1987 election, becoming the largest opposition bloc in the legislature.[46] Shortly thereafter, the group endorsed the candidacy of Mubarak for a second presidential term.[47]

As the Muslim Brotherhood made its presence increasingly felt in public life, the political landscape was undergoing significant changes. The dynamics of the crowding-out process underlay these shifts. The Brotherhood's expanding role in national politics elevated the significance of national identity issues. As a result, distributive issues, especially those shaped by economic liberalization measures, lost salience in national debates. This effect was evident in the changing platforms of parties collaborating with the Muslim Brotherhood as well as in the policies Brotherhood MPs prioritized in parliament between 1987 and 1990.

Shifting Programmatic Priorities of Muslim Brotherhood Allies

The crowding-out effects of the Muslim Brotherhood's 1980s political engagement were visible in the platforms of political parties then allied with the movement. The policy changes these parties experienced as a result of collaborating with the Brotherhood exemplify one aspect of crowding out, the increasing salience of national identity.

One revealing case is that of Al-Wafd Party, which entered into an electoral alliance with the Muslim Brotherhood in 1984. In contrast with the party's 1977 official platform, the program Al-Wafd adopted in the 1984 legislative election displayed a deeper interest in the implementation of Sharia. Unlike the 1977 program, which designated Sharia as "a fundamental source of legislation," the 1984 edition affirmed Sharia as "the principal source of legislation." Additionally, the 1984 version contained a new section outlining a vision for the role of religion in public life, advocating for greater media promotion of Islamic norms and arguing for increasing religious instruction in public schools.[48] By contrast, the 1977 program limited its discussion of Sharia to a few sentences at the end of a section about political liberties.[49]

For some longtime supporters of the party, the new religious dimension in Al-Wafd's program and the party's alliance with the Muslim Brotherhood were at odds with Al-Wafd's historical commitment to national unity and to an inclusive state that did not discriminate on the basis of religion. Although Wafidist leaders supporting the alliance pledged that it did not alter the party's core values, the evidence suggests otherwise. Consider, for example, the account of Salah Abu-Ismail, then an Islamist affiliate of Al-Wafd and the chief interlocutor brokering the party's alliance with the Brotherhood. According to Abu-Ismail, just as the alliance between the Brotherhood and Al-Wafd was taking form, he demanded that Wafdist leader Fouad Serageddin issue a statement distancing the party from the "secular" ideas some of its members advocated in public. "Otherwise," he warned, "Islamists would have nothing to do with Al-Wafd." Eventually, Serageddin obliged, issuing a statement affirming that Al-Wafd supported the implementation of Sharia in accordance with the constitution and that it did not advocate secularism.[50] Shortly thereafter, Al-Wafd released an electoral program reiterating these positions in detail. In other words, Al-Wafd purposely reconfigured its party platform to accommodate an alliance with the Muslim Brotherhood.

Arguably, the effects of the Muslim Brotherhood's expanding political engagement were greater within the SLP than in Al-Wafd. Changes in both parties' platforms during the 1980s evidenced the increasing salience of national identity. The SLP's experience, however, demonstrated that the

elevation of national identity issues was accompanied by the diminish-
ment of economic ones.

During the 1987 electoral campaign, the SLP, in conjunction with the LSP,
formed an alliance with the Muslim Brotherhood. This electoral list ("The
Islamic Alliance") ran on the slogan "Islam is the solution" and prioritized
implementing the principles of Sharia in the political and social spheres.[51]

As detailed later, the SLP's alliance with the Muslim Brotherhood, and
the party's embrace of Islamist policies during the 1980s, alienated many
of its high-ranking members. Pro-Islamist SLP leaders insisted that promoting Sharia had always been a core element of their agenda. Critics
countered that such claims distorted the party's history. They further
charged that the SLP's alliance with the Brotherhood upended the party's
policy priorities and disregarded its fundamental principles.

Evidence suggests that the SLP's 1987 alliance did alter the party's professed political agenda. The alliance elevated concerns about the state's
religious character at the expense of the distributive justice issues that
once anchored the SLP's platform. As table 5.1 indicates, the 1987 election

TABLE 5.1 SOCIALIST LABOR PARTY PROGRAMS ORDER OF PRIORITIES

ORDER	FOUNDING PROGRAM	1984 ELECTION PROGRAM	1987 ELECTION PROGRAM
1	Creating a suitable environment for work and production (democracy, virtue, integrity, and accountability)	Improving economic conditions	Reforming the political system
2	Developing the national economy	Addressing popular grievances	Implementing Sharia
3	Achieving social justice	Purging the country of corruption and establishing a virtuous society	Promoting virtue and eliminating sources of corruption
4	Facilitating the provision of social services to citizens	Reforming the political system by establishing a just democracy	Reforming culture and media
5	Preserving Egypt's image as a great civilization	Rebuilding Egypt's Arab and foreign relations	Addressing popular grievances
6	Realizing liberation and unity	N/A	Pursuing economic development
7	Ensuring national security and foreign relations	N/A	N/A

Source: Reproduced and translated from Awad and Tawfiq, Al-Ikhwan al-Muslimun, 310.

platform downgraded economic and social issues. The party's founding and 1984 programs made economy-related issues their first two priorities, whereas economic development was demoted to the sixth priority in the 1987 program. Notably, the 1987 version set political reform and the implementation of Sharia as its first and second priorities, respectively, and moved the section on "addressing popular grievances" from the second to the fifth priority. Most relevantly, the 1987 program contained two sections absent from previous editions, one on implementing Sharia and the other on culture and media. The latter section called for aligning the content of cultural and media production with religious norms. It is telling that much of the SLP's 1987 program echoed the priorities articulated in the Muslim Brotherhood's open letter to the president published that same year (discussed later). The two documents' similarities strongly suggest that the Brotherhood was behind changes in the SLP's programmatic priorities.[52]

The Legislative Priorities of the Muslim Brotherhood

Crowding out was also apparent in the actions of Muslim Brotherhood members of parliament (MPs) between 1987 and 1990. As the largest opposition bloc in the legislature, the Brotherhood played a major role in setting the tone and priorities of national political debates at a point in which the country confronted intense domestic and international pressure for economic liberalization. Thus, an analysis of its affiliates' parliamentary conduct illuminates the policy issues that the group helped prioritize (or deprioritize) during this critical period.

The evidence indicates that in national public policy debates, the movement privileged issues of national identity, paying particular attention to the state's compliance with Islamic values and directives. Meanwhile, it devoted little attention to issues of wealth distribution or to the government's efforts to erode the Nasserist social pact. In other words, the Muslim Brotherhood's participation in the 1987 parliament displayed the mechanisms of crowding out.

Muslim Brotherhood in the 1987 Legislature

An analysis of Muslim Brotherhood–affiliated MPs' legislative priorities can follow many possible approaches. One obvious approach is to examine all their documented interventions in parliament to assess their contributions to various policy issues. Such an approach might be useful for assessing the Brotherhood's position on particular issues.[53] Yet for the purpose of determining the relative significance the group attributed to various policy fields, this approach falls short. For example, it fails to distinguish between Brotherhood MPs' interventions in debates they did not initiate and interventions they specifically made to raise issues the movement deemed significant. Put simply, the concern is not the Brotherhood MPs' responses to questions posed by others but, rather, to the questions they opted to pose and the order in which they presented them. Thus, one logical strategy is to focus on the laws proposed by the movement's MPs. While sound in theory, this approach is not feasible because Brotherhood-affiliated MPs did not introduce a single new law during the period in question.[54] A viable and appropriate approach employed in this study is to examine the oversight motions Brotherhood MPs initiated. Such motions seek to hold the government accountable by posing to cabinet ministers questions about specific policies and their implementation. This approach maintains exclusive focus on the Brotherhood MPs' agenda-setting actions, revealing the issues that had the highest priority to the movement.

The oversight motions Muslim Brotherhood MPs pursued in the 1987 parliament fall into the categories: questions, information requests, and interpellations. *Su'al* ("a question") is a general query submitted to a cabinet member regarding his/her ministry's policies and practices. *Talab ihatah* ("an information request") is an urgent query submitted to a cabinet member requiring a prompt response. Questions and information requests do not imply an accusation against the addressed cabinet member. In contrast, *istijwab* ("an interpellation") is a motion submitted for the purpose of holding a cabinet member (or members) accountable for suspected negligence, wrongdoing, or violations of law. An interpellation could potentially end with a vote of no confidence in a cabinet member or in the entire government. Table 5.2 provides a breakdown of all oversight motions that Muslim Brotherhood legislators submitted between fall 1987 and summer 1990.

During this period, Brotherhood MPs submitted fifty-seven questions (compared with twenty-five by Al-Wafd and thirty-five in total by both the SLP and LSP combined), ten information requests (compared with six by Al-Wafd and six in total by the SLP and LSP combined), and eleven interpellations (compared with eleven by Al-Wafd, and ten in total by the SLP and LSP combined).[55] Identifying the ministries to which Brotherhood motions were submitted provides important clues about the policy fields that held the most importance to the Brotherhood.

Brotherhood MPs directed more than half of their questions to the Ministries of Information, Culture, and Education, bodies tasked with administering cultural policies and supervising expressions of the state's religious identity. The highest number of information requests and interpellations went to the Ministry of Interior, which implements domestic security policies and manages the police. Together, ministries concerned with cultural issues and the Ministry of Interior received more than 60 percent of all questions, information requests, and interpellations. In other words, Brotherhood MPs focused their efforts on the cultural sphere and the conduct of domestic security agencies. Ministries tasked with economic responsibilities received three of the eleven interpellations Brotherhood MPs initiated; however, none of these motions was directed at the ministries tasked with setting the macroeconomic policies, such as the Ministry of Economy, Planning, or Finance.

One could argue that coding motions by ministry title or responsibility fails to capture the core topic of every intervention. For example, a motion submitted to the Ministry of Education does not necessarily entail cultural affairs, and a motion submitted to the Ministry of Manpower may have little to do with the economy. Others might argue that the data set is too heterogenous or that it includes motions expressing parochial concerns that reveal little about the Brotherhood's public policy priorities. Such parochial motions include those addressing the local needs of constituents and those protesting specific Ministry of Interior actions affecting Brotherhood affiliates and supporters.

To address these concerns, the last set of rows in Table 5.2 ("Non-Interior Motions") excludes motions directed to the Ministry of Interior and places the remainder in either of two categories: national and regional/local. The category "National Motions" includes those displaying an interest in promoting religiously informed norms (or "Value-Based"), as well as those addressing the distribution of state resources and benefits.[56] According to this coding scheme, "Value-Based" motions constituted more than half of the nationally oriented questions, information requests, and interpellations the Muslim Brotherhood MPs submitted. Distribution-based motions

TABLE 5.2 BREAKDOWN OF LEGISLATIVE OVERSIGHT MOTIONS SUBMITTED BY
MUSLIM BROTHERHOOD MPS, 1987–1990

TYPE	MINISTER	QUESTIONS	INFORMATION REQUESTS	INTERPELLATIONS
Cultural Ministries	Information	17	0	0
	Culture	8	0	1
	Education	6	1	1
	Total	**31**	**1**	**2**
	% of total motions	**54.39**	**10**	**18.18**
Security Ministries	Interior	5	7	5
	% of total motions	**8.77**	**70**	**45.45**
Economy Ministries	Subsidies	3	0	0
	Insurance and Social Affairs	0	0	2
	Manpower and Immigration	1	0	0
	Industry	2	0	1
	Total	**6**	**0**	**3**
	% of total motions	**10.53**	**0**	**27.27**
Social Services Ministries	Transport	3	1	0
	Water Resources and Irrigation	5	0	0
	Housing	4	0	0
	Health	0	1	0
	State for Administrative Affairs	2	0	0
	Total	**14**	**2**	**0**
	% of total motions	**24.56**	**20**	**0**
Other	Prime Minister	1	0	1
	% of total motions	**1.75**	**0**	**9.09**
	Total	**57**	**10**	**11**
Noninterior Motions*	Regional/Local	10	1	0
	National	42	2	6
	Value-Based	23	1	4
	Value-based motions as % of National motions	54.76	50	66.67

Source: Awad and Tawfiq, *Al-Ikhwan al-Muslimun*.
*Coded and calculated by author.

constituted less than a quarter of all nationally oriented questions and none of the information requests or interpellations in the same category.

The evidence shows that the Muslim Brotherhood's interventions in the 1987 parliament focused on domestic security bodies and government institutions regulating official expressions of national identity. Consistent with this study's understanding of "crowding out," ministries responsible for economic and social policies received relatively less attention. Similar findings arise when focusing exclusively on nationally oriented motions, which exhibited greater interest in promoting religious values than in contesting the distribution of resources and benefits. A closer look at the substance of these motions and the debates they instigated reinforces this conclusion.

The remainder of this section provides an overview of major policy issues Muslim Brotherhood MPs raised between 1987 and 1990. Tables 5.3, 5.4, and 5.5 (at the end of this section) describe Brotherhood-affiliated legislators' questions, information requests, and interpellations, respectively.[57] These motions, along with the debates they raised, highlight the crowding-out effects of Islamist incorporation policies.

Two prefatory observations are in order. First, contrary to the conventional image of a powerless opposition trapped within an authoritarian legislature, Muslim Brotherhood lawmakers did in fact influence the tone and content of parliamentary debates. Whenever relevant policy issues arose, they were able to overcome procedural barriers and make their voices heard. Second, Brotherhood MPs' most frequent and intense battles centered on the state's compliance with Sharia, as well as police violations, especially ones committed against the group's members and supporters. Less attention was afforded to the effects of state economic policies on distributive justice.

The Economy and Social Policy

Muslim Brotherhood MPs' oversight motions concerning the economy and social policies were relatively limited in scope and did not evince the same degree of interest as motions addressed to cultural ministries or police and security agencies.[58] For example, when Egypt's negotiations with IFIs were receiving extensive media coverage, none of the Brotherhood's motions addressed national economic concerns. Nonetheless, some of the

Brotherhood MPs' interventions displayed awareness of economic issues like inquiries about food shortages and the losses incurred by a state-owned company. As detailed next, however, such issues were pursued far less aggressively than security service abuses or issues of national identity. In fact, some of the motions submitted to ministries with economic responsibilities were not inspired solely by economic concerns. For example, a question submitted to the minister of industry argued that assigning female employees long shifts at textile factories could undermine family cohesion by keeping women away from their homes for long durations of time. Similarly, an interpellation addressing the Ministry of Insurance and Social Affairs expressed concerns that inadequate state oversight of nongovernmental organizations might be enabling morally unsound conduct.[59] In other words, although these motions were addressed to "economic affairs ministries," their primary concern was the preservation of cultural norms. Finally, most Brotherhood legislative motions addressed to social services ministries, raised local—rather than national—issues like the inadequate provision of services in certain towns and villages.[60]

In addition to oversight motions, Muslim Brotherhood MPs engaged with economic issues in the legislative chamber's periodic responses to government reports. Collectively, these interventions did not always display a unified vision, which conforms to previous observations (see chapter 2) about the ambiguity of the Brotherhood's stated positions on economic issues. For example, some Brotherhood MPs called for higher wages and greater rights for public sector workers,[61] whereas others warned that raising wages could increase the budget deficit and result in inflationary spending.[62]

When Brotherhood lawmakers collectively adopted clear positions on economic issues, they rarely contested the bases of the government's economic liberalization program.[63] If anything, they encouraged such liberalization. For example, Mamoun Al-Houdaiby called for removing state barriers to private investment by Egyptians living abroad.[64] Saif Al-Islam Hassan Al-Banna proposed the sale of some public sector companies to finance investments without resorting to "Islamically objectionable" interest-bearing loans.[65]

Brotherhood legislators were vocal in criticizing a bill proposing to regulate the activities of Islamic investment companies. Al-Houdaiby objected to a provision of the bill mandating a minimum and maximum capital requirement for such companies, arguing that the measure would discourage investment.[66] As noted in chapter 2, Brotherhood networks and economic interests had close ties to companies affected by the law in question.

Police Transgressions

In contrast to their relative ambivalence to many economic issues, Muslim Brotherhood MPs were aggressive in protesting police abuses and scrutinizing state compliance with religious traditions in cultural, media, and educational spheres. Many of the Muslim Brotherhood's oversight motions sought to expose and condemn the Ministry of Interior's repressive tactics or the actions of notorious Minister Zaki Badr. One memorable showdown occurred in November 1987, when Muslim Brotherhood MPs Mukhtar Nouh and Mohamed Mahfouz Helmy took Badr to task in two interpellations. The MPs presented evidence of police torture and forced confessions, and condemned security force intrusions into mosques. Badr countered that torture allegations were often fabricated and that security personnel entered mosques only when "radical elements" or weapons were concealed within.

The exchange grew heated, as Badr repeatedly insinuated that the lawmakers submitting the interpellations were sympathizers of "violent Islamic groups." The showdown ended with Brotherhood MPs proposing an unsuccessful motion of no confidence in the minister.[67] This story illustrates how decisively and forcefully the Brotherhood could act when addressing issues of central concern like police and security force abuses.

The Muslim Brotherhood repeatedly challenged Badr's policies, eroding his credibility and perhaps contributing to his dismissal in early 1990.[68] On February 19, 1989, the Brotherhood ambushed him with three questions, four information requests, and one interpellation. Most of the motions alleged security force violations of citizens' rights at police stations and in the course of so-called counterterrorism operations. In an emotional response, Badr, yet again, accused the Brotherhood of supporting terrorists before launching animated, personal attacks on his critics.[69] The session ended with a memorable physical altercation between Badr and Wafdist MP Talaat Raslan. As a result of this incident, Raslan was ejected from the chamber and Badr subjected the entire assembly to a profane diatribe.

Brotherhood members and supporters were frequent victims of the police abuses in question. Thus, it is unsurprising that its MPs' legislative battles with the Ministry of Interior were well informed and coordinated, as in the session just described.[70] In March 1988, the Brotherhood's parliamentary bloc and its allies reacted angrily to a police officer's alleged assault on Brotherhood MP Essam El-Erian.[71] In yet another attempt to put Badr in the hot seat, the Brotherhood submitted three information requests and a petition for an interpellation.[72]

Sharia and Expressions of National Identity

Although Muslim Brotherhood MPs' interactions with the interior minister were quite adversarial, they went even further when engaging with the issue of state policy and Sharia. The conformity of state institutions to the principles of Sharia, per Article 2 of the constitution, was a pervasive concern for Muslim Brotherhood MPs.[73] Mamoun Al-Houdaiby, then spokesperson for the Brotherhood's parliamentary bloc, designated Sharia as "the most important issue for us," preceding other "important" concerns like greater political freedoms and the abolition of the emergency law.[74] Thus, the impulse to enact Sharia was central to many Muslim Brotherhood–led initiatives that addressed a range of government agencies and policy spheres.[75] The issues in question ranged from interest-based banking to the production of alcoholic beverages in state-owned enterprises and the lack of "prayer breaks" for government employees.[76]

Because Brotherhood lawmakers' efforts aimed to make Egypt's social climate amenable to the implementation of Sharia, they devoted considerable attention to officials responsible for public education, the media, and cultural production.[77] One such official was the minister of education (and later speaker of parliament) Ahmed Fathi Sorour, who was the target of MP Mukhtar Nouh's May 1989 interpellation. Nouh complained that public school curricula emphasized Egypt's Pharaonic history at the expense of its Islamic identity. Brotherhood MPs also pressed Sorour to address reports that Islamists were excluded from teaching positions as a matter of policy.[78]

Muslim Brotherhood MPs displayed remarkable unity and coordination when addressing the political aspects of Egyptian media. On April 2, 1988, seventeen Brotherhood legislators (almost half of their parliamentary bloc) submitted questions to Minister of Information Safwat Al-Sherif demanding he disclose the content of public television programming scheduled for the month of Ramadan. The incident was noteworthy, as it featured the greatest number of Brotherhood MPs participating in an oversight effort during the 1987 parliament. Significantly, it was also the only occasion in which four of these seventeen lawmakers submitted an oversight motion during their term in office.[79] In other words, the prospect of broadcasting religiously objectionable programming on public television was the only issue that motivated these four otherwise-passive MPs to pose questions to the government.

These motions came at a time when Muslim Brotherhood leaders were demanding the elimination of what was considered to be risqué Ramadan programming that undermined efforts to cultivate piety during the holy month. In addition to its religious significance, Ramadan is also renowned for the variety and quality of its television productions. During this era, a perennial favorite of Ramadan programming was the prime-time musical series *Fawazir*, which featured pop culture icon Sherihan. According to Muslim Brotherhood legislators, Sherihan's suggestive dancing and immodest costumes not only offended conservative religious sensibilities but also distracted many Muslims from practicing nighttime Ramadan prayers and Quranic recitations known as *tarawih*. Thus, a long-standing demand of Muslim Brotherhood was rescheduling broadcasts of *Fawazir* to a time that did not conflict with the practice of *tarawih*.

Information Minister Al-Sherif responded to such critiques rather defensively. On one occasion he asserted that he had overseen significant changes in public television programming content, introducing a wide variety of religious programming. Al-Sherif further noted that many inappropriate scenes, like those featuring kissing, had been deleted from films broadcast on state television. He also claimed that, out of respect for the public's religious feelings, shows airing during Ramadan were modified under his leadership.[80]

State television programming's compliance with mainstream values at any time of the year remained a pressing issue for Muslim Brotherhood lawmakers. Their interventions on the subject were uncharacteristically blunt, forceful, and performative. This was certainly the case with MP Hassan Al-Gamal's January 1989 response to the government address: "Are dancing and [moral] looseness among the traits of good media? |....| The minds setting television [programming] are clearly imported and are not Egyptian ones, because Egyptian minds would have known what Egyptian morals look like. We are descending into the illicit, my brethren in Islam."[81]

The Brotherhood's abiding focus on media was grounded in the belief that a precondition for the establishment of a so-called Islamic society was the use of media and other cultural institutions to instill religious norms and lead the public by example. Then MP (and later general guide) Mohamed Mahdi Akef articulated this line of reasoning during a parliamentary session:

As you can imagine, the *tarbawiyya* [educational] process needs the public, the mosque, the Ministry of Information, and the Ministry of Culture. If we all set a single guiding principle on which we could cooperate to finally realize a sound educational process, the result would be great. But what the Ministry of Education is doing is being destroyed by the public's perversion and by the Ministries of Information and Culture. It really is a strange thing, because I wonder, why don't we all agree on one philosophy and admit that Islam's Sharia is the sound law that could achieve this goal for us. I am with those who say that Sharia is not a law to be enacted, but rather a behavior. Sharia is ethics [. . . .] The government must announce that it will implement Sharia, and then we can enact it behaviorally in the confines of government so that this behavior can be transferred to the people by example.[82]

The vital importance the Muslim Brotherhood attached to cultural institutions was also evident in their lawmakers' aggressive contestation of Ministry of Culture policies. MP Hassan Al-Husseiny's interpellation on April 2, 1989, was a case in point. Al-Husseiny's interpellation, during which he provided R-rated descriptions of films' erotic content, revealed the lengths to which Brotherhood lawmakers would go to influence state-sponsored cultural production. No other Brotherhood-led legislative battle—including those probing the government's handling of economic and social issues—featured such bold, sensationalist tactics.

Al-Husseiny's interpellation, which was accompanied by three questions submitted by fellow Brotherhood MPs, addressed films screened in conjunction with the annual Cairo International Film Festival. At the time, films screened at international festivals were not subjected to ordinary government censorship. Thus, some of these films retained nudity, sexual content, or other religiously offensive scenes. Muslim Brotherhood legislators took Minister of Culture Farouk Hosni to task over this issue, demanding that films with themes contradicting religious sensibilities not be screened in any venue.

Speaking for more than forty minutes, Al-Husseiny complained that the films the official censorship bureau deemed inappropriate for public viewing were nevertheless being shown at the Cairo Film Festival:

> This interpellation concerns the Minister of Culture's approval, verbally and in writing through the first undersecretary of the Ministry of Culture, to allow forty movies to play in public theaters during the eleventh Cairo Film Festival in November 1987, despite the objections of the censorship authority to these films. Among the five hundred films screened at the festival, I will present copies of the censorship authority's reports | . . .| for some of them are examples of films that have raised the ire of all those who care about morality and Islam. Yet dozens of these films, which were watched by more than two hundred thousand young men and women according to statistics published in the official festival bulletins, contain distasteful stories, morbid, valueless ideas, hardcore sex scenes, violence, and mockery. The most serious of these films contained mockery of God and his prophets and mocked Christian clergy and symbols of the Islamic religion.[83]

Al-Husseiny adopted this confrontational and provocative stance to embarrass the minister of culture. Quite meticulously, he detailed the objectionable content of movies screened at the festival, prompting an unusually heated debate in parliament:

> The first film: in the censorship authority's report on the movie "The Veiled Man," the censor says, "The film is sympathetic to Christians and tries to portray Lebanese Muslims who live in France in a very negative light." Prayers and recitals of the Quran were exploited by the film in the worst possible ways, and that in itself is a transgression against Islam and is sufficient grounds for rejecting [the request for] a screening license | . . . .| and from the censor's description of the film's scenes | . . . .| "one girl completely naked in the bathroom. Two bare chested girls jump in a round pool."[84]

As Al-Husseiny graphically described the films' objectionable scenes, fellow MPs shouted objections at Speaker of Parliament Rifaat Al-Mahgoub. Despite the uproar and persistent pleas that Al-Mahgoub stop Al-Husseiny's long (and detailed) account of several films' adult content, the MP continued:

> The content that aroused your sense of shame and anger would have been better not displayed in front of the nation's youth. It was presented to the wise ones of the nation and aroused their resentment. How could one display two Muslims men praying in an incorrect way . . . a man who is completely naked . . . and a woman lying down and bathing naked while a man is kissing her body . . . And listen to this: two women completely naked playing in the snow while their genitals are showing. A man lying on the ground and a woman sitting on him as they are having sex. All this was presented to the *ummah*: a girl with a naked posterior running. A girl nude from her back rinsing in the dark; the boy recounts in his own mind the scene of the two women. This is really disgusting.[85]

At this point, fellow lawmakers were standing in protest and demanding Al-Mahgoub put an end to Al-Husseiny's ribald presentation. Al-Mahgoub continually pleaded with the MP to stop, noting the irony of Al-Husseiny effectively screening the very films he wished to ban. Al-Husseiny, however, persisted in his tirade:

> A Swedish film with English subtitles entitled "Amorosa" is set in the first half of this century. Agnes is the protagonist and central character. In order to save time, I will also mention the censorship authority's objections to this film. Hear the insults to the men of religion: an insane woman in torn clothing |. . . .| Two naked young women in the water kissing each other passionately. A lustful woman lies in bed moaning while a man embraces her. A brothel containing naked women. Sexual situations and people having sex |. . .| a man in priest's garments chases after Agnes. A lady dressed as a nun disrobes and shows her breasts.[86]

Soon, Al-Mahgoub's interruptions became more assertive, declaring that Al-Husseiny had made his point, eliminating the need for additional examples. Yet, Al-Husseiny powered through, reading graphic descriptions of film scenes screened at the festival. Eventually, almost forty minutes into his remarks, Al-Husseiny stated his formal objections:

> Tell me, dear sirs: For whose benefit does the state adopt this matter and accept the screening of movies that destroy respect for Christian clerics and Islamic clerics through the display of images of deviance? For whose benefit does the state adopt this? Why do we need these strange and outrageous arts? Why does Egypt need such destruction? We are not seeing people overcoming their own impure desires. We want arts that show people triumphing over their impure desires, people who get up when they fall, people who repent to God and ask for his forgiveness |. . . .| The state puts together advertisements and there are advertisements that are published—and that are permitted to be published—inviting people to watch these films and that contain descriptions of sex scenes to encourage people to go watch them. That is by all standards a crime and I am confident that this honorable legislature will adopt a position that would satisfy God Almighty on the day of the great judgment. And in all this are wrongdoings, as I mentioned to you, that violate Article 2 of the Constitution and Article 12 of the Constitution, that violate Law No. 430 of 1955, and also that violate Articles 1, 2, 3, and 4 of Law No. 95 of 1980.[87]

Al-Husseiny's invocation of Article 2 of the constitution, which stated that Sharia was the principal source of legislation, highlights the underlying logic of the Muslim Brotherhood's legislative strategy during the 1980s. Brotherhood oversight motions focused on holding the state to its word, as codified in the constitution, that Sharia was the law of the land. Thus, in the mid-1980s, one of the Brotherhood's first legislative efforts was an attempt to resume the work of the Sadat-era committee tasked with revising key legal codes to reconcile them with Sharia. MP Hassan Al-Gamal explained the logic behind this strategy:

> During the parliament headed by Dr. Sufi Abu-Taleb, specialized committees of scholars, legal counselors, and law professors drafted thirteen Islamic legal codes |. . . .| Our utmost wish—our firm intention—is to implement one code each year, for we do not believe in the sudden implementation of Sharia without first preparing society for it |. . . .| We believe

that it is necessary to understand this [fact] and carry out [this prepara-
tion] through various media like radio, television, and cinema, and that
this [preparation] must be included in the curricula of the colleges of law
and Sharia.[88]

Al-Gamal's explanation also sheds light on why the Brotherhood's parliamentary bloc concentrated its efforts on influencing the conduct and
policies of media, cultural, and educational institutions. These institutions
were deemed essential for the realization of a so-called true Islamic society. They provided a channel for promoting Islamic values in the public
sphere and building popular support for the implementation of Islamic
law in government and daily life.

The cultural and educational spheres were deemed more crucial to realizing this vision than the issues surrounding economic liberalization. Thus,
it is unsurprising that the latter issues were addressed with less urgency.
Furthermore, Brotherhood parliamentarians' relative inattention to economic and social issues is consistent with the movement's long-standing
practice of eschewing concrete stances on economic issues, as described in
chapter 2. This prioritization is also informed by a belief that the Islamiza-
tion of Egyptian society is a prerequisite to solving the country's economic
problems.

This vision is apparent in Muslim Brotherhood General Guide Mohamed
Hamed Abul-Nasr's February 1987 open letter to President Mubarak. The
letter, which appeared in the SLP's mouthpiece *Al-Shaab* several weeks
before the legislative election, outlined political and social reforms the
Muslim Brotherhood proposed to the president. The first half of the letter addressed Cairo's policy toward the Soviet occupation of Afghanistan
and the suffering of Palestinians under Israeli occupation. Abul-Nasr
urged the government to play a more prominent role in supporting the
Muslims enduring these hardships. The second half of the letter addressed
domestic policy issues. Abul-Nasr asserted that implementing the rulings
of Sharia in accordance with Article 2 of the constitution would solve all of
Egypt's existing problems:

I think, Mr. President, if we operationalize Article 2 of the Constitution,
we will find under the principles of Islamic Sharia and in the light of
Islam the best solutions to all of our current problems. This is not simply

a statement driven by religious passion. Rather it is a fact that is upheld by basic logic and supported by reasonable researchers in the East and the West and at the highest levels.[89]

Abul-Nasr's letter echoed an argument that dominated *Al-Dawa* magazine's editorial line throughout the 1970s, namely that Egypt's economic problems were fundamentally moral problems and, thus, soluble only through moral reform:

> This [economic] crisis cannot be attributed to some instability, for the conditions have been stable, praise be to God, for the last five years. Neither can it be attributed, as others claim, to the increase in population relative to the rate of increase in the gross national product | . . .| Rather, the crisis at its core is a moral crisis. As a result of the very low levels of virtue and the deterioration in morality, most [economic] producers have shifted away from useful production, because they found it to be difficult. This has caused honorable producers a crisis of confidence |. . . .| So whatever plans the government tries to put together and whatever policies and efforts they make will not lead to significant progress as long as the moral component is missing entirely from the nation, whether at the governmental or popular level.[90]

Abul-Nasr proposed two sets of recommendations to the problems he identified. The first entailed permitting greater political freedoms and liberties in accordance with the principles of Islam. Interestingly, many of these recommendations echoed the Brotherhood's parliamentary efforts to oppose police and security force repression. The second set of recommendations concerned measures promoting "virtue" inside state institutions. These included ensuring that the actions of public officials conform to the principles of Sharia, granting government employees sufficient breaks to carry out their prayers, and strengthening expressions of religious values in education, cultural institutions, and public media outlets.

This letter, in other words, summarized the priorities Brotherhood lawmakers would pursue in parliament: precedence was given to exposing and condemning police abuses of Islamist activists and encouraging expressions of religious identity in government policies and institutions. Economic and social problems were relegated to secondary status, as

TABLE 5.3 QUESTIONS SUBMITTED BY MUSLIM BROTHERHOOD MPS, 1987–1990

TYPE	MINISTER	MP	QUESTION	SESSION #	DATE
Cultural Ministries	Information	Essam El-Erian	Ministry's plans for scheduling Ramadan television programming to respect the holy month's sanctity	81	4/2/88
	Information	Mohamed Habib	Ministry's plans for Ramadan television programming that is consistent with the guidance and teachings of Islam	81	4/2/88
	Information	Hassan Al-Husseiny Mohamed Abdel-Rahman	Ministry's plans to schedule Ramadan television and radio programming that respects the holy month's sanctity	81	4/2/88
	Information	Bassouni Ibrahim Bassouni	Ministry's plans for programming during the month of Ramadan	81	4/2/88
	Information	Ahmed Al-Bes	Ministry's plans for programming during the month of Ramadan	81	4/2/88
	Information	Lasheen Abdullah Shanab	Ministry's plans for Ramadan television programming that respects the holy month's sanctity	81	4/2/88
	Information	Mostafa Al-Wardani	Ministry's plans for Ramadan television programming that respects the holy month's sanctity	81	4/2/88
	Information	Mukhtar Nouh	Ministry's plans to ban Ramadan programming content that is inconsistent with the month's sanctity	81	4/2/88
	Information	Mohamed Mohamed Al-Shishtany	Ministry's plans for Ramadan programming	81	4/2/88
	Information	Mohamed Fouad Abdel-Medguid Yousef	Ministry's plans for Ramadan television programming that respects the holy month's sanctity	81	4/2/88
	Information	Mohy Eissa	Ministry's plans to prevent the airing of Ramadan programming content contradicting Islamic values	81	4/2/88
	Information	Abdel-Aziz Ashri Hassan Ghobari	Ministry's preparations to broadcast suitable Ramadan programs consistent with Islamic Sharia	81	4/2/88
	Information	Bashir Ibrahim Abdel-Fattah	Ministry's plans to revise Ramadan programming to prevent content contradicting Islamic values	81	4/2/88
	Information	Ibrahim Abu-Taleb	Ministry's plans for Ramadan programming	81	4/2/88
	Information	Mohamed Abdelhakeem Abdel-Salam	Ministry's plans for programming during the month of Ramadan	81	4/2/88
	Information	Ezz Al-Arrab Fouad Hafiz	Ministry's plans for programming during the holy month of Ramadan	81	4/2/88
	Information	Mostafa Ramadan Mahgoub	Ministry's plans to ensure television and radio programming suitable for Ramadan	81	4/2/88
	Culture	Essam El-Erian	Rules governing screening of movies at the Cairo Film Festival, how they differ from general standards governing film screenings, and why the festival screened sexual content previously banned by censors	44	4/2/89

Culture	Mohamed Mahfouz Helmy	Why obscene films were screened at the eleventh Cairo Film Festival despite news reports that they were rejected by the censorship bureau	44	4/2/89
Culture	Bassouni Ibrahim Bassouni	Why the minister approved the screening of films that attack Islam (including the "Veiled Man") at the Cairo Film Festival	44	4/2/89
Culture	Mohy Eissa	The truth behind the screening of movies that contradict mainstream and Islamic values at the Cairo Film Festival of 1987 despite the objections of the censorship bureau, and the screening of obscene content at the 1988 festival	44	4/2/89
Culture	Ezz Al-Arab Fouad Hafiz	Regarding updates on the Pyramids renovation initiative in accordance with the experts' reports presented to the People's Assembly in 1977/1978	52	5/5/90
Culture	Hassan Al-Husseiny Mohamed Abdel-Rahman	The reasons why a piece fell from the shoulder of the Great Sphinx	40	3/6/90
Culture	Hassan Al-Husseiny Mohamed Abdel-Rahman	The reasons behind the fall of a piece from the shoulder of the Great Sphinx	52	5/5/90
Culture	Mohamed Ahmed Abdel-Hamid Al-Manafe	The truth behind reports of Islamic monuments in Cairo collapsing	40	3/6/90
Education	Hassan Al-Gamal	Regarding the Ministry's decision to hold only two sessions of elementary schools—are students formerly enrolled in the third session now enrolled in new schools or added to the frequently overcrowded first and second sessions	65	2/7/88
Education	Mostafa Al-Wardani	Why Al-Moneera Al-Gharbiya does not have elementary schools for boys and girls despite a population of over two hundred thousand people who lack public services	65	2/7/88
Education	Mohamed Ahmed Abdul-Hamid Nafee	Bases of policies for curriculum development and the portion devoted to religious education	73	3/6/88
Education	Essam El-Erian	Truth behind reports regarding the elimination of the university matching office and the Ministry's plans for eliminating illiteracy by the year 2000, and the specific date for voiding the accreditation of the English G.C.E degree	57	5/14/89
Education	Mohamed Mahfouz Helmy	Regarding the Ministry's plan for eliminating illiteracy	46	4/9/90
Education	Mohamed Fouad Abdel-Megiud Yousef	Regarding the efforts of the Ministry to fight illiteracy	46	4/9/90

(cont.)

TABLE 5.3 QUESTIONS SUBMITTED BY MUSLIM BROTHERHOOD MPS, 1987–1990 (CONT.)

TYPE	MINISTER	MP	QUESTION	SESSION #	DATE
Security Ministries	Interior	Essam El-Erian	Details about Ms. Hoda Abdel-Moneim's disappearance and flight from the country, and measures taken by the Ministry to arrest her	48	12/28/87
	Interior	Abdel-Hay Hussein Al-Faramawy	Reasons for the spread of drug addiction and the Ministry's plans to protect youth from this danger	76	3/19/88
	Interior	Mohamed Mahfouz Helmy	Regarding those detained in the Ain Shams events and police treatment of them	33	2/19/89
	Interior	Lasheen Abdullah Shanab	The truth behind events occurring in Ain Shams that led to the death of a police officer	33	2/19/89
	Interior	Mohy Eissa	Causes of tension between police personnel and residents, and the clashes in Ain Shams and Al-Minya that negatively impacted police-community relations	33	2/19/89
Economy Ministries	Subsidies	Mohamed Mahfouz Helmy	Reasons for market shortages of cooking oil and soap	71	2/23/88
	Subsidies	Hassan Al-Husseiny Mohamed Abdel-Rahman	Ministry's policies to provide cooking oil to the public and to eliminate black markets	71	2/23/88
	Subsidies	Lasheen Abdullah Shanab	Ministry's plans to address cooking oil and soap shortages in the market	71	2/23/88
	Manpower and Immigration	Mohamed Ahmed Abdel-Hamid Al-Manafe	Regarding the failure of some government agencies to comply with laws requiring 5 percent of all employees to be persons with special needs	42	3/24/90
	Industry	Mohamed Mahfouz Helmy	The reasons for employing female textile workers for three shifts despite that system's proven failure and its negative social impact	43	4/2/89
	Industry	Mohamed Habib	The reasons for transferring ten employees from Al-Mahalla Textile Factory to rural areas, including Aswan, Safaga, and Hurghada, despite a court ruling exonerating them of all charges	61	5/21/89
Social Services Ministries	Transportation	Mohamed Mahfouz Helmy	The reasons why engineers on the ship Anfoushi were detained in Hamburg, harming the reputation of the Egyptian fleet	68	2/20/88
	Transportation	Bassouni Ibrahim Bassouni	Reasons for the freight train crash between Shablikha and Banha on 12/25/1987, which caused many casualties	68	2/20/88
	Transportation	Bassouni Ibrahim Bassouni	Ministry's plan to meet increasing demand for telephone lines by connecting cables in the Semouha district of Alexandria	51	5/5/90

Ministry	Name	Description	Number	Date
Water Resources and Irrigation	Mohamed Mahfouz Helmy	Ministry's plans to manage agricultural water needs	42	12/12/87
Water Resources and Irrigation	Essam El-Erian	Regarding reports of Ethiopian plans to build a dam threatening Egypt's water resources	44	3/26/90
Water Resources and Irrigation	Mohamed Mahfouz Helmy	Regarding ministry measures to protect stream bridges from vandalism	16	1/2/90
Water Resources and Irrigation	Bassouni Ibrahim Bassouni	Government actions regarding reports that Ethiopia and Israel are coordinating plans to build dams affecting water flow to Egypt and the Sudan	44	3/26/90
Water Resources and Irrigation	Mohamed Mohamed Al-Shishtani	Regarding the suspicious relationship between Israel and Ethiopia and its potential impact on Egypt's water access	44	3/26/90
Housing	Abdel-Gaber Othman Mohamed Hassan	Reasons why the city of Malawi has no sewage system	51	4/17/89
Housing	Mohamed Habib	Regarding the failure to build a sewage system in regions in Assiut	55	5/19/90
Housing	Abdel-Gaber Othman Mohamed Hassan	Ministry's plans for sewage systems in Malawi	55	5/19/90
Housing	Mostafa Al-Wardani	Regarding the Ministry's plans for sewage systems in schools and residential buildings in the Wardan and Imbaba districts of Giza	55	5/19/90
State for Administrative Affairs	Hassan Al-Gamal	Regarding the Ministry's plans to fight pollution especially in the factory district south of Cairo	13	12/30/89
State for Administrative Affairs	Bassouni Ibrahim Bassouni	Regarding plans for protecting the waters of Lake Mariout in Alexandria from factory waste pollution	13	12/30/89
Prime Minister	Essam El-Erian	Reasons why the National Council for Treating and Countering Drug Addiction has not convened since the adoption of presidential decree number 480/1986 establishing it	76	3/19/88
Other				

Source: Compiled and translated from Awad and Tawfiq, *Al-Ikhwan al-Muslimun.*

TABLE 5.4 INFORMATION REQUESTS SUBMITTED BY MUSLIM BROTHERHOOD MPS, 1987–1990

TYPE	MINISTER	MP	INFORMATION REQUEST	SESSION #	DATE
Cultural Ministries	Education	Mohamed Fouad Abdel-Medguid Yousef	Regarding depriving teachers of their salaries and preventing them from teaching without disclosing reasons; or subjecting teachers to investigation without them committing acts warranting such action	67	5/14/89
Security Ministries	Interior	Mohy Eissa	Police assault on MP Essam El-Erian and their barring him from entering the city of Suez	79	3/21/88
	Interior	Mukhtar Nouh	Police assault on MP Essam El-Erian and their barring him from entering the city of Suez	79	3/21/88
	Interior	Mohamed Mahfouz Helmy	Police assault on MP Essam El-Erian and their barring him from entering the city of Suez	79	3/21/88
	Interior	Essam El-Erian	Central Security Forces beating residents of Al-Koum Al-Ahmar village in Al-Giza and vandalizing their property	33	2/19/89
	Interior	Hassan Al-Gamal	Police harassment in Cairo markets and shops, and the arrest, detention, and mistreatment of citizens with no evidence. What measures has the Ministry taken to prevent such illegal acts?	33	2/19/89
	Interior	Mostafa Ramadan Mahgoub	Regarding security forces' actions in Al-Minya that are unconstitutional and contrary to the law	33	2/19/89
	Interior	Mohamed Fouad Abdel-Medguid Yousef	Regarding the five-day siege that security forces imposed on the village of Abu Omar in Kafr Al-Sheikh on 11/6/1988, and the actions causing the death of a citizen and the arrest of twenty-two others	33	2/19/89
Social Services Ministries	Transportation	Abdel-Rahman Al-Sayid Ahmed Al-Rasd	The 12/25/1987 crash of freight train #1341 between Shablikha and Al-Aziziya that caused serious losses	68	2/20/88
	Health	Mohamed Mahfouz Helmy	The spread of meningitis	40	3/18/89

Source: Compiled and translated from Awad and Tawfiq, *Al-Ikhwan al-Muslimun*.

TABLE 5.5 INTERPELLATIONS SUBMITTED BY MUSLIM BROTHERHOOD MPS, 1987–1990

TYPE	MINISTER	MP	INTERPELLATION	SESSION #	DATE
Cultural Ministries	Culture	Hassan Al-Husseiny Mohamed Abdel-Rahman	Regarding the November 1987 screening of films at the Cairo Film Festival despite the censorship bureau's judgment that they were obscene, as well as the statement attributed to the minister of culture threatening the sacred beliefs of society	44	4/2/89
	Education	Mukhtar Nouh	Regarding the unconstitutional policy of making the appointment of university teaching assistants contingent upon security background checks; and regarding the declining profile of Islamic studies, Islamic history, and Islamic philosophy in some curricula	57	5/14/89
Security Ministries	Interior	Mukhtar Nouh	Regarding interior minister decisions that violate the constitution, the minister's abuse of power, and his refusal to implement court rulings and orders	33	2/19/89
	Interior	Mukhtar Nouh	Allegations of torture practiced on political detainees	41	11/30/87
	Interior	Mohamed Mahfouz Helmy	Police forces' violations of human rights	41	11/30/87
	Interior	Mukhtar Nouh	Police forces' unconstitutional practices	81	4/2/88
Economy Ministries	Industry	Bassouni Ibrahim Bassouni	Regarding financial losses at the Tersana Maritime Company	31	2/18/89
	Insurance and Social Affairs	Hassan Al-Gamal	Regarding Article 27 of Law 32/1965, which would eliminate oversight of nongovernmental organizations (NGOs), allowing some to engage in activities hostile to Egyptian society and its values	40	3/18/89
	Insurance and Social Affairs	Hassan Al-Gamal	Regarding violation of Article 27 of Law 32/1965 concerning NGOs, specifically the failure to provide mandated oversight, allowing some NGOs to engage in activities destructive to the values of Egyptian society	30	2/12/90
Other	Prime Minister	Lasheen Abdullah Shanab	Regarding the violation of Articles 2, 19, 84, and 85 of Law 103/1961 with respect to the reorganization of Al-Azhar and its subsidiary bodies, and the neglect of oversight responsibilities, the decline of Al-Azhar's moral and cultural influence	21	1/27/90
	Industry, Interior, Manpower, Prime Minister	Essam El-Erian	The prime minister's approval of the industry minister's decision to transfer employees of the Mahalla Textile Factory to other regions, as well as the interior minister's decision to detain the employees after they were freed by court order	61	5/21/89

Source: Compiled and translated from Awad and Tawfiq, *Al-Ikhwan al-Muslimun*.

restoring society's commitment to Islamic values would ensure their resolution.[91] In some ways Abul-Nasr's letter anticipated the crowding-out effects produced by the movement's political ascendancy, a significant factor contributing to Egypt's arrival at the politics of "more identity, less class."

CROWDING OUT, AL-TAGAMMU, AND THE RISE OF THE ANTI-ISLAMIST LEFT

Meanwhile, as the Brotherhood's electoral gains introduced unique debates and created new fault lines within the opposition, a complementary process was unfolding within Al-Tagammu. The reorientation of politics away from distributional conflicts and toward the question of national identity was a transformational shift for Al-Tagammu. Once the principal political force opposing de-Nasserization and chief advocate of economic liberalization's victims, it became the party of the intellectual left supporting the Mubarak regime's battle with political Islam. In this sense, crowding out captures the process by which important segments of the Egyptian left withdrew from sites of political contestation like factories, unions, universities, and public squares, opting instead to enter state-sponsored intellectual forums and cultural institutions.

A critical juncture in this process occurred in 1987, when Brotherhood members became the largest opposition bloc in parliament, instigating internal disagreements about Al-Tagammu's appropriate response to this development. Eventually, a pragmatist wing eager to cooperate with the ruling party in countering Islamist movements triumphed. Paradoxically, Al-Tagammu's capitulation to the Mubarak regime occurred just as the government was advancing economic liberalization policies inimical to the party's core mission. As Al-Tagammu was proceeding on a new set of priorities, privileging culture wars and national identity over the costs of economic liberalization, these policies had lost relevance for the party. In other words, identity conflicts crowded out the politics of distribution by provoking significant political realignments that neutralized opposition to economic liberalization policies. Herein lies the distinction between the Al-Tagammu Party that rejected Sadat's infitah and the one that supported the Mubarak regime until its final moments in February 2011.

The New President and Signs of Discord Inside Al-Tagammu

Mubarak's assumption of the presidency marked a new era for Al-Tagammu. Until that moment, the party had been largely unified in its opposition to the policies of the Sadat regime—economic liberalization, close alliance with the Western powers, and peace with Israel. Sadat's frequent attacks on Al-Tagammu left no room for accommodation. In contrast, Mubarak began his term of office displaying a more tolerant attitude toward all political forces, manifested by his order to release hundreds of political figures imprisoned by Sadat. The new president also pledged to revise Sadat's infitah policies and took steps to end Egypt's isolation within the Arab world.

In the face of this conciliatory approach, Al-Tagammu's leadership became divided over the party's proper response to the new regime. Whereas a pragmatic camp saw Mubarak's rise as an opportunity to mend relations with the authorities, an opposing consensus rejected this idea, arguing that Mubarak was maintaining Sadat's exclusionary economic policies and was determined to maintain relations with Israel.[92] This disagreement was evident in the party's contradictory postures toward the new president. In public, Al-Tagammu rejected Mubarak's presidential bid, and its mouthpiece *Al-Ahaly* unremittingly criticized the government. Yet, in private, some party leaders assured the president that they had no personal animosity toward him and were prepared to make a fresh start with the regime.[93]

Validating the pragmatists' position was an intellectual shift occurring within Egypt's communist movement, which, as explained in chapter 4, was well represented inside Al-Tagammu. Specifically, a new, slowly emerging consensus advocated for operating within the confines of the state-managed political arena, as evidenced by the Communist Party of Egypt's (CPE) participation in the 1987 legislative election. Before Mubarak's assumption of power, the CPE had already begun to adopt a more modest political agenda. In 1980, it announced that its immediate priority was no longer building socialism but, rather, the less ambitious goal of resisting regressive policies.[94] With Sadat out of the way, the CPE's official proclamations began focusing on the need to cooperate with other political forces to achieve Egypt's political and economic sovereignty and make "an all-embracing turn toward democracy."[95] The imperatives of creating a democratic political system and protecting existing (albeit limited), "democratic gains" would later be cited to justify opposition to Islamists, who allegedly presented a serious obstacle to democratic change.[96]

Meanwhile, an accompanying shift in Al-Tagammu's political positions became evident under Mubarak, reflecting greater willingness to work within the limitations of the existing political system and economic order. For example, the party's 1984 election platform retreated from its previous position demanding the abrogation of infitah legislation, calling instead for reorienting economic liberalization toward productive sectors and for reducing Egypt's trade deficit.[97] In part, this policy change stemmed from a belief that "parasitic" and "nationalist" capitalists inside the ruling coalition were in conflict and that the "nationalist" forces were potential Al-Tagammu allies who offered opportunities to change the system from within.[98] This conclusion evoked 1970s communist leaders' arguments that the Sadat regime harbored progressive elements amenable to outreach and cooperation (see chapter 4).

The softening of Al-Tagammu's opposition to the Mubarak regime demonstrated the extent to which many Marxists had embraced the possibility of building socialism through the ballot box. In other words, working within the existing political system became a viable strategy to achieve socialist transformation. By the early 1990s, this view had become one of the cornerstones of Al-Tagammu's program: "The party believes that building a socialist society depends on the acceptance of the majority of the people of socialism and expressing that through free and fair democratic elections."[99] Rifaat Al-Said elaborated on this perspective, arguing that Lenin's expressed aversion to "democracy" was in fact a distortion of classical Marxism. Even if dismantling class hierarchies required the brief application of authoritarian measures, Al-Said maintained, Marx's vision of a just society was fundamentally consistent with democratic governance.[100]

This was the context in which Al-Said formulated the concept of *al-asquf al-munkhafidah* ("lowered ceilings"). The term encapsulates the pragmatic posture Al-Tagammu Party adopted in relation to the ruling party during the 1990s. The concept required Al-Tagammu to base its program, not on rigid ideological commitments, but on the political realities the party confronted and the opportunities these realities offered—that is, the "ceiling" under which it operated. This pragmatic view acknowledged the futility of attempting to overturn the status quo and effect socialist transformation when economic liberalization has become a fait accompli. According to this argument, a more viable approach would focus on realistic proposals like preserving the public sector or instituting legal protections for vulnerable social groups.[101]

Although Al-Said's lowered ceilings thesis ultimately would prevail and establish the intellectual foundation of Al-Tagammu's alliance with the regime, the process yielding this outcome was anything but seamless. A community of "rejectionist" Marxist activists resisted the party's turn to the right. Initially, some of these activists had opposed the party's seemingly lenient stance toward the regime and thus refused to join it.[102] The influence of this current was evident in the party's appointment of Hussein Abdel-Razek as editor in chief of Al-Ahaly.[103] Both the ruling party and pragmatic elements within Al-Tagammu objected to this move, arguing that Abdel-Razek expressed hardline antiregime viewpoints that would deepen rifts with the ruling establishment.

The differing visions of pragmatists and rejectionists pulled Al-Tagammu in opposing directions. One vision advocated a more accommodating posture in response to Mubarak's limited gestures of reconciliation. The other vision adopted a more confrontational approach, sparing no opportunity to criticize the government and its policies in the pages of Al-Ahaly.[104] Under these circumstances, the newspaper remained a major target of regime attacks throughout the 1980s. Whenever Al-Ahaly heightened its criticism of the ruling party or ran articles deemed subversive, proregime media outlets disparaged the publication and its editors.[105]

The pragmatists' opposition to Al-Ahaly's editorial line began appearing early in Mubarak's first term in office. For example, some members of the General Secretariat opposed Hussein Abdel-Razek's appointment as editor in chief of Al-Ahaly, fearing that this move would destroy the party's already precarious relationship with the government.[106] Within Al-Tagammu, there was more general discomfort about the apparent autonomy Al-Ahaly had established under the leadership of Abdel-Razek. Some party members perceived obvious contradictions between the paper's editorial line and the party's official positions. In fact, many claimed that a coterie of hardline Marxists was exercising undue influence over the publication. First on the list was Abdel-Razek, followed by editors Farida Al-Naqqash (Abdel-Razek's wife) and Salah Eissa, a respected leftist writer whom Abdel-Razek recruited into the editorial team. Eissa was

married to editor Amina Al-Naqqash, who was Farida's sister. These famil-
ial connections lent credence to detractors' complaints that *Al-Ahaly*'s editorial staff was a cabal of like-minded, tightly linked individuals isolated
from the leadership and masses of the party.

At a meeting held in the aftermath of Al-Tagammu's unsuccessful 1984
election campaign, such concerns were openly aired.[107] Hussein Shalan
registered his objections to the antigovernment tone of recent editorials.
The paper, he asserted, had assumed the appearance of a revolutionary
mouthpiece, which contradicted Al-Tagammu's profile as a progressive
democratic party. He also charged that some editorial decisions, like
declining to interview presidential adviser Osama Al-Baz, were made without sufficient consultation of the editorial board.[108] Similarly, Philip Gallab
complained that *Al-Ahaly*'s line was more appropriate for an underground
movement bulletin than a licensed party newspaper. Furthermore, Gallab charged that Abdel-Razek and his close associates were unreceptive to
opinions less critical of the ruling establishment.[109]

This meeting did not result in changes to the editorial leadership of *Al-
Ahaly*. Yet for Abdel-Razek, the incident signaled the emergence of a clear
internal division over *Al-Ahaly*'s appropriate posture toward the regime:

> It seemed clear to me after that meeting and in subsequent meetings that
> there was a unified position bringing together Philip Gallab and Hus-
> sein Shalan, who were often joined by Mohamed Sid-Ahmed, though he
> always emphasized not wanting to be seen as part of any one bloc. These
> colleagues were always keen to register their disagreement with the line
> that I tried to maintain in *Al-Ahaly*, especially regarding any positions sig-
> naling fundamental opposition to the policies of the National Democratic
> Party and those of the president. Under different pretexts and grounds,
> they sought to resist any fundamental opposition to the regime, spe-
> cifically toward the president. And so, efforts to stir up differences, and
> sometimes minor altercations, between Philip Gallab and my colleagues
> Salah Eissa and Farida Al-Naqqash continued.[110]

Such conflict soon expanded beyond the internal deliberations of the
editorial board, promoting divisions within Al-Tagammu's wider leadership circle.[111] For Abdel-Razek, these conflicts were not the product of
personal animosities, or of divisions between radical Marxists and more

"moderate" party members, as some have claimed. Rather, they were manifestations of a deeper, more fundamental cleavage within Al-Tagammu about the party's response to a seismic shift within the opposition favoring political Islam at the expense of the progressive left. Did the perceived threat of Islamist movements justify an alliance with a regime pursuing social and economic policies inimical to Al-Tagammu's stated mission?[112] It was not long before these tensions turned into a real political confrontation over the party line. Ultimately, the faction motivated by fears of religious fundamentalism emerged triumphant, paving the way for a political alliance between the regime and Al-Tagammu. The political ascendancy of the Muslim Brotherhood and the growing salience of identity politics resulting from crowding out tipped the balance in favor of these factions.

April 1987: The Challenge of Political Islam and the Problem of *Al-Ahaly*

The 1987 legislative election was a humiliating setback for Al-Tagammu. The party captured a mere 2 percent of the national vote, far less than the 8 percent threshold required for representation in parliament. Because other opposition lists, including those of the Islamic Alliance (SLP-LSP-Muslim Brotherhood) and Al-Wafd, won numerous seats, many Al-Tagammu leaders concluded that the party's ignominious defeat could not be attributed exclusively to fraud. Rather, they argued, this failure was the product of poor strategy, and thus it warranted an honest discussion about the need to revise the party's stances. Between April 1987 and May 1988, Al-Tagammu witnessed a series of fierce internal debates about assessing and rectifying the problems underscored by the electoral rout. Ultimately, these arguments resulted in the triumph of the party's pragmatist camp. Thus began Al-Tagammu's close cooperation with the ruling establishment to counterbalance Islamist movements.

These brewing conflicts first came to the surface in late April 1987, when Al-Tagammu's General Secretariat convened to investigate the party's poor showing in the legislative election. Participants generally acknowledged Al-Tagammu's alienation from the electorate, but they disagreed about the cause. For some, the problem was the party's failure to articulate a clear position on religion, which made it extremely difficult to compete with Islamist currents to attract an increasingly pious electorate.[113]

Others pointed to *Al-Ahaly*'s editorial leadership, suggesting that the paper's political line evoked the image of an underground communist group with unrealistic, utopian goals. Fouad Morsi, for example, defined the problem as Al-Tagammu's inability to distinguish itself from the CPE, with which some of its senior members were affiliated.[114] Morsi's assessment was an implicit indictment of *Al-Ahaly* and the radical Marxist views of its editors.[115] It also echoed a viewpoint that the editors were eschewing professional journalistic standards in favor of their ideological commitments, which limited *Al-Ahaly*'s ability to compete with less dogmatic opposition newspapers in attracting a broader base of readers.

For Ismail Sabri Abdallah, who was among the leading communist figures inside Al-Tagammu, these problems, including the commotion about *Al-Ahaly*, stemmed from the party's continued inability to create an internal consensus about its mission. In an internal policy paper, he claimed that Al-Tagammu was torn between two competing camps. Seeing no difference between the Mubarak and the Sadat regimes, the first camp asserted that popular revolution or a return to the Nasserist experiment were the only means by which to effect progressive change. The second camp was convinced that change could be achieved only by working within the existing system to construct a broad cross-class coalition that would pursue the goal of socialist transformation through peaceful democratic means.[116] In some ways, Abdallah was recapitulating Egyptian communists' rationale for embracing the Nasserist establishment in the 1960s: the governing coalition had credible partners for advancing socialist change from within. The deep irony, of course, is that in both instances the left upheld and acted upon this line of reasoning at a moment when the balance of power inside the ruling coalition was tilting rightward.

In a policy paper presented at the same secretariat meeting, Abdel-Razek concurred with Abdallah's assessment but remained critical of the pragmatist faction. This contingent, he claimed, believed that the left's primary enemies were the Muslim Brotherhood and right-wing religious fundamentalists rather than the regime. According to Abdel-Razek, this faction of Al-Tagammu wanted merely to contain the influence of Islamist movements by cooperating with reform-minded elements inside the NDP. In other words, he insinuated that the pragmatists' talk of broadening the left's coalition and cooperating with other national political forces was nothing more than a sugarcoated plea to forge an alliance with the regime. On the other side of the debate, Abdel-Razek asserted, was a faction of activists who viewed the ruling party as the ultimate obstacle to transformative change. This perspective held the ruling party responsible, not only for poor economic conditions and social injustice but also for promoting religious fundamentalism.[117]

Although the outcome of these deliberations was initially unclear, the Central Secretariat ultimately formed a number of committees to evaluate the party's performance in various areas. There were clear signs that the pragmatist camp would use this opportunity to isolate *Al-Ahaly*'s radical editorial leadership. Notably, the committee tasked with assessing *Al-Ahaly*'s performance excluded the publication's editor in chief, Hussein Abdel-Razek. Additionally, the leadership placed on the editorial board individuals with clear proregime sympathies like Gallab. These measures left no ambiguity about the pragmatists' objective. They used the 1987 electoral defeat and the controversies surrounding *Al-Ahaly* as pretexts for marginalizing Al-Tagammu's radical elements and adjusting the party's political line in relation to the ruling party. Not long after, Khaled Mohieddin publicly criticized *Al-Ahaly* in an interview with *Kul Al-Arab* magazine, signaling that the party's most prominent leader supported the effort to contain Abdel-Razek and company.[118]

Summer 1987: Rejectionist Faction Defiance

Nevertheless, the internal conflicts fracturing Al-Tagammu in summer 1987 made it obvious that the party's rejectionist faction would not surrender without a fight. Between July and November, *Al-Ahaly* engaged in a fierce campaign against Mubarak's bid for a second presidential term. This campaign portrayed the president as an extension of Sadat's right-wing administration, dismissing the pragmatists' claim that Mubarak was fighting against corrupt, antireform elements inside the regime. On a different front, opponents of the pragmatist line began openly criticizing their detractors in Al-Tagammu's internal bulletins. In mid-July, Abdel-Razek argued against the efforts of what he described as Al-Tagammu's "right-wingers" to move the party closer to the ruling establishment:

> There is a current inside the party that believes with conviction | . . .| that our dispute with authorities—the president, the government, the National

Democratic Party, and the majority in parliament and local councils—does not make it our main enemy and opponent. That is because authority, by its very nature, is composed of distinct currents and wings that are in political disagreement |. . . .| A distinction, in terms of social class, is made between the parasitic bourgeoisie, and productive capital and middle classes in general, including the bureaucratic bourgeoisie, and, politically, between the National Democratic Party, the government, and the presidency. And the latter—particularly the president, some of his aides, and political figures close to him—are viewed as the wing that is most likely to join the rest of the national forces |. . . .| The second current, to which I am clearly partial, sees that Sadat's absence and subsequent developments and shifts in [the government's] ways and practices do not change the core of social conflict in society, notwithstanding the prevalence of currents and factions and class tensions inside the ruling coalition. Socially, the conflict is between the working class, poor and middle fellahin, small craftsmen, junior bureaucrats, and traders, revolutionary intellectuals, and soldiers, along with middle classes, and national, productive capitalists, and [on the other hand] the alliance of foreign capital, large domestic capital linked to international capital, especially in the fields of construction and trade, and parasitic capitalists—with parasitic capitalism at [the alliance's] core. Politically, the conflict is between Al-Tagammu, the Socialist Arab Nasserist Party, the Communist Party of Egypt, and the national, progressive, and unionist forces more generally, and on the other side, the National Democratic Party, the [Islamic] Alliance (the SLP, the Muslim Brotherhood, and the LSP), religious terrorist groups, and Al-Wafd Party. At the core [of the opposing coalition] is the NDP |. . . .| Thus, the main enemy and adversary is the National Democratic Party and its government, including the president, who is responsible |. . .| for what the country has witnessed over the course of six years of his rule, including greater dependency, the economic crisis, the prevalence of the police state, the social crisis, and the growth of terrorist currents. The existence of contradictions inside the governing coalition is something that cannot be denied or ignored, but it comes as the third or fourth order of priority for us, because it is not the most effective way for change and is not worthy of our efforts.[119]

The pragmatist wing responded to Abdel-Razek in subsequent issues of the bulletin. For example, Ibrahim Saadeddin criticized the idea that the ruling party was Al-Tagammu's primary enemy in absolute terms.[120] In another article, Sherif Hetata implicitly criticized Abdel-Razek by attacking what he described as the futile discourse of radical leftists in Al-Tagammu.[121]

As the fault lines of these debates emerged that summer, it became increasingly apparent that the pragmatist camp was led by the core group of Al-Tagammu leaders who had joined the Arab Socialist Union's (ASU's) Vanguard Organization (VO) during the 1960s, including Khaled Mohieddin, Ismail Sabri Abdallah, Fouad Morsi, Philip Gallab, and Ibrahim Saadeddin. Their plea for cooperation with the Mubarak regime was informed by a long history of collaboration with a ruling establishment that was comparably riddled with former VO affiliates (detailed in chapter 4).

The pragmatists' case for allying with the NDP against Islamists was reinforced during the late 1980s by the increasing use of violence by underground Islamist groups. The Muslim Brotherhood's strident anti-leftist discourse during the same period merely increased such concerns. For example, shortly after the April 1987 legislative election, the Brotherhood's general guide stated in an interview:

> Al-Tagammu Party's philosophy is based on the denial of God and that religions are the opium of the people. Therefore, Al-Tagammu Party can never gain stature in Egypt; maybe in other countries. Egypt has Islam and the feet of Christ walked on its soil, and so Al-Tagammu Party can never have a place among us.[122]

Yet, the editors of *Al-Ahaly* and their allies were not deterred. As the date for the national referendum on Mubarak's nomination for a second presidential term drew near, it became apparent to Al-Tagammu's leaders that Abdel-Razek and his comrades would not back down. In September 1987, *Al-Ahaly* announced the release of a book consisting of previously published articles criticizing the government and opposing Mubarak's bid for a second presidential term. The book's title *This Is Why We Oppose Mubarak* provoked the anger of the pragmatists. "This reads like the bulletins of the underground parties of the old days," Gallab remarked to Abdel-Razek in reference to a slogan then ubiquitous in *Al-Ahaly*'s pages: "No to Mubarak!"[123] State media responded by intensifying their attacks on *Al-Ahaly* and portraying its editors as a rogue element attempting to hijack Al-Tagammu. *Al-Ahaly*'s opposition to the president was so daring and vocal that the authorities invoked a dubious legal pretext to confiscate copies of the October 1987 issue urging the electorate to vote "No to Mubarak" in the referendum.[124]

The battle over Al-Tagammu political line escalated in late October, when the Central Committee adopted a resolution naming the NDP as the party's principal adversary. The resolution was supposed to reflect the outcome of a months-long internal dialogue regarding the party's political line and its relationship with the regime. The resolution seemed carefully crafted to dismiss the pragmatist argument that elements of the ruling establishment were potential allies of the party's reform agenda.[125] Soon thereafter, the pragmatists struck back at the *Al-Ahaly* contingent—this time, decisively.

December 1987–May 1988: Pragmatists Strike Back

A few weeks after the resolution's adoption naming the NDP as the party's principal adversary, discussions about *Al-Ahaly*'s performance resumed inside Al-Tagammu's Central Committee. In December, a new committee was formed to identify the problems confronting the newspaper and submit a report to the General Secretariat. The committee was asked to initiate a wide-ranging dialogue among the parties' central and regional officers and to conduct surveys of party members to assess *Al-Ahaly*'s contributions to the party's mission.

As the committee's work proceeded, it became clear that many regional officers felt that *Al-Ahaly* failed to publicize Al-Tagammu's candidates and their positions during the campaign season. Some argued that *Al-Ahaly* afforded greater coverage to CPE candidates than to those of Al-Tagammu. Others complained about *Al-Ahaly*'s significant decline in circulation in recent years.

Although many of these criticisms appeared objectively valid, the pragmatists appeared to be using them as a pretense to force a change in *Al-Ahaly*'s editorial policy in relation to the ruling party. Well before the committee's work had begun, rumors of Khaled Mohieddin's intention to replace Abdel-Razek with a less contentious figure, like Philip Gallab or Lotfi Al-Khouli, circulated in party ranks.[126] In fact, months after Abdel-Razek's eventual resignation, Mohieddin angrily declared that he had been trying to replace the editor in chief for two years.[127] Put simply, the controversy over *Al-Ahaly* involved more than declining circulation or poor electoral performance.

This observation is supported by leading pragmatists' remarks at General Secretariat and Central Committee meetings, which cited the alteration of *Al-Ahaly*'s posture toward the regime as a significant priority. For example, at one such meeting, Ibrahim Saadeddin argued that *Al-Ahaly* must "transcend the conflict between the government and the opposition" and become "the paper of all the nationalists."[128] Lotfi Al-Khouli complained that *Al-Ahaly* had failed to follow the party line regarding "improving the performance of capitalism."[129] Fouad Morsi expressed similar dissatisfaction with *Al-Ahaly*'s line, citing a recent Abdel-Razek's editorial:

> In last week's issue Hussein wrote an editorial under his own name. He picked up intelligently on basic points from Mubarak's speech on democracy, and identified three mistakes that Mubarak fell into, and explained them with utmost greatness . . . But he then concluded that Mubarak's words "confirm that there is no solution to Egypt's problems without total change." A disaster . . . Is the overthrow [of the system] the solution? What is the meaning of total change but an overthrow? Who said that total change is the solution?! This is the kind of writing that makes the party and its members nervous.[130]

Adopting a similar approach, Mohamed Sid-Ahmed contended that *Al-Ahaly*'s hostility toward the ruling establishment ignored the new political landscape that emerged in post-Sadat Egypt. Specifically, he argued that radical Islamist currents had supplanted the NDP as the party's main enemy:

> *Al-Ahaly*'s current motto took shape under Sadat's reign in the wake of his visit to Jerusalem. And in a reality in which Sadat attacked all national political forces in Egypt, it became impossible to work under the ruling regime. That is to say that the [current] shaming approach [of *Al-Ahaly*] was derived from political imperatives, that is, the impossibility of working under the framework of the political system, such that the shaming battles served the purpose of speeding up the emergence of an alternative regime. The shaming approach was derived from the goal of bringing

down the Sadat regime, even if the necessities for operating legally prevented the explicit verbalization of that goal. That is no longer valid in the same way under Mubarak, because the most significant force on the scene calling for bringing down the system are extremist religious groups that condemn the left at least as fiercely as they condemn the regime itself. This does not mean that the left has abandoned its basic differences with Mubarak and his policies, but that what [Al-Tagammu] stands for is not to bring down the regime through extralegal means, because it is the extremist religious groups that are most prepared to exploit the overturning of legal legitimacy. And most likely, they would use it to physically liquidate the left. Therefore, the shaming language, by itself or in principle, is no longer the most appropriate way to go.[131]

These discussions further confirmed that the pressure to impose changes at *Al-Ahaly* was motivated more by a desire to improve the party's relationship with the ruling establishment than by a desire to increase circulation. Farida Al-Naqqash described and reflected on these realities in a 1988 article appearing in Al-Tagammu's internal bulletin:

This is not the first time, nor will be the last, in which the intense political conflict that is ongoing inside Al-Tagammu Party hides behind the sign of *Al-Ahaly*. And I say it will not be the last, because despite the obvious results of the dialogue regarding the political line of the party, its position toward the regime, and its approach to activism and coalition building; [despite] the unambiguous [adopted party] resolutions | . . .| that validate the newspaper's political line | . . .| one group has continued its attacks against those responsible for the newspaper |. . . .| What that group in the leadership basically wants is to open the door for supporting President Hosni Mubarak one way or another. And it is not surprising that some of these colleagues were calling for—and they have every right to—voting "Yes" for President Hosni Mubarak during the reelection bid. And some of them have abstained from voting when the General Secretariat voted for "No" [for supporting Mubarak]. This has been that group's established position | . . .| They want to force *Al-Ahaly* to adopt that [pro-Mubarak] line, since it is considered one of the party's most visible media outlets. And it is no coincidence that they were always active participants in any attack against *Al-Ahaly* under the pretext that [the publication] deviated from the party's political line and moved radically leftwards.[132]

Intensifying attacks from the regime and from within Al-Tagammu, along with Khaled Mohieddin's overt support for the pragmatist camp, finally caused Abdel-Razek to yield. He submitted his resignation in May 1988, paving the way for a reshuffle in the editorial board of *Al-Ahaly* and a 180-degree turn in the newspaper's editorial policy and, by implication, in the party's political posture.

Meanwhile, pro-Mubarak commentators joyously celebrated the ouster of *Al-Ahaly's* radical leftist contingent. Abdel-Azim Ramadan commended Khaled Mohieddin for effecting this change, which he described as the "end of a sad page in the history of the Egyptian left." Samir Ragab, one of Mubarak's staunchest supporters, was even more gleeful, writing in an article entitled "Bravo, Khaled":

> For the first time I announce my support to Khaled Mohieddin Secretary General of Al-Tagammu Party for to his courage in kicking Hussein Abdel-Razek and Salah Eissa out of *Al-Ahaly* |. . . .| A confrontation ensued between the two, wherein Khaled Mohieddin candidly accused Hussein Abdel-Razek of hijacking the management of the newspaper and imposing an editorial policy that contradicts the policies of the party, which was done for the sake of pitting social classes against each other, whereas the primary goal is reform through the current political system.[133]

With Abdel-Razek and his team out of the way, veteran journalist and former *Rose Al-Yousef* senior editor Mahmoud Al-Maraghi was appointed editor in chief of *Al-Ahaly*, serving in that post until succeeded by Gallab in late 1989. The appointment of Gallab, one of Mubarak's staunchest advocates inside al-Tagammu, was an unambiguous signal that the party was preparing to open a new chapter in its relationship with the regime.

Economic Reform, Terrorism, and Al-Tagammu's Shifting Priorities

The overhaul of *Al-Ahaly* marked the beginning of an evident shift in Al-Tagammu's stance toward the ruling elite. Throughout the battles of the 1980s, Abdel-Razek's detractors within Al-Tagammu had claimed that striking bargains with the regime was not their objective, but the November 1990 legislative election proved otherwise.

One month before voting began, the NDP had failed to implement legal protections—like judicial supervision—necessary for a free and fair election. Thus, all opposition forces, including Al-Wafd, the SLP, the LSP, and the Muslim Brotherhood, announced an electoral boycott. To the relief of the ruling establishment, Al-Tagammu eventually agreed to enter the race, becoming the only opposition group to take part. The party's participation lent the election a veneer of legitimacy, a quality the regime would require when the forthcoming parliament deliberated legislation authorizing the new IMF-sponsored economic reform program.

Although Al-Tagammu had voiced identical objections to the electoral process,[134] the party nevertheless chose to break with other opposition forces and field candidates. The party exercised extraordinary pragmatism by abandoning the boycott. The 1990 electoral campaign was the first in which al-Tagammu's platform featured democratic reform as a top priority.[135] The party's leaders, however, chose to ignore an overwhelming national consensus that the forthcoming election's legal framework was inconducive to a free and fair vote. Ultimately, Al-Tagammu won five seats in the election. One went to Khaled Mohieddin, who entered parliament for the first time since Al-Tagammu's falling out with Sadat caused him to lose his seat in the 1979 election.

Meanwhile, Al-Tagammu modified its policy stances to meet the government halfway on critical issues. In March 1990, the party tempered its formerly unequivocal opposition to privatization, acceding to limited sales of loss-incurring public sector companies. Before this date, Al-Tagammu had opposed on principle any measures that would downsize the public sector.[136] By 1993, Al-Tagammu's platform abandoned its absolute rejection of economic liberalization, focusing instead on measures to protect vulnerable groups from the effects of economic reform, which it now appeared to accept as a fait accompli.[137]

More generally, Al-Tagammu of the 1990s backtracked from the confrontational opposition it had mounted against Sadat and, to a lesser degree, Mubarak. With the pragmatists in control of Al-Ahaly, the party presented itself as a loyal opposition that accepted the political status quo despite its serious limitations. Nothing captures this change better than the title of the new publication in Al-Ahaly's book series documenting Al-Tagammu lawmakers' response to the program Prime Minister Atef Sedky presented to parliament in 1991. Whereas the party published This Is Why We Oppose Mubarak in September of 1987, the new pragmatist Al-Tagammu, in contrast, published This Is Why We Oppose the Government in

1991.[138] Simply put, Al-Tagammu made its peace with the regime, advocating incremental reform from within, rather than revolution from without.

As Al-Tagammu's stance on economic reform moved closer to the center of Egypt's political spectrum, the putative threat of political Islam was elevated to a key priority. Calls for "fighting terrorism" and countering the threat of religious extremism predominated in *Al-Ahaly*, the party's programs, and the actions of its key leaders. By privileging these issues and enhancing its anti-Islamist credentials after 1987, Al-Tagammu, in effect, opened the door for collaboration with the regime. As Egyptian scholar Iman Hassan observes:

> The election results of 1987 | . . .| led to a shift in the balance of power inside Al-Tagammu, whereby the influence of the moderate wing of Al-Tagammu increased. This was reflected in *Al-Ahaly*, which adopted a new stance toward the presidency | . . .| including support for national consensus against terrorism and assigning priority to the conflict against radicalism. That orientation helped broaden channels of communications between Al-Tagammu and ruling circles, and [the party] was no longer under siege or repressed the same way it was under the rule of President Sadat.[139]

In the early 1990s, Al-Tagammu launched a vigorous public campaign against Islamist extremism. During the same period, the party's official program adopted "fighting terrorism" as its second most important priority, just behind "achieving social justice."[140] While holding previous governments, particularly those of the Sadat era, responsible for the rise in political violence, Al-Tagammu's new line validated the Mubarak regime's security crackdown on Islamist groups.[141] For example, the party's new program called for a national democratic front to counter the ideas of so-called extremist religious groups active in media and cultural institutions and demanded the "firm application of the law" against those who practice violence.[142] These calls were issued at a moment when proposals to engage in dialogue with militant Islamist groups were gaining traction among some senior government officials, as explained in chapter 2. It was no coincidence, therefore, that another condition Al-Tagammu placed on its support for Mubarak's third presidential term was the regime's commitment to "fighting terrorism."[143]

Meanwhile, Rifaat Al-Said publicly proposed that all political forces, including the NDP, forge a national coalition against Islamist radicalism, while actively lobbying against proposed alliances between the leftist and Islamist opposition.[144] Al-Said long argued that groups like the Muslim Brotherhood, their professed commitment to nonviolent politics notwithstanding, provided intellectual validation for Islamist perpetrators of violence.[145] Similar ideas appeared in Al-Tagammu's official statements of the early 1990s.[146] Some claimed that Al-Tagammu's campaigns against Islamist movements were not unrelated to its fundraising endeavors. For example, Gamal Assaad Abdel-Malak, an early 1990s member of Al-Tagammu's General Secretariat, claimed that the party capitalized on its anti-Islamist discourse to secure political and financial support from the Egyptian Coptic diaspora.[147]

In sum, crowding out elevated political Islam to Al-Tagammu's primary concern and made the Muslim Brotherhood, rather than the regime, the party's main adversary. Meanwhile, Al-Tagammu and the NDP's consensus on the urgency of containing "Islamist radicalism" relegated issues of economic liberalization to the back burner. Khaled Mohieddin summarized the perspective informing this change:

> Would I ever ally myself with the Muslim Brothers against the regime? No, because they are simply no different from it with respect to their positions toward the International Monetary Fund, privatization, and other such matters. And if they were ever to make it to power, they would simply implement the same policies [as the current regime], but only after putting on a turban to supposedly demonstrate compliance with the Quran and the teachings of the Prophet. And they will fight against us fiercely. I differ with the current regime, which, for example, rigs elections against us. But it does not seek to eliminate our existence. Yet Islamist groups and the Brotherhood will try to eliminate my existence altogether.[148]

Into Hosni's "Barn"

Al-Tagammu and other leftist forces' support for the regime's crackdown on Islamist groups during the 1990s was visible in state cultural institutions. Minister of Culture Farouk Hosni's famous, albeit crude, statement described the new relationship thusly: "I got the intellectuals to enter the barn of the ministry."[149] Hosni was referencing, of course, his successful cooptation of large swaths of a leftist intelligentsia once adamantly opposed to the regime. In other words, he coaxed the regime's wild, disobedient opponents into his ministry (i.e., his "barn"), domesticated them, and bound them in service to the regime.

Hosni pursued this endeavor rather strategically, using his ministry to reward loyal leftist intellectuals with various privileges and benefits, including appointments in the ministry's subsidiary bodies. For example, Hosni appointed Salah Eissa, former Al-Ahaly editor and thorn in the side of the Mubarak regime, editor in chief of the ministry's publication Al-Qahirah.[150] Just as he was about to enter the world of the Ministry of Culture, Eissa began publicly defending the minister against attacks by Islamist opinion makers, most notably the editors of the SLP mouthpiece Al-Shaab.[151] Similarly, Mahmoud Amin Al-Alim, one of Egypt's most prominent Marxist intellectuals, was awarded a senior position on the ministry's Supreme Council of Culture (SCC).[152] Prominent Al-Tagammu figures were also appointed to various state-controlled institutions. A case in point is Amina Shafiq's appointment to the National Council for Women chaired by First Lady Suzanne Mubarak.[153] In addition, President Mubarak appointed Rifaat Al-Said to a seat in the upper house of parliament.[154]

The Ministry of Culture's annual literary awards provided yet another mechanism through which Farouk Hosni could reward leftist writers for toeing the regime line. For example, in 1993, the SCC awarded Al-Tagammu member Lotfi Al-Khouli the State Award of Merit in Literature, the country's foremost literary award.[155] It also became common practice for the state to promote the published works of Al-Tagammu's affiliates at the annual Cairo International Book Fair. A major beneficiary of this practice was Rifaat Al-Said, whose books, particularly those attacking Islamist movements, were prominently displayed at the fair, sometimes bearing a photo of the First Lady printed on the back cover in an implicit endorsement.[156] In turn, Al-Said was never short of flattering words for the First Lady or her contributions to the social and cultural spheres. "Does it seem surprising that I extend my salutations and respects to Mrs. Suzanne Mubarak, even though I came here as a [member of the] opposition," he rhetorically asked at a March 1998 session of the Shura Council. "I think not, for she deserves our fullest respect and appreciation."[157]

Observers also have asserted that Hosni's Ministry of Culture devised numerous means to channel financial rewards to its leftist political allies. It has long been an open secret that the ministry purchased exorbitantly priced advertisement space in publications associated with politically loyal leftist figures.[158] The ministry's frequent practice of awarding lavish contracts to private sector companies also aroused considerable suspicion. It was well known for years that the Ministry of Culture, along with the Ministry of Education, granted lucrative contracts to the privately owned printing facility Al-ʾAmal, reportedly owned, in part, by the families of Al-Tagammu leaders Rifaat Al-Said and Khaled Mohieddin.[159] In 2015, Al-Said admitted that some Al-Tagammu leaders and individuals tied to the party, including his own brother, had once owned shares of Al-ʾAmal. According to Al-Said, Khaled Mohieddin bought out the other partners before transferring ownership to his son Amin.[160] In any case, the irony was obvious to all: Al-Tagammu's leaders had not merely acquiesced to the government's privatization policies. They also were benefiting personally from the privatization of the state's mass printing operations.

Perhaps the leftist intelligentsia's potent influence within the Ministry of Culture explains why the ministry was at the center of so much controversy during the short (2012–2013) rule of President Mohamed Morsi. Having become an influential hub for leftist opinion makers holding negative views of the Islamist movement, the ministry represented one of the state bureaucracy's most formidable sites of potential opposition to the Muslim Brotherhood and its political party, the Freedom and Justice Party.

It is also unsurprising that Farouk Hosni, who served as Minister of Culture from 1987 to 2011, was the longest serving cabinet member of Mubarak's presidency. For Hosni was more than the regime-appointed custodian of the cultural sphere. He was also responsible for maintaining and nurturing the collaborative relationship the ruling establishment forged with the leftist intelligentsia in the 1990s.

The Power of Crowding Out

Officially, Al-Tagammu was founded in 1976. Yet the late Mohamed Sid-Ahmed once argued that the party's real birth occurred in 1965, when communist parties agreed to dissolve themselves and work within the Nasserist establishment.[161] In other words, Al-Tagammu was intellectually conceived the moment communists concluded that working within the existing political system was a viable path to socialist transformation. Sid-Ahmed's claim is given credence by the fact that Al-Tagammu leaders who surrendered the party to Mubarak in 1990 were from the same generation of activists who handed the communist movement to Nasser in 1965.

The leftist capitulation to Nasser, however, occurred under greater pressure and was based on the assumption, however misguided, that the president was pursuing a path toward socialist transformation. Yet those who submitted to Mubarak knew very well that their acquiescence would yield no such outcome. Mubarak, unlike Nasser, had expressed no commitment, however nominal, to socialism in 1990. In fact, the regime was openly reversing the Nasserist era's economic course.

Why then did they submit to Mubarak? The answer lies in the transformative impact of Islamist incorporation policies of the 1970s. I refer specifically to the increasing salience of identity-based politics, and the resulting crowding out of state commitments to the Nasserist social pact and of distributive issues more generally. That shift, or what this study designates as crowding out, rationalized Al-Tagammu's alliance with the ruling establishment in the name of opposing Islamist radicalism, as well as the party's concurrent tempering of its opposition to economic liberalization.

Additionally, Al-Tagammu's transformation from vehement opponent of the regime's economic liberalization measures to a collective of state-allied leftist intellectuals preoccupied with the containment of political Islam reinforced the institutional patterns described in chapter 4. It also solidified the dependent relationship that leftist currents within Al-Tagammu had formed with the ruling establishment after agreeing to operate within the state's burdensome and intrusive legal framework.

Splitting: The Dispersal of Opponents to Economic Liberalization

The concept of "splitting" captures another key mechanism through which Islamist incorporation policies contributed to the politics of "more identity, less class" in Egypt. In this study, the term denotes the appearance of national identity–based divisions among opponents of economic liberalization in response to the increasing salience of Islamist politics.

Put differently, once Islamist incorporation policies elevated discussions of the state's religious identity to the national stage, long-dormant disagreements were activated, dividing "old comrades" along these newly evident fissures. This phenomenon was most pronounced in the SLP during the 1980s, when the issue of collaboration with the Muslim Brotherhood divided the party into pro-Islamist and anti-Islamist camps. Ultimately, disagreements over the ideological bases of the party's agenda led to numerous defections, illuminating the mechanisms through which the process of Islamist incorporation promoted or reanimated divisions among opponents of economic reform.

MISR AL-FATAT: SOCIALISM WITH AN ISLAMIC FACE

The 1978 founding of the SLP was the product of two confluent efforts. The first such effort was Sadat's attempt to establish a new left-wing opposition party to replace Al-Tagammu, which was proving too unruly to play its appointed role of "loyal opposition." The second was an attempt by surviving members of Misr Al-Fatat (or "Young Egypt") to revive their movement, which effectively disappeared from the political scene under the rule of Gamal Abdel-Nasser.

Founded in 1933 by Ahmed Hussein and Fathy Radwan, the Misr Al-Fatat movement originated as a nationalist project advocating Egypt's independent economic development. What distinguished the movement from its contemporaries was its parallel commitment to socialist ideas and to asserting Egypt's Islamic identity as a means of resisting Western influence. Unlike the communists, Misr Al-Fatat displayed a strong affinity to Islamic values; however, unlike the Muslim Brotherhood, it did not deem socialism incompatible with religion.[162]

This unique duality was reflected in the movement's historic evolution. In 1940, the movement launched the National Islamic Party. During the same period, Ahmed Hussein proposed to Muslim Brotherhood founder Hassan Al-Banna that they merge their two organizations. Al-Banna declined, creating tension between the two sides. In 1948, Misr Al-Fatat renamed its party the Socialist Party, whose program advocated free education, social insurance, and land reform. The party produced a biweekly newspaper entitled *Socialism*, which was one of the most vocal anti-palace mouthpieces of the period. The leaders of Misr Al-Fatat were accused of involvement in the January 1952 Cairo fire riots, arrested, and sent to prison, where they remained until after the July 23 Revolution of 1952.[163]

Although Misr Al-Fatat disappeared after the 1953 decree banning political parties, its leaders' ideas retained currency. Some evidence has shown that President Gamal Abdel-Nasser, reportedly a member of Misr al-Fatat in his youth, continued to draw inspiration from the group's policy proposals. For example, the land reforms pursued under Nasser's leadership were similar to those proposed by Misr Al-Fatat members before the July 23 Revolution.[164] Furthermore, party cofounder Fathy Radwan served as Nasser's minister of information for most of the 1950s, and Helmy Murad, another movement affiliate, served as minister of education during the late 1960s.

WHAT WAS "LEFT" IN THE SOCIALIST LABOR PARTY

Misr Al-Fatat's third attempt to launch a political party occurred in 1978. At President Anwar Al-Sadat's request, former Misr Al-Fatat leader Ibrahim Shukri resigned his position as minister of agriculture to form the SLP. It was no secret that the SLP was formed to reestablish the illusion of political competition after Sadat-regime repression caused Al-Tagammu to suspend its political activities. This reality was manifested in several ways. First, signatories to the petition requesting the SLP's legal license included known members of the ruling party, notably Sadat. In fact, the president encouraged the party's growth by urging associates, such as his wife's brother-in-law Mahmoud Abu-Wafya, to join the SLP. Second, state media covered the SLP's formation extensively, while frequently reminding audiences that the party was evidence of the president's determination to effect democratic reform. Third, the ruling party declined to contest a significant number of parliamentary races in the 1979 election, thereby permitting the SLP to secure representation in parliament.[165]

According to one party leader, the SLP's diverse founding coalition produced what he characterized as a "fluid party" lacking a coherent mission or an obvious future. Of course, many Sadat loyalists with no commitment to the SLP's professed mission joined the party out of pure opportunism, contributing to this "fluidity." Nevertheless, many of Misr Al-Fatat's old ideological divisions were present in the SLP's founding coalition. Some Misr Al-Fatat members, particularly those who joined the movement during its late-1940s socialist phase, saw the organization as a European-style social democratic party. In contrast, others deemed the movement's professed Islamic identity genuine, that is, not mere lip service or rhetoric. According to this current, Misr Al-Fatat's socialism was derived from Islamic injunctions to promote social justice, and not from any Marxist principles guiding European political parties. Some Misr Al-Fatat leaders, moreover, had experienced an intellectual evolution that deepened their interest in the Islamic dimensions of social justice.[166]

These internal divisions, however insignificant initially, gained salience in the mid-1980s, when the Islamists' importunate demands to define the state's religious identity could no longer be ignored. Before that time, the SLP's founding platform accommodated the party's diverse political sensibilities by rebranding Misr Al-Fatat's assertions of socialism's compatibility with Islam. For example, the document's guiding principles cited both Islamic traditions and "the socialism that is conceived in our own realities and that seeks to provide prosperity to all the people."[167]

THE SLP OUTSIDE OF THE LOYAL OPPOSITION

The Sadat–SLP honeymoon was brief. By the early 1980s, the party had abandoned its previous support for the peace treaty with Israel and had begun actively opposing measures to normalize relations with the Jewish state. The SLP also launched attacks on Sadat's infitah policies and on the numerous restrictions he had imposed on political rights during his final years in office.[168] In response to this new strict antigovernment posture, many of Sadat's allies left the SLP in protest, thereby significantly reducing the party's representation in parliament.[169] As a result, the SLP felt Sadat's wrath in the fall of 1981. In August, authorities suspended SLP mouthpiece *Al-Shaab's* publishing license. In September, some party members were detained when Sadat ordered sweeping arrests of political dissidents.[170]

As previously described, Mubarak's rise to the presidency in 1982 initially improved relations between the ruling establishment and opposition forces. The president restored the licenses of opposition party publications, including that of the SLP's *Al-Shaab*. In addition, Mubarak's stated policies were nominally in accord with some of the SLP's long-standing demands, like revising economic liberalization policies and restoring Egypt's diplomatic relations with Arab countries. Yet when Mubarak declined to terminate Egypt's state of emergency or revise its pro-U.S. foreign policies, the SLP resumed its criticism.[171]

The outcome of May 1984's legislative election generated great disappointment and controversy within the SLP. Having failed to garner the 8 percent of national vote legally required to enter parliament, the SLP was unable to claim any of the thirty-two seats won by its candidates. Instead, these seats were awarded to the ruling party. The close margin by which the SLP failed to fulfill this requirement—it secured 7.2 percent of votes nationwide—exacerbated the party leadership's frustration.

In the election's aftermath, Mubarak communicated to SLP leaders his willingness to appoint several party members to parliament, per his constitutional prerogative. Many SLP leaders urged rejecting the proposal, fearing that its acceptance would reinforce the widespread perception of the party as the loyal opposition. Given the circumstances of the SLP's formation, this stigma was difficult to erase. Ultimately, the proposal narrowly passed a vote of al-hay'ah al-ʿuliyaa (the party's "Supreme Council"). Thus, the party submitted a list of nine nominees to Mubarak, who appointed four of the nine—Ibrahim Shukri, Mamdouh Qenawy, Ahmed Megahed, and Sayyid Rustom—to parliamentary seats.[172]

Having no choice but to endure the embarrassment of serving as a Mubarak-appointed lawmaker, Shukri entered parliament in an extremely demoralized state, bitterly regretting the SLP's failure to form an electoral coalition with the Muslim Brotherhood.[173] According to a former SLP official, Shukri was convinced that Al-Wafd Party had cleared the 8 percent threshold only because of its electoral alliance with the Brotherhood. Thus, the SLP president came to believe that his political fortunes would not improve in the absence of a cooperative relationship with the movement. "That is why Shukri would always make a point to sit next to Brotherhood MPs during the sessions of [the 1984] parliament," claimed the former SLP official.[174]

SPLITTING INSIDE THE SLP

The 1984 electoral debacle coincided with the rise of new divisions within the SLP. Many felt that leaders like Ibrahim Shukri and Helmy Murad were diverging from the party's established line by emphatically advocating the implementation of Sharia. The party's public events, moreover, began to display an Islamist complexion, proposing Islamic solutions to Egypt's economic problems and social injustice. Such differences, however, did not become confrontational until Adel Hussein appeared on the SLP scene in the mid-1980s.[175]

Hussein spent the early 1980s working as an editor in Beirut.[176] After *Al-Shaab* editor in chief Hamid Zeidan accepted a job in Abu Dhabi in 1985, Hussein was recruited to replace him. A communist activist during the 1950s and 1960s, Hussein, had since experienced a significant ideological transformation. Like Shukri and Murad, Hussein came to believe that Egypt's Islamic identity would be central to any effort resisting external political and economic interference.[177]

Indeed, some dismissed Hussein's embrace of political Islam as a purely opportunistic attempt to pander to an emerging political trend in Egypt.[178] Evidence suggests, however, that Hussein's engagement with political Islam did not entail the utter renunciation of his previous political convictions. This change appeared to stem from Hussein's reconceptualization of independence to encompass cultural (in addition to economic and political) phenomena.

As Egyptian economist Galal Amin explained, Adel Hussein had always shown greater interest in achieving economic independence and resisting imperialism than in issues of economic exploitation and the redistribution of wealth.[179] This was not a unique orientation within the Egyptian communist movement, given the prevalence of nationalist influences within the left. Thus, Hussein's famous study, *The Egyptian Economy from Independence to Dependency 1974-1979*, argued that Egyptian development would remain unachievable until the country eliminated its dependence on the economies of the developed world. Hussein's opus both echoed and critiqued predominant Marxist thought in the 1970s. Specifically, Hussein argued that dependency theorists like Andre Gunder Frank had uncritically adopted Western definitions of modernization and development, as if all residents of the developing world aspired only to be Western European. These leftist scholars, Hussein held, failed to recognize that preserving cultural and civilizational heritage is an essential requisite of development in the societies of the developing world.[180] This sense of cultural pride, he argued, enabled societies to muster the will to resist external forces obstructing independent economic development.[181] Perhaps developments occurring elsewhere in the Muslim world reinforced this conviction. I refer here to the 1979 establishment of the Islamic Republic of Iran. This political experiment rejected both Western and Soviet influences and declared its adopted path as a third way, or alternative, to the superpowers' capitalist and Marxist models of development.

By bringing this perspective to his position at Al-Shaab, the new editor in chief alienated many within the SLP's existing leadership. According to a former SLP leader, Hussein effectively banned socialists from publishing in the paper, while affording space to Islamist contributors, including prominent Muslim Brothers.[182] Many senior members of the SLP complained that Hussein, with Shukri's tacit support, had adopted an Islamist editorial line at Al-Shaab, endorsing positions incompatible with the party's original mission.[183] The escalating conflict between these two camps necessitated a review of the party's political line, which occurred at the party's fourth congress in January 1987.

In preparation for the debate, two positions papers were circulated, one authored by Adel Hussein and another by SLP founding member Mamdouh Qenawy. Qenawy made the case for preserving the party's socialist principles and for refusing to bring religion into politics. He argued that the SLP was home to a community of "socialists with faith" and that the party had no reason to toe the line of political Islam. Hussein, in contrast, argued that the dangers the United States posed to Egypt and the wider region could be averted only by cooperating and building a coalition with Islamist forces. Given that Arab nationalism was now defunct, Hussein claimed, political Islam presented the only real alternative for resisting external interference.[184] Eventually, the fourth congress adopted what observers characterized as a compromise—that is, a political program designed to accommodate these opposing views. This compromise failed to reconcile the two positions in any meaningful way.[185] Thus, it was only a matter of time before this arrangement evaporated.

This conflict over the party line resumed and escalated in the lead-up to the April 1987 legislative race, when the SLP had to decide whether to cooperate with the Muslim Brotherhood during the forthcoming campaign. Initially, the SLP called for forming a collective electoral list representing the entire opposition under the leadership of Al-Wafd Party. This proposal was conceived as a means to confront the regime with a unified political front demanding democratic reform and the suspension of the emergency law. Thus, during the second week of February, Shukri discussed the SLP proposal with various political groups, including Al-Wafd and the Muslim Brotherhood. On February 12, however, Al-Wafd, announced that it would field candidates independently of any electoral coalition.

On the same date, the SLP's Supreme Council convened to discuss potential election strategies, including cooperation with other opposition forces. As the meeting began, a group of Muslim Brotherhood leaders visited the SLP's offices, apparently upon Shukri's invitation. After adjourning the Supreme Council meeting, SLP leaders Ibrahim Shukri, Helmy Murad, Ahmed Megahed, and Mamdouh Qenawy consulted with the Brotherhood delegation, composed of Mamoun Al-Houdaiby, Salah Shadi, and Mustafa Mashhur.[186] The Brotherhood officials disclosed that the movement's Guidance Bureau had authorized them to propose an electoral list with the SLP and the LSP. This offer, however, was conditional on the following: (1) SLP candidates would be limited to one-third of the names on the electoral list, and (2) socialists and Nasserists would be excluded from the list. "We do not want the reds or the yellows," they said in a disparaging reference to socialists and Nasserists. As Mamdouh Qenawy objected to these conditions, the meeting ended inconclusively, but with the agreement to reconvene the following day after the SLP Supreme Council had considered the proposal. Ultimately, the Council agreed in principle to joining a national coalition, and on this basis, SLP leaders began discussions with Brotherhood and LSP representatives.[187] The parties ultimately agreed to form a list allotting 40 percent of candidates to the Brotherhood, 40 percent to the SLP, and 20 percent for the LSP.[188]

During these negotiations, it soon became clear that SLP leaders were submitting the party to a number of the Brotherhood's distasteful conditions. For example, despite the Supreme Council's instruction to devise a national coalition of all political forces, in apparent compliance with the Brotherhood's demands, Shukri excluded Al-Tagammu from the discussions.[189] Similarly, SLP candidates of alleged socialist or Nasserist orientation were moved to the bottom of the electoral lists or eliminated entirely. SLP and Muslim Brotherhood figures independently confirmed that this occurred in response to Brotherhood leaders' insistence that such political leanings had no place in the alliance.[190]

In response, high-ranking SLP officials defected from the party, protesting what they viewed as their leaders' complete submission to the Muslim Brotherhood. Among these defectors was Assistant Secretary General

Mamdouh Qenawy, who publicly attacked the party's leadership. Whereas remaining SLP officials accused the defectors of undermining the alliance at the regime's bidding, Qenawy insisted that the disagreements over the electoral coalition were part of a serious years-long internal conflict over the party's relationship with the Islamist movement.[191] In any event, these defections signaled the beginning of a new stage in the conflict over the SLP's identity.

The alliance members' ultimate decision to adopt a joint platform under the slogan "Islam is the solution" alarmed many SLP members who deemed the platform contradictory to the party's line. Such objections often cited the document's reconfiguration of the SLP's priorities (if not its entire identity) to privilege the implementation of Sharia. Pro-Islamist figures like Shukri and Hussein argued that Islamic principles and Sharia had always been central the SLP's professed mission as well as that of Misr Al-Fatat. Yet, as explained earlier, the 1987 platform marked an obvious break from its predecessors. For example, all previous affirmations of socialist principles and the goals of the July 23 Revolution were absent from the new platform.[192]

The SLP's divisions over the new program's Islamist orientation were reflected in party leaders' contradictory statements. Whereas Shukri made no secret that the implementation of Sharia was the central goal of the program the SLP had devised with other members of the Islamic Alliance, his deputy Ahmed Megahed continued to assert that advancing democratic reform was the principal purpose of the alliance.[193] Such divisions within the party's leadership only increased the anxiety of SLP members objecting to the new Islamist line.

The climax of this conflict occurred in spring 1989 at the party's fifth congress. The new party election resulted in complete victory for proponents of the Islamist line, who assumed control of al-lajnah al-tanfidhiyah (the "executive committee"). This development prompted a new wave of defections from the party, including sitting MPs and senior leaders like Ahmed Megahed, Shawki Khaled, and Gamal Assaad Abdel-Malak. Defectors soon questioned the party election's legitimacy. These defectors accused proponents of the Islamist line of padding voter rosters with the names of outside supporters, thereby permitting ineligible voters to cast ballots. Declaring the newly elected leadership illegitimate, the defectors convened a separate party congress attended by 833 members, or 42 percent of members who attended the official congress.[194] After a long, public exchange of accusations, the defecting coalition dissipated, signaling the triumph of the party's Islamist current.[195] Thus, the splitting of the SLP was achieved.

Conclusion

This chapter explained two important long-term effects Islamist incorporation policies wrought on opposition politics in Egypt. The first is the crowding out of conflicts over wealth distribution by identity politics and culture wars. Crowding out was evident in the shifting policy priorities of all parties that allied themselves with the Brotherhood during the 1980s. It was also apparent in the legislative priorities pursued by the Muslim Brotherhood after it became the largest opposition force in the 1987 parliament. Moreover, the process of crowding out altered the balance of power within Al-Tagammu, thus changing the party's policy priorities during the 1980s and 1990s. These changes drove Al-Tagammu closer to the ruling establishment, even while the government pursued economic reform policies inimical to the party's declared mission. The second long-term effect of Islamist incorporation is splitting, defined as new identity-based divides among opponents of economic liberalization produced by the political ascendancy of Islamist movements. This effect is demonstrated by the SLP's experience throughout the 1980s, which witnessed multiple splits as a result of disagreements over the party's appropriate position in relation to political Islam and its adherents.

Conclusion

Reflections on the Legacies of Islamist Incorporation and the Post-Mubarak Politics

J
ust as the July 2010 meeting at Al-Tagammu's headquarters (see the introduction) commenced, the speaker began to lecture the party's younger cadres about the fundamental principles of socialism and the ways in which they informed the party's mission and platform. The official pontificated for nearly an hour before one seemingly bored activist interrupted. In an innocent, puzzled tone, the young man asked why activists' mere mention of the word "socialism" in conversation with ordinary Egyptians almost always provoked accusations of blasphemy. After a long pause, the speaker responded at length, asserting Egyptian society's lack of preparedness for socialism and observing that the necessary preconditions for socialism take time to form. In the absence of genuine class consciousness, he concluded, the masses will naively follow whoever claims to speak in the name of God. Frequent audience interruptions followed, with the questions growing sharper, more critical, and more accusatory. At some point, members of the audience had ceased posing sincere, interrogative questions. Instead, they were criticizing, rather unsubtly, their party leadership's estrangement from the masses and challenging these leaders' frequent claims that society was not yet equipped to understand the socialist concepts they espoused. "And if society is not ready for socialism," one activist inquired, "why did you join this party in the first place?" To which the speaker swiftly responded: "To clear my conscience."

Months later, several of the young faces I had seen at that meeting were visible on international news broadcasts. These activists played significant roles in advancing the nationwide protests that ousted Hosni Mubarak in February 2011. Thus, they—and the generational cohort they mobilized—were dubbed "the youth of the revolution." It was clear that this younger generation of activists was rejecting the apparent timidity of the Egyptian left's aging leaders and was pushing for meaningful social change. This generation of activists overcame or bypassed the formal opposition's largely coopted leadership, launching the historic series of protests that ignited the January 25 Revolution of 2011.

More than ten years into the post-Mubarak era, however, one thing seems clear. The protesters who successfully defied Mubarak's infamous coercive apparatus were unable to overcome the structural constraints of the political environment they had inherited. Despite the traditional ruling elite's erasure from the scene and the emergence of new political parties and actors, old patterns of Egyptian politics endured. Not long after Mubarak's downfall, identity politics made its return to the political stage, defining once more the parameters of political conflicts and alignments. The polarization engendered by these conflicts enabled senior military officers, Egypt's de facto rulers, to undermine their opponents using the same divide-and-rule tactics employed by Mubarak and Anwar Al-Sadat. In fact, within three years, large swaths of the Egyptian left had returned to the ruling establishment's embrace. As in previous times, this collaboration was justified by reference to the "threat" posed by political Islam.

This concluding chapter offers some reflections on the implications of this study's findings for the politics of the post-Mubarak Egypt. After recapping the argument of the book, the conclusion situates the legacies of Islamist incorporation within Egypt's post–January 25 Revolution political dynamics.

Summary of Argument

As discussed in chapters 1 and 2, Sadat's 1970s Islamist incorporation policies were structurally linked to his attempts to discard the costly and unsustainable Nasserist social pact. Unable to fulfill the commitments of this pact, Sadat used economic liberalization measures to free the state from its role as the guarantor of social and economic rights. Despite his efforts to contain opposition to these policies by pursuing institutional reforms and restructuring the ruling coalition, the tide of opposition appeared unstoppable. Thus, as detailed in chapter 2, the political leadership opted to enlist the support of Islamist currents to offset the efforts of de-Nasserization's leftist opponents. The Muslim Brotherhood and its Islamist student movement partners not only counterbalanced Sadat's leftist opponents but also resolutely avoided contesting the fundamentals of Sadat's economic and social policies. This avoidance is attributable, in part, to the Brotherhood leadership's enduring tendency to eschew engagement with divisive economic questions and to treat such issues as secondary elements of a much broader revivalist project. As described in chapter 3, Sadat's Islamist incorporation policies enabled the Muslim Brotherhood to reconstitute itself at a moment when its future was anything but certain. In contrast, Egypt's leftist activists confronted a much more hostile and restrictive environment, as explained in chapter 4. Thus, despite their numbers, passion, and some notable early successes, the left failed to form a coherent, effective national organization.

This book argues that Islamist incorporation policies had an enduring impact on the structure of Egyptian politics in ways that were profoundly relevant to the politics of economic liberalization. Islamist incorporation shaped the (im)balance of power between leftist and Islamist currents in Egypt. This imbalance ensured that political actors opposed to economic liberalization could not develop an organizational capacity comparable to that of their Islamist counterparts. One of the distinctive features of Islamist incorporation was its provision of state support to the Muslim Brotherhood and its allies within the Islamist student movement without imposing conditions that would compromise their organizational autonomy. This approach placed the Islamist movement on a trajectory of institutional development that was markedly different from that of leftists denied such autonomy. And as a result of state interventions, the Egyptian left remained organizationally dependent on the ruling party of the day. The first such intervention was President Gamal Abdel-Nasser's 1965 compulsory dissolution of communist parties and their members' relegation to subordinate roles within in the ruling Arab Socialist Union (ASU). The second intervention occurred as a result of former communists and their allies' agreement to operate under the constraints of the legal political arena. This decision exposed Al-Tagammu and other political actors to assorted forms of state interference. The Muslim Brotherhood, in contrast, neither agreed to operate under the umbrella of the ruling party, nor did it accede to regime entreaties to form an organization with legal status. In other words, Sadat was unable to obtain from the Brotherhood what Nasser had wrested from the communists, their autonomy. This historical divergence helps explain the contemporary imbalance of power between Egypt's Islamist and leftist political forces.

Islamist incorporation also affected the politics of economic liberalization in various ways. As explained in chapter 5, it facilitated splits within antiliberalization coalitions over issues of national identity and reduced the relative salience of distributive issues. Accordingly, when the state inaugurated an era of far-reaching economic liberalization reforms, the political arena's structure reduced the potential for serious opposition to these policies. In other words, Egyptian politics were now characterized by "more identity, less class."

The Military and the Logic of Islamist Incorporation After 2011

Even after the 2011 downfall of the Mubarak regime, the legacies of Islamist incorporation continued to afflict Egyptian politics in subtle ways. For example, a striking feature of post-Mubarak politics is the enduring logic of Islamist incorporation, despite the ruling National Democratic Party (NDP)'s dissolution. Shortly after Mubarak's resignation, the Egyptian state's provisional executive body, the Supreme Council of the Armed Forces (SCAF), formed a tacit alliance with Islamist currents to resist the popular mobilization confronting the new regime.

Egypt's new military rulers faced an array of revolutionary groups and protest movements populated by a newly emboldened leftist current that took the lead in articulating the movement's goals.[1] These activists espoused a commitment to sweeping reforms of the state bureaucracy—particularly police and security forces[2]—and drastic economic prescriptions,[3] including the restoration of privatized public sector companies to state ownership.[4] Some openly called for a civilian-led transition that excluded the armed forces,[5] greater military accountability and transparency, and the abolition of political and economic privileges army officers had long enjoyed.[6] In other words, their demands for change encroached upon all of the Egyptian political system's sacred cows.

Unable to meet protesters' mounting demands and mushrooming wildcat labor actions,[7] the SCAF made political overtures to Islamist currents, seeking their support in rebuffing this seemingly implacable protest movement. To this end, in the spring of 2011, the military regime made significant gestures to the Muslim Brotherhood. It ensured that the movement's views would be well represented on a committee tasked with drafting the constitutional amendments[8] that would define and govern the remainder of the transitional period.[9] Thus, the Brotherhood became the sole political group with an affiliate serving on the committee, attorney Sobhi Saleh. Furthermore, the body was chaired by a figure widely revered within Islamist circles, retired judge Tariq Al-Bishri, whose political views historically had been accommodating to the Brotherhood.[10]

The SCAF structured and sequenced the transition process in a manner highly beneficial to the Muslim Brotherhood. For example, the military's insistence on swiftly convening the legislative election discreetly handed established, well-organized movements like the Brotherhood a comparative advantage relative to the nascent groups appearing in the wake Mubarak's downfall.[11] Similar favoritism was apparent in the process of drafting a new constitution. Senior officers ignored widespread calls for an inclusive, nonpartisan constitution-drafting process before elections. Many liberal and leftist groups argued that such a process would build a national consensus around the rules governing the new political order and prevent any single party from shaping these rules in its own interests.[12] The SCAF did the exact opposite. It scheduled early parliamentary election and made the composition of the prospective constitution-drafting body, known as the constituent assembly, contingent on the election outcome. That is, the new legislature was expected to form the assembly. Because the Brotherhood was poised to take control of the new parliament,[13] it was embarrassingly obvious that this arrangement would give the group (and partisan political forces, more broadly) undue influence over the drafting of a new constitution.

In addition to structuring and scheduling the transition process in a manner friendly to the Muslim Brotherhood's interests, the military provided Islamist currents considerable latitude to form political organizations and engage in activism. Although SCAF Decree 12/2011 barred political parties from organizing on the basis of religion,[14] authorities overlooked that restriction when permitting the Brotherhood to form the Freedom and Justice Party (FJP) and to advertise the party's connection to the mother organization.[15] Similarly, the SCAF permitted Salafists to establish political parties, including Al-Nour, which was cofounded by the Salafist Call movement of Alexandria.[16] The emergence of a strong Salafist current in national politics facilitated the SCAF's divide-and-rule strategy. In addition to pitting Islamist and secular forces against one other, this new development also enabled the SCAF to employ the Salafists as an Islamist counterweight to the Brotherhood. Finally, as the regime and its media allies investigated the foreign funding of prodemocracy civil society groups, the SCAF ignored evidence that Salafist parties like Al-Nour had received financial support from Arab Gulf donors.[17]

Islamist currents sided with the SCAF in several political battles. For example, Islamists campaigned on behalf of the military-sponsored constitutional amendments,[18] which passed the March 19, 2011, referendum with 77 percent of votes.[19] The Muslim Brotherhood also publicly called for an end to protests,[20] sit-ins,[21] and labor strikes;[22] condemned mobilizational efforts targeting the military;[23] and defended SCAF's management of the transition.[24] In addition, the Brotherhood largely ignored military and security force transgressions.[25] Finally, the movement also supported the military's efforts to preserve its economic and political privileges and shield its personnel from oversight and accountability.[26]

By empowering the Muslim Brotherhood, senior officers did much more than prop up one political force to oppose another. In effect, they marginalized (or more aptly, "crowded out") a particular mode of politics. The military's efforts reoriented national political debates toward traditional conflicts over the state's religious identity and away from popular demands for systemic change. This tactic undermined forces calling for the radical reform of state institutions, enabling the military to implement a more manageable (and manipulatable), elite-guided mode of political contestation.[27] Thus, as the SCAF tacitly and overtly promoted conflicts between Islamist and "secular" currents, the political center of gravity shifted from the domain of Tahrir Square–style popular mobilization to discreet arrangements between military and political elites. Such arrangements routinely favored the interests of the military and its allies within the state bureaucracy.

For example, by allying with Islamist currents in early 2011, the SCAF diverted public discussions of the March 19 constitutional referendum from popular demands for meaningful change inside state institutions to issues surrounding the state's religious identity. Encouraging voters to approve the amendments, Salafists used media and the pulpit to argue that a "No" vote was synonymous with rejecting Article 2 of the 1971 Constitution, which defined Islam as the principal source of legislation.[28] Actually, none of the amendments under consideration touched upon Article 2 or, for that matter, the role of religion in politics. Thus, it became clear that many Islamists were creating a political battle out of thin air to advance the military's agenda. Nevertheless, Islamist opinion makers repeatedly presented the outcome of the referendum as a reaffirmation of Egypt's Islamic identity.[29] Absent from this national identity-centered rhetoric was the pressing issue of the military's continued management (and by implication, manipulation) of the transition, which the March 19 referendum effectively upheld.[30] In other words, as secular and Islamist forces engaged in their usual ideological spats, the SCAF emerged triumphant, with its self-appointed role as the arbiter of politics in the post-Mubarak greatly legitimized.

As the prominence of Islamist currents increased, military leaders also exploited fears of an impending "Islamist takeover" to secure secularist support for their agenda. A case in point was the late-2011 affair surrounding the Al-Selmi document. As concerns arose that the Islamists poised to dominate the constitutional drafting assembly would impose a document that failed to protect religious freedoms or other civil liberties, the SCAF used the occasion to orchestrate a devious power grab. In July 2011, SCAF announced its intention to formulate a series of so-called supraconstitutional principles.[31] The idea, in theory, was to present those drafting the constitution with a set of binding articles protecting civil liberties. The avowed purpose of this measure was guaranteeing that the new constitution would safeguard such fundamental rights regardless of the legislative election's outcome.[32]

This list of supraconstitutional principles was drafted under the supervision of Deputy Prime Minister Ali Al-Selmi—a Wafidst academic who reportedly served in the infamous Vanguard Organization under Nasser.[33] Thus, the document, which was disclosed shortly before the 2011 legislative election, was popularly known as the Al-Selmi document.[34] Some versions of the document foreclosed parliamentary oversight of military budgets and internal policies and designated the armed forces as the guardians of constitutional legitimacy.[35] Thus, it became clear that the supraconstitutional initiative's primary purpose was institutionalizing the military's privileges and prerogatives, rather than protecting civil liberties from the alleged authoritarian inclinations of Islamists. The SCAF, in other words, preserved its interests by exploiting and exacerbating secularist fears of an Islamist victory at the polls.[36] Using a seemingly liberal initiative to advance an illiberal agenda, the SCAF conducted a master class in divide-and-conquer tactics.

Although the Al-Selmi document was withdrawn in the wake of November 2011's popular protests,[37] one of the military's chief goals— autonomy in budgetary and internal affairs—was later enshrined in the Muslim Brotherhood–sponsored constitution.[38] This document was ratified in December 2012 against the backdrop of intensifying strife between Brotherhood-affiliated President Mohamed Morsi and liberal and leftist political forces–conflicts that, once again, affirmed the armed forces' power and authority.

Morsi's opponents alleged that he ruled undemocratically, reneged on his campaign promise to share power with other political forces, and sought to tighten the Brotherhood's grip on state institutions as part of a scheme to keep the FJP in power indefinitely.[39] The president's advocates dismissed these charges as disingenuous and countered that criticisms of Morsi were nothing more than election losers' attempts to overturn the voters' democratically expressed will.[40] It was only a matter of time before a politically enterprising minister of defense intervened in these disputes, pushing large swaths of liberal and leftist Egyptians into the embrace of the same military institution against which they had protested the previous year. These developments paved the way for the July 3, 2013, coup, which deposed Morsi, imprisoned and massacred his supporters, and initiated a new era of military-dominated government.

Central to the military's success were the increasing prevalence of ideological conflicts between Islamists and their adversaries and the sidelining of the revolutionary politics that animated national debates immediately after Mubarak's downfall. The political stage ceased being a domain for addressing the issues raised by the January 25 Revolution—political freedom, economic justice, and popular sovereignty[41]—and instead became a field for contesting the national identity of the state, thereby enabling the reestablishment of authoritarian practices.

In sum, the post-Mubarak era witnessed the restoration of aspects of Islamist incorporation policies. Senior military officers took steps to fuel and exploit conflicts across the Islamist–non-Islamist divide to marginalize demands for revolutionary political change that threatened their privileged position within the state. Ultimately, this strategy was successful, for it permitted the military to portray itself as the indispensable arbiter of political conflict, and thus it was able to institutionally impose itself on Egyptian political life.

Legacies of Islamist Incorporation and the Post-Mubarak Political Arena

The legacies of Islamist incorporation were evident in the political arena that emerged in the aftermath of Mubarak's 2011 downfall. Shaping this field were a set of institutional patterns that, as described in chapters 3 and 4, enabled the rise of a powerful, largely unified Islamist current alongside its fragmented, disorganized leftist counterpart. These asymmetries were visible in the dynamics of 2011 and 2012's electoral campaigns, and in the Muslim Brotherhood's standoff with its non-Islamist rivals between late 2012 and early 2013.

THE ASYMMETRIES OF POWER IN THE 2011–2012 ELECTION

Throughout the Mubarak era, leftist activists complained that state-imposed legal constraints and the authoritarian tendencies of their party leaders made organizing nearly impossible. They had long imagined that their political fortunes would improve dramatically when these restrictions were lifted. Yet when that day came, little actually changed. The left's poor showing in the 2011–2012 legislative election left it as powerless as it had been throughout the Mubarak era.

The following discussion summarizes the political context in which this election occurred, describing how leftist groups organized in the election and examining the outcome of their various efforts. This section also briefly explains how the book's findings can help us understand the left's defeat in that contest. This provisional discussion is not conceived as a substitute for a comprehensive analysis of the election results. It is presented as a reflection on how the findings of this book can inform our understanding of post-Mubarak politics.

The Left on the 2011 Political Map

The relaxation of Mubarak-era constraints on the formation of political parties[42] significantly altered Egypt's political landscape. The left side of the spectrum featured the usual suspects, as well as numerous new groups.[43] Despite suffering many defections attributed to the domineering style of party leader Rifaat Al-Said, Al-Tagammu managed to survive Mubarak's ouster.[44] Although Al-Said's decision to stand by the Mubarak regime during the January 25 uprising severely damaged the party's credibility,[45] Hussein Abdel-Razek and a number of the party's iconic figures opted to remain in the party.[46] Others left to form the Socialist Popular Alliance Party (SPA), which, like Al-Tagammu, served as an umbrella under which a broad range of leftist political forces could unify. In addition to defectors from Al-Tagammu, the SPA housed affiliates of relatively newer leftist currents that had emerged during the Mubarak years. These included the Democratic Left current, which had unsuccessfully attempted to form a political party in the 2000s, and the Socialist Renewal current, an offshoot of the Trotskyist Revolutionary Socialists movement.[47]

Another community of leftist activists participated in the centrist experiment of the Egyptian Social Democratic Party (ESDP), which proclaimed itself an advocate for labor rights and social justice within the framework of a liberal, free market system. Like the SPA, the ESDP encompassed members of the Democratic Left current, as well as activists involved in the National Association for Change, the March 9 Movement for the Independence of Universities, and other prodemocracy movements formed under Mubarak.[48]

A different contingent formed the Democratic Workers Party (DWP), which included members of the Revolutionary Socialists movement. The DWP espoused a more daring vision than its centrist counterparts, advocating, for example, for the renationalization of privatized public sector companies.[49] Finally, in mid-2011, a group of veteran leftists announced the formation of the Socialist Party of Egypt (SPE).[50]

The 1970s generation of leftist activists who rose in opposition to Sadat were well represented within these parties. Prominent examples included Farid Zahran in the ESDP, Kamal Khalil in the DWP, Emad Attia in the SPA, and Ahmed Bahaaeddin Shaaban in the SPE. The younger generation of leftist activists whose energies were long stifled by Mubarak-regime repression and the machinations of Rifaat Al-Said was also represented in these parties. All of these forces now had an opportunity to participate in the formal political process and contest political power—or so it seemed.

The Left in the 2011 Electoral Coalitions

Between the spring and fall of 2011, electoral alliances shifted considerably. Initially, all major political forces agreed to join a new coalition, the Democratic Alliance for Egypt (DAE).[51] This arrangement was conceived as a united front against affiliates of the former ruling party and as a means to ensure that all stakeholders would secure representation in the prospective parliament. This coalition was short-lived, however, because of factional disagreements over the apportionment of candidate rosters and ideological conflicts between the coalition's Islamist and secular participants. It was not long before the DAE transformed into a Muslim Brotherhood–dominated alliance, notwithstanding the participation of smaller organizations like Al-Karama, the Nasserist Party, and the Islamic Labor Party (the former Socialist Labor Party).[52]

The most notable realignment of electoral coalitions occurred after a July 29 rally in Tahrir Square, at which Islamist parties alienated a host of liberal and leftist leaders by chanting slogans demanding the implementation of Sharia.[53] More generally, Islamist groups' remarkable display of mobilizing power at Tahrir Square galvanized ideological divisions within the DEA and stimulated the anxieties of secularists. Soon thereafter, several liberal, social democratic, and leftist parties abandoned the DEA to form an anti-Brotherhood coalition known as the Egyptian Bloc.

The Bloc was equally vulnerable to divisions, as objections to the presence of former NDP affiliates on the coalition's candidate slates caused major defections. On the eve of the parliamentary election, the Bloc consisted of ESDP, Al-Tagammu, and the right-leaning Free Egyptians Party (FEP), which was founded by business tycoon Naguib Sawiris.[54] The Bloc's final composition exemplified the effects of crowding out. The union of

Al-Tagammu's socialists and the FEP's promarket business interests spoke to the alliance's counter-Islamist character and its true motivation—fear of an Islamist victory at the polls.[55] The Egyptian Bloc's composition also demonstrated the increasing salience of national identity issues and the marginalization of economic questions, which many parties had placed on the backburner to focus on the battle with political Islam.

A third electoral coalition, the Revolution Continues Alliance (RCA), featured parties that had defected from the Egyptian Bloc. The SPA led the RCA in partnership with the SPE, the Egyptian Current Party (ECP), and others.[56] The ECP had been founded in 2011 by a group of young defectors from the Muslim Brotherhood and affiliates of the April 6 youth movement.[57]

Thus, leftist representation in the Egyptian Bloc and the RCA was primarily confined to the SPA, Al-Tagammu, and the ESDP.[58] Their notable competitors included the DAE and the Alliance for Egypt (also known as the Islamist Bloc), a coalition of Islamist parties led by Al-Nour and that included the Building and Development Party formed by Al-Gamaʿah Al-Islamiyya.[59] Some parties, like Al-Wafd and Al-Wasat, chose to contest the election independently of coalitions.

The Left and the Election Outcome: The Pre-Voting Problem

The election's outcome was a triumph for Islamist parties. Of the 498 seats in contention,[60] about 45 percent went to the Brotherhood's FJP, 22 percent to Al-Nour, and approximately 8 percent to Al-Wafd. Collectively, leftist parties captured less than 5 percent of available seats, with 3 percent going to the ESDP, 1.4 percent to the SPA, and about half of 1 percent to Al-Tagammu.[61]

Why did the left perform so poorly? It is tempting to seek answers through the analysis of voting patterns and public attitudes. Such an endeavor, of course, would yield important insights. All the evidence, however, suggests that leftist forces had lost the election long before a single ballot was cast. For example, none of these parties contested all of the seats in play. The SPA fielded candidates for approximately 55 percent of the seats,[62] whereas the ESDP contested no more than a third, and Al-Tagammu challenged only 8 percent.[63] This overview suggests that none of the leftist parties actually made a genuine effort to achieve a meaningful victory. Thus, it is unsurprising that they fared so poorly. The three parties securing the most seats, the FJP, Al-Nour, and Al-Wafd, contested somewhere between 80 to 90 percent of the races.[64] By failing to mount a comparable effort, the left surrendered any chance of scoring major gains in the election. That is to say, the left's problems long predated the campaigning and voting processes. One could certainly argue that these parties' unpersuasive platforms, inability to reach voters, ineffective campaigning, and other issues would have made securing meaningful representation a long shot, even if they had fielded candidates for every seat. Nonetheless, the fact remains that these leftist parties made no credible effort to achieve substantial political victories.

Pondering the left's failure to campaign for all contested parliamentary seats brings two important findings of this study into focus. The first finding concerns a critical legacy of authoritarianism: the left's distinctive path of institutional development since the 1970s. The second finding pertains to some leftists' adoption of new policy priorities during the 2011–2012 election campaign, another effect of Mubarak-era crowding out.

The Limitations of the Left's Path of Institutional Development

The context for the left's 2011–2012 election failures is a long history of institutional development that effectively prevented the establishment of strong, autonomous political organizations. As chapter 4 explains, successive waves of repression foreclosed such a possibility, leaving Al-Tagammu's experiment as the primary institutional home for the Egyptian left. Al-Tagammu exemplified a path of institutional development that fostered dependency on the state and facilitated regime intervention. Under these conditions, Al-Tagammu evolved into a state-supervised entity accustomed to negotiating its way into elected bodies and securing representation through the regime's largesse, as opposed to a party contesting elections and seeking to mobilize popular support. Thus, when a relatively free election was held in 2011, the left was in complete disarray, lacking an established base through which it could attract supporters. It is telling that in 2011, the generation of 1970s leftist activists who had opposed Sadat's initial efforts to dismantle the Nasserist social pact were fragmented, isolated, and largely irrelevant, whereas many of their Islamist contemporaries occupied the center stage of Egyptian politics.

The Muslim Brotherhood's success in the 2011–2012 election is partially attributable to the movement's path of institutional development since the Sadat era. This path enabled the Brotherhood to erect organizational structures autonomously from the state and to build a meaningful presence in significant social and political spheres, despite repression under the Mubarak regime. Hence, when the opportune moment arrived, the movement was well equipped and positioned to vie for power.

The Persistence of Crowding Out and the Post-Mubarak Left

The left's feeble performance in the 2011–2012 election highlights Islamist incorporation's role in establishing the asymmetries of the post-Mubarak political arena. It also underscores the significant impact of crowding out on the left's political priorities. The persistent salience of conflicts over Egypt's national identity induced the left to join forces with other secular actors, including some lacking its commitments to social and economic rights.

As pre-election debates on national identity proliferated and increased the polarization of Islamist and secular forces, the left gradually became the subordinate partner to a diverse community of political actors sharing little in common beyond their mutual antipathy to Islamists. The 2011–2012 legislative election was exemplary in this regard, as it featured the Egyptian Bloc coalition of leftists and big business interests. Al-Tagammu's cession of nearly half of the Egyptian Bloc's candidate roster to the party of billionaire Nagiub Sawiris warrants reflection. This surrender underscores a harsh reality: not only had leftist forces been eclipsed by their Islamist counterparts, but also the left had abandoned its identity as the chief advocate of social and economic rights. The Bloc's leftists willingly surrendered the electoral list's leadership to secular free marketeers, all in the name of averting the inherent dangers of political Islam. Put simply, although few would acknowledge it, "culture war leftists" had tacitly adopted the neoliberal commitments of fellow secular collaborators. Some observers might judge this to be a positive development, as it implied the Egyptian left's moderation à la European social democrats. Others might detect yet another manifestation of the left's preoccupation with identity and culture wars, and its concomitant failure to devise cogent policy responses to neoliberal economic prescriptions. Given these realities, a careful observer of the 2011–2012 election must ask: When, precisely, do we date the Egyptian left's defeat? Did it occur on election day? Or did it occur the moment its leadership ceased to define itself as theorists and practitioners of class struggle, opting instead to act as the left of identity politics, of the Ministry of Culture, of Rifaat Al-Said, or—more aptly—of "more identity, less class"?

THE ASYMMETRIES OF POLITICS AND THE 2013 POLITICAL GRIDLOCK

The legacies of Islamist incorporation policies, particularly the asymmetrical political landscape these policies helped fashion, offer a useful lens for analyzing the 2013 political standoff between President Mohamed Morsi and his rivals. This showdown proved central to the collapse of Egypt's brief experiment with competitive electoral politics, as it provided the pretext for the July 3 coup and the establishment of President Abdel-Fattah Al-Sisi's military-backed regime.

When examining what went wrong, some say the problem was President Morsi's insistence on marginalizing his opponents and his refusal to share power with them. For others, the problem lay with the president's opponents, who made the dishonorable and short-sighted decision to endorse—perhaps even encourage—the military's assault on democratic institutions. Focused almost exclusively on individual choice, such judgments overlook the institutional constraints shaping the standoff, particularly the structural legacies of Mubarak-era politics. As explained next, the preexisting (im)balance of power between leftist and Islamist currents reduced competitive parity in the political arena, thereby minimizing the prospect of forging a consensus on the rules governing political competition.[65]

Political theorists posit that procedural democracy is operable only if election losers believe in the possibility of becoming tomorrow's winners. Such a system works because those suffering electoral defeat trust that today's victors will not use the powers of state office to fix future elections. In the absence of such trust, the losing party will have little incentive to respect and comply with electoral outcomes. Scholars call this principle "contingent consent," as the party losing the election *consents* to maintain support for the democratic process *contingent* on the possibility of future victory.[66]

One could interpret the 2013 standoff between the Morsi regime and the opposition as a failure to build contingent consent. Morsi's opponents believed they had little or no chance of achieving political power, because they assumed that future elections would be anything but free and fair. I argue that this view was informed, at least in part, by the perception that the Brotherhood would use its predominant position in the constitutional assembly and its influence on state institutions to establish unfair advantages in future elections. Additionally, the results of successive post-Mubarak elections imparted a sobering truth: Islamist currents held the upper hand in the electoral arena. Thus, even in the absence of Islamist malfeasance, leftist electoral victories would be exceedingly difficult. That is to say, the asymmetrical political arena inherited from the Mubarak era— one affording comparative advantages to Islamist forces—was a significant cause of the 2013 standoff. The imbalance of power between Islamist and leftist political forces sharpened the perception that Morsi's opposition was unequipped to mount serious challenges in future electoral contests. As chapters 3 and 4 explain, this imbalance was largely due to the divergent paths of institutional development created by Islamist incorporation policies. Thus, tracing the role these policies played in shaping the post-Mubarak political arena contributes to our understanding of contingent consent's relative absence from post-2011 Egypt.

This finding, that Islamist incorporation policies produced a political environment inhospitable to the development of contingent consent, is applicable outside the Egyptian context. It demonstrates that some elements of state-managed political contestation undermined the country's transition to representative government by diminishing the probability of reaching an agreement on the rules regulating political competition. This finding also contradicts established scholarly wisdom, which holds that any experience with democratic institutions—like elections and multipartyism—under an authoritarian system tends to facilitate future possibilities for democratic transition and consolidation.

Previous research suggests that elections, however flawed, conducted under authoritarian regimes can play a positive role in advancing democratic transitions,[67] but Egypt's experience suggests otherwise. The country's democratic institutions failed because of (not despite) its experience with limited political contestation. I refer specifically to the long-term polarization and debilitating political imbalances that experience

generated. That is to say, because of Egypt's history of Islamist incorporation, limited political contestation was a curse, rather than a blessing,
for the country's post-Mubarak transition.[68] These conclusions challenge
scholars to think more critically about the role played by authoritarian
elections, or state-managed competition more generally, in advancing
or hindering future democratic transitions. Although some theoretical
perspectives emphasize the democratizing effects of state-constrained
competition,[69] this study reveals the potential negative long-term consequences of such modes of political contestation.[70] Thus, it invites further
in-depth research on the phenomenon.[71]

Indispensable Arbiters: Where to Next?

We look next at where this leaves Egypt and the indispensable arbiters who
currently rule it. Despite the turbulence and dramatic changes following
Mubarak's downfall, the state's long struggle to revise the Nasserist social
pact is, as of yet, unresolved.[72] Furthermore, popular visions of the state
as principal protector of economic and social rights remain evocative.[73]
Yet the regime of Abdel-Fattah Al-Sisi appears intent on shedding these
burdensome responsibilities by reshaping public expectations about the
state's role in economic production and resource distribution.[74] Of course,
Al-Sisi's ultimate success or failure at imposing from above the terms of
a new social pact remains unknown. Al-Sisi appears to be following in
the footsteps of his predecessors by exploiting national identity issues to
define his regime's purpose and enhance its legitimacy.

Indeed, upon deposing President Morsi, Al-Sisi employed violence and
other forms of coercion to drive the Muslim Brotherhood and its Islamist
allies underground once more.[75] Despite the marginalization of Islamist
currents, issues of national identity remain highly contested features of
the political arena. This time, however, such questions are posed by the
Al-Sisi regime rather than by the Islamist opposition. After all, the current president portrayed his ascent to power as an attempt to protect
Egypt's "true identity" from those seeking to impose a social order contrary to the country's "authentic" national character.[76] Unsurprisingly, as
its war against dissent continues, the Al-Sisi regime has adopted the time-
tested tactic of charging political prisoners, regardless of their ideological

commitments, with aiding a "terrorist organization," a term frequently employed as code for the Brotherhood.[77] This practice is consistent with the leitmotif of the regime's ultranationalist narrative: every opponent of President Al-Sisi is, by definition, an enemy of the Egyptian people and their way of life. While touting its self-appointed mission of protecting Egypt's true national identity, the regime has continued to expand its pre-rogatives. On some days, the regime does so under the pretense of urging the official religious establishment to call for *tajdid al-khitab al-diny* ("mod-ernizing religious discourse").[78] On other days, the regime announces new measures regulating public spaces and social media in accordance with an ambiguous moral code it labels "the values of the Egyptian family."[79] That is to say, despite Islamist currents' absence from the center stage of political life, the politicization of national identity continues in Al-Sisi's Egypt. And how could it not? If the anxieties stimulated by such manipula-tion disappeared, Egypt's ruling indispensable arbiters would cease to be indispensable.

APPENDIX I

The Theoretical Argument, Key Concepts, and Central Assumptions

T he following is a summary of this study's theoretical argument, which was developed inductively from the Egyptian case. It clarifies the major concepts and central theoretical assumptions on which this argument rests. Because the discussion that follows is conceived as an abstracted formulation of the argument, names of actors and groups relevant to the Egyptian case detailed in previous chapters have been omitted.

Summary of Argument

The study understands Islamist incorporation to denote a ruling party's deliberate efforts to facilitate Islamist groups' participation in formal political life.[1] Participation could assume multiple forms, including the contestation of elections for national office or the governing bodies of professional syndicates, student organizations, and labor unions. Participation also might include serving in cabinets and legislatures. The degree of Islamist incorporation in a given country may vary across time. Participation is subject to partial or full reversals (henceforth referred to as deincorporation) or deepening. Applying this definition, we can identify countries in which Islamist incorporation occurred in the decades before

2011 (e.g., Egypt and Jordan) and those in which Islamists were largely excluded from political life during this period (e.g., Syria, Tunisia, and Libya). We also can identify temporal variations in the extent of a given country's Islamist incorporation.

What accounts for variation in the levels of Islamist incorporation? The findings of this study demonstrate that Islamist incorporation is structurally linked to the challenges the state confronts when it attempts to steer economic policies away from the tenets of an increasingly expensive distributive social pact. As those harmed by this reorientation rise in opposition to economic liberalization, the state resorts to Islamist incorporation as a means of counterbalancing the influence of such opponents and their allies.

Islamist incorporation also generates a new mode of politics. It introduces a new set of identity-based social conflicts into the political arena, causing distributive demands to lose their salience in both the definition of national political agendas and the configuration of political alliances and coalitions. Because of the ideological gulf separating recently incorporated Islamist currents and advocates of the previous social pact, political forces are realigned in ways favorable to the political status quo. Islamists' entry into political life enables the ruling party to enlist the tacit support of actors who oppose the regime's new economic orientation but who support its efforts to contain Islamist activists and impede the agendas they seek to advance. Moreover, the issues Islamists bring to the political arena reanimate previously dormant identity-based conflicts among advocates of the distributive social pact. Such disagreements promote fragmentation among those advocating for the restoration of the pact, undermining their capacity for collective action. Thus, the growing salience of identity politics relative to distributive conflicts—along with the resulting reconfiguration of ideological space—reinforces the political status quo.

In the long run, opening political space to Islamist currents enables the state to expand its influence over those political forces advocating the previous social pact. Growing competition between Islamists and the ruling party, however, increases the probability of deincorporation—that is, the exclusion of Islamists from political participation. Put simply, the state incorporates Islamists to undermine the left, but it deincorporates Islamists as soon as they achieve sufficient political or economic influence to threaten the ruling establishment. The following sections detail and elaborate on this argument.

Regime Survival, Social Pact, and Economic Crises

This study assumes that regime survival is the primary motive informing and constraining the actions of autocrats, and that survival is contingent upon particular societal groups' (hereafter referred to as "coalition partners") continuing support for the current political order. Thus, to survive, an autocrat must provide various benefits to coalition partners in return for their acquiescence to the status quo. Mediating the relationship between the regime and coalition partners is a "social pact," which institutionalizes the expectations and obligations associated with this understanding through the implementation of social and economic policies.[2] Thus, coalition partners' commitment to the underlying political order is contingent upon the state's ability to maintain a particular economic orientation, one that prioritizes state provision of benefits like social services and welfare (see chapter 1). Most of these benefits are the products of distributive policies (those involving the allocation of resources accrued from external rents) or redistributive policies (those resulting in the transfer of wealth from one group to another). For simplicity's sake, I describe the social pact as "distributive."

Economic challenges limit the ability of the state to meet the social pact's obligations. Macroeconomic changes, coupled with chronic economic downturns, undermine the viability of the economic models on which distributive social pacts are based, and thus they constrain the state's ability to maintain the provision of economic and social benefits to coalition partners.[3] Eager to improve economic performance, the state adopts economic liberalization policies. Even when implemented strategically and selectively, such policies generate a host of social and economic grievances for coalition partners (see chapter 1). These shifts reconfigure the ruling coalition, empowering those with a vested interest in economic liberalization and marginalizing, if not excluding, advocates of the social pact.

As aggrieved advocates of the social pact amplify their expressions of dissent, the state employs repressive measures to contain this opposition. Although such measures may succeed in containing dissent in the short run, their long-term viability depends on the state's ability to control channels of political expression. The feasibility of such strategies varies according to context. In contexts in which repressive measures alone have proved ineffective, the state resorts to Islamist incorporation to undermine political actors who oppose the new economic order designed to replace the old social pact. Aware of long-standing ideological conflicts between Islamists and proponents of the old social pact, the state provides Islamist groups greater political space in the hope that they will curb the influence of those opposing the regime's new economic policies (chapter 2). Such measures divide the political field along new ideological fault lines, fragmenting activists who advocate for a return to the old social pact.

Islamist Incorporation, the Ideological Space, Splitting, and Crowding Out

To elucidate the consequences of Islamist incorporation, this study relies on a concept often employed to analyze political parties' positions on salient policy issues, namely "ideological space."[4] I assume that ideological space is defined by multiple dimensions of conflict, each occurring in a particular domain of politics, such as the organization of the economy, the identity of the state, or the balance of power between regions and the central government. Because the national political arena can simultaneously accommodate a limited number of conflicts, it is assumed that an increase in the salience of one dimension of conflict is accompanied by a reduction in the salience of other dimensions. These dimensions' relative salience in national politics and, by implication, their relative influence on the configuration of political coalitions, vary across time and space. What factors determine which dimension of conflict will predominate in national politics at a given moment? Research on political cleavages suggests that the character of a given party system (i.e., the number and type of parties it encompasses) tends to reflect the configuration and content of social conflicts.[5] Scholars of political institutions, however, have shown that the rules governing political competition and institutional design often play a critical role in determining which cleavages will be represented in, or absent from, formal political competition.[6] Scholars have noted that authoritarian rulers can exercise considerable discretion in determining which social cleavages will manifest themselves in formal politics. This is the case because authoritarian rulers usually control political institutional design and enjoy considerable latitude to permit or forbid a given group's participation in political competition.[7]

In this authoritarian context, Islamist incorporation can be understood as a policy that increases the relative salience of one dimension of ideological conflict—that is, disagreements over the state's identity and religion's role in public affairs. A given ideological space might include an infinite number of such conflict dimensions, but, for the sake of parsimony, this theory considers only two broadly defined dimensions: *identity* and *distribution*.[8] In this study, *identity* is shorthand for one's position on religion's appropriate role in defining the state's identity and its policies. In the Arab world, identity issues have long been the focus of conflicts between Islamist and non-Islamist political actors.[9] *Distribution* is shorthand for one's position on whether the national economy and social policies should be structured to achieve distributive justice.

According to this conception of ideological space, this study argues that Islamist incorporation marginalizes proponents of distribution through two mechanisms: *crowding out* and *splitting*. *Crowding out* denotes how Islamists introduce new political agendas emphasizing issues of national identity and religion's role in political life, effectively pushing distributive issues to the margins of ideological space.[10] Because the distribution dimension thus loses much of its salience to the identity dimension, actors who oppose the state's economic policies, but also oppose the Islamist agenda (i.e., their position on national identity), ultimately opt to support the political status quo. By undermining the salience of distributive demands and promoting conflicts over national identity, Islamists' political ascendance sidelines fundamental disagreements between the state and many proponents of distribution, thereby facilitating the latter's cooptation by the regime (see chapter 5).

Splitting refers to the process by which the identity dimension's newly acquired salience galvanizes previously dormant disagreements between proponents of the previous social pact, undermining their prospects for collective action. Under such conditions, proponents of the social pact defect from groupings that protested the state's waning commitment to providing social and economic benefits. These defectors join forces with actors who share their positions on "identity" but who reject their commitment to distribution. Simply put, in a political field predominated by Islamist-secular contention, the disagreements dividing free market liberals from socialists become irrelevant to the formulation of political alignments and coalitions. Under such circumstances, identity-based issues eclipse distributive demands, which also become diluted within coalitions that feature members with conflicting economic orientations. In some cases, proponents of the old social pact simply capitulate to more resourceful probusiness elements within their new coalitions, agreeing to support platforms that contradict their economic commitments. Even when advocates of the old social pact retain their positions on economic and social policies, such commitments are usually subordinated to questions of national identity (see chapter 5).

Islamist Incorporation, Distribution, and Antiregime Mobilization

The weakening of coalitions advocating redistribution alters the political field, making it more accommodating to economic reform measures that violate the terms of the distributive social pact. In effect, Islamist incorporation tempers the opposition of those bearing the costs of such measures. Advocates of the social pact who do not defect to the Islamist coalition become more supportive of the status quo. Their opposition to the ideological tenets of the newly predominant Islamist project increases their willingness to forge tacit alliances with the ruling coalition.

The prospects for Islamist mobilization around distributive claims are equally unfavorable. The Islamist agenda is supported by individuals of varying economic orientations, ranging from business owners weary of state intervention in the economy to actors committed to redistribution. Therefore, the formulation of strong, coherent, and potentially divisive positions on economic policies is neither desirable nor feasible. Islamist actors sympathetic to distributive demands often provide social services to groups newly denied benefits as a result of the state's restructured economic commitments and priorities. Nonetheless, calling for the state to readopt the original social pact's distributive policies is potentially dangerous for Islamists, as such polarizing declarations would destabilize the movement's internal cohesion (see chapters 2 and 5). Thus, Islamist political currents are more likely to eschew decisive positions on economic and social policies, thereby reinforcing distributive demands' relative decline in national politics.

Tensions and Deincorporation

The state receives a short-term dividend from the adoption of Islamist incorporation policies: it can now advance socially disruptive economic measures enjoying narrow popular support without bearing the customary political price. The Islamist social agenda's divisiveness reinforces disaffected members of the former ruling coalition's reluctance to oppose the regime in any way that might strengthen Islamist actors. In other words, Islamist incorporation insulates the regime from opposition, even while it actively violates the social pact on which the political order rests. This initial benefit aside, Islamist incorporation frequently sows the seeds of its own destruction, as it animates extant tensions, thereby stimulating sufficient opposition to imperil the policy. The political space that incorporation opens to Islamist currents affords them a comparative organizational advantage over their leftist counterparts. At the same time, the Islamist sector's increasing influence is eventually perceived as a challenge to the political and rent-seeking interests of the ruling party. As a result, the ruling party becomes more inclined to contain if not reverse Islamist ascendancy.

Intentionality and Deliberation

The question of intentionality looms large in the theoretical formulation of this study's argument. Do the political actors who adopt Islamist incorporation comprehend the potential consequences of their actions? The evidence presented in this study might prompt some to conclude that states undertake Islamist incorporation in complete awareness of its potential benefits. This study advances a different argument. The evidence presented in this study suggests that the initial motivation for pursuing Islamist incorporation is more modest: regimes seek only to counter the influence of nominally secular opponents by encouraging the efforts of these opponents' ideological rivals. This policy, however, yields a host of unintended consequences, including crowding out, splitting, and a long-term imbalance of power between Islamist and leftist currents. For further discussion of critical junctures and path-dependent patterns, see Appendix II.

APPENDIX II

Critical Junctures and Path-Dependent Institutional Patterns

A ppendix II summarizes this study's understanding of critical junctures and path dependence, explaining how they inform the book's argument about the 1970s emergence of Islamist incorporation policies and these policies' enduring impact on the distribution of power among political groups in Egypt.

This study understands the term *critical juncture* to denote a relatively short period of time during which structural influences over decision making are temporarily relaxed, increasing the probability of actor's choices affecting a given outcome.[1] Path dependence, per Mahoney, "characterizes specifically those historical sequences in which contingent events set into motion institutional patterns or event chains that have deterministic properties."[2]

Critical Juncture, Contingency, and Choices

This book's argument assumes that Anwar Al-Sadat's pursuit of Islamist incorporation policies was structurally linked to the economic challenges confronting the state between the mid-1960s and early 1970s. Thus, Sadat's adoption of Islamist incorporation policies does not automatically signify the incidence of a critical juncture, as he made this decision under structural pressures. However, Sadat's choice of a specific *mode* of Islamist incorporation—one that secured the autonomy of Islamist currents from the state—was not governed by structural conditions. The latter decision, as explained next, displayed the defining characteristics of a critical juncture. The institutional legacies initiated during this juncture—specifically as they relate to the balance of power between Islamist and leftist currents—conform to the logic of path dependence.

I contend that the Sadat presidency (1970–1981) roughly coincided with a critical juncture for shaping the balance of power between Islamist and leftist forces for two reasons. First, the conditions preceding that juncture did not determine the outcome.[3] Second, the decisions leading to the outcome were more contingent on human agency than on structural conditions.[4]

On the first point, the period under study marked the state's reauthorization of multiparty competition after nearly two decades of Gamal Abdel-Nasser's one-party rule. Nasser's repression effectively liquidated long-standing political organizations, ranging from the Muslim Brotherhood to elements of the communist movement (see chapters 1, 3, and 4). That is to say, by permitting multiparty competition during the formative period of the 1970s, Sadat effectively restructured the political field from a relatively clean slate. Extant conditions provided no single political group with a comparative advantage. Nor did such conditions determine which current—leftist or Islamist—would dominate the political opposition in subsequent decades.[5] Thus, Sadat's personal decisions to permit or forbid a particular group's participation in politics and to set the conditions governing such participation were instrumental in shaping the distribution of power among political players in post-Nasser Egypt.

Regarding the issue of contingency, the key decision was Sadat's permitting the Muslim Brotherhood to participate in political life without submitting to state regulations governing the conduct of political parties or becoming a subsidiary organ of the ruling party. Instead, Sadat allowed the group to participate in a manner that preserved its organizational autonomy. Assuming that Sadat enjoyed some meaningful discretion in selecting the mode of Islamist incorporation his regime would sanction, what alternatives did he face? Or stated differently, what paths did Sadat decline to take?

One such path was compelling the Muslim Brotherhood to assume legal status, which, arguably, would have sealed the movement's fate in a manner similar to that of Al-Tagammu. As explained in chapter 4, the legal framework in which Al-Tagammu Party's leftist currents were enmeshed hindered their ability to develop independent political organizations and made them vulnerable to constant state intervention. Obviously, such a path would have been detrimental to the Brotherhood's development.

The second path not taken was coopting Islamist currents into the ruling party as Nasser had done to the communist movement (see chapter 4). Evidence shows that Sadat did, however briefly, entertain that possibility. For example, during the early 1970s, the Sadat regime tried to coax the Islamist student movement into state institutions, an effort that proved logistically untenable (see chapter 2). As an alternative, his administration tacitly supported the Islamic Groups at Universities without demanding their cooptation within the ruling party. Similarly, various Sadat emissaries offered the Muslim Brotherhood integration within the ruling party or independent legal status. The group's leaders shunned such offers, knowing that this path would have precluded the Brotherhood's emergence as an independent political player.

Finally, when assessing the critical juncture framework's applicability to this study's argument, a key question arises: Were the aforementioned decisions permitting the Muslim Brotherhood and its associates to operate without state oversight products of structural pressures or of various unpredictable circumstances? The book's assessment leans toward the latter view. Although the regime's policy of opening political space to Islamists was evidently deliberate and informed by structural factors, none of the firsthand accounts examined in this book indicate that the regime exhibited strong preferences for a specific mode of Islamist political participation. Although Sadat had a general interest in controlling the Muslim Brotherhood's political participation, his pursuit of that goal was largely reactive, affording the movement's leaders considerable freedom of action. Additionally, for much of the 1970s, regime officials focused their attention on leftist currents rather than on the Muslim Brotherhood or the Islamist student movement (see chapters 2 and 3).

Path Dependence and the Reproduction of Institutional Patterns

As explained in chapters 3 and 4, the state's chosen mode of Islamist incorporation placed Islamist and leftist currents on divergent trajectories of institutional development, shaping the balance of power between the two forces for decades. How did path-dependent institutional patterns persist after the end of this critical juncture? Two factors were critical to this process.

First, the intensification of ruling party–Muslim Brotherhood competition made senior regime figures reluctant to grant the group any additional privileges—like legal status as a political party—that might facilitate the movement's expansion of its already threatening political presence. Second, during the 1980s and 1990s, the Brotherhood's internal conflicts empowered a faction fearful that legal status would undermine the movement's autonomy and cohesion (see chapter 3). Accordingly, the Brotherhood maintained its unique status as an organization participating in state-managed politics in the absence of any legal standing. By implication, it was free of the costs accompanying this status (see chapter 4). This singular status only cemented the organization's position on a trajectory of institutional development established during the critical juncture. This trajectory also secured the organization's autonomy from state supervision and interference.

The gradual abandonment of Islamist incorporation policies, and their replacement with waves of anti-Islamist repression in the 1990s and 2000s, did not reverse the Brotherhood's long-established path-dependent institutional patterns. This can be attributed to two factors. First, as an underground organization, the Brotherhood was able to maintain its internal structures, even when subjected to repressive measures. Second, in the long run, repressive measures did not necessarily affect the organization's established presence in important social spheres. Nor did they sever the ties Brotherhood members had forged with various sectors of civil society.

In fact, following Mubarak's 2011 downfall, the Brotherhood formed a licensed political party, the Freedom and Justice Party. Yet, as explained in chapter 3, this party's independence was nominal, and it remained largely subordinate to a mother organization that preserved its insulation from state regulation and oversight. Thus, one could argue that the institutional patterns established in the 1970s persisted until the July 3, 2013, military coup and the subsequent violent crackdown on the Muslim Brotherhood.

Notes

Introduction

1. The party's formal name is *al-Tajammuʿ al-Watany al-Taqadumy al-Wahdawy* or the National Progressive Unionist Rally, but it is popularly known as "Al-Tagammu."

2. For a useful summary of the party's history, see Hesham Sallam, ed., *Egypt's Parliamentary Elections, 2011–2012: A Critical Guide to a Changing Political Arena* (Washington, DC: Tadween, 2013), 60–62; 80.

3. Amr Mohamed Kandil, "Mohieddin: 'Democracy Knight' Dies in Peace," *Egypt Today*, May 7, 2018, https://www.egypttoday.com/Article/1/49468/Mohieddin-'Democracy -knight'-dies-in-peace.

4. Mohieddin's memoirs discuss his affiliation with the communist movement. Khaled Mohieddin, *Walʾan Atakalam* (Al-Qahirah: Markaz al-Ahram li-l-Tarjamah wa-l-Nashr, 1992), 49–59.

5. See, for example, Steven Heydemann, "Social Pacts and the Persistence of Authoritarianism in the Middle East," in *Debating Arab Authoritarianism*, ed. Oliver Schlumberger (Stanford, CA: Stanford University Press, 2007), 19–38.

6. Whereas many observers characterize the economic line that Nasser adopted in the 1960s as "state socialism," others argue that "state capitalism" is a more apt description of the late president's policies. Here, the term "state socialism" refers to Nasser's pursuit of nationalization, central economic planning, state-led industrialization, deepening of land redistribution schemes, and state provision of social services and subsidies. For a useful recap of his policies, see Joel Beinin, "Egypt's Gamal Abdel Nasser Was a Towering Figure Who Left an Ambiguous Legacy," *Jacobin Magazine*, September 28, 2020, https://www.jacobinmag.com/2020/09

/egypt-gamal-abdel-nasser-legacy. On the complexities associated with the use of the term "socialism" in the Nasserist context, see Nazih N. Ayubi, "Withered Socialism or Whether Socialism? The Radical Arab States as Populist-Corporatist Regimes," *Third World Quarterly* 13, no. 1 (1992): 89–105.

7. To institute a state-managed multiparty system, Sadat announced in March 1976 the formation of three "platforms" (*manabir*) inside the ASU, each representing a particular political trend within the organization. Representing the right was the Liberal Socialists Organization, the center was housed in the Egypt Arab Socialist Organization, and representing the left was the National Progressive Unionist Rally Organization headed by Khaled Mohieddin. Within a few years and with the de facto disbandment of the ASU, along with the ratification of a law regulating political parties, these organizations were recognized as independent political parties. Not long after, Sadat formed the National Democratic Party (NDP), which replaced the Egypt Arab Socialist Party as the de facto ruling party.

8. During the 1990s, Al-Said actively participated in the regime's culture wars against Islamist groups. For a summary of his perspective on the imperative for countering Islamist movements, see Rifaat Al-Said, *Did al-Ta'slum* (Al-Qahirah: Al-Ahaly, 1996).

9. During the Sadat and Hosni Mubarak eras, the Muslim Brotherhood was allowed to participate in formal political life without legal status, while periodically subject to repressive measures.

10. Past scholarship has used the term "neoliberalism" to characterize a wide array of social phenomena in the developing world. Here, the term "neoliberal economic reforms" specifically refers to public policies that seek to curb the economic role of the state and promote the private sector. These reforms include privatization, elimination of price and exchange rate controls, trade liberalization, tax benefits for the private sector, and relaxing of government regulation over the economy.

11. Although much of the book focuses on the formative period of the Sadat presidency, it contrasts that experience with some of the policies Nasser pursued in prior decades, especially with respect to his relationship with the communist movement.

12. As Clark and Lipset observe, politics in Western democracies in the second half of the twentieth century have become "organized less by class and more by other loyalties." Terry Nichols Clark and Seymour Martin Lipset, "Are Social Classes Dying?," in *The Breakdown of Class Politics: A Debate on Post-Industrial Stratification*, ed. Terry Nichols Clark and Seymour Martin Lipset, 39–54 (Baltimore, MD: Johns Hopkins University Press, 2001), 52. For critiques of such perspectives, see Geoffrey Evans, ed., *The End of Class Politics?: Class Voting in Comparative Context* (New York: Oxford University Press, 1999). More recent findings from Piketty uphold the thesis that class politics have been declining in Western democracies. Thomas Piketty, *Capital and Ideology* (Cambridge, MA: Harvard University Press, 2020), 721–25.

13. Sheri Berman, "The Lost Left," *Journal of Democracy* 27, no. 4 (October 2016): 70.

14. Francis Fukuyama, *Identity: The Demand for Dignity and the Politics of Resentment* (New York: Farrar, Straus and Giroux, 2018), 74.

15. For more on the decline of leftist parties in Western Europe, see Rob Manwaring and Paul Kennedy, eds., *Why the Left Loses: The Decline of the Centre-Left in Comparative Perspective* (Bristol, UK: Policy Press, 2017). On the decline on class-based voting, see Russell J. Dalton, *Citizen Politics: Public Opinion and Political Parties in Advanced Industrial Democracies*, 6th ed. (Washington, DC: CQ Press, 2014), 162–63. On the rise of inequality in advanced industrial countries, see Thomas Piketty, *The Economics of Inequality* (Cambridge, MA: Harvard University Press, 2014), 19; 31.

16. Fukuyama, *Identity*, 79.

17. See, for example, Herbert Kitschelt and Anthony J. McGann, *The Radical Right in Western Europe: A Comparative Analysis* (Ann Arbor: University of Michigan Press, 1995); Cas Mudde, *Populist Radical Right Parties in Europe* (Cambridge: Cambridge University Press, 2007); and Pippa Norris, *Radical Right: Voters and Parties in the Electoral Market* (Cambridge: Cambridge University Press, 2005).

18. Ronald Inglehart and Pippa Norris, "Trump and the Populist Authoritarian Parties," *Perspectives on Politics* 15, no. 2 (June 2017): 444.

19. Inglehart and Norris, "Trump," 446. More recently, Piketty posited an alternative perspective on the character and origins of these transformations. Traditional left-right cleavages, he argues, have been transformed in recent decades into a cleavage between a "Brahmin Left," which attracts support from the educated and cultural elite, and a "Merchant Right," backed by commercial and financial elite. "[T]he rise of "elitist" political parties," he explains, has contributed to the rise of "populism." Piketty, *Capital and Ideology*, 39.

20. This echoes findings from Stephanie L. Mudge, *Leftism Reinvented: Western Parties from Socialism to Neoliberalism* (Cambridge, MA: Harvard University Press, 2018). Also see Piketty's discussion of the alienation of the "Brahmin Left" from its economically disadvantaged voting base. Piketty, *Capital and Ideology*, 755–59.

21. Sheri Berman, "Populism Is a Symptom Rather Than a Cause: Democratic Disconnect, the Decline of the Center-Left, and the Rise of Populism in Western Europe," *Polity* 51, no. 4 (October 2019): 666. Also see Berman, "The Lost Left," and Sheri Berman and Maria Snegovaya, "Populism and the Decline of Social Democracy," *Journal of Democracy* 30, no. 3 (July 2019): 5–19.

22. Declining polarization on economic affairs, Dennis Spies argues, afforded extreme right-wing parties "a favorable political opportunity structure to mobilize voters on their non-material core issues." Dennis Spies, "Explaining Working-Class Support for Extreme Right Parties: A Party Competition Approach," *Acta Politica* 48 (2013): 317.

23. For instance, Daniel Oesch argues that among production and service workers, cultural grievances over immigration rather than economic concerns drive support for extreme right-wing parties. Partisans of the extreme right, he shows, "appear more afraid of immigrants' negative influence on the country's culture than on the country's economy." Daniel Oesch, "Explaining Workers' Support for Right-Wing Populist Parties in Western Europe: Evidence from Austria, Belgium, France, Norway, and Switzerland," *International Political Science Review* 29, no. 3 (2008): 370.

Also see Simon Bornschier and Hanspeter Kriesi, "The Populist Right, the Working Class, and the Changing Face of Class Politics," in *Class Politics and the Radical Right*, ed. Jens Rydgren (New York: Routledge, 2013), 10–30; and Elisabeth Ivarsflaten, "What Unites Right-Wing Populists in Western Europe? Re-Examining Grievance Mobilization Models in Seven Successful Cases," *Comparative Political Studies* 41, no. 1 (2008): 3–23.

24. In voting for such parties, Elisabeth Ivarsflaten explains, blue-collar workers and small business owners discount their opposing economic views and focus instead on what they agree upon, namely "immigration, law and order, the European Union and government corruption." Elisabeth Ivarsflaten, "The Vulnerable Populist Right Parties: No Economic Realignment Fuelling their Electoral Success," *European Journal of Political Research* 44 (2005): 482.

25. The latter argument is widely dubbed "What's the matter with Kansas," in reference to the title of a 2004 book by journalist and historian Thomas Frank that explains why working-class voters in the United States support the Republican Party even though its policies hurt their economic interests. The ascendancy of culture wars in the United States, Frank argues, has made many working-class voters abandon their material self-interest and vote for the Republican Party in support of its conservative social stances on such things as abortion and gay marriage. Thomas Frank, *What's the Matter with Kansas? How Conservatives Won the Heart of America* (New York: Metropolitan Books, 2004). For a critique, see Larry M. Bartels, "What's the Matter with What's the Matter with Kansas?," *Quarterly Journal of Political Science* 1, no. 22 (March 2006): 201–26. For more on the intersection of identity and class in the 2016 presidential election, see Brian F. Schaffner, Matthew Macwilliams, and Tatishe Nteta, "Understanding White Polarization in the 2016 Vote for President: The Sobering Role of Racism and Sexism," *Political Science Quarterly* 133, no. 1 (Spring 2018): 9–34; and John Sides, "Race, Religion, and Immigration in 2016: How the Debate Over American Identity Shaped the Election and What It Means for a Trump Presidency," *Democracy Fund Voter Study Group Report*, June 2017), 12, https://www.voterstudygroup.org/publication/race-religion-immigration-2016.

26. See Margit Tavits and Natalia Letki, "From Values to Interests? The Evolution of Party Competition in New Democracies," *Journal of Politics* 76, no. 1 (January 2014): 246–58; and John D. Huber, *Exclusion by Elections: Inequality, Ethnic Identity, and Democracy* (Cambridge: Cambridge University Press, 2017). Other studies have shown that religious identity can sideline economic voting in the advanced industrial world. See Ana L. De La O and Jonathan A. Rodden, "Does Religion Distract the Poor? Income and Issue Voting Around the World," *Comparative Political Studies* 41, no. 4–5 (April 2008): 437–76; and John E. Roemer, "Why the Poor Do Not Expropriate the Rich: An Old Argument in New Garb," *Journal of Public Economics* 70, no. 3 (December 1998): 399–424.

27. Certainly, this is not to deny that there are contexts in which identity and culture are central to class, per Antonio Gramsci's theorization of the role of culture in mediating class relations. Also, there are indeed economic issues, like trade and immigration, in which identity conflicts can be pronounced. This study acknowledges these

nuances (see discussion of the Muslim Brotherhood's economic orientation in chapter 2) but still recognizes the evident tensions between the two sets of dimensions even in contexts in which they do intersect (see findings in chapter 5).

28. That view is consistent with the notion of equifinality, or the idea that "different causal patterns can lead to similar outcomes." See Alexander George and Andrew Bennett, *Case Studies and Theory Development in the Social Science* (Cambridge, MA: MIT Press, 2005), 161.

29. See, for example, Ellen Lust-Okar, *Structuring Conflict in the Arab World: Incumbents, Opponents, and Institutions* (Cambridge: Cambridge University Press, 2005), and Lisa Blaydes, *Elections and Distributive Politics in Mubarak's Egypt* (New York: Cambridge University Press, 2010).

30. Amr Adly, *Cleft Capitalism: The Social Origins of Failed Market Making in Egypt* (Stanford, CA: Stanford University Press, 2020), 99.

31. Fouad Morsi, *Hadha al-Infitah al-Iqtisady* (Al-Qahirah: Dar al-Thaqafa al-Jadidah, 1976), 166.

32. Morsi, *Hadha al-Infitah*, 164.

33. Fouad Morsi articulates this argument clearly in his book, especially with regard to reforms that ended the public sector's monopoly on imports and acting as agents of foreign companies. Morsi, *Hadha al-Infitah*, 121–22.

34. Adly, *Cleft Capitalism*, 101–3.

35. Angela Joya reports that inflation peaked in 1986 at 23.9 percent and that employment reached 14.7 percent that same year. See Angela Joya, *The Roots of Revolt: A Political Economy of Egypt from Nasser to Mubarak* (Cambridge: Cambridge University Press, 2020), 73.

36. On inflation taxes, see Samer Soliman, *Al-Nizam al-Qawy wa-l-Dawlah al-Da'ifah* (Al-Jizah: Al-Dar li-l-Nashr wa-l-Tawziʿ, 2006), 181–87. For subsidy spending data, see Gouda Abdel-Khalek and Karima Korayem, *Fiscal Policy Measures in Egypt: Public Debt and Food Subsidy* (Cairo, Egypt: American University in Cairo Press, 2000), 71.

37. See Ragui Assaad, "The Effects of Public Sector Hiring and Compensation Policies on the Egyptian Labor Market" (Economic Research Forum Working Paper No. 9517, Cairo, Egypt, 1995), 4, https://idl-bnc-idrc.dspacedirect.org/bitstream/handle/10625/34292/126351.pdf?sequence=1.

38. On the details of Egypt's talks with the IMF during the mid-1980s, see Bessma Momani, *IMF-Egyptian Debt Negotiations* (Cairo, Egypt: American University in Cairo Press, 2005), esp. 24–25.

39. Steven Greenhouse, "Half of Egypt's $20.2 Billion Debt Being Forgiven by U.S. and Allies," *New York Times*, May 27, 1991, https://www.nytimes.com/1991/05/27/business/half-of-egypt-s-20.2-billion-debt-being-forgiven-by-us-and-allies.html.

40. Momani, *IMF-Egyptian Debt*, 50.

41. Momani, *IMF-Egyptian Debt*, 62–63.

42. Adam Hanieh reports that during the 1990s the government sold more than 40 percent of state-owned enterprises eligible for privatization. Quoted in Adly, *Cleft Capitalism*, 105.

43. The percentage of the population holding subsidized ration cards decreased from 89 percent in 1989 to 69 percent in 1997. See Abdel-Khalek and Korayem, *Fiscal Policy*, 75.

44. The government began implementing a far-reaching sales tax in 1991. For details, see Soliman, *Al-Nizam al-Qawy*, 196–201.

45. Rent controls for new housing were legally eliminated in 1996. Omnia Khalil, "Old Rent: Survival Tactics to Live in the City," *Marsad Omran*, June 26, 2018, http://marsadomran.info/en/policy_analysis/2018/06/1582. In 1992 the government passed a law removing agricultural land rent controls, which was implemented in 1997. Joya, *The Roots of Revolt*, 196.

46. See Adly, *Cleft Capitalism*, 111–22.

47. Also noteworthy in this discussion is Piketty's account of the rise of the "Brahmin Left" parties of educated elites in Western democracies. Piketty, *Capital and Ideology*, 848 and esp. chap. 15.

48. Certainly, there are contexts in which identity-based cleavages and class-based demands can coexist in harmony rather than tension. This is not the context under examination in this study, which finds that these two dimensions of conflict have coexisted in tension, as explained in chapters 2 and 4.

49. A recent contribution underscoring the complex role of neoliberal reforms and globalization in contributing to the rise of Islamist movements is Khalid Mustafa Medani, *Black Markets and Militants: Informal Networks in the Middle East and Africa* (New York: Oxford University Press, 2021).

50. See Samuel P. Huntington, "The Clash of Civilizations?," *Foreign Affairs* 72, no. 3 (Summer 1993): 31–32; and Daniel Pipes, *In the Path of God: Islam and Political Power* (New York: Basic Books, 1983).

51. See Edward W. Said, "The Clash of Ignorance," *The Nation*, October 4, 2001, https://www.thenation.com/article/archive/clash-ignorance.

52. See Fouad Ajami, *The Arab Predicament: Arab Political Thought and Practice Since 1967* (Cambridge: Cambridge University Press, 1981); and John L. Esposito, *Islam and Politics* (Syracuse, NY: Syracuse University Press, 1984), 153–54.

53. See, for example, Nazih N. M. Ayubi, *Political Islam: Religion and Politics in the Arab World* (London: Routledge, 1991), 176. This perspective is partially echoed in the finding of Grewal et al. that economic strain increases support for Islamist parties. Sharan Grewal, Amaney A. Jamal, Tarek Masoud, and Elizabeth R. Nugent, "Poverty and Divine Rewards: The Electoral Advantage of Islamist Political Parties," *American Journal of Political Science* 63, no. 4 (October 2019): 859–74. Janine Clark, however, finds that Islamic charities tend to benefit members of the middle class, rather than the poor. Janine A. Clark, *Islam, Charity, and Activism: Middle-Class Networks and Social Welfare in Egypt, Jordan, and Yemen* (Bloomington: Indiana University Press, 2004), 4.

54. See the discussion and works reviewed in Quintan Wiktorowicz, ed., *Islamic Activism: A Social Movement Theory Approach* (Bloomington: Indiana University Press, 2004), 6–11. The literature on the provision of social services by Islamist groups

is vast. See, for example, Clark, *Islam, Charity, and Activism*; Melani Cammett and Sukriti Issar, "Bricks and Mortar Clientelism: Sectarianism and the Logics of Welfare Allocation in Lebanon," *World Politics* 62, no. 3 (July 2010): 381–421; Steven Brooke, *Winning Hearts and Votes: Social Services and the Islamist Political Advantage* (Ithaca, NY: Cornell University Press, 2019); Jane Harrigan and Hamed El-Said, *Economic Liberalisation, Social Capital and Islamic Welfare Provision* (New York: Palgrave Macmillan, 2009); and Mona Atia, *Building a House in Heaven: Pious Neoliberalism and Islamic Charity in Egypt* (Minneapolis: University of Minnesota Press, 2013).

55. For a critical overview of the literature, see Melani Cammett and Pauline Jones Luong, "Is There an Islamist Political Advantage?," *Annual Review of Political Science* 17 (May 2014): 187–206.

56. Carrie Rosefsky Wickham, *Mobilizing Islam: Religion, Activism, and Political Change in Egypt* (New York: Columbia University Press, 2002), 13.

57. Brooke, *Winning Hearts and Votes*, 51–52.

58. Nathan J. Brown, *When Victory Is Not an Option: Islamist Movements in Arab Politics* (Ithaca, NY: Cornell University Press, 2012), 2–3. Wickham discusses the tendency for self-restraint in the context of Egypt's Muslim Brotherhood. See Carrie Rosefsky Wickham, *The Muslim Brotherhood: Evolution of an Islamist Movement* (Princeton, NJ: Princeton University Press, 2013).

59. Tarek E. Masoud, *Counting Islam: Religion, Class, and Elections in Egypt* (New York: Cambridge University Press, 2014), 10.

60. On the specific case of Egypt's Muslim Brotherhood, see Khalil al-Anani, *Inside the Muslim Brotherhood: Religion, Identity, and Politics* (New York: Oxford University Press, 2016); Hazem Kandil, *Inside the Brotherhood* (Cambridge: Polity Press, 2015); Hossam Tammam, *Tahawulat al-Ikhwan al-Muslimin: Tafakuk al-Aydiulujiyya wa Nahayat al-Tanzim* (Al-Qahirah: Maktabat Madbuly, 2009); and Samer Shehata and Joshua Stacher, "The Brotherhood Goes to Parliament," *Middle East Report* 240 (Fall 2006): 32–39. Mona El-Ghobashy emphasizes the Brotherhood's success in managing internal differences. Mona El-Ghobashy, "The Metamorphosis of the Egyptian Muslim Brothers," *International Journal of Middle East Studies* 37, no. 3 (August 2005): 391.

61. Not reviewed here is a wider literature on Islamist "moderation," which, in part, addresses the strategic and ideological reasons why Islamist groups choose to participate in peaceful political competition. See, for example, Vickie Langohr, "Of Islamists and Ballot Boxes: Rethinking the Relationship Between Islamists and Electoral Politics," *International Journal of Middle East Studies* 33, no. 4 (November 2001): 591–610; Wickham, *Mobilizing Islam*; Jillian Schwedler, *Faith in Moderation: Islamist Parties in Jordan and Yemen* (Cambridge: Cambridge University Press, 2006); Jillian Schwedler, "Can Islamists Become Moderates? Rethinking the Inclusion-Moderation Hypothesis," *World Politics* 63, no. 2 (April 2011): 347–76; and Janine A. Clark, "The Conditions of Islamist Moderation: Unpacking Cross-Ideological Cooperation in Jordan," *International Journal of Middle East Studies* 38, no. 4 (November 2006): 539–60.

62. For instance, Nathan Brown acknowledges that regime-imposed limits do affect the strategies and evolution of Islamist movements. Brown, *When Victory*, 15–19.

63. An exception to this trend is Steven Brooke's study, which theorizes why regimes tolerate Islamist groups' provision of social services. Brooke, *Winning Hearts and Votes*, 11.

64. A notable exception is Tarek Masoud's groundbreaking study on religion and class in Egypt, which incorporates structured comparisons of the Brotherhood's and Al-Tagammu's respective electoral performances and public support. Masoud, *Counting Islam*.

65. See, for example, John Waterbury, "The Political Management of Economic Adjustment Reform," in *Fragile Coalitions: The Politics of Economic Adjustment*, ed. Joan M. Nelson (New Brunswick, Canada: Transaction Books, 1989), 39–56; Hector E. Schamis, "Distributional Coalitions and the Politics of Economic Reform in Latin America," *World Politics* 51, no. 2 (January 1999): 236–68; and Joel Hellman, "Winners Take All: The Politics of Partial Reform in Postcommunist Transitions," *World Politics* 50, no. 2 (January 1998): 203–34.

66. Heydemann makes this critique in the context of building a case for studying the politics of economic reform through the lens of "networks" rather than through the lens of competition between distributive coalitions. Steven Heydemann, "Networks of Privilege: Rethinking the Politics of Economic Reform in the Middle East," in *Networks of Privilege in the Middle East: The Politics of Economic Reform Revisited*, ed. Steven Heydemann (Hampshire, UK: Palgrave Macmillan, 2004), 23–27.

67. See Gary W. Cox and Mathew D. McCubbins, "The Institutional Determinants of Economic Policy Outcomes," in *Presidents, Parliaments, and Policy*, ed. Stephan Haggard and Matthew D. McCubbins (New York: Cambridge University Press, 2001), 21–63; and Torsten Person and Guido Tabellini, "Constitutions and Economic Policy," *Journal of Economic Perspectives* 18, no. 1 (Winter 2004): 75–98.

68. See Conor O'Dwyer and Branislav Kovalčík, "And the Last Shall Be First: Party System Institutionalization and Second-Generation Economic Reform in Postcommunist Europe," *Studies in Comparative International Development* 41 (2007): 3–26.

69. See M. Steven Fish, "The Determinants of Economic Reform in the Post-communist World," *East European Politics and Societies* 12, no. 1 (December 1997): 31–78; and Steven A. Block, "Political Business Cycles, Democratization, and Economic Reform: The Case of Africa," *Journal of Development Economics* 67, no. 1 (February 2002): 205–28.

70. See Stephan Haggard and Robert R. Kaufman, *The Political Economy of Democratic Transitions* (Princeton, NJ: Princeton University Press, 1995); and Adam Przeworski, *Democracy and the Market*: Political and Economic Reforms in Eastern Europe and Latin America (New York: Cambridge University Press, 1991).

71. See James Raymond Vreeland, *The IMF and Economic Development* (New York: Cambridge University Press, 2003).

72. Steven Heydemann, "Taxation Without Representation: Authoritarianism and Economic Liberalization in Syria," in *Rules and Rights in the Middle East: Democracy, Law, and Society*, ed. Ellis Goldberg, Resat Kasaba, and Joel S. Migdal (Seattle: University of Washington Press, 1993), 69–101.

73. See Daniel Brumberg, "Authoritarian Legacies and Reform Strategies in the Arab World," in *Political Liberalization and Democratization in the Arab World Volume 1:*

Theoretical Perspectives, ed. Rex Brynen, Bahgat Korany, and Paul Noble, 229–260 (Boulder, CO: Lynne Rienner, 1995).

74. See Lust-Okar, *Structuring Conflict*.

75. See Soliman, *Al-Nizam al-Qawy*; Giacomo Luciani, "Linking Economic and Political Reform in the Middle East: The Role of the Bourgeoisie," in *Debating Arab Authoritarianism*, ed. Oliver Schlumberger (Stanford, CA: Stanford University Press, 2007), 161–76; and Stephen J. King, *The New Authoritarianism in the Middle East and North Africa* (Bloomington: Indiana University Press, 2009).

76. This line of inquiry speaks to growing interest in understanding how various forms of sociocultural diversity can affect economic outcomes pertaining to development, growth, and distribution. See, for example, William Easterly and Ross Levine, "Africa's Growth Tragedy: Policies and Ethnic Divisions," *Quarterly Journal of Economics* 112, no. 4 (November 1997): 1203–50; Alberto Alesina, Reza Baqir, and William Easterly, "Public Goods and Ethnic Divisions," *Quarterly Journal of Economics* 114, no. 4 (November 1999): 1243–84; Brad Lian and John Oneal, "Cultural Diversity and Economic Development," *Economic Development and Cultural Change* 46, no. 1 (October 1997): 61–78; Daniel Nettle, "Linguistic Fragmentation and the Wealth of Nations: The Fishman-Pool Hypothesis Reexamined," *Economic Development and Cultural Change* 48, no. 2 (January 2000): 335–48; David Throsby, *Economics and Culture* (New York: Cambridge University Press, 2001); Daniel Nettle, James B. Grace, Marc Choisy, Howard V. Cornell, Jean-François Guégan, and Michael E. Hochberg, "Cultural Diversity, Economic Development and Societal Instability," *PLoS ONE* 2, no. 9 (September 2007): e929; James Habyarimana, Macartan Humphreys, Daniel N. Posner, and Jeremy M. Weinstein, "Why Does Ethnic Diversity Undermine Public Goods Provision?," *American Political Science Review* 101, no. 4 (November 2007): 709–25.

77. See, for example, Bassam Haddad, *Business Networks in Syria: The Political Economy of Authoritarian Resilience* (Stanford, CA: Stanford University Press, 2011); King, *The New Authoritarianism*; and Joya, *The Roots of Revolt*.

78. See, for example, Marsha Pripstein Posusney, *Labor and the State in Egypt: Workers, Unions, and Economic Restructuring* (New York: Columbia University Press, 1997); Joel Beinin, *Workers and Thieves: Labor Movements and Popular Uprisings in Tunisia and Egypt* (Stanford, CA: Stanford University Press, 2016); and Dina Bishara, *Contesting Authoritarianism: Labor Challenges to the State in Egypt* (Cambridge: Cambridge University Press, 2018).

79. See, for example, Bjørn Olav Utvik, *Islamist Economics in Egypt: The Pious Road to Development* (Boulder, CO: Lynne Rienner, 2006) and contributions in the *Politics and Religion* 2020 symposium on "Islamism, Islamist Parties, and Economic Policy-Making in the Neo-Liberal Age," especially Francesco Cavatorta and Samir Amghar, "Symposium—Islamism, Islamist Parties, and Economic Policy-Making in the Neo-Liberal Age," *Politics and Religion* 13, no. 4 (2020): 685–94; Khalil al-Anani, "Devout Neoliberalism?! Explaining Egypt's Muslim Brotherhood's Socioeconomic Perspective and Policies," *Politics and Religion* 13, no. 4 (2020): 748–67; Francesco Cavatorta and Valeria Resta, "Beyond Quietism: Party Institutionalisation,

Salafism, and the Economy," *Politics and Religion* 13, no. 4 (2020): 796–817; and Maryam Ben Salem, " 'God Loves the Rich.' The Economic Policy of Ennahda: Liberalism in the Service of Social Solidarity," *Politics and Religion* 13, no. 4 (2020): 695–718.

80. A full review of this literature is beyond the scope of this study. For more, see Muhammad Nejatullah Siddiqi, *Muslim Economic Thinking: A Survey of Contemporary Literature* (Leicester, UK: Produced by the Islamic Foundation for the International Centre for Research in Islamic Economics, King Abdul Aziz University, 1981); and Ahmed Abdel-Fattah El-Ashker and Rodney Wilson, *Islamic Economics: A Short History* (Leiden, The Netherlands: Brill, 2006). For a critical perspective on Islamic economics, see Timur Kuran, *Islam and Mammon: The Economic Predicaments of Islamism* (Princeton, NJ: Princeton University Press, 2004).

81. One exception to that trend is Lust-Okar's *Structuring Conflict*, which studies the impact of autocrats' engineering of rules of political contestation on the incentives of opposition actors to mobilize against the political status quo during periods of economic crises. That said, this book is less interested in the impact of regime-imposed rules on opposition incentives than in the effect of regime policies on the development and evolution of different opposition actors, as well the relative salience of various policy agendas.

82. Appendix I provides an abstracted formulation of the book's argument, including a breakdown of the theoretical concepts and assumptions on which it rests.

83. Sven Steinmo and Kathleen Thelen, "Historical Institutionalism in Comparative Politics," in *Structuring Politics: Historical Institutionalism in Comparative Analysis*, ed. Sven Steinmo, Kathleen Thelen, and Frank Longstreth (Cambridge: Cambridge University Press, 1992), 3. For more on historical institutionalism, see Peter A. Hall and Rosemary C. R. Taylor, "Political Science and the Three New Institutionalisms," *Political Studies* 44, no. 5 (December 1996): 936–57; and Kathleen Ann Thelen and James Mahoney, *Explaining Institutional Change: Ambiguity, Agency, and Power* (Cambridge: Cambridge University Press, 2010).

84. Giovanni Capoccia and R. Daniel Kelemen, "The Study of Critical Junctures: Theory, Narrative, and Counterfactuals in Historical Institutionalism," *World Politics* 59, no. 3 (2007): 343.

85. James Mahoney, "Path Dependence in Historical Sociology," *Theory and Society* 29, no. 4 (August 2000): 507. For more on path dependence, see Paul Pierson, "Increasing Returns, Path Dependence, and the Study of Politics," *American Political Science Review* 94, no. 2 (2000): 251–67. Appendix II examines in greater detail the relevance of these features to this book.

86. George and Bennett, *Case Studies*, 75.

87. See Gary King, Robert O. Keohane, and Sidney Verba, *Designing Social Inquiry: Scientific Inference in Qualitative Research* (Princeton, NJ: Princeton University Press, 1994); Barbara Geddes, *Paradigms and Sand Castles: Theory Building and Research Design in Comparative Politics* (Ann Arbor: University of Michigan Press, 2003); and discussion in David Collier and James Mahoney, "Insights and Pitfalls: Selection Bias in Qualitative Research," *World Politics* 49, no. 1 (October 1996): 56–91.

88. George and Bennett, *Case Studies*; and Henry E. Brady and David Collier, eds., *Rethinking Social Inquiry: Diverse Tools, Shared Standards* (Lanham, MD: Rowman & Littlefield, 2010).

89. For George and Bennett, "Heuristic case studies inductively identify new variables, hypotheses, causal mechanisms, and causal paths. 'Deviant' or 'outlier' cases may be particularly useful for heuristic purposes, as by definition, their outcomes are not what traditional theories would anticipate. Also, cases where variables co-vary as expected but are at extremely high or low values may help uncover causal mechanisms." George and Bennett, *Case Studies*, 75. The debate on case studies and their contribution to theory building is rich. See, for example, Harry Eckstein, "Case Studies and Theory in Political Science," in *Strategies of Inquiry*, ed. Fred I. Greenstein, and Nelson W. Polsby (Reading, MA: Addison-Wesley, 1975), 79–138; Arend Lijphart, "Comparative Politics and the Comparative Method," *American Political Science Review* 65, no. 3 (September 1971): 682–93; Geddes, *Paradigms and Sand Castles*; John Gerring, "What Is a Case Study and What Is It Good for?," *American Political Science Review* 98, no. 2 (May 2004): 341–54; and John Gerring, "Case Selection for Case-Study Analysis: Qualitative and Quantitative Techniques," in *The Oxford Handbook of Political Methodology*, ed. Janet M. Box-Steffensmeier, Henry E. Brady, and David Collier (Oxford: Oxford University Press, 2008), 645–84.

90. There is wide consensus on the strategy of selecting cases that experience extreme values on the dependent variable to theorize the origins of a given phenomenon. See, for example, George and Bennett, *Case Studies*; Evan S. Lieberman, "Nested Analysis as a Mixed-Method Strategy for Comparative Research," *American Political Science Review* 99, no. 3 (August 2005): 435–52; Eckstein, "Case Studies"; and Jason Seawright and John Gerring, "Case Selection Techniques in Case Study Research: A Menu of Qualitative and Quantitative Options," *Political Research Quarterly* 61, no. 2 (June 2008): 294–308.

91. For more on the central importance of contemporaneous firsthand testimonies when researching questions related to the issue of cooptation, see Sofia Fenner, "Recovering Lost Futures: Contemporaneous Sources and the Study of Past Possibilities," *APSA Comparative Democratization Newsletter* 29, no. 2 (Fall 2019): 12–17.

92. See Andrew Bennett and Jeffrey T. Checkel, eds., *Process Tracing: From Metaphor to Analytic Tool* (Cambridge: Cambridge University Press, 2014); George and Bennett, *Case Studies*; James Mahoney, "The Logic of Process Tracing Tests in the Social Sciences," *Sociological Methods and Research* 41, no. 4 (March 2012): 570–97. For a summary of types of process-tracing observations, see James Mahoney, "After KKV: The New Methodology of Qualitative Research," *World Politics* 62, no. 1 (January 2010): 120–47.

93. See Ian S. Lustick, "History, Historiography, and Political Science: Multiple Historical Records and the Problem of Selection Bias," *American Political Science Review* 90, no. 3 (September 1996): 605–18; and Cameron G. Thies, "A Pragmatic Guide to Qualitative Historical Analysis in the Study of International Relations," *International Studies Perspectives* 3, no. 4 (November 2002): 351–72.

1. Inheriting Nasser's Debts: The Rise and Fall of the Nasserist Social Pact

1. A full review of the political economy of the Nasser era is beyond the scope of this chapter. Works that have examined that subject include John Waterbury, *The Egypt of Nasser and Sadat: The Political Economy of Two Regimes* (Princeton, NJ: Princeton University Press, 1983); Mahmoud Abdel-Fadil, *The Political Economy of Nasserism: A Study in Employment and Income Distribution Policies in Urban Egypt, 1952-72* (Cambridge: Cambridge University Press, 1980); Nazih N. M. Ayubi, *Bureaucracy and Politics in Contemporary Egypt* (London: Published for the Middle East Centre, St. Antony's College by Ithaca Press, 1980); Anouar Abdel-Malek, *Egypt: Military Society; the Army Regime, the Left, and Social Change Under Nasser*, trans. Charles Lam Markmann (New York: Random House, 1968); Mahmoud Hussein, *Class Conflict in Egypt, 1945-1970* (New York: Monthly Review Press, 1973); and Hassan (Samir) Riad (Amin), *L'Egypte Nasserienne* (Paris: Editions de Minuit, 1964).

2. Reforms were codified in Law 178/1952. For a summary of the law, see Abdel-Malek, *Egypt*, 71-72.

3. Landowners who exceeded the limit had the option of selling, which benefited the middle peasants who had the means to purchase more land. As Reem Abou El-Fadl points out, "the redistributive aspect of the reform was limited and its implementation undermined by bureaucratic inefficiency and nepotism." Reem Abou El-Fadl, "Nasserism," in *The Oxford Handbook of Contemporary Middle-Eastern and North African History*, ed. Amal Ghazal and Jens Hanssen (Oxford: Oxford University Press, 2016), 5. The maximum landownership was further reduced in 1961 to one hundred feddans per household and fifty feddans per individual. M. Riad El-Ghonemy, *Anti-Poverty Land Reform Issues Never Die: Collected Essays on Development Economics in Practice* (New York: Routledge, 2009), 152.

4. Rent could not exceed seven times the tax value of the land.

5. Nasser senior aide Sami Sharaf's memoirs report that the state invited domestic and foreign private investors to contribute to industrial development but that it remained "an unanswered invitation." Sami Sharaf, *Sanawat wa Ayam Maʿa Jamal ʿAbd al-Nasir*, 5 vols. (Al-Qahirah: Al-Maktab al-Misry al-Hadith, 2014), 3:765. For a recap of the Free Officers' relations with private business in the 1950s, see Raymond William Baker, *Egypt's Uncertain Revolution Under Nasser and Sadat* (Cambridge, MA: Harvard University Press, 1978), 49-50.

6. Fouad Morsi offers a close examination of the shortcomings of private investments during that period. Fouad Morsi, *Hadha al-Infitah al-Iqtisady* (Al-Qahirah: Dar al-Thaqafa al-Jadidah, 1976), 57-72.

7. Abdel-Malek, *Egypt*, 102-3.

8. Galal Amin, "The Egyptian Economy and the Revolution," *Egypt Since the Revolution*, ed. P. J. Vatikiotis (New York: Praeger, 1968), 41. Also see Abou El-Fadl, "Nasserism," 6.

9. Peter Mansfield, "Nasser and Nasserism," *International Journal* 28, no. 4 (Autumn 1973): 681.

10. Richards notes that education had already been declared free at the primary and secondary levels in 1936 and 1950, respectively. Alan Richards, "Higher Education in Egypt" (World Bank Policy Research Working Paper 862, World Bank, Washington, DC, 1992), 7. Even though education had been technically free at various levels before Nasser's rule, the late president is credited with making it widely accessible and delivering it to large swaths of previously underserved communities. For a summary, see Alia Eid, "Man Tabaq li-Awwal Marrah Majaniyat al-Taʿlim fi Misr?," *Ultrasawt*, November 17, 2016, https://www.ultrasawt.com ‏/من-طبّق-لأول-مرة-مجانية-التعليم-في-مصر؟/علياء-عيد/طلبة/‎.

11. For details of these measures, see Waterbury, *The Egypt of Nasser*, 219–36.

12. Akhter U. Ahmed et al., *The Egyptian Food Subsidy System: Structure, Performance, and Options for Reform* (Washington, DC: International Food Policy Research Institute, 2001), 6.

13. Betsy Birns McCall, "The Effects of Rent Control in Egypt: Part I," *Arab Law Quarterly* 3, no. 3 (May 1988): 158–59.

14. For example, the late Samer Soliman writes: "Certain researchers in Egyptian policy believe that Nasser established an unwritten contract between the state and society stipulating the state's commitment to extend services to the population in return for acceptance of the political regime and abandonment of political rights and participation in politics. That is, Nasser's regime bartered social rights in exchange for political rights." Samer Soliman, *The Autumn of Dictatorship: Fiscal Crisis and Political Change in Egypt Under Mubarak* (Stanford, CA: Stanford University, 2011), 27. This thesis is also articulated in numerous studies on the political economy of the Middle East. See, for example, Steven Heydemann, "Social Pacts and the Persistence of Authoritarianism in the Middle East," in *Debating Arab Authoritarianism*, ed. Oliver Schlumberger (Stanford, CA: Stanford University Press, 2007), 19–38; and Tarik M. Yousef, "Development, Growth and Policy Reform in the Middle East and North Africa since 1950," *Journal of Economic Perspectives* 18, no. 3 (Summer 2004): 91–115.

15. For more on Al-Wafd Party's pre-1952 history, see Mohamed Farid Hashish, *Hizb al-Wafd* (Al-Qahirah: Al-Hayʾah al-ʿAmah li-l-Kitab, 1999).

16. For background on political party life before the July 23 Revolution of 1952, see Younan Labib Rizk, *Al-Ahzab al-Misriyya ʿabr Miʾat ʿAm* (Al-Qahirah: Al-Hayʾah al-ʿAmah li-l-Kitab, 2006), 23–174.

17. Abou El-Fadl, "Nasserism," 4.

18. This narrative is informed by Harik, who summarizes the evolution of the one-party state under Nasser's rule. Iliya Harik, "The Single Party as a Subordinate Movement: The Case of Egypt," *World Politics* 26, no. 1 (October 1973): 80–105. It is also informed by Hamada Hosni's study on the ASU's Vanguard Organization, which describes the development of various state-sponsored parties and organizations under Nasser's rule. Hamada Hosni, *ʿAbd al-Nasir wa-l-Tanzim al-Taliʿiy al-Sirry 1971–1963* (Al-Qahirah: Maktabat Bayrut, 2007), 27–42.

19. See chapters 1 and 2 in Hazem Kandil, *Soldiers, Spies, and Statesmen: Egypt's Road to Revolt* (London: Verso, 2012).

20. For background on state control of the media during the Nasserist era, see Munir K. Nasser, *Egyptian Mass Media Under Nasser and Sadat: Two Models of Press Management and Control* (Columbia, SC: Association for Education in Journalism and Mass Communication, 1990); and Douglas A. Boyd, "Development of Egypt's Radio: Voice of the Arabs under Nasser," *Journalism Quarterly* 52, no. 4 (December 1975): 645–53.

21. The regime repressed a labor strike in Kafr Al-Dawwar in August 1952 and referred its participants to a military tribunal, which sentenced two of its members, Mohamed Mostafa Khamis and Mohamed Abdel-Rahman Al-Baqary, to death. See Joel Beinin and Zachary Lockman, *Workers on the Nile: Nationalism, Communism, Islam and the Egyptian Working Class, 1882–1954* (London: Tauris, 1988), 421–26.

22. Howaida Adly, *Al-ʿUmmal wa-l-Siyasah: al-Dawr al-Siyasy li-l-Harakah al-ʿUmmaliyya fi Misr min 1952–1981* (Al-Qahirah: Kitab al-Ahaly, 1993), 159.

23. Free Officers member Khaled Mohieddin describes the details of these contacts in his memoir. Khaled Mohieddin, *Walʾan Atakalam* (Al-Qahirah: Markaz al-Ahram li-l-Tarjamah wa-l-Nashr, 1992), 43–47. Muslim Brotherhood figure Ahmed Adil Kamal narrates the Brotherhood's relationship with the Free Officers movement before 1952. Ahmad Adil Kamal, *Al-Nuqqat fawq al-Huruwf: al-Ikhwan al-Muslimun wa-l-Nizam al-Khas* (Al-Qahira: al-Zahraʾ li-l-Iʿlam al-ʿAraby, Qism al-Nashr, 1989), 369–76. Also see Salah Shadi's insider account of the history of the Muslim Brotherhood. Salah Shadi, *Safahat min al-Tarikh: Hisad al-ʿUmr* (Al-Qahirah: Al-Zahraʾ li-l-Iʿlam al-ʿAraby, Qism al-Nashr, 1987), 159–201.

24. The text of the statement is reprinted in full in volume 3 of Mahmoud Abdel-Halim's insider account of the Muslim Brotherhood's history. Mahmoud Abdel-Halim, *Al-Ikhwan Al-Muslimun: Ahdath Sanʿat al-Tarikh: Ruʾyah min al-Dakhil, al-Juzʾ al-Thalith* (Al-Iskandariyya: Dar al-Daʿwah li-l-Tabʿ wa-l-Nashr, 2004), 285–94.

25. Barbara Zollner, "Prison Talk: The Muslim Brotherhood's Internal Struggle During Gamal Abdel Nasser's Persecution, 1954 to 1971," *International Journal of Middle East Studies* 39, no. 3 (August 2007): 413.

26. See Barbara H. E. Zollner, *The Muslim Brotherhood: Hasan al-Hudaybi and Ideology.* (New York: Routledge, 2009), 39–43.

27. For more on Sayyid Qutb's writings and their influence, see Sherif Younis, *Sayid Qutb wa-l-Usuliyya al-Islamiyya* (Al-Qahirah: Dar Tibah li-l-Dirasah wa-l-Nashr, 1995); Hala Mostafa, *Al-Islam al-Siyasy fi Misr: Min Harakat al-Islah ila Jamaʿat al-ʿUnf* (Al-Qahirah: Markaz al-Mahrusah, 1998), 139–51; Helmy Al-Nemnem, *Sayid Qutb wa Thawrat Yulyu* (Cairo: Mirit li-l-Nashr, 1999); and Andrew F. March, "Taking People as They Are: Islam as a 'Realistic Utopia' in the Political Theory of Sayyid Qutb," *American Political Science Review* 104, no. 1 (February 2010): 189–207.

28. For a recap of the rise and fall of the 1965 organization, see Zollner, "Prison Talk," 418–21.

29. See, for example, Richard Paul Mitchell, *The Society of the Muslim Brothers* (London: Oxford University Press, 1969), 105–50; Abdel-Halim, *Al-Ikhwan Al-Muslimun*, 187–280; Fouad Allam, *Al-Ikhwan wa Ana: Min al-Manshiyah ila al-Manasah* (Al-Qahirah: Akhbar al-Yawm, 1996), 107–9; Salah Shadi, *Safahat min al-Tarikh*, 213–360.

30. Wahid Abdel-Meguid, *Al-Ikhwan al-Muslimun bayn al-Tarikh wa-l-Mustaqbal: Kayf Kanat al-Jama'ah wa-Kayf Takun* (Al-Qahirah: Markaz al-Ahram l-il-Nashr w-al-Tarjamah wa-l-Tawzi', 2010), 30–31.

31. World Bank data show that the GDP per capita growth rate fell from 8.6 percent in 1964 to less than 3 percent each year until 1970. Growth rates were negative in 1967 and 1968. "GDP per Capita Growth (Annual %)—Egypt, Arab Republic," World Bank, accessed April 16, 20221, https://data.worldbank.org/indicator/NY.GDP.PCAP.KD .ZG?end=1970&locations=EG&start=1961. For more on the decline in state investments in the second half of the 1960s, see the study by Aly Al-Geretly, an economist who served as minister of finance under Nasser. Aly Al-Geretly, *Khamsah wa 'Ishrun 'Aman: Dirasah Tahliliyya li-l-Siyasat al-Iqtisadiyya fi Misr* (Al-Qahirah: Al-Hay'ah al-Misriyya al-'Amah li-l-Kitab, 1977), 21–22.

32. K. V. Nagarajan, "Egypt's Political Economy and the Downfall of the Mubarak Regime," *International Journal of Humanities and Social Science* 3, no. 10 (May 2013): 24.

33. According to Mohamed Mekky, the average balance of trade deficit increased from 4.7 percent of GDP in the period from 1956 to 1960 to 8 percent in from 1961 to 1966. Mohamed Fakhry Mekky, "Al-Taghayyurat al-Haykaliyya fi Mizan al-Madfu'at al-Misry 1952–1976," in *Al-Iqtisad al-Misry fi-Rub' Qarn, 1952–1977*, ed. Ismail Sabri Abdallah, Gouda Abdel-Khalek, and Ibrahim Al-Issawi (Al-Qahirah: Al-Hay'ah al-Misriyya al-'Amah li-l-Kitab, 1978), 324.

34. Waterbury, *The Egypt of Nasser*, 96.

35. See, for example, Malik Mufti, "The United States and Nasserist Pan-Arabism," in *The Middle East and the United States: A Historical and Political Reassessment*, ed. David W. Lesch (Boulder, CO: Westview Press, 2003), 168–87.

36. Nasser himself articulated that logic to close confidants. See Baker, *Egypt's Uncertain Revolution*, 45–46.

37. In 1963, Egypt became the world's largest per capita consumer of American food aid, wherein the United States was responsible for 99 percent of Egypt's wheat imports and 53 percent of net supply. Jean-Jacques Dethier and Kathy Funk, "The Language of Food," *Middle East Report* 17, no. 145 (March–April 1987): 23.

38. Al-Geretly, *Khamsah wa 'Ishrun 'Aman*, 18.

39. Dethier and Funk, "The Language of Food," 24.

40. Waterbury, *The Egypt of Nasser*, 97.

41. See Kandil for an account of the lead-up to the war and how internal regime rivalries shaped the events that sparked the attack. Kandil, *Soldiers, Spies*, 69–83.

42. Baker, *Egypt's Uncertain Revolution*, 116–17. Fouad Morsi discusses the burdens successive war efforts imposed on the Egyptian economy. Morsi, *Hadha al-Infitah*, 203–4. Ibrahim Al-Issawi and Mohamed Nassar offer a detailed assessment of the direct and indirect losses the country incurred as a result of the 1967 War. Ibrahim Al-Issawi and Mohamed Ali Nassar, "Muhawalah li Taqdir al-Khasa'ir al-Iqtisadiyya Alaty Alhaqtiha al-Harb al-'Arabiyya al-Isra'iliyya bi-Misr Munthu 'Udwan 1967," in *Al-Iqtisad al-Misry fi-Rub' Qarn, 1952–1977*, ed. Ismail Sabri Abdallah, Gouda Abdel-Khalek, and Ibrahim Al-Issawi (Al-Qahirah: Al-Hay'ah al-Misriyya al-'Amah

li-l-Kitab, 1978), 127–56. Sami Sharaf does not cite the war as the primary cause of Egypt's economic woes but claims that the five-year industrialization plan of 1965–1970 was never implemented because of the general hostility of the international environment, particularly with respect to U.S. policies toward Egypt. Sharaf, *Sanawat wa Ayam*, 3:753.

43. Nahid Ezzeddin Abdel-Fattah, *Al-ʿUmmal wa-Rijal al-Aʿmal: Tahawulat al-Furas al-Siyasiyya fi Misr* (Al-Qahirah: Markaz al-Dirasat al-Siyasiyya wa-l-Istiratijiyya bi-l-Ahram, 2003), 34.

44. In his interview with Abdullah Imam, Aly Sabri discussed the difficult trade-offs that were involved in economic planning at the time, indicating that Nasser's eagerness to fulfill consumer demands and to deliver services like free education directly challenged and limited the scope of state-led industrialization plans. Abdullah Imam, *ʿAly Sabry Yatadhakar* (Al-Qahirah: Ruz al-Yusuf, 1987), 70–71.

45. Nazih N. M. Ayubi, *Over-Stating the Arab State: Politics and Society in the Middle East* (London: Tauris, 1995), 299. Also see, Baker, *Egypt's Uncertain Revolution*, 70–73.

46. Echoing a similar perspective, Waterbury writes, "The crisis that overtook Egypt in 1965–66 was first felt in 1964 and was exacerbated, but not caused, by Egypt's military defeat in 1967. It was also not caused by MNCs pumping Egypt's foreign exchange reserves dry through remitted profits, nor by deteriorating terms of international trade, nor by unchecked consumption of luxury imports for the middle classes, nor, finally by the international capitalist banking community. It was caused by the gross inefficiencies of a public sector called upon to do too many things: sell products at cost or at a loss, take on labor unrelated to production needs, earn foreign exchange, and satisfy local demand." Waterbury, *The Egypt of Nasser*, 100.

47. In fact, Aly Sabri says that after the conclusion of the first five-year plan in 1965, Nasser sided with the demands of "orthodox economists" to curtail the size of the following plan and postpone its implementation for at least two years. Quoted in Imam, *ʿAly Sabry*, 75–76.

48. Ghali Shukri, *Al-Thawrah al-Mudadah fi Misr* (Al-Qahirah: Kitab al-Ahaly, 1987), 355.

49. Esmail Hosseinzadeh, "How Egyptian State Capitalism Reverted to Market Capitalism," *Arab Studies Quarterly* 10, no. 3 (Summer 1988): 311–12.

50. Abdel-Fattah, *Al-ʿUmmal*, 34. In fact, after the 1967 defeat, Nasser allowed private companies a role in reconstruction efforts around the Suez Canal region. Although the state's monopoly on the imports sector was not broken until the advent of Sadat's infitah, in 1969, Nasser did allow some private companies limited importation privileges. See Samia Imam, *Man Yamluk Misr? Dirasah Tahliliyya li-l-Usul al-Ijtimaʿiyya li-Nukhbit al-Infitah al-Iqtisady fi-l-Mujtamaʿ al-Misry, 1974–1980* (Al-Qahirah: Dar al-Mustaqbal al-ʿAraby, 1986), 100.

51. Gouda Abdel-Khalek, "Al-Taʿrif bi-l-Infitah wa Tatawuruh," in *Al-Infitah: al-Judhur, al-Hisad, wa-l-Mustaqbal*, ed. Gouda Abdel-Khalek (Al-Qahirah: Al-Markaz al-ʿAraby lil-Bahth wa-al-Nashr, 1982), 36. The full text of the law is available on Laweg, Egypt's Gateway to Law and the Judiciary, accessed November 30, 2020, http://www.laweg.net/Default.aspx?action=ViewActivePages&ItemID=29881&Type=6.

52. The full text of the law is available on Manshurat Qanuniyya, accessed November 30, 2020, https://manshurat.org/node/32294.

53. Morsi, Hadha al-Infitah, 8. A longtime communist activist, Morsi served as minister of trade under Sadat in the early 1970s. He was among the cofounders of Al-Tagammu in 1976.

54. See Shukri, Al-Thawrah al-Mudadah, 40–47.

55. Imam, Man Yamluk, 75–77.

56. While critical of nationalization and Nasser, Osman acknowledges the exception the government made to allow him to continue running his company. Osman Ahmed Osman, Safahat min Tajribaty (Al-Qahirah: Al-Maktab al-Misry al-Hadith, 1981), 304–5; 313–14

57. Shukri, Al-Thawrah al-Mudadah, 46.

58. See Joel Beinin, Workers and Thieves: Labor Movements and Popular Uprisings in Tunisia and Egypt (Stanford, CA: Stanford University Press, 2016), 17–19.

59. Hosseinzadeh, "How Egyptian State," 317. Galal Amin echoes that perspective. For Amin, the inflection point that paved the way for Egypt's experiment with economic liberalization was not the advent of the Sadat presidency in 1970. Rather, it was the suspension of U.S. aid in the mid-1960s, along with a number of setbacks that followed. Successive crises, he argues, put Egypt's economy in virtual paralysis in a way that necessitated a fundamental change in course. Galal Amin, "Al-Tahawul ila al-Infitah: al-ʿAwamil al-Kharijiyya," in Al-Infitah: al-Judhur, al-Hisad, wa-l-Mustaqbal, ed. Gouda Abdel-Khalek (Al-Qahirah: Al-Markaz al-ʿAraby lil-Bahth wa-al-Nashr, 1982), 93–98.

60. As Soliman writes, "The dire need for resources placed the regime before two equally difficult choices: closer alliance with the Soviet Union at the external level and more socialist policy internally, or movement westward (especially toward the United States) at the external level and toward private capitalist development at the internal level." Soliman, The Autumn of Dictatorship, 28.

61. Aly Sabri asserts that Nasser had considered formalizing various "wings" inside the ASU, along the lines of Sadat's short experiment with manabir. This suggests that structural pressures had already been steering the ruling establishment toward such reforms before Sadat's assumption of power. Quoted in Imam, ʿAly Sabry, 32–33. In his memoirs, Sami Sharaf presents evidence that after the 1967 war, Nasser openly discussed the prospect of legalizing an opposition political party. For example, Sharaf published transcripts of ASU deliberations dated August 4, 1967, in which Nasser proposed this measure. For the meeting transcripts, see Sharaf, Sanawat wa Ayam, 3:717–36.

62. As explained in chapter 2, some of Sadat's earliest gestures toward the Muslim Brotherhood were mediated through Saudi Arabia.

63. Egyptian writer and Sadat confidant Musa Sabri recounts these differences in Musa Sabri, Wathaʾiq 15 Mayu (Al-Qahirah: Al-Maktab al-Misry al-Hadith, 1976), 49–58.

64. Kandil outlines the chronology of these events in Kandil, Soldiers, Spies, 99–111.

65. Anthony McDermott, "Sadat and the Soviet Union," The World Today 28, no. 9 (September 1972): 404.

66. Jason Brownlee, *Democracy Prevention: The Politics of the U.S.-Egyptian Alliance* (New York: Cambridge University Press, 2012), 19–22.

67. Jeremy M. Sharp, *Egypt: Background and U.S. Relations* (Washington, DC: Congressional Research Service, 2009), 5–6.

68. Dilip Hiro, *Inside the Middle East* (New York: McGraw-Hill, 1982), 262–63.

69. Andrej Kreutz, *Russia in the Middle East: Friend or Foe?* (Westport, CT: Praeger Security International, 2007), 115.

70. In fact, "the Arab Cold War" was the term that the late Malcolm Kerr had coined to denote the growing conflicts and tensions between Egypt and Saudi Arabia. Malcolm H. Kerr, *The Arab Cold War: Gamal ʾAbd Al-Nasir and His Rivals, 1958–1970* (London: Published for the Royal Institute of International Affairs by Oxford University Press, 1971).

71. Candice Stevens, "The Mineral Industry in Egypt," in *Minerals Yearbook Area Reports: International 1976*, Vol. 3 (Washington, DC: Bureau of Mines, 1976), 359.

72. Abdel-Fattah, *Al-ʿUmmal*, 48.

73. Stevens, "The Mineral Industry," 359.

74. Osama Hamed notes that 56 percent of the tourists that visited Egypt in 1976 were from Arab countries. Osama Hamed, "Egypt's Open Door Economic Policy: An Attempt at Economic Integration in the Middle East," *International Journal of Middle East Studies* 13, no. 1 (February 1981): 5.

75. Tarek Osman, *Egypt on the Brink: From Nasser to Mubarak* (New Haven, CT: Yale University Press, 2013) 89.

76. For example, in 1976, Egyptian migrant workers in the Gulf sent home a total of $756 million in remittances. Hamed, "Egypt's Open Door," 5.

77. Brownlee, *Democracy Prevention*, 15.

78. As Samia Imam argues, Sadat was also laying the groundwork for encouraging investments from the traditional capitalist class that was marginalized in the wake of the July 23 Revolution and the 1961 nationalization drive. Imam, *Man Yamluk*, 57.

79. Although Law 34 was formally issued in 1971, Sadat had ordered it in as early as December 1970, only a few months after Nasser's death. Abdullah Shalaby, *Al-Din wa-l-Siraʿ al-Siyasy fi Misr: 1970–1985* (Al-Qahirah: Kitab al-Ahaly, 2000), 55.

80. The government also signed a number of international agreements protecting against property sequestration, including the International Convention for the Settlement of Investment Disputes. Authorities initiated legal steps toward either returning properties it had confiscated during the previous decade or compensating their owners. Abdel-Fattah, *Al-ʿUmmal*, 114–15.

81. See Abdel-Khalek, "Al-Taʿrif," 36.

82. Morsi, *Hadha al-Infitah*, 10.

83. For more on the growth of proreform elements inside the Egyptian bureaucracy and publics sector, see Ibrahim Al-Issawi, "Al-Tahawul ila al-Infitah: al-ʿAwamel al-Dakhiliyya," in *Al-Infitah: al-Judhur, al-Hisad, wa-l-Mustaqbal*, ed. Gouda Abdel-Khalek (Al-Qahirah: Al-Markaz al-ʿAraby lil-Bahth wa-al-Nashr, 1982), 71–89.

84. On a related issue, Robert Springborg alludes to the idea that the there was some affinity between the affluent leadership of the Muslim Brotherhood and the pursuit of infitah under Sadat. Robert Springborg, *Mubarak's Egypt: Fragmentation of the Political Order* (Boulder, CO: Westview Press, 1989), 236.

85. Abdel-Fattah, *Al-ʿUmmal*, 345.

86. In 1977, the government extended these same privileges to Egyptian private investors through Law 32, which superseded Law 43/1974.

87. Gouda Abdel-Khalek, "Aham Dalalat Siyasat al-Infitah al-Iqtisady bi-l-Nisbah li-l-Tahwulat al-Haykaliyya fi-l-Iqtisad al-Misry 1971–1977," in *Al-Iqtisad al-Misry fi-Rubʿ Qarn, 1952-1977*, ed. Ismail Sabri Abdallah, Gouda Abdel-Khalek, and Ibrahim Al-Issawi (Al-Qahirah: Al-Hayʾah al-Misriyya al-ʿAmah li-l-Kitab, 1978), 367–68.

88. Waterbury, *The Egypt of Nasser*, 131.

89. Abdel-Fattah, *Al-ʿUmmal*, 336.

90. Marsha Pripstein Posusney, *Labor and the State in Egypt: Workers, Unions, and Economic Restructuring* (New York: Columbia University Press, 1997), 178. For Gouda Abdel-Khalek, Law 111, in effect, allowed public sector companies to behave like private enterprises. Abdel-Khalek, "Aham Dalalat," 373–74.

91. For example, in a public speech at the University of Alexandria on April 3, 1973, Sadat denied that selling the public sector was under consideration, adding that "[t]he role of the public sector in the coming period is extremely important, because in light of the policies of infitah and promoting the private sector and Arab and foreign investments, the public sector remains the main political tool for implementing any developmental plan and it is what will lead the major projects, which none other than [the public sector] will undertake." A summary of the speech with excerpts can be found in Mohamed Khaled, *Al-Harakah al-Niqabiyya bayn al-Mady wa-l-Hadir* (Al-Qahirah: Dar al-Taʿawun, 1975).

92. See discussion in Amr Adly, *Cleft Capitalism: The Social Origins of Failed Market Making in Egypt* (Stanford, CA: Stanford University Press, 2020), 100.

93. In 1980, the government circulated a bill that included privatization measures.

94. Morsi, *Hadha al-Infitah*, 11

95. Law 39/1974 allowed private individuals to act as agents of foreign companies, a privilege previously reserved for the public sector. Law 118/1975 broke the public sector's monopoly on imports, although Ministry of Trade Decree 1058 restricted private sector imports of basic food goods, fuel and energy, and defense products. Abdel-Khalek, "Aham Dalalat," 369.

96. See discussions in Morsi, *Hadha al-Infitah*, 121–22; 166–77. Another opinion held that the public sector had limited chances of competing profitably without state investment in industrial infrastructure and equipment. See, for example, Sharaf, *Sanawat wa Ayam*, 3:789.

97. That is, companies under the authority of the Ministry of Industry.

98. Heba Handoussa, "Maʾal al-Qitaʿ al-ʿAm," in *Al-Infitah: al-Judhur, al-Hisad, wa-l-Mustaqbal*, ed. Gouda Abdel-Khalek (Al-Qahirah: Al-Markaz al-ʿAraby li-l-Bahth wa-l-Nashr, 1982), 453.

99. Quoted in Morsi, *Hadha al-Infitah*, 175.

100. The counter argument holds that even when incurring loses, public sector enterprises can still play a critical role, like manufacturing products necessary for industrial development—an endeavor private investors customarily eschew because it does not yield quick profits. Sami Sharaf articulates this point of view in his memoirs. Sharaf, *Sanawat wa Ayam*, 3:818–19.

101. Heba Handoussa questions the claim that the losses of state-owned companies were primarily the result of factors internal to the public sector. Their losses, she explains, cannot be attributed exclusively to poor performance and are related to state-imposed conditions that have increased the likelihood of losses. Among them are inefficiencies resulting from having to comply with state-sponsored guaranteed employment schemes and government-mandated price controls. In addition, the flight of experienced cadres from the public sector because of its inability to offer competitive salaries also has contributed to losses. Handoussa, "Maʾal al-Qitaʿ,", 454–61.

102. Morsi, *Hadha al-Infitah*, 177. For more on 1960s and 1970s debates concerning public sector reform in Egypt, see Malak Labib, "Re-shaping the 'Socialist Factory' in Egypt in the Late 1960s–1970s," *Forum Transregionale Studien*, April 30, 2021, https://trafo.hypotheses.org/28429.

103. Abdel-Fattah, *Al-ʿUmmal*, 348.

104. Abdel-Khalek, "Aham Dalalat," 370–73; 379.

105. Adel Hussein, *Al-Iqtisad al-Misry min al-Istiqlal ila al-Tabʾiyya* (Bayrut: Dar al-Kalimah, 1981).

106. Mark N. Cooper, *The Transformation of Egypt*. Baltimore, MD: Johns Hopkins University Press, 1982), 101–2.

107. These committees were composed of members of the ASU and the agricultural cooperatives and were specifically designed to alleviate the legal costs of these disputes for poor farmers. Abdel-Baset Abdel-Moaty, *Al-Tabaqat al-Ijtimaʿiyya wa Mustaqbal Misr* (Al-Qahirah: Mirit, 2002), 143.

108. Waterbury, *The Egypt of Nasser*, 285–86.

109. Abdel-Moaty, *Al-Tabaqat*, 143.

110. See Hussein Abdel-Razek, *Misr fi 18 wa 19 Yanayir* (Al-Qahirah: Dar Al-Kalimah, 1985), 85.

111. Many such elements had roots in the landowning families.

112. Imam, *Man Yamluk*, 77.

113. Abaza also hailed from a wealthy landowning family in the governorate of Al-Sharqia.

114. Imam, *Man Yamluk*, 93–109.

115. Samia Imam characterizes these elements as "parasitic capitalists." Imam, *Man Yamluk*, 135–41.

116. See Adly, *Cleft Capitalism*, 99; and Kandil, *Soldiers, Spies*, 181–85. For more on the history of the military's economic role, see Zeinab Abul-Magd, *Militarizing the Nation: The Army, Business, and Revolution in Egypt* (New York: Columbia University Press, 2017).

117. The two laws came into being shortly before Sadat's assassination. Sadat signed Law 143/1981 on August 30, 1981, and Decree 531/1981 on September 29, 1981. The full text of Law 143/1981 is available on Manshurat Qanuniyya, accessed December 3, 2020, https://manshurat.org/node/259. The full text of Decree 531/1981 is available on Manshurat Qanuniyya, accessed December 3, 2020, https://www.manshurat .org/node/12906.

118. Abdel-Fattah Barayez, " 'This Land Is Their Land': Egypt's Military and the Economy," *Jadaliyya*, January 25, 2016, https://www.jadaliyya.com/Details/32898.

119. See discussion in Ahmed Abdalla Rozza, *Al-Talabah w-al-Siyasah fi Misr* (Al-Qahirah: Sinaʿ li-l-Nashr, 1991), 271.

120. Abdel-Khalek, "Aham Dalalat," 389.

121. Shalaby, *Al-Din wa-l-Siraʿ*, 65.

122. See Adly, *Cleft Capitalism*, esp. 98–105. Certainly, even if such reforms had been pursued, there would have still been winners and losers. But there likely would have been a broader base of winners reaping the benefits of economic liberalization.

123. Morsi, *Hadha al-Infitah*, 166.

124. Shukri, *Al-Thawrah al-Mudadah*, 338.

125. Hussein, *Al-Iqtisad al-Misry*, 38–41.

126. Waterbury, *The Egypt of Nasser*, 417.

127. Cooper, *The Transformation*, 236.

128. Nasser "argued that relations between these different socioeconomic segments of the population should be peaceful |. . . .| With the implementation of social and political reforms, the whole nation was being prepared for unity under the banner of the official party." Harik, "The Single Party," 87.

129. See Joel Beinin, *Was the Red Flag Flying There? Marxist Politics and the Arab-Israeli Conflict in Egypt and Israel, 1948-1965* (Berkeley: University of California Press, 1990), 208–12. For more on the history of communist movements in Egypt, see Tareq Y. Ismael and Rifaat El-Saʿid, *The Communist Movement in Egypt, 1920-1988* (Syracuse, NY: Syracuse University Press, 1990) and works reviewed in Joel Beinin, "Essential Readings on Marxism and the Left in Egypt," *Jadaliyya*, August 10, 2020, https:// www.jadaliyya.com/Details/41550.

130. Some have noted that the absorption of members of dissolved communist movements into the ASU was mainly limited to the elite level, and the actual number of communist activists who entered the ASU was much lower than many had anticipated and was mainly concentrated in the Vanguard Organization. Sherif Younis, *Nidaʾ al-Shaʿb: Tarikh Naqdy li-l-Aydiulujiyya al-Nasiriyya* (Al-Qahirah: Dar al-Shuruq, 2012), 580.

131. For instance, the paper argued: "The multiplicity of social forces that constitute the alliance [of working forces] must be reflected in the diversity of currents inside the [Arab] Socialist Union. Otherwise, the political organization will cease to represent the nature of the alliance. And the issue here is not limited to individual opinions that could be resolved in the course of discussions." Quoted in Iman Hassan, *Wazaʾif al-Ahzab al-Siyasiyya fi Nuzum al-Taʿadudiyya al-Muqayadah: Dirasat Halat Hizb al-Tajammuʿ fi Misr 1976-1991* (Al-Qahirah: Al-Ahaly, 1995), 109.

132. The background presented in this paragraph is informed by Hassan, *Wazaʾif al-Ahzab*, 108–11.

133. These measures would later be enshrined in Article 30 of the infamous Law 40/1977 (also known as the Political Parties Law). A copy of the Law 40/1977 can be found on Manshurat Qanuniyya, accessed December 5, 2020, https://manshurat.org /node/1708.

134. Ahmed Hafez, "Al-Hizb al-Watany: Min al-Inqilab ʿala al-Ishtrakiyya ila Tajdid Qiyadatihi al-Siyasiyya," *Al-Ahram*, February 6, 2011, https://gate.ahram.org.eg/News /37231.aspx.

135. Hazem Kandil captures the spirit of this transformation eloquently: "So while the ASU was officially dissolved, in reality what happened was that its six million members simply transferred to the new party. In fact, the NDP was described as a carbon copy of the ASU |. . . .| The primary difference, of course, was that after the methodical housecleaning occasioned by the transformation of the ASU to the NDP, the ruling-party elite was no longer composed of political functionaries, but rather state-nurtured businessmen. The ruling party and the parliament, which it controlled, began to cater to the needs of the rising capitalist class." Kandil, *Soldiers, Spies*, 165–66.

136. Adly, *Al-ʿUmmal wa-l-Siyasah*, 221.

137. A summary of labor leaders' remarks at parliamentary hearings, the texts of the ETUF statement, and Gharib's op-ed are available in Khaled, *Al-Harakah al-Niqabiyya.*

138. Adly, *Al-ʿUmmal wa-l-Siyasah*, 223.

139. In November 1970, the head of ETUF Abdel-Latif Bultiya was tapped for the Ministry of Manpower. Bultiya's ETUF successors Salah Gharib and Saad Mohamed Ahmed also served as ministers of manpower under Sadat. Toward the end of Gharib's tenure as ETUF president, however, Bultiya returned to the post of minister of manpower.

140. Abdel-Fattah, *Al-ʿUmmal*, 122.

141. Adly, *Al-ʿUmmal wa-l-Siyasah*, 165.

142. Adly, *Al-ʿUmmal wa-l-Siyasah*, 297.

143. For more details, see Posusney, *Labor and the State*, 99–104.

144. These powers were further solidified by Law 95/1980. Adly, *Al-ʿUmmal wa-l-Siyasah*, 307.

145. Abdel-Fattah, *Al-ʿUmmal*, 121–22; 221–22.

146. Posusney, *Labor and the State*, 109–13.

147. Author interview, August 8, 2010, Cairo, Egypt.

148. For more on government officials' and protesters' portrayals of the uprising, see Sherene Seikaly, "A Protest of the Poor: On the Political Meaning of the People," in *The Aesthetics and Politics of Global Hunger*, ed. Anastasia Ulanowicz and Manisha Basu, 135–155 (Cham, Switzerland: Palgrave Macmillan, 2017). For a critical analysis of leftist accounts of the uprising, see Mélanie Henry, "International Monetary Fund Riots or Nasserian Revolt? Thinking Fluid Memories: Egypt 1977," *International Review of Social History* 66, no. S29 (2021): 161–80.

149. Kandil, *Soldiers, Spies*, 169.

150. The first protesters were the workers of the Misr Helwan Spinning and Weaving Company and those of Alexandria's Naval Arsenal. University students joined them shortly thereafter and took the lead in directing the chanting and inviting wider participation. Abdel-Razek, *Misr*, 80–81; 84.

151. Shukri, *Al-Thawrah al-Mudadah*, 348.

152. Abdel-Razek, *Misr*, 95.

153. Chants translated from Abdel-Razek, *Misr*. For an analysis of popular slogans during this period and their connections to politically active poets, see Elliott Colla, "Egyptian Movement Poetry," *Journal of Arabic Literature* 51, no. 1–2 (2020): 53–82.

154. Rozza, *Al-Talabah*, 184–86.

155. These were collections of opinion articles and reports that various students produced and put up on public display on campus.

156. Mustapha Kamel Al-Sayyid, *Al-Mujtamaʿ wa-l-Siyasah fi Misr: Dawr Jamaʿat al-Masalih fi al-Nizam al-Siyasy al-Misry, 1952-1981* (Al-Qahirah: Dar al-Mustaqbal al-ʿAraby, 1983), 28. The state, however, added more restrictions on student activism in the aftermath of a subsequent student uprising in November of that same year.

157. Ahmed Bahaaeddin Shaaban, *Inhaztu li-l-Watan: Shahadah min Jil al-Ghadab: Safahat min Tarikh al-Harakah al-Wataniyya al-Dimuqratiyya li-Tulab Misr, 1967-1977* (Al-Qahirah: Markaz al-Mahrusah, 1998), 88.

158. Rozza, *Al-Talabah*, 213.

159. Al-Sayyid, *Al-Mujtamaʿ wa-l-Siyasah*, 30.

160. Although some sources narrating these events refer to Abul-Magd as the minister of youth, he was appointed to that post only in September 1972. See text of Abul-Magd's official appointment decree at the Library of Alexandria's Sadat archive, accessed April 16, 2021, http://sadat.bibalex.org/TextViewer.aspx?TextID=DC_23401.

161. Shaaban, *Inhaztu li-l-Watan*, 71.

162. That assessment is consistent with the firsthand testimony of then-student activist Kamal Khalil, who details the slogans and issues that animated the 1972 student mobilization. Kamal Khalil, *Hikayat min Zaman Fat: Sirah Dhatiyya min khilal al-Ahdath* (Al-Jizah: Bayt al-Yasmin li-l-Nashr wa-l-Tawziʿ, 2012), 91–100.

163. This narrative is based on Rozza, *Al-Talabah*, 215–25.

164. Al-Sayyid Abdel-Sattar Al-Meleegy, "Tajribaty maʿa al-Ikhwan," *IkhwanWiki*, November 26, 2012, https://www.ikhwanwiki.com/index.php?title=الدعوة_إلى_التنظيم_السري _.تجربتي_مع_الإخوان_من_

165. More details on the events that led to the mobilization can be found in Shukri, *Al-Thawrah al-Mudadah*, 122–24.

166. Rozza, *Al-Talabah*, 232–39.

167. Al-Ahram Center, *Al-Taqrir Al-Istratijy Al-ʿAraby 1987* (Al-Qahirah: Markaz al-Dirasat al-Siyasiyya wa-l-Istratijiyya, 1988), 371; 377. Wael Othman's firsthand testimony suggests that communists were a dominant force in the student mobilization. Wael Othman, *Asrar Al-Harakah al-Tulabiyya Handasat al-Qahirah 1968-1975* (Al-Qahirah: Al-Sharikah al-Misriyya li-l-Tibaʿah wa-l-Nashr, 1976), 59–62.

168. Rozza, *Al-Talabah*, 221.

169. Al-Sayyid, *Al-Mujtamaᶜ wa-l-Siyasah*, 34.

170. Shaaban, *Inhaztu li-l-Watan*, 42–43.

171. Shaaban, *Inhaztu li-l-Watan*, 59–60.

172. Rozza, *Al-Talabah*, 276.

173. For example, one of the early mobilizations started at Ain Shams University Faculty of Engineering with about three hundred students. That same evening, some students from Cairo University's Imbaba dorms were reportedly protesting. Al-Sayyid, *Al-Mujtamaᶜ wa-l-Siyasah*, 37.

174. Abdel-Razek, *Misr*, 297.

175. Rozza, *Al-Talabah*, 276.

176. Al-Sayyid, *Al-Mujtamaᶜ wa-l-Siyasah*, 40–41.

177. Even though the ASU was effectively the only legal political organization, prior constitutions never stated that explicitly. Shukri, *Al-Thawrah al-Mudadah*, 393.

178. In 1973, Mustafa Kamel Murad cochaired a parliamentary committee that drafted a document setting forth a vision for economic liberalization entitled "Changing the Primary Fundamentals of the Egyptian Economy." Morsi, *Hadha al-Infitah*, 11.

179. Al-Tagammu held four seats in the 1976 parliament.

180. The source of the figure is Khaled Mohieddin. See Abdel-Razek, *Misr*, 193. The number Mohieddin cites is consistent with the circulation rates of *Al-Ahaly* during the early 1980s. The figure is not insignificant given that Al-Tagammu's membership was estimated at twenty-two thousand in 2007, and no more than sixty-five thousand in 2014. Eissa Sudoud, "ᶜAbd al-ᶜAal: La Yujad Inqisam fi Misr," *Vetogate*, April 15, 2014, http://www.vetogate.com/957769. While allies of the Sadat regime often claimed that Al-Tagammu members did not exceed a few hundred, shortly after the 1977 Bread Uprising, the state-owned *Akhbar Al-Youm* published hundreds of names of Al-Tagammu members who left the party, which apparently amounted to only 1.5 percent of its total membership. Shukri, *Al-Thawrah al-Mudadah*, 416.

181. Rozza, *Al-Talabah*, 276.

182. Rifaat Al-Said, *Mujarad Dhikrayat al-Juzuᵓ al-Thalith* (Dimashq: Dar Al-Mada, 2000), 142–43.

183. Hassan, *Wazaᵓif al-Ahzab*, 125–26.

184. Adly, *Al-ᶜUmmal wa-l-Siyasah*, 328.

185. Al-Tagammu's 1980 program, quoted in Hassan, *Wazaᵓif al-Ahzab*, 210–12.

186. Al-Tagammu's 1980 program, quoted in Hassan, *Wazaᵓif al-Ahzab*, 197.

187. See Al-Said, *Mujarad Dhikrayat*, 167. The statement involved a telex message from Al-Tagammu leaders to their local offices nationwide and was scheduled for release the evening of January 18. The first draft message included language that called upon Al-Tagammu regional representatives to organize peaceful protests. Because of the objections of ASU officials, who feared that this particular sentence might spark further unrest, Al-Tagammu official Rifaat Al-Said agreed to delete it. However, as message (#91) was still in transmission reaching Aswan and Assiut only, a new message (#115) was sent instructing recipients to ignore the previous message

with all its directives. Except for Al-Tagammu officials in Assiut and Aswan, none of the intended recipients had received the initial message (#91). Prosecutors tried to use the text of message #91 as evidence that Al-Tagammu was in fact guilty of inciting violent unrest. See Abdel-Razek, *Misr*, 114–18.

188. This figure was cited by Al-Tagammu leader Khaled Mohieddin in an interview with *Rose Al-Yousef* magazine published on March 7, 1977. The interview is reprinted in full in Abdel-Razek, *Misr*, 191.

189. Al-Said, *Mujarad Dhikrayat*, 150.

190. Hassan, *Waza'if al-Ahzab*, 332.

191. Shukri, *Al-Thawrah al-Mudadah*, 416.

192. Iman Hassan, *Hizb al-Tajammuʿ* (Al-Qahirah: Markaz al-Dirasat al-Siyasiyya wa-l-Istratijiyya), 58.

193. For example, see discussion in Hassan, *Waza'if al-Ahzab*, 340.

194. Al-Said, *Mujarad Dhikrayat*, 240.

195. Abdel-Fattah, *Al-ʿUmmal*, 339.

196. Quoted in Hassan, *Hizb al-Tajammuʿ*, 58–59.

197. Al-Said, *Mujarad Dhikrayat*, 240–41.

198. Hassan, *Waza'if al-Ahzab*, 232–33. Also see Al-Said, *Mujarad Dhikrayat*, 153–55.

199. Lotfi Al-Khouli claims that *Al-Gumhuria* and *Al-Akhbar* falsely reported his resignation at the behest of Al-Sibai. Al-Khouli denied it and asked the papers to set the record straight, but they refused to take action. Eventually, Al-Khouli was told that Al-Sibai replaced him with Salah Galal. Thanaa Al-Karas, "Lutfy al-Khuly Yahky Qisat Ighlaq Majlat al-Taliʿah," *Vetogate*, April 15, 2014, https://vetogate.com/961256.

200. Shukri, *Al-Thawrah al-Mudadah*, 402–5.

201. The law is 35/1978, commonly known as the "Law for Protecting the Domestic Front and Social Peace." Shukri, *Al-Thawrah al-Mudadah*, 418.

202. Mahmoud Fawzi, *Al-Nabawy Ismaʿil wa Judhur Manasat al-Sadat* (Al-Qahirah: Bayt al-Lughat Al-Dawliyya, 2007), 47–48.

203. Al-Said, *Mujarad Dhikrayat*, 140.

204. Indeed, the term "organized labor" encompasses a host of diverse interests that are not always in sync as they span a wide range of economic sectors. Thus, it is important to approach the concept with a critical view. This study considers the term to be analytically useful, because the analysis centers on economic reforms threatening workers across a wide range of sectors, such as reductions in price subsidies, dissolution of state-owned enterprises, and relaxing enforcement of labor laws.

205. Maye Kassem, *Egyptian Politics: The Dynamics of Authoritarian Rule* (Boulder, CO: Lynne Rienner, 2004), 100. At that point Helwan had already been a hotbed for subversive labor activities. A few years earlier in 1968, military factory workers in the same city had sparked national demonstrations calling for bringing to justice officials suspected of criminal negligence during the 1967 war. Workers in Helwan would also organize actions in solidarity with the university student uprisings in 1972. Abdel-Fattah, *Al-ʿUmmal*, 214.

206. Shukri, *Al-Thawrah al-Mudadah*, 62–64.
207. Adly, *Al-ʿUmmal wa-l-Siyasah*, 268.
208. Abdel-Fattah, *Al-ʿUmmal*, 334–36.
209. Posusney, *Labor and the State*, 174–75.
210. Adly, *Al-ʿUmmal wa-l-Siyasah*, 268.
211. Posusney, *Labor and the State*, 142–43.
212. Posusney, *Labor and the State*, 177–80.
213. Adly, *Al-ʿUmmal wa-l-Siyasah*, 268–69.
214. Kassem, *Egyptian Politics*, 100.
215. Adly, *Al-ʿUmmal wa-l-Siyasah*, 269.
216. Abdel-Fattah, *Al-ʿUmmal*, 228.
217. Morsi, *Hadha al-Infitah*, 155; 159.
218. This is according to Hassan Abu-Basha, who headed the State Security Investigations Service at the time. Hassan Abu-Basha, *Fi al-Amn wa-l-Siyasah* (Al-Qahirah: Dar al-Hilal, 1990), 38.
219. Adly, *Al-ʿUmmal wa-l-Siyasah*, 269–70. Ghali Shukri has reported strikes in Helwan, Al-Sharqia, Alexandria, and Port Said. Shukri, *Al-Thawrah al-Mudadah*, 345.
220. Posusney, *Labor and the State*, 107.
221. Shalaby, *Al-Din wa-l-Siraʿ*, 67.
222. Adly, *Al-ʿUmmal wa-l-Siyasah*, 270–71.
223. Adly, *Al-ʿUmmal wa-l-Siyasah*, 264–67.
224. See, for example, Abdel-Razek, *Misr*, 150. Earlier that morning Helwan factories halted operations and ten thousand workers announced a strike, while demanding the government reverse its decision. Adly, *Al-ʿUmmal wa-l-Siyasah*, 271.
225. Al-Sayyid, *Al-Mujtamaʿ wa-l-Siyasah*, 75–76.
226. Abdel-Fattah, *Al-ʿUmmal*, 339–43.
227. Abdel-Razek, *Misr*, 113.
228. Shukri, *Al-Thawrah al-Mudadah*, 415.
229. Kandil, *Soldiers, Spies*, 170.
230. Mustapha Kamel Al-Sayyid notes that the ETUF was silent on the state's intervention in union elections in 1978. Al-Sayyid, *Al-Mujtamaʿ wa-l-Siyasah*, 84.
231. Law 33/1978 allowed the socialist public prosecutor to veto the candidacy of individuals whose ideas violate religious principles or adhere to subversive ideologies. Adly, *Al-ʿUmmal wa-l-Siyasah*, 306–7.
232. For details, see Posusney, *Labor and the State*, 110–12.
233. Abdel-Fattah, *Al-ʿUmmal*, 446.
234. Adly, *Al-ʿUmmal wa-l-Siyasah*, 273.
235. For example, spending on bread and oil subsidies increased every year between 1977 and 1982. Between 1977 and 1982, total food subsidy spending as a percentage of government expenditures increased from 10.9 to 19.5. See figures cited in Gouda Abdel-Khalek and Karima Korayem, *Fiscal Policy Measures in Egypt: Public Debt and Food Subsidy* (Cairo, Egypt: American University in Cairo Press, 2000), 71.
236. Abdel-Fattah, *Al-ʿUmmal*, 338.

237. There is no doubt that many of the allegations in these documents are questionable, especially as the court eventually acquitted the vast majority of the suspects
in these cases. Additionally, it took prosecutors over a month to present arrested
suspects with formal charges, some of which were absurd. More pertinently, the
accounts of these documents reveal the regime's perspective on the threats that
various opposition players constituted, even if they fail to convey with any accu-
racy these players' actions in January 1977. More specifically, these documents'
value lies in what they reveal about the security establishment's own assumptions
regarding: (1) how antiregime mass mobilization comes about; and, based on such
an understanding, (2) what roles, if any, could leftist political activists play in such
a context? Close reading of these documents yields a fine-grained understanding
of the regime's hypotheses (however false or unproven) about the type of dangers
that various actors posed to its own stability. By constructing a fuller picture of the
threats that were haunting the regime during that period, such an analysis contributes to our understanding of what drove Sadat to pursue Islamist incorporation
policies.

238. Unlike others who occupied that post under Sadat, Salem commanded a great deal
of influence and was one of the cornerstones of the ruling establishment. The president had entrusted him with the Ministry of Interior in May 1971 in the wake of
a dramatic showdown with Nasser's powerful associates, including Salem's predecessor Sharawi Gomaa. With intensifying labor unrest in the spring of 1975, Sadat
fired Prime Minister Abdel-Aziz Hegazy, and replaced him with Salem. By early
1977, Salem was not only the prime minister but also the head of the ruling Egypt
Arab Socialist Party. Thus, Salem's words displayed a perspective that was firmly
rooted within the core of the regime.

239. Abdel-Razek, *Misr*, 139–40.

240. Abdel-Razek, *Misr*, 143–44.

241. Abdel-Razek, *Misr*, 145–48.

242. Abdel-Razek, *Misr*, 128–29.

243. Abdel-Razek, *Misr*, 149.

244. The State Security Investigations Service is an Interior Ministry intelligence
agency known to engage in the surveillance of opposition political activists and
take measures to contain them. After Mubarak's downfall, it was rebranded the
"National Security Agency."

245. Abdel-Razek, *Misr*, 114.

246. Abdel-Razek, *Misr*, 212; 215.

247. Abdel-Razek, *Misr*, 204.

248. Abdel-Razek, *Misr*, 206.

249. Abdel-Razek, *Misr*, 209.

250. Abdel-Razek, *Misr*, 132.

251. Abdel-Razek, *Misr*, 153.

252. Abdel-Razek, *Misr*, 132.

253. Abdel-Razek, *Misr*, 136.

254. Abdel-Razek, *Misr*, 137–38.

255. Abdel-Razek, *Misr*, 148–50.

256. Abdel-Razek, *Misr*, 203.

2. Islamist Incorporation in the State of Science and Faith

1. Atef Abdel-Ghany, *Muhamad ʿUthman Ismaʿil Yatadhakar: al-Wazir Aladhy Kalafahuh al-Sadat bi-Takwiyn al-Jamaʿat al-Islamiyya* (Al-Qahirah: ʿAtif ʿAbd al-Ghany, 2000), 17–19.

2. Although *Al-Dawa* officially advertised itself a weekly magazine, its post-1976 issues stated that it was temporarily publishing on a monthly schedule.

3. Wael Othman, *Asrar Al-Harakah al-Tulabiyya Handasat al-Qahirah 1968–1975* (Al-Qahirah: Al-Sharikah al-Misriyya li-l-Tibaʿah wa-l-Nashr, 1976), 102.

4. Abdullah A. Al-Arian, *Answering the Call: Popular Islamic Activism in Sadat's Egypt* (New York: Oxford University Press, 2014), 87.

5. Mustafa Mahmoud, *Limadha Rafadtu al-Markisiyya* (Al-Qahirah: Dar al-Maʿarif, 1984), 5.

6. Al-Masry Al-Youm, "Mustafa Mahmud . . . Qalb al-Faylasuf la Yazal Yanbud," *Al-Masry Al-Youm*, June 12, 2008, https://to.almasryalyoum.com/article2.aspx?ArticleID=108880.

7. Nazih N. M. Ayubi, *Political Islam: Religion and Politics in the Arab World* (London: Routledge, 1991), 460–61.

8. For example, he criticized Al-Tagammu leader Khaled Mohieddin in 1975 for suggesting that Islam and socialism are compatible. Their exchange is reprinted in Mahmoud, *Limadha Rafadtu*. Also see Khalid Mohieddin, *Al-Din wa-l-Ishtrakiyya* (Al-Qahirah: Dar al-Thaqafah Al-Jadidah, undated).

9. Thanaa Al-Karas, "Mustafa Mahmud ʿan Intifadat Yanayir: Al-Sadat Qudwah li-man la Qudwatu Lahu," *Vetogate*, January 19, 2014, http://www.vetogate.com/815105.

10. Malika Zeghal, "Religion and Politics in Egypt: The Ulema of al-Azhar, Radical Islam, and the State (1952–94)," *International Journal of Middle East Studies* 31, no. 3 (August 1999): 381. For more on Mahmoud's thoughts on Islam and communism, see Mustafa Mahmoud, *Al-Markisiyya wa-l-Islam* (Al-Qahirah: Dar al-Maʿarif, 1975).

11. Ghali Shukri, *Al-Thawrah al-Mudadah fi Misr* (Al-Qahirah: Kitab al-Ahaly, 1987), 326; 418.

12. Mohamed Hassanein Heikal, *Khariyf al-Ghadab: Qisat Bidayat wa Nahayat ʿAsr al-Sadat* (Al-Qahirah: Markaz al-Ahram l-il-Tarjamah wa-l-Nashr, 2006), 254.

13. Tamir Moustafa, "Conflict and Cooperation between the State and Religious Institutions in Contemporary Egypt," *International Journal of Middle East Studies* 32 (2000): 7.

14. See excerpts of his March 15, 1959, speech in Amr Sabeh, "Qiraʾah Muwajazah li-Mwaqif ʿAbd al-Nasir min al-Shiuʿiyyin, wa min Muʾasasat al-Azhar," *Elw3yalarabi*, May 24, 2018, https://elw3yalarabi.org/elw3y/2018/05/24/لمواقف-عبد-الناصر-من-الشيو قراءة-موجزة-.

15. Saeed Serageddin, *Aqsamt An Arwy Haqaʾiq wa Mawaqif al-Barlamany al-Thaʾir Salah Abu-Ismaʿil* (Al-Qahirah: Dar al-Fikr al-Islamy, 1991), https://www.ikhwanwiki.com /index.php?title=إسماعيل_أبو_الثائر_البرلماني_ومواقف_حقائق.

16. Abdullah Shalaby, *Al-Din wa-l-Siraʿ al-Siyasy fi Misr: 1970-1985* (Al-Qahirah: Kitab al-Ahaly, 2000), 68. For a draft of the law, see Shukri, *Al-Thawrah al-Mudadah*, 490–91.

17. Shalaby, *Al-Din wa-l-Siraʿ*, 77; Shukri, *Al-Thawrah al-Mudadah*, 313. U.S. State Department records indicate that ruling party MP Gamal Al-Oteify told U.S. officials in the winter of 1979 that the purpose behind the government-led drive to make Egyptian laws consistent with Sharia is to preempt any effort by "extremists" to introduce more radical bills, which would be difficult for the ruling party to oppose publicly. Embassy Cairo to Department of State. "Telegram 02824," February 7, 1979, 1979CAIRO02824, Central Foreign Policy Files, 1973–79/Electronic Telegrams, RG 59: General Records of the Department of State, U.S. National Archives, https://aad .archives.gov/aad/createpdf?rid=83071&dt=2776&dl=2169. Wickham writes that Sadat specifically wanted to undermine Brotherhood proposals for implementing Sharia by "allowing them to become tied up in parliamentary subcommittees." Carrie Rosefsky Wickham, *The Muslim Brotherhood: Evolution of an Islamist Movement* (Princeton, NJ: Princeton University Press, 2013), 32.

18. Wickham advances a similar interpretation. Wickham, *The Muslim Brotherhood*, 33.

19. Egyptian Sociologist Abdullah Shalaby's study on religion and social conflict in Egypt between 1970 and 1985 is sympathetic to that perspective. Shalaby, *Al-Din wa-l-Siraʿ*.

20. Badr Mohamed Badr's account of the Islamist student movement in the 1970s is a case in point. Badr Mohamed Badr, *Al-Jamaʿah al-Islamiyya fi-l-Jamiʿat* (Badr Mohamed Badr, 1989).

21. For example, Sadat's Prime Minister Mustafa Khalil said in a 2000 interview with Egyptian writer Belal Fadl that he never felt that Sadat ever tried to pit Islamist movements against the left. He also denied having any knowledge of MOI's support for Islamist groups at universities, adding that he would have intervened to stop such an initiative had he known about it. Belal Fadl, "Hadith al-Mubadrah Maʿa Muwazaf li-kul al-ʿUsur (3)," *Al-Arabi Al-Jadeed*, November 21, 2018, https://www .alaraby.co.uk/3-3-العصور-لكل-موظف-مع-المبادرة-حديث.

22. Whether or not regime leaders knew that some IGU elements were tied to armed groups in Upper Egypt is subject to debate and is a question outside of the scope of this study.

23. MOI discusses his own background in his memoirs. See Abdel-Ghany, *Muhamad ʿUthman*, esp. 10–25.

24. Abdel-Ghany, *Muhamad ʿUthman*, 31.

25. Abdel-Ghany, *Muhamad ʿUthman*, 33–36. "Communism in its essence," MOI argues, "does not recognize religions. In their countries, communists and those who follow them pretend to respect religion [. . .] and argue that Communism and Marxism are but economic principles. But aren't they the advocates of the principle: 'Religion is the opium of the people?!' " (70–71).

26. Abdel-Ghany, *Muhamad ʿUthman*, 59.

27. Shukri, *Al-Thawrah al-Mudadah*, 75.

28. Adel Hammouda, *Qanabil wa Masahif: Qisat Tanzim al-Jihad* (Al-Qahirah: Sinaʾ li-l-Nashr, 1985), 121–22.

29. Abdel-Ghany, *Muhamad ʿUthman*, 62–3. According to MOI, his father was concerned about his behavior before college because it "began veering toward violence and the practice of some forms of bullying" (15).

30. MOI details his involvement in approving these decisions. He claims that the decisions were not his alone and that he voiced reservations about taking disciplinary action against suspected dissidents without adequate investigations. Abdel-Ghany, *Muhamad ʿUthman*, 66–68.

31. Abdel-Ghany, *Muhamad ʿUthman*, 60–61.

32. In his memoirs, he denies having any sectarian inclinations and claims he had long enjoyed a good relationship with Copts in Assiut. He acknowledges that he clashed with Coptic religious leaders on some occasions, but attributes this to personal differences rather than sectarian bias. Abdel-Ghany, *Muhamad ʿUthman*, 114–16. In 1977, Bishop Samuel, who headed the Coptic Orthodox Church's Ecumenical and Social Services, told U.S. officials privately that the Coptic community in Assiut are hoping that Sadat would replace MOI because of increasing intersectarian conflict under his watch. Embassy Cairo to Department of State, "Telegram 17485," October 21, 1977, 1977CAIRO17485, Central Foreign Policy Files, 1973–79/Electronic Telegrams, RG 59: General Records of the Department of State, U.S. National Archives, https://aad.archives.gov/aad/createpdf?rid=245706&dt=2532&dl=1629.

33. Abdel-Ghany, *Muhamad ʿUthman*, 134–35.

34. For instance, according to one widely quoted story, MOI said at least on two occasions that "Egypt's enemies are three: Christians first, communists second, and Jews third." Shukri, *Al-Thawrah al-Mudadah*, 76. In a 1975 interview, MOI denies having ever said that, adding that it is plausible that he could have said that about communists and Jews but that it would be outrageous for him to say something like that about Christians given that they are "our brethren." Quoted in Abdel-Ghany, *Muhamad ʿUthman*, 6.

35. Othman, *Asrar Al-Harakah*, 101–3; 129–30.

36. See, for example, Abdel-Moneim Abdul-Fetouh's account in Hossam Tammam, *Shahid ʿala Tarikh al-Harakah al-Islamiyya fi Misr: 1970-1984* (Al-Qahirah: Dar al-Shuruq, 2010), 52–56; Badr, *Al-Jamaʿah al-Islamiyya*, 13–15; and Essam El-Erian, "Shahadat al-Duktur ʿIsam al-ʿIryan ʿan Nashʾat al-Tayyar al-Islamy bi-l-Jamiʿat al-Misriyya," *Ikhwanonline*, December 13, 2008, https://web.archive.org/web/20120308152435/http://ikhwanwayonline.maktoobblog.com/1508320. Also see various testimonies in Sameh Eid, *Al-Islamiyyun Yatahadathun* (Al-Jizah: Dar Hala, 2013).

37. See the testimony of State Security Investigations Service Inspector Mamdouh Kedwani in *Al-Ahram*, March 6, 1983. Also see the testimony of the Deputy Head of Security of Assiut General Hassan Soliman. *Al-Ahram* February 27, 1983, and March 1, 1983.

38. Quoted in Hammouda, *Qanabil wa Masahif*, 129–30.
39. Ghali Shukri's scathing critique of the Sadat presidency in *The Counter-Revolution in Egypt*, which was first published in 1978, mentions MOI's support for Islamist groups at universities, but stops short of offering details or citing sources. Shukri, *Al-Thawrah al-Mudadah*.
40. Sadat's last Minister of Interior Al-Nabawi Ismail claimed to have criticized the state's policy of counterbalancing political forces at an NDP convention in either 1979 or 1980. See Mahmoud Fawzi, *Al-Nabawy Ismaʿil wa Judhur Manasat al-Sadat* (Al-Qahirah: Bayt al-Lughat Al-Dawliyya, 2007), 133–34.
41. Al-Zayyat, once an adviser to Sadat, was the first secretary of the ASU's Central Committee until replaced by Sayyid Marei in early 1972. He continued to serve as deputy prime minister in the government of Aziz Sedky. After falling out of Sadat's favor, Al-Zayyat became a vocal opponent of economic liberalization policies until losing his parliamentary seat in the 1976 election. He was a staunch critic of the peace treaty with Israel and supported the activities of Al-Tagammu Party. He was jailed in September 1981 as part of Sadat's infamous crackdown on opposition figures.
42. It appeared in *Al-Ahaly* on May 23, 1983. See Ahmed Abdalla Rozza, *Al-Talabah w-al-Siyasah fi Misr* (Al-Qahirah: Sinaʿ li-l-Nashr, 1991), 250.
43. Mohamed Abdel-Salam Al-Zayyat, *Al-Sadat al-Qinaʿ wa-l-Haqiqah* (Al-Qahirah: Kitab al-Ahaly, 1989).
44. Al-Tagammu's publishing house released numerous books critiquing Sadat's policies during the 1980s. They republished Ghali Shukri's *The Counter-Revolution in Egypt* in 1987. Also, see Mohamed Ibrahim Kamel, *Al-Salam al-Daʾiʿ fi Kamb Difid* (Al-Qahirah: Kitab al-Ahaly, 1987); Lotfi Al-Khouli, *Madrasat al-Sadat al-Siyasiyya wa-l-Yasar al-Misry* (Al-Qahirah: Kitab al-Ahaly, 1986); and Ibrahim Al-Issawi, *Fi Islah ma Afsadahu al-Infitah* (Al-Qahirah: Kitab al-Ahaly, 1984). Muslim Brotherhood General Guide Omar Al-Tilmisani published his own account of Sadat's relationship with the Brotherhood in *Days with Sadat*. Omar Al-Tilmisani, *Ayam maʿa al-Sadat* (Al-Qahirah: Dar Al-Iʿtisam, 1984). In *Memories Not Memoirs*, Al-Tilmisani offered some additional insights about the Brotherhood's relationship with authorities. Omar Al-Tilmisani, *Dhikrayat La Mudhakarat* (Al-Qahirah: Dar Al-Iʿtisam, 1985). Transcripts of his September 1981 postarrest interrogations were published by Brotherhood-affiliated attorney Mukhtar Nouh, revealing more details about the Brotherhood's dealings with regime officials. Mukhtar Nouh, *Mawsuʿat al-ʿUnf fi-l-Harakat al-Islamiyya al-Musalahah: 50 ʿAman min al-Dam* (Al-Qahirah: Sama li-l-Nashr wa-l-Tawziʿ, 2014), 383–407.
45. Another example of this perspective is found in Hammouda, *Qanabil wa Masahif*.
46. Heikal, *Khariyf al-Ghadab*, 228–29. Adel Hammouda repeats the same stories. Hammouda, *Qanabil wa Masahif*, 121–25. Muslim Brotherhood General Guide Omar Al-Tilmisani offered some insights into Osman's mediating role. Al-Tilmisani, *Dhikrayat La Mudhakarat*, 114–15. Former Muslim Brotherhood activist Abul-Ela Madi disclosed the firsthand account of Brotherhood leader Helmy Abdel-Meguid, who reported

meeting with Sadat and Osman to discuss the group's legal status. Abul-Ela Madi, "Al-Muhandis ʿUthman Ahmad ʿUthman wa-l-Ikhwan (2)," *Al-Wasat Party*, February 5, 2018, http://web.archive.org/web/20200219145756/https://www.alwasatparty.com /window/شخ--2الإخوان-وا-عثمان-أحمد-عثمان-المهندس.

47. The Muslim Brotherhood secured seats in the 1984 and 1987 parliamentary elections through alliances with Al-Wafd Party (in 1984), Socialist Labor Party, and Liberal Socialists Party (in 1987).

48. Hassan Abu-Basha, *Fi al-Amn wa-l-Siyasah* (Al-Qahirah: Dar al-Hilal, 1990), 135; 181. Abu-Basha also faults Sadat for being too reliant on repressive security measures and for lacking the foresight to address political grievances through democratic processes.

49. That said, he vehemently rejects the repressive option, arguing that "radical" Islamism must be confronted and defeated intellectually through dialogue. Abu-Basha, *Fi al-Amn*, 127–33; 154.

50. That perspective is clearly articulated in Ghali Shukri's *The Culture of the Arbitrary Order*, published by Al-Tagammu's publishing house in 1994. Ghali Shukri, *Thaqafat al-Nizam al-ʿAshwaʾy* (Al-Qahirah: Kitab al-Ahaly, 1994), 244–71.

51. Former Prime Minister Kamal Al-Ganzouri confirms this in his memoirs. Kamal Al-Ganzouri, *Tariqy: Sanawat al-Hulm wa-l-Sidam wa-l-ʿUzlah min al-Qariyah ila Riʾasat Majlis al-Wizaraʾ* (Al-Qahirah: Dar al-Shuruq, 2012), 86–87. In his interview with Makram Mohamed Ahmed, Karam Zohdy of Al-Gamʿah Al-Islamiyya stated that some prominent state-linked figures like Mohamed Metwalli Al-Sharawi and Ahmed Kamal Abul-Magd tried to mediate between the government and his group in the early 1990s. Makram Mohamed Ahmed, *Muʾamarah am Murajaʿah: Hiwar maʿa Qadat al-Tataruf fi Sijn al-ʿAqrab* (Al-Qahirah: Dar al-Shuruq, 2002), 52.

52. I am grateful for Belal Fadl's firsthand insights in elucidating the context of *Rose Al-Yousef*'s interest in the subject of Sadat and the genealogy of the Islamist insurgency.

53. Citing an *Al-Gumhuria* article by Ahmed Kamal Abul-Magd, Salem stated that Abul-Magd advised Sadat to engage in dialogue with students in a "faith-based way." See *Rose Al-Yousef*, July 13, 1992.

54. MOI also denied ever saying that "communists, Christians, and Israelis" were Egypt's enemies. *Rose Al-Yousef*, August 31, 1992.

55. See, for example, Magdy Derbala's report in *Rose Al-Yousef* on violence in Malawy on January 2, 1995, and Nabil Sharafeddin's report on militants in Assiut on January 30, 1995.

56. Allam said in a 2019 interview that his 1995 collaboration with *Rose Al-Yousef* was motivated by alarm at reports that the Muslim Brotherhood might form a political party. See Ahmed Abu-Saleh, "Al-Luwaʾ Fuʾad ʿAllam: 25 Yanayir Karithah ʿala Amn Misr," *Al-Wafd*, June 5, 2019, https://alwafd.news/كارثة-يناير-25-علام-فؤاد-اء اللو/2401679-وحوارات-تحقيقات-مصر-أمن-على .

57. During this period, a similar editorial line is evident in *Al-Ahaly*. See, for example, articles by Rifaat Al-Said republished in Rifaat Al-Said, *Did al-Taʾslum* (Al-Qahirah: Al-Ahaly, 1996), 120–22; 129–31.

58. A physician by training, Gamee was a close friend and confidant of Sadat, who he reportedly knew through family connections since the 1940s. Thanks to his former affiliation with the Muslim Brotherhood, Gamee was involved in mediating between the group's exiled leaders and Sadat during the early 1970s. The journalist Mohamed Abbas claims that Gamee had ties to SSIS and mediated between security officials and IGUs. Belal Fadl, "Shahadah Ghariybah ʿala ʿAsr Aghrab (6)," *Al-Arabi Al-Jadeed*, January 13, 2021, https://www.alaraby.co.uk/blogs /6-شهادة-غريبة-على-عصر-أغرب.

59. He later published an expanded version of his testimony in Fouad Allam, *Al-Ikhwan wa Ana: Min al-Manshiyah ila al-Manasah* (Al-Qahirah: Akhbar al-Yawm, 1996).

60. For example, MOI denied the allegation that he was a member of the Muslim Brotherhood.

61. *Rose Al-Yousef*, July 24, 1995.

62. See Mahmoud Gamee, ʿArift al-Sadat (Al-Qahirah: Al-Maktab al-Misry Al-Hadith, 2004). The first edition of the book was published in November 1998.

63. Abdel-Ghany claims that the memoirs were in the works for more than three years, and that MOI requested they be published posthumously. Abdel-Ghany, *Muhamad ʿUthman*, 5.

64. For example, Allam writes that MOI was tasked with forming "Brotherhood cells" at universities. Allam, *Al-Ikhwan wa Ana*, 250.

65. Al-Zayyat does quote exchanges with Sadat that cite MOI's role in sponsoring anti-leftist student activism, but he did not elucidate the conversations and conditions informing that decision. Al-Zayyat, *Al-Sadat al-Qinaʿ*, 298.

66. For instance, some claim that Osman Ahmed Osman and Mahmoud Gamee were involved in setting up Islamist student groups, which apparently confuses Sadat's support for student activism with his rapprochement with the Muslim Brotherhood. See Allam, *Al-Ikhwan wa Ana*, 250; and Heikal, *Khariyf al-Ghadab*, 252.

67. Ismail had served as the director of Mamdouh Salem's office in the early 1970s when the latter was minister of interior.

68. The interview was transcribed and published in Fawzi, *Al-Nabawy Ismaʿil*.

69. One notable contribution came in 2015, when Mohy Eissa, Muslim Brotherhood figure and former leader of Al-Minya University's Islamic Group, began publishing his own memoirs on social media. His testimony disclosed previously unknown details pertaining to the activities of the IGUs in Middle and Upper Egypt and students' clashes with authorities. His testimony offers a perspective different from that of the Cairo-centered accounts of the rise of the Muslim Brotherhood and Islamic Groups at Universities during the 1970s. The entries are available on Eissa's Facebook personal page, accessed April 17, 2021, https://www.facebook.com/profile.php?id=100006418533527. For more on the importance of incorporating geographically diverse sources and narratives, see the recent roundtable in *International Journal for Middle East Studies* on "decentering Egyptian historiography," especially Lucia Carminati and Mohamed Gamal-Eldin, "Decentering Egyptian Historiography: Provincializing Geographies, Methodologies, and Sources," *International Journal of Middle East Studies* 53, no. 1 (2021): 107–11.

70. That was the political climate in which Abdel-Reheem Aly released his book *The Muslim Brotherhood: The Crisis of the Renewal Current*, which compiled a host of first-hand testimonies of former Islamist student leaders who went on to become Muslim Brotherhood members. Abdel-Reheem Aly, *Al-Ikhwan al-Muslimun: Azmat Tayar al-Tajdid* (Al-Qahirah: Markaz al-Mahrusah, 2004). Wickham outlines these divisions and their genealogy in her seminal study on the Muslim Brotherhood. Wickham, *The Muslim Brotherhood*, esp. chap. 3, 4, and 5.

71. See, for example, the account of Al-Sayyid Abdel-Sattar Al-Meleegy. He presents the history of the Muslim Brotherhood since the 1970s as a struggle between the student movement generation that helped revive the group after its decades-long absence and a set of dogmatic leaders who wanted to control the group through covert, parallel structures operating alongside the movement's formal apparatus. Al-Sayyid Abdel-Sattar Al-Meleegy, *Tajribaty maʿa al-Ikhwan* (Al-Qahirah: Al-Markaz al-ʿIlmy li-l-Buhuth wa-l-Dirasat, 2009). An electronic version of the book published by *IkhwanWiki* contains some details not included in the print version. Al-Sayyid Abdel-Sattar Al-Meleegy, "Tajribaty maʿa al-Ikhwan," *IkhwanWiki*, November 26, 2012, https://www.ikhwanwiki.com/index.php?title =تجربتي_مع_الإخوان_من_الدعوة_إلى_التنظيم_السري. Abdel-Moneim Aboul-Fotouh is more diplomatic in his account of the 1970s student movement and its role in rebuilding the Muslim Brotherhood. Although he argues that the Brotherhood survived only because of the student activists who joined it in the 1970s, he refrains from Al-Meleegy's ad hominem attacks against senior leaders. See, for example, Aboul-Fotouh's remarks about Mustafa Mashhur in Tammam, *Shahid ʿala Tarikh*, 80–81.

72. Hassanein Koroum, *Al-Taharukat al-Siyasiyya li-l-Ikhwan al-Muslimin 1971-1987* (Al-Qahirah: al-Markaz al-ʿAraby al-Dawly li-l-Iʿlam, 2012).

73. Abu-Ruqayiq's firsthand account of the period complements others offered by Brotherhood leaders, like that of Al-Tilmisani. Al-Tilmisani, *Dhikrayat La Mudhakarat*. Al-Tilmisani, *Ayam maʿa al-Sadat*.

74. These include conversations with Tawfiq Oweida, a ruling party figure and longtime head of the Supreme Council for Islamic Affairs (SCIA), regarding his efforts to promote Islamic groups at public universities.

75. Documents are publicly accessible at the U.S. National Archives, accessed February 4, 2021, https://aad.archives.gov/aad.

76. Rozza, *Al-Talabah*, 150–57. Sami Sharaf attributes the political leadership's inconsistent support for the Youth Organization under Nasser to internal regime conflicts. For more details, see Sami Sharaf, *Sanawat wa Ayam Maʿa Jamal ʿAbd al-Nasir*, 5 vols. (Al-Qahirah: Al-Maktab al-Misry al-Hadith, 2014), 5:1186–90.

77. Al-Zayyat, *Al-Sadat al-Qinaʿ*, 288–89.

78. Al-Nabawi Ismail also cites the Tahrir Square sit-in as a key motivator to Sadat's decision to mobilize Islamist groups. Quoted in Fawzi, *Al-Nabawy Ismaʿil*, 133–34.

79. Abu-Basha concludes that the YO was not a viable instrument for Sadat because it contained too many Marxist elements. Abu-Basha, *Fi al-Amn*, 31. Although the YO continued to exist on paper for a few more years, Sadat officially disbanded it in 1975. Sharaf, *Sanawat wa Ayam*, 5:1190.

80. See Hassan Abu-Basha's interview in *Rose Al-Yousef*, February 24, 1997. The occupation of Tahrir Square occurred hours after security units stormed Cairo University and forced an end to an anti-Sadat sit-in. See Rozza, *Al-Talabah*, 218–19.

81. Quoted in Fawzi, *Al-Nabawy Isma'il*, 133.

82. Although the existence of this initiative became evident only toward the end of 1972, Sadat's posturing to pit Islamist currents against his leftist challengers was on display in January of that year. In a January 25 speech condemning the unrest, Sadat made a point of reading a purported letter of support from the Religious Association of Ain Shams University. The letter belittlingly described the anti-Sadat protesters as "foolish clowns" and the "pioneers of the cafeterias." See Shaaban, *Inhaztu li-l-Watan*, 135.

83. Replacing him at the ASU was Sayyid Marei.

84. Abdel-Ghany, *Muhamad 'Uthman*, 76–77.

85. Abdel-Ghany, *Muhamad 'Uthman*, 78–79. MOI's account is largely consistent with Gamee's: "He [Sadat] did in fact ask Mohamed Othman Ismail to form and promote Islamist groups at universities and support them using the funds allocated for youth development. Sadat was not really thinking about bringing Islamists back, but he wanted to form Islamist institutions and organizations that could confront both communists and Nasserists. He had told me once that communists and Nasserists are spreading throughout the state [apparatus] and they are bothering him and will continue to do so unless there are strong groups and stronger institutions that could rein them in, beat them, and break their back." Gamee, *'Arift al-Sadat*, 173–74. Presenting a similar account, Hassan Abu-Basha, quoted in Amr Al-Leithy, *Ikhtiraq: Kashf al-Sitar 'an Akhtar al-Asrar* (Al-Qahirah: Dar al-Shuruq, 2003), 139–40, says that the ASU backed these groups with the "personal support and recommendation of the president." Finally, in the fall of 1975, Tawfiq Oweida, the secretary general of the Supreme Council on Islamic Affairs, told a U.S. official that Sadat intended to use religiously oriented students to respond to leftist criticism of the government. Embassy Cairo to Department of State, "Telegram 10283," October 15, 1976, 1975CAIRO10283, Central Foreign Policy Files, 1973–79/Electronic Telegrams, RG 59: General Records of the Department of State, U.S. National Archives, https://aad.archives.gov/aad/createpdf?rid=284958&dt=2476&dl=1345.

86. Abdel-Ghany, *Muhamad 'Uthman*, 80–81.

87. Abdel-Ghany, *Muhamad 'Uthman*, 81.

88. Abdel-Ghany, *Muhamad 'Uthman*, 88.

89. Abdel-Ghany, *Muhamad 'Uthman*, 98.

90. These groups' expenditures on printing raised eyebrows among students and reinforced the perception that the ASU was backing them. Wael Othman, an engineering student engaged in Islamist activism at the time, recalls encountering seemingly well-funded religious groups from other faculties with unknown sponsors. He cites an incident when a student from one such group offered to print more than ten thousand copies of a joint statement he coauthored. Othman, *Asrar Al-Harakah*, 118.

91. Kamal Khalil, who was a student at the Faculty of Engineering, recalls this incident in his memoirs and reports that leftist activist Ahmed Bahaaeddin Shaaban was

beaten up by Youth of Islam members and Ministry of Interior undercover agents. Kamal Khalil, *Hikayat min Zaman Fat: Sirah Dhatiyya min khilal al-Ahdath* (Al-Jizah: Bayt al-Yasmin li-l-Nashr wa-l-Tawziʿ, 2012), 126.

92. Rozza, *Al-Talabah*, 232–33. Othman reports that a Cairo University "communist march" was intercepted by a group that self-identified as the "Youth of Islam Faculty of Law chapter." Othman, *Asrar Al-Harakah*, 91.

93. Allam, *Al-Ikhwan wa Ana*, 251.

94. Abdel-Ghany, *Muhamad ʿUthman*, 86–87. Gamee counters that ASU funds were directed only at peaceful endeavors, such as students' summer camps and Muslim pilgrimage trips (quoted in Allam, *Al-Ikhwan wa Ana*, 263–64).

95. In narrating that incident in his memoirs, Abu-Basha did not disclose MOI's name. Abu-Basha, *Fi al-Amn*, 30. He did so, however, in a 1997 interview. See *Rose Al-Yousef*, February 24, 1997.

96. Quoted in Rozza, *Al-Talabah*, 230.

97. Al-Zayyat, *Al-Sadat al-Qinaʿ*, 292.

98. Abdel-Ghany, *Muhamad ʿUthman*, 83.

99. Othman, *Asrar Al-Harakah*, 129–30.

100. Othman, *Asrar Al-Harakah*, 102.

101. Abdel-Moneim Aboul-Fotouh, who was then active in a rival Islamist group, suggests that the YOI may have been a regime implant. Tammam, *Shahid ʿala Tarikh*, 55–56. Essam El-Erian states, "There was a pro-government current present in the group of Youth of Islam which was formed by Mohamed Othman Ismail inside the Faculty of Engineering, and their role was always to counter communist thought." El-Erian, "Shahadat al-Duktur." Also see Badr, *Al-Jamaʿah al-Islamiyya*, 14–15.

102. Othman, *Asrar Al-Harakah*, 130.

103. For example, various groups and activists operating under the name of YOI began appearing on Cairo University campus, often employing hostile tactics to antagonize leftist members of the student body. YOI's leaders also report pressure from affiliates who belonged to other schools at Cairo University to join in confrontations with leftist students. They report that one such affiliate reworded a YOI statement to give it a clear anticommunist bent without their knowledge. Othman, *Asrar Al-Harakah*, 105; 119; 124. Also see Al-Arian, *Answering the Call*, 62–63.

104. Othman, *Asrar Al-Harakah*, 158.

105. Abdel-Ghany, *Muhamad ʿUthman*, 80.

106. Othman, *Asrar Al-Harakah*, 102.

107. Othman, *Asrar Al-Harakah*, 103.

108. Othman, *Asrar Al-Harakah*, 129–30.

109. For example, former Cairo University Islamic Group leader Abdel-Moneim Aboul-Fotouh recounts how he often saw YOI affiliates speaking casually with female students, which made him suspect that they were regime informants rather than sincere activists who were committed to conservative social norms. Tammam,

Shahid ʿala Tarikh, 54–56. In fact, a 1973 report that students submitted to a parliamentary fact-finding commission openly identified YOI as an ASU-backed organization. Othman, *Asrar Al-Harakah*, 105.

110. See Al-Arian, *Answering the Call*, 67–69.

111. Note on terminology: the term IGUs is used to reference the entire network of Islamic Groups at public universities. The term Islamic Group (IG) is used to describe any specific university or college level chapter of the IGUs. The Arabic name *al-Gamʿa al-Islamiyya* (GI) is used to describe the militant movement that emerged from the networks of the IGUs and that led an insurgency against the Egyptian government.

112. In his insider account of the IGUs, Muslim Brotherhood–affiliated journalist Badr Mohamed Badr suggests that officials tried but failed to coopt the student networks that eventually formed the IGUs: "Indeed, officials have tried to contain these religious associations, and to exploit this Islamic revival trend for the interests of those in power, but these attempts failed at the outset, and authorities' enticements did not succeed in persuading the 'principled ones' to work on their behalf." Badr, *Al-Jamaʿah al-Islamiyya*, 13.

113. For example, Al-Nabawi Ismail, who was then the Minister of Interior's office manager, claims that SSIS submitted reports expressing reservations about this policy. Al-Leithy, *Ikhtiraq*, 140.

114. Allam writes, "One of the orders we received decreed that no security actions would be taken against these plans," and no attempts would be made to infiltrate these organizations. Allam, *Al-Ikhwan wa Ana*, 250. He emphasizes that oversight of Islamist groups, more generally, was limited for most of the 1970s (270).

115. Abdel-Ghany, *Muhamad ʿUthman*, 88.

116. Embassy Cairo to Department of State, "Telegram 06893," May 19, 1976, 1976CAIRO06893, Central Foreign Policy Files, 1973–79/Electronic Telegrams, RG 59: General Records of the Department of State, U.S. National Archives, https://aad.archives.gov/aad/createpdf?rid=257824&dt=2082&dl=1345. In another 1976 exchange with the Embassy, Oweida said that the government was financing Islamic groups on campuses to discourage subversive activities. Embassy Cairo to Department of State, "Telegram 04727," April 9, 1976, 1976CAIRO04727, Central Foreign Policy Files, 1973–79/Electronic Telegrams, RG 59: General Records of the Department of State, U.S. National Archives, https://aad.archives.gov/aad/createpdf?rid=22799&dt=2082&dl=1345.

117. Gamee, *ʿArift al-Sadat*, 240–41.

118. Embassy Cairo to Department of State, "Telegram 18508," September 11, 1979, 1979CAIRO18508, Central Foreign Policy Files, 1973–79/Electronic Telegrams, RG 59: General Records of the Department of State, U.S. National Archives, https://aad.archives.gov/aad/createpdf?rid=301299&dt=2776&dl=2169.

119. On July 7, 1979, at one such site, the "Abu-Bakr Al-Siddiq Summer Camp," Sadat gave an address emphasizing the importance of Islamic values in the foundation of the individual. Anwar Al-Sadat, "Kalimat al-Raʾis Muhamad Anwar al-Sadat li-Shabab al-Hizb al-Watany bi Muʿaskar Abu Bakr al-Al-Sidiqbi-l-Iskandariyya,"

The *Library of Alexandria Sadat Archives*, July 7, 1979, http://sadat.bibalex.org /TextViewer.aspx?TextID=SP_884.

120. Gamee, *ʿArift al-Sadat*, 241.

121. Shalaby, *Al-Din wa-l-Siraʿ*, 110.

122. For background on the GI, see Hala Mostafa, *Al-Islam al-Siyasy fi Misr: Min Harakat al-Islah ila Jamaʿat al-ʿUnf* (Al-Qahirah: Markaz al-Mahrusah, 1998), 216–28; and Salwa Mohamed Al-Awwa, *Al-Jamaʿah al-Islamiyya al-Musalahah fi Misr, 1974–2004* (Al-Qahirah: Maktabat al-Shuruq al-Dawliyya, 2006).

123. For more on the Alexandrian Salafist Call movement, see Ahmed Zaghloul Shalata, "Al-Daʿwah al-Salafiyya al-Sakandariyya: Masarat al-Tanzim wa Maʾalat al-Siyasah," *Al-Mustaqbal Al-ʿAraby* 443 (2016): 128–40.

124. Aboul-Fotouh points out that, before 1973, the group was officially called the "Committee for Religious Awareness." Tammam, *Shahid ʿala Tarikh*, 40.

125. See El-Erian, "Shahadat al-Duktur"; Tammam, *Shahid ʿala Tarikh*, 33; and Badr, *Al-Jamaʿah al-Islamiyya*, 11. Al-Meleegy states that the IG at Ain Shams University originated from the "Religious Society." Al-Meleegy, *Tajribaty*, 60. Salah Hashem, one of the founders of the IG at Assiut University also locates the IG's roots in the "Religious Society." Quoted in Al-Bayan, "Kitab al-Jamaʿat al-Islamiyya Tuʿlin Tawbatuha, al-Halaqah al-Thalithah," *Al-Bayan*, February 9, 2002, https://www.albayan .ae/one-world/2002-02-09-1.1310027.

126. Tammam, *Shahid ʿala Tarikh*, 41–42.

127. Badr, *Al-Jamaʿah al-Islamiyya*, 12.

128. Tammam, *Shahid ʿala Tarikh*, 47.

129. See Essam El-Erian's testimony in Eid, *Al-Islamiyyun Yatahadathun*, 87. Ahmed Bahaaeddin Shaaban, who at the time was a prominent leftist student activist at Cairo University's Faculty of Engineering, acknowledges that leftist organizers focused on social services far less than their Islamist counterparts. Shaaban, *Inhaztu li-l-Watan*, 65.

130. Badr, *Al-Jamaʿah al-Islamiyya*, 27–32. IG Assiut leader Aly Al-Sherif describes a similar array of services offered at Assiut University. Aly Al-Sherif, "Li-Awal Marah al-Mujaz Tanshur Mudhakirat Qaʾid al-Tanzim al-Musalah li-l-Jamaʿah al-Islamiyya bi-Khat Yaduh," *Elmogaz*, December 21, 2012, https://www.elmogaz.com/60135.

131. El-Erian, "Shahadat al-Duktur."

132. In 1973, Islamic student camps were held at Cairo and Ain Shams universities. In 1974, camps were held at Cairo, Ain Shams, and Al-Azhar universities. In 1975, new camps were convened at Mansoura, Zaqaziq, and Tanta universities. In 1976, all the same universities, plus Alexandria, Assiut, and Al-Minya universities, held camps. In 1977, camps were held in almost all universities. Al-Meleegy, "Tajribaty."

133. According to Badr, a typical day at these camps began with *fajr* (dawn) prayers, followed by readings of the Quran and important texts authored by such figures as Hassan Al-Banna, followed by an exercise session, and seminars featuring prominent religious thinkers and preachers. These camps, he reports, were designed to help students "get used to Islamic behavior and Islamic life" and "had a notable

effect on the behavior, make-up, and development of IG members during that period." Badr, *Al-Jamaʿah al-Islamiyya*, 30. A full schedule of a typical camp can be found in Al-Meleegy, "Tajribaty."

134. Abdullah Shalaby, who attended one such camp at Ain Sham University, writes, "These camps were a revival of the summer camps that youth of the Muslim Brotherhood used to convene before the dissolution of the group | . . .| And it was effectively a school for preparing future cadres for the Islamist movement. The daily program at the camp was an attempt to simulate an Islamic society built around the idea of isolation from the society outside of the camp." Shalaby, *Al-Din wa-l-Siraʿ*, 89.

135. Mohy Eissa, one of the leaders of the Al-Minya University IG, says that the first attempt to bring all the various IG chapters together was made at a 1975 summer camp held in Cairo. Mohy Eissa, personal Facebook page post, Facebook, February 19, 2015, https://www.facebook.com/permalink.php?story_fbid=161942836494776 6&id=100006418533527.

136. Eissa cites a 1977 exchange with Abdel-Moneim Aboul-Fotouh, who explained that gaining control of the unions would give IGUs a stronger legal and political standing and would force the state to take them seriously. Mohy Eissa, personal Facebook page post, Facebook. March 4, 2015, https://www.facebook.com/permalink .php?story_fbid=1623679997855936&id=100006418533527.

137. Abul-Ela Madi, "Hikayaty maʿa al-Ikhwan wa Qisat al-Wasat," *Masress*, January 4, 2006, http://www.masress.com/almesryoon/9998.

138. Mohy Eissa notes that by the late 1970s, IGUs were engaged in setting up markets for selling subsidized household goods. Mohy Eissa, personal Facebook page post, Facebook, April 28, 2015, https://www.facebook.com/permalink.php?story_fbid=1 646287168928552&id=100006418533527.

139. See Tammam, *Shahid ʿala Tarikh*, 50–51.

140. Badr, *Al-Jamaʿah al-Islamiyya*, 33. Ibrahim Al-Zafarani, one of the leaders of the IG at Alexandria University, says that the first public Eid prayer was organized in the city in the 1975–76 academic year. Ibrahim Al-Zafarani, "Hikayat al-Zaʿfarany," *Ikhwanwiki*, December 9, 2017, http://www.ikhwan.wiki/index.php?title=حكايات_الزعفراني.

141. Othman, *Asrar Al-Harakah*, 160.

142. Badr, *Al-Jamaʿah al-Islamiyya*, 34.

143. Shaaban writes, "They do not refrain from practicing all kinds of 'religious' terrorism, sectarian discrimination, and attacks against male and female colleagues, and even against the faculty members, at 'the Faculty of Medicine.' The matter even came to the point of imposing separation between male and female students through barbaric force, suspending all artistic, cultural and sports student activities in some faculties, and monopolizing the student union budget for the benefit of their group alone on grounds that every thought that does not stem from Islam or any activity that directly leads to disbelief and delusion should be eliminated, along with those who believe in it." Shaaban, *Inhaztu li-l-Watan*, 47.

144. IG Assiut leader Aly Al-Sherif recounts devising a system of gender segregation at auditoriums, and admits to intervening to separate unmarried couples, sometimes

at knifepoint. Aly Al-Sherif, "ʿIlaqat al-Jamaʿah al-Islamiyya bi-l-Aqbat Kanat Sayiʾah Jidan wa Kuna Nuwajih Tajawuzatuhum bi-l-Shiddah wa-l-ʿUnf," *Elmogaz*, December 28, 2012, https://www.elmogaz.com/60873.

145. Shalaby, *Al-Din wa-l-Siraʿ*, 107. Some reports claim that the IGUs followed similar practices outside campus walls. During his time at Al-Minya University, Al-Sayyid Abdel-Sattar Al-Meleegy claims that IG banned local stores from playing music. Al-Meleegy, *Tajribaty*, 79–90.

146. A faculty member at Assiut University cites an incident when IG students held Coptic students hostage during a days-long sit-in protesting the arrest of fellow IG students at Al-Minya University. See Nabil Omar's account in *Sabah Al-Khair*, November 19, 1981. Al-Sayyid Abdel-Sattar Al-Meleegy reports a 1977 incident at Al-Minya University, where IG students, who were surrounded by security forces, held Coptic students hostage and demanded that the police end its siege. He writes that the hostages were sympathetic to the IG captors. Al-Meleegy, *Tajribaty*, 75. Aly Al-Sherif reports that the "IG in Assiut used to stand up to Christian transgressions with ferocity and violence." Aly Al-Sherif, "ʿIlaqat al-Jamaʿah." Also see Shalaby, *Al-Din wa-l-Siraʿ*, 108.

147. Mohy Eissa, personal Facebook page post, Facebook, February 19, 2015, https://www.facebook.com/permalink.php?story_fbid=1619423841614885&id=100006418533527; Mohy Eissa, personal Facebook page post, Facebook, March 2, 2015, https://www.facebook.com/permalink.php?story_fbid=1623030801254189&id=100006418533527; Mohy Eissa, personal Facebook page post, Facebook, March 3, 2015, https://www.facebook.com/permalink.php?story_fbid=1623333867890549&id=100006418533527; Mohy Eissa, personal Facebook page post, Facebook, April 7, 2015, https://www.facebook.com/photo/?fbid=1637890666434869&set=a.1578510872372849.

148. In interpreting these claims, bear in mind that the term "IGUs" encompasses a variety of different groups with diverse histories and experiences. In other words, it is entirely possible that the regime's influence on Islamist student activism varied from institution to institution.

149. Tammam, *Shahid ʿala Tarikh*, 52. Essam El-Erian states, "We came to control the student union but there was no guidance from any party or deals. Everything was just moving naturally." El-Erian, "Shahadat al-Duktur."

150. See Abul-Ela Madi's account in Eid, *Al-Islamiyyun Yatahadathun*, 16–17.

151. Quoted in Ahmed Mawlana, *Al-Jamaʿah al-Islamiyya: Istiratijyat Mutaʿaridah* (Istanbul: Al-Maʿhad al-Misry li-l-Dirasat, 2018), 4.

152. Abbas Al-Sisi, *Min al-Madhbahah ila Sahat al-Daʿwah* (Al-Qahirah: Dar al-Tawziʿ wa-l-Nashr al-Ismaliyya, 2003), 109–10.

153. See Tammam, *Shahid ʿala Tarikh*, 47–50; also see Al-Arian, *Answering the Call*, 120.

154. Tammam, *Shahid ʿala Tarikh*, 55. Similarly, Badr explains that IG members were expected to "adhere to Islamic behavior" and follow a religious education curriculum. Badr, *Al-Jamaʿah al-Islamiyya*, 23; 31–32.

155. Many such students embraced conservative practices that are said to have gained visibility in Egypt during the 1970s. Thus, IGU activists were shocked at the realization that some of the same Muslim Brotherhood leaders they had long admired

from afar did not object to watching sports, listening to music, or keeping clean-shaven. Tammam, *Shahid ʿala Tarikh*, 83, 96; and see El-Erian's testimony in Eid, *Al-Islamiyyun Yatahadathun*, 92.

156. Tammam, *Shahid ʿala Tarikh*, 40. In one such incident, leftist students provoked Islamist activists by displaying on their wall magazines feminist writer Amina Al-Said's article criticizing the practice of veiling. See El-Erian's testimony in Eid, *Al-Islamiyyun Yatahadathun*, 99.

157. Tammam, *Shahid ʿala Tarikh*, 102.

158. Badr, *Al-Jamaʿah al-Islamiyya*, 51–52.

159. Quoted in Shaaban, *Inhaztu li-l-Watan*, 46.

160. Among such exceptions was Al-Minya University IG leader Mohy Eissa, who was jailed after joining the January 17 protest. Mohy Eissa, personal Facebook page post, Facebook, February 18, 2015, https://www.facebook.com/permalink.php?story_fbid=1619008188323117&id=100006418533527.

161. Tammam, *Shahid ʿala Tarikh*, 59. Quoted in Al-Leithy, *Ikhtiraq*, 225, Essam El-Erian denies that IGUs were involved in these events and recalls using his authority as a student union official to deter students from joining the protests.

162. Quoted in Shaaban, *Inhaztu li-l-Watan*, fn2, 47.

163. Aboul-Fotouh says, "Although we used to enter into confrontations with the communists at the university, some of which escalated to the use of physical violence, they were spontaneous, voluntary confrontations governed by the logic of conflict between a genuine, hardline religious current that does not have a disciplined approach, and a current that was always directing mockery and criticism toward Islamic fundamentals; which made these confrontations a natural matter, neither intended nor plotted by the regime." Tammam, *Shahid ʿala Tarikh*, 52–53.

164. Quoted in Badr, *Al-Jamaʿah al-Islamiyya*, 113. Aboul-Fotouh acknowledges that during his years of activism at Cairo University, senior administrators openly voiced expectations that the IG would intervene to disrupt subversive activities by leftist students. He cites an exchange with the then vice president of Cairo University Sufi Abu-Taleb, who expressed disappointment that the IG failed to stop communist student protests. Tammam, *Shahid ʿala Tarikh*, 53; Essam El-Erian corroborates Aboul-Fotouh's account of the exchange. Eid, *Al-Islamiyyun Yatahadathun*, 98.

165. Al-Meleegy, for example, recounts that Islamic camps were permitted at Ain Shams University primarily because the administrators and authorities wanted a counterweight to the annual Pan-Arab Nasserist conference that featured participants from all over the Arab world. Al-Meleegy, "Tajribaty."

166. Al-Meleegy, "Tajribaty." He also argues that the university administrators gave IGUs "free reign" in organizing their activities.

167. Badr, *Al-Jamaʿah al-Islamiyya*, 85. Mohy Eissa's testimony conveys a similar viewpoint, but is more praiseful of Sadat and the impact his policies had on the Islamist movement. Mohy Eissa, personal Facebook page post, Facebook, April 5, 2015, https://www.facebook.com/photo/?fbid=1637245606499375&set=a.1578510872372849.

168. Tammam, *Shahid ʿala Tarikh*, 54.

169. Tammam, *Shahid ʿala Tarikh*, 56–57.

170. According to Aboul-Fotouh, Islamist currents were more successful because of Egyptian society's deeply ingrained sense of religiosity. Tammam, *Shahid ʿala Tarikh*, 56–57. In his seminal study of the 1970s Islamist student movement in Egypt, Abdullah Al-Arian presents a complementary perspective: "Given the severe restrictions on independent student activism strictly enforced by the Nasser regime, the relative freedom provided by Sadat could easily be viewed through the lens of his narrow political objectives. But if that were the case, many student leaders argue, the regime would have placed barriers before other political movements and would have created space in which only the Islamic movement would be allowed to operate. In reality Sadat granted equal freedom to all ideological trends." Al-Arian, *Answering the Call*, 127–28.

171. Echoing this view, an activist involved in Cairo University's Islamist student groups during the 1970s recounts that he never encountered a single security official in his entire college experience, whereas several of the leftists he knew experienced arrests and intimidation. Author interview, August 9, 2010, Cairo, Egypt. Mustapha Kamel Al-Sayyid attributes Islamist success in student union elections, at least partially, to state interventions that effectively shut leftists out of university politics. Mustapha Kamel Al-Sayyid, *Al-Mujtamaʿ wa-l-Siyasah fi Misr: Dawr Jamaʿat al-Masalih fi al-Nizam al-Siyasy al-Misry, 1952–1981* (Al-Qahirah: Dar al-Mustaqbal al-ʿAraby, 1983), 41.

172. For example, Mohy Eissa recalls in his memoirs that the IG at Al-Minya University contested the student union election per an agreement with security officials. The agreement stipulated that the IG would nominate Abul-Ela Madi (and not Eissa) for the presidency of the university-wide student union and that Madi would select a security approved nominee to serve as his deputy. Mohy Eissa, personal Facebook page post, Facebook, March 7, 2015, https://www.facebook.com/photo/?fbid=1624 698064420796&set=a.1428496920707579.

173. See Tammam, *Shahid ʿala Tarikh*, 46; and El-Erian's testimony in Eid, *Al-Islamiyyun Yatahadathun*, 89.

174. Al-Meleegy, "Tajribaty."

175. Al-Sisi, *Min al-Madhbahah*, 118.

176. Abdel-Ghany, *Muhamad ʿUthman*, 83.

177. Tammam, *Shahid ʿala Tarikh*, 110.

178. Helmy Al-Gazzar, "Al-Nahdah al-Tulabiyya al-Islamiyya fi Hiwar li-l-Mawqiʿ maʿa Duktur Hilmy al-Jazar," *Ikhwanonline*, November 2, 2003, https://ikhwanonline.net/article/3165. Badr and El-Erian confirm the cooperation of IGUs with Al-Nabawi Ismail in calming down volatile situations. Badr, *Al-Jamaʿah al-Islamiyya*, 89. El-Erian, "Shahadat al-Duktur." Ismail confirms that he called upon IGUs leaders, among others, to intervene in sectarian clashes at Al-Zaywa Al-Hamra in 1981. See his account Fawzi, *Al-Nabawy Ismaʿil*, 104.

179. Quoted in Badr, *Al-Jamaʿah al-Islamiyya*, 89.

180. Abdel-Ghany, *Muhamad ʿUthman*, 90.

181. Abdel-Ghany, *Muhamad ʿUthman*, 82.
182. Tammam, *Shahid ʿala Tarikh*, 33; 41; 49; also see Essam El-Erian's comments in Eid, *Al-Islamiyyun Yatahadathun*, 86–87.
183. El-Erian's account in Eid, *Al-Islamiyyun Yatahadathun*, 103.
184. Eid, *Al-Islamiyyun Yatahadathun*, 97.
185. Eid, *Al-Islamiyyun Yatahadathun*, 85.
186. Montasser Al-Zayat testimony in Eid, *Al-Islamiyyun Yatahadathun*, 33.
187. Badr notes that the student union budget on which the IG relied only amounted to several thousand Egyptian pounds, which could not have conceivably covered all these expenses without some additional backing from the university. Badr, *Al-Jamaʿah al-Islamiyya*, 26. For instance, El-Erian acknowledges that the university paid for all the meals served at the IG camps. El-Erian, "Shahadat al-Duktur."
188. According to Al-Gazzar, the camps were held under the joint oversight of the student union and the university administration. Al-Gazzar, "Al-Nahdah al-Tulabiyya."
189. Tammam, *Shahid ʿala Tarikh*, 46. In outlining the procedures for organizing these camps, Al-Meleegy reveals the central role the university administration played in supporting such events: "The [procedure for] organizing an Islamic camp begins with a petition by one of the emirs [or leaders] of the Islamic Group submitted to the director of the university and requesting permission for convening the camp on campus using [university] rooms and food halls, along with a preliminary budget outlining the financial support needed from the university, which was submitted to the campus administration. Included with the petition were the daily program of the camp, and the lists of speakers and student organizers. And a professor was usually selected from among faculty members as a general supervisor for the camp. There was never one incident in which the university objected to the convening of camps, which were attended by 500–800 people on average for ten days." Al-Meleegy, "Tajribaty." El-Erian notes that these camps, sometimes featured up to one thousand five hundred male students, as well as many female students who sometimes attended daytime events. El-Erian, "Shahadat al-Duktur."
190. That is, according to Assiut IG leader Salah Hashem. Quoted in Ahmed Mawlana, *Al-Jamaʿah al-Islamiyya*, 4.
191. El-Erian's testimony in Eid, *Al-Islamiyyun Yatahadathun*, 87.
192. Montasser Al-Zayat testimony in Eid, *Al-Islamiyyun Yatahadathun*, 33.
193. Tammam, *Shahid ʿala Tarikh*, 111.
194. Tammam, *Shahid ʿala Tarikh*, 57.
195. On that day, eighteen armed militants tried to storm the MTC. Their unsuccessful attempt left dozens of casualties and injuries. It was later revealed that the attackers belonged to an underground Islamist group known as "Mohamed's Youth." For more on the group, which media outlets later dubbed the Military Institute Group, see Mostafa, *Al-Islam al-Siyasy*, 191–201.
196. Anwar Al-Sadat, "Hadith al-Raʾis Muhamad Anwar al-Sadat al-Awal ila Aʿdaʾ al-Muʿtamar al-Qiady li-Shabab al-Hizb al-Watany," *The Library of Alexandria Sadat Archives*, January 31, 1979, http://sadat.bibalex.org/TextViewer.aspx?TextID=SP_817.

197. Sadat reiterated that same point in speeches on March 1 and April 5, 1979. Anwar Al-Sadat, "Hadith al-Raʾis Muhamad Anwar al-Sadat maʿa Asatidhat Jamiʿat al-Iskandariyya," *The Library of Alexandria Sadat Archives*, March 1, 1979, http://sadat .bibalex.org/TextViewer.aspx?TextID=SP_827. Anwar Al-Sadat, "Khitab al-Raʾis Muhamad Anwar al-Sadat fi-l-Jalsa al-Khasah bi-Majlis al-Shaʿb," *The Library of Alexandria Sadat Archives*, April 5, 1979, http://sadat.bibalex.org/TextViewer .aspx?TextID=SP_846.

198. Anwar Al-Sadat, "Kalimat al-Raʾis Muhamad Anwar al-Sadat khilal Liqaʾih bi-ʿUmmal al-Naql bi-l-Iskandariyya," *The Library of Alexandria Sadat Archives*, February 28, 1979, http://sadat.bibalex.org/TextViewer.aspx?TextID=SP_826. Anwar Al-Sadat, "Khitab al-Raʾis Muhamad Anwar al-Sadat fi-Jamiʿat ʿAyn Shams," *The Library of Alexandria Sadat Archives*. April 16, 1979, http://sadat.bibalex.org/Text -Viewer.aspx?TextID=SP_851. Anwar Al-Sadat, "Kalimat al-Raʾis Muhamad Anwar al-Sadat maʿa Qiyadat al-Suwais," *The Library of Alexandria Sadat Archives*, April 29, 1979, http://sadat.bibalex.org/TextViewer.aspx?TextID=SP_854.

199. A text of the letter is published in Badr, *Al-Jamaʿah al-Islamiyya*, 54–58.

200. Abul-Ela Madi, "Al-Ustadh ʿUmar al-Tilmisany (2)," *Al-Wasat Party*, January 7, 2018, http:// web.archive.org/web/20180120145640/http://www.alwasatparty.com/window/الأستاذ عمر-التلمساني-2-.

201. Abul-Ela Madi suggests that the arrests happened because of antipeace treaty protests (Madi, "Al-Ustadh ʿUmar."), but Mohy Eissa says that the immediate pretext for their arrest was their taking Christian students hostage during a showdown with security forces. The confrontation ended with the IG leaders' surrender. Eissa, personal Facebook page post, Facebook, April 7, 2015.

202. Anwar Al-Sadat, "Hiwar al-Raʾis Muhamad Anwar al-Sadat maʿa Qiyadat al-Hizb al-Watany bi-l-Ismaʿiliyya," *The Library of Alexandria Sadat Archives*, April 22, 1979, http://sadat.bibalex.org/TextViewer.aspx?TextID=SP_852.

203. Madi, "Al-Ustadh ʿUmar."

204. Student unions were forbidden to form national or campus-wide bodies, restricting their operations to individual colleges. See Rozza, *Al-Talabah*, 277.

205. Around that same time, Assiut and Al-Minya universities began erecting walls around university buildings and elsewhere, presumably to enable greater security force containment of student unrest. See Al-Meleegy, "Tajribaty"; and Aly Al-Sherif, "ʿIlaqat al-Jamaʿah."

206. See Badr, *Al-Jamaʿah al-Islamiyya*, 79–83.

207. Division in the Alexandria IG between supporters of the Muslim Brotherhood and advocates of a Salafist tendency happened years prior and came to the surface in as early as 1975, according to Al-Zafarani, "Hikayat al-Zaʿfarany."

208. It is interesting to note that both Abul-Ela Madi and Mohy Eissa claim that their decision to join the Brotherhood and break with would-be GI leaders like Karam Zohdy and others came about during their imprisonment in 1979. See Madi, "Al-Ustadh ʿUmar."; and Mohy Eissa, Personal Facebook page post, Facebook, April 13, 2015, https://www .facebook.com/permalink.php?story_fbid=1639865552904047&id=100006418533527.

209. Aly Al-Sherif details how that break happened and how he and fellow IG members decided to join forces with Mohamed Abdel-Salam Farag and select Omar Abdel-Rahman as their emir. Aly Al-Sherif, "ʿIlaqat al-Jamaʿah."

210. See, for example, a 1977 U.S. Embassy in Cairo telegram conveying some of these sentiments. Embassy Cairo to Department of State, "Telegram 17485."

211. The story is recounted in Osman Ahmed Osman's memoirs. Osman Ahmed Osman, *Safahat min Tajribaty* (Al-Qahirah: Al-Maktab al-Misry al-Hadith, 1981), 632–34. Although Osman does not date the exchange, the details he shares regarding individuals in attendance permit us to conclude that the meeting occurred sometime between October 1973 and September 1974.

212. In his memoirs, Osman makes some damning allegations about corruption involving Nasser. This provoked responses from many Nasserists, including the journalist Abdullah Imam, who disputed many of Osman's claims. Abdullah Imam, *Tajribat ʿUthman: al-Rad ʿala Kitab al-Muhandis ʿUthman Ahmad ʿUthman* (Al-Qahirah: Dar al-Mawqif al-ʿAraby, 1981).

213. A March 1979 cable from the U.S. Embassy in Cairo recounts Prime Minister Mustafa Khalil's frustrations with Osman Ahmed Osman's excessive influence over the president. Embassy Cairo to Department of State, "Telegram 05969," March 23, 1979, 1979CAIRO05969, Central Foreign Policy Files, 1973–79/Electronic Telegrams, RG 59: General Records of the Department of State, U.S. National Archives, https://aad.archives.gov/aad/createpdf?rid=199832&dt=2776&dl=2169.

214. Osman, *Safahat min Tajribaty*, 354.

215. Osman, *Safahat min Tajribaty*, 359.

216. Osman, *Safahat min Tajribaty*, 362.

217. The U.S. Embassy Cairo reported in 1976 that Osman donated money to Cairo University's Faculty of Engineering to support the regime's antileftist campaigns on campus. Embassy Cairo to Department of State, "Telegram 04727."

218. For example, Abdel-Salam Al-Zayyat recalls that in a June 1971 conversation, Secretary of Youth Kamal Abul-Magd implied that he was tasked with seeking reconciliation with the Muslim Brotherhood. He writes, "I found out later that [Abul-Magd's mission] was seeking to win Sadat the backing of the Muslim Brotherhood." Al-Zayyat, *Al-Sadat al-Qinaʿ*, 165.

219. Heikal, *Khariyf al-Ghadab*, 228.

220. Gamee, *ʿArift al-Sadat*, 173.

221. Wickham, *The Muslim Brotherhood*, 30.

222. *Al-Ahram*, March 13, 1974.

223. Abdel-Ghany, *Muhamad ʿUthman*, 78–79.

224. As Carrie Wickham notes, sources differ on when exactly Al-Tilmisani became general guide, but she acknowledges that he emerged as the de facto leader and spokesperson of the group in the aftermath of Hassan Al-Houdaiby's death in 1973. Wickham, *The Muslim Brotherhood*, 30. According to allegations, for a period of time during the 1970s and before Al-Tilmisani's leadership was officially recognized, the Brotherhood was secretly led by Helmy Abdel-Meguid. See, for example, Abul-Ela Madi, "Al-Muhandis ʿUthman."

225. Al-Arian, *Answering the Call*, 90; 95–101. Al-Meleegy summarizes these internal deliberations. Al-Meleegy, *Tajribaty*, 91–93.

226. Koroum, *Al-Taharukat al-Siyasiyya*, 31–39.

227. Al-Tilmisani, *Dhikrayat La Mudhakarat*, 114–15.

228. Abul-Ela Madi, "Al-Muhandis ʿUthman."

229. Al-Tilmisani, *Dhikrayat La Mudhakarat*, 178.

230. Embassy Cairo to Department of State, "Telegram 18347," November 4, 1977, 1977CAIRO18347, Central Foreign Policy Files, 1973–79/Electronic Telegrams, RG 59: General Records of the Department of State, U.S. National Archives, https://aad .archives.gov/aad/createpdf?rid=254863&dt=2532&dl=1629.

231. Al-Tilmisani recounts the incident in his memoirs but does not name the prime minister. Given that *Al-Dawa* was restarted in 1976, the offer had to have been made by either Mamdouh Salem or Mustafa Khalil. Al-Tilmisani, *Dhikrayat La Mudhakarat*, 40–41.

232. In late 1977, Al-Tilmisani personally told U.S. diplomats that the magazine's priority was "combatting communism and atheism." Embassy Cairo to Department of State, "Telegram 18347."

233. Embassy Cairo to Department of State, "Telegram 16440," November 26, 1976, 1976CAIRO16440, Central Foreign Policy Files, 1973–79/Electronic Telegrams, RG 59: General Records of the Department of State, U.S. National Archives, https://aad .archives.gov/aad/createpdf?rid=275931&dt=2082&dl=1345.

234. Omar Al-Tilmisani, "Min Kalimat al-Ustadh ʿUmar al-Tilmisany ila al-Shabab," *Ikhwanonline*, September 2, 2012, https://www.ikhwanonline.com/article/118751.

235. Al-Tilmisani, *Dhikrayat La Mudhakarat*, 176.

236. Tammam, *Shahid ʿala Tarikh*, 80; and Al-Zafarani, "Hikayat al-Zaʿfarany."

237. Quoted in Nouh, *Mawsuʿat al-ʿUnf*, 384.

238. Quoted in "Omar Al-Tilmisani in the Business School of Cairo University," *Al-Dawa*, February 1981.

239. Allam, *Al-Ikhwan wa Ana*, 249–50. When he was interrogated in September 1981, Al-Tilmisani revealed the extent to which authorities were involved in facilitating his contacts with the leaders of the IGUs who subsequently joined the Brotherhood. University administrators preapproved every invitation Al-Tilmisani received to speak at any university IG event. In addition, the IGUs public conferences at which he spoke were preauthorized by the Ministry of Interior. See transcripts of interrogation in Nouh, *Mawsuʿat al-ʿUnf*, 395–401.

240. For example, Abbas Al-Sisi, a longtime Muslim Brotherhood leader in Alexandria, notes that in the lead-up to the 1976 legislative election, the police were uncharacteristically respectful of campaign marches that featured Islamist slogans and signs. Al-Sisi, *Min al-Madhbahah*, 112–13.

241. It is unclear whether these discussions were related to Ahmed Al-Malt's formation of the Islamic Medical Association in 1977.

242. Koroum, *Al-Taharukat al-Siyasiyya*, 31–39.

243. According to Sadat, the group sent Prime Minister Mamdouh Salem a letter conveying the same claims listed in the lawsuit. Anwar Al-Sadat, "Kalimat al-Raʾis Muhamad Anwar al-Sadat khilal Liqaʾihi bi-Rijal al-Din wa-l-Fikr al-Islamy," *The Library of Alexandria Sadat Archives*, August 20, 1979, http://sadat.bibalex.org/TextViewer .aspx?TextID=SP_897. The case would remain in courts for more than a decade, outliving Al-Tilmisani himself. Eventually, the court ruled against the Muslim Brotherhood in 1992, arguing that the Revolutionary Command Council's decisions were immune from court challenges. See summary of the case's history in Akhbar Al-Youm, "Nakshif Kawalis Muhawalat Majlis al-Dawlah li-Hal Wasat al-Ikhwan wa Qatᶜ Dhiraᶜaha al-Siyasy," *Akhbar Al-Youm*, August 29, 2013, https://akhbarelyom .com/news/newdetails/271057/1/وسط-لحل-الدولة-مجلس-محاولات-كواليس-نكشف.

244. That same wariness was also reflected in the fact that in relaunching *Al-Dawa* in 1976, the group did not apply for a license and instead relied on a publishing license issued before the July 23 Revolution of 1952 in the name of longtime Brotherhood leader Saleh Ashmawy. See Al-Tilmisani's testimony in Nouh, *Mawsuᶜat al-ᶜUnf*, 387; and Al-Tilmisani, *Ayam maᶜa al-Sadat*, 67.

245. Aly Al-Sherif of Assiut University's IG recounts turning down Mustafa Mashhur's offer to join the Muslim Brotherhood in an adversarial meeting. Aly Al-Sherif, "ᶜIlaqat al-Jamaᶜah." Essam El-Erian reports failing to recruit into the Brotherhood student leaders from Al-Minya and Assiut Universities. El-Erian, "Shahadat al-Duktur."

246. Mohy Eissa, personal Facebook page post, Facebook, March 31, 2015, https://www .facebook.com/photo/?fbid=1635207340036535&set=a.1578510872372849.

247. Badr notes that publications promoted in IGUs exhibits, curricula, and summer camps included many works authored by Muslim Brotherhood figures. Badr, *Al-Jamaᶜah al-Islamiyya*, 28–29; 31–32. Saleh Wardani reports that an IGUs booklet entitled "Peace Per the American Way" was copied verbatim from *Al-Dawa* magazine. Saleh Wardani, *Al-Harakah al-Islamiyya fi Misr: Al-Waqiᶜ wa-l-Tahadiyat min al-Khamsiniyat ila al-Tisᶜiniyat* (Al-Qahirah: Dar al-Kalimah, 2000), 98.

248. Quoted in Aly, *Al-Ikhwan al-Muslimun: Azmat Tayar*, 73. Essam El-Erian says that IGUs leaders would often criticize the Brotherhood in public to conceal the fact that they had pledged loyalty to the group. El-Erian, "Shahadat al-Duktur."

249. For example, Al-Tilmisani told a U.S. diplomat in the fall of 1978 that the Muslim Brotherhood opposed negotiations with Israel on religious grounds, but that it would not stand in Sadat's way because it recognized that such "agreements are all [the president] can get." Embassy Cairo to Department of State, "Telegram 22969," October 16, 1978, 1978CAIRO22969, Central Foreign Policy Files, 1973–79/Electronic Telegrams, RG 59: General Records of the Department of State, U.S. National Archives, https://aad.archives.gov/aad/createpdf?rid=254487&dt=2694&dl=2009.

250. See, for example, the September 1979 issue of *Al-Dawa*, which was tilted "The Impossible Peace Between Egypt and Israel," and the October 1979 issue, which was entitled "Those Are the Jews, They Have No Covenant or Integrity."

251. Al-Tilmisani, *Ayam maʿa al-Sadat*, 19. Egyptian officials suspected that the document was part of a Libyan-Soviet hoax, but they were unable to produce hard evidence. Embassy Cairo to Department of State, "Telegram 01470," January 22, 1979, 1979CAIRO01470, Central Foreign Policy Files, 1973–79/Electronic Telegrams, RG 59: General Records of the Department of State, U.S. National Archives, https://aad .archives.gov/aad/createpdf?rid=118439&dt=2776&dl=2169.

252. A document generated by the U.S. Embassy in Cairo provides then vice president Hosni Mubarak's account of the incident. Mubarak said that Ismail met with Al-Tilmisani to "lay down the law" per Sadat's order and convey the government's refusal to tolerate any such misconduct in the future. According to the document, Al-Tilmisani promised that such incidents would not recur. Embassy Cairo to Department of State, "Telegram 02033," January 29, 1979, 1979CAIRO02033, Central Foreign Policy Files, 1973–79/Electronic Telegrams, RG 59: General Records of the Department of State, U.S. National Archives, https://aad.archives.gov/aad/createp df?rid=125296&dt=2776&dl=2169.

253. The magazine also published a response from the purported author of the document, U.S. historian Richard P. Mitchell, who denied the document's authenticity. See the February 1979 issue of *Al-Dawa*. That said, the U.S. Embassy reported that *Al-Dawa*'s coverage of the U.S. government became increasingly negative following the incident. Embassy Cairo to Department of State, "Telegram 02033," January 29, 1979, 1979CAIRO02033, Central Foreign Policy Files, 1973–79/Electronic Telegrams, RG 59: General Records of the Department of State, U.S. National Archives, https:// aad.archives.gov/aad/createpdf?rid=125296&dt=2776&dl=2169.

254. Sadat made this allegation in several of his speeches. See, for example, transcripts of his town hall meeting with Assiut and Al-Minya universities faculty members on April 14, 1979. Anwar Al-Sadat, "Hiwar al-Raʾis Muhamad Anwar al-Sadat wa Asatidhat Jamiʿatay Asyut wa-l-Minya," *The Library of Alexandria Sadat Archives*, April 14, 1979, http://sadat.bibalex.org/TextViewer.aspx?TextID=SP_850. Also see transcripts of his August 20, 1979, address to religious figures in Ismailia in Al-Sadat, "Kalimat al-Raʾis Muhamad Anwar al-Sadat khilal Liqaʾihi bi-Rijal al-Din."

255. Fawzi, *Al-Nabawy Ismaʿil*, 36. Al-Tilmisani also claims that the article contributed to Sadat's decision to imprison him in 1981. Al-Tilmisani, *Ayam maʿa al-Sadat*, 19.

256. Aly, *Al-Ikhwan al-Muslimun: Azmat Tayar*, 73. According to Al-Meleegy, around that same time, the Muslim Brotherhood's IG affiliates in Middle and Upper Egypt began clashing publicly with their opponents. Al-Meleegy, *Tajribaty*, 104–5.

257. Al-Sadat, "Hadith al-Raʾis Muhamad Anwar al-Sadat maʿa Asatidhat Jamiʿat al-Iskandariyya."

258. Al-Sadat, "Hadith al-Raʾis Muhamad Anwar al-Sadat maʿa Asatidhat Jamiʿat al-Iskandariyya."

259. The text of the statement is reprinted in Badr, *Al-Jamaʿah al-Islamiyya*, 44–47.

260. Not long after Sadat's public showdown with Al-Tilmisani in Ismailia in August 1979, the IGUs began distributing pamphlets denying their ties to the Muslim Brotherhood. According to a U.S. Embassy cable, one such pamphlet stated that

the IGUs did not have "ties with any past or present religious organizations inside Egypt or abroad" and that "its reprinting of articles from certain publications (presumably a reference to Ikhwani "*Al-Dawa*") should not be interpreted as indicating they are under any external control." Embassy Cairo to Department of State, "Telegram 17425," August 28, 1979, 1979CAIRO17425, Central Foreign Policy Files, 1973–79/Electronic Telegrams, RG 59: General Records of the Department of State, U.S. National Archives, https://aad.archives.gov/aad/createpdf?rid=42802&dt=2776&dl=2169.

261. A text of Law 44/1979 is available at Laweg, Egypt's Gateway to Law and the Judiciary, accessed April 19, 2021, http://www.laweg.net/Default.aspx?action=ViewActivePages&ItemID=39951&Type=6. The law was issued through a presidential decree while parliament was in recess. It was judged unconstitutional in May 1985. For more, see Huda Abdel-Fattah, "Qawaniyn Jihan, al-Bahth ʿan Dhaat al-Marʾah," *Al-Wafd*, March 1, 2011, https://alwafd.news/-البحث-جيهان-قوانين20095/-هى20%و20%هو .عن-ذات-المرأة

262. Al-Sadat, "Kalimat al-Raʾis Muhamad Anwar al-Sadat khilal Liqaʾihi bi-Rijal al-Din."

263. Sadat prefaced these remarks recounting his own confrontation with Abdel-Moneim Aboul-Fotouh in a meeting with university student leaders organized in the aftermath of the 1977 Bread Uprising.

264. Al-Tilmisani, *Ayam maʿa al-Sadat*, 35.

265. One issue that seemed to have bothered Sadat and that often animated his public attacks against the Muslim Brotherhood in 1979 is his suspicion that the movement joined forces with Nasserists, communists, and Wafdists during the 1978 lawyers syndicate election to support an antigovernment candidate critical of Sadat's peace talks with Israel. See, for example, his speech on August 20, 1979 in Al-Sadat, "Kalimat al-Raʾis Muhamad Anwar al-Sadat khilal Liqaʾihi bi-Rijal al-Din." Al-Tilmisani may have excited such fears by disclosing in his retort to Sadat that he had been approached by "communists" about potential collaboration but rejected such offers. See summary of his remarks in Mohamed Habib, *Dhikrayat Duktur Muhamad Habib: ʿAn al-Hayah wa-l-Daʿwah wa-l-Siyasah wa-l-Fikr* (Al-Qahirah: Dar Al-Shuruq, 2012), 148.

266. Al-Tilmisani, *Dhikrayat La Mudhakarat*, 222.

267. Al-Tilmisani initially expressed his reluctance to discuss such a matter with a woman (Amal Othman), prompting Sadat to suggest meeting instead with Minister of Interior Al-Nabawi Ismail or Minister of Information Mansour Hassan.

268. Al-Tilmisani, *Ayam maʿa al-Sadat*, 16. Al-Tilmisani said in a 1982 interview, "I opposed it, because under the law of social associations, the Ministry of Social Affairs has the right to dissolve any association at any time, as well as to appoint its officials and subject it to managerial and budgetary scrutiny." Quoted in Al-Arian, *Answering the Call*, 173. On that particular point, Mamoun Al-Houdaiby confirmed in a 1998 interview that Sadat did make this offer, noting that such an arrangement would have given the government excessive discretion to intervene in the Brotherhood's internal affairs. Al-Ansary, *Al-Ikhwan al-Muslimun*, 42. During interrogations

in 1981, Al-Tilmisani told authorities that the president promised a solution to the movement's legal problems, but said he was not at liberty to disclose the details of that meeting. Nouh, *Mawsuʿat al-ʿUnf*, 385.

269. Al-Tilmisani reiterates that point in his memoirs, boasting that he had always been in close touch with Ministry of Interior officials, and that he never let them down whenever they asked him to calm unrest on university campuses. He also expressed pride that the Minister of Interior Al-Nabawi Ismail had personally asked him to help defuse the clashes of Al-Zawya Al-Hamra, one of the most high-profile cases of sectarian violence that Cairo witnessed under Sadat. Al-Tilmisani, *Dhikrayat La Mudhakarat*, 116; 176–77. When interrogated in 1981, Al-Tilmisani revealed that he was in close contact with the minister of interior, obtaining his approval to participate in conferences or hold meetings with foreign diplomats. Nouh, *Mawsuʿat al-ʿUnf*, 386.

270. Ismail reveals that he tried to convince the president that Al-Tilmisani was useful in combating radical Islamist currents, but Sadat would not hear of it: "I did not share with this man [Al-Tilmisani] any friendship, but he was combating Islamist groups and used to go to the university and attack them, and try to correct their understandings. The president told me: 'He is helping you to counter these children, but is he not responsible for *Al-Dawa*, Nabawi, where it was said that there is an Egyptian-American plot to eliminate Islam in Egypt? You are the minister of interior, now are you aware of that plot?' I told him: 'No, sir, Al-Tilmisani is just the head of the board. He has nothing to do with the editorial line. He is not responsible for it.'" Quoted in Fawzi, *Al-Nabawy Ismaʿil*, 35–36.

271. This was the second publication of *Al-Dawa*. It was published on a monthly basis between November 1976 and September 1981. Ibrahim reports the magazine's circulation at one hundred thousand. Saad Eddin Ibrahim, "An Islamic Alternative in Egypt: The Muslim Brotherhood and Sadat," *Arab Studies Quarterly* 4, no. 1–2 (Spring 1982): 81. Aboul-Fotouh estimates it at eighty-five thousand. Tammam, *Shahid ʿala Tarikh*, 103. Al-Tilmisani told U.S. diplomats in 1977 that circulation is somewhere between seventy and eighty thousand. Embassy Cairo to Department of State, "Telegram 18347."

272. "The Secret History of Communism in Egypt," *Al-Dawa*, June 1977; "Heikal and the Communist Mohamed Sid-Ahmed and the American National Security Envoy on a Television Panel," *Al-Dawa*, April 1979.

273. Tammam, *Shahid ʿala Tarikh*, 101–2.

274. "A Curious Question," *Al-Dawa*, December 1976.

275. See, for example, "Debating Atheists in the Soviet Union," in *Al-Dawa*, January 1977; "Islamic Affairs at the Bolshevik Seminar," *Al-Dawa*, December 1976; and "Muslim Youth and Atheism," *Al-Dawa*, November 1976.

276. "The Baath Party and Its Role," *Al-Dawa*, November 1976; "The Crisis of God's Preachers Under the Red Authority," *Al-Dawa*, March 1977; "And the Mask Has Fallen off the Face of Communism in Indo-China," *Al-Dawa*, February 1979; "Under the Rule of Socialist Revolutionary Regimes," *Al-Dawa*, September 1979; "The Fateful

Baathist Conspiracy Against Islam," *Al-Dawa*, September 1979; "That Communism: Until When?," *Al-Dawa*, February 1981; and "The Afghan Events and the Red Attacks Against Islamic Bases," *Al-Dawa*, July 1978. Additionally, *Al-Dawa* published a regular section entitled "Our Islamic Homeland," which was devoted to brief reports about the state of Muslims around the world and often featured stories about communist regimes' persecution of Muslims.

277. See, for example, "When Faith Disappears: Highest Suicide Rates in Hungary and East Germany," *Al-Dawa*, February 1979.

278. These usually appeared in a section entitled *Safahat min al-Ams* ("Pages from the Past"), which was devoted to documenting the Brotherhood's history. Also see "A Benevolent Tree, the Muslim Brotherhood," *Al-Dawa*, April 1979.

279. See "Muslims on the Road," *Al-Dawa*, March 1977; "The Massacre of the Brothers in Tora Prison," *Al-Dawa*, June 1977; and "I Accuse!!," *Al-Dawa*, August 1977.

280. "The Reasons for the June Defeat," *Al-Dawa*, June 1977; Al-Tilmisani reiterates the same point in his memoirs. Al-Tilmisani, *Dhikrayat La Mudhakarat*, 211.

281. See "We Do Not Declare a Muslim *Kafir* Based on a View or a Sin," *Al-Dawa*, January 1977. This is not to deny the revolutionary orientations of members of the student movement that were forging ties with the Brotherhood at the time. Aboul-Fotouh, for example, reports participating in protests during the 1977 Bread Uprising, and he even acknowledges that the use of violence as an instrument of change was an unresolved question for many Islamist students. Yet, it must be emphasized that the formal ties between these student elements and the Muslim Brotherhood were not publicized until the late phases of the Sadat presidency. Additionally, as Aboul-Fotouh himself states, the mentorship of Brotherhood leaders was critical to the students' rejection of revolutionary action. Tammam, *Shahid 'ala Tarikh*, 65; 68–69.

282. Al-Tilmisani, *Dhikrayat La Mudhakarat*, 214.

283. "This Ruthless Campaign Against the Muslim Brotherhood . . . Is It Not Time for It to End?," *Al-Dawa*, March 1977.

284. "When Do We Target Religion and the Nation," *Al-Dawa*, February 1979. Interestingly, when the general guide made the same argument in a meeting with Sadat later that year, a reassured president told Al-Tilmisani to continue writing. Al-Tilmisani, *Dhikrayat La Mudhakarat*, 222.

285. See, for example, "Members of Parliament Demand the Return of the Muslim Brotherhood," *Al-Dawa*, December 1976; "Do Not Block the Way for Those Who Preach for God," *Al-Dawa*, January 1977; "Where Are Prayers in the State of Faith and Science," *Al-Dawa*, March 1977; "On Legislating Sharia and Intellectual Opening," *Al-Dawa*, September 1978; "People Are Demanding the Implementing of Sharia," *Al-Dawa*, September 1978; and "The Death Penalty," *Al-Dawa*, October 1979.

286. Examples include "Why Has Talk of Implementing Sharia Disappeared?," *Al-Dawa*, June 1980; "Is There an Islamic Constitution," *Al-Dawa*, September 1979; "Do Not Raise Your Voice Over the Voice of the Prophet," *Al-Dawa*, September 1979; "Legislating Sharia and the Dreams of the Shallow Ones," *Al-Dawa*, September 1979; "This Government Must Resign or Get Fired," *Al-Dawa*, November 1980; "Once Again, the

Personal Status Law," *Al-Dawa*, October 1979; and "Conspiracy: What Is Being Plot-ted Against Sharia," *Al-Dawa*, April 1979.

287. See, for example, "How to Prepare the Environment for Implementing Sharia," *Al-Dawa*, December 1976.

288. See "What Are the Judges Waiting For?," *Al-Dawa*, February 1981; "Women and Assuming the Position of Judge," *Al-Dawa*, July 1978; and "The Types of Courts," *Al-Dawa*, April 1979.

289. See "An Islamic Perspective on the Problem of Education," *Al-Dawa*, January 1977; "The Most Dangerous Conspiracy Against Education in the Islamic World," *Al-Dawa*, November 1980.

290. See "The Problem of Education in Egypt: Education is Pitting Religion against Sci-ence," *Al-Dawa*, November 1976; "The Necessity of Rewriting Biological Science from an Islamic Perspective," *Al-Dawa*, March 1977; "The Tragedy of Literary Stud-ies in School Curricula," *Al-Dawa*, September 1978; and "Science that Guides Toward Faith," *Al-Dawa*, February 1979.

291. "Why Was the Quran and Sunnah Course Canceled in the Arabic Department at the School of Humanities of Cairo University," *Al-Dawa*, June 1977.

292. See, for example, "When the Event Happened, We Called for a Return to Islam," *Al-Dawa*, March 1977; and "A Healthy Phenomenon at Universities: Head of Sharia Department at Cairo University Insists on Segregating Male and Female Students During Lectures," *Al-Dawa*, December 1976.

293. See, for example, "I Grew My Beard and They Kicked Me out of School," *Al-Dawa*, July 1978, and "A Professor at Cairo University Mocks the Niqab," *Al-Dawa*, June 1980.

294. See, for example, "Candid Interview with Dr. Fahham," *Al-Dawa*, December 1976; "A Scientific Plan for a Comprehensive Renaissance at Al-Azhar," *Al-Dawa*, August 1977; "Rectifying the Conditions of the Wise Ones," *Al-Dawa*, July 1978; "There Needs to Be an Azhar University in Alexandria," *Al-Dawa*, April 1979; and "Al-Azhar, The Fortress of Islam: Where to?," *Al-Dawa*, November 1980.

295. See, for example, "This Is What People Think, Mr. Minister of Information," *Al-Dawa*, August 1977; and "Egyptian Television and Exploiting Women's Bodies Dur-ing Ramadan," *Al-Dawa*, September 1978.

296. See, for example, "Dignity, Humiliation: Between Tourism and Art," *Al-Dawa*, Sep-tember 1978; "Theatrical Arts and the Destructive Plot," *Al-Dawa*, December 1976; and "The Sources of Destruction and Demolition," *Al-Dawa*, January 1977.

297. For example, a May 1981 editorial reads: "The United States is the leader of the inter-national crusade and neocolonialism." Quoted in Ibrahim, "An Islamic Alternative," 89; see also "The Crusader West and the Muslim World," *Al-Dawa*, April 1979.

298. "Communism, Crusaderism, and Zionism do not hate anyone as much as they hate 'Hassan Al-Banna' and the Muslim Brotherhood," writes Omar Al-Tilmisani. Al-Tilmisani, *Dhikrayat La Mudhakarat*, 50. An editorial in Al-Dawa states, "The war of the Communist East and the Crusader West against the Muslim Brotherhood is an extension of their war against Islam." "The Muslim Brotherhood in the American Press," *Al-Dawa*, December 1976.

299. "The Muslim Brotherhood in the American Press," *Al-Dawa*, November 1976.

300. See, for example, the regular feature "Our Islamic Homeland," in the November 1976, December 1976, January 1977, March 1977, and May 1977 issues of *Al-Dawa*; also see "Until When? The Attack Campaigns Against Islam," *Al-Dawa*, March 1977; and "World Health Organization Cooperates in a Dangerous Way with Missionaries in the Muslim World," *Al-Dawa*, February 1979.

301. A May 1981 editorial states: "The Muslim world in general and the Arab region in particular are considered a prime target for American designs because of their energy resources, strategic location, and tremendous markets. The United States would not permit competition from any rival in its quest to monopolize the pillage of Islamic wealth. It may allow other partners a small share so long as they enhance the strategic objectives of the American imperialist crusade against Islam and the Muslims." Quoted in Ibrahim, "An Islamic Alternative," 89; see also "An American Book Reveals the Role of the United States in Spreading Hunger Around the World," *Al-Dawa*, February 1981.

302. See, for example, "Peace the American Way," *Al-Dawa*, January 1977; "Hafez Al-Asad Says That Mediation Must Be Led by the United States," *Al-Dawa*, December 1976.

303. See the cover of *Al-Dawa*, July 1978.

304. See, for example, "Israel: The Present and the Future," *Al-Dawa*, November 1976; and "Begin Is Israel's True Face," *Al-Dawa*, June 1977.

305. See, for example, "From the Pages of the Past," in the January 1977, September 1979, June 1980, and February 1981 issues of *Al-Dawa*.

306. See, for example, "Warning, the Jews Are Coming: The Impossible Peace Between Egypt and Israel," *Al-Dawa*, September 1979; "The Path to Palestine Must Be Islamic," *Al-Dawa*, September 1979; "Those Jews Have No Word or Integrity," *Al-Dawa*, October 1979; "Be Just to Yourself Before Israel Commits Injustice Against You," *Al-Dawa*, July 1978; "Israel That We Want to Wage a Settlement With!!," *Al-Dawa*, September 1978; "When Do We Target Religion and the Nation," *Al-Dawa*, February 1979; "Palestine Question: Where to?," *Al-Dawa*, June 1980; "Israel: The Biggest Mistake," *Al-Dawa*, November 1980; "Women and Liberating Palestine," *Al-Dawa*, February 1981; and "What Is the Alternative," *Al-Dawa*, February 1981.

307. Based on an analysis of *Al-Dawa*'s coverage of Egyptian-Israeli peace, Saad Eddin Ibrahim concluded: "The MB arguments revolve around the impossibility of peaceful coexistence with the Jewish State. It is an aggressor villain on the abode of Islam. It is directly or indirectly behind the major calamities befalling Muslims everywhere, especially in Palestine. It has desecrated Muslim shrines in the Holy Land." Ibrahim, "An Islamic Alternative," 86.

308. Consistent with this assessment, Ibrahim concludes that criticism of Sadat's economic policies and the question of democratization were not as central as coverage of Egypt's peace with Israel and alliance with the West. Ibrahim, "An Islamic Alternative," 80.

309. The article states: "*Al-Dawa* magazine posed a question to a number of Egypt's sons: What is the most dangerous problem or issue in the lives of Muslims? And

despite the diversity in the profiles of respondents, who included Islamic scholars, students, and workers, all of them agreed that it is the distance from God's law." The article presents these opinions as reflective of a widespread consensus, even though some of the individuals surveyed, such as Yusuf Al-Qaradawi and Helmy Al-Gazzar, had known ties with the Muslim Brotherhood. See "What Is the Most Dangerous Problem in the Lives of Muslims?," *Al-Dawa*, October 1979.

310. See, for example, "The Only Way to Establish a Real Renaissance," *Al-Dawa*, November 1976; "Muslim Rulers: Uphold God and He Shall Uphold You," *Al-Dawa*, September 1978.

311. Following a similar line of reasoning, Saleh Ashmawy argued that delay in implementing Sharia has contributed to a rise in incidents of theft, kidnapping, and rape, suggesting that parliament could have prevented many such crimes by delivering on its previous pledge to implement Islamic law. See "Why Has Talk of Implementing Sharia Disappeared?," *Al-Dawa*, June 1980.

312. For example, even while attacking the government's poor management of the economy, Abdel-Moneim Aboul-Fotouh, writes: "The declared slogan of the regime of "science and religious faith" has remained empty. People kept waiting for its implementation behaviorally by rulers but to no avail. Instead, poisonous corruption is enveloping new generations, which do not know anything about Islam except the name." Quoted in Ibrahim, "An Islamic Alternative," 83.

313. "The Man of the Street Speaks: The Solution to Egypt's Problems Is the Islamic System," *Al-Dawa*, March 1977.

314. "When the Event Happened, We Called for a Return to Islam," *Al-Dawa*, March 1977.

315. Articles on public health, for example, usually focused on habits and practices that Islamic texts inspire or stipulate, especially with respect to mental well-being and reproductive health. Some examples include, "Birth Control Is a Religiously Forbidden Idea," *Al-Dawa*, August 1977; "Islam and the Prioritization of Child Health," *Al-Dawa*, June 1980; "Humanity Moves Toward Religion," *Al-Dawa*, February 1979; "Is What Happened Not Enough?!," *Al-Dawa*, February 1981; "Regarding Women's Sterilization," *Al-Dawa*, February 1979; and "Birth Control: Truths and Goals," *Al-Dawa*, October 1979.

316. Al-Feki told the story on *Al-Nahar TV*. His remarks can be viewed on YouTube, accessed February 6, 2021, https://www.youtube.com/watch?v=c--tZ36vCMg.

317. Mona Atia, *Building a House in Heaven: Pious Neoliberalism and Islamic Charity in Egypt* (Minneapolis: University of Minnesota Press, 2013), xvi.

318. Hazem Kandil echoes a similar perspective on the Muslim Brotherhood's reluctance to adopt concrete positions on a variety of issues: "Whether in parliament or in the presidency, Brothers adopted eclectic reform proposals from here and there, without clearly communicating what was distinctive about Islamism as a transformative ideology." Hazem Kandil, *Inside the Brotherhood* (Cambridge: Polity Press, 2015), 42.

319. Khalil al-Anani, *Inside the Muslim Brotherhood: Religion, Identity, and Politics* (Oxford: Oxford University Press, 2016), 13.

320. The term dominated *Al-Dawa*'s coverage of economic issues during the 1970s. In a regular feature entitled "Toward an Islamic Economy," contributors discussed ways in which Islamic principles could inform economic public policy, as well as the microeconomic conduct of individuals, private companies, and financial institutions.

321. See Timur Kuran, "Islamic Economics and the Islamic Subeconomy," *Journal of Economic Perspectives* 9, no. 4 (Fall 1995): 155–73; and Timur Kuran, *Islam and Mammon: The Economic Predicaments of Islamism* (Princeton, NJ: Princeton University Press, 2004).

322. Another frequent contributor to *Al-Dawa*'s economy section was the well-published theorist of Islamic Economics, Yousef Kamal. For a summary of his views on the subject, see Bjørn Olav Utvik, *Islamist Economics in Egypt: The Pious Road to Development* (Boulder, CO: Lynne Rienner, 2006), 81–101.

323. Al-Ghazali states that he helped draft Al-Houdaiby's program and that the 2004 document borrowed from the program. Abdel-Hamid Al-Ghazali, *Al-Fikr al-Iqtisady ʿind al-Ikhwan al-Muslimin* (Al-Qahirah: Dar al-Nashr li-l-Jamiʿat, 2007), 92, fn3; 108, fn2.

324. Compare for example Al-Ghazali, *Al-Fikr al-Iqtisady*, 297–99 and Freedom and Justice Party, *Barnamaj Hizb al-Hurriyah wa-l-ʿAdalah* (Al-Qahirah: Dar al-Tibaʿah wa-l-Nashr al-Islamiyya, 2011), 86–88.

325. Quoted in Al-Ghazali, *Al-Fikr al-Iqtisady*, 24.

326. Al-Ghazali, *Al-Fikr al-Iqtisady*, 82–86.

327. Adel Al-Ansary, *Al-Ikhwan al-Muslimun: 60 Qadiyah Sakhinah* (Al-Qahirah: Dar al-Tawziʿ wa-l-Nashr al-Islamiyya, 1998), 52. In response to the accusation that the Brotherhood has shown little interest in tackling corruption, Al-Houdaiby stated that they would do so if provided proof of government corruption, while adding that "we also focus on the primary issues, such as calling for the implementation of the rulings of Sharia" (14).

328. Reflecting on the appeal of political Islam to contradictory economic interests, Joel Beinin notes, "Islamism appeals to both the losers and the winners of global neoliberal economic restructuring." Joel Beinin, "Political Islam and the New Global Economy: The Political Economy of an Egyptian Social Movement," *CR: The New Centennial Review* 5, no. 1 (Spring 2005): 115.

329. I thank Mohamed Gad for bringing this point to my attention.

330. See Freedom and Justice Party, *Barnamaj*, 83–102.

331. Ahram Online, "Egypt Brotherhood Businessman: Manufacturing Is Key," *Ahram Online*, October 28, 2011, http://english.ahram.org.eg/NewsContent/3/12/25348/Business/Economy/Egypt-Brotherhood-businessman-Manufacturing-is-key.aspx.

332. Rebecca M. Nelson and Jeremy M. Sharp, *Egypt and the IMF: Overview and Issues for Congress* (Washington, DC: Congressional Research Service, 2013), 6, https://www.files.ethz.ch/isn/164704/209246.pdf. According to Egyptian economic researcher Wael Gamal, the Egyptian government also committed to raising energy prices and public services. Wael Gamal, "Lost Capital: The Egyptian Muslim Brotherhood's

Neoliberal Transformation" (Carnegie Endowment for International Peace Work-ing Paper, Washington, DC, February 2019), 4, https://carnegieendowment.org /files/2-1-19_Gamal_Muslim_Brotherhood.pdf. The Morsi administration's eco-nomic policies cannot be simply reduced to an expression of the Brotherhood's preferences. It reflects broader structural pressures and legacies that shape eco-nomic public policy making in Egypt. For a discussion of these pressures, see Amr Adly, "Between Social Populism and Pragmatic Conservatism," in *Egypt's Revolutions: Politics, Religion, and Social Movements*, ed. Bernard Rougier and Stéphane Lacroix (New York: Palgrave Macmillan, 2016), 66–77.

333. For more on this issue and development of the Brotherhood-led Egyptian Busi-ness Development Association (EBDA), see Amr Adly, "Too Big to Fail: Egypt's Large Enterprises After the 2011 Uprising" (Carnegie Endowment for International Peace Working Paper, Washington, DC, March 2017), 14–17, https://carnegieendowment .org/files/CMEC_65_Adly_Final_Web.pdf.

334. Hesham Sallam, ed., *Egypt's Parliamentary Elections, 2011–2012: A Critical Guide to a Changing Political Arena* (Washington, DC: Tadween, 2013), 55–57.

335. Al-Thawra Mostamera, *Barnamijna al-Intikhaby li-Majlis al-Sha'b*, Al-Thawra Mostamera, 2011, 9–10; 19, https://thawramostamera.files.wordpress.com/2011/11/program1 .pdf.

336. Khaled Mohieddin, *Wal'an Atakalam* (Al-Qahirah: Markaz al-Ahram li-l-Tarjamah wa-l-Nashr, 1992), 44–45.

337. Otto Kirchheimer, "The Catch-all Party," in *The West European Party System*, ed. Peter Mair (Oxford: Oxford University Press, 1990), 50–60.

338. Beyond catch-all tendencies, Rovny argues that parties competing in multidimen-sional space have a strong incentive to blur their positions on relatively low-stake issues. Jan Rovny, "Who Emphasizes and Who Blurs? Party Strategies in Multidi-mensional Competition," *European Union Politics* 13, no. 2 (2012): 269–92.

339. The point is not unique to Islam. A century ago, for example, Gramsci noted the contradictory socioeconomic interests that the Italian People's Party harbored under its Catholic-inspired banner. See discussion in Daniela Saresella, "Gramsci and the Issue of Religion: Catholic Modernism and the Italian Partito Popolare," *History of European Ideas* 45, no. 8 (2019): 1148–49.

340. Ibrahim El-Houdaiby, "Al-Islam Huwa al-Hal wa Misr li Kul al-Misryyin," *Ibrahim El-Houdaiby* (blog), May 29, 2007, http://web.archive.org/web/20120313055301 /http://ihoudaiby.blogspot.com/2007_05_01_archive.html. Ibrahim El-Houdaiby's source was his grandfather, General Guide Mamoun Al-Houdaiby (personal com-munication with the author, April 27, 2014). Islamist activist Khaled Al-Zafarani recounts that Hussein took the slogan from the title of an essay written in the late-1970s and republished in the mid-1980s. See Al-Zaafarani's interview with Nageh Ibrahim. Nageh Ibrahim, "Ana Umathil al-Tayar al-Islamy al-Sha'by: Hiwar ma'a Khalid al-Za'farany al-Murashah li-Majlis al-Sha'b," *Al-Jamaa Al-Islamiyya*, accessed April 21, 2021, https://web.archive.org/web/20120307194418/http://www.egyig .com/Public/articles/interview/6/41119056.shtml.

341. For a summary of Adel Hussein's intellectual contributions, see Utvik, *Islamist Economics*, 67–68; 101–19.

342. Author interview, June 10, 2008, Cairo, Egypt.

343. Author interview, June 10, 2008, Cairo, Egypt.

344. It is important to mention that the Misr Al-Fatat, a political movement that was active in Egypt between 1933 and 1953 and whose leaders played a lead role in forming the SLP, was a strong advocate of the post-1952 land reforms. In fact, they had adopted that position well before the July 23 Revolution. In contrast, the Muslim Brotherhood generally was opposed to these measures, which was one of the factors that contributed to the rift between the movement and Nasser. Thus, it is not surprising that when the Mubarak regime began reversing these reforms in the 1990s, the Brotherhood was tacitly supportive, whereas the Labor Party strongly opposed these moves. Mahmoud Abdel-Halim explains these differences in greater detail. Mahmoud Abdel-Halim, *Al-Ikhwan Al-Muslimun: Ahdath Sanʿat al-Tarikh: Ruʾyah min al-Dakhil, al-Juzʾ al-Thalith* (Al-Iskandariyya: Dar al-Daʿwah li-l-Tabʿ wa-l-Nashr, 2004), 107–24; 146; 189–96.

345. Author interview, September 28, 2011, Cairo, Egypt.

346. Tarek E. Masoud, *Counting Islam: Religion, Class, and Elections in Egypt* (New York: Cambridge University Press, 2014), 126.

347. Masoud also finds that survey respondents identified the Muslim Brotherhood's party as one of the most left-leaning parties. Masoud, *Counting Islam*, 147.

348. In explaining the merits of Islamic economics, Al-Ghazali's takes the notion of private ownership as given, implying that disparities in wealth and social class differences are a natural occurrence.

349. That conception overlaps to an extent with Tocquevillian interpretations of the role of religion in politics. See, for example, discussion in Joshua Mitchell, *The Fragility of Freedom: Tocqueville on Religion, Democracy, and the American Future* (Chicago: University of Chicago Press, 1995), 85–87.

350. See, for example, the fifty-point demand that the Muslim Brotherhood issued in 1936. Aly Abdel-Halim Mahmoud, *Wasaʾil al-Tarbiyah ʿind al-Ikhwan al-Muslimin: Dirasah Tahliliyya Tarikhiyya* (Al-Mansurah: Dar al-Wafaʾ, 1989), 71–74. In addition, see the Muslim Brotherhood's full statement dated August 2, 1952, published in Abdel-Halim, *Al-Ikhwan Al-Muslimun*, 141–49. See 1954 article by Mahmoud Abu-Seoud on Islamic economics in the Muslim Brotherhood magazine "Our Islamic Economy," *Al-Ikhwan Al-Muslimun*, June 24, 1954, 13.

351. See, for example, Mahmoud Abu-Seoud's article lauding the establishment of an Islamic bank in Dubai and calling on the Egyptian government to approve pending requests to form a similar bank in Egypt. "In the Field of Islamic Economy," *Al-Dawa*, December 1976.

352. "The Attempt to Allow Interest: A Tune of a Single Maestro in Different Places," *Al-Dawa*, September 1979; and "An Open Letter to the Minister of Finance," *Al-Dawa*, June 1980. On one occasion, Yousef Kamal devoted an entire article to critiquing an Al-Azhar graduate student's dissertation because, he claimed, its argument

endorsed interest. "Al-Azhar Gives Global Fame to Those who Endorse Interest?,"
Al-Dawa, April 1979.

353. See, for example, "Comments on the Law on Islamic Finance Companies," *Liwaa Al-Islam*, June 1988.

354. Ahram Online, "Egypt's President Signs Islamic Bonds Bill," *Ahram Online*, May 9, 2013, http://english.ahram.org.eg/News/71025.aspx. Nevertheless, as al-Anani notes, Morsi diverged from that long-standing stance on ribaa by negotiating with the IMF in 2012. Al-Anani, *Inside the Muslim Brotherhood*, 11–12.

355. Al-Ghazali, *Al-Fikr al-Iqtisady*, 236.

356. Al-Ghazali, *Al-Fikr al-Iqtisady*, 300.

357. See, for example, Janine A. Clark, *Islam, Charity, and Activism: Middle-Class Networks and Social Welfare in Egypt, Jordan, and Yemen* (Bloomington: Indiana University Press, 2004); Jane Harrigan and Hamed El-Said, *Economic Liberalisation, Social Capital and Islamic Welfare Provision* (New York: Palgrave Macmillan, 2009); and Steven Brooke, *Winning Hearts and Votes: Social Services and the Islamist Political Advantage* (Ithaca, NY: Cornell University Press, 2019).

358. This practice is definitely central to the abovementioned claim that a society of devout Muslims will never experience class strife, because Islam ordains the redistribution of wealth through zakat.

359. Freedom and Justice Party, *Barnamaj*, 89–90; 110. A similar trend is found in Al-Tilmisani's discussion of the "Islamic economy." See Al-Tilmisani, *Ayam maʿa al-Sadat*, 94.

360. Al-Ghazali, *Al-Fikr al-Iqtisady*, 303.

361. Freedom and Justice Party, *Barnamaj*, 112.

362. Abdel-Halim, *Al-Ikhwan Al-Muslimun*, 145.

363. Beinin and Lockman write on the Muslim Brotherhood's position on labor during that same period: "Most of the [Muslim Brotherhood] Society's writings on labor affairs suffered from ambiguity, inconsistency, and programmatic unclarity." Joel Beinin and Zachary Lockman, *Workers on the Nile: Nationalism, Communism, Islam and the Egyptian Working Class, 1882–1954* (London: Tauris, 1988), 393.

364. Freedom and Justice Party, *Barnamaj*, 110.

365. This may seem like a minor issue, yet in the Egyptian context, such seemingly benign qualifiers have important implications. Consider, for example, the issue of health care. According to the 2012 Muslim Brotherhood-sponsored constitution, the state is obligated to provide free treatment to *ghayr al-qadiriyn* ("those who are incapable"), a term that is commonly used to denote members of low-income households. In practice, only those holding documentation from the government certifying low-incomes status can qualify for such benefits. It is exceedingly difficult for a poor (let alone ill) person to complete the complicated, time-consuming steps associated with obtaining such documentation, which the media has famously dubbed "the certificate of poverty."

366. In discussing the means to achieve social justice, Mamoun Al-Houdaiby is equally vague about the state's role in the redistribution of wealth: "Any system or law that leads to the concentration of money in a limited number of hands is unacceptable.

The basic rule in earning money legitimately is that it occurs through *halal* [Islamically acceptable] means, and this rule ensures that there would be no loopholes that allow a person to suddenly become a millionaire or more. Secondly, spending money in *halal* ways. Thirdly, fulfilling religious obligations. Distributing money that way would not lead to the concentration of money in a limited number of hands." Al-Ansary, *Al-Ikhwan al-Muslimun*, 71.

367. Author interview, July 10, 2010, Cairo, Egypt. The Revolutionary Socialists voice a similar critique in Revolutionary Socialists, *Al-Ishtirakiyya Allaty Nudafiʿ ʿAnha* (Al-Qahirah: Markaz al-Dirasat al-Ishtirakiyya, 2006), 36.

368. See, for example, Wael Gamal, "The Brotherhood's One Percent." *Jadaliyya*, July 19, 2012, http://www.jadaliyya.com/pages/index/6483/the-brotherhoods-one -percent/; and Wael Gamal, "Lost Capital."

369. In 2007, Al-Ghazali argued that the state could accept interest-bearing loans from international financial institutions if such loans were absolutely necessary. Al-Ghazali, *Al-Fikr al-Iqtisady*, 304.

370. Al-Ghazali, *Al-Fikr al-Iqtisady*, 305. Al-Ghazali's ideas are consistent with Hossam Tammam's conclusion that by the 2000s, the Muslim Brotherhood resembled a center-right party with liberal leanings on economic and social issues, as evidenced by its "acceptance of or non-opposition to the changes that happened in the country with respect to enacting policies of economic transformation and the adoption of market economics based on privatization, structural adjustment, free trade, and state withdrawal." Hossam Tammam, *Tahawulat al-Ikhwan al-Muslimin: Tafakuk al-Aydiulujiyya wa Nahayat al-Tanzim* (Al-Qahirah: Maktabat Madbuly, 2009), 10.

371. Al-Ansary, *Al-Ikhwan al-Muslimun*, 68.

372. "An Open Letter to the Minister of Finance," *Al-Dawa*, June 1980.

373. In the opening article of the September 1978 issue, for example, Al-Tilmisani complained that the draft constitution described Egypt as a socialist democracy, even though socialist models have proven ineffective. "And on Amending the Constitution, We Have an Opinion," *Al-Dawa*, September 1979; Abdel-Hamid Al-Ghazali expressed similar views in the Mohamed Abdel-Quddous editorial, "Why Wasn't Prosperity Achieved in the Year 1980?," *Al-Dawa*, February 1981; also see Al-Tilmisani's memoirs, in which he attacks Nasser for allowing Marxism to spread in Egypt. Al-Tilmisani, *Dhikrayat La Mudhakarat*, 210.

374. During the 1970s, moreover, *Al-Dawa*'s articles expressed dismay at the government's continuing role in setting prices, arguing that agricultural produce must be sold at international market prices. "So a Crisis Does Not Ensue the Government Must Reconsider Crop Prices," *Al-Dawa*, September 1978.

375. Beinin, "Political Islam," 120; in his memoirs, Al-Tilmisani attacks Nasser's agricultural reform law, and calls it "agricultural corruption law." Al-Tilmisani, *Dhikrayat La Mudhakarat*, 126–27.

376. Author interview, August 5, 2010, Cairo, Egypt. The first bill for that legislation was introduced in 1986. Sayyid Ashmawy, *Al-Falahun wa-l-Sultah* (Al-Qahirah: Mirit, 2001), 218.

377. Author interview, August 3, 2010, Cairo, Egypt.
378. Rafiq Zahran, "Al-Harakah al-Falahiyya wa Qanun Tard al-Musta'jiriyn," *Revsoc*, September 1, 1997, http://revsoc.me/workers-farmers/lhrk-lflhy-wqnwn-trd-lmstjryn.
379. Author interview, July 27, 2010, Cairo, Egypt.
380. Al-Ansary, *Al-Ikhwan al-Muslimun*, 70.
381. Al-Ghazali, *Al-Fikr al-Iqtisady*, 304. A similar view is evident in *Al-Dawa*'s coverage of the early phases of infitah, which, the magazine argued, resulted in the concentration of foreign investments in consumerist rather than productive sectors. See, for example, "Why Wasn't Prosperity Achieved in the Year 1980?," *Al-Dawa*, February 1981.
382. Al-Ghazali, *Al-Fikr al-Iqtisady*, 304; 318.
383. Al-Ghazali, *Al-Fikr al-Iqtisady*, 312.
384. See, for example, "Between the Pyramids and the Cabarets of Al-Haram Street," *Al-Dawa*, July 1978; and "Dignity, Humiliation: Between Tourism and Art," *Al-Dawa*, September 1978.
385. Kandil, *Inside the Brotherhood*, 42–47.
386. Utvik notes Islamist discourse since the 1950s more generally has "moved to a decidedly more liberal position." Utvik, *Islamist Economics*, 145.
387. A case in point is Mohamed Al-Ghazali's *Islam and Socialist Curricula*, which was first published in 1947. Mohamed Al-Ghazali, *Al-Islam wa-l-Manahij al-Ishtrakiyya* (Al-Jizah: Nahdat Misr, 2005).
388. I thank Amr Adly for bringing that point to my attention.
389. Tammam, *Tahawulat al-Ikhwan*, 14–15. Utvik makes similar observations. Utvik, *Islamist Economics*, 74.
390. Angela Joya, *The Roots of Revolt: A Political Economy of Egypt from Nasser to Mubarak* (Cambridge: Cambridge University Press, 2020), 139–40.
391. A case in point is Abdel-Azim Luqma, whose family business eventually expanded into a variety of sectors, including maritime development and fiberglass pipes manufacturing.
392. Brotherhood figures, including Ahmed Adel Kamal, Abdel-Hamid Al-Ghazali, and Khairat El-Shater, played prominent management roles in the Faisal Bank and the International Islamic Bank for Investment and Development. Hesham Al-Awadi, *Sira' 'ala al-Shar'iyah: al-Ikhwan al-Muslimun wa Mubarak 1982-2007* (Bayrut: Markaz Dirasat al-Wihdah al-'Arabiyya, 2009), 116.
393. Sami Zubaida, "The Politics of the Islamic Investment Companies in Egypt," *British Society for Middle Eastern Studies. Bulletin* 17, no. 2 (1990): 152–61.
394. Al-Awadi, *Sira' 'ala al-Shar'iyah*, 114–17; 156–59.
395. For example, even at a time when allegations of corruption were haunting Islamic investment companies, an article in the Muslim Brotherhood–linked magazine *Liwaa Al-Islam* came to their defense, arguing that the vast majority of such firms adhered to Islamic principles "The Lost Truths, and the Confused Papers in the Question of Islamic Investment Companies," *Liwaa Al-Islam*, January 1989. For more on the history of Islamic investment companies, see Abdel-Qadir Shuheib, *Al-Ikhtiraq: Qisat Sharikat Tawziyf al-Amwal* (Al-Qahira: Sina' li-l-Nashr, 1989).

396. Khaled Mahmoud, "Sisi's Grab for Brotherhood Assets," *Sada*, October 5, 2018, https://carnegieendowment.org/sada/77427. Ahmed Abdel-Hay, Khairy Omar, Abdel-Hafiz Al-Sawy, and Wesam Fouad, *Al-Muʿaradah al-Mustabahah* (Al-Jizah: Markaz Sawasiyah li-Huquq al-Insan, 2008).

3. Sadat's Brothers: Islamist Incorporation and the Autonomous Path

1. Wael Othman, *Asrar Al-Harakah al-Tulabiyya Handasat al-Qahirah 1968–1975* (Al-Qahirah: Al-Sharikah al-Misriyya li-l-Tibaʿah wa-l-Nashr, 1976), 166.

2. According to Al-Sayyid Abdel-Sattar Al-Meleegy, Brotherhood figures have acknowledged these gestures in various accounts. Al-Sayyid Abdel-Sattar Al-Meleegy, *Tajribaty maʿa al-Ikhwan* (Al-Qahirah: Al-Markaz al-ʿIlmy li-l-Buhuth wa-l-Dirasat, 2009), 106–7.

3. Hossam Tammam, *Shahid ʿala Tarikh al-Harakah al-Islamiyya fi Misr: 1970–1984* (Al-Qahirah: Dar al-Shuruq, 2010), 74–75.

4. Essam El-Erian, "Shahadat al-Duktur ʿIsam al-ʿIryan ʿan Nashʾat al-Tayyar al-Islamy bi-l-Jamiʿat al-Misriyya," *Ikhwanonline*, December 13, 2008, https://web.archive.org/web/20120308152435/http://ikhwanwayonline.maktoobblog.com/1508320.

5. See El-Erian's account in Sameh Eid, *Al-Islamiyyun Yatahadathun* (Al-Jizah: Dar Hala, 2013), 91.

6. Tammam, *Shahid ʿala Tarikh*, 80. Mohy Eissa also underscored the central role Brotherhood intellectuals and preachers played in mentoring IGU cadres during that period. Mohy Eissa, personal Facebook page post, Facebook, March 27, 2015, https://www.facebook.com/permalink.php?story_fbid=1634057436818192&id=100006418533527.

7. Ibrahim Al-Zafarani, "Hikayat al-Zaʿfarany," *Ikhwanwiki*, December 9, 2017, http://www.ikhwan.wiki/index.php?title=حكايات_الزعفراني. See also, Badr Mohamed Badr, *Al-Jamaʿah al-Islamiyya fi-l-Jamiʿat* (Badr Mohamed Badr, 1989), 18. Mohamed Habib described a similar experience at Assiut University, where longtime Brotherhood members were connecting with student activists as early as 1975. Mohamed Habib, *Dhikrayat Duktur Muhamad Habib: ʿAn al-Hayah wa-l-Daʿwah wa-l-Siyasah wa-l-Fikr* (Al-Qahirah: Dar Al-Shuruq, 2012), 124.

8. Tammam, *Shahid ʿala Tarikh*, 88; Al-Zafarani reports that the Alexandria contingent's decision to join the Brotherhood came in the wake of a 1975 meeting between IG student leaders, including Khaled Daoud, Hamed Al-Dafrawi, and himself, and Brotherhood elders at the home of Abbas Al-Sisi. Al-Zafarani, "Hikayat al-Zaʿfarany."

9. Also see El-Erian's account in Eid, *Al-Islamiyyun Yatahadathun*, 97.

10. Badr Mohamed Badr indicates that the books of Hassan Al-Banna and Sayyid Qutb were included in the curriculum of these summer camps and other IGU-related endeavors. Badr, *Al-Jamaʿah al-Islamiyya*, 18; 30–32. In fact, some observers have argued that the camps resembled the Muslim Brotherhood's pre-1954 youth camps.

See, for example, Abdullah Shalaby, *Al-Din wa-l-Sira' al-Siyasy fi Misr: 1970–1985* (Al-Qahirah: Kitab al-Ahaly, 2000), 89.

11. Mohy Eissa, personal Facebook page post, Facebook, March 31, 2015, https://www .facebook.com/photo/?fbid=1635207340036535&set=a.1578510872372849.

12. The structure is detailed in Badr, *Al-Jama'ah al-Islamiyya*, 24.

13. Hossam Tammam, *Al-Ikhwan al-Muslimun: Sanawat ma Qabl al-Thawrah* (Al-Qahirah: Dar al-Shuruq, 2012), 43–45, 157.

14. Mohy Eissa recalls that in late 1977, Aboul-Fotouh, El-Erian and Al-Zafarani met with him in Al-Minya for the purpose of "testing the waters" regarding cooperation with the Muslim Brotherhood. Mohy Eissa, personal Facebook page post, Facebook, March 29, 2015, https://www.facebook.com/permalink.php?story_fbid=163458493 6765442&id=100006418533527.

15. See Abul-Ela Madi's remarks in Abdel-Reheem Aly, *Al-Ikhwan al-Muslimun: Azmat Tayar al-Tajdid* (Al-Qahirah: Markaz al-Mahrusah, 2004), 169.

16. Many IG elements in Middle and Upper Egypt refused to follow suit and eventually chose to form a separate group, Al-Gama'ah Al-Islamiyya (GI).

17. Fouad Allam writes that regime directives impeded the security establishment's attempts to infiltrate Islamist groups at the time. Fouad Allam, *Al-Ikhwan wa Ana: Min al-Manshiyah ila al-Manasah* (Al-Qahirah: Akhbar al-Yawm, 1996), 250. This is consistent with the testimony of security officers at the trials of those charged with orchestrating an insurrection after Sadat's assassination. Summaries of these testimonies are available on page 6 of *Al-Ahram* on February 27, March 1, and March 6, 1983. Also see discussion in Abdel-Reheem Aly, *Al-Hisad al-Mur: al-Dawlah wa Jama'at al-'Unf al-Diny fi Misr* (Al-Qahirah: al-Mahrusah, 2005), 121.

18. Al-Sayyid Abdel-Sattar Al-Meleegy, "Tajribaty ma'a al-Ikhwan," *IkhwanWiki*, November 26, 2012, https://www.ikhwanwiki.com/index.php?title=التنظيم_السري_إلى _تجربتي_مع_الإخوان_من_الدعوة. Longtime Brotherhood leader Farid Abdel-Khaleq makes a similar claim. Farid Abdel-Khaleq, *Al-Ikhwan al-Muslimun fi Mizan al-Haq* (Al-Qahirah: Dar al-Sahwah li-l-Nashr, 1987), 134. In fact, according to Al-Tilmisani, the Brotherhood's decision to participate in the parliamentary election in 1984 came only after authorities banned *Al-Dawa*, thereby depriving the movement of its voice in public affairs. Al-Tilmisani raised this issue in a December 1985 interview with Muslim Brotherhood historian Gomaa Amin. The interview is available online: You-Tube, February 5, 2013, https://www.youtube.com/watch?v=73jUyXzoPQw.

19. Al-Tilmisani reports that with the exception of himself and Saleh Ashmawy, the magazine's editorial team was composed entirely of students or recent graduates from the Faculty of Mass Communication. Omar Al-Tilmisani, *Dhikrayat La Mudha-karat* (Al-Qahirah: Dar Al-I'tisam, 1985), 180.

20. Tammam, *Shahid 'ala Tarikh*, 103. Abbas Al-Sisi also notes the role of *Al-Dawa* in encouraging Islamic Group youth in Alexandria to forge ties with the Muslim Brotherhood. Abbas Al-Sisi, *Min al-Madhbahah ila Sahat al-Da'wah* (Al-Qahirah: Dar al-Tawzi' wa-l-Nashr al-Ismaliyya, 2003), 111.

21. El-Erian, "Shahadat al-Duktur."

22. See, for example, Naguib Sawiris' remarks in a recent interview; summarized in Amer Mostafa, "Sawiris li 'CNN': Mubarak Wafaq ʿala Fatrah Intiqaliyya Walakin al-Ikhwan wa Asdiqaʾ al-Suʾ Rafadu," Youm7, November 13, 2020, https://www.youm7.com /story/2020/11/13/ـلـساويرس-CNN-الإخوان-ولكن-انتقالية-فترة-على-وافق-مبارك/5066178.

23. Abdullah A. Al-Arian, *Answering the Call: Popular Islamic Activism in Sadat's Egypt* (New York: Oxford University Press, 2014), 104; 109; 140; "The student leaders," he explains, "made up the base of the newly established Muslim Brotherhood" (17); Al-Arian concludes: "In due course, the youth members of the organization, who had successfully held the banner of popular activism during their college years, would take the reins of leadership and determine the Muslim Brotherhood's program for the coming decades" (219).

24. Tammam, *Shahid ʿala Tarikh*, 91–92.

25. Quoted in Aly, *Al-Ikhwan al-Muslimun: Azmat Tayar*, 169. Other firsthand accounts acknowledge that the Brotherhood lacked any meaningful organizational structures by the end of the 1970s. See, for example, Mohy Eissa, personal Facebook page post, Facebook, June 8, 2015, https://www.facebook.com/photo/?fbid=165801 9797755289&set=a.1578510872372849.

26. Carrie Rosefsky Wickham, *Mobilizing Islam: Religion, Activism, and Political Change in Egypt* (New York: Columbia University Press, 2002), 97. Also see a similar interpretation of the Brotherhood's gains in parliament and professional syndicates in Mona El-Ghobashy, "The Metamorphosis of the Egyptian Muslim Brothers," *International Journal of Middle East Studies* 37, no. 3 (August 2005): 373–95. Al-Anani acknowledges the significance of the 1970s generation in rebuilding the Brotherhood's organizational structures and advancing the movement's reemergence into political life. Khalil al-Anani, *Inside the Muslim Brotherhood: Religion, Identity, and Politics* (New York: Oxford University Press, 2016), 147.

27. See Steven Brooke, *Winning Hearts and Votes: Social Services and the Islamist Political Advantage* (Ithaca, NY: Cornell University Press, 2019), esp. chap. 3, 4, and 7. Also see Janine Clark seminal book on the subject. Janine A. Clark, *Islam, Charity, and Activism: Middle-Class Networks and Social Welfare in Egypt, Jordan, and Yemen* (Bloomington: Indiana University Press, 2004).

28. Tarek E. Masoud, *Counting Islam: Religion, Class, and Elections in Egypt* (New York: Cambridge University Press, 2014), xiv, 40.

29. At the mosque, Eissa and his collaborators would convene religious study groups, and sometimes they would "illegally" lead the Friday prayer sermon. Mohy Eissa, personal Facebook page post, Facebook, June 7, 2015, https://www.facebook.com /photo/?fbid=1657770001113602&set=a.1578510872372849.

30. This was not an easy endeavor, Eissa explains, because affiliates of Al-Gamaʿah Al-Islamiyya were also competing to establish their own influence at Al-Minya mosques. Mohy Eissa, personal Facebook page post, Facebook, June 18, 2015, https://www .facebook.com/permalink.php?story_fbid=1661027684121167&id=100006418533527. Mohy Eissa, personal Facebook page post, Facebook, April 25, 2015, https://www .facebook.com/permalink.php?story_fbid=1645502839006985&id=100006418533527.

31. Mohy Eissa, personal Facebook page post, Facebook, July 11, 2015, https://www
.facebook.com/permalink.php?story_fbid=1667221230168479&id=100006418533527.

32. According to Al-Meleegy, by 1985, the Brotherhood's basic organizational structures, including major administrative and regional departments, were in place. Al-
Meleegy, *Tajribaty*, 334.

33. Al-Meleegy reports that the members of that committee were Omar Al-Tilmisani,
Gaber Rizk, Ahmed Al-Malt, Mohamed Salim, Mohamed Habib, Mamdouh Al-Diri,
Al-Sayyid Abdel-Sattar Al-Meleegy, Abdel-Moneim Aboul-Fotouh, and Anwar She-
hata. Al-Meleegy, *Tajribaty*, 121–22. See, also, Habib, *Dhikrayat*, 170.

34. Al-Zafarani, "Hikayat al-Za'farany."

35. Mohy Eissa, personal Facebook page post, Facebook, June 8, 2015.

36. Al-Meleegy, *Tajribaty*, 130–31.

37. See Aboul-Fotouh's comments in Aly, *Al-Ikhwan al-Muslimun: Azmat Tayar*, 163. For
more details, see Wickham, *Mobilizing Islam*, 176–203.

38. See al-Anani, *Inside the Muslim Brotherhood*, 7; 46.

39. Hassanein Koroum, *Al-Taharukat al-Siyasiyya li-l-Ikhwan al-Muslimin 1971-1987* (Al-
Qahirah: al-Markaz al-ʿAraby al-Dawly li-l-Iʿlam, 2012), 114.

40. Author interview, August 3, 2010, Cairo, Egypt.

41. For further elaboration of this point, see Hesham Al-Awadi, *Siraʿ ʿala al-Sharʿiyah:
al-Ikhwan al-Muslimun wa Mubarak 1982-2007* (Bayrut: Markaz Dirasat al-Wihdah
al-ʿArabiyya, 2009), 209–19.

42. Brooke, *Winning Hearts and Votes*, 51.

43. The same assessment appears in an unpublished Muslim Brotherhood strategy paper entitled "The Extended Crisis: The Relationship between the Egyptian
Regime with the Muslim Brotherhood," which is reprinted in Al-Awadi, *Siraʿ ʿala
al-Sharʿiyah*, 338.

44. Months before his assassination, Foda debated, among others, Muslim Brotherhood
senior figure Mamoun Al-Houdaiby at the Cairo International Book Fair on the
appropriate role of Islamic principles in politics and state policy. For the transcript
of this debate, see Khaled Mohsen, *Misr bayn al-Dawlah al-Islamiyya wa-l-Dawlah
al-ʿIlmaniyya* (Al-Qahirah: Markaz Al-Iʿlam Al-ʿAraby, 1992).

45. Quoted in Habib, *Dhikrayat*, 344.

46. Habib, *Dhikrayat*, 338.

47. These documents were published in Abdel-Reheem Aly, *Kashf al-Bahtan: Al-Ikhwan
al-Muslimun, Waqaʾiʿ al-ʿUnf wa Fatawy al-Takfir* (Al-Qahirah: Al-Markaz al-ʿAraby li-l-
Buhuth wa-l-Dirasat, 2010), 155–68.

48. Mohamed Habib, *Dhikrayat*, 341–42. Some observers have argued that the targeting of Salsabeel had little to do with national security, and everything to do with
regime-allied business figures' rising concerns about competition from Brotherhood-linked businesses. Hassan Malek claims that the raid was prompted by
Salsabeel's formal complaint that it was illicitly denied a government contract ultimately awarded to a company connected to Ahmed Rasekh, a retired police officer
whose niece Heidy Rasekh was married to President Mubarak's son Alaa. Haytham

Al-Boraei, "Al-Watan Tanshur Nas Tahqiqat al-Niyabah Maʿa Rajul al-Aʿmal Hasan Malik fi Qadiyat al-Idrar bi-l-Iqtisad," *Al-Watan*, February 8, 2018, https://www.elwatannews.com/news/details/3077816.

49. Al-Meleegy, *Tajribaty*, 132–33.
50. Hossam Tammam presents a similar interpretation. Hossam Tammam, *Tahawulat al-Ikhwan al-Muslimin: Tafakuk al-Aydiulujiyya wa Nahayat al-Tanzim* (Al-Qahirah: Maktabat Madbuly, 2009), 161.
51. For a summary of this escalation, see Carrie Rosefsky Wickham, *The Muslim Brotherhood: Evolution of an Islamist Movement* (Princeton, NJ: Princeton University Press, 2013), 76–81.
52. Mohamed Habib, *Dhikrayat*, 425–29.
53. For a full list of the suspects and the court sentences, see Abdel-Reheem Aly, *Al-Ikhwan al-Muslimun: Min Hasan al-Bana ila Mahdy ʿAkif* (Al-Qahirah: Al-Markaz al-ʿAraby li-l-Buhuth wa-l-Dirasat, 2007), 334–40.
54. Wickham, *Mobilizing Islam*, 200–202.
55. El-Ghobashy, "The Metamorphosis," 384.
56. Only one known affiliate of the Brotherhood secured a seat.
57. Tammam, *Al-Ikhwan*, 177.
58. Joel Beinin, "Popular Social Movements and the Future of Egyptian Politics," *Middle East Report Online*, March 10, 2005, https://merip.org/2005/03/popular-social-movements-and-the-future-of-egyptian-politics/; and Mona El-Ghobashy, "Egypt Looks Ahead to Portentous Year," *Middle East Report Online*, February 2, 2005, https://merip.org/2005/02/egypt-looks-ahead-to-portentous-year.
59. Hesham Sallam, "The New Iraq and Arab Political Reform: Drawing New Boundaries (and Reinforcing Old Ones)," in *Iraq, Its Neighbors, and the United States: Competition, Crisis, and the Reordering of Power*, ed. Henri J. Barkey, Scott Lasensky, and Phebe Marr (Washington, DC: U.S. Institute of Peace, 2011), 199–205.
60. Brotherhood officials have acknowledged that they had reached an understanding of sorts with security agencies before the vote. See Ahmed Antar, "Muhamad Habib: al-Ikhwan ʿAqadat Safqah maʿa Amn al-Dawlah fi Intikhabat al-Barlaman ʿAm 2005," *Al-Watan*, April 29, 2014, https://www.elwatannews.com/news/details/472134; Hani Zayed, "Ghuzlan: al-Ikhwan Lam Yadkhulu Safqah Intikhabiyya maʿa Nizam Mubarak," *Al-Watan*, June 8, 2012, https://www.alwatan.com.sa/article/140871; and Al-Masry Al-Youm, "ʿAbd al-Hamid al-Ghazaly Mustashar Murshid al-Ikhwan li-l-Misry al-Yawm: Naʿam ʿAqadna Safqah maʿa al-Amn fi Intikhabat 2005 Walakin al-Nizam Naqadha," *Al-Masry Al-Youm*, October 29, 2009, https://www.almasryalyoum.com/news/details/72648.
61. Author interview, August 7, 2010, Cairo, Egypt.
62. Joshua Stacher offers a micro-level view of state intervention in the 2005 election. Joshua Stacher, "Damanhour by Hook and by Crook," *Middle East Report* 238 (Spring 2006): 26–27. See, also, Samer Shehata's firsthand accounts of election rigging in 2005. Samer Shehata, "Political Daʿwa: Understanding the Muslim Brotherhood's Participation in Semi-Authoritarian Elections," in *Islamist Politics*

in the Middle East Movements and Change, ed. Samer Shehata (New York: Routledge, 2012), 121–22.

63. Nathan J. Brown, *When Victory Is Not an Option: Islamist Movements in Arab Politics* (Ithaca, NY: Cornell University Press, 2012), 85.

64. Joshua Stacher and Samer Shehata, "Boxing in the Brothers," *Middle East Report Online*, August 8, 2007, https://merip.org/2007/08/boxing-in-the-brothers.

65. Mona El-Ghobashy, "The Liquidation of Egypt's Illiberal Experiment," *Middle East Report Online*, December 29, 2010, https://merip.org/2010/12/the-liquidation-of -egypts-illiberal-experiment.

66. The state's standoff with the Brotherhood happened against the backdrop of a project that reduced the regime's tolerance for political dissent more generally: preparing the political arena for a smooth transition to the presidency of Hosni Mubarak's son Gamal. Nominating the younger Mubarak to become Egypt's next president and organizing a convincing multiparty election that guaranteed his victory necessitated NDP domination of the political arena, leaving little room for opposition voices not firmly under regime control. It, therefore, was not surprising that the Muslim Brotherhood's political presence, however limited, was one of the first casualties of the succession project.

67. Author interview, August 7, 2010, Cairo, Egypt.

68. Recent notable works on this subject include al-Anani, *Inside the Muslim Brotherhood*, Wickham, *The Muslim Brotherhood*; Hazem Kandil, *Inside the Brotherhood* (Cambridge: Polity Press, 2015); Tammam, *Tahawulat al-Ikhwan*; Tammam, *Al-Ikhwan*; and El-Ghobashy, "The Metamorphosis." See, also, Egypt sections in Brown, *When Victory Is Not an Option*.

69. As will be clear in the discussion that follows, the old–new distinction is not entirely helpful as it conceals the fact that both sets of antagonists include "young" and "old" elements. Characterizing the divide as one between those favoring or opposing political participation is a step in the right direction. Yet it overlooks the idea that the disagreement was not about whether to participate in politics, but rather over the acceptable terms and risks under which the Brotherhood should do so. The conservative–reformist binary is useful. But it lends itself to confusion, because the so-called reformists sometimes adopt conservative stances on social and cultural issues. These reformists were often equally conservative when discussing strategies to avoid provoking the ruling establishment.

70. See chapters 5 and 6 in al-Anani, *Inside the Muslim Brotherhood*.

71. Kandil, *Inside the Brotherhood*, 5.

72. Brown, *When Victory Is Not an Option*, 141.

73. Brown, *When Victory Is Not an Option*, 138.

74. Mustafa Mashhur mirrors this perspective in a 2002 interview in which he explains that transforming the movement into a political party would limit its activities to the political sphere, whereas turning it into an NGO would restrict its political activism. Aly, *Al-Ikhwan al-Muslimun: Azmat Tayar*, 155. See, also, discussion in Shehata, "Political Da'wa," 123.

75. Tammam, *Tahawulat al-Ikhwan*, 138. See, also, Tammam, *Al-Ikhwan*, 21.

76. Aly, *Al-Ikhwan al-Muslimun: Azmat Tayar*, 81–83.

77. Al-Anani, *Inside the Muslim Brotherhood*, 151.

78. Al-Meleegy, *Tajribaty*, 337.

79. Mohy Eissa, personal Facebook page post, Facebook, June 21, 2015, https://www.face book.com/permalink.php?story_fbid=1661984550692147&id=100006418533527.

80. Abdel-Rahman Abul-Ela, "Sa'd al-Katatny," *Al-Jazeera*, January 23, 2012, https:// www.aljazeera.net/news/reportsandinterviews/2012/1/23/2-محمد-سعد-الكتاتني. Subsequently, Al-Katatni would serve as leader the Brotherhood's bloc in the 2005 parliament, speaker of parliament when the group won a plurality of the 2012 legislature, and head of its political party, the Freedom and Justice Party in the same year.

81. El-Ghobashy, "The Metamorphosis," 386.

82. Mohy Eissa, personal Facebook page post, Facebook, June 23, 2015, https://www .facebook.com/photo/?fbid=1662478997309369&set=a.1578510872372849.

83. Al-Meleegy, *Tajribaty*, 135–36.

84. Salah Eddin Hassan, "Rashad Bayumy al-Rajul al-Samit," *Al-Watan*, December 29, 2012, https://www.elwatannews.com/news/details/104926.

85. See discussion in Al-Meleegy, *Tajribaty*, 134.

86. For more on the subject, see the firsthand accounts of Ahmed Adil Kamal, *Al-Nuqqat fawq al-Huruwf: al-Ikhwan al-Muslimun wa-l-Nizam al-Khas* (Al-Qahira: al-Zahra' li-l-I'lam al-'Araby, Qism al-Nashr, 1989) and Salah Shadi, *Safahat min al-Tarikh: Hisad al-'Umr* (Al-Qahirah: Al-Zahra' li-l-I'lam al-'Araby, Qism al-Nashr, 1987).

87. For more on the influence of these ideas, see chapter 2 in Barbara H. E. Zollner, *The Muslim Brotherhood: Hasan al-Hudaybi and Ideology* (New York: Routledge, 2009). On the nuances and problems raised by the use of the term "Qutbist," see discussion in Andrew Hammond, "The Egyptian Uprising Through the Lens of the Muslim Brotherhood," *Maydan*, January 28, 2021, https://themaydan.com/2021/01/the -egyptian-uprising-through-the-lens-of-the-muslim-brotherhood.

88. Mohy Eissa's memoirs offer some insight into how greatly the rogue elements in Al-Minya's IG troubled Mashhur. Eissa recalls that during his 1979 recruitment meeting with Mustafa Mashhur, the latter candidly stated that he did not want any of the IG's *kalakiy'* ("obstructive elements") in the Brotherhood. Mohy Eissa, personal Facebook page post, Facebook, April 18, 2015, https://www.facebook.com /permalink.php?story_fbid=1642207529336516&id=100006418533527. Aly Al-Sherif of the Assiut IG mentions the poor rapport he and his peers had with Mashhur. Aly Al-Sherif, "'Ilaqat al-Jama'ah al-Islamiyya bi-l-Aqbat Kanat Sayi'ah Jidan wa Kuna Nuwajih Tajawuzatuhum bi-l-Shiddah wa-l-'Unf," *Elmogaz*, December 28, 2012, https://www.elmogaz.com/60873.

89. Mashhur noted in a 2002 interview that despite the Muslim Brotherhood's condemnation of violence during the Sadat era, the regime attributed the transgressions of the IGUs to the Brotherhood, which, he laments, cut all channels of dialogue with the regime and led to showdowns with the security apparatus. Aly, *Al-Ikhwan al-Muslimun: Azmat Tayar*, 155.

90. Al-Meleegy writes that before voting for the Guidance Bureau commenced, Brotherhood leaders added thirty members by appointment to an eighty-five-member Shura Council. Al-Meleegy, *Tajribaty*, 142.
91. El-Ghobashy, "The Metamorphosis," 386.
92. For an excellent recap of that showdown and its outcome, see Wickham, *The Muslim Brotherhood*, 81–95.
93. Even though the 1995 military court rulings did not spare members of the guardianist camp like Ezzat and El-Shater, many remained free. Notably, even when the state started investigating El-Shater's company, Salsabeel, in the early 1990s, it eventually dropped the case and never referred it to court.
94. Tammam, *Tahawulat al-Ikhwan*, 32–34; 82–86.
95. According to Malek, El-Shater was then a teaching assistant, and was involved in the campus IG.
96. See transcripts of Hassan Malek's 2015 interrogation by authorities in Al-Boraei, "Al-Watan Tanshur."
97. Tammam, *Tahawulat al-Ikhwan*, 84–85.
98. Al-Anani, *Inside the Muslim Brotherhood*, 149–52.
99. For an overview of the Brotherhood's internal politics during that era, see chapter 5 in Wickham, *The Muslim Brotherhood*.
100. Al-Anani, *Inside the Muslim Brotherhood*, 153–54.
101. For example, the bylaws state that a membership application could be rejected on the basis of evidence that the applicant is not committed to the principles and identity of the party.
102. Although Essam El-Erian was a strong advocate of the institutionalist positions throughout much of his career, he became, as Hossam Tammam puts it, "amenable to understandings" toward the end of the Mubarak era. Tammam, *Al-Ikhwan*, 28.

4. Nasser's Comrades: State Guardianship and the Dependent Path

1. For the sake of simplicity, I use the term "state socialism" to describe this era of Nasser's rule. As many have observed, however, the term "state capitalism" is a more apt description of his actual policies, as there is no evidence that Nasser had any intention of allowing the working class any meaningful power.
2. The story was told by Sami Sharaf in his memoirs. Sami Sharaf, *Sanawat wa Ayam Ma'a Jamal 'Abd al-Nasir*, 5 vols. (Al-Qahirah: Al-Maktab al-Misry al-Hadith, 2014), 4:917–19. To my knowledge, there are three different editions of Sharaf's memoirs. In addition to this five-volume edition that was published by Al-Maktab al-Misry al-Hadith starting 2014, a two-volume edition was published by Al-Firsan li-l-Nashr in 2005. An earlier edition of the book also was published online on Sharaf's personal website. The three editions have slight differences. Unless otherwise stated, I rely on the Al-Maktab al-Misry edition.
3. Rifaat Al-Said, *Mujarad Dhikrayat al-Juzu' al-Thalith* (Dimashq: Dar Al-Mada, 2000), 42.

4. Born to a Russian family in Beirut, Rosenthal migrated to Egypt in 1899. Although there have been discrepancies in reporting on Rosenthal's origins, Al-Said confirms that both official British and Egyptian government documents identify him as Russian. Rifaat Al-Said, *Tarikh al-Harakah al-Shiu'iyya al-Misriyya 1900–1940* (Al-Qahirah: Dar al-Thaqafah al-Jadidah, 1987), 364–65.

5. For details, see Gennaro Gervasio, *Al-Harakah al-Markisiyya fi Misr (1967–1981)* (Al-Qahirah: Al-Markaz al-Qawmy li-l-Tarjamah, 2010), 173–75.

6. Talaat Romiah, *Ma'ziq al-Harakah al-Shiu'iyya al-Misriyya: al-Judhur al-Tarikhiyya wa-l Khiyarat al-Mustaqbaliyya* (Al-Qahirah: Markaz al-Ahram lil-Nashr wa-l-Tarjamah wal-Tawzi', 2010), 46. Sources vary greatly on the party's membership numbers.

7. For more details on that history, see Tareq Y. Ismael and Rifaat El-Sa'id, *The Communist Movement in Egypt, 1920–1988* (Syracuse, NY: Syracuse University Press, 1990), 12–31.

8. A list of all communist organizations and the years of their founding appears in Ahmed Al-Gebaly, Hassan Abul-Kheir, Sayyid Abdel-Wahab Nada, et al., *Al-'Ummal fi-l-Haraka al-Shiu'iyya al-Misriyya hata 'Aam 1965* (Al-Qahirah: Dar al-Amin, 2011), 88–92. For more detailed background on communist intellectual circles during the interwar period, see Gervasio, *Al-Harakah al-Markisiyya*, 185–89.

9. Rami Ginat, *A History of Egyptian Communism: Jews and Their Compatriots in Quest of Revolution* (Boulder, CO: Lynne Rienner, 2011), 277–83.

10. Ismael and El-Sa'id, *The Communist Movement*, 67.

11. Joel Beinin, "Henri Curiel and the Egyptian Communist Movement," *Radical History Review* 45 (1989): 157.

12. Ismael and El-Sa'id estimate Hadeto's membership at three thousand in 1952 (Ismael and El-Sa'id, *The Communist Movement*, 69), compared with one thousand four hundred reported by Curiel in 1947 (quoted in Ginat, *A History of Egyptian Communism*, 279). Fouad Morsi estimates the size of the entire communist movement in 1952 at about five thousand individuals (quoted in Romiah, *Ma'ziq al-Harakah al-Shiu'iyya*, 45).

13. Ismael and El-Sa'id, *The Communist Movement*, 69–70.

14. The groups were the Popular Vanguard for Liberation and the People's Liberation Movement. Al-Gebaly et al., *Al-'Ummal fi-l-Haraka al-Shiu'iyya al-Misriyya hata 'Aam 1965*, 88–89.

15. Joel Beinin, *Was the Red Flag Flying There? Marxist Politics and the Arab-Israeli Conflict in Egypt and Israel, 1948–1965* (Berkeley: University of California Press, 1990), 63; 185.

16. A confounding issue in these discussions is the tendency of some commentators to use the terms "foreigners" and "Jews" interchangeably, implying that Egyptian Jews were not truly Egyptian or that they were loyal to states other than Egypt. See, for example, Tariq Al-Bishri's talk of a "political foreign Jewish presence" inside the second wave of the communist movement. At points he refers to this presence as "foreign Jews," "foreigners," and "foreigners and Jews," and attributing their presence within the communist movement, at least in part, to growing Zionist influence in the region. Tariq Al-Bishri, *Al-Muslimun wa-l-Aqbat fi Itar al-Jama'ah al-Wataniyya* (Al-Qahirah: Al-Hay'ah al-'Amah li-l-Kitab, 1981), 642–43; 665. Bashir Al-Sibai critiques Al-Bishri's interpretation. Bashir Al-Sibai, "Al-Yahud wa-l-Harakah

al-Shiu'iyya: Radan 'ala Tariq al-Bishry," *Mabdaa Al-Amal*, April 11, 2011, http://mabda-alamal.blogspot.com/2011/04/blog-post_11.html.

17. See Fouad Morsi's remarks in Beinin, *Was the Red Flag Flying*, 103. For more on debates about the participation of Jewish people in the communist movement, see Rami Ginat, "Remembering History: The Egyptian Discourse on the Role of Jews in the Communist Movements," *Middle Eastern Studies* 49, no. 6 (2013): 919–40. Other firsthand accounts appear in Albert Arie , Janet Shirazi, Suad Zoheer, et al., *Al-Ajanib fi-l-Harakah al-Shiu'iyya al-Misriyya hata 'Am 1965* (Al-Qahirah: Markaz al-Buhuth al-'Arabiyya li-l-Dirasat al-'Arabiyya wa-l-Afriqiyya, 2002).

18. As a condition for unity with the other parties, Al-Raya demanded the exclusion of Jewish people from WPCP leadership positions, and the severing of all ties between UECP members and Hadeto's contingent of exiles known as "the Rome Group." Beinin, *Was the Red Flag Flying*, 185.

19. Ismael and El-Sa'id, *The Communist Movement*, 85–89.

20. For more details, see Ismael and El-Sa'id, *The Communist Movement*, 109–21.

21. According to Beinin, by the end of 1959, "two to three thousand left-wing opponents of the regime were jailed, including one to two thousand members of both the CPE and [the CPE-Hadeto]." Beinin, *Was the Red Flag Flying*, 207.

22. Aly Sabri reiterates the same points in Abdullah Imam, *'Aly Sabry Yatadhakar* (Al-Qahirah: Ruz al-Yusuf, 1987), 35–36.

23. Beinin, *Was the Red Flag Flying*, 205–6. For insight into the extent of the torture experienced by communist activists in prison, see Tahir Abdel-Hakim, *Al-Aqdam al-'Ariyah: al-Shiu'iyyin al-Misriyyin, Khamas Sanawat fi al-Sijun wa Mu'askarat al-Ta'thib* (Bayrut: Dar Ibn Khaldun, 1978).

24. See Abdel-Nasser's July, 2 1962, remarks in Adel Al-Ashwah, *Haqiqat al-Tanzim al-Tali'y wa Inqilab al-Sadat 'ala Thawrat Yulyu* (Al-Qahirah: Al-Markaz al-'Araby al-Dawly li al-I'lam, 2016), 19.

25. Iliya Harik, "The Single Party as a Subordinate Movement: The Case of Egypt," *World Politics* 26, no. 1 (October 1973): 92.

26. Esmail Hosseinzadeh, "How Egyptian State Capitalism Reverted to Market Capitalism," *Arab Studies Quarterly* 10, no. 3 (Summer 1988): 302–3.

27. Hazem Kandil describes the dynamics of this rivalry in his study of the Egyptian security establishment. Hazem Kandil, *Soldiers, Spies, and Statesmen: Egypt's Road to Revolt* (London: Verso, 2012), 43–97; In his account of the lead-up to the 1971 Corrective Revolution, Musa Sabri writes that by the early 1960s, Amer exercised influence over appointments to ranking posts inside the bureaucracy, public sector enterprises, and even local councils. Musa Sabri, *Watha'iq 15 Mayu* (Al-Qahirah: Al-Maktab al-Misry al-Hadith, 1976), 17.

28. Sherif Younis, *Nida' al-Sha'b: Tarikh Naqdy li-l-Aydiulujiyya al-Nasiriyya* (Al-Qahirah: Dar al-Shuruq, 2012), 388.

29. Kandil, *Soldiers, Spies*, 63. In fact, as Musa Sabri reports, following his return from Syria, Amer called for democracy and the return of multiparty life. Sabri, *Watha'iq 15 Mayu*, 17.

30. Nasser referenced many of these fears in his speech of October 16, 1961, which came in the immediate aftermath of Syria's secession from the UAR. He portrayed the coup as a failure to anticipate and defend against alliances between private capitalists and external forces: "We saw in Syria how capitalist, feudalist, and opportunist forces have partnered with colonialism to eliminate the gains of the masses, hit the socialist revolution, and recover all of their privileges, even using, if necessary, armed force and bloodshed." Gamal Abdel-Nasser, "Khitab al-Raʾis Jamal ʿAbd al-Nasir min al-Qasr al-Jumhury bi-l Qahirah ʿaqib al-Infisal," *Library of Alexandria Gamal Abdel-Nasser Archives*, October 16, 1961, http://nasser.bibalex.org/Speeches/browser.aspx?SID=1002.

31. Abdel-Nasser, "Khitab al-Raʾis."

32. Aly Sabri (quoted in Imam, ʿAly Sabry, 28) reiterates this rationale for the VO's formation.

33. Abdel-Nasser, "Khitab al-Raʾis."

34. See, for example, the accounts of Ahmed Hamroush, *Thawrat 23 Yulyu* (Al-Qahirah: Al-Hayʾah al-ʿAmah li-l-Kitab, 1992); Ahmed Fouad in Ahmed Hamroush, *Shuhud Thawrat Yulyu* (Al-Qahirah: Maktabat Madbuly, 1984), 51–55; and Aly Sabri in Imam, ʿAly Sabry.

35. See Hesham Sallam, "From the State of Vanguards to the House of Kofta: Reflections on Egypt's Authoritarian Impasse," *Jadaliyya*, October 26, 2020, https://www.jadaliyya.com/Details/41912.

36. See Sharaf, *Sanawat wa Ayam*, 3. Sharaf's account of the VO in his memoirs was in part based on an interview with Abdallah Imam and that was published in Abdullah Imam, ʿAbd al-Nasir Hakadha Kan Yahkum Misr (Al-Qahirah: Maktabat Madbuly al-Saghir, 1996). An electronic version of Sharaf's book—published on his own personal website—named public figures and officials involved in the VO. Sami Sharaf, "ʿAbd al-Nasir wa-l-Tanzim al-Siyasy," *Sanawat wa Ayam Maʿa Jamal ʿAbd al-Nasir, al-Juzʿ Al-Thany*, accessed April 15, 2015, http://hakaek-misr.com/yahiaalshaer.com/SAMY/Book-2-POLORG-XX.html.

37. These sources include minutes of closed ASU and VO meetings, relevant documents from the Ministry of Justice archives, and unpublished accounts of former senior officials. See Hamada Hosni, ʿAbd al-Nasir wa-l-Tanzim al-Taliʿiy al-Sirry 1971-1963 (Al-Qahirah: Maktabat Bayrut, 2007). Hazem Kandil's study on the evolution of the Egyptian military and the domestic security apparatus placed the VOs formation within the context of growing competition between Nasser and the army's leadership. Kandil, *Soldiers, Spies*.

38. In addition to his position as minister of interior, Gomaa also served the secretary general of the VO.

39. Al-Ashwah, *Haqiqat al-Tanzim*. Another important contribution is Amin Iskandar, *Al-Tanzim al-Sirry li-Jamal ʿAbd al-Nasir: Taliʿat al-Ishtrakiyyin, al-Mawlid al-Masar al-Masir* (Al-Qahirah: Al-Mahrusah, 2016).

40. Sharaf, *Sanawat wa Ayam*, 3:648–58; Sharaf's own assessment of the ruling party's shortcomings echoed Nasser's (3:692–96). Also see Nasser's August 6, 1966, remarks, as quoted in Al-Ashwah, *Haqiqat al-Tanzim*, 20.

41. Atef Abdel-Ghany, *Muhamad ʿUthman Ismaʿil Yatadhakar: al-Wazir Aladhy Kalafahuh al-Sadat bi-Takwin al-Jamaʿat al-Islamiyya* (Al-Qahirah: ʿAtif ʿAbd al-Ghany, 2000), 76–77.

42. Nasser acknowledged the existence of the secret VO in August 1966. See Hamroush, *Thawrat 23 Yulyu*, 613.

43. Details of this discussion appear in two independent firsthand accounts, including those of Sharaf, *Sanawat wa Ayam*, 3:687–90; and Ahmed Fouad in Hamroush, *Shuhud Thawrat Yulyu*, 55.

44. Whereas Sharaf reports that the meeting was held on September 3, 1963, Hamroush claims the date of the meeting was June 1963 and does not list Abbas Radwan as one of the participants. Sharaf, *Sanawat wa Ayam*, 3:687. Hamroush, *Thawrat 23 Yulyu*, 611. Fouad's testimony in Hamroush dates the meeting to the summer of 1963 "in the presence of Hassan Ibrahim, Mohamed Hassanein Heikal, Aly Sabri, and Sami Sharaf." *Shuhud Thawrat Yulyu*, 55.

45. Sharaf, *Sanawat wa Ayam*, 3:690.

46. As Gennaro Gervasio points out, there had already been some stirrings of "dethawing" relations with Marxist intellectuals in the early 1960s. Gervasio, *Al-Harakah al-Markisiyya*, 211.

47. Quoted in Hamroush, *Shuhud Thawrat Yulyu*, 55.

48. Hamroush, *Thawrat 23 Yulyu*, 611. This reasoning is apparent in Nasser's remarks at the second meeting of the VO group. Sharaf, *Sanawat wa Ayam*, 3:689–90.

49. Sharaf, *Sanawat wa Ayam*, 3:687.

50. According to Hamroush, Nasser confided to Ahmed Fouad that he thought Sabri and Heikal were undergoing an intellectual transformation that brought them closer to socialist ideas. Hamroush, *Thawrat 23 Yulyu*, 613.

51. Sharaf, "ʿAbd al-Nasir wa-l-Tanzim al-Siyasy."

52. Sharaf, "ʿAbd al-Nasir wa-l-Tanzim al-Siyasy."; Ibrahim Saadeddin's account confirmed his participation in that cell. Hamroush, *Shuhud Thawrat Yulyu*, 22.

53. Hamroush, *Thawrat 23 Yulyu*, 614. Aly Sabri estimates that the VO's total membership peaked at a hundred thousand. Imam, *ʿAly Sabry*, 30.

54. Hosni, *ʿAbd al-Nasir wa-l-Tanzim*, 68.

55. Shatta's name cited in Ismael and El-Saʿid, *The Communist Movement*, 123; Tiba and Abdel-Halim are cited in Hosni, *ʿAbd al-Nasir wa-l-Tanzim*, 52; 205.

56. Exemplifying that trend is the veteran Nasserist activist and legal scholar Hossam Eissa, who served as the minister of higher education in the government formed immediately after the July 2013 coup. Hosni, *ʿAbd al-Nasir wa-l-Tanzim*, 53.

57. Quoted in Ismael and El-Saʿid, *The Communist Movement*, 128.

58. Details of the contacts between leaders of the CPE and Nasser are provided, unless otherwise stated, by Sami Sharaf's account. Sharaf, *Sanawat wa Ayam*, 4:917–33.

59. Before his meeting with Nasser, Morsi met with Sami Sharaf and Aly Sabri to offer feedback on the ASU's organizational structures and components. Imam, *ʿAbd al-Nasir*, 185.

60. Sharaf, *Sanawat wa Ayam*, 4:919–20.

61. Sharaf, *Sanawat wa Ayam*, 4:920.

62. Sharaf, *Sanawat wa Ayam*, 4: 920–21.
63. Sharaf reports that some communists demanded they collectively receive a "special status" inside the ASU, but Nasser insisted that they join the ruling party only as individuals. Sharaf, *Sanawat wa Ayam*, 4:921.
64. Sharaf, *Sanawat wa Ayam*, 4:922.
65. A scanned copy of the handwritten letter appears in the Al-Fisran edition of Sharaf's memoirs. Sami Sharaf, *Sanawat wa Ayam Maʿa Jamal ʿAbd al-Nasir*, 2 vols. (Al-Qahirah: al-Firsan li-l-Nashr, 2005), 2:776–82.
66. See Rami Ginat, *Egypt's Incomplete Revolution: Lutfi Al-Khuli and Nasser's Socialism in the 1960s* (London: Frank Cass, 1997), 28.
67. Ismael and El-Saʿid, *The Communist Movement*, 123.
68. The text of the letter is taken from Ismael and El-Saʿid, *The Communist Movement*, 124, except for the last sentence, which is translated from the original telegram. A scanned copy of the telegram is available in Sharaf, *Sanawat wa Ayam*, 4:922.
69. See Fouad Morsi's remarks in Ismael and El-Saʿid, *The Communist Movement*, 125.
70. Hamroush articulates this point of view. Hamroush, *Thawrat 23 Yulyu*, 615.
71. See, for example, the discussion in Ismael and El-Saʿid, *The Communist Movement*, 123–25, especially the comments of Fakhri Labib and Saad Rahimi. Al-Said says that pressure came from "former" Marxist writers who were involved in *Al-Ahram* and later *Al-Talia*. Rifaat Al-Said, *Al-Tayarat al-Siyasiyya fi Misr, Ruʾyah Naqdiyya: Al-Markisiyyun, al-Ikhwan, al-Nasiryyun, al-Tajammuʿ* (Al-Qahirah: al-Hayʾah al-ʿAmah li-l-Kitab, 2002), 81. Sharaf reports that would-be *Al-Talia* editorial leaders Lotfi Al-Khouli and Mohamed Sid-Ahmed were involved in negotiating communists' entry into the ASU. Sharaf, *Sanawat wa Ayam*, 4:921.
72. See discussion in Beinin, *Was the Red Flag Flying*, 248–55.
73. See Younis, *Nidaʾ al-Shaʿb*, 577–78. See, also, Joel Beinin, *Workers and Thieves: Labor Movements and Popular Uprisings in Tunisia and Egypt* (Stanford, CA: Stanford University Press, 2016), 27.
74. Beinin, *Was the Red Flag Flying*, 249.
75. Younis, *Nidaʾ al-Shaʿb*, 576.
76. A similar line of reasoning also allowed the Soviet Union to forge alliances with countries like Egypt.
77. Roel Meijer, *The Quest for Modernity: Secular Liberal and Left-Wing Political Thought in Egypt, 1945–1958* (London: RoutledgeCurzon, 2002), 194.
78. Meijer, *The Quest for Modernity*, 123.
79. Quoted in Beinin, *Was the Red Flag Flying*, 190–91.
80. Beinin, *Was the Red Flag Flying*, 210. Perhaps for this reason Beinin interprets Morsi's 1957 article as evidence that the intellectual groundwork for dissolving the communist party was laid long before Nasser's socialist reforms of the 1960s.
81. Younis notes that the functionalist reasoning common to Marxist intellectuals rationalized the dissolution of a communist party if another force assumed the mission of advancing historical progress toward socialism. Younis, *Nidaʾ al-Shaʿb*, 577.
82. Beinin, *Was the Red Flag Flying*, 59–65.

83. Beinin, *Was the Red Flag Flying*, 104; Ginat, *A History of Egyptian Communism*, 293–94; Ismael and El-Sa'id, *The Communist Movement*, 68.

84. Reflecting on Egyptian communists' identity predicament, Roel Meijer writes: "[T]he issue of nationalism and therefore the issue of identity were to pose a problem from the very beginning and would constitute one of the main distinctions between communist organizations. HAMITU accepted nationalism not only as an ideology but also as an organizational principle |. . . .| In a sense, the inclusion of nationalism in the communist modernist program was a means of appropriating it politically and neutralizing it |. . . .| The communist movement was perfunctorily involved in the modernist attempt to create a national image." Meijer, *The Quest for Modernity*, 105.

85. Ismael and El-Sa'id, *The Communist Movement*, 87.

86. Meijer analyzes some of these ideas in Fouad Morsi's earliest writings. Meijer, *The Quest for Modernity*, 121–23.

87. Younis, *Nida' al-Sha'b*, 358.

88. A scanned copy of the memo appears in Sharaf, *Sanawat wa Ayam*, 4:1134–39.

89. In the same scanned memo, the president recommended promoting division and conflict inside communist organizations.

90. Younis, *Nida' al-Sha'b*, 359–62.

91. Sharaf, *Sanawat wa Ayam*, 4:921.

92. Younis' analysis of Heikal's article delivers that point decisively: "After the release of the communists in March 1964, and when they were dragging their feet about dissolving [their organizations], Heikal went on to review, what he considers from his perspective, the erroneous stances that the communist movement had adopted toward the regime; specifically its criticism of the policies of the regime at different times. But he also indicated that the movement from the beginning had only a meager following, and described [the movement's essence] as 'a set of fluid, incoherent ideas that were brought together using the seduction of sex and money; sex for the students, and money for the workers. And thus was the beginning [of the communist movement]. And here I speak with utmost candor and objectivity!' And although for him the communist movement, 'objectively,' consisted of a group of pimps, prostitutes, and brothels, he still manages to charge it with failure on a count that is unrelated to the said activities; that is, identifying 'the true engines of revolution in the realities of the entire third world . . . and the unity of the Arab destiny.' Thus, [the communists] have lived in 'isolation . . . from the nationalist movement.' Also 'if these movements had succeeded, even to a limited degree, in mobilizing the popular masses, the persecution they experienced would not have reached the levels [we witnessed]!'|. . . .| In the same article, wherein he decides that the communist movement was built on sex and money, he states, 'the time has come for Egyptian society to look at communists and communism through a normal perspective'|. . .| and he declared that 'they must be left in the sea of society . . . as one opinion among many,' while keeping the coercive solution [on the table] just in case they attempt to 'create a formal or secret political party in Egypt,' or if they tried 'to insult religion.'" Younis, *Nida' al-Sha'b*, 572–73.

93. A scanned copy of the handwritten letter appears in the Al-Firsan edition of Sharaf's memoirs. Sami Sharaf, *Sanawat wa Ayam Maʿa Jamal ʿAbd al-Nasir*, 2 vols. (Al-Qahirah: al-Firsan li-l-Nashr, 2005), 2:776–82.

94. Beinin, *Was the Red Flag Flying*, 191.

95. Al-Said, *Mujarad Dhikrayat*, 42.

96. Karem Yahya, "Faris al-Dimuqratiyya Khalid Muhy al-Din Akhir al-ʿAnqud fi Majlis Qiyadat al-Thawrah," *Al-Ahram*, July 23, 2012, http://digital.ahram.org.eg/articles .aspx?Serial=971306&eid=2406.

97. See the Revolutionary Socialists' 2006 vision for change, which references these decisions. Revolutionary Socialists, *Al-Ishtirakiyya Allaty Nudafiʿ ʿAnha* (Al-Qahirah: Markaz al-Dirasat al-Ishtirakiyya, 2006), 35.

98. Quoted in Ismael and El-Saʿid, *The Communist Movement*, 140.

99. Hamroush, *Thawrat 23 Yulyu*, 615.

100. Hamroush, *Thawrat 23 Yulyu*, 639.

101. Sami Sharaf makes this point emphatically in his memoirs, in which he lists the names of all the figures who occupied prominent positions in state media during the period, noting that only a few of them were in fact communists. Sharaf, *Sanawat wa Ayam*, 4:923–24. Note that the regime continued to crack down on Marxist writers after the dissolution of the communist parties. See Gervasio, *Al-Harakah al-Markisiyya*, 218–19.

102. Hamroush, *Thawrat 23 Yulyu*, 627.

103. Younis, *Nidaʾ al-Shaʿb*, 580.

104. Hosni, *ʿAbd al-Nasir wa-l-Tanzim*, 65.

105. See Kandil, *Soldiers, Spies*, 59–60; Hamroush, *Thawrat 23 Yulyu*, 629; 631.

106. In his interview with Abdullah Imam, Aly Sabri vehemently denied that the VO was tasked with spying on individuals. Imam, *ʿAly Sabry*, 31.

107. On the internal circulation of these reports, see Al-Ashwah, *Haqiqat al-Tanzim*, 57. He also details incidents when VO members were able to "detect" subversive activities and raise them to the attention of relevant officials (58–61). According to Al-Ashwah, after 1967, the VO, much like other Egyptian domestic intelligence agencies, was tasked with nominating appropriate candidates for ranking posts in the bureaucracy and local governance bodies (56). The bylaws of the VO lists under members' duties, "working on uncovering reactionaries, the enemies of socialism, elements of corruption, and opportunists in their place of work and residence" (177). At one point, Al-Ashwah discloses that the VO sent affiliates to East Germany for months-long educational programs to "train them in political work and develop their leadership skills" (56).

108. Hamroush cites evidence in support of this argument. Hamroush, *Thawrat 23 Yulyu*, 621–22.

109. Khalil Abdel-Karim, who heard the story firsthand from Salah Eissa, recounts it in Rifaat Al-Said, Adel Hussein, Mohamed Said Ashmawy, et al., *Al-Muwajahah hawl al-Iʿtidal wa-l-Tataruf bayn Rifʿat al-Saʿid wa ʿAdil Husayn* (Dimishq: Dar al-Taliʿah al-Jadidah, 1996), 98.

110. This list was compiled from Sharaf, "ʿAbd al-Nasir wa-l-Tanzim al-Siyasy." Yousef Wali's collaboration with the VO is cited in Belal Fadl, "Aan Al-Awan Tarjaʿiy ya Dawlat Al-Jawasis (5)," *Mada Masr*, November 2, 2014, https://www.madamasr.com /ar/2014/11/02/opinion/politics/آن-الأوان-ترجعي-يا-دولة-الجواسيس-الحلق.

111. Sami Sharaf told Abdullah Imam in an interview that membership in the VO was an important consideration (albeit not a perquisite) in the selection of candidates for ministerial and governorship posts. It is unclear how that standard evolved in the post-Nasser era. Imam, *ʿAbd al-Nasir*, 198.

112. All of these names appear in Sharaf, "ʿAbd al-Nasir wa-l-Tanzim al-Siyasy," except for Gamal Badawi and Adel Hussein. Badawi is identified as a VO member in Hosni, *ʿAbd al-Nasir wa-l-Tanzim*, 52. Rifaat Al-Said identified Adel Hussein as a member in his own VO cell in Rifaat Al-Said, "Musalsal Al-Jamaʿah (2) . . . Al-Bahth ʿan al-Haq-iqah fi Kumat Qash," *Al-Ahaly*, July 5, 2017, http://webcache.googleusercontent.com /search?q=cache:u4wxCK-w-s0J:alahalygate.com/archives/60571+&cd=11&hl=en& ct=clnk&gl=us&client=safari.

113. For cursory discussion of these issues, see Sallam, "From the State of Vanguards."

114. Hamada Hosni asserts that attempts to recruit imprisoned Muslim Brotherhood fig-ures for the VO failed. He also reports that judges seeking to maintain their indepen-dence from Nasser offered strong resistance to the efforts of VO recruits inside the judiciary. Hosni, *ʿAbd al-Nasir wa-l-Tanzim*, 62; 111–44. Although some claim a VO pres-ence in the army, Kandil reports that Field Marshal Abdel-Hakim Amer gave orders to keep the VO out of the army. Kandil, *Soldiers, Spies*, 59. Adel Al-Ashwah's detailed outline of the organizational structure of the VO and its presence inside various state bodies makes no mention of the army. Al-Ashwah, *Haqiqat al-Tanzim*, 49.

115. Hosni, *ʿAbd al-Nasir wa-l-Tanzim*, 52.

116. The memberships of Gallab, Abdallah, Shokr, and Shafiq are reported in Hosni, *ʿAbd al-Nasir wa-l-Tanzim*, 55–57; Saadeddin acknowledges his own membership in *Shuhud Thawrat Yulyu*, 22; and Fouad Morsi's membership is disclosed in Sharaf, "ʿAbd al-Nasir wa-l-Tanzim al-Siyasy"; Hetata's membership is mentioned in Ismael and El-Saʿid, *The Communist Movement*, 123.

117. Gallab and Mahmoud Al-Maraghi, both former affiliates of the VO, served as *Al-Ahaly*'s editor in chief when Al-Tagammu sought to make the newspaper's editorial line more friendly to the regime.

118. Gervasio, *Al-Harakah al-Markisiyya*, 265.

119. Gervasio, *Al-Harakah al-Markisiyya*, 335.

120. Gervasio, *Al-Harakah al-Markisiyya*, 323.

121. Gervasio, *Al-Harakah al-Markisiyya*, 373.

122. Gervasio acknowledges repression as a significant factor shaping the trajectory of the communist movement in the 1970s: "Finally, any analysis of the radical left must not forget that the parties that were analyzed were all underground and sub-ject to harsh and persistent repression from the security bodies. This basic real-ity does not justify in any case the inability of the "revolutionary" intellectuals to address the masses, but it is a crucial factor if we want to assess objectivity and in a

balanced manner the movement and the intellectual production of this important phase of Egyptian Marxism." Gervasio, *Al-Harakah al-Markisiyya*, 363.

123. A smaller contingent consisting of CPE-Hadeto remnants opposing the dissolution decision was known as the Revolutionary Current. This group would later become the Democratic Communist Party. Al-Said, *Al-Tayarat al-Siyasiyya*, 82. Talaat Romiah asserts that, unlike other "third wave" communist organizations, the Revolutionary Current had no clear organizational structures. Romiah, *Ma'ziq al-Harakah al-Shiu'iyya*, 38. Kamal Khalil notes that the Revolutionary Current had a "nominal presence" at Cairo University starting in 1973. Kamal Khalil, *Hikayat min Zaman Fat: Sirah Dhatiyya min khilal al-Ahdath* (Al-Jizah: Bayt al-Yasmin li-l-Nashr wa-l-Tawzi', 2012), 116.

124. See Rozza's account in Asem Al-Desouki, *'Ummal wa Tulab fi-l-Harakah al-Wataniyya Al-Misriyya: Nadwa 'an Shahadat wa Ru'y Abtal Harakat al-'Ummal wa-l-Talabah, 1946–1977* (Al-Qahirah: Dar al-Mahrusah, 1998), 174.

125. Kamal Khalil provides a list of groups and formations active at Cairo University between 1972 and 1976. In the 1972–73 academic year, the two active communist groups at Cairo University were Al-Sherouk and the COE, the precursors to the CPE and the WCP, respectively. In 1973–74, in addition to the CPE and the WCP, January 8, Al-Matraqqah, and the Revolutionary Current became active on campus. In 1974–75, in addition to the CPE, WCP, January 8, and Al-Matraqqah, the Trotskyist circle was active on campus. In 1975–76, Al-Mutammar, one of the groups that defected from the CPE surfaced on campus. Khalil, *Hikayat min Zaman Fat*, 116.

126. Said Al-Olaimy, "Sirah Dhatiyya li-Shiu'y Misry, Qad Ta'ny aw la Ta'ny Ahadan, Hizb al-'Ummal al-Shiu'y, al-Qism al-Thany," *Al-Hewar Al-Mutamadin*, July 13, 2018, https://www.ahewar.org/debat/show.art.asp?aid=605184.

127. Gervasio, *Al-Harakah al-Markisiyya*, 335.

128. Al-Mirghani, a former member of the WCP and a Cairo University graduate, disputes Gervasio's claim that the WCP was involved in the Club for Progressive Socialist Thought. Ilhamy Al-Mirghani, "Ru'yat Jinaru li-l-Harakah al-Markasiyya al-Thalitha fi Misr," *Al-Hewar Al-Mutamadin*, December 6, 2010, https://www.ahewar.org/debat/show.art.asp?aid=237321. Gervasio, *Al-Harakah al-Markisiyya*, 335. It is worth mentioning that Prime Minister Mamdouh Salem's parliamentary address following the January 1977 Bread Uprising implied that the WCP was involved the Club's November 1976 march to parliament. See his remarks in Hussein Abdel-Razek, *Misr fi 18 wa 19 Yanayir* (Al-Qahirah: Dar Al-Kalimah, 1985), 149.

129. Gervasio, *Al-Harakah al-Markisiyya*, 351.

130. Gervasio, *Al-Harakah al-Markisiyya*, 324–25.

131. Much credit is due to Gennaro Gervasio for unearthing a wealth of data on the previously underexplored experience of the WCP and to Said Al-Olaimy for making available an incredible amount of information about the WCP, including his own account, and those of former party leaders. Gervasio, *Al-Harakah al-Markisiyya*. See Al-Olaimy's page on Al-Hewar Al-Mutamadin, accessed March 5, 2021, https://www.ahewar.org/m.asp?i=5022.

132. See former WCP activist Salah Al-Amrousy's remarks in Al-Olaimy, "Sirah Dhatiyya li-Shiuʿy Misry, Qad Taʿny aw la Taʿny Ahadan, Hizb al-ʿUmmal al-Shiuʿy, al-Qism al-Thany." Even Rifaat Al-Said, whose account of the 1970s communist movement tends to be unflattering to organizations outside of the CPE, acknowledges the important role the WCP played in the 1972–73 student uprising. Al-Said, *Al-Tayarat al-Siyasiyya*, 84.

133. The party's bylaws (first produced in 1970 and amended in 1983) were published online by Said Al-Olaimy. Said Al-Olaimy, "Laʾihat Hizb al-ʿUmmal al-Shiuʿy," *Al-Hewar Al-Mutamadin*, June 24, 2020, https://www.ahewar.org/debat/show.art.asp?aid=682295.

134. See Salah Al-Amrousy's testimony in Al-Olaimy, "Sirah Dhatiyya li-Shiuʿy Misry, Qad Taʿny aw la Taʿny Ahadan, Hizb al-ʿUmmal al-Shiuʿy, al-Qism al-Thany."

135. See, for example, Abul-Ezz Al-Hariri's account in Al-Desouki, *ʿUmmal wa Tulab fi-l-Harakah al-Wataniyya Al-Misriyya*, 178–79. According to Mohamed Abdel-Salam Al-Zayyat, Sadat told an Egyptian Trade Union Federation (ETUF) gathering, "If one or two communists found their way into the ETUF, I ask you to purge your ranks of them without my intervention." Mohamed Abdel-Salam Al-Zayyat, *Al-Sadat al-Qinaʿ wa-l-Haqiqah* (Al-Qahirah: Kitab al-Ahaly, 1989), 210.

136. Salah Al-Amrousy's account appears in Al-Olaimy, "Sirah Dhatiyya li-Shiuʿy Misry, Qad Taʿny aw la Taʿny Ahadan, Hizb al-ʿUmmal al-Shiuʿy, al-Qism al-Thany."

137. Rifaat Al-Said discusses this problem in the context of Al-Tagammu, indicating that the regime was aware of the party's eagerness to recruit labor elements and thus would often plant workers inside the organization as moles. Al-Said, *Mujarad Dhikrayat*, 108–9.

138. Al-Olaimy, "Sirah Dhatiyya li-Shiuʿy Misry, Qad Taʿny aw la Taʿny Ahadan, Hizb al-ʿUmmal al-Shiuʿy, al-Qism al-Thany."

139. Said Al-Olaimy, "Al-Tanzim al-Shiuʿy al-Misry Tshm," *Al-Hewar Al-Mutamadin*, June 3, 2019, https://www.ahewar.org/debat/show.art.asp?aid=639244. According to court records, at least one former defendant in the case later filed a lawsuit alleging torture during their time in prison. Mahkamat Al-Naqd. "Al-Taʿn Raqam 4046 li-Sanat 67 Qadaʾiyya," *Court of Cassation*, November 1, 2010, https://www.cc.gov.eg/judgment_single?id=111290541&ja=98121.

140. Said Al-Olaimy, "Sirah Dhatiyya li-Shiuʿy Misry, Qad Taʿny aw la Taʿny Ahadan, Hizb al-ʿUmmal al-Shiuʿy, al-Qism al-Thalith," *Al-Hewar Al-Mutamadin*, July 15, 2018, https://www.ahewar.org/debat/show.art.asp?aid=605365.

141. Khalil, *Hikayat min Zaman Fat*, 114.

142. Gervasio, *Al-Harakah al-Markisiyya*, 319.

143. A cable from the U.S. Embassy in Cairo states that the number arrested during these events was likely much higher than reported in the Egyptian press, perhaps reaching four hundred. Embassy Cairo to Department of State, "Telegram 00129," January 6, 1975, 1975CAIRO00129, Central Foreign Policy Files, 1973–79/Electronic Telegrams, RG 59: General Records of the Department of State, U.S. National Archives, https://aad.archives.gov/aad/createpdf?rid=124615&dt=2476&dl=1345.

144. For more on those arrested, see Abdel-Razek, *Misr*, 98–99.
145. The U.S. Embassy in Cairo reported extensively about a 1979 wave of arrests against communist activists, once describing it as "part of the pattern of periodic crackdown on the left." Embassy Cairo to Department of State, "Telegram 20510," October 4, 1979, 1979CAIRO20510, Central Foreign Policy Files, 1973–79/Electronic Telegrams, RG 59: General Records of the Department of State, U.S. National Archives, https://aad.archives.gov/aad/createpdf?rid=294588&dt=2776&dl=2169.
146. For more on the case and court proceedings, see Ahmed Nabil Al-Helaly, *Huriyat al-Fikr wa-l-ʿAqidah, Tilk Hiya al-Qadiyah: Murafaʿah Qanuniyya wa Siyasiyya fi Qadiyat al-Hizb al-Shiuʿy al-Misry* (Al-Jizah: Dar al-Misry al-Jadid li-l-Nashr, 1989). Fawzi Habashi writes in his memoirs that preceding the crackdown, CPE leaders rebuffed Sadat's request that they support his peace treaty. Fawzi Habashi, *Muʿtaqal kul al-ʿUsuur: Hayaty fi-l-Watan* (Al-Qahirah: Dar Mirit, 2004), 263–64.
147. Fawzi Habashi details these waves of repression in his own firsthand account in Habashi, *Muʿtaqal*, 247–67.
148. Gervasio, *Al-Harakah al-Markisiyya*, 337; 347; 351.
149. Shukri provides a useful summary of the steps Sadat took to undermine leftist journalists and media outlets. Ghali Shukri, *Al-Thawrah al-Mudadah fi Misr* (Al-Qahirah: Kitab al-Ahaly, 1987), 400–405.
150. Rifaat Al-Said describes the state pressures that led to the publication's suspension in October 1978. Al-Said, *Mujarad Dhikrayat*, 238–44. The publication would not officially return until May 1982.
151. See Prime Minister Mamdouh Salem's January 29, 1977, address to parliament in Abdel-Razek, *Misr*, esp. 148–53.
152. In one memorable incident, Sadat-allied writer Mustafa Mahmoud attacked Al-Tagammu leader Khaled Mohieddin for his article suggesting that socialist ideas were perfectly compatible with Islam. For Mohieddin's writings on the issue, see Khaled Mohieddin, *Al-Din wa-l-Ishtrakiyya* (Al-Qahirah: Dar al-Thaqafah Al-Jadidah, undated). For his exchanges with Mustafa Mahmoud, see Mustafa Mahmoud, *Limadha Rafadtu al-Markisiyya* (Al-Qahirah: Dar al-Maʿarif, 1984).
153. Shukri, *Al-Thawrah al-Mudadah*, 126.
154. Al-Tagammu leaders assert that many centrists friendly to the left were scared away by regime propaganda and repression (quoted in Gervasio, *Al-Harakah al-Markisiyya*, 309).
155. A central, spacious area in downtown Cairo.
156. Author interview, August 7, 2010, Cairo, Egypt.
157. Ibrahim Al-Issawi, "Al-Tajammuʿ fi Aʿqab al-Intikhabat al-Tashriʿyya: Naqd Dhaty wa Tataluʿ li-l-Mustaqbal," in *Hiwarat al-Yasar al-Misry: Min Ajl Nuhud Jadid*, ed. Abdel-Ghaffar Shukr (Al-Qahirah: Maktabat Madbuly, 2006), 46.
158. There were initially attempts to form a Nasserist *minbar* under the leadership of Kamal Ahmed, but ultimately Sadat rejected the idea. See Ahmed Al-Gammal's account of these events. Ahmed Al-Gammal, "Husayn ʿAbd al-Raziq al-Insan," *Al-Ahram*, September 6, 2018, http://gate.ahram.org.eg/daily/NewsQ/669616.aspx.

See, also, Kamal Ahmed's account in Alaa Al-Gaoudi, "Kamal Ahmad: Nazamna Mustabaqat Dumino ʿala al-Maqahy li-l-Hadith fi-l-Siyasah," *Al-Watan*, March 11, 2020, https://www.elwatannews.com/news/details/4635875. Some believe that Sadat wanted the Nasserist currents to join the centrist (ruling) platform, leaving the left platform openly Marxist, and thus easy to attack and discredit. Iman Hassan, *Wazaʾif al-Ahzab al-Siyasiyya fi Nuzum al-Taʿadudiyya al-Muqayadah: Dirasat Halat Hizb al-Tajammuʿ fi Misr 1976-1991* (Al-Qahirah: Al-Ahaly, 1995), 158. A prominent member of Al-Tagammu shares this assessment. Author interview, August 8, 2010, Cairo, Egypt.

159. For more on the currents that participated in Al-Tagammu Party's founding see Hassan, *Wazaʾif al-Ahzab*, 133–46.

160. Al-Said, *Al-Tayarat al-Siyasiyya*, 335; 339.

161. Sadat was particularly alert to the tensions between the party's CPE-affiliated and Nasserist elements. Thus, he tried to provoke the latter by alleging that the CPE was covertly controlling Al-Tagammu. For example, shortly after Al-Tagammu's formation, journalist and staunch Sadat supporter Musa Sabri claimed in an article that communist members were plotting to seize control of the party. "That cunning man," writes Rifaat Al-Said, "rubbed salt on two wounds. He rubbed salt on the wound haunting the consensual vision of Al-Tagammu, one that was averse to Marxists' control. Then he rubbed salt on the wound of Marxists' external associations and the historical controversies they arouse." Al-Said, *Mujarad Dhikrayat*, 142. Al-Said writes that Sabri revealed to him in a personal exchange that he wrote the article at Sadat's direction. Al-Said provides more background on Al-Tagammu's internal splits and divisions, in Al-Said, *Mujarad Dhikrayat*, 77–89.

162. Mohamed Mounir, "Wa Ma Nayl al-Matalib bi-Laʿn al-Ikhwan," *Al-Hewar Al-Mutamadin*, December 18, 2005, https://www.ahewar.org/debat/show.art.asp?aid=52643. Iman Hassan discusses these elements' participation in Al-Tagammu during the 1980s. Hassan, *Wazaʾif al-Ahzab*, 142–43.

163. Vickie Langohr, "Too Much Civil Society, Too Little Politics: Egypt and Liberalizing Arab Regimes," *Comparative Politics* 36, no. 2 (January 2004): esp. 186–88.

164. Text of the law is available on Mashurat Qanuniyya, accessed August 30, 2021, https://manshurat.org/node/1708.

165. Holger Albrecht, *Raging Against the Machine: Political Opposition Under Authoritarianism in Egypt* (Syracuse, NY: Syracuse University Press, 2013), 44.

166. Author interview, July 11, 2010, Cairo, Egypt.

167. Author interview, August 6, 2010, Cairo, Egypt.

168. Shaymaa Abdel-Hady, "Tajmid al-Ahzab . . . ʿArd Mustamir," *Al-Masry Al-Youm*, January 8, 2006, https://www.almasryalyoum.com/news/details/2188382.

169. See discussion of PPC in Tamir Moustafa, *The Struggle for Constitutional Power: Law, Politics, and Economic Development in Egypt* (New York: Cambridge University Press, 2007), 95–96.

170. Al-Bayan, "Al-Hukumah Al-Misriyya Tujamid Nashat Hizb Al-ʿAmal wa Tuʿaliq Sudur Sahifatih," *Al-Bayan*, May 21, 2000, https://www.albayan.ae/last-page/2000-05-21-1.1068098.

171. During the election campaign, Al-Ghad leader Ayman Nour, who was a candidate for president, criticized the president on several occasions, at a time when public criticism of Mubarak remained taboo.

172. Rifaat Al-Said devotes an entire chapter of his memoirs to the question of regime informants, recalling the security services' persistent attempts to place its agents within the ranks of Al-Tagammu: "Besides technological surveillance there was also the poisonous weed that was being grown in our garden. It was amusing to learn that most of such spies we were able to identify were trade union affiliated workers. Security agencies realized we were eager to bring in trade union leaders and incorporate them into our ranks. So, they sent us as many as our heart desired. And this was only the beginning of the cat and mouse game between the two of us." Al-Said, *Mujarad Dhikrayat*, 108–9.

173. Author interview, June 7, 2008, Cairo, Egypt.

174. Author interview, July 24, 2010, Cairo, Egypt.

175. See details in Al-Said, *Mujarad Dhikrayat*, 242–43.

176. Hassan, *Waza'if al-Ahzab*, 236.

177. Author interview, June 7, 2008, Cairo, Egypt.

5. Islamist Incorporation, National Identity, and the Left: A Tale of Two Comrades

1. Rifaat Al-Said, Adel Hussein, Mohamed Said Ashmawy, et al., *Al-Muwajahah hawl al-I'tidal wa-l-Tataruf bayn Rif'at al-Sa'id wa 'Adil Husayn* (Dimishq: Dar al-Tali'ah al-Jadidah, 1996), 13–14.

2. Conversely, in economics, "crowding out" often refers to the crowding out of private investments by government spending.

3. Nahid Ezzeddin Abdel-Fattah, *Al-'Ummal wa-Rijal al-A'mal: Tahawulat al-Furas al-Siyasiyya fi Misr* (Al-Qahirah: Markaz al-Dirasat al-Siyasiyya wa-l-Istiratijiyya bi-l-Ahram, 2003), 50.

4. For example, from 1977 to 1984, food subsidies increased from 10.9 to 18 percent of public expenditures. Gouda Abdel-Khalek and Karima Korayem, *Fiscal Policy Measures in Egypt: Public Debt and Food Subsidy* (Cairo: American University in Cairo Press, 2000), 71.

5. Bessma Momani, *IMF-Egyptian Debt Negotiations* (Cairo: American University in Cairo Press, 2005), 100. Between 1982 and 1986, the budget deficit to GDP ratio grew from 4 to 10 percent. Samer Soliman, *Al-Nizam al-Qawy wa-l-Dawlah al-Da'ifah* (Al-Jizah: Al-Dar li-l-Nashr wa-l-Tawzi', 2006), 62.

6. Abdel-Fattah, *Al-'Ummal*, 50.

7. Momani, *IMF-Egyptian Debt*, 96.

8. Abdel-Khalek and Korayem, *Fiscal Policy*, 55.

9. Robert Springborg observes that most of Sadat's power brokers were "put on the shelf" during Mubarak's first decade in office. Robert Springborg, *Mubarak's Egypt: Fragmentation of the Political Order* (Boulder, CO: Westview Press, 1989), 38.

10. Marsha Pripstein Posusney, *Labor and the State in Egypt: Workers, Unions, and Economic Restructuring* (New York: Columbia University Press, 1997), 184.

11. Soliman, *Al-Nizam al-Qawy*, 41.

12. According to Soliman, "The year 1986 marked a turning point for the Egyptian treasury. Petroleum prices dropped by nearly 50 percent, causing petroleum revenues to fall to $1.2 billion, down from $2.26 billion the year before, and Suez Canal revenues fell from $1 billion to $900 million. Egypt could no longer finance its imports. To make matters worse, Washington decided to hold back $265 million worth of aid until Cairo undertook the reforms prescribed by the IMF." Samer Soliman, *The Autumn of Dictatorship: Fiscal Crisis and Political Change in Egypt Under Mubarak* (Stanford, CA: Stanford University, 2011), 44.

13. Abdel-Fattah, *Al-ʿUmmal*, 51.

14. Author interview, July 17, 2010, Cairo, Egypt.

15. Momani, *IMF-Egyptian Debt*, 15. Momani reports that Mubarak told European officials that the proposed IMF reforms could "lead to a wave of unrest similar to that of 1977" (17).

16. See Abdel-Fattah, *Al-ʿUmmal*, 55.

17. Momani, *IMF-Egyptian Debt*, 14; 20. Soliman reports that the government consented to limiting public spending and liquidating loss-incurring public sector companies. Soliman, *Al-Nizam al-Qawy*, 54

18. Posusney, *Labor and the State*, 199. According to Abdel-Khalek and Korayem, the percentage of state spending devoted to food subsidies dropped during this period, from 18 percent in 1984 to 5 percent in 1991. Abdel-Khalek and Korayem, *Fiscal Policy*, 71.

19. As Soliman notes, no similar measures were implemented to offset the losses of the less organized (and hence less politically threatening) urban poor. Soliman, *Al-Nizam al-Qawy*, 78–82.

20. Soliman, *Al-Nizam al-Qawy*, 54.

21. Angela Joya reports that inflation reached 23 percent in 1986. Angela Joya, *The Roots of Revolt: A Political Economy of Egypt from Nasser to Mubarak* (Cambridge: Cambridge University Press, 2020), 73.

22. Springborg notes that the U.S. Agency for International Development, the IMF, and the World Bank coordinated their efforts to "exert pressure on Egypt to adopt policies consistent with the new orthodoxy of development in exchange for debt rescheduling." Springborg, *Mubarak's Egypt*, 259.

23. Posusney, *Labor and the State*, 185; 194–95.

24. Momani, *IMF-Egyptian Debt*, 29.

25. Momani, *IMF-Egyptian Debt*, 24.

26. For a summary of Egypt's worsening debt situation during that period, see Momani, *IMF-Egyptian Debt*, 28–31.

27. Momani, *IMF-Egyptian Debt*, 33.

28. Posusney, *Labor and the State*, 210–11.

29. Galal A. Amin, *Egypt's Economic Predicament: A Study in the Interaction of External Pressure, Political Folly, and Social Tension in Egypt, 1960-1990* (Leiden, The Netherlands: Brill, 1995), 33.

30. Posusney, *Labor and the State*, 211.

31. Momani, *IMF-Egyptian Debt*, 34.

32. Momani, *IMF-Egyptian Debt*, 37-38.

33. Ragui Assaad, "The Effects of Public Sector Hiring and Compensation Policies on the Egyptian Labor Market" (Economic Research Forum Working Paper No. 9517, Cairo, Egypt, 1995), 80.

34. Joya, *The Roots of Revolt*, 196.

35. Maryse Louis, Alia El Mahdy, and Heba Handoussa, "Foreign Direct Investment in Egypt," in *Investment Strategies in Emerging Markets*, ed. Saul Estrin and Kalus E. Meyer (Northampton, UK: Edward Elgar, 2004), 53.

36. Privatization Coordination Support Unit (PCSU), *Privatization in Egypt Quarterly Review April-June 2002* (Cairo: CARNA Corporation, 2002), 28.

37. Joel Beinin, *Justice for All: The Struggle for Worker Rights in Egypt* (Washington, DC: Solidarity Center, 2010), 13-14. See, also, Amr Adly, *Cleft Capitalism: The Social Origins of Failed Market Making in Egypt* (Stanford, CA: Stanford University Press, 2020), 111-16.

38. For more on the evolution and state containment of labor opposition to privatization, see Posusney, *Labor and the State*, 223-37.

39. Beinin, *Justice for All*, 47-48.

40. Beinin, *Justice for All*, 28.

41. This is not to deny the periodic expressions of opposition to these reforms by various stakeholders, including public sector labor and state bureaucrats. The issue of concern is why these expressions have failed to leave their mark on national politics and opposition parties.

42. Al-Sananiri's death causes antiregime resentment among Brotherhood members to this day. Security officials claimed that Al-Sananiri committed suicide in his prison cell. See, for example, Fouad Allam's account in Khaled Soliman, *Dhikrayat la Mudhakarat: al-Luwaʾ Fuʾad ʿAllam Yatahadath* (Al-Qahirah: Dar al-Ahmady, 2007), 91-99. Many Brotherhood leaders reject such claims, alleging that Al-Sananiri died as a result of severe police torture. See, for example, Abdel-Moneim Abul-Fetouh's account in Hossam Tammam, *Shahid ʿala Tarikh al-Harakah al-Islamiyya fi Misr: 1970-1984* (Al-Qahirah: Dar al-Shuruq, 2010), 122-24.

43. For example, Muslim Brotherhood General Guide Omar Al-Tilmisani lamented the fact that Mubarak never met with him after assuming the presidency. Omar Al-Tilmisani, *Dhikrayat La Mudhakarat* (Al-Qahirah: Dar Al-Iʿtisam, 1985), 196-97. Minister of Interior Hassan Abu-Basha suggests that Mubarak permitted the Brotherhood to operate but ceased displaying the favoritism practiced by Sadat. Hassan Abu-Basha, *Fi al-Amn wa-l-Siyasah* (Al-Qahirah: Dar al-Hilal, 1990), 181; 186.

44. Huda Ragheb Awad and Hassanein Tawfiq, *Al-Ikhwan al-Muslimun wa-l-Siyasah fi Misr* (Al-Qahirah: Markaz al-Mahrusah, 1995), 181–82. Sources differ on the precise figures, as candidate affiliations did not appear on Al-Wafd's electoral list.

45. Mohamed Habib, *Dhikrayat Duktur Muhamad Habib: ʿAn al-Hayah wa-l-Daʿwah wa-l-Siyasah wa-l-Fikr* (Al-Qahirah: Dar Al-Shuruq, 2012), 254–60.

46. Awad and Tawfiq, *Al-Ikhwan al-Muslimun*, 346.

47. According to Mohamed Habib, the endorsement came at the encouragement of Parliamentary Speaker Rifaat Al-Mahgoub. Habib, *Dhikrayat*, 324.

48. Awad and Tawfiq, *Al-Ikhwan al-Muslimun*, 173–74.

49. Awad and Tawfiq, *Al-Ikhwan al-Muslimun*, 126.

50. See Abu-Ismail's account in Hassanein Koroum, *Al-Taharukat al-Siyasiyya li-l-Ikhwan al-Muslimin 1971–1987* (Al-Qahirah: al-Markaz al-ʿAraby al-Dawly li-l-Iʿlam, 2012), 86.

51. See chapter 2 for the economic considerations that rationalized this slogan.

52. Awad and Tawfiq, *Al-Ikhwan al-Muslimun*, 304–15.

53. Utvik employs this approach very effectively, using Muslim Brotherhood and SLP MPs' contributions to parliamentary debates on economic policies to elucidate Islamist economics. Bjørn Olav Utvik, *Islamist Economics in Egypt: The Pious Road to Development* (Boulder, CO: Lynne Rienner, 2006).

54. Awad and Tawfiq confirm this. Awad and Tawfiq, *Al-Ikhwan al-Muslimun*, 372. Mohamed Mahfouz Helmy (quoted in Mohsen Radi, *Al-Ikhwan al-Muslimun taht Qubbat al-Barlaman* (Al-Qahirah: Dar al-Tawziʿ wa-l-Nashr al-Islamiyya, 1990), 97), stated in a June 1987 intervention that the group planned to introduce laws for implementing Sharia, as did Mamoun Al-Houdaiby in an interview with *Liwaa Al-Islam* on March 19, 1988.

55. Awad and Tawfiq compiled the Muslim Brotherhood data using official legislative records. Awad and Tawfiq, *Al-Ikhwan al-Muslimun*. The data for other parties were provided in Ammar Aly Hassan, "Adaʾ al-Tahaluf al-Islamy fi Majlis al-Shaʿb khilal al-Fasl al-Tashriʿy al-Khamis," in *Al-Tatawwur Al-Siyasy fi Misr 1982-1992*, ed. Mohamed Safieeddin Khaarboush (Al-Qahirah: Markaz Al-Buhuth wa-l-Dirasat al-Siyasiyya, 1995), 113–60.

56. They also include motions that are neither value nor distribution based (i.e., "other").

57. These data were compiled from Awad and Tawfiq, *Al-Ikhwan al-Muslimun*.

58. This is consistent with Ammar Aly Hassan's assessment of the Islamic Alliance's performance in parliament. Hassan quotes SLP leader Magdy Hussein as follows: "The Labor Party is totally attuned to social issues, but its representation inside the [Islamic] Alliance was smaller compared to the Muslim Brotherhood. And the Muslim Brotherhood gives priority to other issues." Hassan, "Adaʾ al-Tahaluf," 159.

59. For a summary of Al-Gamal's objections, see the May 6, 1989, issue of *Liwaa Al-Islam*.

60. One notable exception was a set of questions submitted to the Ministry of Water Resources and Irrigation expressing concern over Ethiopia's reported plans to build a dam with the potential to limit Egyptian access to Nile waters—an issue that proved critical decades later.

61. See MPs quoted in Utvik, *Islamist Economics*, 165, and Mohamed Mahfouz Helmy's response to the government report on June 24, 1987, quoted in Radi, *Al-Ikhwan*, 103.

62. See Hassan Al-Husseiny's response to the government report in 1987, quoted in Radi, *Al-Ikhwan*, 109.

63. This observation is consistent with Mohamed Al-Taweel's evaluation of Brotherhood MPs' interventions on economic affairs. Al-Taweel, who argued that the Brotherhood's parliamentary bloc focused on removing barriers to private investments and upholding free market principles, laments that the government never responded to the group's vision for reform, even though its MPs advocated measures similar to those the IFIs imposed on Egypt years later. Mohamed Al-Taweel, *Al-Ikhwan fi-l-Barlaman* (Al-Qahirah: Al-Maktab al-Misry al-Hadith, 1992), 248.

64. See Mamoun Al-Houdaiby's January 9, 1988, response to the government address, quoted in Radi, *Al-Ikhwan*, 82–83.

65. See Saif Al-Islam Hassan Al-Banna's June 24, 1987, response to the government address, quoted in Radi, *Al-Ikhwan*, 93.

66. Al-Taweel, *Al-Ikhwan*, 332–34.

67. For summaries of these interpellations, see Awad and Tawfiq, *Al-Ikhwan al-Muslimun*, 380–82 and Al-Taweel, *Al-Ikhwan*, 135–47.

68. Brotherhood MPs' responses to government addresses frequently included critiques of emergency laws. See, for example, Mamoun Al-Houdaiby's June 3, 1987, response to the government report, quoted in Radi, *Al-Ikhwan*, 48. See, also, responses by Abdel-Azim Al-Maghrabi on January 24, 1988 (190) and by Saif Al-Islam Hassan Al-Banna on June 24, 1987 (92).

69. For a summary, see Al-Taweel, *Al-Ikhwan*, 149–65.

70. Ammar Aly Hassan notes that the Islamic Alliance's criticism of the Ministry of Interior in parliament tended to focus on abuses experienced by Islamist activists. Hassan, "Ada' al-Tahaluf," 146.

71. Awad and Tawfiq, *Al-Ikhwan al-Muslimun*, 379. See, also, Al-Taweel, *Al-Ikhwan*, 127–33.

72. The interpellation was mooted because the MP submitting the request was not present on the day it was scheduled. Awad and Tawfiq, *Al-Ikhwan al-Muslimun*, 380.

73. That assessment is shared across multiple sources. See, for example, Hassan, "Ada' al-Tahaluf," 156; Awad and Tawfiq, *Al-Ikhwan al-Muslimun*, 364.

74. These remarks appeared in an interview in the April 22, 1987 issue of *Akhir Saa*, quoted in Al-Taweel, *Al-Ikhwan*, 46.

75. See, for example, Mamoun Al-Houdaiby's January 9, 1988, response to the government address, quoted in Radi, *Al-Ikhwan* (72); Mohamed Mahfouz Helmy's June 25, 1987, response to the government address (97–98); and Mohamed Hussein Eissa's January 25, 1988, response to the government address (209–10).

76. Awad and Tawfiq, *Al-Ikhwan al-Muslimun*, 365.

77. Awad and Tawfiq, *Al-Ikhwan al-Muslimun*, 367; 401.

78. The issue arose during Nouh's interpellation. See the summary in Hassan, "Ada' al-Tahaluf," 148–49. During the same session, Mohamed Mahfouz Helmy submitted an

information request motion concerning the same issue. For details of the interpellation, see Al-Taweel, *Al-Ikhwan*, 214–22.

79. The four MPs in question are Ahmed Al-Bes, Abdel-Aziz Ashri Hassan Ghobari, Bashir Ibrahim Abdel-Fattah, and Ibrahim Abu-Taleb. Two other participants, Mohamed Habib and Ezz Al-Arab Fouad Hafiz, submitted only one additional oversight motion each during that parliamentary term.

80. Al-Taweel, *Al-Ikhwan*, 174–78.

81. Al-Taweel, *Al-Ikhwan*, 181.

82. Quoted in Radi, *Al-Ikhwan*, 56. MP Mohy Eissa reiterates Akef's same points in a response to a government address (148).

83. Al-Taweel, *Al-Ikhwan*, 195.

84. Al-Taweel, *Al-Ikhwan*, 195–96.

85. Al-Taweel, *Al-Ikhwan*, 196–97.

86. Al-Taweel, *Al-Ikhwan*, 197.

87. Al-Taweel, *Al-Ikhwan*, 201.

88. Al-Taweel, *Al-Ikhwan*, 46–47. Mamoun Al-Houdaiby reiterated this priority and discussed the legal codes prepared under leadership of Sufi Abu-Taleb. *Liwaa Al-Islam*, March 19, 1988.

89. Mohamed Hamed Abul-Nasr, "Risalah min al-Ikhwan al-Muslimun li-l-Raʾis Mubarak," *Al-Shaab*, February 17, 1987.

90. Abul-Nasr, "Risalah."

91. That viewpoint was also reflected in the editorial line of *Liwaa Al-Islam*, which often attributed economic problems to the absence of the "Islamic solution." See, for example, reports by Mohamed Abdel-Quddous on rising prices in the magazine's issues dated August 13, 1988, and March 9, 1989.

92. Following the 1987 election, Ismail Sabri Abdallah articulated this vision in a paper presented to Al-Tagammu's General Secretariat. Hussein Abdel-Razek, *Al-Ahaly: Sahifah taht al-Hisar* (Al-Qahirah: Dar al-ʿAlam al-Thalith, 1994), 457–58.

93. See, for example, Khaled Mohieddin's comments in Iman Hassan, *Wazaʾif al-Ahzab al-Siyasiyya fi Nuzum al-Taʿadudiyya al-Muqayadah: Dirasat Halat Hizb al-Tajammuʿ fi Misr 1976–1991* (Al-Qahirah: Al-Ahaly, 1995), 162.

94. This position was stated in the program produced at the CPE's first congress of September 1980. Tareq Y. Ismael and Rifaat El-Saʿid, *The Communist Movement in Egypt, 1920–1988* (Syracuse, NY: Syracuse University Press, 1990), 138.

95. Ismael and El-Saʿid, *The Communist Movement*, 141.

96. For discussion of the CPE's adoption of a combative stance toward Islamist groups at its third congress in 1992, see Rifaat Al-Said, *Al-Yasar, al-Dimuqratiyya wa-l-Taʾslum* (Al-Qahirah: Al-Ahaly, 1998), 44–46.

97. Hassan, *Wazaʾif al-Ahzab*, 311.

98. Hassan, *Wazaʾif al-Ahzab*, 166–67.

99. Al-Tagammu, *Barnamijna li-l-Taghyir* (Al-Qahirah: Al-Ahaly, 1993).

100. Rifaat Al-Said, *Al-Tayarat al-Siyasiyya fi Misr, Ruʾyah Naqdiyya: Al-Markisiyyun, al-Ikhwan, al-Nasiryyun, al-Tajammuʿ* (Al-Qahirah: Al-Hayʾah al-ʿAmah li-l-Kitab, 2002),

107–18; see also Rifaat Al-Said, *Al-Dimuqratiyya wal-Taʿadudiyya: Dirasah fi al-Masafah bayn al-Nazariyah wal-Tadbiyq* (Al-Qahirah: Al-Hayiʾah al-ʿAmah li-l-Kitab, 2005), 97–152.

101. Aziza Sami, "Rifaat El-Said: Which Way Will He Bend Next?," *Ahram Weekly*, July 7–13, 2005, http://web.archive.org/web/20141007182250/http://weekly.ahram.org .eg/2005/750/profile.htm. Al-Said elaborated on this line of reasoning: "Perhaps the most logical thing for the party to propose are non-radical, or partial, demands for immediate implementation, without ruling out the possibility of proposing a maximalist program as an ultimate demand . . . or, more accurately, as an ultimate ambition or even dream." Al-Said, *Al-Tayarat*, 122.

102. Hassan, *Wazaʾif al-Ahzab*, 151–52.

103. The view that Abdel-Razek led a radical Marxist faction is limited to Al-Tagammu's leadership circle and *Al-Ahaly*'s proregime critics. For Egypt's actual radical communists, he was merely a prominent member of a status-quo party.

104. For more on *Al-Ahaly*'s coverage of foreign policy issues, including peace with Israel and relations with Washington, see Hassan, *Wazaʾif al-Ahzab*, 164–65; 237–42. *Al-Ahaly* criticized government proposals to reverse post-1952 land reforms, and assailed the deterioration of state social services and rising prices, attributing such problems to economic liberalization policies. The newspaper also broke stories about unreported government plans to dissolve public sector enterprises and regime efforts to intervene in ETUF elections. Posusney, *Labor and the State*, 184–45; 116; 124; 143; 191.

105. On one occasion, state-owned media launched a fierce attack on *Al-Ahaly* when it published excerpts from Mohamed Hassanein Heikal's book *The Autumn of Fury*, which included a host of harsh critiques of Sadat. The regime also resorted to censorship, ordering the removal of controversial issues from newsstands. Abdel-Razek, *Al-Ahaly*, 141–43; 189–202; 280–84; 321–22.

106. Yehia Al-Gamal, one of the dissenters, argued that, as authorities had accused Abdel-Razek of membership in the Communist Party of Egypt, his appointment would be interpreted as a direct challenge to the regime. Abdel-Razek, *Al-Ahaly*, 104. Al-Gamal's assessment was not misplaced, as senior presidential aide Osama Al-Baz would later express his reservations about the appointment in a personal call to Khaled Mohieddin. Hassan, *Wazaʾif al-Ahzab*, 244.

107. The meeting was between Al-Tagammu leaders and *Al-Ahaly*'s editorial board.

108. Abdel-Razek, *Al-Ahaly*, 256–57.

109. Abdel-Razek, *Al-Ahaly*, 257.

110. Abdel-Razek, *Al-Ahaly*, 258.

111. Abdel-Razek details the rise of these divisions. Abdel-Razek, *Al-Ahaly*, 261–78.

112. In a 1987 memo he prepared for a party leadership meeting, Abdel-Razek elaborated on these divisions: "There are those who believe that the enemy and the main danger comes from extremist and violent religious currents, including the Muslim Brotherhood, the Islamic Jihad, and Al-Takfir Wal-Hijra, and from any potential military coups linked to these currents or to the right more generally. Accordingly,

they believe that our battle is not with the regime and the National Democratic Party—notwithstanding their responsibility for the growth of that current and its hatred of the left—and that we must seek to ally ourselves with the more rational wing inside the regime against the dangers of a military coup and against religious fundamentalism, as part of a broad national front |. . . .| And then there are those who believe that the main opponent is the ruling National Democratic Party." Abdel-Razek, *Al-Ahaly*, 462.

113. See remarks by Khaled Mohieddin and Rifaat Al-Said in Abdel-Razek, *Al-Ahaly*, 467–72.

114. Abdel-Razek, *Al-Ahaly*, 465–66.

115. Echoing a similar concern, Gouda Abdel-Khalek, a prominent economist who was then serving on Al-Tagammu's Central Committee, bluntly criticized *Al-Ahaly* and its seemingly pro-Soviet coverage of the war in Afghanistan, which, he thought, diverged from mainstream consensus on the subject. For a summary of a paper he prepared for a General Secretariat meeting convened in April 1987, see Abdel-Razek, *Al-Ahaly*, 453.

116. Abdel-Razek, *Al-Ahaly*, 457–58.

117. Abdel-Razek, *Al-Ahaly*, 462.

118. Abdel-Razek, *Al-Ahaly*, 500.

119. Abdel-Razek, *Al-Ahaly*, 506–7.

120. Abdel-Razek, *Al-Ahaly*, 507.

121. Abdel-Razek, *Al-Ahaly*, 508.

122. Quoted in Awad and Tawfiq, *Al-Ikhwan al-Muslimun*, 263.

123. Abdel-Razek, *Al-Ahaly*, 483–84; see, also, Gallab's remarks in Abdel-Razek, *Al-Ahaly*, 512–13.

124. Abdel-Razek, *Al-Ahaly*, 489.

125. The resolution read, "The existing authority represents the Egyptian bourgeoisie broadly speaking under the leadership of its large parasitic factions, and the bureaucracy. The large bourgeoisie and productive capital and middle classes with all their diversity exist inside of all the parties of the right: The National Democratic Party, the New Wafd Party, and the Tripartite [Islamic] Alliance. The National Democratic Party represents the leading party or the main adversary inside the ruling class coalition, by virtue of its control of state authority, and all decision-making institutions. This was confirmed by actual experiences since the founding of the National Democratic Party, including the last six years." Abdel-Razek, *Al-Ahaly*, 508.

126. In fact, Abdel-Rahman Al-Sharqawi quoted Mohieddin saying as much in a September 1987 article. Abdel-Razek, *Al-Ahaly*, 499.

127. Abdel-Razek, *Al-Ahaly*, 560.

128. Abdel-Razek, *Al-Ahaly*, 548.

129. Abdel-Razek, *Al-Ahaly*, 549. This expression conveyed the party's new priority of reforming the capitalist system to better serve the underprivileged rather than rejecting the current system in its entirely.

130. Abdel-Razek, *Al-Ahaly*, 554.

131. Abdel-Razek, *Al-Ahaly*, 537–38.

132. Abdel-Razek, *Al-Ahaly*, 539.

133. Abdel-Razek, *Al-Ahaly*, 564.

134. For example, in the summer of 1990, Al-Tagammu was among the parties proposing a new elections law to replace the ruling party's allegedly undemocratic legislation. Awad and Tawfiq, *Al-Ikhwan al-Muslimun*, 412.

135. Peaceful democratic change, the program argued, was the best means for achieving the party's long-term vision of socialist transformation. Iman Hassan, *Hizb al-Tajammuʿ* (Al-Qahirah: Markaz al-Dirasat al-Siyasiyya wa-l-Istratijiyya, 2005), 134.

136. Hassan, *Wazaʾif al-Ahzab*, 216.

137. Al-Tagammu, *Barnamijna*, 23–27. Al-Tagammu endorsed Mubarak's candidacy for a third presidential term on four conditions, including a reduction of the hardships imposed on low-income households by economic reform. Manar El-Shorbagy, "Al-Qadaya al-Dusturiyya wal-Qanuniyya fi Fatrat Riʾasat Mubarak al-Thaniyah," in *Al-Tatawwur Al-Siyasy fi Misr 1982-1992*, ed. Mohamed Safieeddin Khaarboush, 38–70 (Al-Qahirah: Markaz al-Buhuth wa-l-Dirasat al-Siyasiyya, 1995), 44. In an interview published in 1992, Philip Gallab stated that Al-Tagammu's program no longer upheld a socialist vision, focusing instead on managing the capitalist system and reducing the influence of parasitic capitalists seeking to undermine national economic development. Amr Abdel-Samie, *Al-Nasarah: Hiwarat hawl al-Mustaqbal* (Al-Qahirah: Maktabat al-Turath al-Islamy, 1992).

138. Khaled Mohieddin, Lutfi Waked, Mukhtar Gomaa, et al., *Lihadha Nuʿarid al-Hukumah* (Al-Qahirah: Al-Ahaly, 1991).

139. Hassan, *Hizb al-Tajammuʿ*, 100.

140. Al-Tagammu, *Barnamijna*, 21.

141. In fact, Al-Tagammu's MPs supported the government's controversial 1992 terrorism law, voicing only minor reservations. El-Shorbagy, "Al-Qadaya," 57–58.

142. Al-Tagammu, *Barnamijna*, 28.

143. El-Shorbagy, "Al-Qadaya," 44.

144. See, for example, Al-Said's September 15, 1995, interview with *Al-Watan Al-Arabi*, appearing in Rifaat Al-Said, *Did al-Taʾslum* (Al-Qahirah: Al-Ahaly, 1996), 209–17. See, also, Al-Said's 1995 debate with Adel Hussein, in Al-Said et al., *Al-Muwajahah*, 41.

145. See Al-Said, *Did al-Taʾslum*; Al-Said, *Al-Yasar*; and Al-Said et al., *Al-Muwajahah*.

146. See party statements quoted in Al-Said, *Al-Yasar*, 22–23.

147. Assaad claimed that members of the Egyptian Coptic diaspora channeled funds to Al-Tagammu during the 1990s and encouraged community members to subscribe to *Al-Ahaly*, presenting it as an advocate for the rights of Egyptian Copts. Gamal Assaad, *Iny Aʿtarif Kawalis al-Kanisah wa-l-Ahzab wa-l-Ikhwan al-Muslimun* (Al-Qahirah: Dar al-Khayal, 2001), 69. Rifaat Al-Said brushed off such claims, arguing that the party defended Egyptian national unity rather than Copts. Al-Said, *Al-Yasar*, 138. Whereas Assaad claimed that Al-Tagammu cynically exploited the plight of

Egyptian Copts for political gain, his detractors alleged that his criticism of the Coptic Orthodox Church and Pope Shenouda III provided ammunition to sectarian Islamist commentators. Ghali Shukri made similar insinuations, but without naming Assaad. Ghali Shukri, *Thaqafat al-Nizam al-ʿAshwaʾy* (Al-Qahirah: Kitab al-Ahaly, 1994), 247. Assaad has long believed that the church inappropriately sought to act as the principal political representative of Egyptian Copts. Gamal Assaad, *Man Yumathil al-Aqbat? Al-Dawlah? Am al-Baba?* (Publisher unknown, 1993).

148. Mohieddin offered these remarks in an address to Al-Tagammu's spring 1998 Central Committee meeting. Al-Said, *Al-Yasar*, 26.

149. See Hosni's remarks about this widely quoted statement in Abdallah Kamal, "Faruq Husny Yaftah Qalbah li-ʿAbdallah Kamal," *Donia Al-Watan*, November 23, 2003, https://pulpit.alwatanvoice.com/articles/2003/11/23/1154.html.

150. Salama Abdel-Hamid, "Salah ʿIsa, Nahayat Rihlah min al-Yasar ila al-Sultah," *Al-Arabi Al-Jadeed*, December 25, 2017, https://www.alaraby.co.uk/-حلة-من-اليسار-إلى-السلطة صلاح-عيسى-نهاية-ر.

151. Farouk Hosni's former aide Mohamed Abdel-Wahed described the events surrounding Eissa's appointment. Mohamed Abdel-Wahed, *Muthaqafun taht al-Talab* (Al-Qahirah: Dar Ghirnatah, 2005), 79–90; 323–25.

152. Reuters, "Wafat al-Katib al-Misry Mahmud Amin al-ʿAlim," Reuters, January 10, 2009, https://www.reuters.com/article/oegen-egypt-writer-at1-idARACAE5090OP20090110.

153. Ayaa Al-Meleegy, "10 Maʿlumat ʿan Aminah Shafiq baʿd Takrimaha fi Hafl al-Um al-Mithaliyah," *Honna*, March 21, 2018, https://honna.elwatannews.com/news/details/1958597/10--في-حفل-الأم-المثالية-صحفية-ارتدت-زي-الصياديين معلومات-عن-أمينة-شفيق-بعد-تكريمها.

154. In accordance with the constitution, the president was responsible for appointing a third of the upper house members.

155. Ahmed Ibrahim Al-Sherif, "Lutfy al-Khuly, Sahib Raʾy wa Katib Masrahy wa Qisasy wa Saniʿ Sinima," *Youm7*, March 23, 2021, https://www.youm7.com/story/2021/3/23/-لطفي5253984/الخولى-صاحب-رأى-وكاتب-مسرحى-وقصصى-وصانع-سينما.

156. Al-Said, *Al-Tayarat*; Al-Said, *Al-Dimuqratiyya*; Rifaat Al-Said, *Al-Libraliyya al-Misriyya* (Al-Qahirah: Al-Hayʾah al-Misriyya al-ʿAmah li-l-Kitab, 2007).

157. Quoted in Mohamed Farag, *Al-Tajammuʿ fi-l-Barlaman: Difaʿan ʿan al-Watan, Difaʿan ʿan al-Muwatinin* (Al-Qahirah: Kitab al-Ahaly, 2000), 91.

158. See, for example, the discussion of this in Abdel-Wahed, *Muthaqafun*, 156–57.

159. Hamdi Abu-Galeel reports that a Greek entrepreneur founded the company, originally named "Murvetli," (name transliterated from Arabic) in 1898. According to Abu-Galeel, the company was purchased in the 1970s by a group of investors that included Khaled Mohieddin and Rifaat Al-Said. Al-ʾAmal, he adds, was commissioned to print Ministry of Education, Ministry of Culture, Supreme Council of Culture, and various cultural and cinematic festival publications. He also states that Mohieddin's son Amin comanaged Al-ʾAmal. Hamdi Abu-Galeel, *Al-Qahirah: Shawariʿ wa Hikayat* (Al-Qahirah: al-Hayʾah al-Misriyya al-ʿAmah li-l-Kitab, 2008), 132–33.

160. Al-Said's remarks came in response to accusations of corruption leveled by Adel Al-Rifai, a former Al-Tagammu member. He claimed that Al-Tagammu used to own a share in Al-ʾAmal, albeit under the name of party leaders and their

associates. Al-Rifai alleged that in 1994 Al-Said and others bought Al-Tagammu out to seize control over Al-ʾAmal and its lucrative government contracts. Ramy Said, "Nanshur Nas Istiqalat ʿUdu bi-l-Tajammuʿ wa Yantaqid Mawqif Qadat Al-Hizb," Youm7, November 6, 2015, https://www.youm7.com/story/2015/11/6 /2426625/الحزب-قادة-موقف-وينتقد-التجمع-بـ-عضو-استقالة-نص-ننشر. Al-Said countered that Al-Tagammu never owned Al-ʾAmal and that Khaled Mohieddin bought out the other partners, including Al-Said's own brother, but he did not specify a date for the alleged transaction. Moataz Al-Khosousy, "Amin al-Tajammuʿ Yatahim al-Saʿid bi-l-Istilaʾ ʿala Matbaʿat al-Hizb," Sada Al-Balad, November 17, 2015, https://www .elbalad.news/1799952.

161. Quoted in Abdel-Razek, Al-Ahaly, 548.

162. Tariq Al-Bishri, Al-Harakah al-Siyasiyya fi Misr 1945-1953 (Al-Qahirah: Dar al-Shuruq, 2002), 476–77.

163. Younan Labib Rizk, Al-Ahzab al-Misriyya ʿabr Miʾat ʿAm (Al-Qahirah: Al-Hayʾah al-ʿAmah li-l-Kitab, 2006), 172–73.

164. A former associate of party cofounder Ahmed Hussein claimed that Nasser admitted as much in private. Author interview, June 10, 2008, Cairo, Egypt.

165. Amr El-Shobaki, Hizb al-ʿAmal (Al-Qahirah: Markaz al-Dirasat al-Siyasiyya wa-l-Istratijiyya, 2005), 22–24.

166. Author interview, June 10, 2008, Cairo, Egypt.

167. El-Shobaki, Hizb al-ʿAmal, 25.

168. El-Shobaki, Hizb al-ʿAmal, 27.

169. El-Shobaki, Hizb al-ʿAmal, 26.

170. El-Shobaki, Hizb al-ʿAmal, 30.

171. El-Shobaki, Hizb al-ʿAmal, 35.

172. Author interview, August 6, 2010, Cairo, Egypt.

173. According to both Ibrahim Shukri and Mamoun Al-Houdaiby, SLP and Brotherhood members discussed the possibility of forming a joint electoral list. The Brotherhood ultimately declined, citing Ibrahim Shukri's visit to Syria shortly after the regime killed thousands of Muslims, including members of the Syrian Muslim Brotherhood, in the city of Hama. Koroum, Al-Taharukat al-Siyasiyya, 56; 138.

174. Author interview, June 9, 2008, Cairo, Egypt.

175. Iman Noureddin, "Athar al-Inshiqaq ʿala al-Adaʾ al-Siyasy li-Hizb al-ʿAmal," in Al-Tatawur al-Siyasy fi Misr 1982-1992, ed. Mohamed Safieeddin Khaarboush (Al-Qahirah: Markaz al-Buhuth wa-l-Dirasat al-Siyasiyya, 1995), 351–52.

176. Hussein worked at the Center for Arab Unity Studies (CAUS), where he served as editor of the Center's journal Al-Mustaqbal Al-Araby. George Ishaq, Adel Hussein, Nahid Youssef, et al., Al-Faris Alladhi Marra min Huna: ʿAdil Husayn fi ʿUyun man ʿArafuh (Publisher unknown, 2007), 9.

177. Rifaat Al-Said attributes Hussein's intellectual transformation to his involvement at CAUS; quoted in Amr Abdel-Samie, Baʿd min Dhikrayat (Al-Qairah: Sama li-l-Nashr wa-l-Tawziʿ, 2016), 368–69.

178. For an example of this cynical perspective, see Khalil Abdel-Karim's contribution to Al-Said et al., Al-Muwajahah, 89–111.

179. Galal Amin, "Hadha al-Nabil fi Markisiyyatihi wa Islamihi," *Al-Araby*, April 8, 2001.
180. Adel Hussein, *Al-Iqtisad al-Misry min al-Istiqlal ila al-Tabʿiyya* (Bayrut: Dar al-Kalimah, 1981), fn97, 943–44.
181. Hussein, *Al-Iqtisad al-Misry*, 773–84. This perspective was clearly articulated in the last study Hussein published before passing away in 2001. Adel Hussein, *Al-Istiqlal al-Watany wa-l-Qawmy* (Al-Qahirah: al-Markaz al-ʿAraby Li-l-Dirasat, 2004), esp. 13–21. See, also, Adel Hussein, *Al-Tanmiyah al-Ijtimaʿiyya bi-l-Gharb? Am bi-l-Islam?* (Al-Qahirah: Nahdat Misr, 1999).
182. Author interview, June 9, 2008, Cairo, Egypt.
183. Author interview, June 10, 2008, Cairo, Egypt.
184. Author interview, August 6, 2010, Cairo, Egypt.
185. Noureddin, "Athar," 352; 357.
186. Koroum, *Al-Taharukat al-Siyasiyya*, 140–41.
187. Author interview, August 6, 2010, Cairo, Egypt.
188. Koroum, *Al-Taharukat al-Siyasiyya*, 142.
189. Shukri claimed after said meeting he contacted Khaled Mohieddin, inviting Al-Tagammu to join the alliance. Koroum, *Al-Taharukat al-Siyasiyya*, 143. Yet Shukri's actions show that this supposed invitation was issued in bad faith, because Al-Tagammu was never included in the initial talks and the invitation was extended only after the SLP had already reached an agreement with the Brotherhood and the LSP over the division of seats. One SLP leader claims that upon hearing of the talks, Mohieddin said, "It seems that Ibrahim [Shukri] is not taking us into account." Author interview, August 6, 2010, Cairo, Egypt.
190. Ibrahim Khalil, "ʿAsifah fi Hizb al-ʿAmal bi-Sabab al-Tahaluf maʿa al-Ikhwan," *Rose Al-Yousef*, February 17, 1987.
191. Akhir Saʿa, "Asrar Safqat al-Tahaluf Yakshufha al-Mafsulun min Hizb al-ʿAmal," *Akhir Saʿa*, April 22, 1987.
192. Awad and Tawfiq, *Al-Ikhwan al-Muslimun*, 313.
193. Khalil, "ʿAsifah"; Awad and Tawfiq, *Al-Ikhwan al-Muslimun*, 274.
194. Noureddin, "Athar," 352–55; 359–60.
195. The defecting MPs remained in parliament and formed a separate caucus. According to Gamal Assaad Abdel-Malak, Mubarak made attempts to coopt defecting members. For example, the president appointed Mamdouh Qenawy to the Shura Council. Gamal Assaad Abdel-Malak, "Shahid ʿala al-ʿAsr (18) Maʾsat Inshiqaq al-ʿAmal wa-l-Sidq al-Mustankar fi-l-Tajammuʿ," *ElMashhad*, September 11, 2020, https://www.elmashhad.online/Post/details/127195/شاهد-على-العصر.

Conclusion: Reflections on the Legacies of Islamist Incorporation and the Post-Mubarak Politics

1. For an analysis of the challenges confronting the military during SCAF's rule and the military's response to these challenges, see Atef Said, "The Paradox of Transition to

'Democracy' Under Military Rule," *Social Research* 79, no. 2 (Summer 2012): 397–434. For more on the evolution of Egyptian politics between 2011 and 2013, see Adel Iskandar, *Egypt in Flux: Essays on an Unfinished Revolution* (Cairo: American University in Cairo Press, 2013); H. A. Hellyer, *A Revolution Undone: Egypt's Road Beyond Revolt* (New York: Oxford University Press, 2016); Amy Austin Holmes, *Coups and Revolutions: Mass Mobilization, the Egyptian Military, and the United States from Mubarak to Sisi* (New York: Oxford University Press, 2019); Jack Shenker, *The Egyptians: A Radical History of Egypt's Unfinished Revolution* (New York: New Press, 2016); and Neil Ketchley, *Egypt in a Time of Revolution: Contentious Politics and the Arab Spring* (Cambridge: Cambridge University Press, 2017).

2. See, for example, Mahmoud Gomaa, "Daʿwah li-Thawrat Ghadab Jadidah bi Misr," *Al-Jazeera*, May 19, 2011, https://www.aljazeera.net/news/reportsandinterviews /2011/5/19/ دعوة-لـ-ثورة-غضب-جديدة-بمصر.

3. For example, then finance minister Hazem Al-Beblawi acknowledged that the government's nominal interest in designating a maximum salary for state employees was largely the product of popular pressure, even though wage discrepancies in the state sector were, in his assessment, relatively small. Hazem Al-Beblawi, *Arbaʿat Shuhur fi Qafas al-Hikumah* (Al-Qahira: Dar Al-Shuruq, 2012), 31; 36.

4. For example, multiple lawsuits demanding the reversal of public sector enterprises' privatization were filed in the wake of the January 25 Revolution of 2011. Reda Mawi, "Misr: Daʿawy li-Istirdad Sharikat ʿAmah min al-Qitaʿ al-Khas," *BBC News*, June 7, 2011, https://www.bbc.com/arabic/middleeast/2011/06/110607_egypt_privatisation.

5. Imam Ahmed, "Inqadh al-Thawrah: al-ʿAskary Faqad al-Sharʿiyah wa Nahtaj li-Majlis Riʾasy Madany," *Masrawy*, December 17, 2011, https://www.masrawy.com /news/news_egypt/details/2011/12/17/97629/-فقد-العسكري-الثورة-إنقاذ-مدني-رئاسي-مجلس -الشرعية-ونحتاج-لـ.

6. Mohamed Hamdy and Mohamed Soliman, "Al-Taʾsisiyya: Shabab al-Thawrah Yuhathirun min Wadʿ Khas li-l-Jaysh wa Yuhadidun bi-l-Insihab," *Al-Watan*, August 11, 2012, https://www.elwatannews.com/news/details/36611.

7. Al-Bayan, "Al-Idrabat al-ʿUmmaliyya Tatasiʿ wa Tatajahal Tahdhirat al-Jaysh," *Al-Bayan*, February 17, 2011, https://www.albayan.ae/one-world/arabs/2011-02-17-1 .1386704.

8. Adel Al-Dargali, Nashwa Al-Houfy, Monir Adib, et al., "Al-Bishry Raʾisan li-Lajnat Taʿdil al-Dustur wa Ikhtiyar Ikhwany bayn al-Aʿdaʾ," *Al-Masry Al-Youm*, February 15, 2011, https://www.almasryalyoum.com/news/details/113986.

9. In what Nathan Brown and Kristen Stilt described as a "haphazard constitutional compromise," the SCAF promulgated a sixty-three-article Constitutional Declaration, despite the fact that the referendum gave the electorate the opportunity to vote on only nine amendments to the 1971 Constitution. Nathan Brown and Kristen Stilt, "A Haphazard Constitutional Compromise," *Carnegie Endowment for International Peace*, April 11, 2011, https://carnegieendowment.org/2011/04/11 /haphazard-constitutional-compromise-pub-43533. The March 30 Constitutional Declaration named the SCAF as de facto ruler of Egypt, handing it executive and

legislative powers (Article 56) until an elected president assumed office and a parliament was in session (Article 61).

10. As Mohamed Naeem notes, although observers often described Al-Bishri as an Islamist, given his role on the 2011 committee drafting constitutional amendments, that rather simplistic characterization ignores the complexity found in his intellectual production. Mohamed Naeem, "Tariq al-Bishry: ʿArrab al-Wataniyya al-Misriyya wa Tirkatuh," *Mada Masr*, March 18, 2021, https://www.madamasr.com /ar/2021/03/18/opinion/u/طارق-عرّاب-الوطنية-المصرية-البشري.

11. Scholar and founding member of the Egyptian Social Democratic Party Samer Soliman expressed this opinion at an April 2011 conference at Stanford University. CDDRL, "CDDRL Conference on Democratic Transition in Egypt," *Center on Democracy, Development, and the Rule of Law*, accessed April 22, 2021, https://fsi-live.s3.us -west-1.amazonaws.com/s3fs-public/Egypt_Conference_Report.pdf.

12. This point of view was articulated in a June 2011 statement jointly issued by seven Egyptian human rights organizations. CIHRS, "ʿAla Khatiy al-Thawrah al-Tunisiyya al-Dustur Awalan," *CIHRS*, June 8, 2011, https://cihrs.org/أولا-الدستور-التونسية-ة الثور-خطى-على . Shortly thereafter, the Muslim Brotherhood declared its opposition to altering the SCAF-designed transitional framework. Al-Quds Al-Arabi, "Misr: Al-Ikhwan Yuhadidun bi-l-Tasady li-l-Majlis al-ʿAskary Idha Wafaq ʿala Wadiʿ al-Dustur qabl al-Intikhabat," *Al-Quds Al-Arabi*, June 27, 2011, https://www.alquds.co.uk /ال-للمجلس-بالتصدي-يهددون-الاخوان-مصر.

13. Ahmed Hassan, "Tawaquʿat bi-Husul Ikhwan Misr ʿala al-Ghalibiyah fi al-Intikhabat al-Muqbilah," *Elaph*, October 29, 2011, https://elaph.com/Web/news /2011/10/692437.html.

14. For a text of the decree, see Dandarawy Al-Hawari, "Nanshur Nas Marsum al-Qanun al-Khas bi-Taʾsis wa Tanzim al-Ahzab al-Siyasiyya," *Youm 7*, March 28, 2011, https:// www.youm7.com/story/2011/3/28//السياسية-الأحزاب-وتنظيم-بتأسيس-الخاص-القانون-سوم مر-نص-نشر 378865.

15. Interestingly, this issue was raised in the court order dissolving the Freedom and Justice Party in 2014. Mohamed Al-Omda, "Haythiyat Hal al-Huriyyah wa-l-ʿAdalah," *Al-Watan*, August 10, 2014, https://www.elwatannews.com/news/details /536077. Additionally, despite pledges to bar such practices, election authorities ignored the use of religious slogans during electoral campaigns. See Mohamed Abul-Enein, "Li-l-Iflat min Dawabit al-Daʿayah: Lafitat al-Islam Huwa al-Hal Tuhit bi al-Hurriyah wa-l-ʿAdalah," *Al-Masry Al-Youm*, November 8, 2011, https://www .almasryalyoum.com/news/details/124427; and Camilia Maqroun, "Intihaʾ al -Jawlah al-Uwla min al-Marhalah al-Thaniyah wa Intiqadat li-l-Islamiyyin bi -Istiʿmal al-Din fi-l-Daʿayah al-Siyasiyya," *France24*, December 15, 2011, https:// www.france24.com/ar/20111215--السلفيين-المسلمين-الإخوان-التشريعية-الانتخابات-مصر السياسية-الدعاية-الدين-استعمال-انتخابية-حملة-الثانية-المرحلة. See also the Carter Center report on the 2011–2012 legislative elections. Carter Center, *Final Report of the Carter Center Mission to Witness The 2011–2012 Parliamentary Elections in Egypt* (Atlanta, GA: Carter Center, 2012), 131.

16. Stéphane Lacroix details Al-Nour and the Salafist Call's evolving relationship. Stéphane Lacroix, "Egypt's Pragmatic Salafis: The Politics of Hizb al-Nour" (working paper, Carnegie Endowment for International Peace, Washington, DC, November 2016), 6–10.

17. For example, a December 2011 Ministry of Justice report alleged that charities linked to Salafist political parties received hundreds of millions of Egyptian pounds from Arab Gulf donors. Khaled Mohamed Aly, "83 Milyun Dular Tamwilat Kharijiyya li-l-Ta'thir fi al-Intikhabat al-Misriyya," *Emarat Al-Youm*, December 15, 2011, https://www.emaratalyoum.com/politics/reports-and-translation/2011-12-15-1.445238. The Carter Center report on the 2011–2012 legislative election cites reports that certain parties have received funds from "charities that in turn have received foreign funding." Carter Center, *Final Report*, fn66, 131. Years later, when the Sisi regime was seeking to contain the influence of Salafist parties, progovernment commentators began to take seriously allegations that these parties were recipients of foreign funding. See Saeed Aly, Mahmoud Al-Emari, Ghada Mohamed Al-Sherif et al., "Masadir: Wafd Salafy fi al-Su'udiyya li-Tamwil al-Nur," *Al-Masry Al-Youm*, June 21, 2015, https://www.almasryalyoum.com/news/details/758574.

18. Amira Fouad, "Hamalat li-l-Salafiyyin wa-l-Ikhwan wa Nushata' al-Faysbuk Ta'yidan li-Ta'dilat al-Dustur al-Misry," *Al-Arabiya*, March 15, 2011, https://www.alarabiya.net/articles/2011%2F03%2F15%2F141681.

19. Istiftaa Misr, "Al-Natiyjah: Na'am bi-Nisbat 77.3%," *Referendum2011*, 2011, https://referendum2011.elections.eg/84-slideshow/155-result.html.

20. Heba Abdel-Sattar, "Manshit al-Hurriyah wa-l-'Adalah hawl Bandita Yuthir Mawjah min al-Sukhriyah wa-l-Hujum 'ala al-Ikhwan," *Al-Ahram*, January 21, 2012, https://gate.ahram.org.eg/News/162728.aspx.

21. Radio Sawa, "Al-Shurtah al-Misriyya Taqtahim Maydan al-Tahrir fi Muhawalah li-Fad al-I'tisam fih," *Radio Sawa*, April 9, 2011, https://www.radiosawa.com/archive الاعتصام-فيه-الشرطة-المصرية-تقتحم-ميدان-التحرير-في-محاولة-لفض/2011/04/09/.

22. Mahmoud Omar, Hind Ibrahim, and Mohamed Farghali, "Al-Ikhwan Yahshidun al-Ahaly li-Fad Idrab al-Mu'alimin bi-l-Munufiyya," *Al-Masry Al-Youm*, September 20, 2011, https://www.almasryalyoum.com/news/details/112297.

23. For General Guide Mohamed Badie's reaction to security forces' April 9, 2011, use of force to end the Tahrir Square sit-in, see Al-Ahram, "Murshid al-Ikhwan: La Safaqat Ma'a al-Jaysh wa Lan Nasmah b-il-Waq'iyah baynahu wa bayn al-Sha'b," *Al-Ahram*, April 13, 2011, https://gate.ahram.org.eg/News/59818.aspx.

24. Yasser Abu-Maaylaq, "Takhminat hawl Safqah bayn al-Jaysh wa-l-Ikhwan 'ala Hisab Maydan al-Tahrir," *DW*, May 26, 2011, https://www.dw.com/ar/حول-صفقة-بين-الجيش-والإخوان-على-حساب-ميدان-التحرير تخمينات/a-15109881.

25. See, for example, General Guide Mohamed Badie's comments on the October 2011 Maspero massacre in Youm7, "Murshid al-Ikhwan: Fulul al-Watany wara' Ahdath Masbiru," *Youm7*, October 12, 2011, https://www.youm7.com/story/2011/10/12 الإخوان-فلول-الوطنى-وراء-أحداث-ماسبيرو مرشد-/510960/. For background on SCAF's violent repression of protests, see Wael Eskandar, "Year of the SCAF: A Timeline of

Mounting Repression," *Jadaliyya*, March 9, 2012, https://www.jadaliyya.com/Details/24604.

26. The two sides fell out in the spring of 2012, resulting in the disqualification of Brotherhood leader Khairat El Shater's presidential candidacy and the dissolution of parliament. Eventually the military and the Brotherhood were able to find common ground and carve out an arrangement whereby the military ceded to the Brotherhood nominal control of the presidency and the civilian bureaucracy, and the Brotherhood committed to protecting the military's autonomy from civilian politics.

27. I discuss the distinctions between these two realms of politics in Hesham Sallam, "Post-Elections Egypt: Revolution or Pact?," *Jadaliyya*, February 10, 2012, https://www.jadaliyya.com/Details/25249. Joshua Stacher makes a similar argument about the SCAF's use of elections to "wear down popular mobilization and minimize the power it projected." Joshua Stacher, *Watermelon Democracy: Egypt's Turbulent Transition* (Syracuse, NY: Syracuse University Press, 2020), 67.

28. Salma Shukrallah and Yassin Gaber, "What Was Religion Doing in the Debate on Egypt's Constitutional Amendments?," *Ahram Online*, March 22, 2011, https://english.ahram.org.eg/NewsContent/1/64/8267/Egypt/Politics-/What-was-religion-doing-in-the-debate-on-Egypts-Co.aspx.

29. Omar Al-Hadi, "Muhamad Husayn Yaʿqub: Intasarna fi Ghazwat al-Sanadiq wa al-Balad Baladna wa-l-Shaʿb Qal Naʿam li-l-Din," *Al-Masry Al-Youm*, March 21, 2011, https://www.almasryalyoum.com/news/details/120575.

30. See discussion in Hesham Sallam, "Reflections on Egypt After March 19," *Jadaliyya*, May 31, 2011, https://www.jadaliyya.com/Details/24050. Throughout the transition period, the SCAF often invoked the legitimacy it allegedly garnered through the March 19 referendum to justify its problematic policies. For example, when faced with widespread November 2011 protests calling for the military to hand off power to a civilian-led interim council, Field Marshal Mohamed Hussein Tantawi repeatedly claimed in a November 22 speech that the SCAF was merely abiding by the people's wishes as expressed in the March 19 popular referendum and that it could not relinquish power before another national referendum. For a complete transcript of the speech, see Al-Ahram, "Nas Bayan al-Mushir Tantawy Radan ʿala al-Aahdath al-Jariyah bi-Maydan al-Tahrir," *Al-Ahram*, November 22, 2011, https://gate.ahram.org.eg/News/140523.aspx.

31. Shaaban Hediya, Nermin Abdel-Zaher, Mohamed Ismail, et al., "Al-Yawm al-Sabiʿ Yanshur Malamih Wathiqat al-Mabadiʾ al-Hakimah li-l-Dustur al-Jadid," *Youm7*, July 13, 2011, https://www.youm7.com/story/2011/7/13/-ملامح-وثيقة-المبادئ-الحاكمة-للدستور-الجديد-المجلس454325/ اليوم-السابع-ينشر-.

32. Some versions of the document also included guidelines for the selection of constituent assembly members.

33. Sami Sharaf named Al-Selmi, among others, as Vanguard Organization members at public universities. Sami Sharaf, "ʿAbd al-Nasir wa-l-Tanzim al-Siyasy," *Sanawat*

wa Ayam Maʿa Jamal ʿAbd al-Nasir, al-Juzʿ Al-Thany, accessed April 15, 2015, http://
hakaek-misr.com/yahiaalshaer.com/SAMY/Book-2-POLORG-XX.html.

34. Al-Selmi contextualized the process of negotiating supraconstitutional principles
in his book. Ali Al-Selmi, *Al-Tahawul al-Al-Dimuqraty wa-Ishkaliyat Wathiqat al-Mabadiʾ
al-Dusturiyya* (Al-Qahirah: Al-Masry al-Youmm, 2012).

35. See Article 9 in the November 1, 2011, version in Al-Selmi, *Al-Tahawul,* 175. Also see
Mohamed Abdel-Qadir, "Al-Karamah Yatahafaz ʿala Wathiqat al-Silmy wa Yatrah
Ruʾyatih li-l-Mabadiʾ al-Dusturiyya," *Al-Masry Al-Youm,* November 17, 2011, https://
www.almasryalyoum.com/news/details/126665.

36. This argument appears in a November 2011 statement by the Cairo Institute for
Human Rights Studies. Ahmed Mostafa, "27 Munazamah Huquqiyya Tatliq Mubadarat
al-Hal al-Wasat li-Inqadh Wathiqat al-Silmy," *Youm7,* November 4, 2011, https://www
.youm7.com/story/2011/11/4/27-منظمة-حقوقية-تطلق-مبادرة-الحل-الوسط-لإنقاذ-وثيقة-السلمى
/526995.

37. Hossam Al-Soweify, "20 Hizban wa Iʾtilafan Thawriyyan Yasharikun fi Jumʿat
al-Matlab al-Wahid," *Al-Wafd,* November 16, 2011, https://alwafd.news/-122648
20-حزباً-وائتلافا-ثوريا-يشاركون-في-جمعة-المطلب-الواحدالشارع-السياسي. Although the Muslim
Brotherhood publicly opposed the Al-Selmi Document in mid-November, Ali Al-
Selmi claimed that Freedom and Justice Party leaders participated in the drafting
and negotiating process until November 1, when they opted to boycott one of the
drafting committee meetings. Al-Selmi noted that the controversial Article 9 protecting the military's unusual privileges had not been introduced as of that date,
suggesting that the Brotherhood's opposition was unrelated to that particular
article. Al-Selmi, *Al-Tahawul,* 172–73.

38. See Lina Attalah, "The Draft Constitution: Some Controversial Stipulations," *Jadaliyya,* December 1, 2012, https://www.jadaliyya.com/Details/27520, 2021. Additionally, the Muslim Brotherhood turned a blind eye to allegations of atrocities
committed by military officials. See France24, "Egypt's Morsi Promotes Generals to Ease Tensions," *France24,* December 4, 2013, https://www.france24.com/en
/20130412-egypt-morsi-promotes-army-generals-tensions.

39. On fears surrounding the Brotherhood's control of state institutions, see Ziad
Bahaaeddin, "Ma Hiya Akhwanat al-Dawlah? Wa Limadha Nakhshaha," *Al-Shorouk,*
September 11, 2012, https://www.shorouknews.com/columns/view.aspx?cdate
=10092012&id=d8962c68-7416-4ce4-b733-672a9a1dc5e1.

40. For a summary of this perspective, see Mohamed Elmasry, "Unpacking Anti-Muslim
Brotherhood Discourse," *Jadaliyya,* June 28, 2013, https://www.jadaliyya.com
/Details/28855.

41. For more on the theme of contending visions of sovereignty in Egypt's 2011 "revolutionary situation," see Mona El-Ghobashy, *Bread and Freedom: Egypt's Revolutionary Situation* (Stanford, CA: Stanford University Press, 2021). For more on the
impact of the January 25 Revolution on popular political consciousness, see Paul
Amar, "Egypt," in *Dispatches from the Arab Spring: Understanding the New Middle East,*

ed. Paul Amar and Vijay Prashad (Minneapolis: University of Minnesota Press, 2013), 24–64.

42. Dalia Othman, "Al-Majlis al-Aʿla li-l-Quwat al-Musalahah Yuʿlin Idkhal 15 Taʿdilan ʿala Qanun al-Ahzab," *Al-Masry Al-Youm*, March 28, 2011, https://www.almasry alyoum.com/news/details/121914.

43. The following discussion is informed by *Jadaliyya-Ahram Online* joint coverage and analysis of the 2011–2012 legislative election, as compiled and edited in Hesham Sallam, ed., *Egypt's Parliamentary Elections, 2011–2012: A Critical Guide to a Changing Political Arena* (Washington, DC: Tadween, 2013). For a useful overview of leftist forces operating in 2011, as well as their origins, see diagram in Brecht De Smet, *The Prince and the Pharaoh: The Collaborative Project of Egyptian Workers and Their Intellectuals in the Face of Revolution* (PhD diss., Ghent University, 2012), 10.

44. Mohamed Ismail, "Rifʿat al-Saʿid: La Ahad Yastatiyʿ an Yuzahzihany min al-Tajammuʿ," *Youm7*, March 13, 2011, https://www.youm7.com/story/2011/3/13 /368818/لا-أحد-يستطيع-أن-يزحزحنى-من-التجمع-رفعت-السعيد-.

45. Mohamed Ismail, "Al-Tajammuʿ Yarfud al-Tazahur Yawm 25 Yanayir," *Youm7*, January 23, 2011, https://www.youm7.com/story/2011/1/23/342011/التظاهر-يوم-25-يناير-التجمع-يرفض.

46. Mohamed Abdel-Quddous, "Husayn ʿAbd al-Raziq wa-l-Munshaqun ʿan al-Tajammuʿ," *Al-Mada*, October 21, 2012, https://almadapaper.net/view.php?cat=1142.

47. Sallam, *Egypt's Parliamentary Elections*, 80–81. Many of the Democratic Left and Socialist Renewal elements subsequently left the SPA to form the Bread and Freedom Party. Ilhamy Al-Mirghani, "Intikhabat al-Riʾasah al-Misriyya wa Azmat al-Quwa al-Ishtirakiyya," *Al-Hewar Al-Mutamadin*, April 18, 2014, https://www.ahewar .org/debat/show.art.asp?aid=410909.

48. Sallam, *Egypt's Parliamentary Elections*, 23.

49. Sallam, *Egypt's Parliamentary Elections*, 13–17

50. Al-Ahram, "Iʿlan Taʾsis al-Hizb al-Ishtiraky al-Misry," *Al-Ahram*, June 18, 2011, https://gate.ahram.org.eg/News/84113.aspx. Some members of the SPE joined the SPA in October 2012. Iman Aly and Mahmoud Othman, "Aʿdaʾ min al-Ishtiraky al-Misry Tuʿlin Indimamaha li-Hizb al-Tahaluf al-Shaʿby," *Youm7*, October 7, 2012, https://www.youm7.com/story/2012/10/7/-المصرى-تعلن-انضمامها-لحزب-التحالف-الشعبى-وسكرتارية/808288أعضاء-من-الاشتراكى.

51. Hammam Sarhan, "Misr: ʿAqabat fi Tariq al-Tahaluf al-Al-Dimuqraty," *Swissinfo*, June 27, 2011, https://www.swissinfo.ch/ara/30538450/-طريق--التحالف-الديمقراطي--في-عقبات---مصر.

52. Sallam, *Egypt's Parliamentary Elections*, 102–4.

53. Al-Quds Al-Arabi, "Jumʿat Lam al-Shaml Karasat al-Inqisamat baʿd Insihab al-ʿAlmaniyyin Ihtijajan ʿala al-Shiʿarat al-Diniyya," *Al-Quds Al-Arabi*, July 29, 2011, https://www.alquds.co.uk/ا-بعد-الانقسامات-كرّست-الشمل-لمّ-جمعة.

54. Sallam, *Egypt's Parliamentary Elections*, 105–6.

55. Mohamed Al-Fiqi, "Al-Kutlah Badaʾat al-Harb ʿala al-Ikhwan," *Al-Shorouk*, November 3, 2011, https://www.shorouknews.com/news/view.aspx?cdate=03112011&id =10425738-3603-4d67-b86b-0d82506ecd2d.

56. Sallam, *Egypt's Parliamentary Elections*, 109–10.

57. Sallam, *Egypt's Parliamentary Elections*, 18–19.

58. Months earlier, the DWP announced that it would boycott the vote because emergency laws, antistrike laws, and military trials of civilians had rendered the political environment inhospitable to free elections. Sallam, *Egypt's Parliamentary Elections*, 14–15.

59. Sallam, *Egypt's Parliamentary Elections*, 106.

60. The 2012 lower house had 508 seats, ten of which were filled by presidential appointments. Sallam, *Egypt's Parliamentary Elections*, 136.

61. For full results, see Sallam, *Egypt's Parliamentary Elections*, 153–72. Results are also summarized in chapter 4 in El-Ghobashy, *Bread and Freedom*.

62. Some candidates ran without disclosing an official party affiliation or under a party affiliation other than their own, specifically the affiliation of the leading party in their respective coalitions. I rely, therefore, on each coalition's or party's self-reporting on how many candidates they fielded and, in the case of coalitions, what the share of each coalition partner was on the joint candidate roster. The RCA claimed candidates for 306 seats. It reported that most of the candidates belonged to the SPA with about thirty-two belonging to the Egyptian Current Party. Thus, the SPA contested no more than 274 candidates. Sallam, *Egypt's Parliamentary Elections*, 109.

63. The Egyptian Bloc claimed 412 candidates, half of them belonging to the Free Egyptians, 40 percent to ESDP, and 10 percent to Al-Tagammu. Thus, ESDP and Al-Tagammu ran about 165 and forty-one candidates, respectively.

64. The FJP reported fielding four hundred candidates for the lower house election. Gamal Essam El-Din, "Parliamentary Mix and Match," *Ahram Weekly*, October 27, 2011, http://web.archive.org/web/20111101135020/http://weekly.ahram.org.eg/2011/1070/fr1.htm. Al-Nour contested approximately 90 percent of the seats. Al-Wafd claimed 428 candidates in lower house races. Sallam, *Egypt's Parliamentary Elections*, 69; 90.

65. Additional discussion of this issue appears in Hesham Sallam, "Nasser's Comrades and Sadat's Brothers: Institutional Legacies and the Downfall of the Second Egyptian Republic," in *Egypt and the Contradictions of Liberalism: Illiberal Intelligentsia and the Future of Egyptian Democracy*, ed. Dalia F. Fahmy and Daanish Faruqi, 57–64 (London: Oneworld, 2017).

66. Guillermo O'Donnell and Philippe C. Schmitter, *Transitions from Authoritarian Rule: Tentative Conclusions About Uncertain Democracies* (Baltimore, MD: Johns Hopkins University Press, 1986), 59. Przeworski reiterates this point: "Political forces comply with present defeats, because they believe that the institutional framework that organizes the democratic competition will permit them to advance their interests in the future." Adam Przeworski, *Democracy and the Market* (New York: Cambridge University Press, 1991), 19.

67. See, for example, Michael Bratton and Nicolas Van de Walle, *Democratic Experiments in Africa: Regime Transitions in Comparative Perspective* (New York: Cambridge University Press, 1997); Jason Brownlee, "Portents of Pluralism: How Hybrid Regimes Affect Democratic Transitions," *American Journal of Political Science* 53, no. 3 (July

2009): 515–32; and Staffan I. Lindberg, ed., *Democratization by Elections: A New Mode of Transition* (Baltimore, MD: Johns Hopkins University Press, 2009).

68. Interestingly, exactly a year before the outbreak of the Arab Uprisings, scholars began to discuss the long-term negative effects of state-managed competition, or what Daniel Brumberg has characterized as "liberalized autocracy" in the Arab context. Daniel Brumberg, "Democratization in the Arab World? The Trap of Liberalized Autocracy," *Journal of Democracy* 13, no. 4 (October 2002): 56–68. Consider the following excerpt from a 2010 report issued by a U.S. Institute of Peace working group: "In the short term, state-managed political liberalization can provide one means of securing domestic political stability and security. However, in the long run, tactical liberalization does not endow parliaments with real authority or accountability. Nor does it offer an effective arena for negotiating social or identity disputes. At best, state-managed liberalization allows for cycles of liberalization and de-liberalization. Over time, these cycles widen the gap between society and the state, robbing regimes of what little legitimacy they once enjoyed. State-managed liberalization can facilitate regime survival, but at the cost of making regimes vulnerable to domestic social conflicts, internal succession struggle, and regional disputes." Daniel Brumberg, *In Pursuit of Democracy and Security in the Greater Middle East* (Washington, DC: U.S. Institute of Peace, 2010), 17.

69. See, for example, Andreas Schedler, "The Nested Game of Democratization by Elections," *International Political Science Review* 23, no. 1 (January 2002): 103–22; Marc Morje Howard and Philip G. Roessler, "Liberalizing Electoral Outcomes in Competitive Authoritarian Regimes," *American Journal of Political Science* 50, no. 2 (April 2006): 365–81; Susan Hyde, "The Observer Effect in International Politics: Evidence from a Natural Experiment," *World Politics* 60, no. 1 (October 2007): 37–63; Beatriz Magaloni, "The Game of Electoral Fraud and the Ousting of Authoritarian Rule," *American Journal of Political Science* 54, no. 3 (July 2010): 751–65; Staffan I. Lindberg, *Democracy and Elections in Africa* (Baltimore, MD: Johns Hopkins University Press, 2006); Daniela Donno, "Elections and Democratization in Authoritarian Regimes," *American Journal of Political Science* 57, no. 3 (July 2013): 703–16; Amanda B. Edgell, Valeriya Mechkova, David Altman, Michael Bernhard, and Staffan I. Lindberg, "When and Where Do Elections Matter? A Global Test of the Democratization by Elections Hypothesis, 1900–2010," *Democratization* 25, no. 3 (2018): 424–44.

70. Similar conclusions appear in Kim's analysis of the determinants of democratization. Kim observes that all other things being equal, prior experience with repeated multiparty elections exhibit a negative correlation with levels of democracy. Kim calls on scholars to "investigate mechanisms in which elections in non-democratic regimes negatively affect democratic qualities." Nam Kyu Kim, "Reassessing the Relationship Between Elections and Democratization," *International Political Science Review* 41, no. 3 (2020): 318.

71. Certainly, scholars have highlighted the stabilizing role that elections play in authoritarian settings. See, for example, Ellen Lust-Okar, "Elections Under

Authoritarianism: Preliminary Lessons from Jordan," *Democratization* 13, no. 3 (July 2006): 455–70; Lisa Blaydes, *Elections and Distributive Politics in Mubarak's Egypt* (New York: Cambridge University Press, 2010); Andreas Schedler, ed., *Electoral Authoritarianism: The Dynamics of Unfree Competition* (Boulder, CO: Lynne Rienner, 2006). They have not, however, adequately investigated the impact of authoritarian elections on subsequent regime "transitions."

72. Beesan Kassab, "Farewell to Worker Participation in the Management of the Public Business Sector," *Mada Masr*, September 17, 2020, https://www.madamasr.com/en/2020/09/17/feature/economy/farewell-to-worker-participation-in-the-managemen-of-the-public-business-sector/, 2021. Sisi's attempts to reshape the social pact speaks to a region-wide trend noted by Steven Heydemann. Since the advent of the Arab Uprisings, he observes, many authoritarian regimes in the region have sought to erect "repressive-exclusionary social pacts," as distinct from the more inclusive social pacts that prevailed in prior decades. Steven Heydemann, "Rethinking Social Contracts in the MENA Region: Economic Governance, Contingent Citizenship, and State-Society Relations After the Arab Uprisings," *World Development* 135 (November 2020).

73. See Amr Adly, "Ma baʿd al-Nasiriyya," *Jadaliyya*, March 18, 2014, https://www.jadaliyya.com/Details/30401/ما-بعد-الناصرية, and Amr Adly, "Ma baʿd al-Nasiriyya al-Juzʾ al-Thany," *Jadaliyya*, August 14, 2014, https://www.jadaliyya.com/Details/31100/ما-بعد-الناصرية-الجزء-الثاني.

74. See, for example, the summary of Sisi's 2018 public address marking the fifth anniversary of the June 30 protests in Al-Araby, "Al-Sisy Yaʿtarif bi Qaswat al-Ijraʾat wa Yatmasak bi al-Islah al-Iqtisady," *Al-Araby*, July 1, 2018, https://alarab.co.uk/بقسوة-الإجراءات-ويتمسك-بالإصلاح-الاقتصادي-السيسي-يعترف-.

75. Nathan J. Brown and Michelle Dunne, "Unprecedented Pressures, Uncharted Course for Egypt's Muslim Brotherhood" (working paper, Carnegie Endowment for International Peace, Washington, DC, July 2015), https://carnegieendowment.org/files/CP248-EgyptMB_BrownDunne_final.pdf.

76. See CNN, "Fi-l-Dhikra al-Sabiʿah, al-Sisy: 30 Yunyu Hafazat ʿala Hawiyat Misr min al-Ikhtitaf," *CNN*, June 30, 2020, https://arabic.cnn.com/middle-east/article/2020/06/30/egypt-president-30-june-al-sisi; and Sawt Al-Balad, "Al-Sisy: 30 Yunyu Qamat min ʾAjl al-Difaʿ ʿan al-Hawiyah al-Misriyya," *Sawt Al-Balad*, August 24, 2014, http://baladnews.com/?p=920.

77. See, for example, Al-Quds Al-Arabi, "Itiham Muham wa Sahafiyyin Misriyyin bi-Silat maʿa Jamaʿah Irhabiyya," *Al-Quds Al-Arabi*, November 29, 2019, https://www.alquds.co.uk/اتهام-محام-وصحافيين-مصريين-بصلات-مع-جم.

78. Mohamed Nassar, "Kayf Tahadath al-Sisy ʿan Tatwir al-Khitab al-Diny fi 16 Munasabah," *Masrawy*, January 28, 2020, https://www.masrawy.com/news/news_egypt/details/2020/1/28/1713739/-16-مناسبةكيف-تحدث-السيسي-عن-تطوير-الخطاب-الديني-في-.

79. Basil El-Dabh, "Ijraʾat Sarimah Did al-Tiktok fi Misr bi-Daʿwat al-Hifaz ʿala Qiam al-Usrah," *Tahrir Institute for Middle East Policy*, December 11, 2020, https://timep.org/عربي/إجراءات-صارمة-ضد-التيك-توك-في-مصر-بدعو.

Appendix I: The Theoretical Argument, Key Concepts, and Central Assumptions

1. Building on an existing scholarly consensus, I define "Islamist group" as any political organization whose stated policies and objectives are derived from the principle that Islamic values and traditions provide important guidance on matters of governance. For discussions of conceptual issues, see Carrie Rosefsky Wickham, *Mobilizing Islam: Religion, Activism, and Political Change in Egypt* (New York: Columbia University Press, 2002); and Jillian Schwedler, *Faith in Moderation: Islamist Parties in Jordan and Yemen* (Cambridge: Cambridge University Press, 2006).

2. This arrangement reflects Heydemann's definition of a social pact as "a set of [formal and informal] norms or shared expectations about the appropriate organization of a political economy." Steven Heydemann, "Social Pacts and the Persistence of Authoritarianism in the Middle East," in *Debating Arab Authoritarianism*, ed. Oliver Schlumberger (Stanford, CA: Stanford University Press, 2007), 25. Yousef describes the emergence of a "social contract" in the Middle East and North Africa during the 1950s and 1960s, as follows: "The welfare gains also helped cement an 'authoritarian bargain,' with citizens of the Middle East effectively trading restrictions on political participation in exchange for economic security and the public provision of social services and welfare." Tarik M. Yousef, "Development, Growth and Policy Reform in the Middle East and North Africa Since 1950," *Journal of Economic Perspectives* 18, no. 3 (Summer 2004): 91–115.

3. David Harvey explained the origins of the neoliberal turn thusly: "Towards the end of the 1960s global capitalism was falling into disarray. Serious recession occurred in early 1973—the first since the great slump of the 1930s. The oil embargo and oil price hike that occurred later that year in the wake of the Arab–Israeli war exacerbated already serious problems. It was clear that the 'embedded capitalism' of the postwar period with its heavy emphasis upon some sort of uneasy compact between capital and labour brokered by an interventionist state that paid great attention to the social (i.e. welfare state) as well as the individual wage, was no longer working." David Harvey, "Neo-Liberalism as Creative Destruction," *Geografiska Annaler: Series B, Human Geography* 88, no. 2 (2006): 149.

4. See, for example, Kenneth Benoit and Michael Laver, *Party Policy in Modern Democracies* (London: Routledge, 2006); Michael A. Bailey, "Comparable Preference Estimates Across Time and Institutions for the Court, Congress, and Presidency," *American Journal of Political Science* 51, no. 3 (July 2007): 433–48; Simon Franzmann and André Kaiser. "Locating Political Parties in Policy Space: A Reanalysis of Party Manifesto Data," *Party Politics* 12, no. 2 (March 2006): 163–88.

5. See, for example, Seymour Martin Lipset and Stein Rokkan, "Cleavage Structures, Party Systems, and Voter Alignment: An Introduction," in *Party Systems and Voter Alignments: Cross-national Perspectives*, ed. Seymour Martin Lipset and Stein Rokkan (New York: Free Press, 1967), 1–64.

6. See Octavio Amorim Neto and Gary W. Cox, "Electoral Institutions, Cleavage Structures, and the Number of Parties," *American Journal of Political Science* 41, no. 1 (January 1997): 149–74; Arend Lijphart, *Democracy in Plural Societies: A Comparative Exploration* (New Haven, CT: Yale University Press, 1977); and Arend Lijphart, *Patterns of Democracy: Government Forms and Performance in Thirty-Six Countries* (New Haven, CT: Yale University Press, 1999).

7. See Ellen Lust-Okar, *Structuring Conflict in the Arab World: Incumbents, Opponents, and Institutions* (Cambridge: Cambridge University Press, 2005); and Marsha Pripstein Posusney, "Multi-Party Elections in the Arab World: Institutional Engineering and Oppositional Strategies," *Studies in Comparative International Development* 36 (2002): 34–62.

8. I recognize that this simplification may not be applicable to every context.

9. Although this understanding of identity applies to the Egyptian case, I recognize that definitions of *identity* and of *identity conflicts* vary across contexts.

10. This formulation rests on two assumptions about Islamist groups: (1) they rarely adopt definitive positions on economic policies; and (2) when diverging from this pattern, they assume conservative, right-wing stances on issues of distribution. These assumptions are informed, of course, by the example of the Muslim Brotherhood in Egypt (see chapter 2) and are by no means universally valid.

Appendix II: Critical Junctures and Path-Dependent Institutional Patterns

1. Giovanni Capoccia and R. Daniel Kelemen, "The Study of Critical Junctures: Theory, Narrative, and Counterfactuals in Historical Institutionalism," *World Politics* 59, no. 3 (2007): 343; 348.

2. James Mahoney, "Path Dependence in Historical Sociology," *Theory and Society* 29, no. 4 (August 2000): 507.

3. According to Mahoney, "[I]n a path-dependent sequence, early historical events are contingent occurrences that cannot be explained on the basis of prior events or 'initial conditions.'" Mahoney, "Path Dependence," 511.

4. According to Capoccia and Kelemen, "[I]n institutional analysis critical junctures are characterized by a situation in which the structural (that is, economic, cultural, ideological, organizational) influences on political action are significantly relaxed for a relatively short period, with two main consequences: the range of plausible choices open to powerful political actors expands substantially and the consequences of their decisions for the outcome of interest are potentially much more momentous. Contingency, in other words, becomes paramount." Capoccia and Kelemen, "The Study of Critical Junctures," 343.

5. Capoccia and Kelemen, "The Study of Critical Junctures," 342.

Bibliography

Abdel-Fadil, Mahmoud. *The Political Economy of Nasserism: A Study in Employment and Income Distribution Policies in Urban Egypt, 1952–72.* Cambridge: Cambridge University Press, 1980.

Abdel-Fattah, Huda. "Qawaniyn Jihan, al-Bahth ʿan Dhaat al-Marʾah." *Al-Wafd*, March 1, 2011. https://alwafd.news/أة-المر-ذات-عن-البحث-جيهان-قوانين/20095-هى%20و%20. هو.

Abdel-Fattah, Nahid Ezzeddin. *Al-ʿUmmal wa-Rijal al-Aʿmal: Tahawulat al-Furas al-Siyasiyya fi Misr.* Al-Qahirah: Markaz al-Dirasat al-Siyasiyya wa-l-Istiratijiyya bi-l-Ahram, 2003.

Abdel-Ghany, Atef. *Muhamad ʿUthman Ismaʿil Yatadhakar: al-Wazir Aladhy Kalafahuh al-Sadat bi-Takwin al-Jamaʿat al-Islamiyya.* Al-Qahirah: ʿAtif ʿAbd al-Ghany, 2000.

Abdel-Hady, Shaymaa. "Tajmid al-Ahzab . . . ʿArd Mustamir." *Al-Masry Al-Youm*, January 8, 2006. https://www.almasryalyoum.com/news/details/2188382.

Abdel-Hakim, Tahir. *Al-Aqdam al-ʿAriyah: al-Shiuʿiyyin al-Misriyyin, Khamas Sanawat fi al-Sijun wa Muʿaskarat al-Taʿthib.* Bayrut: Dar Ibn Khaldun, 1978.

Abdel-Halim, Mahmoud. *Al-Ikhwan Al-Muslimun: Ahdath Sanʿat al-Tarikh: Ruʾyah min al-Dakhil, al-Juzʾ al-Thalith.* Al-Iskandariyya: Dar al-Daʿwah li-l-Tabʿ wa-l-Nashr, 2004.

Abdel-Hamid, Salama. "Salah ʿIsa, Nahayat Rihlah min al-Yasar ila al-Sultah." *Al-Arabi Al-Jadeed*, December 25, 2017. https://www.alaraby.co.uk/السلطة-إلى-اليسار-من-رحلة-نهاية-عيسى-صلاح.

Abdel-Hay, Ahmed, Khairy Omar, Abdel-Hafiz Al-Sawy, and Wesam Fouad. *Al-Muʿaradah al-Mustabahah.* Al-Jizah: Markaz Sawasiyah li-Huquq al-Insan, 2008.

Abdel-Khalek, Gouda. "Aham Dalalat Siyasat al-Infitah al-Iqtisady bi-l-Nisbah li-l-Tahwulat al-Haykaliyya fi-l-Iqtisad al-Misry 1971-1977." In *Al-Iqtisad al-Misry fi-Rubʿ Qarn, 1952-1977*, ed. Ismail Sabri Abdallah, Gouda Abdel-Khalek, and Ibrahim Al-Issawi, 363–402. Al-Qahirah: Al-Hayʾah al-Misriyya al-ʿAmah li-l-Kitab, 1978.

Abdel-Khalek, Gouda. "Al-Taʿrif bi-l-Infitah wa Tatawuruh." In *Al-Infitah: al-Judhur, al-Hisad, wa-l-Mustaqbal*, ed. Gouda Abdel-Khalek, 23–69. Al-Qahirah: Al-Markaz al-ʿAraby lil-Bahth wa-al-Nashr, 1982.

Abdel-Khalek, Gouda, and Karima Korayem. *Fiscal Policy Measures in Egypt: Public Debt and Food Subsidy*. Cairo, Egypt: American University in Cairo Press, 2000.

Abdel-Khaleq, Farid. *Al-Ikhwan al-Muslimun fi Mizan al-Haq*. Al-Qahirah: Dar al-Sahwah li-l-Nashr, 1987.

Abdel-Malak, Gamal Assaad. "Shahid ʿala al-ʿAsr (18) Maʾsat Inshiqaq al-ʿAmal wa-l-Sidq al-Mustankar fi-l-Tajammuʿ." *ElMashhad*, September 11, 2020. https://www.elmashhad .online/Post/details/127195/شاهد-على-العصر.

Abdel-Malek, Anouar. *Egypt: Military Society; the Army Regime, the Left, and Social Change under Nasser*. Translated by Charles Lam Markmann. New York: Random House, 1968.

Abdel-Meguid, Wahid. *Al-Ikhwan al-Muslimun bayn al-Tarikh wa-l-Mustaqbal: Kayf Kanat al-Jamaʿah wa-Kayf Takun*. Al-Qahirah: Markaz al-Ahram l-il-Nashr w-al-Tarjamah wa-l-Tawziʿ, 2010.

Abdel-Moaty, Abdel-Baset. *Al-Tabaqat al-Ijtimaʿiyya wa Mustaqbal Misr*. Al-Qahirah: Mirit, 2002.

Abdel-Nasser, Gamal. "Khitab al-Raʾis Jamal ʿAbd al-Nasir min al-Qasr al-Jumhury bi-l Qahirah ʿaqib al-Infisal." *Library of Alexandria Gamal Abdel-Nasser Archives*, October 16, 1961. http://nasser.bibalex.org/Speeches/browser.aspx?SID=1002.

Abdel-Qadir, Mohamed. "Al-Karamah Yatahafaz ʿala Wathiqat al-Silmy wa Yatrah Ruʾyatih li-l-Mabadiʾ al-Dusturiyya." *Al-Masry Al-Youm*, November 17, 2011. https://www .almasryalyoum.com/news/details/126665.

Abdel-Quddous, Mohamed. "Husayn ʿAbd al-Raziq wa-l-Munshaqun ʿan al-Tajammuʿ." *Al-Mada*, October 21, 2012. https://almadapaper.net/view.php?cat=1142.

Abdel-Razek, Hussein. *Al-Ahaly: Sahifah taht al-Hisar*. Al-Qahirah: Dar al-ʿAlam al-Thalith, 1994.

Abdel-Razek, Hussein. *Misr fi 18 wa 19 Yanayir*. Al-Qahirah: Dar Al-Kalimah, 1985.

Abdel-Samie, Amr. *Al-Nasarah: Hiwarat hawl al-Mustaqbal*. Al-Qahirah: Maktabat al-Turath al-Islamy, 1992.

Abdel-Samie, Amr. *Baʿd min Dhikrayat*. Al-Qairah: Sama li-l-Nashr wa-l-Tawziʿ, 2016.

Abdel-Sattar, Heba. "Manshit al-Hurriyah wa-l-ʿAdalah hawl Bandita Yuthir Mawjah min al-Sukhriyah wa-l-Hujum ʿala al-Ikhwan." *Al-Ahram*, January 21, 2012. https://gate .ahram.org.eg/News/162728.aspx.

Abdel-Wahed, Mohamed. *Muthaqafun taht al-Talab*. Al-Qahirah: Dar Ghirnatah, 2005.

Abou El-Fadl, Reem. "Nasserism." In *The Oxford Handbook of Contemporary Middle-Eastern and North African History*, ed. Amal Ghazal and Jens Hanssen. Oxford: Oxford University Press, 2016.

Abu-Basha, Hassan. *Fi al-Amn wa-l-Siyasah*. Al-Qahirah: Dar al-Hilal, 1990.

Abu-Galeel, Hamdi. *Al-Qahirah: Shawariʿ wa Hikayat*. Al-Qahirah: al-Hayʾah al-Misriyya al-ʿAmah li-l-Kitab, 2008.

Abu-Maaylaq, Yasser. "Takhminat hawl Safqah bayn al-Jaysh wa-l-Ikhwan ʿala Hisab Maydan al-Tahrir." *DW*, May 26, 2011. https://www.dw.com/ar/بين-الجيش-والإخوان-على- حساب-ميدان-التحرير تخمينات-حول-صفقة/a-15109881.

Abu-Saleh, Ahmed. "Al-Luwaʾ Fuʾad ʿAllam: 25 Yanayir Karithah ʿala Amn Misr." *Al-Wafd*, June 5, 2019. https://alwafd.news/تحقيقات-وحوارات/1679-/2401اللواء-فؤاد-علام-25-يناير-كارثة-على-أمن-مصر.

Abul-Ela, Abdel-Rahman. "Saʿd al-Katatny." *Al-Jazeera*, January 23, 2012. https://www .aljazeera.net/news/reportsandinterviews/2012/1/23/محمد-سعد-الكتاتني.

Abul-Enein, Mohamed. "Li-l-Iflat min Dawabit al-Daʿayah: Lafitat al-Islam Huwa al-Hal Tuhit bi al-Hurriyah wa-l-ʿAdalah." *Al-Masry Al Youm*, November 8, 2011. https://www .almasryalyoum.com/news/details/124427.

Abul-Magd, Zeinab. *Militarizing the Nation: The Army, Business, and Revolution in Egypt*. New York: Columbia University Press, 2017.

Abul-Nasr, Mohamed Hamed. "Risalah min al-Ikhwan al-Muslimun li-l-Raʾis Mubarak." *Al-Shaab*, February 17, 1987.

Adly, Amr. "Between Social Populism and Pragmatic Conservatism." In *Egypt's Revolutions: Politics, Religion, and Social Movements*, ed. Bernard Rougier and Stéphane Lacroix, 61–78. New York: Palgrave Macmillan, 2016.

Adly, Amr. *Cleft Capitalism: The Social Origins of Failed Market Making in Egypt*. Stanford, CA: Stanford University Press, 2020.

Adly, Amr. "Ma baʿd al-Nasiriyya." *Jadaliyya*, March 18, 2014. https://www.jadaliyya.com /Details/30401/ما-بعد-الناصرية.

Adly, Amr. "Ma baʿd al-Nasiriyya al-Juzʾ al-Thany." *Jadaliyya*, August 14, 2014. https:// www.jadaliyya.com/Details/31100/ما-بعد-الناصرية-الجزء-الثاني.

Adly, Amr. "Too Big to Fail: Egypt's Large Enterprises After the 2011 Uprising." Carnegie Endowment for International Peace Working Paper, Washington, DC, March 2017. https://carnegieendowment.org/files/CMEC_65_Adly_Final_Web.pdf.

Adly, Howaida. *Al-ʿUmmal wa-l-Siyasah: al-Dawr al-Siyasy li-l-Harakah al-ʿUmmaliyya fi Misr min 1952–1981*. Al-Qahirah: Kitab al-Ahaly, 1993.

Ahmed, Akhter U., Tamar Gutner, Hans Lofgren, and Howarth E. Bouis. *The Egyptian Food Subsidy System: Structure, Performance, and Options for Reform*. Washington, DC: International Food Policy Research Institute, 2001.

Ahmed, Imam. "Inqadh al-Thawrah: al-ʿAskary Faqad al-Sharʿiyah wa Nahtaj li-Majlis Riʾasy Madany." *Masrawy*, December 17, 2011. https://www.masrawy.com/news/news _egypt/details/2011/12/17/97629/إنقاذ-الثورة-العسكري-فقد-الشرعية-ونحتاج-لـمجلس-رئاسي-مدني.

Ahmed, Makram Mohamed. *Muʾamarah am Murajaʿah: Hiwar maʿa Qadat al-Tataruf fi Sijn al-ʿAqrab*. Al-Qahirah: Dar al-Shuruq, 2002.

Ahram Online. "Egypt Brotherhood Businessman: Manufacturing Is Key." *Ahram Online*, October 28, 2011. http://english.ahram.org.eg/NewsContent/3/12/25348/Business /Economy/Egypt-Brotherhood-businessman-Manufacturing-is-key.aspx.

Ahram Online. "Egypt's President Signs Islamic Bonds Bill." *Ahram Online*, May 9, 2013. http://english.ahram.org.eg/News/71025.aspx.

Ajami, Fouad. *The Arab Predicament: Arab Political Thought and Practice Since 1967*. Cambridge: Cambridge University Press, 1981.

Akhbar Al-Youm. "Nakshif Kawalis Muhawalat Majlis al-Dawlah li-Hal Wasat al-Ikhwan wa Qatʿ Dhiraʿaha al-Siyasy." *Akhbar Al-Youm*, August 29, 2013. https://akhbarelyom .com/news/newdetails/271057/1/نكشف-كواليس-محاولات-مجلس-الدولة-لحل-وسط.

Akhir Sa'a. "Asrar Safqat al-Tahaluf Yakshufha al-Mafsulun min Hizb al-ʿAmal." *Akhir Sa'a*, April 22, 1987.

Al-Ahram. "Iʿlan Taʾsis al-Hizb al-Ishtiraky al-Misry." *Al-Ahram*, June 18, 2011. https://gate.ahram.org.eg/News/84113.aspx.

Al-Ahram. "Murshid al-Ikhwan: La Safaqat Maʿa al-Jaysh wa Lan Nasmah b-il-Waqʿiyah baynahu wa bayn al-Shaʿb." *Al-Ahram*, April 13, 2011. https://gate.ahram.org.eg/News/59818.aspx.

Al-Ahram. "Nas Bayan al-Mushir Tantawy Radan ʿala al-Aahdath al-Jariyah bi-Maydan al-Tahrir." *Al-Ahram*, November 22, 2011. https://gate.ahram.org.eg/News/140523.aspx.

Al-Ahram Center. *Al-Taqrir Al-Istratijy Al-ʿAraby 1987*. Al-Qahirah: Markaz al-Dirasat al-Siyasiyya wa-l-Istratijiyya, 1988.

Al-Anani, Khalil. "Devout Neoliberalism?! Explaining Egypt's Muslim Brotherhood's Socio-economic Perspective and Policies." *Politics and Religion* 13, no. 4 (2020): 748–67.

Al-Anani, Khalil. *Inside the Muslim Brotherhood: Religion, Identity, and Politics*. New York: Oxford University Press, 2016.

Al-Ansary, Adel. *Al-Ikhwan al-Muslimun: 60 Qadiyah Sakhinah*. Al-Qahirah: Dar al-Tawziʿ wa-l-Nashr al-Islamiyya, 1998.

Al-Araby. "Al-Sisy Yaʿtarif bi Qaswat al-Ijraʾat wa Yatmasak bi al-Islah al-Iqtisady." *Al-Araby*, July 1, 2018. https://alarab.co.uk/السيسي-يعترف-بقسوة-الإجراءات-ويتمسك-بالإصلاح-الاقتصادي.

Al-Arian, Abdullah A. *Answering the Call: Popular Islamic Activism in Sadat's Egypt*. New York: Oxford University Press, 2014.

Al-Ashwah, Adel. *Haqiqat al-Tanzim al-Taliʿy wa Inqilab al-Sadat ʿala Thawrat Yulyu*. Al-Qahirah: Al-Markaz al-ʿAraby al-Dawly li al-Iʿlam, 2016.

Al-Awadi, Hesham. *Siraʿ ʿala al-Sharʿiyah: al-Ikhwan al-Muslimun wa Mubarak 1982–2007*. Bayrut: Markaz Dirasat al-Wihdah al-ʿArabiyya, 2009.

Al-Awwa, Salwa Mohamed. *Al-Jamaʿah al-Islamiyya al-Musalahah fi Misr, 1974–2004*. Al-Qahirah: Maktabat al-Shuruq al-Dawliyya, 2006.

Al-Bayan. "Al-Hukumah Al-Misriyya Tujamid Nashat Hizb Al-ʿAmal wa Tuʿaliq Sudur Sahi-fatih." *Al-Bayan*, May 21, 2000. https://www.albayan.ae/last-page/2000-05-21-1.1068098.

Al-Bayan. "Al-Idrabat al-ʿUmmaliyya Tatasiʿ wa Tatajahal Tahdhirat al-Jaysh." *Al-Bayan*, February 17, 2011. https://www.albayan.ae/one-world/arabs/2011-02-17-1.1386704.

Al-Bayan. "Kitab al-Jamaʿat al-Islamiyya Tuʿlin Tawbatuha, al-Halaqah al-Thalithah." *Al-Bayan*, February 9, 2002. https://www.albayan.ae/one-world/2002-02-09-1.1310027.

Al-Beblawi, Hazem. *Arbaʿat Shuhur fi Qafas al-Hikumah*. Al-Qahira: Dar Al-Shuruq, 2012.

Al-Bishri, Tariq. *Al-Harakah al-Siyasiyya fi Misr 1945–1953*. Al-Qahirah: Dar al-Shuruq, 2002.

Al-Bishri, Tariq. *Al-Muslimun wa-l-Aqbat fi Itar al-Jamaʿah al-Wataniyya*. Al-Qahirah: Al-Hayʾah al-ʿAmah li-l-Kitab, 1981.

Al-Boraei, Haytham. "Al-Watan Tanshur Nas Tahqiqat al-Niyabah Maʿa Rajul al-Aʿmal Hasan Malik fi Qadiyat al-Idrar bi-l-Iqtisad." *Al-Watan*, February 8, 2018. https://www.elwatannews.com/news/details/3077816.

Adel Al-Dargali, Nashwa Al-Houfy, Monir Adib, Hany Al-Waziri. "Al-Bishry Raʾisan li-Lajnat Taʿdil al-Dustur wa Ikhtiyar Ikhwany bayn al-Aʿdaʾ." *Al-Masry Al-Youm*, February 15, 2011. https://www.almasryalyoum.com/news/details/113986.

Al-Desouki, Asem. ʿUmmal wa Tulab fi-l-Harakah al-Wataniyya Al-Misriyya: Nadwa ʿan Shahadat wa Ruʾy Abtal Harakat al-ʿUmmal wa-l-Talabah, 1946–1977. Al-Qahirah: Dar al-Mahrusah, 1998.

Al-Fiqi, Mohamed. "Al-Kutlah Badaʾat al-Harb ʿala al-Ikhwan." Al-Shorouk, November 3, 2011. https://www.shorouknews.com/news/view.aspx?cdate=03112011&id=10425738-3603-4d67-b86b-0d82506ecd2d.

Al-Gammal, Ahmed. "Husayn ʿAbd al-Raziq al-Insan." Al-Ahram, September 6, 2018. http://gate.ahram.org.eg/daily/NewsQ/669616.aspx.

Al-Ganzouri, Kamal. Tariqy: Sanawat al-Hulm wa-l-Sidam wa-l-ʿUzlah min al-Qariyah ila Riʾasat Majlis al-Wizaraʾ. Al-Qahirah: Dar al-Shuruq, 2012.

Al-Gaoudi, Alaa. "Kamal Ahmad: Nazamna Mustabaqat Dumino ʿala al-Maqahy li-l-Hadith fi-l-Siyasa." Al-Watan, March 11, 2020. https://www.elwatannews.com/news/details/4635875.

Al-Gazzar, Helmy. "Al-Nahdah al-Tulabiyya al-Islamiyya fi Hiwar li-l-Mawqiʿ maʿa Duktur Hilmy al-Jazar." Ikhwanonline, November 2, 2003. https://ikhwanonline.net/article/3165.

Ahmed Al-Gebaly, Hassan Abul-Kheir, Sayyid Abdel-Wahab Nada, Shehata Abdel-Halim, Taha Saad Othman, Atiyya Al-Serafy, Fathallah Mahrous, Nagaty Abdel-Megiud, and Youssef Darwish. Al-ʿUmmal fi-l-Haraka al-Shiuʿiyya al-Misriyya hata ʿAam 1965. Al-Qahirah: Dar al-Amin, 2011.

Al-Geretly, Aly. Khamsah wa ʿIshrun ʿAman: Dirasah Tahliliyya li-l-Siyasat al-Iqtisadiyya fi Misr. Al-Qahirah: Al-Hayʾah al-Misriyya al-ʿAmah li-l-Kitab, 1977.

Al-Ghazali, Abdel-Hamid. Al-Fikr al-Iqtisady ʿind al-Ikhwan al-Muslimin. Al-Qahirah: Dar al-Nashr li-l-Jamiʿat, 2007.

Al-Ghazali, Mohamed. Al-Islam wa-l-Manahij al-Ishtrakiyya. Al-Jizah: Nahdat Misr, 2005.

Al-Hadi, Omar. "Muhamad Husayn Yaʿqub: Intasarna fi Ghazwat al-Sanadiq wa al-Balad Baladna wa-l-Shaʿb Qal Naʿam li-l-Din." Al-Masry Al-Youm, March 21, 2011. https://www.almasryalyoum.com/news/details/120575.

Al-Hawari, Dandarawy. "Nanshur Nas Marsum al-Qanun al-Khas bi-Taʾsis wa Tanzim al-Ahzab al-Siyasiyya." Youm7, March 28, 2011. https://www.youm7.com/story/2011/3/مرسوم-القانون-الخاص-بتأسيس-وتنظيم-الأحزاب-السياسية/378865-ننشر-نص-/28/.

Al-Helaly, Ahmed Nabil. Huriyat al-Fikr wa-l-ʿAqidah, Tilk Hiya al-Qadiyah: Murafaʿah Qanuniyya wa Siyasiyya fi Qadiyat al-Hizb al-Shiuʿy al-Misry. Al-Jizah: Dar al-Misry al-Jadid li-l-Nashr, 1989.

Al-Issawi, Ibrahim. "Al-Tahawul ila al-Infitah: al-ʿAwamel al-Dakhiliyya." In Al-Infitah: al-Judhur, al-Hisad, wa-l-Mustaqbal, ed. Gouda Abdel-Khalek, 71–89. Al-Qahirah: Al-Markaz al-ʿAraby lil-Bahth wa-al-Nashr, 1982.

Al-Issawi, Ibrahim. "Al-Tajammuʿ fi Aʿqab al-Intikhabat al-Tashriʿyya: Naqd Dhaty wa Tataluʿ li-l-Mustaqbal." In Hiwarat al-Yasar al-Misry: Min Ajl Nuhud Jadid, ed. Abdel-Ghaffar Shukr, 43–52. Al-Qahirah: Maktabat Madbuly, 2006.

Al-Issawi, Ibrahim. Fi Islah ma Afsadahu al-Infitah. Al-Qahirah: Kitab al-Ahaly, 1984.

Al-Issawi, Ibrahim, and Mohamed Ali Nassar. "Muhawalah li Taqdir al-Khasaʾir al-Iqtisadiyya Alaty Alhaqtiha al-Harb al-ʿArabiyya al-Israʾiliyya bi-Misr Munthu ʿUdwan

1967." In *Al-Iqtisad al-Misry fi-Rub' Qarn, 1952–1977*, ed. Ismail Sabri Abdallah, Gouda Abdel-Khalek, and Ibrahim Al-Issawi, 127–56. Al-Qahirah: Al-Hay'ah al-Misriyya al-'Amah li-l-Kitab, 1978.

Al-Karas, Thanaa. "Lutfy al-Khuly Yahky Qisat Ighlaq Majlat al-Tali'ah." *Vetogate*, April 15, 2014. https://vetogate.com/961256.

Al-Karas, Thanaa. "Mustafa Mahmud 'an Intifadat Yanayir: Al-Sadat Qudwah li-man la Qudwatu Lahu." *Vetogate*, January 19, 2014. http://www.vetogate.com/815105.

Al-Khosousy, Moataz. "Amin al-Tajammu' Yatahim al-Sa'id bi-l-Istila' 'ala Matba'at al-Hizb." *Sada Al-Balad*, November 17, 2015. https://www.elbalad.news/1799952.

Al-Khouli, Lotfi. *Madrasat al-Sadat al-Siyasiyya wa-l-Yasar al-Misry*. Al-Qahirah: Kitab al-Ahaly, 1986.

Al-Leithy, Amr. *Ikhtiraq: Kashf al-Sitar 'an Akhtar al-Asrar*. Al-Qahirah: Dar al-Shuruq, 2003.

Al-Masry Al-Youm. "'Abd al-Hamid al-Ghazaly Mustashar Murshid al-Ikhwan li-l-Misry al-Yawm: Na'am 'Aqadna Safqah ma'a al-Amn fi Intikhabat 2005 Walakin al-Nizam Naqadha." *Al-Masry Al-Youm*, October 29, 2009. https://www.almasryalyoum.com/news/details/72648.

Al-Masry Al-Youm. "Mustafa Mahmud . . . Qalb al-Faylasuf la Yazal Yanbud." *Al-Masry Al-Youm*, June 12, 2008. https://to.almasryalyoum.com/article2.aspx?ArticleID=108880.

Al-Meleegy, Al-Sayyid Abdel-Sattar. *Tajribaty ma'a al-Ikhwan*. Al-Qahirah: Al-Markaz al-'Ilmy li-l-Buhuth wa-l-Dirasat, 2009.

Al-Meleegy, Al-Sayyid Abdel-Sattar. "Tajribaty ma'a al-Ikhwan." *IkhwanWiki*, November 26, 2012. https://www.ikhwanwiki.com/index.php?title=تجربتي_مع_الإخوان_من_الدعوة_إلى_التنظيم_السري.

Al-Meleegy, Ayaa. "10 Ma'lumat 'an Aminah Shafiq ba'd Takrimaha fi Hafl al-Um al-Mithaliyah." *Honna*, March 21, 2018. https://honna.elwatannews.com/news/details/1958597/10-معلومات-عن-أمينة-شفيق-بعد-تكريمها-في-حفل-الأم-المثالية-صحفية-ارتدت-زي-الصيادين.

Al-Mirghani, Ilhamy. "Intikhabat al-Ri'asah al-Misriyya wa Azmat al-Quwa al-Ishtirakiyya." *Al-Hewar Al-Mutamadin*, April 18, 2014. https://www.ahewar.org/debat/show.art.asp?aid=410909.

Al-Mirghani, Ilhamy. "Ru'yat Jinaru li-l-Harakah al-Markasiyya al-Thalitha fi Misr." *Al-Hewar Al-Mutamadin*, December 6, 2010. https://www.ahewar.org/debat/show.art.asp?aid=237321.

Al-Nemnem, Helmy. *Sayid Qutb wa Thawrat Yulyu*. Cairo: Mirit li-l-Nashr, 1999.

Al-Olaimy, Said. "Al-Tanzim al-Shiu'y al-Misry Tshm." *Al-Hewar Al-Mutamadin*, June 3, 2019. https://www.ahewar.org/debat/show.art.asp?aid=639244.

Al-Olaimy, Said. "La'ihat Hizb al-'Ummal al-Shiu'y." *Al-Hewar Al-Mutamadin*, June 24, 2020. https://www.ahewar.org/debat/show.art.asp?aid=682295.

Al-Olaimy, Said. "Sirah Dhatiyya li-Shiu'y Misry, Qad Ta'ny aw la Ta'ny Ahadan, Hizb al-'Ummal al-Shiu'y, al-Qism al-Thalith." *Al-Hewar Al-Mutamadin*, July 15, 2018. https://www.ahewar.org/debat/show.art.asp?aid=605365.

Al-Olaimy, Said. "Sirah Dhatiyya li-Shiu'y Misry, Qad Ta'ny aw la Ta'ny Ahadan, Hizb al-'Ummal al-Shiu'y, al-Qism al-Thany." *Al-Hewar Al-Mutamadin*, July 13, 2018. https://www.ahewar.org/debat/show.art.asp?aid=605184.

Al-Omda, Mohamed. "Haythiyat Hal al-Huriyyah wa-l-ʿAdalah." *Al-Watan*, August 10, 2014. https://www.elwatannews.com/news/details/536077.

Al-Quds Al-Arabi. "Itiham Muham wa Sahafiyyin Misriyyin bi-Silat maʿa Jamaʿah Irhabiyya." *Al-Quds Al-Arabi*, November 29, 2019. https://www.alquds.co.uk/اتهام-محام-وصحافيين-مصريين-بصلات-مع-جم.

Al-Quds Al-Arabi. "Jumʿat Lam al-Shaml Karasat al-Inqisamat baʿd Insihab al-ʿAlmaniyyin Ihtijajan ʿala al-Shiʿarat al-Diniyya." *Al-Quds Al-Arabi*, July 29, 2011. https://www.alquds.co.uk/ا-بعد-الانقسامات-كرّست-الشمل-جمعة-لمّ.

Al-Quds Al-Arabi. "Misr: Al-Ikhwan Yuhadidun bi-l-Tasady li-l-Majlis al-ʿAskary Idha Wafaq ʿala Wadiʿ al-Dustur qabl al-Intikhabat." *Al-Quds Al-Arabi*, June 27, 2011. https://www.alquds.co.uk/ال-للمجلس-بالتصدي-يهددون-الاخوان-مصر.

Al-Sadat, Anwar. *Al-Bahth ʿan al-Dhaat*. Al-Qahirah: Al-Maktab al-Misry al-Hadith, 1978.

Al-Sadat, Anwar. "Hadith al-Raʾis Muhamad Anwar al-Sadat al-Awal ila Aʿdaʾ al-Muʿtamar al-Qiady li-Shabab al-Hizb al-Watany." *The Library of Alexandria Sadat Archives*, January 31, 1979. http://sadat.bibalex.org/TextViewer.aspx?TextID=SP_817.

Al-Sadat, Anwar. "Hadith al-Raʾis Muhamad Anwar al-Sadat maʿa Asatidhat Jamiʿat al-Iskandariyya." *The Library of Alexandria Sadat Archives*, March 1, 1979. http://sadat.bibalex.org/TextViewer.aspx?TextID=SP_827.

Al-Sadat, Anwar. "Hiwar al-Raʾis Muhamad Anwar al-Sadat maʿa Qiyadat al-Hizb al-Watany bi-l-Ismaʿiliyya." *The Library of Alexandria Sadat Archives*, April 22, 1979. http://sadat.bibalex.org/TextViewer.aspx?TextID=SP_852.

Al-Sadat, Anwar. "Hiwar al-Raʾis Muhamad Anwar al-Sadat wa Asatidhat Jamiʿatay Asyut wa-l-Minya." *The Library of Alexandria Sadat Archives*, April 14, 1979. http://sadat.bibalex.org/TextViewer.aspx?TextID=SP_850.

Al-Sadat, Anwar. "Kalimat al-Raʾis Muhamad Anwar al-Sadat khilal Liqaʾihi bi-Rijal al-Din wa-l-Fikr al-Islamy." *The Library of Alexandria Sadat Archives*, August 20, 1979. http://sadat.bibalex.org/TextViewer.aspx?TextID=SP_897.

Al-Sadat, Anwar. "Kalimat al-Raʾis Muhamad Anwar al-Sadat khilal Liqaʾih bi-ʿUmmal al-Naql bi-l-Iskandariyya." *The Library of Alexandria Sadat Archives*, February 28, 1979. http://sadat.bibalex.org/TextViewer.aspx?TextID=SP_826.

Al-Sadat, Anwar. "Kalimat al-Raʾis Muhamad Anwar al-Sadat li-Shabab al-Hizb al-Watany bi Muʿaskar Abu Bakr al-Al-Sidiqbi-l-Iskandariyya." *The Library of Alexandria Sadat Archives*, July 7, 1979. http://sadat.bibalex.org/TextViewer.aspx?TextID=SP_884.

Al-Sadat, Anwar. "Kalimat al-Raʾis Muhamad Anwar al-Sadat maʿa Qiyadat al-Suwais." *The Library of Alexandria Sadat Archives*, April 29, 1979. http://sadat.bibalex.org/TextViewer.aspx?TextID=SP_854.

Al-Sadat, Anwar. "Khitab al-Raʾis Muhamad Anwar al-Sadat fi-l-Jalsa al-Khasah bi-Majlis al-Shaʿb." *The Library of Alexandria Sadat Archives*, April 5, 1979. http://sadat.bibalex.org/TextViewer.aspx?TextID=SP_846.

Al-Sadat, Anwar. "Khitab al-Raʾis Muhamad Anwar al-Sadat fi-Jamiʿat ʿAyn Shams." *The Library of Alexandria Sadat Archives*, April 16, 1979. http://sadat.bibalex.org/TextViewer.aspx?TextID=SP_851.

Al-Said, Rifaat. *Al-Dimuqratiyya wal-Taʿadudiyya: Dirasah fi al-Masafah bayn al-Nazariyah wal-Tadbiyq*. Al-Qahirah: Al-Hayiʾah al-ʿAmah li-l-Kitab, 2005.

Al-Said, Rifaat. *Al-Libraliyya al-Misriyya*. Al-Qahirah: Al-Hayʾah al-Misriyya al-ʿAmah li-l-Kitab, 2007.

Al-Said, Rifaat. *Al-Tayarat al-Siyasiyya fi Misr, Ruʾyah Naqdiyya: Al-Markisiyyun, al-Ikhwan, al-Nasiryyun, al-Tajammuʿ*. Al-Qahirah: Al-Hayʾah al-ʿAmah li-l-Kitab, 2002.

Al-Said, Rifaat. *Al-Yasar, al-Dimuqratiyya wa-l-Taʾslum*. Al-Qahirah: Al-Ahaly, 1998.

Al-Said, Rifaat. *Did al-Taʾslum*. Al-Qahirah: Al-Ahaly, 1996.

Al-Said, Rifaat. *Mujarad Dhikrayat al-Juzuʾ al-Thalith*. Dimashq: Dar Al-Mada, 2000.

Al-Said, Rifaat. "Musalsal Al-Jamaʿah (2) . . . Al-Bahth ʿan al-Haqiqah fi Kumat Qash." *Al-Ahaly*, July 5, 2017. http://webcache.googleusercontent.com/search?q=cache:u4wxCK-w-s0J:alahalygate.com/archives/60571+&cd=11&hl=en&ct=clnk&gl=us&client=safari.

Al-Said, Rifaat. *Tarikh al-Harakah al-Shiuʿiyya al-Misriyya* 1900–1940. Al-Qahirah: Dar al-Thaqafah al-Jadidah, 1987.

Al-Said, Rifaat, Adel Hussein, Mohamed Said Ashmawy, Nasr Hamid Abu-Zeid, Khalil Abdel-Karim, Mustafa Aasy, Magdy Qurqur, and Salah Adly. *Al-Muwajahah hawl al-Iʿtidal wa-l-Tataruf bayn Rifʿat al-Saʿid wa ʿAdil Husayn*. Dimishq: Dar al-Taliʿah al-Jadidah, 1996.

Al-Sayyid, Mustapha Kamel. *Al-Mujtamaʿ wa-l-Siyasah fi Misr: Dawr Jamaʿat al-Masalih fi al-Nizam al-Siyasy al-Misry, 1952–1981*. Al-Qahirah: Dar al-Mustaqbal al-ʿAraby, 1983.

Al-Selmi, Ali. *Al-Tahawul al-Al-Dimuqraty wa-Ishkaliyat Wathiqat al-Mabadiʾ al-Dusturiyya*. Al-Qahirah: Al-Masry al-Youmm, 2012.

Al-Sherif, Ahmed Ibrahim. "Lutfy al-Khuly, Sahib Raʾy wa Katib Masrahy wa Qisasy wa Saniʿ Sinima." *Youm7*, March 23, 2021. https://www.youm7.com/story/2021/3/23 /صاحب-رأى-وكاتب-مسرحى-وقصصى-وصانع-سينما/5253984 لطفى-الخولى-.

Al-Sherif, Aly. "ʿIlaqat al-Jamaʿah al-Islamiyya bi-l-Aqbat Kanat Sayiʾah Jidan wa Kuna Nuwajih Tajawuzatuhum bi-l-Shiddah wa-l-ʿUnf." *Elmogaz*, December 28, 2012. https://www.elmogaz.com/60873.

Al-Sherif, Aly. "Li-Awal Marah al-Mujaz Tanshur Mudhakirat Qaʾid al-Tanzim al-Musalah li-l-Jamaʿah al-Islamiyya bi-Khat Yaduh." *Elmogaz*, December 21, 2012. https://www.elmogaz.com/60135.

Al-Sibai, Bashir. "Al-Yahud wa-l-Harakah al-Shiuʿiyya: Radan ʿala Tariq al-Bishry." *Mabdaa Al-Amal* (blog), April 11, 2011. http://mabda-alamal.blogspot.com/2011/04/blog-post_11.html.

Al-Sisi, Abbas. *Min al-Madhbahah ila Sahat al-Daʿwah*. Al-Qahirah: Dar al-Tawziʿ wa-l-Nashr al-Islamiyya, 2003.

Al-Soweify, Hossam. "20 Hizban wa Iʾtilafan Thawriyyan Yasharikun fi Jumʿat al-Matlab al-Wahid." *Al-Wafd*, November 16, 2011. https://alwafd.news/حزبا-20-122648/الشارع-السياسي .وائتلافا-ثوريا-يشاركون-في-جمعة-المطلب-الواحد.

Al-Tagammu. *Barnamijna li-l-Taghyir*. Al-Qahirah: Al-Ahaly, 1993.

Al-Taweel, Mohamed. *Al-Ikhwan fi-l-Barlaman*. Al-Qahirah: Al-Maktab al-Misry al-Hadith, 1992.

Al-Thawra Mostamera. *Barnamijna al-Intikhaby li-Majlis al-Shaʿb*. *Al-Thawra Mostamera*, 2011. https://thawramostamera.files.wordpress.com/2011/11/program1.pdf.

Al-Tilmisani, Omar. *Ayam maʿa al-Sadat*. Al-Qahirah: Dar Al-Iʿtisam, 1984.

Al-Tilmisani, Omar. *Dhikrayat La Mudhakarat*. Al-Qahirah: Dar Al-Iʿtisam, 1985.

Al-Tilmisani, Omar. "Min Kalimat al-Ustadh ʿUmar al-Tilmisany ila al-Shabab." *Ikhwanonline*, September 2, 2012. https://www.ikhwanonline.com/article/118751.

Al-Zafarani, Ibrahim. "Hikayat al-Zaʿfarany." *Ikhwanwiki*, December 9, 2017. http://www .ikhwan.wiki/index.php?title=حكايات_الزعفراني.

Al-Zayyat, Mohamed Abdel-Salam. *Al-Sadat al-Qinaʿ wa-l-Haqiqah*. Al-Qahirah: Kitab al-Ahaly, 1989.

Albrecht, Holger. *Raging Against the Machine: Political Opposition Under Authoritarianism in Egypt*. Syracuse, NY: Syracuse University Press, 2013.

Alesina, Alberto, Reza Baqir, and William Easterly. "Public Goods and Ethnic Divisions." *Quarterly Journal of Economics* 114, no. 4 (November 1999): 1243–84.

Allam, Fouad. *Al-Ikhwan wa Ana: Min al-Manshiyah ila al-Manasah*. Al-Qahirah: Akhbar al-Yawm, 1996.

Aly, Abdel-Reheem. *Al-Hisad al-Mur: al-Dawlah wa Jamaʿat al-ʿUnf al-Diny fi Misr*. Al-Qahirah: al-Mahrusah, 2005.

Aly, Abdel-Reheem. *Al-Ikhwan al-Muslimun: Azmat Tayar al-Tajdid*. Al-Qahirah: Markaz al-Mahrusah, 2004.

Aly, Abdel-Reheem. *Al-Ikhwan al-Muslimun: Min Hasan al-Bana ila Mahdy ʿAkif*. Al-Qahirah: Al-Markaz al-ʿAraby li-l-Buhuth wa-l-Dirasat, 2007.

Aly, Abdel-Reheem. *Kashf al-Bahtan: Al-Ikhwan al-Muslimun, Waqaʾiʿ al-ʿUnf wa Fatawy al-Takfir*. Al-Qahirah: Al-Markaz al-ʿAraby li-l-Buhuth wa-l-Dirasat, 2010.

Aly, Iman, and Mahmoud Othman. "Aʿdaʾ min al-Ishtiraky al-Misry Tuʿlin Indimamaha li-Hizb al-Tahaluf al-Shaʿby." *Youm7*, October 7, 2012. https://www.youm7.com/story/2012 /10/7/وسكرتارية/808288 أعضاء-من-الاشتراكى-المصرى-تعلن-انضمامها-لحزب-التحالف-الشعبى.

Aly, Khaled Mohamed. "83 Milyun Dular Tamwilat Kharijiyya li-l-Taʾthir fi al-Intikhabat al-Misriyya." *Emarat Al-Youm*, December 15, 2011. https://www.emaratalyoum.com /politics/reports-and-translation/2011-12-15-1.445238.

Aly, Saeed, Mahmoud Al-Emari, Ghada Mohamed Al-Sherif. "Masadir: Wafd Salafy fi al-Suʿudiyya li-Tamwil al-Nur." *Al-Masry Al-Youm*, June 21, 2015. https://www.almasry alyoum.com/news/details/758574.

Amar, Paul. "Egypt." In *Dispatches from the Arab Spring Understanding the New Middle East*, ed. Paul Amar and Vijay Prashad, 24–64. Minneapolis: University of Minnesota Press, 2013.

Amin, Galal. "Al-Tahawul ila al-Infitah: al-ʿAwamil al-Kharijiyya." In *Al-Infitah: al-Judhur, al-Hisad, wa-l-Mustaqbal*, ed. Gouda Abdel-Khalek, 91–121. Al-Qahirah: Al-Markaz al-ʿAraby lil-Bahth wa-al-Nashr, 1982.

Amin, Galal. "The Egyptian Economy and the Revolution." *Egypt Since the Revolution*, ed. P. J. Vatikiotis, 40–49. New York: Praeger, 1968.

Amin, Galal A. *Egypt's Economic Predicament: A Study in the Interaction of External Pressure, Political Folly, and Social Tension in Egypt, 1960–1990*. Leiden, The Netherlands: Brill, 1995.

Amin, Galal. "Hadha al-Nabil fi Markisiyyatihi wa Islamihi." *Al-Araby*, April 8, 2001.

Angela, Joya. *The Roots of Revolt: A Political Economy of Egypt from Nasser to Mubarak*. Cambridge: Cambridge University Press, 2020.

Antar, Ahmed. "Muhamad Habib: al-Ikhwan ʿAqadat Safqah maʿa Amn al-Dawlah fi Intikhabat al-Barlaman ʿAm 2005." *Al-Watan*, April 29, 2014. https://www.elwatannews .com/news/details/472134.

Arie, Albert, Janet Shirazi, Suad Zoheer, Saad Al-Taweel, Sherif Hetata, Marcel Shirazi, Mohamed Al-Gendy, Mohamed Sid-Ahmed, and Youssef Darwish. *Al-Ajanib fi-l-Harakah al-Shiuʿiyya al-Misriyya hata ʿAm 1965*. Al-Qahirah: Markaz al-Buhuth al-ʿArabiyya li-l-Dirasat al-ʿArabiyya wa-l-Afriqiyya, 2002.

Ashmawy, Sayyid. *Al-Falahun wa-l-Sultah*. Al-Qahirah: Mirit, 2001.

Assaad, Gamal. *Iny Aʿtarif Kawalis al-Kanisah wa-l-Ahzab wa-l-Ikhwan al-Muslimun*. Al-Qahirah: Dar al-Khayal, 2001.

Assaad, Gamal. *Man Yumathil al-Aqbat? Al-Dawlah? Am al-Baba?* Publisher unknown, 1993.

Assaad, Ragui. "The Effects of Public Sector Hiring and Compensation Policies on the Egyptian Labor Market." Economic Research Forum Working Paper No. 9517, Cairo, Egypt, 1995. https://idl-bnc-idrc.dspacedirect.org/bitstream/handle/10625/34292/126351 .pdf?sequence=1.

Atia, Mona. *Building a House in Heaven: Pious Neoliberalism and Islamic Charity in Egypt*. Minneapolis: University of Minnesota Press, 2013.

Attalah, Lina. "The Draft Constitution: Some Controversial Stipulations." *Jadaliyya*, December 1, 2012. https://www.jadaliyya.com/Details/27520.

Awad, Huda Ragheb, and Hassanein Tawfiq. *Al-Ikhwan al-Muslimun wa-l-Siyasah fi Misr*. Al-Qahirah: Markaz al-Mahrusah, 1995.

Ayubi, Nazih N. M. *Bureaucracy and Politics in Contemporary Egypt*. London: Published for the Middle East Centre, St. Antony's College by Ithaca Press, 1980.

Ayubi, Nazih N. M. *Over-Stating the Arab State: Politics and Society in the Middle East*. London: Tauris, 1995.

Ayubi, Nazih N. M. *Political Islam: Religion and Politics in the Arab World*. London: Routledge, 1991.

Ayubi, Nazih N. "Withered Socialism or Whether Socialism? The Radical Arab States as Populist-Corporatist Regimes." *Third World Quarterly* 13, no. 1 (1992): 89–105.

Badr, Badr Mohamed. *Al-Jamaʿah al-Islamiyya fi-l-Jamiʿat*. Badr Mohamed Badr, 1989.

Bahaaeddin, Ziad. "Ma Hiya Akhwanat al-Dawlah? Wa Limadha Nakhshaha." *Al-Shorouk*, September 11, 2012. https://www.shorouknews.com/columns/view.aspx?cdate =10092012&id=d8962c68-7416-4ce4-b733-672a9a1dc5e1.

Bailey, Michael A. "Comparable Preference Estimates Across Time and Institutions for the Court, Congress, and Presidency." *American Journal of Political Science* 51, no. 3 (July 2007): 433–48.

Baker, Raymond William. *Egypt's Uncertain Revolution Under Nasser and Sadat*. Cambridge, MA: Harvard University Press, 1978.

Barayez, Abdel-Fattah. " 'This Land Is Their Land': Egypt's Military and the Economy." *Jadaliyya*, January 25, 2016. https://www.jadaliyya.com/Details/32898.

Bartels, Larry M. "What's the Matter with What's the Matter with Kansas?" *Quarterly Journal of Political Science* 1, no. 22 (March 2006): 201–26.

Beinin, Joel. "Egypt's Gamal Abdel Nasser Was a Towering Figure Who Left an Ambiguous Legacy." *Jacobin Magazine*, September 28, 2020. https://www.jacobinmag.com/2020 /09/egypt-gamal-abdel-nasser-legacy.

Beinin, Joel. "Essential Readings on Marxism and the Left in Egypt." *Jadaliyya*, August 10, 2020. https://www.jadaliyya.com/Details/41550.

Beinin, Joel. "Henri Curiel and the Egyptian Communist Movement." *Radical History Review* 45 (1989): 157–63.

Beinin, Joel. *Justice for All: The Struggle for Worker Rights in Egypt*. Washington, DC: Solidarity Center, 2010.

Beinin, Joel. "Political Islam and the New Global Economy: The Political Economy of an Egyptian Social Movement." *CR: The New Centennial Review* 5, no. 1 (Spring 2005): 111–39.

Beinin, Joel. "Popular Social Movements and the Future of Egyptian Politics." *Middle East Report Online*, March 10, 2005. https://merip.org/2005/03/popular-social-movements-and-the-future-of-egyptian-politics.

Beinin, Joel. *Was the Red Flag Flying There? Marxist Politics and the Arab-Israeli Conflict in Egypt and Israel, 1948-1965*. Berkeley: University of California Press, 1990.

Beinin, Joel. *Workers and Thieves: Labor Movements and Popular Uprisings in Tunisia and Egypt*. Stanford, CA: Stanford University Press, 2016.

Beinin, Joel, and Zachary Lockman. *Workers on the Nile: Nationalism, Communism, Islam and the Egyptian Working Class, 1882-1954*. London: Tauris, 1988.

Ben Salem, Maryam. "God Loves the Rich. The Economic Policy of Ennahda: Liberalism in the Service of Social Solidarity." *Politics and Religion* 13, no. 4 (2020): 695–718.

Bennett, Andrew, and Jeffrey T. Checkel, eds. *Process Tracing: From Metaphor to Analytic Tool*. Cambridge: Cambridge University Press, 2014.

Benoit, Kenneth, and Michael Laver. *Party Policy in Modern Democracies*. London: Routledge, 2006.

Berman, Sheri. "The Lost Left." *Journal of Democracy* 27, no. 4 (October 2016): 69–76.

Berman, Sheri. "Populism Is a Symptom Rather than a Cause: Democratic Disconnect, the Decline of the Center-Left, and the Rise of Populism in Western Europe." *Polity* 51, no. 4 (October 2019): 654–67.

Berman, Sheri, and Maria Snegovaya. "Populism and the Decline of Social Democracy." *Journal of Democracy* 30, no. 3 (July 2019): 5–19.

Bishara, Dina. *Contesting Authoritarianism: Labor Challenges to the State in Egypt*. Cambridge: Cambridge University Press, 2018.

Blaydes, Lisa. *Elections and Distributive Politics in Mubarak's Egypt*. New York: Cambridge University Press, 2010.

Block, Steven A. "Political Business Cycles, Democratization, and Economic Reform: The Case of Africa." *Journal of Development Economics* 67, no. 1 (February 2002): 205–28.

Bornschier, Simon, and Hanspeter Kriesi. "The Populist Right, the Working Class, and the Changing Face of Class Politics." In *Class Politics and the Radical Right*, ed. Jens Rydgren, 10–30. New York: Routledge, 2013.

Boyd, Douglas A. "Development of Egypt's Radio: Voice of the Arabs Under Nasser." *Journalism Quarterly* 52, no. 4 (December 1975): 645–53.

Brady, Henry E., and David Collier, eds. *Rethinking Social Inquiry: Diverse Tools, Shared Standards*. Lanham, MD: Rowman & Littlefield, 2010.

Bratton, Michael, and Nicolas Van de Walle. *Democratic Experiments in Africa: Regime Transitions in Comparative Perspective*. New York: Cambridge University Press, 1997.

Brooke, Steven. *Winning Hearts and Votes: Social Services and the Islamist Political Advantage.* Ithaca, NY: Cornell University Press, 2019.

Brown, Nathan J. *When Victory Is Not an Option: Islamist Movements in Arab Politics.* Ithaca, NY: Cornell University Press, 2012.

Brown, Nathan J., and Michelle Dunne. "Unprecedented Pressures, Uncharted Course for Egypt's Muslim Brotherhood." Carnegie Endowment for International Peace Working Paper, Washington, DC, July 2015. https://carnegieendowment.org/files/CP248 -EgyptMB_BrownDunne_final.pdf.

Brown, Nathan, and Kristen Stilt. "A Haphazard Constitutional Compromise." Carnegie Endowment for International Peace, April 11, 2011. https://carnegieendowment. org/2011/04/11/haphazard-constitutional-compromise-pub-43533.

Brownlee, Jason. *Democracy Prevention: The Politics of the U.S.-Egyptian Alliance.* New York: Cambridge University Press, 2012.

Brownlee, Jason. "Portents of Pluralism: How Hybrid Regimes Affect Democratic Transitions." *American Journal of Political Science* 53, no. 3 (July 2009): 515–32.

Brumberg, Daniel. "Authoritarian Legacies and Reform Strategies in the Arab World." In *Political Liberalization and Democratization in the Arab World.* Vol. 1, *Theoretical Perspectives,* ed. Rex Brynen, Bahgat Korany, and Paul Noble, 229–60. Boulder, CO: Lynne Rienner, 1995.

Brumberg, Daniel. "Democratization in the Arab World? The Trap of Liberalized Autocracy." *Journal of Democracy* 13, no. 4 (October 2002): 56–68.

Brumberg, Daniel. *In Pursuit of Democracy and Security in the Greater Middle East.* Washington, DC: U.S. Institute of Peace, 2010. https://www.usip.org/sites/default/files /Reform%20and%20Security%20WP%201.21.pdf.

Cairo Institute for Human Rights Studies (CIHRS). "ʿAla Khatiy al-Thawrah al-Tunisiyya al-Dustur Awalan." CIHRS, June 8, 2011. https://cihrs.org/اولا-الدستور-التونسية-الثورة-خطى-على.

Cammett, Melani, and Sukriti Issar. "Bricks and Mortar Clientelism: Sectarianism and the Logics of Welfare Allocation in Lebanon." *World Politics* 62, no. 3 (July 2010): 381–421.

Cammett, Melani, and Pauline Jones Luong. "Is There an Islamist Political Advantage?" *Annual Review of Political Science* 17 (May 2014): 187–206.

Capoccia, Giovanni, and R. Daniel Kelemen. "The Study of Critical Junctures: Theory, Narrative, and Counterfactuals in Historical Institutionalism." *World Politics* 59, no. 3 (2007): 341–69.

Carminati, Lucia, and Mohamed Gamal-Eldin. "Decentering Egyptian Historiography: Provincializing Geographies, Methodologies, and Sources." *International Journal of Middle East Studies* 53, no. 1 (2021): 107–11.

Carter Center. *Final Report of the Carter Center Mission to Witness the 2011–2012 Parliamentary Elections in Egypt.* Atlanta, GA: Carter Center 2012. https://www.cartercenter.org /resources/pdfs/news/peace_publications/election_reports/egypt-2011-2012-final -rpt.pdf.

Cavatorta, Francesco, and Samir Amghar. "Symposium—Islamism, Islamist Parties, and Economic Policy-Making in the Neo-Liberal Age." *Politics and Religion* 13, no. 4 (2020): 685–94.

Cavatorta, Francesco, and Valeria Resta. "Beyond Quietism: Party Institutionalisation, Salafism, and the Economy." *Politics and Religion* 13, no. 4 (2020): 796–817.

Center on Democracy, Development, and the Rule of Law (CDDRL). "CDDRL Conference on Democratic Transition in Egypt." Center on Democracy, Development, and the Rule of Law, Stanford University, Stanford, CA. Accessed April 22, 2021. https://fsi-live.s3.us-west-1.amazonaws.com/s3fs-public/Egypt_Conference_Report.pdf.

Clark, Janine A. "The Conditions of Islamist Moderation: Unpacking Cross-Ideological Cooperation in Jordan." *International Journal of Middle East Studies* 38, no. 4 (November 2006): 539–60.

Clark, Janine A. *Islam, Charity, and Activism: Middle-Class Networks and Social Welfare in Egypt, Jordan, and Yemen.* Bloomington: Indiana University Press, 2004.

Clark, Terry Nichols, and Seymour Martin Lipset. "Are Social Classes Dying?" In *The Breakdown of Class Politics: A Debate on Post-Industrial Stratification*, ed. Terry Nichols Clark and Seymour Martin Lipset, 39–54. Baltimore, MD: Johns Hopkins University Press, 2001.

CNN. "Fi-l-Dhikra al-Sabiʿah, al-Sisy: 30 Yunyu Hafazat ʿala Hawiyat Misr min al-Ikhtitaf." *CNN*, June 30, 2020. https://arabic.cnn.com/middle-east/article/2020/06/30/egypt-president-30-june-al-sisi.

Colla, Elliott. "Egyptian Movement Poetry." *Journal of Arabic Literature* 51, no. 1–2 (2020): 53–82.

Collier, David, and James Mahoney. "Insights and Pitfalls: Selection Bias in Qualitative Research." *World Politics* 49, no. 1 (October 1996): 56–91.

Cooper, Mark N. *The Transformation of Egypt.* Baltimore, MD: Johns Hopkins University Press, 1982.

Cox, Gary W., and Mathew D. McCubbins. "The Institutional Determinants of Economic Policy Outcomes." In *Presidents, Parliaments, and Policy*, ed. Stephan Haggard and Matthew D. McCubbins, 21–63. New York: Cambridge University Press, 2001.

Dalton, Russell J. *Citizen Politics: Public Opinion and Political Parties in Advanced Industrial Democracies.* 6th ed. Washington, DC: CQ Press, 2014.

De La O, Ana L., and Jonathan A. Rodden. "Does Religion Distract the Poor? Income and Issue Voting Around the World." *Comparative Political Studies* 41, no. 4–5 (April 2008): 437–76.

De Smet, Brecht. *The Prince and the Pharaoh: The Collaborative Project of Egyptian Workers and Their Intellectuals in the Face of Revolution.* PhD diss., Ghent University, 2012. https://biblio.ugent.be/publication/3220354/file/4336128.pdf.

Dethier, Jean-Jacques, and Kathy Funk. "The Language of Food." *Middle East Report* 17, no. 145 (March-April 1987): 22–27.

Donno, Daniela. "Elections and Democratization in Authoritarian Regimes." *American Journal of Political Science* 57, no. 3 (July 2013): 703–16.

Easterly, William, and Ross Levine. "Africa's Growth Tragedy: Policies and Ethnic Divisions." *Quarterly Journal of Economics* 112, no. 4 (November 1997): 1203–50.

Eckstein, Harry. "Case Studies and Theory in Political Science." In *Strategies of Inquiry*, ed. Fred I. Greenstein, and Nelson W. Polsby, 79–138. Reading, MA: Addison-Wesley, 1975.

Edgell, Amanda B., Valeriya Mechkova, David Altman, Michael Bernhard, and Staffan I. Lindberg. "When and Where Do Elections Matter? A Global Test of the Democratization by Elections Hypothesis, 1900–2010." *Democratization* 25, no. 3 (2018): 424–44.

Eid, Alia. "Man Tabaq li-Awwal Marrah Majaniyat al-Taʿlim fi Misr?" *Ultrasawt*, November 17, 2016. https://www.ultrasawt.com/طلبة-عيد-علياء؟/في-مصر-التعليم-مجانية-مرة-لأول-طبّق-من.

Eid, Sameh. *Al-Islamiyyun Yatahadathun.* Al-Jizah: Dar Hala, 2013.

Eissa, Mohy. Personal Facebook page post. Facebook. February 18, 2015. https://www.facebook.com/permalink.php?story_fbid=1619008188323117&id=100006418533527.

Eissa, Mohy. Personal Facebook page post. Facebook. February 19, 2015. https://www.facebook.com/permalink.php?story_fbid=1619423841614885&id=100006418533527.

Eissa, Mohy. Personal Facebook page post. Facebook. February 19, 2015. https://www.facebook.com/permalink.php?story_fbid=1619428364947766&id=100006418533527.

Eissa, Mohy. Personal Facebook page post. Facebook. March 2, 2015. https://www.facebook.com/permalink.php?story_fbid=1623030801254189&id=100006418533527.

Eissa, Mohy. Personal Facebook page post. Facebook. March 3, 2015. https://www.facebook.com/permalink.php?story_fbid=1623333867890549&id=100006418533527.

Eissa, Mohy. Personal Facebook page post. Facebook. March 4, 2015. https://www.facebook.com/permalink.php?story_fbid=1623679997855936&id=100006418533527.

Eissa, Mohy. Personal Facebook page post. Facebook. March 7, 2015. https://www.facebook.com/photo/?fbid=1624698064420796&set=a.1428496920707579.

Eissa, Mohy. Personal Facebook page post. Facebook. March 27, 2015. https://www.facebook.com/permalink.php?story_fbid=1634057436818192&id=100006418533527.

Eissa, Mohy. Personal Facebook page post. Facebook. March 29, 2015. https://www.facebook.com/permalink.php?story_fbid=1634584936765442&id=100006418533527.

Eissa, Mohy. Personal Facebook page post. Facebook. March 31, 2015. https://www.facebook.com/photo/?fbid=1635207340036535&set=a.1578510872372849.

Eissa, Mohy. Personal Facebook page post. Facebook. April 5, 2015. https://www.facebook.com/photo/?fbid=1637245606499375&set=a.1578510872372849.

Eissa, Mohy. Personal Facebook page post. Facebook. April 7, 2015. https://www.facebook.com/photo/?fbid=1637890666434869&set=a.1578510872372849.

Eissa, Mohy. Personal Facebook page post. Facebook. April 13, 2015. https://www.facebook.com/permalink.php?story_fbid=1639865552904047&id=100006418533527.

Eissa, Mohy. Personal Facebook page post. Facebook. April 18, 2015. https://www.facebook.com/permalink.php?story_fbid=1642207529336516&id=100006418533527.

Eissa, Mohy. Personal Facebook page post. Facebook. April 25, 2015. https://www.facebook.com/permalink.php?story_fbid=1645502839006985&id=100006418533527.

Eissa, Mohy. Personal Facebook page post. Facebook. April 28, 2015. https://www.facebook.com/permalink.php?story_fbid=1646287168928552&id=100006418533527.

Eissa, Mohy. Personal Facebook page post. Facebook. June 7, 2015. https://www.facebook.com/photo/?fbid=1657770001113602&set=a.1578510872372849.

Eissa, Mohy. Personal Facebook page post. Facebook. June 8, 2015. https://www.facebook.com/photo/?fbid=1658019797755289&set=a.1578510872372849.

Eissa, Mohy. Personal Facebook page post. Facebook. June 18, 2015. https://www.face book.com/permalink.php?story_fbid=1661027684121167&id=100006418533527.

Eissa, Mohy. Personal Facebook page post. Facebook. June 21, 2015. https://www.face book.com/permalink.php?story_fbid=1661984550692147&id=100006418533527.

Eissa, Mohy. Personal Facebook page post. Facebook. June 23, 2015. https://www.face book.com/photo/?fbid=1662478997309369&set=a.1578510872372849.

Eissa, Mohy. Personal Facebook page post. Facebook. July 11, 2015. https://www.face book.com/permalink.php?story_fbid=1667221230168479&id=100006418533527.

Eissa, Mohy. Personal Facebook page. Facebook. Accessed April 17, 2021. https://www .facebook.com/profile.php?id=100006418533527.

El-Ashker, Ahmed Abdel-Fattah, and Rodney Wilson. *Islamic Economics: A Short History.* Leiden, The Netherlands: Brill, 2006.

El-Dabh, Basil. "Ijra'at Sarimah Did al-Tiktok fi Misr bi-Da'wat al-Hifaz 'ala Qiyam al-Usrah." *Tahrir Institute for Middle East Policy,* December 11, 2020. https://timep.org / عربی/اجراءات-صارمة-ضد-التیك-توك-فی-مصر-بدعو .

El-Erian, Essam. "Shahadat al-Duktur 'Isam al-'Iryan 'an Nash'at al-Tayyar al-Islamy bi-l-Jami'at al-Misriyya." *Ikhwanonline,* December 13, 2008. https://web.archive.org /web/20120308152435/http://ikhwanwayonline.maktoobblog.com/1508320.

El-Ghobashy, Mona. *Bread and Freedom: Egypt's Revolutionary Situation.* Stanford, CA: Stanford University Press, 2021.

El-Ghobashy, Mona. "Egypt Looks Ahead to Portentous Year." *Middle East Report Online,* February 2, 2005. https://merip.org/2005/02/egypt-looks-ahead-to-portentous-year.

El-Ghobashy, Mona. "The Liquidation of Egypt's Illiberal Experiment." *Middle East Report Online,* December 29, 2010. https://merip.org/2010/12/the-liquidation-of-egypts -illiberal-experiment.

El-Ghobashy, Mona. "The Metamorphosis of the Egyptian Muslim Brothers." *International Journal of Middle East Studies* 37, no. 3 (August 2005): 373–95.

El-Ghonemy, M. Riad. *Anti-Poverty Land Reform Issues Never Die: Collected Essays on Development Economics in Practice.* New York: Routledge, 2009.

El-Houdaiby, Ibrahim. "Al-Islam Huwa al-Hal wa Misr li Kul al-Misryyin." *Ibrahim El-Houdaiby* (blog), May 29, 2007. http://web.archive.org/web/20120313055301/http:// ihoudaiby.blogspot.com/2007_05_01_archive.html.

El-Shobaki, Amr. *Hizb al-'Amal.* Al-Qahirah: Markaz al-Dirasat al-Siyasiyya wa-l-Istratiji-yya, 2005.

El-Shorbagy, Manar. "Al-Qadaya al-Dusturiyya wal-Qanuniyya fi Fatrat Ri'asat Mubarak al-Thaniyah." In *Al-Tatawwur Al-Siyasy fi Misr 1982-1992,* ed. Mohamed Safieeddin Khaarboush, 38–70. Al-Qahirah: Markaz al-Buhuth wa-l-Dirasat al-Siyasiyya, 1995.

Elmasry, Mohamed. "Unpacking Anti-Muslim Brotherhood Discourse." *Jadaliyya,* June 28, 2013. https://www.jadaliyya.com/Details/28855.

Embassy Cairo to Department of State. "Telegram 00129." January 6, 1975, 1975CAIRO00129, Central Foreign Policy Files, 1973–79/Electronic Telegrams, RG 59: General Records of the Department of State, U.S. National Archives. https://aad.archives.gov/aad/creat epdf?rid=124615&dt=2476&dl=1345.

Embassy Cairo to Department of State. "Telegram 04727." April 9, 1976, 1976CAIRO04727, Central Foreign Policy Files, 1973–79/Electronic Telegrams, RG 59: General Records of the Department of State, U.S. National Archives. https://aad.archives.gov/aad /createpdf?rid=22799&dt=2082&dl=1345.

Embassy Cairo to Department of State. "Telegram 06893." May 19, 1976, 1976CAIRO06893, Central Foreign Policy Files, 1973–79/Electronic Telegrams, RG 59: General Records of the Department of State, U.S. National Archives. https://aad.archives.gov/aad /createpdf?rid=257824&dt=2082&dl=1345.

Embassy Cairo to Department of State. "Telegram 10283." October 15, 1976, 1975CAIRO10283, Central Foreign Policy Files, 1973–79/Electronic Telegrams, RG 59: General Records of the Department of State, U.S. National Archives. https://aad .archives.gov/aad/createpdf?rid=284958&dt=2476&dl=1345.

Embassy Cairo to Department of State. "Telegram 16440." November 26, 1976, 1976CAIRO16440, Central Foreign Policy Files, 1973–79/Electronic Telegrams, RG 59: General Records of the Department of State, U.S. National Archives. https://aad .archives.gov/aad/createpdf?rid=275931&dt=2082&dl=1345.

Embassy Cairo to Department of State. "Telegram 17485." October 21, 1977, 1977CAIRO17485, Central Foreign Policy Files, 1973–79/Electronic Telegrams, RG 59: General Records of the Department of State, U.S. National Archives. https://aad.archives.gov/aad /createpdf?rid=245706&dt=2532&dl=1629.

Embassy Cairo to Department of State. "Telegram 18347." November 4, 1977, 1977CAIRO18347, Central Foreign Policy Files, 1973-79/Electronic Telegrams, RG 59: General Records of the Department of State, U.S. National Archives. https://aad .archives.gov/aad/createpdf?rid=254863&dt=2532&dl=1629.

Embassy Cairo to Department of State. "Telegram 22969." October 16, 1978, 1978CAIRO22969, Central Foreign Policy Files, 1973–79/Electronic Telegrams, RG 59: General Records of the Department of State, U.S. National Archives. https://aad.archives.gov/aad /createpdf?rid=254487&dt=2694&dl=2009.

Embassy Cairo to Department of State. "Telegram 01470." January 22, 1979, 1979CAIRO01470, Central Foreign Policy Files, 1973–79/Electronic Telegrams, RG 59: General Records of the Department of State, U.S. National Archives. https://aad.archives.gov/aad /createpdf?rid=118439&dt=2776&dl=2169.

Embassy Cairo to Department of State. "Telegram 02033." January 29, 1979, 1979CAIRO02033, Central Foreign Policy Files, 1973-79/Electronic Telegrams, RG 59: General Records of the Department of State, U.S. National Archives. https://aad .archives.gov/aad/createpdf?rid=125296&dt=2776&dl=2169.

Embassy Cairo to Department of State. "Telegram 02350." February 1, 1979, 1979CAIRO02350, Central Foreign Policy Files, 1973–79/Electronic Telegrams, RG 59: General Records of the Department of State, U.S. National Archives. https://aad.archives.gov/aad /createpdf?rid=102241&dt=2776&dl=2169.

Embassy Cairo to Department of State. "Telegram 02824." February 7, 1979, 1979CAIRO02824, Central Foreign Policy Files, 1973–79/Electronic Telegrams, RG 59: General Records of the Department of State, U.S. National Archives. https://aad.archives.gov/aad /createpdf?rid=83071&dt=2776&dl=2169.

Embassy Cairo to Department of State. "Telegram 05969." March 23, 1979, 1979CAIRO05969, Central Foreign Policy Files, 1973-79/Electronic Telegrams, RG 59: General Records of the Department of State, U.S. National Archives. https://aad.archives.gov/aad /createpdf?rid=199832&dt=2776&dl=2169.

Embassy Cairo to Department of State. "Telegram 17425." August 28, 1979, 1979CAIRO17425, Central Foreign Policy Files, 1973-79/Electronic Telegrams, RG 59: General Records of the Department of State, U.S. National Archives. https://aad.archives.gov/aad /createpdf?rid=42802&dt=2776&dl=2169.

Embassy Cairo to Department of State. "Telegram 18508." September 11, 1979, 1979CAIRO18508, Central Foreign Policy Files, 1973-79/Electronic Telegrams, RG 59: General Records of the Department of State, U.S. National Archives. https://aad .archives.gov/aad/createpdf?rid=301299&dt=2776&dl=2169.

Embassy Cairo to Department of State. "Telegram 20510." October 4, 1979, 1979CAIRO20510, Central Foreign Policy Files, 1973-79/Electronic Telegrams, RG 59: General Records of the Department of State, U.S. National Archives. https://aad.archives.gov/aad /createpdf?rid=294588&dt=2776&dl=2169.

Eskandar, Wael. "Year of the SCAF: A Timeline of Mounting Repression." *Jadaliyya*, March 9, 2013. https://www.jadaliyya.com/Details/24604.

Esposito, John L. *Islam and Politics*. Syracuse, NY: Syracuse University Press, 1984.

Essam El-Din, Gamal. "Parliamentary Mix and Match." *Ahram Weekly*, October 27, 2011. http://web.archive.org/web/20111101135020/http://weekly.ahram.org.eg/2011/1070 /fr1.htm.

Evans, Geoffrey, ed. *The End of Class Politics?: Class Voting in Comparative Context*. New York: Oxford University Press, 1999.

Fadl, Belal. "Aan Al-Awan Tarjaʿiy ya Dawlat Al-Jawasis (5)." *Mada Masr*, November 2, 2014. https://www.madamasr.com/ar/2014/11/02/opinion/politics/الجواسيس-الحلق-آن-الأوان-ترجعي-يا-دولة.

Fadl, Belal. "Hadith al-Mubadrah Maʿa Muwazaf li-kul al-ʿUsur (3)." *Al-Arabi Al-Jadeed*, November 21, 2018. https://www.alaraby.co.uk/حديث-المبادرة-مع-موظف-لكل-العصور-3-3.

Fadl, Belal. "Shahadah Ghariybah ʿala ʿAsr Aghrab (6)." *Al-Arabi Al-Jadeed*, January 13, 2021. https://www.alaraby.co.uk/blogs/6 شهادة-غريبة-على-عصر-أغرب-.

Farag, Mohamed. *Al-Tajammuʿ fi-l-Barlaman: Difaʿan ʿan al-Watan, Difaʿan ʿan al-Muwatinin*. Al-Qahirah: Kitab al-Ahaly, 2000.

Fawzi, Mahmoud. *Al-Nabawy Ismaʿil wa Judhur Manasat al-Sadat*. Al-Qahirah: Bayt al-Lughat Al-Dawliyya, 2007.

Fenner, Sofia. "Recovering Lost Futures: Contemporaneous Sources and the Study of Past Possibilities." *APSA Comparative Democratization Newsletter* 29, no. 2 (Fall 2019): 12–17.

Fish, M. Steven. "The Determinants of Economic Reform in the Post-communist World." *East European Politics and Societies* 12, no. 1 (December 1997): 31–78.

Fouad, Amira. "Hamalat li-l-Salafiyyin wa-l-Ikhwan wa Nushataʾ al-Faysbuk Taʾyidan li-Taʿdilat al-Dustur al-Misry." *Al-Arabiya*, March 15, 2011. https://www.alarabiya.net /articles/2011%2F03%2F15%2F141681.

France24. "Egypt's Morsi Promotes Generals to Ease Tensions." *France24*, December 4, 2013. https://www.france24.com/en/20130412-egypt-morsi-promotes-army-generals-tensions.

Frank, Thomas. *What's the Matter with Kansas? How Conservatives Won the Heart of America*. New York: Metropolitan, 2004.

Franzmann, Simon, and André Kaiser. "Locating Political Parties in Policy Space: A Reanalysis of Party Manifesto Data." *Party Politics* 12, no. 2 (March 2006): 163–88.

Freedom and Justice Party. *Barnamaj Hizb al-Hurriyah wa-l-ʿAdalah*. Al-Qahirah: Dar al-Tibaʿah wa-l-Nashr al-Islamiyya, 2011.

Fukuyama, Francis. *Identity: The Demand for Dignity and the Politics of Resentment*. New York: Farrar, Straus and Giroux, 2018.

Gamal, Wael. "The Brotherhood's One Percent." *Jadaliyya*, July 19, 2012. http://www .jadaliyya.com/pages/index/6483/the-brotherhoods-one-percent.

Gamal, Wael. "Lost Capital: The Egyptian Muslim Brotherhood's Neoliberal Transformation." Carnegie Endowment for International Peace Working Paper, Washington, DC, February 2019. https://carnegieendowment.org/files/2-1-19_Gamal_Muslim_Brotherhood.pdf.

Gamee, Mahmoud. *ʿArift al-Sadat*. Al-Qahirah: Al-Maktab al-Misry Al-Hadith, 2004.

Geddes, Barbara. *Paradigms and Sand Castles: Theory Building and Research Design in Comparative Politics*. Ann Arbor: University of Michigan Press, 2003.

George, Alexander, and Andrew Bennett. *Case Studies and Theory Development in the Social Science*. Cambridge, MA: MIT Press, 2005.

Gerring, John. "Case Selection for Case-Study Analysis: Qualitative and Quantitative Techniques." In *The Oxford Handbook of Political Methodology*, ed. Janet M. Box-Steffensmeier, Henry E. Brady, and David Collier, 645–684. Oxford: Oxford University Press, 2008.

Gerring, John. "What Is a Case Study and What Is It Good for?" *American Political Science Review* 98, no. 2 (May 2004): 341–54.

Gervasio, Gennaro. *Al-Harakah al-Markisiyya fi Misr (1967–1981)*. Al-Qahirah: Al-Markaz al-Qawmy li-l-Tarjamah, 2010.

Ginat, Rami. *Egypt's Incomplete Revolution: Lutfi Al-Khuli and Nasser's Socialism in the 1960s*. London: Frank Cass, 1997.

Ginat, Rami. *A History of Egyptian Communism: Jews and Their Compatriots in Quest of Revolution*. Boulder, CO: Lynne Rienner, 2011.

Ginat, Rami. "Remembering History: The Egyptian Discourse on the Role of Jews in the Communist Movements." *Middle Eastern Studies* 49, no. 6 (2013): 919–40.

Gomaa, Mahmoud. "Daʿwah li-Thawrat Ghadab Jadidah bi Misr." *Al-Jazeera*, May 19, 2011. https://www.aljazeera.net/news/reportsandinterviews/2011/5/19/غضب-جديدة-بمصر-دعوة-لثورة-.

Greenhouse, Steven. "Half of Egypt's $20.2 Billion Debt Being Forgiven by U.S. and Allies." *New York Times*. May 27, 1991. https://www.nytimes.com/1991/05/27/business/half-of -egypt-s-20.2-billion-debt-being-forgiven-by-us-and-allies.html.

Grewal, Sharan, Amaney A. Jamal, Tarek Masoud, and Elizabeth R. Nugent. "Poverty and Divine Rewards: The Electoral Advantage of Islamist Political Parties." *American Journal of Political Science* 63, no. 4 (October 2019): 859–74.

Habashi, Fawzi. *Muʿtaqal kul al-ʿUsuur: Hayaty fi-l-Watan*. Al-Qahirah: Dar Mirit, 2004.

Habib, Mohamed. *Dhikrayat Duktur Muhamad Habib: ʿAn al-Hayah wa-l-Daʿwah wa-l-Siyasah wa-l-Fikr*. Al-Qahirah: Dar Al-Shuruq, 2012.

Habyarimana, James, Macartan Humphreys, Daniel N. Posner, and Jeremy M. Weinstein. "Why Does Ethnic Diversity Undermine Public Goods Provision?" *American Political Science Review* 101, no. 4 (November 2007): 709–25.

Haddad, Bassam. *Business Networks in Syria: The Political Economy of Authoritarian Resilience.* Stanford, CA: Stanford University Press, 2011.

Hafez, Ahmed. "Al-Hizb al-Watany: Min al-Inqilab ʿala al-Ishtrakiyya ila Tajdid Qiyadatihi al-Siyasiyya." *Al-Ahram.* February 6, 2011. https://gate.ahram.org.eg/News/37231.aspx.

Haggard, Stephan, and Robert R. Kaufman. *The Political Economy of Democratic Transitions.* Princeton, NJ: Princeton University Press, 1995.

Hall, Peter A., and Rosemary C. R. Taylor. "Political Science and the Three New Institutionalisms." *Political Studies* 44, no. 5 (December 1996): 936–57.

Hamdy, Mohamed, and Mohamed Soliman. "Al-Taʾsisiyya: Shabab al-Thawrah Yuhathirun min Wadʿ Khas li-l-Jaysh wa Yuhadidun bi-l-Insihab." *Al-Watan.* August 11, 2012. https://www.elwatannews.com/news/details/36611.

Hamed, Osama. "Egypt's Open Door Economic Policy: An Attempt at Economic Integration in the Middle East." *International Journal of Middle East Studies* 13, no. 1 (February 1981): 1–9.

Hammond, Andrew. "The Egyptian Uprising Through the Lens of the Muslim Brotherhood." *Maydan*, January 28, 2021. https://themaydan.com/2021/01/the-egyptian-uprising-through-the-lens-of-the-muslim-brotherhood.

Hammouda, Adel. *Qanabil wa Masahif: Qisat Tanzim al-Jihad.* Al-Qahirah: Sinaʾ li-l-Nashr, 1985.

Hamroush, Ahmed. *Shuhud Thawrat Yulyu.* Al-Qahirah: Maktabat Madbuly, 1984.

Hamroush, Ahmed. *Thawrat 23 Yulyu.* Al-Qahirah: Al-Hayʾah al-ʿAmah li-l-Kitab, 1992.

Handoussa, Heba. "Maʾal al-Qitaʿ al-ʿAm." In *Al-Infitah: al-Judhur, al-Hisad, wa-l-Mustaqbal,* ed. Gouda Abdel-Khalek, 449–72. Al-Qahirah: Al-Markaz al-ʿAraby li-l-Bahth wa-l-Nashr, 1982.

Harik, Iliya. "The Single Party as a Subordinate Movement: The Case of Egypt." *World Politics* 26, no. 1 (October 1973): 80–105.

Harrigan, Jane, and Hamed El-Said. *Economic Liberalisation, Social Capital and Islamic Welfare Provision.* New York: Palgrave Macmillan, 2009.

Harvey, David. "Neo-Liberalism as Creative Destruction." *Geografiska Annaler: Series B, Human Geography* 88, no. 2 (2006): 145–58.

Hashish, Mohamed Farid. *Hizb al-Wafd.* Al-Qahirah: Al-Hayʾah al-ʿAmah li-l-Kitab, 1999.

Hassan, Ammar Aly. "Adaʾ al-Tahaluf al-Islamy fi Majlis al-Shaʿb khilal al-Fasl al-Tashriʿy al-Khamis." In *Al-Tatawwur Al-Siyasy fi Misr 1982–1992,* ed. Mohamed Safieeddin Khaarboush, 113–60. Al-Qahirah: Markaz Al-Buhuth wa-l-Dirasat al-Siyasiyya, 1995.

Hassan, Iman. *Hizb al-Tajammuʿ.* Al-Qahirah: Markaz al-Dirasat al-Siyasiyya wa-l-Istratijiyya, 2005.

Hassan, Iman. *Wazaʾif al-Ahzab al-Siyasiyya fi Nuzum al-Taʿadudiyya al-Muqayadah: Dirasat Halat Hizb al-Tajammuʿ fi Misr 1976–1991.* Al-Qahirah: Al-Ahaly, 1995.

Hassan, Ahmed. "Tawaquʿat bi-Husul Ikhwan Misr ʿala al-Ghalibiyah fi al-Intikhabat al-Muqbilah." *Elaph.* October 29, 2011. https://elaph.com/Web/news/2011/10/692437.html.

Hassan, Salah Eddin. "Rashad Bayumy al-Rajul al-Samit." *Al-Watan*, December 29, 2012. https://www.elwatannews.com/news/details/104926.

Hediya, Shaaban, Nermin Abdel-Zaher, Mohamed Ismail, Mahmoud Hussein. "Al-Yawm al-Sabiʿ Yanshur Malamih Wathiqat al-Mabadiʾ al-Hakimah li-l-Dustur al-Jadid." *Youm7*, July 13, 2011. https://www.youm7.com/story/2011/7/13/-وثيقة-المبادى-الحاكمة- للدستور-الجديد-المجلس-السابع-ينشر-ملامح/454325 .

Heikal, Mohamed Hassanein. *Khariyf al-Ghadab: Qisat Bidayat wa Nahayat ʿAsr al-Sadat*. Al-Qahirah: Markaz al-Ahram l-il-Tarjamah wa-l-Nashr, 2006.

Hellman, Joel. "Winners Take All: The Politics of Partial Reform in Postcommunist Transitions." *World Politics* 50, no. 2 (January 1998): 203–34.

Hellyer, H. A. *A Revolution Undone: Egypt's Road Beyond Revolt*. New York: Oxford University Press, 2016.

Henry, Mélanie. "International Monetary Fund Riots or Nasserian Revolt? Thinking Fluid Memories: Egypt 1977." *International Review of Social History* 66, no. S29 (2021): 161–80.

Heydemann, Steven. "Networks of Privilege: Rethinking the Politics of Economic Reform in the Middle East." In *Networks of Privilege in the Middle East: The Politics of Economic Reform Revisited*, ed. Steven Heydemann, 1–34. Hampshire, UK: Palgrave Macmillan, 2004.

Heydemann, Steven. "Rethinking Social Contracts in the MENA Region: Economic Governance, Contingent Citizenship, and State-Society Relations After the Arab Uprisings." *World Development* 135 (November 2020): 105019.

Heydemann, Steven. "Social Pacts and the Persistence of Authoritarianism in the Middle East." In *Debating Arab Authoritarianism*, ed. Oliver Schlumberger, 29–31. Stanford, CA: Stanford University Press, 2007.

Heydemann, Steven. "Taxation Without Representation: Authoritarianism and Economic Liberalization in Syria." In *Rules and Rights in the Middle East: Democracy, Law, and Society*, ed. Ellis Goldberg, Resat Kasaba, and Joel S. Migdal, 69–101. Seattle: University of Washington Press, 1993.

Hiro, Dilip. *Inside the Middle East*. New York: McGraw-Hill, 1982.

Holmes, Amy Austin. *Coups and Revolutions: Mass Mobilization, the Egyptian Military, and the United States from Mubarak to Sisi*. New York: Oxford University Press, 2019.

Hosni, Hamada. *ʿAbd al-Nasir wa-l-Tanzim al-Taliʿiy al-Sirry 1971–1963*. Al-Qahirah: Maktabat Bayrut, 2007.

Hosseinzadeh, Esmail. "How Egyptian State Capitalism Reverted to Market Capitalism." *Arab Studies Quarterly* 10, no. 3 (Summer 1988): 299–318.

Howard, Marc Morje, and Philip G. Roessler. "Liberalizing Electoral Outcomes in Competitive Authoritarian Regimes." *American Journal of Political Science* 50, no. 2 (April 2006): 365–81.

Huber, John D. *Exclusion by Elections: Inequality, Ethnic Identity, and Democracy*. Cambridge: Cambridge University Press, 2017.

Huntington, Samuel P. "The Clash of Civilizations?" *Foreign Affairs* 72, no. 3 (Summer 1993): 22–49.

Hussein, Adel. *Al-Iqtisad al-Misry min al-Istiqlal ila al-Tabʿiyya*. Bayrut: Dar al-Kalimah, 1981.

Hussein, Adel. *Al-Istiqlal al-Watany wa-l-Qawmy.* Al-Qahirah: al-Markaz al-ʿAraby Li-l-Dirasat, 2004.

Hussein, Adel. *Al-Tanmiyah al-Ijtimaʿiyya bi-l-Gharb? Am bi-l-Islam?* Al-Qahirah: Nahdat Misr, 1999.

Hussein, Mahmoud. *Class Conflict in Egypt, 1945–1970.* New York: Monthly Review Press, 1973.

Hyde, Susan. "The Observer Effect in International Politics: Evidence from a Natural Experiment." *World Politics* 60, no. 1 (October 2007): 37–63.

Ibrahim, Nageh. "Ana Umathil al-Tayar al-Islamy al-Shaʿby: Hiwar maʿa Khalid al-Zaʿfarany al-Murashah li-Majlis al-Shaʿb." *Al-Jamaa Al-Islamiyya,* accessed April 21, 2021. https://web.archive.org/web/20120307194418/http://www.egyig.com/Public/articles/interview/6/41119056.shtml.

Ibrahim, Saad Eddin. "An Islamic Alternative in Egypt: The Muslim Brotherhood and Sadat." *Arab Studies Quarterly* 4, no. 1–2 (Spring 1982): 75–93.

Imam, Abdullah. *ʿAbd al-Nasir Hakadha Kan Yahkum Misr.* Al-Qahirah: Maktabat Madbuly al-Saghir, 1996.

Imam, Abdullah. *ʿAly Sabry Yatadhakar.* Al-Qahirah: Ruz al-Yusuf, 1987.

Imam, Abdullah. *Tajribat ʿUthman: al-Rad ʿala Kitab al-Muhandis ʿUthman Ahmad ʿUthman.* Al-Qahirah: Dar al-Mawqif al-ʿAraby, 1981.

Imam, Samia. *Man Yamluk Misr? Dirasah Tahliliyya li-l-Usul al-Ijtimaʿiyya li-Nukhbit al-Infitah al-Iqtisady fi-l-Mujtamaʿ al-Misry, 1974–1980.* Al-Qahirah: Dar al-Mustaqbal al-ʿAraby, 1986.

Inglehart, Ronald, and Pippa Norris. "Trump and the Populist Authoritarian Parties." *Perspectives on Politics* 15, no. 2 (June 2017): 443–54.

Ishaq, George, et al. *Al-Faris Alladhi Marra min Huna: ʿAdil Husayn fi ʿUyun man ʿArafuh.* Publisher unknown, 2007.

Iskandar, Adel. *Egypt in Flux: Essays on an Unfinished Revolution.* Cairo: American University in Cairo Press, 2013.

Iskandar, Amin. *Al-Tanzim al-Sirry li-Jamal ʿAbd al-Nasir: Taliʿat al-Ishtrakiyyin, al-Mawlid al-Masar al-Masir.* Al-Qahirah: Al-Mahrusah, 2016.

Ismael, Tareq Y., and Rifaat El-Saʿid. *The Communist Movement in Egypt, 1920–1988.* Syracuse, NY: Syracuse University Press, 1990.

Ismail, Mohamed. "Al-Tajammuʿ Yarfud al-Tazahur Yawm 25 Yanayir." *Youm7,* January 23, 2011.https://www.youm7.com/story/2011/1/23/342011/التجمع-يرفض-التظاهر-يوم-25-يناير.

Ismail, Mohamed. "Rifʿat al-Saʿid: La Ahad Yastatiyʿ an Yuzahzihany min al-Tajammuʿ." *Youm7,* March 13, 2011. https://www.youm7.com/story/2011/3/13/-رفعت-السعيد-لا-أحد-يستطيع-أن-يزحزحنى-من-التجمع/368818.

Istiftaa Misr. "Al-Natiyjah: Naʿam bi-Nisbat 77.3%." *Referendum2011,* 2011. https://referendum2011.elections.eg/84-slideshow/155-result.html.

Ivarsflaten, Elisabeth. "The Vulnerable Populist Right Parties: No Economic Realignment Fuelling Their Electoral Success." *European Journal of Political Research* 44 (2005): 465–92.

Ivarsflaten, Elisabeth. "What Unites Right-Wing Populists in Western Europe? Re-Examining Grievance Mobilization Models in Seven Successful Cases." *Comparative Political Studies* 41, no. 1 (2008): 3–23.

Kamal, Abdallah. "Faruq Husny Yaftah Qalbah li-ʿAbdallah Kamal." *Donia Al-Watan*, November 23, 2003. https://pulpit.alwatanvoice.com/articles/2003/11/23/1154.html.

Kamal, Ahmed Adil. *Al-Nuqqat fawq al-Huruwf: al-Ikhwan al-Muslimun wa-l-Nizam al-Khas.* Al-Qahirah: al-Zahraʾ li-l-Iʿlam al-ʿAraby, Qism al-Nashr, 1989.

Kamel, Mohamed Ibrahim. *Al-Salam al-Daʾiʿ fi Kamb Difid.* Al-Qahirah: Kitab al-Ahaly, 1987.

Kandil, Amr Mohamed. "Mohieddin: 'Democracy Knight' Dies in Peace." *Egypt Today*. May 7, 2018. https://www.egypttoday.com/Article/1/49468/Mohieddin-'Democracy-knight'-dies-in-peace.

Kandil, Hazem. *Inside the Brotherhood.* Cambridge: Polity Press, 2015.

Kandil, Hazem. *Soldiers, Spies, and Statesmen: Egypt's Road to Revolt.* London: Verso, 2012.

Kassab, Beesan. "Farewell to Worker Participation in the Management of the Public Business Sector." *Mada Masr*, September 17, 2020. https://www.madamasr.com/en/2020/09/17/feature/economy/farewell-to-worker-participation-in-the-management-of-the-public-business-sector.

Kassem, Maye. *Egyptian Politics: The Dynamics of Authoritarian Rule.* Boulder, CO: Lynne Rienner, 2004.

Kerr, Malcolm H. *The Arab Cold War: Gamal ʾAbd Al-Nasir and His Rivals, 1958–1970.* London: Published for the Royal Institute of International Affairs by Oxford University Press, 1971.

Ketchley, Neil. *Egypt in a Time of Revolution: Contentious Politics and the Arab Spring.* Cambridge: Cambridge University Press, 2017.

Khaled, Mohamed. *Al-Harakah al-Niqabiyya bayn al-Mady wa-l-Hadir.* Al-Qahirah: Dar al-Taʿawun, 1975. https://www.ikhwanwiki.com/index.php?title= بين_الماضي_والحاضر_الحركة_النقابية.

Khalil, Ibrahim. "ʿAsifah fi Hizb al-ʿAmal bi-Sabab al-Tahaluf maʿa al-Ikhwan." *Rose Al-Yousef*, February 17, 1987.

Khalil, Kamal. *Hikayat min Zaman Fat: Sirah Dhatiyya min khilal al-Ahdath.* Al-Jizah: Bayt al-Yasmin li-l-Nashr wa-l-Tawziʿ, 2012.

Khalil, Omnia. "Old Rent: Survival Tactics to Live in the City." *Marsad Omran*. June 26, 2018. http://marsadomran.info/en/policy_analysis/2018/06/1582.

Kim, Nam Kyu. "Reassessing the Relationship Between Elections and Democratization." *International Political Science Review* 41, no. 3 (2020): 305–20.

King, Gary, Robert O. Keohane, and Sidney Verba. *Designing Social Inquiry: Scientific Inference in Qualitative Research.* Princeton, NJ: Princeton University Press, 1994.

King, Stephen J. *The New Authoritarianism in the Middle East and North Africa.* Bloomington: Indiana University Press, 2009.

Kirchheimer, Otto. "The Catch-all Party." In *The West European Party System*, ed. Peter Mair, 50–60. Oxford: Oxford University Press, 1990.

Kitschelt, Herbert, and Anthony J. McGann. *The Radical Right in Western Europe: A Comparative Analysis.* Ann Arbor: University of Michigan Press, 1995.

Koroum, Hassanein. *Al-Taharukat al-Siyasiyya li-l-Ikhwan al-Muslimin 1971–1987.* Al-Qahirah: al-Markaz al-ʿAraby al-Dawly li-l-Iʿlam, 2012.

Kreutz, Andrej. *Russia in the Middle East: Friend or Foe?* Westport, CT: Praeger Security International, 2007.

Kuran, Timur. *Islam and Mammon: The Economic Predicaments of Islamism.* Princeton, NJ: Princeton University Press, 2004.

Kuran, Timur. "Islamic Economics and the Islamic Subeconomy." *Journal of Economic Perspectives* 9, no. 4 (Fall 1995): 155–73.

Labib, Malak. "Re-shaping the "Socialist Factory" in Egypt in the Late 1960s–1970s." *Forum Transregionale Studien,* April 30, 2021. https://trafo.hypotheses.org/28429.

Lacroix, Stéphane. "Egypt's Pragmatic Salafis: The Politics of Hizb al-Nour." Carnegie Endowment for International Peace Working Paper, Washington, DC, November 2016. https://carnegieendowment.org/files/CP_287_Lacroix_al_Nour_Party_Final .pdf.

Langohr, Vickie. "Of Islamists and Ballot Boxes: Rethinking the Relationship Between Islamists and Electoral Politics." *International Journal of Middle East Studies* 33, no. 4 (November 2001): 591–610.

Langohr, Vickie. "Too Much Civil Society, Too Little Politics: Egypt and Liberalizing Arab Regimes." *Comparative Politics* 36, no. 2 (January 2004): 181–204.

Lian, Brad, and John Oneal. "Cultural Diversity and Economic Development." *Economic Development and Cultural Change* 46, no. 1 (October 1997): 61–78.

Lieberman, Evan S. "Nested Analysis as a Mixed-Method Strategy for Comparative Research." *American Political Science Review* 99, no. 3 (August 2005): 435–52.

Lijphart, Arend. "Comparative Politics and the Comparative Method." *American Political Science Review* 65, no. 3 (September 1971): 682–93.

Lijphart, Arend. *Democracy in Plural Societies: A Comparative Exploration.* New Haven, CT: Yale University Press, 1977.

Lijphart, Arend. *Patterns of Democracy: Government Forms and Performance in Thirty-Six Countries.* New Haven, CT: Yale University Press, 1999.

Lindberg, Staffan I. *Democracy and Elections in Africa.* Baltimore, MD: Johns Hopkins University Press, 2006.

Lindberg, Staffan I., ed. *Democratization by Elections: A New Mode of Transition.* Baltimore, MD: Johns Hopkins University Press, 2009.

Lipset, Seymour Martin, and Stein Rokkan. "Cleavage Structures, Party Systems, and Voter Alignment: An Introduction." In *Party Systems and Voter Alignments: Cross-national Perspectives,* ed. Seymour Martin Lipset and Stein Rokkan, 1–64. New York: Free Press, 1967.

Louis, Maryse, Alia El Mahdy, and Heba Handoussa. "Foreign Direct Investment in Egypt." In *Investment Strategies in Emerging Markets,* ed. Saul Estrin and Kalus E. Meyer, 51–87. Northampton, UK: Edward Elgar, 2004.

Luciani, Giacomo. "Linking Economic and Political Reform in the Middle East: The Role of the Bourgeoisie." In *Debating Arab Authoritarianism,* ed. Oliver Schlumberger, 161–76. Stanford, CA: Stanford University Press, 2007.

Lust-Okar, Ellen. "Elections Under Authoritarianism: Preliminary Lessons from Jordan." *Democratization* 13, no. 3 (July 2006): 455–70.

Lust-Okar, Ellen. *Structuring Conflict in the Arab World: Incumbents, Opponents, and Institutions.* Cambridge: Cambridge University Press, 2005.

Lustick, Ian S. "History, Historiography, and Political Science: Multiple Historical Records and the Problem of Selection Bias." *American Political Science Review* 90, no. 3 (September 1996): 605–18.

Madi, Abul-Ela. "Al-Muhandis ʿUthman Ahmad ʿUthman wa-l-Ikhwan (2)." *Al-Wasat Party*, February 5, 2018. http://web.archive.org/web/20200219145756/https://www.alwasat party.com/window/شخ-2الإخوان-وا-عثمان-أحمد-عثمان-المهندس.

Madi, Abul-Ela. "Al-Ustadh ʿUmar al-Tilmisany (2)." *Al-Wasat Party*, January 7, 2018. http://web.archive.org/web/20180120145640/http://www.alwasatparty.com /window/الأستاذ-2التلمساني-عمر.

Madi, Abul-Ela. "Hikayaty maʿa al-Ikhwan wa Qisat al-Wasat." *Masress*, January 4, 2006. http://www.masress.com/almesryoon/9998.

Magaloni, Beatriz. "The Game of Electoral Fraud and the Ousting of Authoritarian Rule." *American Journal of Political Science* 54, no. 3 (July 2010): 751–65.

Mahkamat Al-Naqd. "Al-Taʿn Raqam 4046 li-Sanat 67 Qadaʾiyya." *Court of Cassation*, November 1, 2010. https://www.cc.gov.eg/judgment_single?id=111290541&ja=98121.

Mahmoud, Aly Abdel-Halim. *Wasaʾil al-Tarbiyah ʿind al-Ikhwan al-Muslimin: Dirasah Tahlili-yya Tarikhiyya*. Al-Mansurah: Dar al-Wafaʾ, 1989.

Mahmoud, Khaled. "Sisi's Grab for Brotherhood Assets." *Sada*. October 5, 2018. https://carnegieendowment.org/sada/77427.

Mahmoud, Mustafa. *Al-Markisiyya wa-l-Islam*. Al-Qahirah: Dar al-Maʿarif, 1975.

Mahmoud, Mustafa. *Limadha Rafadtu al-Markisiyya*. Al-Qahirah: Dar al-Maʿarif, 1984.

Mahoney, James. "After KKV: The New Methodology of Qualitative Research." *World Politics* 62, no. 1 (January 2010): 120–47.

Mahoney, James. "The Logic of Process Tracing Tests in the Social Sciences." *Sociological Methods and Research* 41, no. 4 (March 2012): 570–97.

Mahoney, James. "Path Dependence in Historical Sociology." *Theory and Society* 29, no. 4 (August 2000): 507–48.

Mansfield, Peter. "Nasser and Nasserism." *International Journal* 28, no. 4 (Autumn 1973): 670–88.

Manwaring, Rob, and Paul Kennedy, eds. *Why the Left Loses: The Decline of the Centre-Left in Comparative Perspective*. Bristol, UK: Policy Press, 2017.

Maqroun, Camilia. "Intihaʾ al-Jawlah al-Uwla min al-Marhalah al-Thaniyah wa Intiqadat li-l-Islamiyyin bi-Istiʿmal al-Din fi-l-Daʿayah al-Siyasiyya." *France24*, December 15, 2011. https://www.france24.com/ar/20111215--الثانية-المرحلة-السلفيين-المسلمين-الإخوان-يعية التشر-الانتخابات-مصر-السياسيةمصر-الدعاية-الدين-استعمال-انتخابية-حملة.

March, Andrew F. "Taking People as They Are: Islam as a 'Realistic Utopia' in the Political Theory of Sayyid Qutb." *American Political Science Review* 104, no. 1 (February 2010): 189–207.

Masoud, Tarek E. *Counting Islam: Religion, Class, and Elections in Egypt*. New York: Cambridge University Press, 2014.

Mawi, Reda. "Misr: Daʿawy li-Istirdad Sharikat ʿAmah min al-Qitaʿ al-Khas." *BBC News*, June 7, 2011. https://www.bbc.com/arabic/middleeast/2011/06/110607_egypt _privatisation.

Mawlana, Ahmed. *Al-Jama'ah al-Islamiyya: Istiratijiyat Muta'aridah.* Istanbul: Al-Ma'had al-Misry li-l-Dirasat, 2018. https://eipss-eg.org/wp-content/uploads/2018/02/-الجماعة-الإسلامية-استراتيجيات-متعارضة.pdf.

McCall, Betsy Birns. "The Effects of Rent Control in Egypt: Part I." *Arab Law Quarterly* 3, no. 3 (May 1988): 151–66.

McDermott, Anthony. "Sadat and the Soviet Union." *The World Today* 28, no. 9 (September 1972): 404–10.

Medani, Khalid Mustafa. *Black Markets and Militants: Informal Networks in the Middle East and Africa.* New York: Oxford University Press, 2021.

Meijer, Roel. *The Quest for Modernity: Secular Liberal and Left-Wing Political Thought in Egypt, 1945–1958.* London: RoutledgeCurzon, 2002.

Mekky, Mohamed Fakhry. "Al-Taghayyurat al-Haykaliyya fi Mizan al-Madfu'at al-Misry 1952–1976." In *Al-Iqtisad al-Misry fi-Rub' Qarn, 1952–1977,* ed. Ismail Sabri Abdallah, Gouda Abdel-Khalek, and Ibrahim Al-Issawi, 322–50. Al-Qahirah: Al-Hay'ah al-Misriyya al-'Amah li-l-Kitab, 1978.

Mitchell, Joshua. *The Fragility of Freedom: Tocqueville on Religion, Democracy, and the American Future.* Chicago: University of Chicago Press, 1995.

Mitchell, Richard Paul. *The Society of the Muslim Brothers.* New York: Oxford University Press, 1969.

Mohieddin, Khaled. *Al-Din wa-l-Ishtrakiyya.* Al-Qahirah: Dar al-Thaqafah Al-Jadidah, undated.

Mohieddin, Khaled. *Wal'an Atakalam.* Al-Qahirah: Markaz al-Ahram li-l-Tarjamah wa-l-Nashr, 1992.

Mohieddin, Khaled, Lutfi Waked, Mukhtar Gomaa, Abdel-Aziz Shaaban, and Al-Badri Farghali. *Lihadha Nu'arid al-Hukumah.* Al-Qahirah: Al-Ahaly, 1991.

Mohsen, Khaled. *Misr bayn al-Dawlah al-Islamiyya wa-l-Dawlah al-'Ilmaniyya.* Al-Qahirah: Markaz Al-I'lam Al-'Araby, 1992.

Momani, Bessma. *IMF-Egyptian Debt Negotiations.* Cairo: American University in Cairo Press, 2005.

Morsi, Fouad. *Hadha al-Infitah al-Iqtisady.* Al-Qahirah: Dar al-Thaqafa al-Jadidah, 1976.

Mostafa, Ahmed. "27 Munazamah Huquqiyya Tatliq Mubadarat al-Hal al-Wasat li-Inqadh Wathiqat al-Silmy." *Youm7,* November 4, 2011. https://www.youm7.com/story/2011/11/4/27-526995/منظمة-حقوقية-تطلق-مبادرة-الحل-الوسط-لإنقاذ-وثيقة-السلمى.

Mostafa, Amer. "Sawiris li 'CNN': Mubarak Wafaq 'ala Fatrah Intiqaliyya Walakin al-Ikhwan wa Asdiqa' al-Su' Rafadu." *Youm7,* November 13, 2020. https://www.youm7.com/story/2020/11/13/-ساويرس-لـCNN-مبارك-وافق-على-فترة-انتقالية-ولكن-الإخوان/5066178.

Mostafa, Hala. *Al-Islam al-Siyasy fi Misr: Min Harakat al-Islah ila Jama'at al-'Unf.* Al-Qahirah: Markaz al-Mahrusah, 1998.

Mounir, Mohamed. "Wa Ma Nayl al-Matalib bi-La'n al-Ikhwan." *Al-Hewar Al-Mutamadin,* December 18, 2005. https://www.ahewar.org/debat/show.art.asp?aid=52643.

Moustafa, Tamir. "Conflict and Cooperation Between the State and Religious Institutions in Contemporary Egypt." *International Journal of Middle East Studies* 32 (2000): 3–22.

Moustafa, Tamir. *The Struggle for Constitutional Power: Law, Politics, and Economic Development in Egypt*. New York: Cambridge University Press, 2007.

Mudde, Cas. *Populist Radical Right Parties in Europe*. Cambridge: Cambridge University Press, 2007.

Mudge, Stephanie L. *Leftism Reinvented: Western Parties from Socialism to Neoliberalism*. Cambridge, MA: Harvard University Press, 2018.

Mufti, Malik. "The United States and Nasserist Pan-Arabism." In *The Middle East and the United States: A Historical and Political Reassessment*, ed. David W. Lesch, 168–87. Boulder, CO: Westview Press, 2003.

Naeem, Mohamed. "Tariq al-Bishry: ʿArrab al-Wataniyya al-Misriyya wa Tirkatuh." *Mada Masr*, March 18, 2021. https://www.madamasr.com/ar/2021/03/18/opinion/u/-طارق-البشري عرّاب-الوطنية-المصرية-وت.

Nagarajan, K. V. "Egypt's Political Economy and the Downfall of the Mubarak Regime." *International Journal of Humanities and Social Science* 3, no. 10 (May 2013): 22–39.

Nassar, Mohamed. "Kayf Tahadath al-Sisy ʿan Tatwir al-Khitab al-Diny fi 16 Munasabah." *Masrawy*, January 28, 2020. https://www.masrawy.com/news/news_egypt/details/2020 /1/28/1713739/-عن-تطوير-الخطاب-الديني-في-16-مناسبة كيف-تحدث-السيسي.

Nasser, Munir K. *Egyptian Mass Media Under Nasser and Sadat: Two Models of Press Management and Control*. Columbia, SC: Association for Education in Journalism and Mass Communication, 1990.

Nelson, Rebecca M., and Jeremy M. Sharp. *Egypt and the IMF: Overview and Issues for Congress*. Washington DC: Congressional Research Service, 2013. https://www.files.ethz.ch/isn/164704/209246.pdf.

Neto, Octavio Amorim, and Gary W. Cox. "Electoral Institutions, Cleavage Structures, and the Number of Parties." *American Journal of Political Science* 41, no. 1 (January 1997): 149–74.

Nettle, Daniel. "Linguistic Fragmentation and the Wealth of Nations: The Fishman-Pool Hypothesis Reexamined." *Economic Development and Cultural Change* 48, no. 2 (January 2000): 335–48.

Nettle, Daniel, James B. Grace, Marc Choisy, Howard V. Cornell, Jean-François Guégan, and Michael E. Hochberg. "Cultural Diversity, Economic Development and Societal Instability." *PLoS ONE* 2, no. 9 (September 2007): e929.

Norris, Pippa. *Radical Right: Voters and Parties in the Electoral Market*. Cambridge: Cambridge University Press, 2005.

Nouh, Mukhtar. *Mawsuʿat al-ʿUnf fi-l-Harakat al-Islamiyya al-Musalahah: 50 ʿAman min al-Dam*. Al-Qahirah: Sama li-l-Nashr wa-l-Tawziʿ, 2014.

Noureddin, Iman. "Athar al-Inshiqaq ʿala al-Adaʾ al-Siyasy li-Hizb al-ʿAmal." In *Al-Tatawur al-Siyasy fi Misr 1982-1992*, ed. Mohamed Safieeddin Khaarboush, 343–74. Al-Qahirah: Markaz al-Buhuth wa-l-Dirasat al-Siyasiyya, 1995.

O'Donnell, Guillermo, and Philippe C. Schmitter. *Transitions from Authoritarian Rule: Tentative Conclusions About Uncertain Democracies*. Baltimore, MD: Johns Hopkins University Press, 1986.

O'Dwyer, Conor, and Branislav Kovalčík. "And the Last Shall Be First: Party System Institutionalization and Second-Generation Economic Reform in Postcommunist Europe." *Studies in Comparative International Development* 41 (2007): 3–26.

Oesch, Daniel. "Explaining Workers' Support for Right-Wing Populist Parties in Western Europe: Evidence from Austria, Belgium, France, Norway, and Switzerland." *International Political Science Review* 29, no. 3 (2008): 349–73.

Omar, Mahmoud, Hind Ibrahim, and Mohamed Farghali. "Al-Ikhwan Yahshidun al-Ahaly li-Fad Idrab al-Mu'alimin bi-l-Munufiyya." *Al-Masry Al-Youm*, September 20, 2011. https://www.almasryalyoum.com/news/details/112297.

Osman, Osman Ahmed. *Safahat min Tajribaty*. Al-Qahirah: Al-Maktab al-Misry al-Hadith, 1981.

Osman, Tarek. *Egypt on the Brink: From Nasser to Mubarak*. New Haven, CT: Yale University Press, 2013.

Othman, Dalia. "Al-Majlis al-A'la li-l-Quwat al-Musalahah Yu'lin Idkhal 15 Ta'dilan 'ala Qanun al-Ahzab." *Al-Masry Al-Youm*, March 28, 2011. https://www.almasryalyoum.com/news/details/121914.

Othman, Wael. *Asrar Al-Harakah al-Tulabiyya Handasat al-Qahirah 1968–1975*. Al-Qahirah: Al-Sharikah al-Misriyya li-l-Tiba'ah wa-l-Nashr, 1976.

Person, Torsten, and Guido Tabellini. "Constitutions and Economic Policy." *Journal of Economic Perspectives* 18, no. 1 (Winter 2004): 75–98.

Pierson, Paul. "Increasing Returns, Path Dependence, and the Study of Politics." *American Political Science Review* 94, no. 2 (2000): 251–67.

Piketty, Thomas. *Capital and Ideology*. Cambridge, MA: Harvard University Press, 2020.

Piketty, Thomas. *The Economics of Inequality*. Cambridge, MA: Harvard University Press, 2014.

Pipes, Daniel. *In the Path of God: Islam and Political Power*. New York: Basic Books, 1983.

Posusney, Marsha Pripstein. *Labor and the State in Egypt: Workers, Unions, and Economic Restructuring*. New York: Columbia University Press, 1997.

Posusney, Marsha Pripstein. "Multi-Party Elections in the Arab World: Institutional Engineering and Oppositional Strategies." *Studies in Comparative International Development* 36 (2002): 34–62.

Privatization Coordination Support Unit (PCSU). *Privatization in Egypt Quarterly Review April–June 2002*. Cairo: CARNA Corporation, 2002. http://www1.aucegypt.edu/src/wsite1/Pdfs/Privatization%20in%20Egypt%20-Quarterly%20Review.pdf.

Przeworski, Adam. *Democracy and the Market*: Political and Economic Reforms in Eastern Europe and Latin America. New York: Cambridge University Press, 1991.

Radi, Mohsen. *Al-Ikhwan al-Muslimun taht Qubbat al-Barlaman*. Al-Qahirah: Dar al-Tawzi' wa-l-Nashr al-Islamiyya, 1990.

Radio Sawa. "Al-Shurtah al-Misriyya Taqtahim Maydan al-Tahrir fi Muhawalah li-Fad al-I'tisam fih." *Radio Sawa*, April 9, 2011. https://www.radiosawa.com/archive/2011/04/09/الشرطة-المصرية-تقتحم-ميدان-التحرير-في-محاولة-لفض-الاعتصام-فيه.

Ramzi, Mahmoud and Khaled Al-Shami. "Al-Tajammu' Yu'lin Da'muh Tarashuh al-Sisy li-l-Ri'asah." *Al-Masry Al-Youm*, February 2, 2014. http://www.almasryalyoum.com/news/details/387073.

Reuters. "Wafat al-Katib al-Misry Mahmud Amin al-ʿAlim." Reuters, January 10, 2009. https://www.reuters.com/article/oegen-egypt-writer-at1-idARACAE50900P20090110.

Revolutionary Socialists. Al-Ishtirakiyya Allaty Nudafiʿ ʿAnha. Al-Qahirah: Markaz al-Dirasat al-Ishtirakiyya, 2006.

Riad (Amin), Hassan (Samir). L'Egypte Nasserienne. Paris: Editions de Minuit, 1964.

Richards, Alan. "Higher Education in Egypt." World Bank Policy Research Working Paper 862, World Bank, Washington, DC, 1992.

Rizk, Younan Labib. Al-Ahzab al-Misriyya ʿabr Miʾat ʿAm. Al-Qahirah: Al-Hayʾah al-ʿAmah li-l-Kitab, 2006.

Roemer, John E. "Why the Poor Do Not Expropriate the Rich: An Old Argument in New Garb." Journal of Public Economics 70, no. 3 (December 1998): 399–424.

Romiah, Talaat. Maʾziq al-Harakah al-Shiuʿiyya al-Misriyya: al-Judhur al-Tarikhiyya wa-l Khiyarat al-Mustaqbaliyya. Al-Qahirah: Markaz al-Ahram lil-Nashr wa-l-Tarjamah wal-Tawziʿ, 2010.

Rovny, Jan. "Who Emphasizes and Who Blurs? Party Strategies in Multidimensional Competition." European Union Politics 13, no. 2 (2012): 269–92.

Rozza, Ahmed Abdalla. Al-Talabah w-al-Siyasah fi Misr. Al-Qahirah: Sinaʿ li-l-Nashr, 1991.

Sabeh, Amr. "Qiraʾah Muwajazah li-Mwaqif ʿAbd al-Nasir min al-Shiuʿiyyin, wa min Muʿasasat al-Azhar." Elw3yalarabi, May 24, 2018. https://elw3yalarabi.org/elw3y/2018 قراءة-موجزة-لمواقف-عبد-الناصر-من-الشيو/05/24/.

Sabri, Musa. Wathaʾiq 15 Mayu. Al-Qahirah: Al-Maktab al-Misry al-Hadith, 1976.

Said, Atef. "The Paradox of Transition to 'Democracy' Under Military Rule." Social Research 79, no. 2 (Summer 2012): 397–434.

Said, Edward W. "The Clash of Ignorance." The Nation, October 4, 2001. https://www.thenation.com/article/archive/clash-ignorance.

Said, Ramy. "Nanshur Nas Istiqalat ʿUdu bi-l-Tajammuʿ wa Yantaqid Mawqif Qadat Al-Hizb." Youm7, November 6, 2015. https://www.youm7.com/story/2015/11/6/عضو-بالتجمع-وينتقد-موقف-قادة-الحزب/2426625ننشر-نص-استقالة.

Sallam, Hesham, ed. Egypt's Parliamentary Elections, 2011-2012: A Critical Guide to a Changing Political Arena. Washington, DC: Tadween, 2013.

Sallam, Hesham. "From the State of Vanguards to the House of Kofta: Reflections on Egypt's Authoritarian Impasse." Jadaliyya, October 26, 2020. https://www.jadaliyya.com/Details/41912.

Sallam, Hesham. "Nasser's Comrades and Sadat's Brothers: Institutional Legacies and the Downfall of the Second Egyptian Republic." In Egypt and the Contradictions of Liberalism: Illiberal Intelligentsia and the Future of Egyptian Democracy, ed. Dalia F. Fahmy and Daanish Faruqi, 55–84. London: Oneworld, 2017.

Sallam, Hesham. "The New Iraq and Arab Political Reform: Drawing New Boundaries (and Reinforcing Old Ones)." In Iraq, Its Neighbors, and the United States: Competition, Crisis, and the Reordering of Power, ed. Henri J. Barkey, Scott Lasensky, and Phebe Marr, 189–207. Washington, DC: U.S. Institute of Peace, 2011.

Sallam, Hesham. "Post-Elections Egypt: Revolution or Pact?" Jadaliyya, February 10, 2012. https://www.jadaliyya.com/Details/25249.

Sallam, Hesham. "Reflections on Egypt After March 19." *Jadaliyya*, May 31, 2011. https://www.jadaliyya.com/Details/24050.

Sami, Aziza. "Rifaat El-Said: Which Way Will He Bend Next?" *Ahram Weekly*, July 7–13, 2005. http://web.archive.org/web/20141007182250/http://weekly.ahram.org.eg/2005/750/profile.htm.

Saresella, Daniela. "Gramsci and the Issue of Religion: Catholic Modernism and the Italian Partito Popolare." *History of European Ideas* 45, no. 8 (2019): 1143–55.

Sarhan, Hammam. "Misr: ʿAqabat fi Tariq al-Tahaluf al-Al-Dimuqraty." *Swissinfo*, June 27, 2011. https://www.swissinfo.ch/ara/30538450/--مصر---عقبات-في-طريق--التحالف--الديمقراطي.

Sawt Al-Balad. "Al-Sisy: 30 Yunyu Qamat min ʾAjl al-Difaʿ ʿan al-Hawiyah al-Misriyya." *Sawt Al-Balad*, August 24, 2014. http://baladnews.com/?p=920.

Schaffner, Brian F., Matthew Macwilliams, and Tatishe Nteta. "Understanding White Polarization in the 2016 Vote for President: The Sobering Role of Racism and Sexism." *Political Science Quarterly* 133, no. 1 (Spring 2018): 9–34.

Schamis, Hector E. "Distributional Coalitions and the Politics of Economic Reform in Latin America." *World Politics* 51, no. 2 (January 1999): 236–68.

Schedler, Andreas, ed. *Electoral Authoritarianism: The Dynamics of Unfree Competition*. Boulder, CO: Lynne Rienner, 2006.

Schedler, Andreas. "The Nested Game of Democratization by Elections." *International Political Science Review* 23, no. 1 (January 2002): 103–22.

Schwedler, Jillian. "Can Islamists Become Moderates? Rethinking the Inclusion-Moderation Hypothesis." *World Politics* 63, no. 2 (April 2011): 347–76.

Schwedler, Jillian. *Faith in Moderation: Islamist Parties in Jordan and Yemen*. Cambridge: Cambridge University Press, 2006.

Seawright, Jason, and John Gerring. "Case Selection Techniques in Case Study Research: A Menu of Qualitative and Quantitative Options." *Political Research Quarterly* 61, no. 2 (June 2008): 294–308.

Seikaly, Sherene. "A Protest of the Poor: On the Political Meaning of the People." In *The Aesthetics and Politics of Global Hunger*, ed. Anastasia Ulanowicz and Manisha Basu, 135–55. Cham, Switzerland: Palgrave Macmillan, 2017.

Serageddin, Saeed. *Aqsamt An Arwy Haqaʾiq wa Mawaqif al-Barlamany al-Thaʾir Salah Abu-Ismaʿil*. Al-Qahirah: Dar al-Fikr al-Islamy, 1991. https://www.ikhwanwiki.com/index.php?title=حقائق_ومواقف_البرلماني_الثائر_أبو_إسماعيل.

Shaaban, Ahmed Bahaaeddin. *Inhaztu li-l-Watan: Shahadah min Jil al-Ghadab: Safahat min Tarikh al-Harakah al-Wataniyya al-Dimuqratiyya li-Tulab Misr, 1967-1977*. Al-Qahirah: Markaz al-Mahrusah, 1998.

Shadi, Salah. *Safahat min al-Tarikh: Hisad al-ʿUmr*. Al-Qahirah: Al-Zahraʾ li-l-Iʿlam al-ʿAraby, Qism al-Nashr, 1987.

Shalaby, Abdullah. *Al-Din wa-l-Siraʿ al-Siyasy fi Misr: 1970-1985*. Al-Qahirah: Kitab al-Ahaly, 2000.

Shalata, Ahmed Zaghloul. "Al-Daʿwah al-Salafiyya al-Sakandariyya: Masarat al-Tanzim wa Maʾalat al-Siyasah." *Al-Mustaqbal Al-ʿAraby* 443 (2016): 128–40.

Sharaf, Sami. "ʿAbd al-Nasir wa-l-Tanzim al-Siyasy." *Sanawat wa Ayam Maʿa Jamal ʿAbd al-Nasir, al-Juzʿ Al-Thany*. Accessed April 15, 2015. http://hakaek-misr.com/yahiaalshaer.com/SAMY/Book-2-POLORG-XX.html.

Sharaf, Sami. *Sanawat wa Ayam Maʿa Jamal ʿAbd al-Nasir*. 2 vols. Al-Qahirah: Al-Firsan li-l-Nashr, 2005.

Sharaf, Sami. *Sanawat wa Ayam Maʿa Jamal ʿAbd al-Nasir*. 5 vols. Al-Qahirah: Al-Maktab al-Misry al-Hadith, 2014.

Sharp, Jeremy M. *Egypt: Background and U.S. Relations*. Washington DC: Congressional Research Service, 2009. http://www.dtic.mil/dtic/tr/fulltext/u2/a501061.pdf.

Shehata, Samer. "Political Da'wa: Understanding the Muslim Brotherhood's Participation in Semi-Authoritarian Elections." In *Islamist Politics in the Middle East Movements and Change*, ed. Samer Shehata, 120–45. New York: Routledge, 2012.

Shehata, Samer, and Joshua Stacher. "The Brotherhood Goes to Parliament." *Middle East Report* no. 240 (Fall 2006): 32–39.

Shenker, Jack. *The Egyptians: A Radical History of Egypt's Unfinished Revolution*. New York: New Press, 2016.

Shuheib, Abdel-Qadir. *Al-Ikhtiraq: Qisat Sharikat Tawziyf al-Amwal*. Al-Qahira: Sinaʾ li-l-Nashr, 1989.

Shukrallah, Salma, and Yassin Gaber. "What Was Religion Doing in the Debate on Egypt's Constitutional Amendments?" *Ahram Online*, March 22, 2011. https://english.ahram.org.eg/NewsContent/1/64/8267/Egypt/Politics-/What-was-religion-doing-in-the-debate-on-Egypts-Co.aspx.

Shukri, Ghali. *Al-Thawrah al-Mudadah fi Misr*. Al-Qahirah: Kitab al-Ahaly, 1987.

Shukri, Ghali. *Thaqafat al-Nizam al-ʿAshwaʾy*. Al-Qahirah: Kitab al-Ahaly, 1994.

Siddiqi, Muhammad Nejatullah. *Muslim Economic Thinking: A Survey of Contemporary Literature*. Leicester: Produced by the Islamic Foundation for the International Centre for Research in Islamic Economics, King Abdul Aziz University, 1981.

Sides, John. "Race, Religion, and Immigration in 2016: How the Debate Over American Identity Shaped the Election and What It Means for a Trump Presidency." The Democracy Fund Voter Study Group Report, June 2017. https://www.voterstudygroup.org/publication/race-religion-immigration-2016.

Soliman, Khaled. *Dhikrayat la Mudhakarat: al-Luwaʾ Fuʾad ʿAllam Yatahadath*. Al-Qahirah: Dar al-Ahmady, 2007.

Soliman, Samer. *Al-Nizam al-Qawy wa-l-Dawlah al-Daʿifah*. Al-Jizah: Al-Dar li-l-Nashr wa-l-Tawziʿ, 2006.

Soliman, Samer. *The Autumn of Dictatorship: Fiscal Crisis and Political Change in Egypt Under Mubarak*. Stanford, CA: Stanford University, 2011.

Spies, Dennis. "Explaining Working-Class Support for Extreme Right Parties: A Party Competition Approach." *Acta Politica* 48 (2013): 296–325.

Springborg, Robert. *Mubarak's Egypt: Fragmentation of the Political Order*. Boulder, CO: Westview Press, 1989.

Stacher, Joshua. "Damanhour by Hook and by Crook." *Middle East Report* 238 (Spring 2006): 26–27.

Stacher, Joshua. *Watermelon Democracy: Egypt's Turbulent Transition.* Syracuse, NY: Syracuse University Press, 2020.

Stacher, Joshua, and Samer Shehata. "Boxing in the Brothers." *Middle East Report Online*, August 8, 2007. https://merip.org/2007/08/boxing-in-the-brothers.

Steinmo, Sven, and Kathleen Thelen. "Historical Institutionalism in Comparative Politics." In *Structuring Politics: Historical Institutionalism in Comparative Analysis*, ed. Sven Steinmo, Kathleen Thelen, and Frank Longstreth, 1–32. Cambridge: Cambridge University Press, 1992.

Stevens, Candice. "The Mineral Industry in Egypt." In *Minerals Yearbook Area Reports: International 1976*, 359–70. Vol. 3. Washington, DC: Bureau of Mines, 1976.

Sudoud, Eissa. "ʿAbd al-ʿAal: La Yujad Inqisam fi Misr." *Vetogate*, April 15, 2014. http://www.vetogate.com/957769.

Tammam, Hossam. *Al-Ikhwan al-Muslimun: Sanawat ma Qabl al-Thawrah.* Al-Qahirah: Dar al-Shuruq, 2012.

Tammam, Hossam. *Shahid ʿala Tarikh al-Harakah al-Islamiyya fi Misr: 1970-1984.* Al-Qahirah: Dar al-Shuruq, 2010.

Tammam, Hossam. *Tahawulat al-Ikhwan al-Muslimin: Tafakuk al-Aydiulujiyya wa Nahayat al-Tanzim.* Al-Qahirah: Maktabat Madbuly, 2009.

Tavits, Margit, and Natalia Letki. "From Values to Interests? The Evolution of Party Competition in New Democracies." *The Journal of Politics* 76, no. 1 (January 2014): 246–58.

Thelen, Kathleen Ann, and James Mahoney. *Explaining Institutional Change: Ambiguity, Agency, and Power.* Cambridge: Cambridge University Press, 2010.

Thies, Cameron G. "A Pragmatic Guide to Qualitative Historical Analysis in the Study of International Relations." *International Studies Perspectives* 3, no. 4 (November 2002): 351–72.

Throsby, David. *Economics and Culture.* New York: Cambridge University Press, 2001.

Utvik, Bjørn Olav. *Islamist Economics in Egypt: The Pious Road to Development.* Boulder, CO: Lynne Rienner, 2006.

Vreeland, James Raymond. *The IMF and Economic Development.* New York: Cambridge University Press, 2003.

Wardani, Saleh. *Al-Harakah al-Islamiyya fi Misr: Al-Waqiʿ wa-l-Tahadiyat min al-Khamsiniyat ila al-Tisʿiniyat.* Al-Qahirah: Dar al-Kalimah, 2000.

Waterbury, John. *The Egypt of Nasser and Sadat: The Political Economy of Two Regimes.* Princeton, NJ: Princeton University Press, 1983.

Waterbury, John. "The Political Management of Economic Adjustment Reform." In *Fragile Coalitions: The Politics of Economic Adjustment*, ed. Joan M. Nelson, 39–56. New Brunswick, Canada: Transaction, 1989.

Wickham, Carrie Rosefsky. *Mobilizing Islam: Religion, Activism, and Political Change in Egypt.* New York: Columbia University Press, 2002.

Wickham, Carrie Rosefsky. *The Muslim Brotherhood: Evolution of an Islamist Movement.* Princeton, NJ: Princeton University Press, 2013.

Wickham, Carrie Rosefsky. "The Path to Moderation: Strategy and Learning in the Formation of Egypt's Wasat Party." *Comparative Politics* 36, no. 2 (January): 205–28.

Wiktorowicz, Quintan, ed. *Islamic Activism: A Social Movement Theory Approach.* Bloomington: Indiana University Press, 2004.

Yahya, Karem. "Faris al-Dimuqratiyya Khalid Muhy al-Din Akhir al-ʿAnqud fi Majlis Qiyadat al-Thawrah." *Al-Ahram*, July 23, 2012. http://digital.ahram.org.eg/articles. aspx?Serial=971306&eid=2406.

Youm7. "Murshid al-Ikhwan: Fulul al-Watany waraʾ Ahdath Masbiru." *Youm7*, October 12, 2011. https://www.youm7.com/story/2011/10/12/مرشد-الإخوان-فلول-الوطنى-وراء-أحداث-ماسبيرو 510960.

Younis, Sherif. *Nidaʾ al-Shaʿb: Tarikh Naqdy li-l-Aydiulujiyya al-Nasiriyya.* Al-Qahirah: Dar al-Shuruq, 2012.

Younis, Sherif. *Sayid Qutb wa-l-Usuliyya al-Islamiyya.* Al-Qahirah: Dar Tibah li-l-Dirasah wa-l-Nashr, 1995.

Yousef, Tarik M. "Development, Growth and Policy Reform in the Middle East and North Africa Since 1950." *Journal of Economic Perspectives* 18, no. 3 (Summer 2004): 91–115.

Zahran, Rafiq. "Al-Harakah al-Falahiyya wa Qanun Tard al-Mustaʾjiriyn." *Revsoc*, September 1, 1997. http://revsoc.me/workers-farmers/lhrk-lflhy-wqnwn-trd-lmstjryn.

Zayed, Hani. "Ghuzlan: al-Ikhwan Lam Yadkhulu Safqah Intikhabiyya maʿa Nizam Mubarak." *Al-Watan*, June 8, 2012. https://www.alwatan.com.sa/article/140871.

Zeghal, Malika. "Religion and Politics in Egypt: The Ulema of al-Azhar, Radical Islam, and the State (1952–94)." *International Journal of Middle East Studies* 31, no. 3 (August 1999): 371–99.

Zollner, Barbara H. E. *The Muslim Brotherhood: Hasan al-Hudaybi and Ideology.* New York: Routledge, 2009.

Zollner, Barbara. "Prison Talk: The Muslim Brotherhood's Internal Struggle During Gamal Abdel Nasser's Persecution, 1954 to 1971." *International Journal of Middle East Studies* 39, no. 3 (August 2007): 411–33.

Zubaida, Sami. "The Politics of the Islamic Investment Companies in Egypt." *British Society for Middle Eastern Studies. Bulletin* 17, no. 2 (1990): 152–61.

Index

Abaza, Wagih, 41

Abdallah, Ismail Sabri, 109, 110, 172, 175, 195, 252

Abdel-Ghany, Atef, 85

Abdel-Hadi, Aisha, 49

Abdel-Halim, Kamal, 181, 184

Abdel-Khalek, Gouda, 31, 392n115

Abdel-Malak, Gamal Assaad, 262, 273

Abdel-Maqsoud, Salah, 150

Abdel-Meguid, Esmat, 193

Abdel-Meguid, Helmy, 112

Abdel-Meguid, Wahid, 28

Abdel-Quddous, Mohamed, 150

Abdel-Razek, Hussein, 171, 249, 250, 252–55, 256, 391n105

Aboul-Fotouh, Abdel-Moneim, 101, 106; on *Al-Dawa*, 150; on deals with ruling party, 98; on freedom of Islamist currents, 102; history of Islamist movement and, 151–52; importance of, 95; on institutional links between IGUs and Muslim Brotherhood, 116; Muslim Brotherhood's guardianist camp and, 164, 165; on physical clashes with leftist activists, 99, 100; as president of the Student Union of Cairo University, 96; prison sentence of, 104, 159;

recruitment of, 114; removal of from Guidance Bureau, 167–68; Al-Sadat and, 115, 353n263; Al-Sananiri and, 149; university administrators and, 105

Abu-Basha, Hassan, 82–83, 88, 91, 193

Abu-Galeel, Hamdi, 394n159

Abul-Magd, Kamal, 52, 55, 92

Abul-Nasr, Mohamed Hamed, 164, 165, 238–39, 246

Abu-Ruqayiq, Saleh, 86, 87, 112

Abu-Wafya, Mahmoud, 112, 267

Adly, Amr, 42

Adly, Howaida, 63

Afghanistan, 238, 392n115

Ahaly, Al- (newspaper), 58–59, 82, 84, 194, 201, 210, 247; editorial leadership of, 249–50, 252, 253; hostility toward ruling establishment of, 257; pressure to impose changes at, 258; Al-Tagammu pragmatist wing and, 256, 260; *This Is Why We Oppose Mubarak*, 255, 260

Ahmed, Saad Mohamed, 326n139

Ahram Institution, Al-, 60, 191

Akef, Mohamed Mahdi, 127, 128, 167, 234

Akhbar, Al- (newspaper), 329n199

and, 246, 247, 248, 249, 284; terrorism and, 261
Mubarak, Suzanne, 263
Murad, Helmy, 269, 272
Murad, Mustafa Kamel, 46, 57, 156, 328n178
Murad, Zaki, 180
Muslim Brotherhood, 1, 18, 28, 43, 79, 96, 108, 110, 154–55, 291; agrarian policy of, 138; anti-leftist discourse of, 255; ascendancy of, 212; ASU and, 112; autonomy of, 146, 148, 170, 278; B. M. Badr and, 231; base of, 163; Al-Bishri and, 279; Bread Uprising and, 121; business people affiliated with, 141–42; as center-right party, 363n370; collaboration with, 266; crackdown against, 158, 159; crowding out and, 222, 225; Al-Dawa and, 113; difficulty of infiltration in, 209; on economic issues, 126, 127, 128, 130, 137; economic liberalization and, 16, 126, 131, 140; ECP and, 286; electoral boycott by, 260; electoral successes of, 145, 157, 288, 336n47; engagement in public life, 164; exiled leaders of, 111; FJP and, 168–69; focus on media by, 233–34; gains in parliamentary elections, 156; General Guide of, 103, 113; growing influence of, 161; guardianist camp of, 163; Guidance Bureau of, 158, 165, 167–68; IG and, 150; IGUs and, 116, 119, 150, 151, 352n260, 371n89; impact of, 277; influence of, 152; information requests submitted by, 244; institutional development of, 154, 204, 206; internal divisions in, 161; interpellations submitted by, 245; Islamist advantage of, 153; Islamist incorporation policies and, 122, 148, 153, 277; Islamist movements and, 74; Islamist student activists and, 81, 85; Islamist student movement and, 196; Israel and, 351n249; key figures of, 114; lack of organizational structures, 367n25; leaders of, 117; legislative oversight motions submitted by,

228, 230; legislative priorities of, 225–27; major policy issues raised by, 229; K. Mohieddin on, 262; MOI and, 72, 73; H. Mubarak and, 146, 221; Nada and, 166; Nasserist social pact and, 140; organizational base of, 108; organizational successes of, 197; parliamentary bloc of, 238; political ascendancy of, 251; political marginalization of, 27, 69, 73, 121; Political Parties Law and, 207; private sector and, 167; privatization and, 137–38; public profile of, 11; questions submitted by, 240–43; recruitment efforts of, 115; reemergence on political scene, 148, 216; reluctance to adopt concrete positions, 358n318; rent controls and, 139; return to political life of, 82, 83; return to public life of, 142; Rose Al-Yousef on, 84; ruling party competition with, 304; Al-Sadat and legal status of, 118, 302, 303; Al-Sadat falling out with, 115; SCAF and, 280; Sharia and, 232; SLP and, 131, 271–72; socialism and, 124; state leniency toward, 120; state repression of, 12; on state welfare provision, 135; student elements of, 355n281; VO and, 380n114; Al-Wafd Party and, 222, 223; zakat and, 136

Nada, Youssef, 166
Naksah, Al- ("the setback"), 30
Naqqash, Amina Al-, 250
Naqqash, Farida Al-, 249, 258
Nasser, Gamal Abdel-, 2, 9, 18, 41, 44–45, 109, 321n61, 349n212; anti-imperialism of, 187, 188; attacks on legacy of, 143; communist parties and, 32; "Comrade Khaled" and, 172; death of, 32; demand of full political submission, 189; dissolution of communist organizations under, 172–73, 175, 195, 204, 277; distributive social and economic policies of, 26; eagerness to fulfill consumer demands, 320n44; entitlements gained under, 49; IMF and, 42; on lack of mass organization,

GPSR Authorized Representative: Easy Access System Europe, Mustamäe tee 50, 10621 Tallinn, Estonia, gpsr.requests@easproject.com

www.ingramcontent.com/pod-product-compliance
Lightning Source LLC
Chambersburg PA
CBHW021842020426
42334CB00013B/155